1989

Allegheny County v. American Civil Liberties Union 396
Allegheny Pittsurgh Coal Company v. County Commission 247
Allgeyer v. Louisiana 359
Amerada Hess Corporation v. Division, Director of Taxation . 226
American Federation of Government Employees v. Thornburg . . 150
Arizona v. Hicks 112
Aronson v. Quick Pencil Company 288
Atlas Roofing Co. v. Occupational Safety & Health Review Com..279
Bacheldar v. Maryland 209
Barton v. Barbour 263
Batson v. Kentucky 168
Bell v. Wolfish 161
Biswell v. United States 94
Bivens v. Six Unknown Named Agents 69
Bonito Boats, Inc. v. Thunder Craft Boats, Inc. 283
Brown v. Allen 176
Brown v. Board of Education 17
Burger King v. Rudzewicz 228
Camara v. Municipal Court 90
Chapman v. California 200
Colonnade Catering Company v. United States 94
Commonwealth Edison Company v. Montana 244
Compco Corporation v. Day-Brite Lighting, Inc. 284
Complete Auto Transit, Inc. v. Brady 226
Container Corporation of America v. Franchise Tax Board . . . 235
Corporation of Presiding Bishop v. Amos 388
County of Allegheny v. American Civil Liberties Union 385
Crowell v. Benson 279
Davis v. Michigan Department of Treasury 254
Delaware v. Prouse 96
DeShaney v. Winnebago County Department of Social Services . 53
Donovan v. Dewey 97
Eddings v. Oklahoma 173
Estelle v. Gamble 65
Fay v. Noia 166
Ford v. Wainwright 171
Frank v. Maryland 90
Frazee v. Illinois Department of Employment Security 378
Fullilove v. Klutznick 37
Goldberg v. Kelly 344
Goldberg v. Sweet 226
Goldstein v. California 287
Granfinanciera v. Nordberg 262
Griffin v. Wisconsin 104
Griggs v. Duke Power Company 32
Guiney v. Roache 151
Hamilton v. Regents of the University of California 384
Harmon v. Thornburg 150
Home Telephone and Telegraph Company v. City of Los Angeles . 84
Jones v. Alfred H. Mayer Company 20
Katchen v. Landy 265
Kewanee Oil Company v. Bicron Corporation 288
Kimmelman v. Morrison 185

1989
The Supreme Court Review

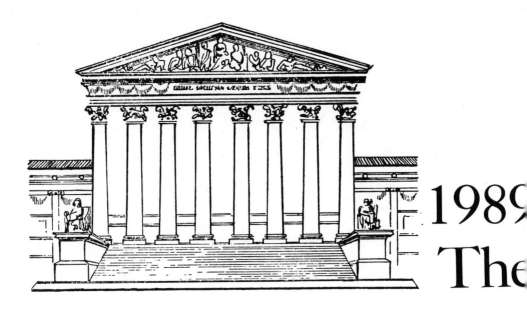

1989
The

"Judges as persons, or courts as institutions, are entitled to
no greater immunity from criticism than other persons
or institutions . . . [J]udges must be kept mindful of their limitations and
of their ultimate public responsibility by a vigorous
stream of criticism expressed with candor however blunt."
—*Felix Frankfurter*

". . . while it is proper that people should find fault when
their judges fail, it is only reasonable that they should recognize the
difficulties. . . . Let them be severely brought to book,
when they go wrong, but by those who will take the trouble
to understand them."
—*Learned Hand*

THE LAW SCHOOL

THE UNIVERSITY OF CHICAGO

upreme Court Review

EDITED BY

GERHARD CASPER

AND DENNIS J. HUTCHINSON

THE UNIVERSITY OF CHICAGO PRESS

CHICAGO AND LONDON

INTERNATIONAL STANDARD BOOK NUMBER: 0-226-09571-1

LIBRARY OF CONGRESS CATALOG CARD NUMBER: 60-14353

THE UNIVERSITY OF CHICAGO PRESS, CHICAGO 60637

THE UNIVERSITY OF CHICAGO PRESS, LTD., LONDON

© 1990 BY THE UNIVERSITY OF CHICAGO, ALL RIGHTS RESERVED, PUBLISHED 1990

PRINTED IN THE UNITED STATES OF AMERICA

The paper used in this publication meets the minimum requirements of American National Standard for Information Sciences—Permanence of Paper for Printed Library Materials, ANSI Z39.48-1984. ∞

TO
PHILIP B. KURLAND

. . . a truly civilized man . . .
confiden[t] in the strength and security
derived from the inquiring mind . . .
unafraid of the uncertitudes.

CONTENTS

PREFACE   ix

PRIVATE DISCRIMINATION AND PUBLIC RESPONSIBILITY:
   PATTERSON IN CONTEXT   1
    Kenneth L. Karst

DUE PROCESS, GOVERNMENT INACTION, AND PRIVATE
   WRONGS   53
    David A. Strauss

ON THE FOURTH AMENDMENT RIGHTS OF THE
   LAW-ABIDING PUBLIC   87
    Stephen J. Schulhofer

THE SUPREME COURT'S NEW VISION OF FEDERAL HABEAS
   CORPUS FOR STATE PRISONERS   165
    Joseph L. Hoffmann

HARMLESS ERROR AND THE VALID RULE REQUIREMENT   195
    Henry P. Monaghan

AFTER PROFESSIONAL VIRTUE   213
    Geoffrey C. Hazard, Jr.

STATE TAXATION AND THE SUPREME COURT   223
    Walter Hellerstein

THE SEVENTH AMENDMENT AND JURY TRIALS
   IN BANKRUPTCY   261
    Douglas G. Baird

BONITO BOATS: UNINFORMED BUT MANDATORY
  INNOVATION POLICY   283
  John Shepard Wiley Jr.

CHANGING CONCEPTS OF CONSTITUTIONALISM: 18TH TO
  20TH CENTURY   311
  Gerhard Casper

LOCHNER ABROAD: SUBSTANTIVE DUE PROCESS AND
  EQUAL PROTECTION IN THE FEDERAL REPUBLIC
  OF GERMANY   333
  David P. Currie

"OF CHURCH AND STATE AND THE SUPREME COURT":
  KURLAND REVISITED   373
  Mark Tushnet

PREFACE

In 1960, setting forth his reasons for bringing another law review into existence, Philip Kurland quoted Professor Henry Hart's lament that there was no "adequate tradition of sustained, disinterested, and competent criticism" of the professional qualities of Supreme Court opinions. What was a well-justified complaint thirty years ago is no longer true. Those who seek to explain this change for the better will readily recognize the role of *The Supreme Court Review*, and that means the role of the founder and sole editor for many years.

Phil has brought to the editorship his own commitment to the concept of the legal profession as a learned profession. After graduating from the Harvard Law School, Phil clerked for two very great judges—Jerome Frank, a graduate of The University of Chicago Law School, and Felix Frankfurter. For three decades, *The Supreme Court Review* has reflected its founding editor's commitment to high standards of practice and of scholarship, his utter distaste for cant, and the catholicity of his interests in political science, history, and theory. Phil's sharp pencil as editor, as well as his own equally sharp pen, have served, rather than hindered, the wide diversity of views, approaches, and conclusions that can be found in the volumes published since 1960.

While Phil's list of authors has always included well-established figures, his most important contribution as editor may have been his willingness to seek not only diversity, but to encourage young scholars. Phil has never shown insecurity when it comes to judgment. This trait, occasionally not fully appreciated by his colleagues, has been one of the great assets of the *Review*. Phil has never withheld his imprimatur from good work by obscure authors. Among the contributors to this volume are two—Kenneth Karst and David Currie—whose names can also be found in the table of contents for the first volume. Professor Karst then had just begun his third year of law teaching; Professor Currie was not even that far along—serving as a law clerk at the United States Court of Appeals for the Second Circuit.

Phil invited Gerhard Casper, in 1977, and Dennis Hutchinson, in 1981, to become his co-editors. Last year Phil told us that he wanted to resign his editorship in order to be relieved of its burdens. Unfortunately, this was not a request, and, therefore, we were not able to refuse it. We were consoled by the fact that Phil will continue as the William R. Kenan, Jr., Distinguished Service Professor at The University of Chicago, and, thereby, continue to comfort us when we vent our frustrations and disappointments. His advice invariably concludes, "Cheer up, things will only get worse." His departure from *The Supreme Court Review*, for once, confirms that tart wisdom.

The first two volumes of *The Supreme Court Review* were dedicated to "The Chief Justice and the Associate Justices of the Supreme Court of the United States." In 1962, the year of Justice Frankfurter's retirement, Phil dedicated *The Review* to Felix Frankfurter. Since then, each volume has been inscribed to different and various victims of the editors' admiration. The choice of this year's dedication goes without saying. The text is the one selected by Phil for the dedication to the 1962 volume.

GERHARD CASPER
DENNIS J. HUTCHINSON

KENNETH L. KARST

PRIVATE DISCRIMINATION AND PUBLIC RESPONSIBILITY: PATTERSON IN CONTEXT

When the Supreme Court in April 1988 ordered reargument of *Patterson v. McLean Credit Union* and asked the parties to consider whether *Runyon v. McCrary*[1] should be overruled, the bitterness of four dissenting Justices was matched by the majority's righteous dudgeon.[2] At issue was the interpretation of a part of the Civil Rights Act of 1866, reenacted in 1870 and now codified in 42 U.S.C. §1981, giving "all persons . . . the same right . . . to make and enforce contracts . . . as is enjoyed by white citizens. . . ." In *Runyon*, decided in 1976, the Court had held that Section 1981 not only required a state to give blacks and whites the same legal rights in contracting, but also forbade private racial discrimination in the making of contracts—in the case at hand, the refusal by two private schools in Virginia to admit black children as pupils. Justices White and Rehnquist dissented.

Kenneth L. Karst is Professor of Law, University of California, Los Angeles.

AUTHOR'S NOTE: I am grateful for the chance to join in saluting Philip Kurland as he lays down his editorial pen—although it is sobering to realize that Phil first applied that pen to my prose in 1960, when this *Review* began. A vital factor in the *Review*'s success during these three decades has been Phil's capacity to edit sympathetically even when the writer's point of view differs from his own. For that kind of editing, and for his own consistently stimulating scholarship on the Court and the Constitution, I offer my thanks and my congratulations.

A number of friends and colleagues have read a draft of this article. For their thoughtful comments I am grateful to Craig Becker, Kimberlé Crenshaw, Julian Eule, Robert Goldstein, Catherine Hancock, Joel Handler, Patrick Patterson, and Jonathan Varat.

[1] 427 U.S. 160 (1976).

[2] 108 S.Ct. 1419 (1988).

Even before *Runyon*, the Court had held that Section 1981 forbade some kinds of racial discrimination by private employers.[3] *Patterson* had initially presented a issue of middling importance: whether Section 1981 should also be interpreted to provide a remedy in damages for a private employer's racial harassment of an employee.[4] The request to reconsider *Runyon* came not from the parties but from the Court itself—or, more specifically, from the two *Runyon* dissenters plus the three Justices who had been appointed by President Reagan. In these circumstances the reargument order strongly suggested that Something Big was about to happen.[5] That expectation would explain the angry tone of the four dissenting Justices—the surviving remnant of the *Runyon* majority[6]—and the huffy response of their five colleagues.

At the time the Court ordered reargument of *Patterson*, two of the three short opinions mainly addressed the principle of stare decisis. Justice Blackmun's dissent argued that *Runyon*'s interpretation of Section 1981 was correct when it was decided, had been consistently followed, had been accepted by Congress, and had been seen as an expression of the Nation's commitment to racial justice.[7] The majority, answering per curiam, blandly argued the legitimacy of overruling statutory precedents. They were guarded about their intention, saying nothing about the substantive interests at stake. Instead, they listed a number of cases in which the Court had asked the parties to argue whether a precedent should be overruled, and a number of cases in which the Court had overruled previous statutory interpretations. The majority concluded with a grand harrumph: the *Runyon*

---

[3]Tillman v. Wheaton-Haugh Recreation Ass'n, Inc., 410 U.S. 431 (1973); Johnson v. Railway Express Agency, Inc., 421 U.S. 454 (1975). See also McDonald v. Santa Fe Trail Trans. Co., 427 U.S. 273 (1976), decided the same day as *Runyon*.

[4]The issue's importance lay in the inadequacy of the remedies for racial harassment offered by Title VII of the Civil Rights Act of 1964. See text at note 97 *infra*. But plaintiffs in actions under Section 1981 have had only modest success, partly because the cases are hard to try. See Eisenberg & Schwab, The Importance of Section 1981, 73 Corn. L. Rev. 596, 600 (1988); Jost, Precedent, Race and The Court, Calif. Lawyer 47, 48 (Jan. 1989).

[5]See, *e.g.*, Jost, *ibid*. Last year in these pages, in a thoughtful analysis of the political setting of the reargument order, Mark Tushnet noted the reaction that was already building outside the Court. Tushnet, Patterson and the Politics of the Judicial Process, 1988 Supreme Court Review 43. The reargument order provoked at least three law review symposia: 87 Mich. L. Rev. 1 (1989); 67 Wash. U.L.Q. 1 (1989); 98 Yale L.J. 521 (1989).

[6]Justices Blackmun and Stevens joined in each other's dissenting opinions, and Justices Brennan and Marshall joined both dissents.

[7]The latter point was the focus of Justice Stevens's dissent. See Tushnet, note 5 *supra*, at 57–60.

precedent was entitled to no special weight just "because it benefited civil rights plaintiffs by expanding liability under the statute." To say otherwise would abandon the sworn duty of federal judges "to administer justice without respect to persons, and to do equal right to the poor and to the rich"[8]—a lofty, if unintentionally ironic, pronouncement.

Who would have thought, in that frosty Spring of 1988, that in the next Term the Court would unanimously reaffirm the *Runyon* precedent?[9] By the time the reaffirmation was announced, however, only its unanimity came as a surprise. At the October 1988 reargument, all three of the Justices appointed by President Reagan had indicated their reluctance to carry through with the threatened overruling.[10] When counsel for the employer argued that the Court in *Runyon* had been mistaken in reading the Civil Rights Act of 1866 to forbid private racial discrimination, Justice Scalia replied, "If that's all you have, Mr. Kaplan, I'm afraid you have nothing."[11] When Justice Kennedy wrote for the majority in June 1989, he made the same point, but less bluntly: some Justices still thought *Runyon* had been decided wrongly, but all agreed the precedent should be followed. On the principle of stare decisis Justice Kennedy's opinion rounded up the usual formulas. In the aggregate those formulas accurately summarize the doctrine: precedent should be followed unless there is a sufficient reason for not following it.[12] The very malleability of the principle suggests that the decision was governed by other considerations.

---

[8]108 S.Ct. at 1421.

[9]Patterson v. McLean Credit Union, 109 S.Ct. 2363 (1989).

[10]Savage, Court May Let Key Rights Rulings Stand, L.A. Times, Oct. 13, 1988, pt. I, p. 14, col. 1.

[11]*Ibid.*

[12]In estimating the authority of precedent, there seems to be far less difference between interpretation of the Reconstruction civil rights laws and constitutional interpretation than one might expect from reading generalized statements about stare decisis in opinions and commentary. See text at note 41 *infra.* The definitive statement of the uncertainty of the role of stare decisis in constitutional law is Monaghan, Stare Decisis and Constitutional Adjudication, 88 Colum. L. Rev. 723 (1988). For valuable commentary on stare decisis in statutory interpretation, see Symposium, Patterson v. McLean, 87 Mich. L. Rev. 1 (1989) (articles by Daniel Farber, Alexander Aleinikoff, and William Eskridge).

The Supreme Court has often treated the Reconstruction civil rights acts as near-relatives of the Civil War Amendments. See text at note 40 *infra.* A by-product of this attitude is the Court's willingness to reconsider its previous interpretations of these laws. One case on the *Patterson* majority's list of statutory reinterpretations was Monell v. New York City Dep't of Social Services, 436 U.S. 658 (1978), a decision dear to the hearts of civil rights advocates.

If *Patterson* left unchanged our understanding of stare decisis, still its reaffirmation of *Runyon* was a civil rights watershed. In hindsight we can see it as the doctrinal consolidation of a broad political consensus already established. No doubt that consensus was brought to the attention of the majority Justices by the clamorous response to their questioning of *Runyon*'s continuing vitality as a precedent. Surely they noticed, for example, that sixty-six United States Senators and 118 Representatives filed a brief urging the Court to reaffirm *Runyon*, as did the attorneys general of forty-seven states.

Patterson shows, however, that consolidation comes with a price tag. The Supreme Court's present majority is not seeking remedies for private racial discrimination. After unanimously confirming *Runyon*'s vitality, the Court went on to rule, 5–4, that Section 1981 does not provide a remedy in damages for an employer's racial harassment. The decision's mixed message exemplifies the current state of civil rights doctrine in the Supreme Court.

In this field of constitutional and statutory law, the homing principle that attracts the Court's present majority is a model of formal racial neutrality that minimizes the remedial responsibilities of both governmental and nongovernmental actors. The model's attractions for the *Runyon* dissenters had been evident in 1976, and the reargument order in *Patterson* itself suggests that those two Justices are not the only members of the Court so attracted. The inadequacy of the model of formal neutrality has been apparent ever since the Supreme Court brought it to life in the *Civil Rights Cases*[13] a century ago. The model has always been unresponsive to the central problem of American race relations: eliminating the stigma of racial caste.[14] One major

---

[13] The basic charter for the model is the opinion in the Civil Rights Cases, 109 U.S. 3 (1883).

[14] See, *e.g.*, Crenshaw, Race, Reform, and Retrenchment: Transformation and Legitimation in Antidiscrimination Law, 101 Harv. L. Rev. 1331 (1988); Lawrence, The Id, the Ego, and Equal Protection: Reckoning with Unconscious Racism, 30 Stan. L. Rev. 317 (1987); Freeman, Legitimizing Racial Discrimination Through Antidiscrimination Law: A Critical Review of Supreme Court Doctrine, 62 Minn. L. Rev. 1049 (1978); Karst, The Supreme Court, 1976 Term—Foreword: Equal Citizenship Under the Fourteenth Amendment, 91 Harv. L. Rev. 1 (1977). In a recent article, Roy Brooks criticizes a public policy of "formal equal opportunity," and shows in impressive detail how this policy, as applied to issues of education, employment, and housing, has failed as "a cure for the American race problem," i.e., racial subordination. Brooks, Racial Subordination Through Formal Equal Opportunity, 25 S. D. L. Rev. 879 (1988). Brooks defines formal equal opportunity as "equal legal treatment," *id.* at 886, and describes the policy's two operational tenets as "racial omission, or what some might call colorblindness," and racial integration. The policy is epitomized by Brown v. Board of Education, 347 U.S. 483 (1954). *Id.* at 890–91. In contrast, the doctrinal model I call formal racial neutrality is a set of preferences emphasizing limited responsibility, private ordering, and

reason is that the model leaves untouched the private discrimination that is, and always has been, central to racial subordination.

By no means are the Justices of the present majority woodenly devoted to the model of formal racial neutrality. They are prepared to live with some significant deviations in the direction of substantive equality, particularly when, as in *Patterson*'s reaffirmation of *Runyon*, these departures from the model can be explained as settled doctrine. Yet, for anyone who recognizes the primacy of private discrimination in the subordination of a race, many of last Term's developments in civil rights doctrine surely represent retrogression. The dismay of civil rights advocates expresses more than their concerns about particular results, or even particular doctrines. They take the recent decisions to indicate a general inclination toward ungenerous readings of civil rights laws, and, more specifically, to reject the idea that private discrimination is a public responsibility.

I. PATTERSON'S PAST AND FUTURE

A. THE PRIMACY OF PRIVATE DISCRIMINATION IN RACIAL SUBORDINATION

To understand the implications of a principle of formal neutrality for race relations in America, we must begin by looking at the central role that private discrimination has played in racial subordination, from the times of slavery to the present day. I have used the term "private discrimination" in its modern sense: racial discrimination that is not directly caused by the acts of government officials. But in the era of slavery, the term had no meaning. Slavery began as the work of nongovernmental actors who used forced labor to maximize the profit on their investment in land. Governmental action, including the substantial body of law that governed slavery, was designed to protect—to legitimize, to institutionalize—private interests that the first slaveholders had created by violence. Slavery was not simply a relationship defined by law; it was a social system, a culture, an amalgam of beliefs and behavior that permeated all segments of society in the slaveholding states.

---

narrowly focused remedies. This model is epitomized by the *Civil Rights Cases*. The model is set out fully in the text following note 84. Brooks and I follow different paths in our discussions, but we agree on the urgency of substantive remedies in response to the persistence of racial subordination.

The defenders of slavery did make a distinction between the public and private spheres of their society. They saw the slaves as members of their masters' households, and argued that government had no business intefering with that private domain.[15] But "private discrimination" was not separate from the larger system of control; the slaves were subject to their masters' paternalistic governance, the defenders argued, because Nature made them incapable of governing themselves. This idea of racial superiority and inferiority became a dogma as private landowners sought a justification for slavery. For individuals who were enslaved, their bondage to private masters was their all-pervasive public status. Their membership in the slave caste indelibly stained every aspect of their lives: work, living conditions, family relations, self-image. In a society that enslaved a race, the distinction between public and private discrimination would never occur to anyone.[16]

After Emancipation, the "customs" of racial caste persisted; the removal of slavery's legal props left much of the system in place. Race remained the central signifier in stratifying southern society, and thus in defining individual identities. The immediate concern of the planters was to maintain a labor force to plant and harvest cotton and other crops. "The dominant theme in the planters' lives became the search for a substitute for slavery."[17] In the earliest post-war days, the vagrancy laws of the Black Codes served, along with a "convict-lease system," to provide black workers for the farms.[18] Even after the Black Codes were suppressed it was clear that formal legal equality was consistent with an extreme degree of real inequality, founded on race. A "contract system" was used to hold black workers on the land in an arrangement that amounted to debt peonage.[19] The law's contribution was the formally neutral enforcement of labor contracts, which typically required personal service to pay off debts. Owners would encourage workers to accept advances of money, the

---

[15]On paternalism, see Genovese, Roll, Jordan, Roll: The World the Slaves Made 3–7, 70–86, 123–49 and *passim* (Vintage ed. 1976).

[16]See generally Jordan, White Over Black: American Attitudes toward the Negro, 1550–1812 (1968); Genovese, note 15 *supra*; Blassingame, The Slave Community: Plantation Life in the Antebellum South (1979).

[17]Daniel, The Metamorphosis of Slavery, 1865–1900, 66 J. Am. Hist. 88 (1979). See also Foner, Reconstruction: America's Unfinished Revolution, 1863–1877 128–42 (1988).

[18]Litwack, Been in the Storm So Long: The Aftermath of Slavery 364–71 (Vintage ed. 1980).

[19]*Id.* 408–20.

debts would gather interest, and the system "would hold [the workers] forever by a constantly strengthening chain."[20]

What was surprising was that some black farmers did manage to keep their heads above the waters of debt. One was Nate Shaw, who found the struggle hard: "I had men turn me down [as a sharecropper], wouldn't let me have the land I needed to work, wouldn't sell me guano, didn't want to see me with anything."[21] Today we call similar refusals to deal—such as the refusal to rent a house to a black tenant—by the name of private discrimination. In the Reconstruction years, however, those acts had no special name. They were an undifferentiated part of a larger social system that excluded blacks from equal citizenship. White supremacy again became governmental policy, but it began in private interests in securing a labor force, private beliefs about racial inferiority, and private fears of status displacement.

For every Nate Shaw there were scores of black workers and tenants who were less fortunate. Slavery, by law and custom, had kept most black people illiterate, a condition that affected three-quarters of the freed slaves as late as the 1880s.[22] If a worker or a sharecropping tenant could not read, how could he dispute the landowner's account book? On many a farm, if a worker complained about his account, he risked a beating for his insolence.[23] Landowners might agree informally among themselves not to pay black workers more than a certain wage. A landowner in difficult straits could avoid paying anything at all by driving workers off the land just before the end of their work contracts and then refusing to pay them.[24] In ensnaring and subordinating black workers, then, "the legal net was formidable. But the new labor system . . . was more than that."[25]

In the same post-Emancipation period, blacks were subjected to a range of personal indignities which also had their origins in the slave system's assumptions about racial superiority and inferiority. Blacks were relegated to lower-class accommodations in streetcars; if they

---

[20]Daniel, note 17 *supra*, at 96.

[21]*Id.* at 98.

[22]*Id.* at 95.

[23]On violence against blacks, including lynchings, as means of maintaining racial subordination, see Foner, note 17 *supra*, at 119–23.

[24]See *id.* at 142; Hyman & Wiecek, Equal Justice under Law: Constitutional Development, 1835–1875 399 (1982).

[25]Daniel, note 17 *supra*, at 96.

were allowed in churches and theaters they were typically required to sit in the back rows; they had access only to a few hotels and restaurants that catered exclusively to black patrons.[26] These behavioral expressions of private prejudice were underpinned by law, from common law powers over property to legislative charters for streetcar companies. The restrictions generally were "understood rather than stated,"[27] but they were powerful customs with deep roots in slavery. In 1867 the editor of a black newspaper in New Orleans saw how these informal modes of private behavior readily translated into discrimination by governmental institutions: "For as long as [racial] distinctions will be kept on in public manners, these discriminations will react on the decisions of juries and courts, and make impartial justice a lie."[28] Later, when Jim Crow arrived, the force of law was explicitly placed behind the customs of exclusion and domination. But Jim Crow was always more than its legal framework. Like slavery, it was a comprehensive system of racial subordination in which private discrimination and the acts and policies of government officials reinforced each other.[29]

If private racial discrimination has presented a difficult problem for legal doctrine, one reason is the ambiguity of the categories "public" and "private." In law the label "public" carries many different meanings, the range of which is suggested by some common terms of our constitutional discourse: public figure, public forum, public purpose, public use. A term is useful when it is adapted to its context. In the field of civil rights, the relevant context is the equal citizenship guaranteed by the Civil War Amendments and their implementing legislation. A century of legal doctrine has trained us, when we think of private discrimination, to draw an implicit distinction between governmental and nongovernmental actors. But in ordinary speech it is also common to distinguish between the public and the private in quite a different way, differentiating our shared public life from our separate private lives. One major source of difficulty for civil rights law, both constitutional and statutory, is the tendency to assume that these two different public-private distinctions are congruent. Everyone understands that law and government are part of the commu-

---

[26]Litwack, note 18 *supra*, at 261–67.

[27]*Id*. at 262.

[28]*Id*. at 263–64. See also Hyman & Wiecek, note 24 *supra*, at 423–26.

[29]See generally Woodward, The Strange Career of Jim Crow (2d rev. ed. 1966); Williamson, The Crucible of Race: Black-White Relations in the American South Since Emancipation (1984); Dollard, Caste and Class in a Southern Town (Anchor ed. 1957).

nity's public life. And the idea that each of us should control his or her own private life has great appeal in a society with a strong tradition of individualism.[30] It is easy, and perhaps also morally convenient, for us to slide from those generalizations into the assumption that our public life consists entirely of dealings with government actors, and that whatever nongovernmental actors do is part of their private lives—their own business and nobody else's.

That assumption is profoundly mistaken. Translated into law, the assumption leads away from the substance of equal citizenship and toward the model of formal racial neutrality, and then to a series of specific legal doctrines. The doctrines begin with the "state action" limitation to the Fourteenth Amendment,[31] but do not end there.[32] Before we turn to those doctrines, it will be helpful to recall the ways in which racial discrimination by nongovernmental actors deforms our public life.

The longest-lasting and most damaging legacy of the system of racial caste is racism. The very word is off-putting to most whites, for it has taken on a connotation that implies the malevolence of the skinhead. The issue is not that simple. The most serious problem of racism is not a problem of evil hearts, but of culture, that is, the meanings that we learn to assign to our experience.[33] Necessarily, we usually assign those meanings without reflecting on what we are doing; life is too short to pause and reflect on everything we see and do. The unreflective meanings that white Americans project on black Americans[34] are the product of multiple aspects of the dominant culture. Our strong individualism trains us to believe that people succeed and fail individually. Yet, without dropping a stitch, we go on from this belief to the assumption that if substantial numbers of blacks do not succeed, the explanation must lie in some failing of

[30]On the potential for the subordination of women in this private sphere, see Powers, Sex Segregation and the Ambivalent Directions of Sex Discrimination Law, 1979 Wis. L. Rev. 55; Olsen, The Family and the Market: A Study of Ideology and Legal Reform, 96 Harv. L. Rev. 1497 (1983).

[31]Discussed in the text at note 53 *infra*.

[32]Other doctrinal implications of the model are discussed in the text at note 88 *infra*.

[33]See Karst, Belonging to America: Equal Citizenship and the Constitution 21–26, 40–42, 64–69, 73–80 (1989).

[34]See generally Lawrence, note 14 *supra*. See also Crenshaw, note 14 *supra*, at 1373 (list of traits historically ascribed by racist ideology to whites and blacks). A Louis Harris poll commissioned by the NAACP Legal Defense and Educational Fund suggests a considerable, but incomplete, departure from these images among American whites over the last generation. See NAACP Legal Defense and Educational Fund, Inc., The Unfinished Agenda on Race in America 1–51 (1989).

blacks as a group. This awkward transition from individualist to group-based assumption is eased by two emotions that lie at the margins of consciousness. First, there is the wish to justify our own status in two contrary ways: as earned, and as the result of some innate qualities. Second, there is fear: the fear of violent response, and the fear of displacement from a favorable status. The entire process is closely tied to the defense of private interests; it is a direct descendant of the race-based apologies for slavery. The main difference is that in our time, the assignment of meanings to our experience of race relations often is unexpressed, even suppressed from conscious thought, and held by people who—genuinely—have the best of will. It is understandable why most of us try to suppress pain and guilt and fear.

In any culture beliefs and behavior reinforce each other. The behavior we call private discrimination is not just the result of racism but the cause of further racism. If you are white and you have no black neighbors, it is hard for you to know any black person well, and easy for your day-to-day assumptions about blacks as a group to be dominated by those acculturated generalizations. The result is not merely the inability of a family to buy a particular home; the cumulative effect of this pattern—which is present in all our cities[35]—is to reinforce a status difference based on race that affects the whole society. It is hard to imagine any result that is more "public" in nature. The harm of private discrimination is not limited to its direct victims. All society suffers.

Given the high level of residential segregation, the workplace becomes our main opportunity for acquaintance across the racial divisions that afflict us all. Furthermore, work in America is a major determinant of individual status. Part of the status-affecting feature of work is the income it produces, and the wealth a family can accumulate. But work is also a way of expressing one's ability in ways that are visible to others. The point is not just self-expression; in this context of race relations, work ranks with schooling in educating us about people of other races and cultures. In the aggregate, these employment opportunities—especially in the private sector—are crucial to the public status of subordinated groups. An incident of racial harassment on the job, of course, is completely antithetical to inte-

---

[35]See Jaynes & Williams, eds., A Common Destiny: Blacks and American Society 78–79, 89–91, 144–46 (1989); Collin & Morris, Racial Inequality in American Cities: An Interdisciplinary Critique, 11 Nat'l Black L.J. 177, 179–86 (1989).

gration of the workplace;[36] multiplied by the hundreds of thousands, it is antithetical to the integration of American society, as is the separation of the races in private employment—whether or not that separation results from the employer's conscious purpose.

What happens in the marketplace and in the workplace, then, has vital consequences for the social status, even the political status, of black people as a group, and therefore the status of every individual black man and woman and child.[37] The history of ethnic integration in America is in great measure an economic history: as the overwhelming majority of a social group come to enter the middle class, individual members of the group come to be recognized as equal citizens.[38] Correspondingly, both in the workplace and in the marketplace, the indignities imposed by private racial discrimination not only hurt people one by one but also impose a "status-harm"[39] on a racial group, reinforcing the group's subordination.

Perhaps this process of reinforcement is easier to understand when one is a member of the subordinated group—such as the editor who remarked in 1867 on the way private discriminatory behavior hindered blacks in their efforts to claim their citizenship. But there is more to the problem of private discrimination than the editor mentioned in the quoted passage. The marketplace and the workplace not only affect the sphere of public life that is governmental; they are themselves a major sphere of public life. To end the effects of racial caste, it will not be enough—it has never been enough—to do away with discriminatory laws. Even without those laws, private discrimination will perpetuate the effects of racial caste; to accomplish that end, all that is needed from government is formal racial neutrality.

B. THE NEAR-CONSTITUTIONAL STATUS OF THE RECONSTRUCTION CIVIL RIGHTS ACTS

From the beginning, the fates of the Reconstruction civil rights laws have been bound up with the fates of the Thirteenth, Fourteenth, and Fifteenth Amendments. For a century and a quarter,

---

[36]See, for example, Brenda Patterson's story, in the text at note 96 *infra*.

[37]For two poignant personal statements by young, successful, upper-middle-class black men, see Walton, Willie Horton and Me, N.Y. Times Magazine, Aug. 20, 1989, p. 52; Standard, A Young Black Man Asks: Will I Be Next?, N.Y. Times, Sept. 2, 1989, p. 13, col. 2.

[38]See Karst, note 33 *supra*, ch. 6.

[39]Fiss, Groups and the Equal Protection Clause, 5 Phil & Pub. Aff. 107, 157 (1976).

their judicial interpretations have waxed and waned together. During the long years when the Supreme Court was imposing restricted meanings on the Civil War Amendments, it was also interpreting the Reconstruction laws narrowly, particularly by denying their application to private racial discrimination.[40] As the Justices came to read those amendments more broadly, they also expanded their interpretations of the civil rights laws to reach more private conduct.[41] The Supreme Court has regularly and properly interpreted the Reconstruction laws as if they had a special near-constitutional status as close relatives of the Civil War Amendments.

If judges and commentators have seen the civil rights acts and the Civil War Amendments as parts of a substantive package, the explanation begins in the circumstances of their adoption. All were adopted within a single decade,[42] with a considerable overlap of sponsorship and authorship. They were all seen as parts of the Nation's continuing effort to end slavery and the subordination of a race, to convert slaves into free citizens. At each step along this legislative path, historians of the present generation have found statements by congressional sponsors that the legislation about to be adopted would secure freedom—not formal freedom but real freedom, the substance of freedom—for those who had been enslaved.[43]

---

[40]Two very early examples are United States v. Cruikshank, 92 U.S. 542 (1876) (1870 act's protection of rights "granted and secured" by the Constitution did not apply to private persons' concerted action in breaking up an assembly of blacks and lynching two men); and United States v. Reese, 92 U.S. 214 (1876) (1870 act given hypertechnical construction, so that it did not apply to the refusal of a Kentucky election inspector to receive the ballot of a black voter).

[41]See, e.g., Note, 66 Harv. L. Rev. 1285 (1953), remarking on the "rediscovery" of the statutes that are now codified in 42 U.S.C. §1983 and 1985(3), and pointing out the steady growth in the number of actions filed under those statutes: from 21 to 166 in fiscal years 1944 and 1952, respectively. Id. 1285 and n.1. This rediscovery took place during the period in which the Supreme Court decided such landmark "state action" cases as Smith v. Allwright, 321 U.S. 649 (1944); Screws v. United States, 325 U.S. 91 (1945); and Shelley v. Kraemer, 334 U.S. 1 (1948). Neil Cogan has shown how the Court's interpretation of the central prohibition in the Ku Klux Klan Act of 1871, now condensed and codified in 42 U.S.C. §1985(3), has followed this pattern. Cogan, Section 1985(3)'s Reconstruction of Equality: An Essay on Texts, History, Progress, and Cynicism, 39 Rutgers L. Rev. 575 (1987). Cogan argues persuasively that the 1871 Act's framers saw Section 1985(3) as a charter of "universal equality," extending well beyond concerns about animus based on race or ethnicity. His discussion of two race cases supports the narrower point I make in the text. Id. at 519–23, 527–32, discussing United States v. Harris, 106 U.S. 629 (1883), and Griffin v. Breckenridge, 403 U.S. 88 (1971).

[42]Here is a chronological list: Thirteenth Amendment (1865), Civil Rights Act of 1866, Fourteenth Amendment (1868), Fifteenth Amendment (1870), Civil Rights Act of 1870 (Enforcement Act), Civil Rights Act of 1871 (Ku Klux Klan Act), Civil Rights Act of 1875.

[43]E.g., Hyman & Wiecek, note 24 supra, ch. 8–12; Foner, note 17 supra, at 244–51, 258. Two recent articles explicitly focused on the Patterson reargument are Sullivan, Historical Reconstruction, Reconstruction History, and the Proper Scope of Section 1981, 98 Yale L.J. 541 (1989), and Kaczorowski, The Enforcement Provisions of the Civil Rights Act of 1866: A Leg-

A good example is the law involved in *Patterson*, the Civil Rights Act of 1866,[44] which was seen by its main sponsors as giving specific content to the Thirteenth Amendment's abolition of slavery. Because slavery had been founded on an assumption of racial inferiority, it had maintained a complete exclusion of black people from the community of citizens.[45] The 1866 Act began with a declaration of citizenship that would include the newly freed slaves, and proceeded to list a number of rights that would attach to them as citizens: the same rights as white citizens to make and enforce contracts, to own or lease or deal with property, to be secure in their persons, to have access to the courts as parties or witnesses. The freed slaves were also to have the same responsibilities as white citizens, not only to be responsible for their contracts and other dealings, but to be subjected to the same penalties in the criminal process. Plainly the framers of the 1866 Act understood that citizenship was more than a formality; it required the underpinnings of substantive rights and responsibilities that added up to participation in the community of free and equal citizens.[46] Yet the framers did not say with any clarity that they intended the act to forbid discrimination by nongovernmental actors.[47]

---

islative History in Light of Runyon v. McCrary, 98 Yale L.J. 565 (1989). A similarly focused argument for a restrictive view of the intentions of the framers of the 1866 Act is presented by McClellan, The Foibles and Fables of Runyon, 67 Wash. U.L.Q. 13 (1989).

[44]14 Stat. 74 (1866). Justice White, dissenting in *Runyon*, argued that §1981 should be considered to be based not on the 1866 Act, which the framers saw as founded on Congress's power to enforce the Thirteenth Amendment, but on the reenactment of almost the same language in the Enforcement Act of 1870; that the 1870 Act was designed to enforce the Fourteenth Amendment, and thus implicitly included a "state action" limitation; and that when the revisers compiled the Revised Statutes (1874), they described §1977, which embodies what is now §1981, as based not on the 1866 Act but on the 1870 Act. This argument is imaginative, but it assumes that Congress in adopting the Revised Statutes meant, without discussion, to repeal the 1866 Act on the basis of the revisers' notes. To call this argument unpersuasive is, of course, not to say that the *Runyon* majority was right in claiming to have discovered a clear purpose of the framers of the 1866 Act to forbid private discrimination. For powerful arguments to the contrary, in the context of *Runyon*'s predecessor decision, see Casper, Jones v. Mayer: Clio, Bemused and Confused Muse, 1968 Supreme Court Review 89; Fairman, VI Holmes Devise History of the Supreme Court: Reconstruction and Reunion, 1864–88 (part one) 1207–59 (1971).

[45]The Supreme Court's decision in Dred Scott v. Sandford, 19 How. 393 (1857), purported to extend this exclusion to free blacks—making clear that the subordination in question was based on race.

[46]See Karst, note 33 *supra*, at 49–51.

[47]The cloudiness of the legislative history on this precise issue has engendered a considerable literature, including many briefs and articles focused on the reargument of *Patterson*. The most persuasive contributions to this debate, in my judgment, are the ones recognizing the difficulties attending strong conclusions about the framers' intentions to forbid or not to forbid what we now call private discrimination. See, *e.g.*, Sullivan, note 43 *supra*; Hyman & Wiecek, note 24 *supra*, ch. 11.

The text of the act, including the "same right . . . to make and en-force contracts," is broad enough to embrace the reading the Su-preme Court gave it in *Runyon v. McCrary*. Furthermore, the act's framers understood that "Freedom was much more than the absence of slavery. It was, like slavery, an evolving, enlarging matrix of both formal and customary relationships rather than a sterile catalog."[48] What we now call private discrimination was certainly a major part of the general problem the framers were addressing: the exclusion of black people from real citizenship.[49] If they did not focus on the question that later divided the Supreme Court in *Runyon v. McCrary*, it is hard to fault them for failing to use the categories of a later time.

The main immediate purpose of the Fourteenth Amendment, pro-posed to the states in 1866 and ratified in 1868, was to "constitu-tionalize" the 1866 Act, not only by authorizing Congress to adopt such legislation but also by putting the act's guarantees into the Con-stitution where they would be secure against the possibility of repeal by a later Congress.[50] The framers of the Fourteenth Amendment did not specifically intend it to forbid some kinds of racial discrimi-nation that we now understand to be wholly inconsistent with equal citizenship—racial segregation, for example. But the framers were aware that the content of equal citizenship might grow in ways that could be recognized by the judges of later generations.[51]

Because the framers of the Reconstruction statutes and the Civil War Amendments saw Congress as the primary agency for develop-ing the content of civil rights, it was natural for the substantive rights of citizens established in the 1866 Act to be closely intertwined with the substantive rights protected by the Thirteenth and Fourteenth Amendments. Given the 1866 Act's near-constitutional status, it was predictable that the act's interpretation would expand along with the growth in the meaning of those two amendments. It is entirely legiti-mate for today's courts to interpret the 1866 Act in ways that outstrip the details of its framers' expectations.[52] Specifically, given the

---

[48]*Id.* at 391–92.

[49]See *id.* at ch. 11; Foner, note 17 *supra*, at 258.

[50]See, *e.g.*, Casper, note 44 *supra*, at 122–23; Fairman, note 44 *supra*, at 1270–1300; Berger, Government by Judiciary 23 (1977).

[51]See Fairman, note 44 *supra*, at 1328; Bickel, The Original Understanding and the Segrega-tion Decision, 69 Harv. L. Rev. 1, 63 (1955); Hyman & Wiecek, note 24 *supra*, ch. 11; Karst, note 33 *supra*, at 51–56.

[52]For the argument that §1985(3) similarly should be read as a "corollary to the equal protec-tion clause," and interpreted with an eye to today's equal protection doctrine, see Gormley,

continuing central role of private discrimination in maintaining the subordination of a race, it lies within the range of permissible interpretations for today's judges to read the act as a broad charter of freedom, forbidding private as well as governmental discrimination. *Runyon* deserved reaffirmation because it was rightly decided.

C. THE "STATE ACTION" BARRIER: INVENTION AND CIRCUMVENTION

In the years immediately following Reconstruction, however, the Supreme Court read both the civil rights acts and the Civil War Amendments narrowly. In 1883 the Court decided the *Civil Rights Cases*,[53] still the most influential source for the doctrinal model of formal racial neutrality. The decision rests on three interpretive assumptions, each of which is highly questionable. First, the Court assumed, the Thirteenth Amendment is limited to slavery itself, and other forms of private discrimination are not "badges of slavery." Second, the Court assumed that the Fourteenth Amendment forbids only "state action," requiring the state only to adopt a formal, official neutrality concerning race relations. So long as the state maintains this formally neutral posture, the substantive inequalities imposed by private discrimination are, from the Constitution's standpoint, not the state's responsibility. The Court's third assumption was that Congress, in enforcing the Fourteenth Amendment, is empowered to reach only "state action," and not private discrimination.

In the last Reconstruction civil rights law, the Civil Rights Act of 1875, Congress sought to advance substantive equality by prohibiting racial discrimination in hotels, theaters, railroads, and other places of public accommodation. One obvious implication is that the law's framers (including some who had been framers of the Civil War Amendments and the 1866 Act) saw no constitutional impediment to congressional regulation of private discrimination. Unfortunately for the cause of equal citizenship, the 1875 Act came along just in time to be steamrollered by the political deal that ended Reconstruction. In the Compromise of 1877, the Democrats conceded the disputed presidential election of 1876 to the Republican candidate, Rutherford B. Hayes, in exchange for the withdrawal of federal troops from the South and the effective end of Reconstruction.[54] A

Private Conspiracies and the Constitution: A Modern Vision of 42 U.S.C. Section 1985(3), 64 Texas L. Rev. 527, 564 and *passim* (1985).

[53] 109 U.S. 3.

[54] See Woodward, Reunion and Reaction: The Compromise of 1877 and the End of Reconstruction (1966).

key member of the commission that produced this settlement was Justice Bradley, and it was not just the luck of the draw that assigned Bradley the Supreme Court's opinion in the *Civil Rights Cases*.[55] Making all three of the restrictive assumptions I have listed, Bradley and the Court held that the 1875 Act exceeded Congress's powers under either the Thirteenth or the Fourteenth Amendment.

To reach the conclusion that private racial discrimination was not a badge of slavery, the Justices had to ignore that slavery had been founded on race, and that a theory of racial inferiority had been the central argument of slavery's defenders. If the Justices were not simply dissembling, they were assigning to formal legal changes an extraordinary power to start the world anew. In this perspective of formal neutrality, the abolition of slavery and the Fourteenth Amendment's declaration of equal citizenship were seen as erasing the history of racial subordination and the continuing effects of that history—as if a culture and a society could be changed at their foundations by the wave of a legal wand.

Frederick Douglass indulged in no such illusions. He understood from his own experience how discrimination by nongovernmental actors continued to reinforce status inequalities in the post-abolition world. In a speech criticizing the decision in the *Civil Rights Cases*, he pointed out the connection between equal citizenship and equal access to privately owned public accommodations. Some of the crucial elements in that connection were states of mind. Private prejudice translated into public humiliation.[56] Although Douglass described the decision as "a painful and bewildering surprise," "a blow from an unexpected quarter,"[57] the Supreme Court had already begun its own retreat from Reconstruction.[58] Surely, too, most members of the Congress sitting in 1883 shared the prevailing political consensus among whites, which accepted the deal that had unified the white North and the white South.

In the generation following the *Civil Rights Cases*, for those who would promote a racial equality that was not just formal but real, things went from bad to worse. Both politics and legal doctrine re-

---

[55]See Scott, Justice Bradley's Evolving Concept of the Fourteenth Amendment from the Slaughterhouse Cases to the Civil Rights Cases, 25 Rutgers L. Rev. 552 (1971).

[56]Douglass, Life and Times of Frederick Douglass 539–53 (1962 reprint of 1892 rev. ed.).

[57]*Id*. at 540.

[58]See Goldstein, Blyew: Variations on a Jurisdictional Theme, 41 Stan. L. Rev. 469 (1989); Hyman & Wiecek, note 24 *supra*, at 496–97.

flected this deterioration, neutralizing the effects of the Civil War Amendments and the Reconstruction civil rights acts. In the South, Jim Crow's culture of subordination remained intact until the eve of the Second World War. The turnaround began in the 1940s, with political changes again matched by changes in constitutional doctrine. The great breakthrough, of course, came in the next decade and was led by the Supreme Court. For the modern constitutional era, as Philip Kurland has said, "At the beginning there was *Brown v. Board of Education.*"[59] By the end of the 1950s the Court had effectively held unconstitutional all forms of state-sponsored racial segregation.

In the 1960s, however, both legislators and judges confronted a discomfiting reality that northern whites had not fully apprehended a decade earlier: the pervasiveness and effectiveness of private discrimination in maintaining the stigma of caste. In the South, Jim Crow's private aspects still flourished, and still included a measure of violence.[60] In the North, where law and government were largely cleansed of explicit racial subordination, a more informal kind of discrimination found its most typical expression in private behavior, from landlords to labor unions. Both North and South, racially discriminatory behavior was intertwined with beliefs about racial inferiority.

It has always been easy for white Americans to look at individual blacks and see an abstraction: the Other, the projection of whites' own negative identities.[61] In these circumstances an end to the stigma of racial caste may be threatening to whites who fear the loss of a status based on whiteness.[62] If there is any iron law of society, it is this: status and substance are mutually reinforcing. Group-based inequalities in the material world of jobs and housing and health reinforce a group's subordinate status: if the Other are treated poorly, so the "stigma-theory"[63] goes, they must be getting what they deserve. In turn, the stigma itself serves to justify further unequal treatment. In North and South alike the achievement of equal citizenship would require not only the protection of formally equal laws but also

[59]Kurland, Politics, the Constitution, and the Warren Court 26 (1970).

[60]Two grisly examples that came before the Supreme Court are found in United States v. Price, 383 U.S. 787 (1966), and United States v. Guest, 383 U.S. 745 (1966). See generally Belknap, Federal Law and Southern Order: Racial Violence and Constitutional Conflict in the Post-Brown South (1987).

[61]See generally Karst, note 33 *supra*, at 21–27.

[62]See *id*. at 148–51; Dollard, note 29 *supra*, *passim* (1957).

[63]Goffman, Stigma: Notes on the Management of Spoiled Identity 5 (1963).

an effort to reduce private fears and change patterns of private behavior.

The desegregation of governmental institutions had been carried on by the courts in the name of the Equal Protection Clause of the Fourteenth Amendment. But that Amendment's jurisprudence, still gripped by the dead hand of the *Civil Rights Cases*, continued to assume that the Amendment forbade only governmental action. Now that private discrimination had come into clearer focus as a major contributor to racial subordination, there was increasing pressure on the "state action" barrier—and the barrier began to crack. In the early 1960s the Warren Court began to solve the "state action" problem by finding "significant state involvement" in a number of private arrangements.[64] Some such circumvention of the *Civil Rights Cases* was necessary to bring the Fourteenth Amendment to bear on various forms of private discrimination that seriously impaired black people's participation in the community of equal citizens. At the same time the Court studiously avoided the question whether the *Civil Rights Cases* should be overruled or radically modified.

The Court was relieved of facing that question when legislative politics took a hand. After President Kennedy's assassination, Congress accelerated its consideration of broad-ranging civil rights legislation, including prohibitions against private racial discrimination by employers and by the operators of hotels, restaurants, and other places of public accommodation. Congress had plenary power to regulate interstate commerce, but some members were concerned about using the commerce power as a pretext for achieving goals of racial equality.[65] Congress's power to enforce the Fourteenth Amendment seemed more to the point, but the "state action" barrier still looked formidable. The public accommodations title of the proposed bill bore a strong resemblance to the 1875 Act that had been held unconstitutional in the *Civil Rights Cases*, and the Supreme Court thus far had been cautious in lowering the barrier. Thus, many in Congress felt uneasy about an effort to rely on the Fourteenth Amendment to regulate private discrimination. After some soul-searching about its own legislative powers, Congress decided to rest the Civil Rights Act

---

[64]The cases are catalogued in Black, The Supreme Court, 1966 Term—Foreword: "State Action," Equal Protection, and California's Proposition 14, 81 Harv. L. Rev. 69 (1987), and in Karst & Horowitz, Reitman v. Mulkey: A Telophase of Substantive Equal Protection, 1967 Supreme Court Review 39.

[65]These doubts were expressed in the Senate hearings, excerpted in Gunther, Constitutional Law 159–62 (11th ed. 1985).

of 1964 on two constitutional bases: on its power to regulate interstate commerce and on a conservative view of its power to enforce the
Fourteenth Amendment. Thus the Act regulated private racial discrimination by public accommodations only to the extent that it
"affect[ed] commerce" or could be brought within conventional definitions of "state action."[66]

Around the same time the Supreme Court began to send new signals to Congress. Even before the 1964 Act became law, some
Justices—including Justice Black, who had resisted finding "state
action" in private conduct that was only tenuously related to governmental action—had hinted that Congress might have the power to
forbid private racial discrimination.[67] And when the Court rushed to
uphold the constitutionality of the 1964 Act under the commerce
power, Justice Douglas's concurring opinion said the law was valid
under Congress's power to enforce the Fourteenth Amendment.[68]
Two years later, in *United States v. Guest*, six Justices agreed in two
separate opinions that Congress could constitutionally protect Fourteenth Amendment rights against private invasion.[69] The clear message was that the Warren Court was nibbling at one of the important
holdings in the *Civil Rights Cases*,[70] and was encouraging Congress to
go ahead with further civil rights legislation.[71] If the Congress was
paying attention to the Court in the 1960s, the Court was itself paying attention to Congress's implicit statements, in the 1964 Act and
in the Voting Rights Act of 1965, that the civil rights cause now had a
broad national constituency. In the civil rights field, this pattern of
Court-Congress interaction has prevailed since Reconstruction. Of
course, both the Court and the Congress were divided on many civil

---

[66]No one in Congress in 1964 seems to have considered seriously what the framers of the
1866 Act would have taken for granted: that the law might be valid under Congress's power to
enforce the Thirteenth Amendment.

[67]Bell v. Maryland, 378 U.S. 226, 343 (1964) (Back, J. dissenting).

[68]Heart of Atlanta Motel v. United States, 379 U.S. 241 (1984); Katzenbach v. McClung,
379 U.S. 294 (1964).

[69]383 U.S. 745 at 762 (Clark, J., concurring), at 777 (Brennan, J., concurring in part and
dissenting in part).

[70]The word "nibbling" is appropriate. A power to protect Fourteenth Amendment rights
against private interference was not a generalized power to remedy private discrimination, but
a power to protect the exercise of rights that could be claimed against the state. For a pre-*Guest*
example of this theory in operation, see Brewer v. Hoxie School Dist. No. 46, 238 F.2d 91 (8th
Cir. 1956) (using federal civil rights law to enjoin private actors who were harassing school
officials involved in desegregating schools under court order).

[71]Around the same time the Court sent further signals in the voting rights cases of South
Carolina v. Katzenbach, 383 U.S. 301 (1966), and Katzenbach v. Morgan, 384 U.S. 641 (1966).

rights issues. All the back-and-forth signaling was mainly important
in giving encouragement to the Justices and legislators who sought to
make good on the promise of freedom in the Civil War Amendments
and the Reconstruction civil rights acts.

Soon after the *Guest* decision the issue of Congress's power under
the Fourteenth Amendment to forbid private racial discrimination
receded from view, for the Court found just such a power in the Thirteenth Amendment. The year was 1968, and the case was *Jones v. Alfred H. Mayer Co.*[72] A private real estate developer had refused to sell
houses and lots to black applicants. The would-be buyers argued
that the developer's conduct constituted "state action," because of the
size of the development (about 1,000 residents), the developer's continuing responsibility within the tract, and the state's regulation of
land development. The Court, however, avoided this opportunity
for further erosion of the "state action" barrier, instead resting
decision for the black applicants on their second—and more far-
reaching—argument.

That argument had two parts, and the Court accepted both of
them. First, the Court held that the developer's refusal to sell violated the provision of the Civil Rights Act of 1866, today codified in
42 U.S.C. §1982, giving "all citizens . . . the same right [as white
citizens] to inherit, purchase, lease, sell, hold, and convey real and
personal property."[73] In so deciding, the Court overruled several of
its own precedents interpreting the 1866 Act, including its dictum in
the *Civil Rights Cases* describing the act as merely "corrective" of
"state laws and proceedings, and customs having the force of law."[74]
The *Jones* Court held that the 1866 Act not only was aimed at legal
disabilities imposed by state law, but also forbade private racial discrimination in dealings with property. Second, the Court held that
such private racial discrimination was a badge of slavery that Congress could eradicate under its power to enforce the Thirteenth
Amendment, a power concededly not subject to any "state action"
limitation. This ruling overruled the narrow (and history-ignoring)
definition of badges of slavery adopted when the Court interpreted
the Thirteenth Amendment in the *Civil Rights Cases*. Justice Harlan,

[72]392 U.S. 409 (1968).

[73]Initially, the plaintiffs had also claimed under §1981, the provision involved in *Patterson*.
See Jones v. Alfred H. Mayer Co., 225 F. Supp. 115 (E.D. Mo. 1966). The Supreme Court,
however, rested decision only on §1982.

[74]109 U.S. at 16.

joined by Justice White, dissented from the Court's interpretation of Section 1982, and expressed strong reservations about Congress's Thirteenth Amendment power to forbid private discrimination.

The "state action" barrier of the Fourteenth Amendment was now circumvented in two ways. First, even if the *Guest* opinions were not to be expanded into a broad Fourteenth Amendment congressional power to forbid private racial discrimination, Congress could do precisely that under its power to enforce the Thirteenth Amendment, which had no "state action" limitation. Second, although the Fourteenth Amendment standing alone (without any congressional enforcement legislation) might still be limited to "state action"—on this score, the *Civil Rights Cases* precedent remains strong even today—Section 1982 filled the gap, supplying a federal cause of action against private discrimination in property dealings.[75]

Once again, the Court's reading of a Reconstruction civil rights law was interwoven with its reading of one of the Civil War Amendments. Now, however, the readings were expansive rather than confining. Given all the agonizing in the 1960s over the possibilities of bringing federal law to bear on private racial discrimination, both of the Court's doctrinal conclusions were of major importance to the civil rights movement. Strenuous labors had been necessary to bring the Court to *Jones's* solution of some of the problems created by the *Civil Rights Cases*. Now those earlier efforts to get around the "state action" barrier were superseded in one grand circumvention. The Supreme Court could stop straining to find state involvement in private discrimination. The cautious limitations built into the public accommodations title of the Civil Rights Act of 1964—reaching only activity affecting commerce or activity that could be called "state action"—could now be eliminated.[76] Such nibbling at the *Civil Rights Cases* as the Justices had done in those two *Guest* opinions was no longer needed. The "state action" barrier still prevented litigants from attacking private racial discrimination on the basis of the Fourteenth Amendment standing alone, but Congress now had a green light.

---

[75]On the kinds of "state action" issues the Supreme Court might have to face if *Runyon* were overruled, and similar causes of action were unavailable under Section 1981, see Rotunda, Runyon v. McCrary and the Mosaic of State Action, 67 Wash. U.L.Q. 47, 54–57 (1989).

[76]Indeed, the courts might have gone back to enforcing the Civil Rights Act of 1875, which was in some ways broader than the public accommodations title of the 1964 Act. See Nimmer, A Proposal for Judicial Validation of a Previously Unconstitutional Law: The Civil Rights Act of 1875, 65 Colum. L. Rev. 1394 (1965).

At least as important, in the long run, was another feature of *Jones*'s recognition of racial discrimination as a badge of slavery. That recognition served as an official declaration about the way private racist beliefs and private discriminatory behavior reinforce each other. And, of course, it was the *Jones* precedent that the Court followed eight years later in *Runyon v. McCrary* in holding that Section 1981 prohibited private discrimination in the making of contracts.

D. THE PATTERSON REAFFIRMATION

All this and more seemed threatened by the suggestion that the *Runyon* precedent was up for grabs. In the end, however, *Patterson*'s reaffirmation turned out to be a civil rights milestone. If *Runyon* had been overruled, it is hard to imagine any persuasive distinction that would protect *Jones* from overruling, at least on its statutory interpretation ground. Indeed, a majority that refused to read the 1866 Act to prohibit private discrimination might also be so attracted by a principle of formal neutrality as to think *Jones* mistaken in its other conclusion: that private discrimination was a badge of slavery subject to Congress's Thirteenth Amendment power.[77] Probably the Justices who ordered the *Patterson* reargument were not looking ahead to a restriction of Congress's constitutional power to reach private discrimination. But if we see the reargument order through the eyes of the civil rights advocates who mobilized the political response, it is hard to call their reaction excessive.[78]

The Justices who voted for reargument, surprised and defensive at the vehemence of the dissenters' objections, went out of their way to say that the reargument order did not mean they had decided to overrule *Runyon*. Perhaps, too, the majority Justices were surprised by the strength of the bipartisan political outcry against their order. An impressively wide range of amici curiae filed briefs asking the Court not to overrule *Runyon*: not only all those Senators and Representatives and state attorneys general, but scores of organizations from the Na-

---

[77]For one such suggestion that reached print, see Kushner, The Fair Housing Amendments Act of 1988: The Second Generation of Fair Housing, 42 Vand. L. Rev. 1049, 1112 (1989). But see Farber, Statutory Interpretation, Legislative Inaction, and Civil Rights, 87 Mich. L. Rev. 2, 5–6 (1989) (validity of *Jones* precedent probably was not in issue). Justice White, who had joined in Justice Harlan's *Jones* dissent expressing doubt about congressional power, had been no more reassuring in his *Runyon* dissent: "I do not question *at this point* the power of Congress or a state legislature to ban racial discrimination in private school admissions decisions. . . ." 427 U.S. at 193 n.2 (emphasis added).

[78]For a sample of some of the expressions of alarm, see Farber, note 77 *supra*, at 2 n.3 (1988).

tional Lawyers Guild to the American Bar Association. Almost certainly the majority Justices did not see themselves as wreckers out to destroy the fabric of civil rights law governing private discrimination, so laboriously constructed over the past quarter-century. More probably they had thought something like this: Well, yes, the interpretation in *Runyon* may well have gone beyond the intentions of the framers of the 1866 Act. We should think about that question before we go on to decide whether Section 1981 should be extended[79] to provide still another remedy, one that Congress chose not to include in Title VII of the 1964 Act.

When the shouting was over, the majority drew back, and instead polished the doctrine of stare decisis anew. But something had been added. The Court's previous interpretations of the 1866 Act and of Congress's Thirteenth Amendment power had seemed vulnerable to revision by the Court's new majority. Yet both the *Runyon* dissenters and all three of the Justices appointed in the 1980s joined in the reaffirmance of *Runyon*. Two important doctrinal propositions now seem secure for the indefinite future. First, the 1866 Act (in Sections 1981 and 1982) stands as a generalized prohibition against many forms of private racial discrimination in contract and property dealings. Second, Congress's power to enforce the Thirteenth Amendment includes a broad power to prohibit private racial discrimination. The *Jones-Runyon* circumvention of the "state action" barrier is now confirmed by a unanimous Court.

For civil rights advocates this development is not just the absence of bad news. The judicial climate for civil rights is markedly more chilly than it was in 1968, when *Jones* was decided. As *Patterson* itself indicates, nowadays civil rights advocates must look to Congress for the extension—even for the maintenance—of civil rights remedies. Surely they cannot look for the recently reconstituted federal judiciary[80] to be sympathetic to those ends. It is all the more remarkable, then, that the Supreme Court has renewed its invitation to Congress

---

[79]In referring to an extension of §1981, I am imagining someone else's thinking here. The lower courts, until the Fourth Circuit's decision in *Patterson*, had assumed that §1981 did provide a damages remedy for a private employer's racial harassment. *E.g.*, Goodman v. Lukens Steel Co., 580 F. Supp. 1114 (E.D. Pa. 1984), aff'd without explicitly addressing the harassment issue, 482 U.S. 656 (1987); Taylor v. Jones, 653 F.2d 1193 (8th Cir. 1981); Williamson v. Handy Button Mach. Co., 817 F.2d 1290 (7th Cir. 1987). The Supreme Court's conclusion to the contrary in *Patterson* effectively changed existing law.

[80]See Goldman, Reagan's Second-term Judicial Appointments: The Battle at Midway, 70 Judicature 324 (1987); Wermiel, Reagan Choices Alter the Makeup and Views of the Federal Courts, Wall St. Journal, Feb. 1, 1988, p. 1, col. 1.

to use the power of federal law to eradicate the private discrimination that perpetuates the effects of the racial caste system.

II. From Formal Neutrality to Public Responsibility

Many of the civil rights issues that have recently divided the Supreme Court can be seen as modern versions of the general questions that were at stake in the *Civil Rights Cases*: questions about formal and substantive neutrality, and about responsibility for remedying inequalities. A century ago the Court opted in all respects for formal racial neutrality and limited responsibility. These preferences have never been completely submerged, not even while the Warren Court was giving new life to the principle of equal citizenship. Indeed, the Warren Court's earliest civil rights achievements can be seen as a redefinition of formal equality that placed "separate but equal" outside the constitutional pale. Yet, from the 1950s to the 1970s, the need for remedying a wide variety of forms of private discrimination was also recognized: for example, by the Warren Court's decisions relaxing the "state action" barrier,[81] by the Burger Court's acceptance of group remedies,[82] and by both Courts' generous construction of federal civil rights laws.[83] These civil rights decisions served to nourish a counter-tradition of public responsibility, not just to avoid perpetuating the effects of racial caste but to take positive action to end those effects.

Against this background, the 1980s have been a decade of discontinuity. In their civil rights opinions last Term, including *Patterson*, the Justices of the current majority sounded several of the Rehnquist Court's main civil rights themes: (1) Formal racial neutrality is the central command of the Civil War Amendments and the civil rights acts. (2) Already-established departures from that command, authorizing remedies against practices that perpetuate the effects of past discrimination, are under persistent attack within the Court, but those attacks are only occasionally successful; more often the prece-

[81]Reitman v. Mulkey, 387 U.S. 369 (1967), is a good example. The most satisfying explanation for the decision would be the recognition of a state responsibility for remedying private housing discrimination. See Karst and Horowitz, note 64 *supra*.

[82]*E.g.*, Griggs v. Duke Power Co., 401 U.S. 424 (1971), discussed in text at note 105 *infra* (private employment discrimination); Fullilove v. Klutznick, 448 U.S. 448 (1980), discussed in text at note 123 *infra* (affirmative action in federal spending program for local government contracting).

[83]*E.g.*, the *Jones* and *Runyon* decisions discussed at length above.

dents will be preserved. (3) New judicial interpretations in that direction, in the pattern of *Jones* and *Runyon*, are generally (but not always) to be avoided. When such departures are made, they are to be explained in the language of formal neutrality. (4) Congress, on the other hand, has wide legislative discretion to remedy substantive inequalities. In the pages that follow we shall look at the principle of formal racial equality, and at its recent uses by the Justices in two areas of civil rights law: private employment discrimination and affirmative action.

A. THE GRAVITATIONAL PULL OF THE MODEL OF FORMAL NEUTRALITY

Even today the Supreme Court does not interpret the Civil War Amendments and federal civil rights laws as if they wholly incorporated a doctrinal model of formal neutrality. Yet, such a model appears to be central in some Justices' vision of racial equality, and to enjoy varying degrees of appeal for other Justices.[84] What I am calling a model is a cluster of preferences. First is the preference for limited governmental responsibility, in which government's only legal duty is to avoid purposeful discrimination of its own. Second, the model embodies a preference for private ordering, and a corresponding aversion to governmental intervention in private decisions—in short, a preference for deregulation. To promote this preference, the courts should hold that the Constitution imposes no limitation on private discrimination and no responsibility on government to remedy private discrimination. Furthermore, congressional remedies for private discrimination should be narrowly interpreted, absent clear statement by Congress to the contrary. For example, the federal antidiscrimination laws should reach only purposeful racial discrimination. Third, even when governmental or private discrimination is proved, the model embodies a preference for individualized remedies.[85] This view favors two kinds of limits on civil rights remedies. First, a remedy should benefit only those who can prove that they are the direct victims of specifically identified acts of discrimination. Second, a remedy should burden only persons who have deliberately engaged in those acts or persons directly benefited by that wrongdo-

---

[84]The model doesn't explain anything; models never do. I offer this one as a perspective on issues concerning private racial discrimination.

[85]Alan Freeman, note 14 *supra*, explores a number of doctrinal and practical consequences of this preference, which he calls "the perpetrator perspective."

ing. Group remedies—remedies that take race into account in allocating burdens or benefits—are strongly disfavored.

In this model of formal neutrality, every arguably discriminatory act is evaluated without reference to its general societal context, as if history began this morning. The presumption is that present conditions—whatever they are—represent equilibrium, or race-neutrality. That presumption stands until a specific transgression of the norm of race-neutrality is proved by a claimant who satisfies a demanding burden of proof. Thus, every race-conscious remedy, imposed either by a legislative body or by a court, violates the norm unless it is a narrowly focused remedy for a previous (and particularly identified) violation. In the model of formal neutrality, nobody is responsible to remedy the present effects of slavery and Jim Crow and the myriad deformations of our public life produced by the stigma of caste. Indeed, an effort to remedy past societal discrimination is, under the model, a violation of the principle of race neutrality. The model of formal neutrality is a formula for avoiding public responsibility for private discrimination.

It can be argued that these doctrines represent not so much substantive preference as judicial self-limitation. A judge may believe that deference to Congress implies a refusal to "fill in the gaps" of a statute, on the assumption that a "gap" is just a legislative compromise by another name. Some years ago Frank Easterbrook offered a sensitive account of this position.[86] The broad language of many of our civil rights laws illustrates one of Judge Easterbrook's propositions: there may be more than one plausible answer to the question, Should this statute be "construed" as to the issue before the court or is there simply "no law on the subject"?[87] It seems clear that substantive preferences have considerable influence on judges' answers to this question. In particular, the preferences I have called the model of formal racial neutrality seem to have influenced a number of Justices, both in "construing" civil rights laws and in perceiving that Congress has chosen to enact "no law."

The model, in its pure form, would produce a number of legal doctrines. Some of these doctrines, invented in the *Civil Rights Cases*, are no longer embodied in present law: (i) the "state action" limitation on the power of Congress to enforce the Fourteenth Amendment

---

[86]Easterbrook, Statutes' Domains, 50 U. Chi. L. Rev. 533 (1987).

[87]*Id.* at 534–36.

(doubtful after *Guest*[88] and presumably finished off by *Richmond v. J. A. Croson Co.*[89]); (ii) limitation of Congress's power to enforce the Thirteenth Amendment to the abolition of slavery itself, excluding any power to forbid racial discrimination apart from slavery (after *Jones*, no longer good law); (iii) interpretation of the 1866 Civil Rights Act to require no more than equal state laws, thus rejecting any interpretation of the Act to forbid private discrimination (after *Jones*, *Runyon*, and *Patterson*, no longer good law). As this list shows, even for the members of the present Supreme Court majority who are most devoted to the model of formal neutrality, the influence of those preferences can be overcome by other considerations.

Yet the preferences retain considerable vitality, influencing decisions, or judicial rhetoric, or both, in several related doctrinal areas: (iv) the "state action" limitation on the Fourteenth Amendment's self-executing commands (still good law); (v) interpretation of the Civil War Amendments to forbid only purposeful racial discrimination, and to leave untouched other practices that produce racially disparate impacts (still good law); (vi) a similar interpretation of federal civil rights acts (partly good law and partly not, with the current majority pushing the law of private employment discrimination in the direction of the model of formal neutrality); and (vii) constitutional and statutory interpretations prohibiting affirmative action except as a highly particularized remedy for identifiable acts of discrimination (a view highly influential in current law, which nonetheless permits some significant departures from the model of formal neutrality).

The factor that most clearly distinguishes the doctrines that have been accepted from those that have not is, of course, congressional power. Some Justices who are disinclined for the Court to expand the reach of substantive civil rights and their corresponding remedies nonetheless support a broad power in Congress to do so.[90] It is entirely consistent for those Justices to refuse to recognize either rights or remedies in federal civil rights laws unless Congress has spoken with considerable clarity. Perhaps, as Owen Fiss suggested, some Justices are more comfortable in intruding into areas governed by

[88]Note 69 *supra*, discussed at pp. 38–46 *infra*.

[89]109 S.Ct. 706 (1989).

[90]Some of them are also receptive to state antidiscrimination legislation. See, *e.g.*, California Federal Savings and Loan Ass'n v. Guerra, 479 U.S. 272 (1984) (rejecting claim of federal preemption of state pregnancy discrimination law).

private ordering when they have the political backing of Congress.[91]
The clear statement requirement, however, suggests more than judicial reticence; private ordering itself is a value dear to the hearts of
some Justices. Alternatively, a willingness to defer to Congress may
reflect the awareness that Congress has a unique capability to allay
the fears of persons who feel threatened by group remedies, by
spreading the burdens of those remedies among all Americans.[92]
Like any other set of judicial preferences, the ones I call the model of
formal neutrality appear to have their strongest influence in cases
perceived by today's majority Justices as doctrinally marginal. One
way to characterize the gravitational pull of these preferences is to
say that they keep the margins of our civil rights law from expanding;
but the model's preferences are also capable of pulling the doctrinal
frontiers inward, and here—as in the employment discrimination
cases—it is appropriate to speak of civil rights retrenchment.

B. EMPLOYMENT DISCRIMINATION AND CIVIL RIGHTS DEREGULATION

When the Supreme Court in *Patterson* refused to read Section 1981
to forbid racial harassment by a private employer, the majority said
that the law's protection of the "same right . . . to make or enforce
contracts" forbade racial discrimination at the point of formation of a
contract (such as a race-based refusal to deal) and at the point of enforcement (such as a race-based denial of access to court), but not racial discrimination during a contract's performance. This distinction
is at odds with a basic norm of the law of contracts. One of the central
insights in that field of law has been the recognition that a contract—
especially a labor contract—is not just a text, not just an agreement,
but the totality of interrelations between the contracting parties
throughout the term of the contract's performance and enforcement.[93] Suppose the private schools involved in the *Runyon* case, hav-

---

[91]Fiss, Racial Discrimination, 3 Encyc. of Am. Const. 1500, 1503–04 (Levy, Karst & Ma-
honey, eds. 1986).

[92]Justice Scalia properly invoked The Federalist No. 10 (Madison) as another justification
for distinguishing between congressional power and state power. The idea was (and is) that in
the national legislature "factions" with strong local influence would tend to cancel each other.

[93]As Ian Macneil has perceptively written, one of the "primal roots" of contract law is the
"social matrix" of an agreement. Macneil, The Many Futures of Contracts, 47 So. Cal. L. Rev.
691. 710–12 (1974). See further *id*. at 710; 810. See also Uniform Commercial Code §1–201
(11), 1–201(3), and 1–205 (defining, respectively, "Contract," "Agreement," and "Course of
Dealing and Usage of Trade"). The law of labor contracts, from the common law to the National Labor Relations Act, has been especially sensitive to these concerns. See, for example,
Atleson, Values and Assumptions in American Labor Law 11 (1983).

ing admitted black pupils, now deliberately segregate them behind a bar in the back of each classroom. Are we to assume that Section 1981 provides no remedy? The Court's strained distinction is evidence that more was at work than an effort to parse the words of the statute.

The *Patterson* majority admitted as much, ultimately defending its interpretation on the ground that interpreting Section 1981 to cover "postformation conduct unrelated to an employee's right to enforce her contract" would "undermine the detailed and well-crafted procedures for conciliation and resolution of Title VII claims."[94] The Court reads Title VII of the 1964 Act as prohibiting an employer's racial harassment of an employee.[95] However, consider the remedies available in a Title VII case—chiefly injunction against further harassment, reinstatement, and back pay—in the light of Brenda Patterson's testimony. She testified in excruciating detail about her white supervisor's differential treatment of white and black employees in such matters as workload, training, and promotion opportunities. But the hurt of racial harassment goes beyond such material concerns. Patterson also testified that her supervisor

- criticized white employees in private or, in staff meetings, without referring to individuals, but criticized the two black employees by name in meetings;
- assigned her, but no other clerical worker, to dust and sweep;
- repeatedly suggested that a white would be able to do her job better than she could; and
- said to her on several occasions that "blacks are known to work slower than whites by nature"—once putting the same idea in these words: "some animals [are] faster than other animals."[96]

If you were in Brenda Patterson's circumstances, would you see an injunction as an adequate remedy for these harms?

The Title VII remedies offer no compensation at all for the main harms caused by harassment, such as humiliation. It takes real resolution for a victim of harassment to go through the ordeal of prosecuting a Title VII claim in order to make the harassing employer behave—even (if she has been demoted or fired) with the inducement of back pay.[97] It is here that the majority's preference for civil

---

[94]109 S.Ct. at 2374.

[95]*Id.*, drawing on Meritor Savings Bank v. Vinson, 477 U.S. 57 (1986) (sexual harassment violates Title VII).

[96]These examples are taken from Justice Brennan's dissenting opinion in *Patterson*, 109 S.Ct. at 2391–93.

[97]A computer search some weeks after *Patterson* showed that thirteen racial harassment cases in federal district courts had been dismissed. Hayes, Job-Bias Litigation Wilts Under High

rights deregulation made itself felt. Rather than construe Section 1981 (as a number of courts of appeals had done) to provide the one common-sense remedy for the harm of harassment, the *Patterson* majority fell back on formal neutrality's preference for narrow construction. With none of the concern for stability in the law that characterized its reaffirmation of *Runyon*, the majority now argued that Congress in Title VII had worked out a "delicate balance between employee and employer rights," which the courts ought not to disturb by allowing a damages award in an action under Section 1981.[98] We are left to wonder how the majority would answer two questions. First, what "employer right" is being exercised in a case of racial harassment? Second, how could Congress's "delicate balance" in 1964 place racial harassment in the scales, given that racial harassment as a Title VII violation first emerged in the 1970s—not in an act of Congress but in the interpretations of administrators and judges?[99]

The contrast between the *Patterson* and *Jones* majorities is striking. In *Jones*, Justice Harlan, dissenting, argued that Congress in the recently enacted Civil Rights Act of 1968[100] had similarly balanced the rights of would-be buyers and sellers of houses, and that the Court should not disturb that balance. The *Jones* majority responded by saying that the two acts served a number of different purposes, and that Section 1982 in no way diminished the importance of the 1968 law. The majority, however, saw the case as an occasion to repair some of the damage that the Court itself had done in the *Civil Rights Cases*. Furthermore, the Justices saw the need to find a way around the "state action" barrier; they understood how that barrier had pro-

---

Court Ruling, Wall St. Journal, Aug. 22, 1989, p. B1. And at least one federal judge has enthusiastically embraced the decision for all it can possibly be worth, holding that §1981 has nothing to say about racially discriminatory employee evaluations, compensation, or discharges, and that a racially discriminatory refusal to promote would be forbidden, if at all, only when the promotion in question amounted to an entirely new employer/employee relation. Greggs v. Hillman Distributing. Co., 58 U.S.L. Week 2088 (S.D. Texas 1989).

[98] 109 S.Ct. at 2375 n.4.

[99] Title VII does speak of discrimination concerning the "conditions" of employment, but the major lawmaking events concerning racial harassment took place in 1971, when the EEOC adopted a guideline concerning racial harassment, and Judge Goldberg of the Fifth Circuit spelled out a similar theory in Rogers v. EEOC, 454 F.2d 234, 238 (5th Cir. 1971). As late as 1975 at least one federal judge had not received the message. See Howard v. National Cash Register Co., 388 F. Supp. 603 (S.D. Ohio 1975). By the late 1970s, however, application of the principle had become widespread. See the decisions cited in EEOC v. Murphy Motor Freight Lines, Inc., 488 F. Supp. 381, 384 (D. Minn. 1980).

[100] The bill became law after oral argument of *Jones* but before decision.

tected the private discrimination that was disfiguiring our public life by excluding people from equal citizenship.

A similar recognition eluded the *Patterson* majority, who confronted a deliberate and particularly harmful form of racial discrimination, and then fell back on the preference for narrow construction, even at the cost of contortion. The more serious cost is that the Court's reading leaves employer racial harassment without any sensible remedy—although, for one strongly attracted to formal neutrality's preference for private ordering, that result is racial justice. Now, as in 1968, Congress retains the option to convert dissenting views into law by amending the relevant statutes. But in all seasons legislative bodies at rest tend to remain at rest. The political difference between the post-*Jones* and post-*Patterson* situations is that the burden of overcoming congressional inertia is now placed on civil rights advocates. In the meantime, private employers can ignore racial harassment in their workplaces—or even practice it themselves—knowing that the costs will be slight.

Perhaps the *Patterson* majority saw its decision as a compromise, resisting the pull of formal neutrality toward overruling *Runyon*, but responding to that pull in refusing to find a damages remedy in Section 1981 for an employer's racial harassment. No such compromise was visible in *Wards Cove Packing Co., Inc. v. Atonio*,[101] decided ten days before *Patterson*, where the same majority moved decisively and unambiguously in the direction of that doctrinal model. Of all the civil rights decisions in the 1988 Term, *Wards Cove* seems the most serious setback for the civil rights cause.

In the pure version of the model of formal neutrality, the only recognizable violations of constitutional or statutory rights to racial equality are specifically identifiable acts of purposeful discrimination that directly cause harm to individuals. This view—along with the idea that past societal discrimination is irrelevant, and the presumption that present conditions constitute race-neutral equilibrium—makes the model almost completely unresponsive to one of the most obvious facts of American life: that racism affects the members of a racial group as a group.[102] The implication of that fact for our race relations law, as I have argued elsewhere, is plain: "either we

---

[101]109 S.Ct. 2115 (1989).

[102]See generally Crenshaw, note 14 *supra*; Fiss, Groups and the Equal Protection Clause, 5 Phil. and Pub. Aff. 107 (1976); Karst, note 33 *supra*, at 21–27 and ch. 9.

use group remedies for past discrimination, or we give up the pretense that a remedy is what we seek."[103]

During the past two decades our courts have persistently confronted the question of group remedies for racial wrongs. Part of that large issue is cast in the language of substantive rights: Should we limit the notion of discrimination to acts that are purposefully discriminatory, or should we also include those acts which produce disparate impacts on racial groups? The model of formal racial neutrality calls for limiting responsibility to purposeful wrongs, and for rejecting group remedies. In cases presenting constitutional challenges to governmental action, the Supreme Court in 1976 followed the model, limiting the idea of discrimination to direct, purposefully disadvantaging acts. The case was *Washington v. Davis*,[104] and Justice White wrote for the Court.

In defining employment discrimination under Title VII of the 1964 Act, however, the Court in the 1971 case of *Griggs v. Duke Power Co.*[105] had departed from the model of formal neutrality, recognizing that facially neutral employment practices could also produce many of the harmful effects of deliberate discrimination. An employer's intentional racial discrimination, of course, violates Title VII. But, the Court held in *Griggs*, even absent a showing of discriminatory purpose, an employer's practice amounted to a prima facie violation of Title VII if it produced a disparate impact on a racial group. The employer could overcome the presumption of a violation by showing the business necessity of the practice. Chief Justice Burger wrote for a unanimous Court. Subsequent decisions reinforced the rule that, once the plaintiff proved a disparate impact, the employer had the burden of proving business necessity.[106]

The *Griggs* formula responded to the idea of a broad public responsibility for ending the effects of racial caste. First, it recognized that racism often lurks at the margins of consciousness, affecting behavior without ripening into anything that can be identified—even by the actor—as purpose. Second, the formula recognized the public effects of widespread racial segregation in private employment,

---

[103]*Id.* at 151. See also Freeman, note 14 *supra*.

[104]426 U.S. 229 (1976).

[105]401 U.S. 424 (1971).

[106]Justice Stevens, dissenting in *Wards Cove*, recounted the history of this doctrine. 109 S.Ct. at 2128–33 and 2130 n.14.

effects that seriously impede the integration of American society, whether or not the segregation be intended. Third, by placing on employers the burden of justifying the behavior that produced those segregating effects, *Griggs* admonished employers to take responsibility for examining their practices and acting to minimize the harms of segregation.

Even so, the *Griggs* scheme did not wholly abandon the model of formal neutrality. Rather the Court sought to accommodate that model's preference for private ordering with another substantive goal: to avoid perpetuating the effects of past systematic racial discrimination. True, in its rules for establishing a prima facie violation of Title VII *Griggs* did recognize group harms and seek to remedy them. But it did not press an employer to adopt a racial "proportionate representation" principle in hiring and promoting workers.[107] Rather the doctrine accommodated the concern for private autonomy by allowing the employer to show that the challenged practice was necessary in running its business. There is nothing unusual in this allocation of burdens of proof; typically the law places such burdens on the party who has the better access to the evidence.

Wards Cove signals a major retreat from the *Griggs* scheme. Two changes in the law are especially ominous for employment discrimination plaintiffs. First—and here the Court follows an argument made by a plurality of four Justices the year before[108]—to establish a prima facie case of disparate impact, a plaintiff now must show more than a statistical racial disparity between the employer's work force and the relevant pool of qualified persons.[109] The plaintiff must identify a specific employment practice, and explain the mechanism by which that practice has caused the disparate racial impact. The *Griggs* plaintiffs had satisfied this requirement, for they were complaining of the disparate effects of a clear-cut employment standard: a high school diploma or passage of two written tests. Where the employer's standard is subjective or multifactored or otherwise imprecise, the burden of proof established by *Wards Cove* will be

---

[107]This concern seemed to be driving the *Wards Cove* majority. See *id*. at 2122.

[108]Watson v. Fort Worth Bank & Trust Co., 108 S.Ct. 2777, 2788–90 (1988) (plurality opinion of O'Connor, J.).

[109]In the case at hand, the employer's unskilled cannery workers were essentially all Filipino or Alaska Natives; workers in skilled jobs, almost all of whom were better paid than the cannery workers, were predominantly white. The two groups of workers—as fate would have it—were housed in separate dormitories and ate in separate dining halls.

extremely hard for plaintiffs to carry.[110] The *Griggs* Court was aware that, in the area of race relations, the interplay of beliefs and behavior is often hard to detect, and yet is capable of inflicting serious group harms. In *Wards Cove* this awareness gives way to the preference for narrowly focused definitions of harm and remedy—and, not incidentally, the preference for private ordering.

This latter preference is even more clearly visible in the Court's second major change in the *Griggs* doctrine. Even when a plaintiff succeeds in proving how an employer's practice has caused a racially disparate impact, *Wards Cove* radically reduces the value of that prima facie case[111] by turning upside down the burden of proof on the question of business necessity. Now, the employer's only burden is to produce some evidence of a business justification for the challenged practice. Then it is up to the employee to prove that the practice does not serve, "in a significant way, the legitimate employment goals of the employer." Not only is this substantive standard a far cry from one of "necessity"; the burden on the plaintiff to prove the required negative is extremely heavy.

At the end of his opinion, Justice White tosses a bone to employment discrimination plaintiffs. If, as seems likely, the plaintiff cannot prove the absence of any significant business justification, the plaintiff can still win a "disparate impact" case by converting it into a case of intentional discrimination. The plaintiff can win by showing that some other employment practice would serve the employer just as well, without causing the racial disparity in the work force. This line of argument, which Justice White properly identifies as proof of an employer's "pretext" for discrimination, has been available to plaintiffs all along—and, not surprisingly, it has been a consistent loser.[112] One reason for this lack of success is that the standard of proof is explicitly designed to maximize the autonomy of private em-

---

[110]Justice White sought to answer this argument by saying that liberal discovery rules would permit plaintiffs to gain access to employers' hiring records. No such records were kept by the employer in *Wards Cove*, perhaps because the relevant record-keeping guidelines of the Equal Employment Opportunity Commission exempt seasonal employment from any such requirement.

[111]Judge Richard Posner recently made this point in his opinion for the Seventh Circuit in Allen v. Seidman, 881 F.2d. 375 (7th Cir. 1989). This opinion and its companion opinion in Evans v. City of Evanston, 881 F.2d 382 (7th Cir. 1989), deserve to be published in an instruction booklet for civil rights lawyers. It is a model for careful analysis of prima facie cases in post-*Wards Cove* actions under Title VII based on the disparate impact theory.

[112]See Note, 67 N.C.L. Rev. 725, 738–39 and n.125 (1989).

ployers: "Courts are generally less competent than employees to re-structure business practices."[113]

The result of Justice White's opinion in *Wards Cove* is that a considerable number of Title VII plaintiffs are effectively forced out of the disparate-impact mode, requiring them to prove purposeful discrimination. The author of the Court's opinion in *Washington v. Davis*,[114] having succeeded in 1982 in reading that decision's limitations into the 1866 Act,[115] has scored once more for private ordering, for narrowly focused individual remedies, for narrow construction—in short, for a vision of racial equality as formal neutrality.

The influence of the model of formal neutrality comes into sharper focus when we consider *Wards Cove* and *Patterson* together. In *Patterson* the majority uses the availability of an unsuitable Title VII remedy as a reason for an ungenerous reading of Section 1981, narrowly confining its use in employment discrimination cases. In *Wards Cove* the Court drastically limits the reach of Title VII in a type of case outside the scope of Section 1981. Both decisions, in the name of private ordering, slight the importance of the workplace in the integration of American public life. Together, *Patterson* and *Wards Cove* actively promote the cause of civil rights deregulation.

C. AFFIRMATIVE ACTION: THE FORMAL USES OF FORMAL EQUALITY

One obvious way to provide a partial remedy for the continuing effects of past discrimination, both governmental and private, is to adopt a program of affirmative action, taking race into account in facilitating minority representation in employment, or higher education, or government contracting. In the aggregate these programs promote the integration of American society, the inclusion of the members of subordinated groups as equal citizens.[116] Because these group remedies are race-conscious, affirmative action programs are frequently challenged as violations of federal civil rights laws, or the Constitution, or both. The challengers appeal to the ideals of individualized justice and formal equality. The defenders of affirmative action respond that group remedies are necessary to remedy the

[113]109 S.Ct. at 2127, quoting Furnco Constr. Corp. v. Waters, 438 U.S. 567, 578 (1978).

[114]Note 104 *supra*.

[115]See Memphis v. Greene, 451 U.S. 100, 135 (1981) (White, J., concurring). Justice White's view was adopted in General Bldg. Contractors Ass'n v. Pennsylvania, 458 U.S. 375 (1982).

[116]See generally Karst, note 33 *supra*, at 158–72.

harms that racism has visited on individuals because of their membership in a racial group. [117]

If the Supreme Court were to embrace a pure version of the model of formal neutrality as constitutional doctrine and statutory construction, affirmative action programs would be forbidden, for they directly confront the preferences for limited public responsibility and for narrowly focused remedies. Although these preferences have influenced the Court's affirmative action decisions, the Court has never come close to the position that all race-conscious programs are presumptively illegal. Underlying the major opinions specifying the conditions of validity for affirmative action is an awareness that mostly goes unspoken: the best long-term remedy for the private beliefs and behavior that perpetuate the effects of racial caste is the integration of our public life, from school to workplace to marketplace. The most striking feature of the opinions that have shaped the constitutional law governing affirmative action is that they permit the effectuation of these civil rights goals while using the rhetoric of formal equality.

1. *Confronting the Model of Formal Neutrality.* The easiest case for race-conscious relief, all the Justices now seem to agree, is the case in which a court is called on to remedy systematic past discrimination by some governmental agency or private employer. The pattern was set in the early school busing cases[118] and in cases of systematic employment discrimination,[119] both of which seemed to require group-based relief. From these situations it is only a short step to the case in which a public or private institution admits the errors of its past behavior and voluntarily adopts a program of race-conscious remedy—

---

[117]My repeated references to racial discrimination grow out of the racial context of the 1988 Term decisions I have discussed. They should not obscure the applicability of these remarks to remedies for discrimination based on ethnicity or sex. Although a case can be made for treating sex-discrimination challenges to affirmative action more leniently than the courts treat racial-discrimination challenges, see Associated General Contractors of Calif. v. City and County of San Francisco, 813 F. 2d 922 (9th Cir. 1987), it now seems that the constitutional standards for affirmative action are the same whether the beneficiaries of the plans be women or members of racial or ethnic minorities. See Johnson v. Transportation Agency, 480 U.S. 616, 627, 632 (1987) (opinion of the Court); 480 U.S. at 652 (O'Connor, J., concurring); Wygant v. Jackson Board of Education, 476 U.S. 267, 286 (1986) (O'Connor, J., concurring, suggesting that the difference between "compelling" and "important" state interests is negligible); Richmond v. J. A. Croson Co., 109 S.Ct. at 721–22, 725 (opinion of the Court) (mentioning "the close examination of legislative purpose we have engaged in when reviewing classifications based either on race or gender," and citing indiscriminately decisions concerning race-based and sex-based affirmative action).

[118]*E.g.*, Swann v. Charlotte-Mecklenburg Board of Education, 402 U.S. 1 (1971).

[119]*E.g.*, Griggs v. Duke Power Co., note 105 *supra*.

and the Supreme Court was willing to take that step. In 1971 the Court unanimously endorsed the power of a school board, as a matter of educational policy, to take voluntary affirmative action to remedy school segregation, whether or not the segregation had resulted from any violation of federal rights.[120] And in *United Steelworkers v. Weber*[121] in 1979, over a scathing dissent by Justice Rehnquist, the Court upheld the legality (under Title VII) of a private employer's voluntary affirmative action plan, adopted to cure "conspicuous racial imbalance in traditionally segregated job categories."[122]

The very next year a 6–3 Court took a much longer step, extending the reach of permissible affirmative action far beyond remedying identifiable misbehavior. *Fullilove v. Klutznick*[123] upheld an act of Congress appropriating funds to aid local public works projects and requiring that 10 percent of the money be used to hire minority contractors. Chief Justice Burger emphasized that it was permissible for Congress to conclude that minority businesses had been disadvantaged in obtaining public works contracts "by procurement practices that perpetuated the effects of prior discrimination."[124] Thus the Chief Justice endorsed a broad congressional power to go beyond formal neutrality in remedying the present effects of past societal discrimination. Justice Powell added an opinion that emphasized the statute's narrow tailoring to the purposes of remedying the effects of past public or private discrimination against minority contractors.

The critics of *Weber* and *Fullilove* include not only the contemporary dissenters but some widely read commentators and two Justices who have joined the Court more recently. Justice Scalia would overrule *Weber*,[125] and last Term Justice Kennedy said he was not yet willing to endorse *Fullilove*.[126] The critics have made several points,

---

[120]Dictum in *Swann*, note 118 *supra*, at 28.

[121]443 U.S. 109 (1979).

[122]443 U.S. at 209. In Johnson v. Transportation Agency, note 117 *supra*, the Justices debated whether *Weber*'s approval of voluntary affirmative action was limited to the case in which an employer seeks to remedy its own previous deliberate discrimination.

[123]448 U.S. 448 (1980).

[124]448 U.S. at 477–78 (Burger, C.J., for three Justices). Justice Marshall, writing for three additional Justices, offered an even broader view of congressional power.

[125]See his dissent in Johnson v. Transportation Agency, 480 U.S. at 677. In *Croson*, note 117 *supra*, he accepted a greater role for Congress than for state and local governments in remedying the effects of discrimination; he might even accept the *Fullilove* result.

[126]Concurring in Richmond v. J.A. Croson Co., note 117 *supra*, 109 U.S. at 734. Other Justices have changed positions. Justice White, who concurred in *Weber*, now would overrule it; Chief Justice Rehnquist, who dissented in *Fullilove*, accepts it in *Croson*. Justice Stevens now seems generally more receptive to affirmative action than he was in *Bakke* or *Fullilove*.

all of which are variations on the theme of formal racial neutrality. *Weber*'s race-conscious remedy was called "reverse discrimination" that pointed toward a rule of "pervasive dispersion" of jobs among ethnic groups.[127] In accepting racial imbalance as a basis for affirmative action, said Justice Scalia, *Weber* "replace[s] the goal of a discrimination-free society with the quite incompatible goal of proportionate representation by race . . . ."[128] Even a "benign" racial quota, said Justice Rehnquist, is "a creator of castes, a two-edged sword that must demean one in order to prefer another."[129] In the vision that equates racial equality with formal neutrality, caste is not something that results from a history of systematic racial subordination, but a formal status that might attach just as easily to whites as to blacks. In this view caste is divorced from history and from culture; it becomes a synonym for race-conscious law.

Justice Stewart, dissenting in *Fullilove*, offered a different criticism. He chided Congress for "implicitly teach[ing] the public that the apportionment of rewards and penalties can legitimately be made according to race" and encouraging people to "view themselves and others in terms of their racial characteristics."[130] Remedies focused on racial groups, say the critics, not only raise the spectre of proportional representation but also threaten to stigmatize the preferences' intended beneficiaries and to foist on the legislative process "a new generation of racial spoils."[131] These concerns were revisited by several Justices last Term in *Richmond v. J. A. Croson Co.*,[132] when the Court struck down a city's contracting set-aside program modeled on the congressional statute upheld in *Fullilove*. Justice Kennedy, concurring, encapsulated in one sentence a decade's worth of disquiet among the critics of affirmative action: "The moral imperative of racial neutrality is the driving force of the Equal Protection Clause."[133]

The quoted jeremiads against *Fullilove* and *Weber* not only capture the combative mood that has pervaded much of the ongoing debate

---

[127]Kitch, The Return of Color-Consciousness to the Constitution: Weber, Dayton, and Columbus, 1979 Supreme Court Review 1, 5–6.

[128]Dissenting in Johnson v. Transportation Agency, 480 U.S. at 658.

[129]Dissenting in United Steelworkers v. Weber, note 121 *supra*, 443 U.S. at 254, borrowing Alexander Bickel's language, which is echoed by Justice Scalia in *Croson*, note 117 *supra*, 109 S.Ct. at 739.

[130]448 U.S. at 532.

[131]Van Alstyne, Rites of Passage: Race, the Supreme Court, and the Constitution, 46 U. Chi. L. Rev. 775, 809 (1979).

[132]109 S.Ct. 706 (1989).

[133]109 S.Ct. at 734.

over affirmative action since the late 1970s, but also suggest the all-or-nothing spirit that has characterized the positions of several Justices on both sides. Against Justice Scalia's powerful advocacy of formal equality and limited responsibility[134] is ranged the moral imperative of the substantive equality essential to integrate American public life and remedy the effects of racial caste.[135] Justices Brennan, Marshall, and Blackmun would transpose this concern into a broad charter to provide remedies when significant substantive inequalities are manifested in racial imbalance.[136]

Threading their way through this crossfire, Justice Powell and Justice O'Connor have looked for a middle path to a basis for affirmative action that will allow significant movement toward integration of higher education, work forces, and marketplaces without abandoning the individualist values of formal racial neutrality. They have succeeded so well that their views have become law in spite of the Court's persistent fragmentation in affirmative action cases. If these two Justices have been prepared to uphold some race-conscious group remedies, surely one unstated reason is that an uncompromising adherence to formal neutrality is a recipe for perpetuating a racial group's past systematic deprivation of equal citizenship. In short, they have understood that the threat of a caste system subordinating whites and men is entirely theoretical, and that the real burdens of caste in our country continue to weigh on women and minorities. But that sort of reasoning will not fit into the doctrinal model of formal racial neutrality. In their affirmative action opinions Justices Powell and O'Connor have contributed to a resolution of this tension between theory and life by encasing the substance of substantive equality in the forms of formal equality.

2. *Croson's Invitations.* The *Croson* decision disheartened some civil rights advocates, who rightly saw Justice O'Connor's opinion for the Court as establishing rigorous requirements for state and local governments' affirmative action programs. That opinion is, indeed, written in the vocabulary of formal racial neutrality. Thus: (1) There is no such thing as "benign" racial discrimination; every affirmative action plan must be subjected to strict judicial scrutiny to assure that

---

[134]His opinions in the *Johnson* and *Croson* cases were foreshadowed by an article he wrote while he was a law teacher, Scalia, The Disease as Cure: "In Order to Get Beyond Racism, We Must First Take Account of Race," 1979 Wash. U.L.Q. 147.

[135]And its parallels in the subordination of ethnic groups and of women.

[136]See these Justices' opinions in *Fullilove, Johnson,* and *Croson*—and, before that, in Regents of University of California v. Bakke, 438 U.S. 265 (1978).

it is narrowly tailored to the achievement of governmental purposes that are compelling. (2) Remedying identifiable discrimination may be such a compelling purpose, but state and local governments cannot justify racial preferences as remedies for past societal discrimination. (3) To be narrowly tailored to their permissible remedial purposes, state and local government affirmative action plans must be a last resort after alternative race-neutral measures have been considered, must not employ percentage goals unless they are carefully attuned to the permissible remedial purpose, must be flexible and of limited duration, and must not unduly burden innocent third parties (such as white contractors and subcontractors who might seek to work on the City of Richmond's projects).

These limitations on state and local government affirmative action plans are directly traceable to Justice Powell's opinions in *Regents of University of California v. Bakke*[137] and in *Fullilove*; and to the opinions of Justices Powell and O'Connor in *Wygant v. Jackson Board of Education*.[138] The limitations are troublesome for the sponsors of affirmative action. But civil rights advocates will miss some important opportunities if they look only at *Croson's* limitations. For the civil rights cause the decision is also part of the good news in a time when the road goes mostly uphill. The case marks the culmination of the efforts of Justices Powell and O'Connor to establish a solid constitutional base for affirmative action. *Croson* confirms what *Bakke* began.

Of the Court's four major constitutional decisions in this area, only *Fullilove* upheld an affirmative action plan. Justice O'Connor's *Croson* opinion treats *Fullilove* as a special case, resting on Congress's broad power under the Fourteenth Amendment to remedy past societal discrimination. This far-reaching interpretation of congressional power, endorsed by at least six of the Justices, is the most important pronouncement the Supreme Court has ever made on the subject of affirmative action. *Croson* and *Patterson* together recognize in Congress a sweeping power to legislate in the interest of the racial integration of the workplace, the marketplace, and all other areas of our public life.[139]

---

[137]*Ibid.* A fragmented Supreme Court there held invalid a minority quota for admissions to the medical school of the University of California, Davis.

[138]Note 117 *supra*. The Court held unconstitutional a local school board's voluntary affirmative action plan, insofar as it gave minority teachers with low seniority greater protection against layoffs than it gave to white teachers with higher seniority.

[139]At the end of this article I discuss the Court's sweeping invitation to Congress to take action to remedy the effects of private discrimination. See text at note 161 *infra*.

The prevailing opinions in the Court's other three major constitutional decisions—*Bakke*, *Wygant*, and now *Croson*—were written by
Justices Powell and O'Connor. Those opinions not only recognize
that race-conscious remedies may be constitutional but teach state
and local governments how to lead their affirmative action safely
through the valley of the shadow of strict scrutiny.

In retrospect it does not seem accidental that Justices Powell and
O'Connor provided their affirmative action instruction manuals for
state and local governments in three decisions that invalidated the
plans before the Court. In building the present consensus within the
Court, these two Justices have had to gain the support of some colleagues who are powerfully attached to the model of formal neutrality, and whose tolerance for affirmative action is distinctly
limited. For example, it is arguable that even under the formulations
of Justices Powell and O'Connor in *Wygant* the affirmative action aspects of the school board's layoff plan[140] might have been upheld if
the case had been remanded for further development of the record to
show in more detail the board's past discrimination. But it is doubtful
in the extreme that Chief Justice Burger and Justice Rehnquist
would have joined in Justice Powell's formulation if it had offered the
prospect of displacing white teachers with seniority to make room for
black teachers recently hired. Similarly, it is doubtful that Chief Justice Rehnquist and Justice White would have joined in *Croson*'s pro-
nouncements consolidating various affirmative action gains if the
Court had been validating an instrument so blunt as the city's 30 percent quota.

In their affirmative action opinions Justice Powell and Justice
O'Connor are particularly clear in expressing one major purpose of
the doctrines they announce: to avoid a "politics of racial hostility."[141] If Justice O'Connor in *Croson* is concerned to prevent the
emergence of a new round of racial spoils,[142] she is tracing a path
cleared by Justice Powell's *Bakke* opinion, where he took account of
white resentment.[143] Both Justices seem concerned that politics will

---

[140]See note 138 *supra*.

[141]Richmond v. J.A. Croson Co., 109 S.Ct. at 721.

[142]*Id*. at 722. Black people can be forgiven if they react less than charitably when they are
instructed about the divisiveness of ethnic politics by people bearing surnames recalling the
ethnic politics that played so important a role in group integrations now largely completed. See
Karst, Paths to Belonging: The Constitution and Cultural Identity, 64 N.C. L. Rev. 303, 325–
36 (1986).

[143]See Karst & Horowitz, The Bakke Opinions and Equal Protection Doctrine, 14 Harv.
C.R.-C.L. L. Rev. 7, 13–15 (1979). Derrick Bell, commenting on *Bakke*, pointed out how typi-

destroy efforts to remedy past discrimination unless affirmative action is defined as formal equality.

They may be right. Before the *Bakke* decision the legislative process was on the verge of wiping out racial preferences in state university admissions. Once Alan Bakke was admitted to medical school, and racial admission quotas were declared unlawful, the political scene changed. Although Justice Powell wrote only for himself, his opinion set the pattern for affirmative action's doctrinal future. He insisted on strict judicial scrutiny of race-conscious remedies, and then found a "compelling" interest in the educational advantages of a diverse student body—on the basis of scrutiny that was anything but strict.[144] He rejected "past societal discrimination" as a basis for state and local government affirmative action remedies, and then handed the universities a lawsuit-proof means of assuring a significant minority presence in their professional schools. "Diversity" programs sprang up all over the land, and the permissibility of minority preferences in university admissions moved out of the political spotlight and into the wings. "Diversity" admissions offer the politics of racial hostility no handle to grasp.[145]

In *Wygant* Justices Powell and O'Connor combined to make clear how a state or local government could adopt a voluntary affirmative action plan in its capacity as employer—again in opinions written in the language of formal equality. Both Justices distinguished between remedying societal discrimination, which would not pass the test of strict scrutiny, and remedying identifiable discrimination, which would. In this public employment context, identifiable discrimination meant past discrimination by the agency that had adopted the race-conscious plan. But the agency need not confess any specific wrongdoing in order to adopt an affirmative action remedy; all it need do is have "a strong basis in evidence for its conclusion that remedial action was necessary," that is, "that there has been prior discrimination."[146] And what sort of evidence would suffice? Justice O'Connor offered one example: "a disparity between the percentage

---

cal is the insistence that remedies for the effects of racial discrimination not be too burdensome on whites. Bell, Bakke, Minority Admissions, and the Usual Price of Racial Remedies, 67 Cal. L. Rev. 3 (1979).

[144]See Karst & Horowitz, note 143 *supra*, at 7–20.

[145]*Id.* at 27–29.

[146]476 U.S. at 277 (plurality opinion of Powell, J.). The burden remains on the challengers to the plan to show the absence of such a "basis in evidence." Herman Schwartz has pointed out how this approach softens the strictness of "strict scrutiny." Schwartz, The 1986 and 1987 Affirmative Action Cases: It's All Over But the Shouting, 86 Mich. L. Rev. 524, 561–66 (1987).

of qualified blacks on a school's teaching staff and the percentage of qualified minorities in the relevant labor pool sufficient to support a prima facie Title VII . . . claim."[147]

Wygant reminds us that one factor encouraging an employer to adopt an affirmative action plan may be the desire to avoid being a defendant in a Title VII action. In this respect private and governmental employers are in similar positions.[148] Although affirmative action in these circumstances replaces one group remedy with another, a Title VII action looks backward at questions of fault or justification or both, while affirmative action offers a chance to look forward to integration.[149] In the case of a private employer's voluntary affirmative action plan, the values of workplace integration go hand in hand with the values of private ordering—reinforced by the version of stare decisis invoked in reaffirming *Runyon*—and it would be surprising if the Supreme Court were to follow the lead of Justices who now say they would overrule *Weber*. From the standpoint of those who see the segregation of workplaces as a critical factor in the perpetuation of the effects of racial caste, private employment and government employment alike are part of our public life. Government contracting can be seen in a similar perspective. It was natural for the Civil Rights Act of 1964 to look toward integrated hotels and restaurants as well as integrated work forces. Not just our places of

---

[147]476 U.S. at 292 (concurring opinion), repeated by Justice O'Connor in her *Johnson* concurrence, 480 U.S. at 651.

Charles Fried has recently suggested that *Wards Cove*, by further encumbering Title VII plaintiffs, changed the definition of the "identifiable discrimination" that, according to *Croson*, will justify affirmative action. Fried, Affirmative Action after City of Richmond v. J.A. Croson Co.: A Response to the Scholars' Statement, 99 Yale L.J. 155 (1989). This argument ignores Justice O'Connor's approving references to a Sixth Circuit decision using statistical evidence alone to justify affirmative action in government contracting. See text at note 154 *infra*. More broadly, the argument is unpersuasive even in the employment context. The *Wards Cove* formula, requiring identification of a specific employment practice that has caused a statistical racial disparity, is taken from Justice O'Connor's own plurality opinion in the *Watson* case decided a year before. See note 108 *supra*. *Croson* came after *Watson*, and yet Justice O'Connor repeatedly invoked her *Wygant* opinion, quoted above in the text, as the guide to permissible affirmative action. If Fried is right, a school board in the *Wygant* situation could not adopt an affirmative action plan without focusing on (and thus confessing to) particularized wrongdoing—a result that Justice O'Connor in *Wygant* specifically disavowed. There is no indication whatever that Justice O'Connor saw her *Croson* opinion as working a covert change in the doctrinal structure for affirmative action that she had so carefully developed in *Wygant*.

[148]The indirect suggestion in Johnson v. Transportation Agency, 480 U.S. at 620 n.2, that the Title VII standard may differ from the constitutional standard applicable to public employers, seems unlikely to survive.

[149]See Sullivan, Sins of Discrimination: Last Term's Affirmative Action Cases, 100 Harv. L. Rev. 78, 96–98 (1986). Still, *Croson*'s renewed emphasis on "identifiable discrimination" also implies some looking backward. See *id*. at 91–96.

public accommodation but the marketplace in general is part of the public life that defines our citizenship, even though it is under private management.[150]

This is not the place to examine the *Croson* decision in detail. For our purposes it is enough to notice that Justice O'Connor has now succeeded in writing into an opinion of the Court[151] the views that she and Justice Powell expressed in *Wygant*.[152] By specifying the constitutional defects in Richmond's contracting plan, the Court has legitimized affirmative action programs for state and local government contracting. Furthermore, it has provided still another set of how-to-do-it instructions. The rules are rigorous, but the requirements— such as statistical showings about past discrimination, careful adjustment of racial preferences to the remedial goals suggested by those figures, and a waiver procedure of the kind mentioned in *Fullilove*— do not seem beyond the capacity of most communities to meet.[153]

In one respect, *Croson* extends the range of permissible state and local government affirmative action beyond *Wygant*. The Fourth Circuit, very much under the influence of the model of formal neutrality, had applied *Wygant* literally, holding that a city could use affirmative action in contracting only for the purpose of remedying its own past discrimination. Justice O'Connor, joined by Chief Justice Rehnquist and Justice White, rejected this limitation, making clear that the city can accept its share of the public responsibility for remedying private discrimination, using its spending powers to remedy discrimination in the local construction industry.

The key to affirmative action's permissible purposes, whether the city be remedying its own discrimination or private discrimination, is the idea of "identifiable discrimination." Here, too, general princi-

---

[150]For that matter, it does not seem unreasonable for legislators to conclude that minority contractors are more likely than white contractors to employ minority employees. (I do not suggest that the present majority of the Supreme Court would agree with this view. Congress, however, might.)

[151]Parts II-B and IV of her opinion are the only parts that are the opinion of the Court.

[152]476 U.S. at 277–84 (Powell, J.); *id.* at 284–94 (O'Connor, J.).

[153]Just such an ordinance has been proposed in San Francisco, supported by an impressive statistical study. See also Greenberg & Lee, For Affirmative Action, Richmond Decision Is a Detour, Not a Dead End, L.A. Times, Feb. 8, 1989, pt. II, p. 7, col. 1. Some communities, however, may be disabled from adopting plans that are effective. The very discrimination that motivates affirmative action also inhibits the formation of contracting firms, thus reducing the pool of "qualified" minority contractors. In some communities the number of such firms may be so small that the apparent racial disparity, measured as prescribed by *Croson*, will be negligible. Using one form of discrimination to justify another may not be new, see, *e.g.*, Rostker v. Goldberg, 453 U.S. 57 (1981), but it does not promote the principle of equal citizenship.

ples announced in *Wygant* are consolidated in the opinion for the Court. To make clear the availability of statistical showings of minority underrepresentation, Justice O'Connor twice cites with approval the Sixth Circuit's decision in *Ohio Contractors Assn. v. Keip*,[154] which upheld a statewide affirmative action program based on a disparity between the percentage of minority businesses in the state and the percentage of state purchasing contracts awarded to minority businesses. Similarly, the required "narrow tailoring" of the affirmative action remedy closely follows the pattern set by Justices Powell and O'Connor in *Fullilove* and *Wygant*.

Both as to the permissible ends and the permissible means of affirmative action, there is much to be said for Justice Marshall's dissent. To ask for proof of past discrimination in the construction industry in Richmond does seem a little like asking someone to prove that Jim Crow had racially discriminatory effects. But, consider today's political setting for affirmative action. Because group remedies employing affirmative action for women and minorities are often seen by whites and males as individually threatening, they touch not only interests but emotions, fears, the sense of identity.[155] In no state will the abstract principle of affirmative action win a statewide election. In a legislature, of course, minority interests are part of a larger process of bargaining on a series of issues. But about half the states authorize legislation (including amendments of state constitutions) through initiative measures and other forms of popular voting.[156] When race-focused measures appear on statewide ballots, minorities lose. (Justice Marshall, when he was Solicitor General, once argued this point with great effectiveness.[157])

Suppose you were a Justice who believed that the states (and cities) ought to be allowed to employ affirmative action remedies to avoid perpetuating the effects of racial discrimination. Given the always-precarious political position of affirmative action in the states, you might be concerned about the possible effects of validating a plan like Richmond's on the basis of what everyone knows about Jim Crow. You might believe that such an explanation would set in motion a political backlash—all in the name of formal racial equality—that

---

[154]713 F.2d 167, 171 (6th Cir. 1983).

[155]See Karst, note 33 *supra*, at 21–27, 148–51.

[156]See Eule, Judicial Review of Direct Democracy, 99 Yale L.J. (forthcoming 1990).

[157]The occasion was the oral argument of Reitman v. Mulkey, 387 U.S. 369 (1967). See Arguments Before the Court, 35 U.S.L. Week 3337, 3339 (Mar. 28, 1967).

could destroy affirmative action by state and local government institutions, at least in the states that permit legislation by initiative. On the other hand, the model of formal neutrality offers a rhetoric for upholding race-conscious remedies, not for the threatening-sounding purpose of advancing the conditions of a minority group as a group, but to remedy acts of discrimination. For a Justice who accepts this view of the politics of affirmative action, *Croson*, like *Bakke*, may be intended not as a "giant step backward"[158] but as a step toward civil rights consolidation. These speculations may or may not reflect Justice O'Connor's actual thoughts in approaching *Croson*, but some lateral support for that view can be found in her sweeping endorsement of congressional power. The Constitution's framers wisely gave us no national process for legislation via the initiative measure.

III. Congress's Power and Responsibility

In one perspective *Croson* looks like a simple allocation of legislative jurisdiction. Cities and states can use affirmative action programs only as remedies for discrimination within their own regions.[159] Congress, on the other hand, is empowered to enforce the Fourteenth Amendment by remedying discrimination throughout the country. But the congressional power consolidated in *Croson* is not merely the power to remedy "identifiable" discrimination. Justice O'Connor recognizes a broad power in Congress "to define situations which *Congress* determines threaten equality and to adopt prophylactic rules to deal with those situations."[160] To avoid any mistake about the implications of this expansive principle for affirmative action, Justice O'Connor specifies that "Congress may identify and redress the effects of society-wide discrimination . . . ."[161] If the effects of private discrimination hurt all Americans,[162] Congress does seem the most appropriate body to recognize these harms and to remedy them.

Not only by these comments but also by her approving citation of two sweeping Warren Court endorsements of congressional power—

---

[158]109 S.Ct. at 740 (Marshall, J., dissenting).

[159]Perhaps a city will be allowed to seek to remedy discrimination in its immediate suburbs as well as within its borders.

[160]109 S.Ct. at 719 (emphasis in original).

[161]*Ibid*.

[162]See text at notes 33–39 *supra*.

not incidentally, two opinions taken at the time to be go-ahead signals to Congress[163]—Justice O'Connor brings off the Supreme Court's most important confirmation of civil rights gains in the 1980s. Perhaps because confirmation doesn't seem to be "news," this feature of the decision received little attention in the press. Thus *Fullilove*, which has always seemed vulnerable to a civil rights counterrevolution within the Court,[164] now rests on a base that is firm both doctrinally and (within the Court) politically.[165]

If *Fullilove* was a departure from the model of formal neutrality, *Croson* is a greater departure still. The decision consolidates in the Congress a power extending beyond the powers recognized in *Jones* (and now *Patterson*),[166] in the separate opinions in *Guest*,[167] or in *Fullilove* itself. Congress's power to define an inequality and provide a remedy is not limited to the spending of federal money.[168] It is not limited to affirmative action programs. It is not limited to the promotion of racial equality. It is not limited to the correction of "state action."[169] It is broad enough, for example, to support an act of Congress forbidding private discrimination against lesbians and gay men, irrespective of any connection with interstate commerce or "state action."

One explanation for this development might lie in a concern that is more institutional than substantive: deference to Congress on a subject of political moment. Surely the model of formal racial neutrality is far from dead. For the present majority of the Supreme Court, the model's substantive preferences are full of vigor, most visibly in their interpretations of the federal civil rights laws. As *Patterson* illus-

---

[163]Katzenbach v. Morgan, note 71 *supra*; South Carolina v. Katzenbach, note 71 *supra*.

[164]See Days, Fullilove, 96 Yale L.J. 453 (1987).

[165]At least six Justices are now on record as reaffirming *Fullilove*: Justice O'Connor's opinion on this point was joined by Chief Justice Rehnquist and Justice White. To this group we can add Justices Marshall, Brennan, and Blackmun, who dissented in *Croson*. It is not clear that any of the other three Justices would actually vote to overrule *Fullilove*, even though Justice Stevens dissented in that case and concurred in the judgment in *Croson*, and Justice Kennedy in *Croson* criticized the distinction between congressional and state legislative power to adopt affirmative action remedies.

[166]See text at notes 72–76 *supra*.

[167]See text at note 69 *supra*.

[168]Even if Congress's affirmative action remedies were confined to the spending power, there is much that Congress can achieve by placing conditions on grants of money to state and local governments. See McCoy & Friedman, Conditional Spending: Federalism's Trojan Horse, 1988 Supreme Court Review 85.

[169]The two separate opinions in *Guest*, note 69 *supra*, supporting congressional power to protect Fourteenth Amendment rights against private intereference, now seem not only reaffirmed but surpassed.

trates, the majority's operative principle for interpreting these statutes is, in effect, a rule of "clear statement": in cases they see as
doctrinally marginal, the preferences for private ordering and limited responsibility are followed unless Congress rather explicitly
commands a different result. For Congress itself, however, the
model of formal racial equality has little or no restraining force. Justice O'Connor's discussion of the flexibility of the act of Congress upheld in *Fullilove* is a hint that congressional power to engage in
affirmative action (or to authorize state and local governments to do
so) may be limited in similar ways, to avoid undue effects on "innocent third persons."[170] But even this limit is of uncertain dimensions;
throughout Justice O'Connor's discussion of congressional power the
watchword is deference. The principal limits on congressional action
to promote equal citizenship now lie not in constitutional doctrine
but in politics.

Thus both doctrine and politics have come full circle. The defining values of Congressional Reconstruction centered on the substantive conditions of equal citizenship, and Congress was assumed to be
the main engine of civil rights advance.[171] Then, during the much
longer era epitomized by the *Civil Rights Cases*, when the doctrinal
model of formal neutrality reached the peak of its influence in the
Court, Congress, too, had no interest in racial equality. Eventually,
Brown v. Board of Education gave new impetus to the modern civil
rights movement. When, in turn, the movement dramatized the connections between substantive equality and equal citizenship, Congress awoke to its civil rights responsibilities, and constitutional
doctrine responded with expanded interpretations of the Civil War
Amendments and of Congress's enforcement powers.[172]

Politics and constitutional doctrine also went hand in hand from
the late 1960s through the 1970s, when a broad bipartisan consensus
about civil rights reigned in the national government. Even during
the 1980s much of the consensus endured, despite the active hostility
of the White House and the Department of Justice.[173] Only a few

---

[170]Compare Shapiro v. Thompson, 394 U.S. 618, 641 (1969) ("Congress may not authorize
the states to violate the Equal Protection Clause").

[171]See, *e.g.*, Bickel, note 51 *supra*.

[172]See Tushnet, The NAACP's Legal Strategy Against Segregated Education, 1925–1950
(1987); Karst, note 33 *supra*, at 69–80.

[173]On Executive branch hostility, see Caplan, The Tenth Justice: The Solicitor General and
the Rule of Law 53–60, 81–95, 108–12, 202–09, 239–41 (1987); Days, Turning Back the
Clock: The Reagan Administration and Civil Rights, 19 Harv. C.R.-C.L. L. Rev. 309 (1984);
Days, The Courts' Response to the Reagan Civil Rights Agenda, 42 Vand. L. Rev. 1003 (1989);

days before President Bush was inaugurated, he offered reassurance that the civil rights consensus once again included the Executive Branch: "What becomes of Martin Luther King's dreams is up to us. We must not fail him. We must not fail ourselves. And we must not fail the nation he loved so much and gave his life for."[174] The congressional reaction to the reargument of the *Patterson* case was cut from the same political cloth. In short, the time is again ripe for Congress to review its responsibilities for doing substantive justice in the civil rights field.

Several of the Court's recent rulings call for Congress to engage in some "clear statement" that can be heard across the street. The starting point could well be a statutory "overruling" of two aspects of the *Wards Cove* decision: its highly particularized "causation" rule for proving the racially disparate impact that establishes a prima facie case of employer discrimination, and its radical revision of the burden of proof on the business justifications for an employer's practice.[175] A second ruling ripe for revision is the determination in *Patterson* that, in effect, denies any real remedy for the major harms of private employers' racial harassment. Such a revision should amend Title VII, to assure a damages remedy for sexual harassment; it should also amend Section 1981, to make damages available throughout a contract's duration—for example, to minority pupils who might be segregated in private schools.

In the field of state and local government contracting, *Croson* invites federal legislation to authorize affirmative action plans as remedies for past societal discrimination, both public and private. In support of such a law Congress could reasonably make at least two findings about the reasons why there are relatively few minority contractors and subcontractors in a city with a history like Richmond's. One explanation lies in the continuing effects of a system of education that, for generations following Emancipation, was defined around the demands of a system of racial subordination. Another lies in the very discrimination at issue in *Croson*: the public and private

Crenshaw, note 14 *supra*, at 1336–46; Kennedy, Pesuasion and Distrust: A Comment on the Affirmative Action Debate, 99 Harv. L. Rev. 1327 (1986); Guinier, Keeping the Faith: Black Voters in the Post-Reagan Era, 24 Harv. C.R.-C.L. L. Rev. 393 (1989). On the bipartisan consensus, see the impressive number of statutes enacted by Congress to "overrule" the Supreme Court's restrictive interpretations of federal civil rights laws, listed in Tushnet, note 5 *supra*, at 57 n.42.

[174]N.Y. Times, Jan. 17, 1989, pt. I, p. 1, col. 3.

[175]See text at notes 105–14 *supra*. A few weeks after the *Wards Cove* decision, Senator Metzenbaum introduced such a bill, S. 1261, 101st Cong., 1st Sess.

discrimination in the contracting business that powerfully discouraged minority entry. Beyond the decisions I have discussed, others of the 1988 Term further illustrate the need for Congress to reconsider the latest round of civil rights deregulation.[176]

One reason for Congress to respond quickly to undo the damage wrought last Term would be to send the sort of signal to the Supreme Court that Congress sent in the 1964 and 1965 Acts, telling the Justices that a national political consensus supports genuine efforts to reduce the harms of private racial discrimination. Although there is no reason to assume that the Justices of the current majority will respond sympathetically to such a signal when they next interpret a civil rights statute, Justice O'Connor's opinion in *Croson* suggests that there is reason to hope.

The substantive objective in pursuing such group-based remedies as affirmative action and an effective "disparate impact" rule in Title VII cases is not merely to create minority jobs or an enlarged minority middle class—although those are goals that ultimately seem essential to national integration. The objective is, more broadly, to create the conditions for effective interaction of people of every race and ethnicity in the public life of our communities. If we are to address the fears of the Other that are the seedbed of private discrimination and public neglect, we must know people as individuals and not as the abstract projection of a negative identity that must be repressed. Formal racial neutrality does little to achieve that understanding. What matters is our day-to-day interaction with each other—and each Other—in the workplace, in the university, in the world of business.[177] As Brenda Patterson's testimony illustrates, racial harassment stains that interaction, prevents the sharing of a community's public life.

Integration is a form of acculturation. Legislation can change attitudes by changing behavior. A major success story of our time can be found in the integration of southern hotels and restaurants in the quarter-century since the Civil Rights Act of 1964. The sight of black and white patrons being served alongside each other at a dime

---

[176]One of the most pressing of these would seem to be Lorance v. AT&T Technologies, Inc., 109 S.Ct. 2261 (1989), which constructs a statute-of-limitations trap for unwary employees who must now anticipate, when a seniority system is adopted by an employer and a union, that one day, under circumstances they cannot now foresee, they may have reason to challenge the system under Title VII because it is discriminatory. The limitations period, in other words, begins to run not when the employee is hurt, but when the plan is established.

[177]I have discussed this point at length in Karst, Boundaries and Reasons: Freedom of Expression and the Subordination of Groups, 1989 U. Ill. L. Rev. (forthcoming).

store lunch counter in Atlanta would have been astounding in 1950. Today, no one blinks. "The normative power of the factual,"[178] which long promoted separation and subordination, is also capable of promoting integration and racial equality. The positive side of the current civil rights consolidation, evident in *Patterson*'s reaffirmation of *Runyon* and in *Croson*'s invitations, is that the Supreme Court at last has rebuilt a lasting and solid constitutional basis for Congress to carry out the public responsibility to redress the effects of racial caste. Now we shall see whether the Congress will reclaim its historic leadership in defining and creating the substantive conditions of equal citizenship.

---

[178]Jellinek, Allgemeine Staatslehre (General Theory of the State) 338 (1929). (For assurance that the proper translation is "factual" rather than "actual," I am indebted to Frederick Smith.)

DAVID A. STRAUSS

DUE PROCESS, GOVERNMENT INACTION, AND PRIVATE WRONGS

Whatever else the government is supposed to do, it is supposed to protect citizens against violence by other citizens. Whatever else the social contract requires, it at least requires this much. Last Term, in *DeShaney v. Winnebago County Department of Social Services*,[1] the Supreme Court appeared to rule that this most basic duty of government is not enforceable as a matter of constitutional law. "As a general matter," the Court said, "a State's failure to protect an individual against private violence simply does not constitute a violation of the Due Process Clause."[2]

The idea is familiar: government actions can violate the Constitution, but government failures to act against private wrongdoers cannot.[3] Notwithstanding its sweeping language, however, *DeShaney* should not be read as a broad holding that there is never a constitutional right to government protection against private wrongs. More important, the distinction between action and inaction has no place in determining the government's duties under the Due Process Clause.

The Court's approach is mistaken on at least three levels. First, even assuming that there is such a thing as government inaction, it is

---

David A. Strauss is Professor of Law, The University of Chicago, and Visiting Professor of Law, Georgetown University Law Center, 1989–90.

AUTHOR'S NOTE: I am grateful to Cass Sunstein, Geoffrey Stone, Benna Solomon, and Richard Posner for their comments on an earlier draft.

[1] 109 S.Ct. 998 (1989).

[2] *Id.* at 1004.

[3] See, *e.g.*, Currie, Positive and Negative Constitutional Rights, 53 U. Chi. L. Rev. 864 (1986).

wrong to say that a failure to act cannot constitute a violation of the Due Process Clause. There are core violations of the Due Process Clause that consist of inaction indistinguishable from the official conduct in *DeShaney*. Second, private wrongdoing is never simply the product of government inaction. Government action—in the sense in which the Court itself used the term in *DeShaney*—exists every time an individual is the victim of private violence. Third, and most fundamental, the distinction between action and inaction can be coherently defined only by importing common law notions into constitutional law, specifically by making constitutional litigation a species of common law litigation. There is no legitimate basis for assigning such a role to the common law.

The Court's distinction between action and inaction is also unnecessary. The proposition that the government has some duty to protect individuals against private wrongs—that the Constitution forbids the government from withdrawing all protection against private wrongdoing—is far from novel, and presents neither practical nor theoretical difficulties. Once the government has established a program designed to protect individuals against private wrongdoing, the Due Process Clause, as the Court has often said, prohibits officials charged with administering that program from abusing their power. Wrongfully withholding protection—no less than "actively" injuring a person—can constitute an abuse of power.

I

Joshua DeShaney, a four-year-old boy, was the victim of the particularly barbarous private acts of violence that led to the *DeShaney* litigation. The perpetrator was Joshua's father, Randy De-Shaney, who was awarded custody of Joshua following a divorce. Between January 1982 and March 1984, various employees of Winnebago County, Wisconsin, where the DeShaneys lived, received information suggesting that Joshua was the victim of child abuse. For example, on several occasions Joshua was treated at county hospitals for injuries that hospital employees thought might be the product of child abuse; on her visits to the DeShaney home, a social services agency caseworker noticed a number of suspicious injuries; and on her last two visits before March 1984, the caseworker was not allowed to see Joshua. The caseworker meticulously recorded the information but the county did not seek to have Joshua removed from his father's home. The caseworker also made notes in her files, and comments to others, suggesting that she believed that Joshua was the victim of child abuse.

In March 1984, after Joshua was beaten so severely that he fell into a coma, doctors who operated on him discovered evidence of repeated blows to the head over a long period of time. The result of the beatings was that Joshua is severely brain damaged and will spend the rest of his life in an institution for the profoundly retarded. Randy DeShaney was convicted of child abuse and sentenced to prison.

Joshua and his mother sued Winnebago County, its Department of Social Services, and several county employees and officials. They alleged that the county's failure to protect Joshua from his father violated Joshua's constitutional rights. They based their claim on 42 U.S.C. §1983 and the Due Process Clause of the Fourteenth Amendment.

The Supreme Court upheld a grant of summary judgment for the defendants. The Court concluded, on the basis of text and precedent, that the Due Process Clause does not, in general, require the government to protect individuals against private wrongs. The Court acknowledged one exception to this rule: "when the State takes a person into its custody and holds him there against his will, the Constitution imposes upon it a corresponding duty to assume some responsibility for his safety."[4] Accordingly, the Court said, the government would be responsible for providing protection against private violence to state prisoners and involuntary patients in state hospitals. The Court left open the possibility that the state would have a similar obligation to children in state-operated foster homes. But since Joshua was injured while in his father's custody, not the State's, the Court ruled that this exception was inapplicable.[5]

II

Notwithstanding this categorical language, the holding of *De-Shaney* is in fact limited. The Court characterized the plaintiffs' claim as "one invoking the substantive rather than the procedural component of the Due Process Clause."[6] The Court left open the possibility

---

[4]109 S.Ct. at 1005. In fact, the state was not a defendant in *DeShaney*. Quern v. Jordan, 440 U.S. 332 (1979), held that the Eleventh Amendment bars a §1983 damages action against a state in federal court, and last Term the Court held that states are not "persons" under §1983, Will v. Michigan Department of State Police, 109 S.Ct. 2304 (1989), and therefore cannot be sued under §1983 in either state or federal court. The Court in *DeShaney* nonetheless referred to "the State," and for clarity I will do likewise.

[5]109 S.Ct. at 1005–6 & n.9.

[6]*Id.* at 1003.

that persons in Joshua's position might recover under the procedural component if they could show that state law created "an 'entitlement' to receive protective services in accordance with the terms of [a] statute."[7] The plaintiffs did not raise, and the Court did not consider, any arguments under the Equal Protection Clause.[8]

Less obvious but perhaps more important, the holding in *DeShaney* is narrower than might appear because the state in *DeShaney* did not deny all protection to the victim of the private wrongdoing. Only the state's child protective services were alleged to have failed. The plaintiffs did not suggest that there was a breakdown in the state's criminal or tort law enforcement systems. Indeed, the state imposed a criminal penalty on the private wrongdoer. A damages remedy in tort was also available in theory; while it seems unlikely that Joshua could have recovered any substantial sum, the existence of an effectively enforced tort remedy (there was no allegation that it was not effectively enforced),[9] like the criminal remedy, could be expected to have some deterrent effect.

If the state had withdrawn those remedies in *DeShaney*, the case would have had an entirely different complexion. It seems quite doubtful that the broad language the Court used in *DeShaney* was directed to such a situation. Indeed, at one point the Court suggested that it was holding only that the Due Process Clause "does not require the State to provide its citizens with *particular* protective services."[10] *DeShaney* therefore should not be taken to resolve the question whether a state is free to withdraw tort and criminal law remedies, either in principle or in practice.

III

While the holding of *DeShaney*, properly understood, is therefore narrow, the reasoning that the Court used has broad implications and reflects a distinct theoretical orientation toward consti-

---

[7]*Id.* at 1003 n.2. The Court declined to consider such a claim on the ground that it had not been raised in the Court of Appeals. *Ibid.* Procedural due process arguments for holding officials liable in cases of state inaction are developed in Note, 53 U. Chi. L. Rev. 1048, 1063–72 (1986).

[8]See 109 S. Ct. at 1003 n.3.

[9]Wisconsin limits the tort liability of government agencies and their employees to $50,000, Wis. Stat. Ann. 893.80 (West 1983), but this limitation does not impair the effectiveness of the tort remedies against private wrongdoers.

[10]109 S.Ct. at 1004 (emphasis added).

tutional litigation. The same reasoning has persuaded many lower court judges as well.[11] The idea has a simple allure: the Due Process Clause only forbids the government from actively injuring people. It does not require the government to protect people from private wrongs. So long as the government is not acting, it cannot violate the Due Process Clause. The Constitution is a charter of "negative rather than positive liberties" designed to protect people from the government rather than from each other.[12]

This reasoning is wrong in several respects, and the theoretical approach it reflects is utterly inadequate. First, there are forms of government "inaction," indistinguishable from the conduct of the defendants in *DeShaney* (at least as the Court viewed that conduct), that unquestionably violate the Due Process Clause. Second, *DeShaney* presented a form of undoubted state action that arguably caused the injury to Joshua; the Court did not explain why that state action was not sufficient to establish a claim under the Due Process Clause. Third, the Court's exception for "custodial" arrangements such as prisons and state hospitals is not really an exception at all. The principle underlying that exception implies that the government has "affirmative" duties not only to persons in custody but to someone in Joshua DeShaney's situation and, in fact, to every person in society. Finally, the distinction between action and inaction cannot be defined at all unless one borrows common law notions: the implicit definition of government "action" used by the Court is that government action occurs when the government invades common law interests. This definition cannot be justified.

1. Even assuming that separate categories of government action and inaction can be identified, the principle that the government is liable only for the former and not for the latter produces implausible results.

a) Suppose that police officers learn that a murder is about to occur that they can prevent with minimal cost. Ordinarily they would intervene without hesitation. But in this case they decide not to do so

---

[11]See, *e.g.*, Washington v. District of Columbia, 802 F.2d 1478, 1481 (D.C. Cir. 1986); Estate of Gilmore v. Buckley, 787 F.2d 714, 719–21 (1st Cir.), cert. denied, 464 U.S. 864 (1983); Doe v. New York Department of Social Services, 649 F.2d 134, 141 (2d Cir. 1981), cert. denied, 464 U.S. 864 (1983); Fox v. Custis, 712 F.2d 84, 86–88 (4th Cir. 1983); Rankin v. City of Wichita Falls, 762 F.2d 444, 449 (5th Cir. 1985); Archie v. City of Racine, 847 F.2d 1211 (7th Cir. 1988) (en banc); Jones v. Phyfer, 761 F.2d 642 (11th Cir. 1985).

[12]Jackson v. City of Joliet, 715 F.2d 1200, 1203 (7th Cir. 1983), cert. denied, 465 U.S. 1049 (1984).

because the targeted victim is someone whom they believe is guilty of another crime. The officers would rather see him killed by private persons than brought to trial where, they fear, he might escape with an acquittal or a light sentence.

This must be a case of government inaction, assuming there is such a thing. The police officers did not instigate or facilitate the murder in any way, except to refrain from intervening. They did not make the victim worse off than he would have been if the officers had never become aware of his predicament.

But it seems clear that this kind of government failure to act violates the Due Process Clause. A summary execution of a suspect by the authorities would be the clearest possible violation of the Due Process Clause. The hypothetical example is no different except for the fortuity that there were private persons who planned to do the murder. The *DeShaney* approach would allow the existence of that fortuity to make the difference between a flagrant violation of the Due Process Clause and an action that is not a constitutional violation at all. There is no reason to attach such significance to a fortuity.

This hypothetical case is indistinguishable from *DeShaney*, at least as the Supreme Court viewed that case. In *DeShaney* social services workers, instead of police officers, failed to intervene to prevent private violence; that difference is immaterial. Of course, in *DeShaney* the state of mind of the government officials was different. There was no allegation that they acted out of a desire to see Joshua injured. Had the Supreme Court decided *DeShaney* on the ground that the state officials lacked the necessary state of mind to violate the Constitution, the holding would be less vulnerable to criticism, and much less significant.[13]

But the Court explicitly declined to decide the case on that ground. It followed the court of appeals in assuming that the defendants' state of mind was sufficiently culpable to violate the Constitution.[14] It ruled in favor of the officials on the ground that they had only engaged in inaction, not action. That does not distinguish *DeShaney*

---

[13]The Court had previously ruled that negligent government action does not constitute a "depriv[ation]" within the meaning of the Due Process Clause, Daniels v. Williams, 474 U.S. 327 (1986); Davidson v. Cannon, 474 U.S. 344 (1986), and there are sound bases for the conclusion that routine negligent actions (or inactions) by government officials do not constitute violations of the Constitution. See pages 82–86 *infra*.

[14]109 S.Ct. at 1007 n.10; see DeShaney v. Winnebago County Department of Social Services, 812 F.2d 298, 302 (7th Cir. 1987).

from the hypothetical police inaction case. To put the point another
way, under *DeShaney*, child protective services employees would not
violate the Due Process Clause even if they deliberately refused to
intervene because they wanted to see a child harmed (because of a
grudge against a family or out of a bizarre belief that child abuse constitutes proper discipline, for example).[15]

b) The Due Process Clause requires that a judge be impartial. That
requirement applies to suits between private parties, as well as suits
against the government. Plaintiffs, as well as defendants, are protected by this requirement. None of these propositions has ever been
seriously disputed.

But the plaintiff in a private action is, by definition, seeking to have
the government act against alleged private wrongdoing.[16] A plaintiff
who loses a private suit is the victim of private harm and government
inaction —the government failure to stop or correct the harm—just
like the victim in *DeShaney*.

Suppose a plaintiff seeking, say, to enjoin a trespass by a private
party, loses his or her case because the judge is biased. (Suppose the
judge has a financial interest aligned with the defendant.) That is a
clear violation of the Due Process Clause. In what sense, however, is
this an instance of government action, as opposed to inaction? The
case is just like *DeShaney* (again leaving state of mind aside), except
that the official who refused to intervene against the private wrongdoing is a judge instead of a social worker. Thus the *DeShaney* approach leads to a wholly implausible conclusion in connection with
an issue that goes to the core of the Due Process Clause, the right to
trial before an impartial judge.

---

[15]It might be thought that the police inaction in this hypothetical constitutes a violation not
of the Due Process Clause but of the Equal Protection Clause. If so, then the defendants' action
in *DeShaney* also violates the Equal Protection Clause; as the Court analyzed *DeShaney* (that is,
leaving the officials' state of mind aside), the only difference between *DeShaney* and the police
inaction hypothetical is that the former concerned social service workers and the latter involved
the police.

In addition, it is by no means clear that it violates the Equal Protection Clause for the police
to refuse to provide protection to a suspect. The Equal Protection Clause is ordinarily concerned not with the nature or magnitude of the burden the government places on a group but
with whether the government has an appropriate basis for treating that group less favorably
than another. There is no question that the government may treat persons suspected of crimes
less favorably than others in a variety of ways (including ways that are not specifically authorized by the Fourth and Fifth Amendments). Therefore it is difficult to see how the government offends the Equal Protection Clause when it affords less protection to suspects.

[16]I leave aside complications such as declaratory judgments.

There appear to be four possible (and related) arguments against this conclusion, but none is successful. First, it might be said that this is not a case of inaction because the judge has affirmatively acted by dismissing the complaint or entering judgment against the plaintiff. But if a judge's dismissing a complaint counts as action, so does the *DeShaney* defendants' "refusal" to intervene. In both instances a state official has declined to intervene to prevent an alleged private wrong. The notions of action and inaction are notoriously manipulable in this way. Many actions can be recharacterized as inaction, and vice versa.[17] Indeed there is a serious question whether action and inaction can be coherently differentiated. (I suggest below that they can be coherently defined in the *DeShaney* context only by giving common law notions an unjustifiably prominent role.) But however the terms are defined, it cannot matter whether the state functionary who refuses to try to prevent private wrongdoing is a judge or a social worker.

Second, it might be said that the hypothetical case of the biased judge is different from *DeShaney* because procedural and not substantive due process is at stake. Again, however, if this is a case of procedural due process, so is *DeShaney*. In *DeShaney*, as the Court decided the case, the government employees' failure to provide relief could have been caused by the impermissible influence of a pecuniary interest or another equally illegitimate personal interest (such as a desire to maximize their leisure time). More generally, as I will explain below, the distinction between substantive and procedural due process is blurred in cases of this kind; it does not stretch the notion unduly to call *DeShaney*, like the biased judge hypothetical, a case involving procedural due process. Neither the Court nor the plaintiffs characterized it that way, but the characterization should not dictate the way in which the case is analyzed, and there is no indication in the opinion that it did affect the Court.

Third, it might be said that the biased judge affirmatively acts by depriving the plaintiff of a cause of action—a valuable property right established by state law. But what warrant is there for saying, in the hypothetical case, that state law has established a "cause of action"?

---

[17]"The clever law student is able to turn commissions into omissions by arguing, for example, that negligent driving is nothing more than the failure to brake." Levmore, Waiting for Rescue: An Essay on the Evolution and Incentive Structure of the Law of Affirmative Obligations, 72 Va. L. Rev. 879, 879 (1986).

In the example I gave—a suit to enjoin a trespass—the plaintiff would be entitled to an unbiased judge even if state law had never recognized an injunctive remedy for trespass. Indeed, even if no common law interest is at stake and the state law leaves a determination entirely to the discretion of the judge—so that there is no "entitlement" in the usual sense—the Due Process Clause still requires that the plaintiff have an impartial judge. Similarly, in the police inaction case I described, the conduct of the police would violate the Constitution even if (as is usually the case) state law did not create any entitlement to police protection in specific cases (because state law explicity left the deployment of police resources to the discretion of police officials).

Finally, it might be said that the jurisdictional statutes that establish the judge's position and empower him or her to decide cases somehow alter the situation by implicitly creating a right to an unbiased decision. As I will argue more elaborately below, the premise of this argument is correct. The jurisdictional statutes do create an entitlement to a fair determination; a judge who issues a biased decision deprives a litigant of this interest. But this does not distinguish the judge's case from *DeShaney*. The equivalent of a jurisdictional statute exists for all government officials. Some statute or set of statutes establishes their positions and empowers them to act in certain situations. If jurisdictional statutes are the source of the judge's obligation to be impartial, the equivalent statutes are the source of a parallel obligation for other government officials.

I will argue below that in all three cases—the two hypotheticals and *DeShaney* itself—the government has indeed deprived an individual of a state-created right, not one of the traditional common law interests. When the government establishes a program of services that protects citizens against private wrongdoing—courts, police, or child protective services—it implicitly creates a right to a fair determination (a term that of course must be defined) of when those services should be provided.

2. Even under the Court's premise—that the government can be held liable only for action, not for inaction—the state should not have been absolved of liability in *DeShaney*. The state established a comprehensive program designed to protect children from abuse. There is no question that this constitutes state action, not state inaction. The defendants' "inaction"—the failure to protect Joshua DeShaney—took place against a background of this form of state action. Before ruling in favor of the state, the Court should have

explained why this pattern of state action did not make the state liable.[18]

In his dissent in *DeShaney*, Justice Brennan urged that this government action contributed to Joshua's injuries. His argument was that by establishing such a program, the government discouraged others—private persons and other government agencies—from intervening to protect Joshua. This argument reflects the tort rule that an individual has no obligation to attempt the rescue of a person endangered by another's conduct, but can be held liable if the rescue attempt is carried out negligently. The theory is that the rescue attempt may have worsened the victim's situation by causing the victim to forgo other sources of aid or by discouraging other potential rescuers from coming to the victim's aid.[19]

It is difficult—for many reasons—to know whether, as an empirical matter, Justice Brennan's argument is correct. Certainly the existence of some government services discourages private rescue. For example, if the government establishes an emergency telephone service for people to call when they need medical care, people are discouraged from calling on private sources for help. If the emergency service then gives bad advice, the government's action has unquestionably caused any resulting injury.[20] *DeShaney* is a more difficult case, because it is less obvious that private rescuers would have appeared if there were no state protective services.

In *DeShaney*, it is not implausible to say, as the court of appeals did, that it is too "conjectural" to argue that others would have rescued Joshua had they not relied on the social service agencies to do so.[21] But the court of appeals' solution does not justify the Supreme Court's sweeping statement that the government generally cannot be

---

[18]The Court's only discussion of this point begged the question. The Court noted that the state's action (in establishing and then incompetently administering a protective program) might be tortious, then asserted— correctly—that not every tort by a state employee violates the Due Process Clause. 109 S.Ct. at 1006–7. But some torts by state employees obviously violate the Due Process Clause, so the question remains whether this tort was one of them. The Court said: "Because . . . the State had no constitutional duty to protect Joshua against his father's violence, its failure to do so . . . simply does not constitute a violation of the Due Process Clause." *Id*. at 1007. But even if there was no *general* "duty to protect Joshua against his father's violence," the state may have a duty not to establish a protective regime that discourages private assistance and then administer it incompetently.

[19]Restatement (Second) of Torts §§314, 323, 324 (1965); see Section 323, comment c.

[20]See Archie v. City of Racine, 847 F.2d at 1225 (Posner, J., concurring).

[21]DeShaney v. Winnebago County Department of Social Services, 812 F.2d 298, 302 (7th Cir. 1987). See Restatement (Second) of Torts, §323, comment e.

held liable in cases of "inaction." In some such cases, for example that involving the emergency telephone service, the causal connection will not be conjectural at all.

The more important implication of this line of argument, however, is that it would be better to adopt an approach that avoids assessing this causal connection at all. In the case of a discrete act by an individual rescuer—such as stopping to give aid to an accident victim on a busy highway—it will sometimes be possible to imagine what might have happened had the rescuer not intervened. But when the "rescue" consists of an elaborate government program, such a counterfactual inquiry will often be highly problematic. The existence of government programs affects private behavior in ways that are very difficult to assess. For example, if there were no police departments or social services agencies, private parties would undoubtedly establish rough equivalents to some extent. But one can only speculate about what form those private equivalents would take or how effective they would be—let alone whether they would have been successful in any individual case.

Any approach that requires the courts to make such a determination is to that extent unsatisfactory. But such an approach is necessary only if constitutional wrongs are assimilated to torts. As I will suggest presently, it is a mistake to transfer common law notions into the interpretation of the Due Process Clause in this way.

3. To its general rule that "inaction" does not violate the Due Process Clause, the *DeShaney* Court established an exception, for instances in which "the State takes a person into custody and holds him there against his will." For example, *Youngberg v. Romeo*[22] held that the Due Process Clause guarantees mental patients who are involuntarily committed to a state hospital a right to the services that are needed to ensure their "reasonable safety" from attacks by others. *Estelle v. Gamble*[23] held that prisoners' constitutional rights are violated when prison authorities show deliberate indifference toward their serious medical needs.[24] The Court in *DeShaney* explicitly left

---

[22]457 U.S. 307 (1982).

[23]429 U.S. 97 (1976).

[24]*Id.* at 105–6. Although Estelle v. Gamble was based on the Eighth Amendment, the *DeShaney* Court treated it as if it were a case under the Due Process Clause, perhaps because Whitley v. Albers, 475 U.S. 312 (1986), suggested that a similar standard would apply to substantive due process claims. See *id.* at 326–27; *DeShaney*, 109 S.Ct. at 1005 n.5.

open the possibility that the state might have "an affirmative duty to protect" a child in Joshua DeShaney's situation if the child were in a "foster home operated by [state] agents."[25]

The basis for this exception is unclear. The Court seemed to say that the government's duty to act arises in these cases because the government has taken an individual into custody against his or her will. The courts of appeals have generally held that a state has a duty to provide some degree of protection against private wrongdoing only when the state has either "put a [person] in a position of danger from private persons"[26] or has "cut[] off sources of private aid."[27] For example, the Court of Appeals for the Seventh Circuit has held that state employees may be liable for arresting the driver of a car containing small children and leaving the children alone on a major highway.[28]

Whatever the basis for this exception, it cannot be confined to exceptional cases such as prisons. Joshua DeShaney's situation did not differ in any relevant respect from the situation of the persons to whom this exception applies. And what is true of Joshua DeShaney in this respect is equally true of every person. As I will show, the "exception," applied in a principled way, swallows up the rule and establishes that the government has a general duty to provide some level of protection against private wrongdoing.

a) The state was, to a significant degree, responsible for the fact that Joshua was in a family unit with his father. Even leaving aside the fact that Joshua lived with his father because of a court decree[29]— assuming that he had lived from birth with both biological parents

---

[25]109 S.Ct. at 1006 n.9. See Taylor v. Ledbetter, 818 F.2d 791 (11th Cir. 1987) (en banc); Doe v. New York City Department of Social Services, 649 F.2d 134 (2d Cir. 1981), cert. denied, 464 U.S. 864 (1983).

[26]Bowers v. De Vito, 686 F.2d 616, 618 (7th Cir. 1982); see, e.g., Escamilla v. City of Santa Ana, 796 F.2d 266, 269 (9th Cir. 1986); Wideman v. Shallowford Commuunity Hospital, 826 F.2d 1030, 1035, 1037 (11th Cir. 1987). The Supreme Court seemed to endorse this approach at one point in the *DeShaney* opinion. After one of the early incidents in which state employees saw evidence that Joshua was being abused, the state took custody of Joshua for three days and then returned him to his father. See 109 S.Ct. at 1001. The Court said that this action by the state did not create an obligation to protect Joshua against private violence because "when [the state] returned him to his father's custody, it placed him in no worse position than that in which he would have been had it not acted at all." *Id.* at 1006.

[27]Archie v. City of Racine, 847 F.2d at 1222–23.

[28]White v. Rochford, 592 F.2d 381 (1979).

[29]In *DeShaney* the decree awarding custody to the father was entered by a Wyoming state court before the father and Joshua moved to Wisconsin. See 109 S.Ct. at 1001. Wyoming officials were not named as defendants, but nothing in the opinion suggests that the outcome would have been different if they had been named.

without any judicial intervention—the family unit is to a significant extent the product of state action.

The government actively supports the family unit in countless ways. State law imposes support obligations on parents and gives them vast rights to control and direct their children's lives. State law bars strangers from intervening in the family except in extraordinary circumstances. Many state laws—those concerning marriage and divorce, property, testamentary disposition, taxation, intra-family immunities—are designed to promote the establishment and maintenance of families. Through schools and many other media, the government promotes the family unit and reinforces the authority of the parents.

In all of these ways, the state "put [Joshua] in a position of danger from [a] private person"—his father—and "cut off his sources of private aid" just as it does to a prison inmate. If there were no presumption that children stay with their families; if the barriers to adoption or termination of parental rights were lower; if relatives could intervene in the family more easily; if his father would not have faced criminal penalties for abandoning the child; if (in the case of a child older than Joshua) the state made it easier for a child to run away; if the state did not reinforce parental authority by various means; Joshua might not have been subjected to his father's violence or might have been able to obtain private aid. Under the logic of the "exception," therefore, the state owed Joshua a duty of care against private violence from his father.

The point is not that these acts by the state—acts that promote the family and that increased the likelihood that Joshua would be in a family unit with his father—were in themselves wrongful. In *Estelle v. Gamble*, is was not wrongful for the state to confine the inmate to prison after a trial; in *Youngberg*, it was not wrongful for the state involuntarily to commit the patient to the state hospital. What is wrongful under the Due Process Clause, according to the opinion in *DeShaney*, is to establish such institutions without taking care to protect those who are "confined" within them. Since the state plays a role in establishing the family, it owes a duty of care to persons in Joshua DeShaney's position as well.

It is also not an answer that children in a "natural" family are not held in state custody against their will. The fact that the state has placed someone in the custody of a private party instead of in the custody of a state employee has no bearing on whether the state has placed the person in danger or has cut off that person's sources of private aid. And it is pointless, and probably meaningless, to ask whether an infant is in a family against his or her will.[30] If it is meaningful, then children in a foster home are not ordinarily there against their wills. And whether it is meaningful or not, the notion that Joshua was in the family unit with his father in accordance with his will is truly Orwellian.[31]

It is true that natural families are not entirely the creation of the state. Parents and children are held together in part by bonds of affection and dependency that we feel confident would exist even without the state. But parents and children are not always united by such bonds; if they were, there would be no need for the many government institutions that enforce parents' obligations. Moreover, the other institutions are not entirely the creation of the state: foster homes can be created and held together by the same bonds as conventional families, and foster homes, prisons, and mental hospitals might all be established by private arrangement without the state. Nor is it helpful to try to determine which kind of institution is "more" the product of state actions.[32]

It might be objected that placing children in family units does not in itself increase their exposure to acts of private violence. Indeed, if the state had not done so much to promote the family, Joshua might have ended up a homeless child on the streets of a city, and he could have been more vulnerable to private violence (although he could hardly have been much worse off). But it is also doubtful that foster children or patients in state hospitals are better off outside of these institutions. Prisoners may or may not be more exposed to private violence inside prison; they are confined in the company of criminals, but their extraordinarily controlled environment provides greater protection from crime.

b) This argument can be extended beyond Joshua to every member

---

[30]It also makes little sense to speak of an incompetent being held against his or her will in a mental institution; the premise of involuntary commitment in such cases is that what the patient wills is of reduced, or no, significance.

[31]Inexplicably, the Court's opinion twice used terms like this to refer to Joshua's situation when he was in his father's custody. See 109 S.Ct. at 1006 ("the dangers Joshua faced in the free world"); *id.* at 1006 n.9 ("free society").

[32]That determination would require utterly unwieldy counterfactual speculation. For example: If the government did not require parents to support their children, what private protective organizations would develop? What would happen if the government allowed free–wheeling intervention by concerned private citizens where family abuse was suspected? If the government determined that children were to be raised in communal settings, to what extent would nuclear families survive? On the other side of the equation, if the government did not establish prisons, what comparable institutions would private parties develop?

of society. If, as the Court said in *DeShaney*, the principle that inaction cannot violate the Due Process Clause is inapplicable to persons in state custody, then it is inapplicable everywhere.

This point is significant because the intuition underlying the Court's exception for "custodial" institutions is strong; every court of appeals that has addressed the issue has adopted a comparable exception.[33] When the state is obviously, visibly responsible for a person's vulnerability to private violence, no court has denied that the state ought to provide some protection against the private wrongs that the person suffers. The concern seems to be that while private action was the immediate cause of the injury—to the prisoner or involuntary patient injured by another inmate, for example, or to the child injured by the foster parent—state action is present in the background; the state's action placed the victim in a position where he or she could be injured.[34]

But state action is always present in the background in this sense. State action contributes to the condition in which all members of society—not just persons in state custody, and not just children in families—find themselves. In most instances, the state action takes the form of enforcing, for example, common law rules of contract and property.

These forms of state action will often have the effect of exposing people to private violence and cutting them off from private sources of assistance. A poor person living in a high-crime area is exposed to private violence and cut off (because of both geography and poverty) from many private sources of protection. That person's situation is at least partly the result of the state's enforcement of various rules that establish and regulate the market and that distribute and redistribute resources. We are so accustomed to that set of state rules—they are the background of so much of ordinary life—that they tend to become invisible. But the enforcement of those rules is indisputably state action, and it has the effect of placing many people in a position where they are vulnerable to private violence and cannot escape.

Of course, the state rules are not the sole cause of most individuals' vulnerability to private violence. Poverty can be the result of a person's lacking the attributes that the market values (or, less benignly, of unfair discrimination, irrationality, or chance). But state law is not

---

[33]See cases cited in notes 25–27 *supra*.

[34]See, *e.g.*, Archie v. City of Racine, 847 F.2d 1211, 1222–23 (7th Cir. 1988); Wideman v. Shallowford Community Hospital, Inc., 826 F.2d 1030, 1034–36 (11th Cir. 1987).

the sole cause of an inmate's imprisonment, either. In fact, a person living in poverty in a high-crime area is much less likely to be the author of his or her own fate than a person living in prison.

Thus the logic of the Court's exception for "custodial" situations extends not only to a person in Joshua DeShaney's situation but to all members of society. All members of society—not just state prisoners, involuntarily committed patients, and foster children—owe their position in some measure to the actions of the government. To the extent they are exposed to private violence or cut off from private assistance, they are in that position partly because the state put them there—just like state prisoners. If the state adopted different arrangements, they might be better protected against private violence or not as well protected; that, too, is true of state prisoners. It is true that prisoners are in custody, but there is no apparent reason that this should matter. If, as every court has agreed, the state owes prisoners a duty of care in protecting them against private violence, then it owes this duty to all citizens.

4. The underlying logic of the Court's ruling in *DeShaney*—and its fundamental inadequacy—can be better understood if one sees the Court's reasoning as implicitly based on a particular approach to constitutional litigation. This approach is coherent, and it has venerable roots. But it has now been thoroughly, and correctly, rejected. Indeed, it is flatly inconsistent with Section 1983.

This underlying view is that a plaintiff may not bring an action alleging a violation of the Constitution unless he or she can also show that a common law interest was invaded. The Court did not consider what the defendants in *DeShaney* did to be "action" because the defendants did not infringe any common law interests of Joshua De-Shaney. The Court said at one point: "it is well to remember . . . that the harm was inflicted not by the State of Wisconsin, but by Joshua's father."[35] This sentence (which the Court thought obvious) is true only if the terms are given common law meanings: if "inflicted" means an actual touching and the only "harm" is the battery. But if causation is expanded beyond physical invasion, or "harm" includes the deprivation of a fair opportunity for state protection, the statement is not obviously true.

Similarly, the Court established a separate category for "custodial" institutions, because the individuals inhabiting them have suf-

---

[35] 109 S.Ct. at 1007.

fered an infringement of a common law interest at the hands of the
state. That is why the Court saw state action when the state placed an
individual in a prison, state hospital, or (perhaps) foster home. In
those cases, the state did something that, if done by a private person,
would constitute an invasion of a common law interests. But the
Court does not see state action when the state helps establish and
maintain conventional family relations, and it certainly does not see
state action when the state maintains property, contract, and other
rules that effectively confine people in certain economic and social
positions. That is because in those cases there is no infringement of
common law interests.

Thus the Court explained its treatment of "custodial" institutions
by saying that "it is the State's affirmative act of restraining the individual's freedom to act on his own behalf—through incarceration,
institutionalization, or other similar restraint of personal liberty—
which is the 'deprivation of liberty' triggering the protections of the
Due Process Clause . . . ."[36] As the dissent pointed out, this assertion is incorrect on its face. The prisoner or involuntary patient who
sues because he was injured while institutionalized is complaining
about the injury, not about the decision to institutionalize him; that
initial decision conformed to the Due Process Clause.[37] But one can
make sense of the Court's statement if one views it as reflecting an
implicit assimilation of constitutional to common law wrongs. At
common law, taking custody of a person creates an obligation to exercise due care in protecting that person's safety.[38]

It appears, therefore, that the Court in *DeShaney* is implicitly requiring plaintiffs raising constitutional claims to establish that the
state has invaded some common law interest. The roots of this approach are in what Justice Harlan called (in the course of rejecting it
in his opinion in *Bivens v. Six Unknown Named Agents*[39]) the "'state-
created right—federal defense' model" of constitutional litigation.
Under this model, the Constitution creates no implied rights of ac-

[36]*Id.* at 1006.
[37]*Id.* at 1008–9 (Brennan, J., dissenting).
[38] See Restatement (Second) of Torts §314A(4): "One who . . . voluntarily takes the custody
of another under circumstances such as to deprive the other of his normal opportunities for
protection is under" a duty "to take reasonable action . . . to protect [the other] against unreasonable risk of physical harm." See also *DeShaney*, 109 S.Ct. at 1006 n.8: "[T]he protections of
the Due Process Clause . . . may be triggered when the State . . . subjects an involuntarily
confined individual to deprivations of liberty which are not among those generally authorized
by his confinement."
[39]403 U.S. 388, 400 n.3 (1971) (concurring opinion).

tion. A constitutional right therefore cannot be the basis for a plaintiff's claim. Constitutional rights can still be enforced in a variety of ways, notably as defenses in actions brought by the government. But a plaintiff cannot bring suit on the basis of a constitutional right alone.

Instead, under this model, a plaintiff seeking to enforce a constitutional right must bring a common law action against the allegedly culpable official. For example, a plaintiff seeking damages for an illegal search must sue in trespass. The constutitutional issue enters the case if the official defends on the ground that his or her action was privileged because it was authorized by law. At that point, if the plaintiff can show that the action was unconstitutional—and therefore could not be privileged—the plaintiff can prevail. But the constitutional claim does not itself give rise to the cause of action. It operates only to defeat a defense of official privilege. Therefore a plaintiff who alleges a constitutional violation cannot sue unless he or she can also show that a common law interest has been invaded.

The best way to make sense of the *DeShaney* opinion is to view it as having implicitly adopted this approach. That would at least give the Court a possible way to deal with the biased judge hypothetical (since that Due Process Clause claim can be raised on appeal, without an implied right of action),[40] and it would explain why the Court did not perceive the state action involved in establishing and maintaining the family (since that state action invades no common law interests). It would of course explain why the Court did not perceive the state action that is at the root of every ordinary citizen's situation, since much of that state action takes the form of enforcing, not infringing, common law interests. It would not explain the Court's refusal to consider the "botched rescue" argument, although that claim was not particularly strong on the facts of *DeShaney*. And it seems to provide no help with the police inaction hypothetical.

But the problem with the "state right–federal defense" approach—that is, with the notion that a plaintiff complaining of a constitutional violation must also show an invasion of a common law interest—is that it has been thoroughly and deservedly repudiated. Section 1983 explicitly authorizes actions based on the Constitution alone against state officials. *Bivens* removed any doubt that constitu-

---

[40]Even this is not entirely clear. Ultimately it might be necessary to seek mandamus or prohibition to enforce the right to an impartial judge, and an implied right of action would be needed to ground those suits.

tional rights can ground actions against federal officials, even in the absence of a common law wrong.[41] Many clear constitutional violations—ranging from racial discrimination to illegal mail openings—do not always involve the invasion of common law interests and commonly will go unremedied unless the victim can bring suit directly under the Constitution. To the extent that the *DeShaney* Court's distinction between action and inaction implicitly required a common law invasion as a prerequisite for a suit to enforce constitutional rights—and that seems to be a reasonable account of what the Court was doing—the Court's action reflects an outmoded and inappropriately restrictive view of constitutional litigation.

IV

How should the problem of government obligations to protect against private wrongs be addressed? The broad language of the *DeShaney* opinion blurs two distinct issues. The first is whether the government must provide some absolute minimum level of protection against private wrongdoing. The second is whether, assuming that the government has established a program designed to protect citizens against private wrongs, a government official's improper conduct in administering the program can violate the Due Process Clause even when that conduct takes the form of inaction rather than action. These issues are analytically independent: the resolution of one does not depend on the answer to the other.

A

The question whether the government owes its citizens some absolute level of protection against private wrongdoing is one of substantive, rather than procedural, due process.[42] That is because the claim

---

[41]*Bivens* held that a plaintiff may bring an action for damages directly under the Constitution. See also Bell v. Hood, 327 U.S. 678, 684 (1946). Actions for injunctions directly under the Constitution date at least from Ex parte Young, 209 U.S. 123 (1908). See generally Bator *et al.*, Hart & Wechsler's The Federal Courts and the Federal System 1180–82 (3d ed. 1988).

The *DeShaney* Court's (implicit) incorporation of common law notions into §1983 litigation is also at odds with the Court's repeated insistence, in other cases, that §1983 and state tort law protect different interests. See, *e.g.*, Paul v. Davis, 424 U.S. 693, 701 (1976); Baker v. Mc-Collum, 443 U.S. 137, 146 (1979); Martinez v. California, 444 U.S. 277, 285 (1980); Parratt v. Taylor, 451 U.S. 527, 544 (1981); Daniels v. Williams, 474 U.S. 327, 332 (1986).

[42]It is possible to view the issue as arising not under the Due Process Clause at all but under the Fourth Amendment's prohibition against unreasonable searches and seizures and the Fifth Amendment's prohibition against uncompensated takings. See pages 72–76 *infra*. But *DeShaney* viewed the issue as one of substantive due process.

is that there exists a minimum level of protection against private wrongs that the government must provide, irrespective of the procedures the government affords. As I explained earlier, *DeShaney* did not present the question whether the government may withhold all protection against private wrongs. There was no allegation in *De-Shaney* that the state denied all protection to Joshua. In fact the state enforced the criminal law against his father, and there is no reason to doubt that it stood ready to enforce a damages remedy in tort.

Nonetheless, the opinion contains sweeping language suggesting that the Due Process Clause does not require a state to provide even "minimal levels of safety and security." The "purpose" of the Due Process Clause, the Court said, "was to protect the people from the State, not to ensure that the State protected them from each other."[43] The Court also relied on the language of the Clause—the word "deprive," it asserted, referred to government action, not to the government's failure to protect against private action—and on cases that asserted that the Due Process Clause creates "no affirmative right to governmental aid."[44]

None of the arguments I have made so far draws this aspect of *De-Shaney* into question. In fact, there is no basis for criticizing the Court's holding (as opposed to its language) on this aspect of *De-Shaney*. But the Court's broad language is incorrect. The best interpretation of the Due Process Clause is that it requires the states to provide some level of protection against private violence.

This conclusion should not be surprising. In fact, the view suggested by the language of *DeShaney*—that the government has no duty at all to protect citizens against private wrongs—is novel. It has generally been assumed that the states have some obligation to maintain common law remedies, or their equivalent, to some degree. Apparently no state has ever sought to deny all protection against private wrongs. And when the states have rescinded particular common law remedies, the Supreme Court, in upholding the action, has relied on the fact that the state provided an adequate alternative remedy.[45]

1. The Takings Clause prohibits the government from seizing pri-

---

[43] 109 S.Ct. at 1003.

[44] *Id.* at 1003–4. *E.g.*, Harris v. McRae, 448 U.S. 297, 317–18 (1980); Lindsey v. Normet, 405 U.S. 56, 74 (1972).

[45] See, *e.g.*, Duke Power Co. v. Carolina Environmental Study Group, 438 U.S. 59, 88 (1978); New York Central R. Co. v. White, 243 U.S. 188, 201 (1917). See generally Pruneyard Shopping Center v. Robins, 447 U.S. 74, 93–95 (1979) (Marshall, J., concurring).

vate property without just compensation, at least in certain circumstances. The Takings Clause of course applies when the government
itself takes title to private property. But the Takings Clause must also
be intepreted to require the government to provide property owners
with some protection—for example, an action in trespass—against
other private parties.

That is because often the power of eminent domain is exercised
not so that the government itself can use the property but in order to
vest title to the property in another private party, such as a private
developer or, in the last century, a railroad.[46] If there were no requirement that the government provide any remedy against private
invasion, owners would not have to be compensated in such cases.
The government could simply abrogate the owner's tort remedy
against the private party who sought the land. Thus in some circumstances the Takings Clause does not just forbid the government from
itself seizing private property. It also requires the government to provide a remedy against invasions by other private parties.[47]

DeShaney did not involve an invasion of property, but it did involve
an invasion of another interest protected by the common law, the interest in physical integrity (in the sense of freedom from battery). It
is difficult to see why that interest should receive less constitutional
protection than the interest in property. The common law interest in
freedom from battery is surely at least as important as the interest in
property. And for some purposes, at least, that common law interest
is unquestionably an aspect of "liberty" within the meaning of the
Due Process Clause; no one would deny that state officials themselves may not commit an unjustified battery against a person. Since
the language of the Due Process Clause seems to place the "liberty"
interest in being free from battery on a par with the "property" interest in being free from trespass, both interest should receive protection against private invasion. That is, just as the state may not withdraw all trespass remedies, it may not withdraw all remedies against
battery.

This is not to say that the Constitution requires the state to protect
against invasion all of the interests that were protected at common
law.[48] Such a view would severely restrict the power of the state, in

---

[46]See, *e.g.*, Berman v. Parker, 348 U.S. 26 (1954).
[47]*Cf.* Truax v. Corrigan, 257 U.S. 312 (1921). For an illuminating discussion of this issue, see
Currie, note 3 *supra*, at 876–78.
[48]Nor is it to say that the state is liable for every tort that does occur. See pages 76–77 *infra*.

much the way that (although to an even greater extent than) *Lochner v. New York*[49] restricted it. Not all common law interests are sacrosanct.[50] But the argument based on the Takings Clause demonstrates that the state is also not free to abrogate all common law interests.[51] Unless the liberty interest in freedom from battery is to receive less protection than property interests, it follows that the state must provide some protection against private batteries.

2. There seem to be two possible answers to this argument. First, it might be objected that there is a fundamental difference between liberty and property. Property, it might be said, is necessarily a creation of law. No one has a property right unless the government protects it against private invasion. Therefore the withdrawal of such protection deprives a person of property. But liberty, it might be said, is not a legal creation. It is simply the right to do as one wants without government restrictions. Thus, it might be said, my parallel fails.

This argument is misconceived. Property and liberty alike have both a governmentally created component and a "natural" component. In the case of property, the "natural" component is simple possession. If liberty is defined as the right to do as one wants free of government restrictions, and does not include protection against private invasion, then property should be defined as the right to possession, free of government interference but not including protection against private invasions of the possessory interest. If property includes protection against private invasions of possession, then liberty should include those protections as well. There is no reason to treat the two notions asymmetrically.

The second possible objection is a strict incorporationist view reminiscent of Justice Black.[52] On this view, the Due Process Clause protects only two classes of rights: those that are distinctively procedural, and those that are specifically enumerated in the first eight amendments. The right to a minimum level of protection against battery does not fall into either category. It is not procedural, and unlike the right to a minimum level of protection against trespass, it

---

[49]198 U.S. 45 (1905).

[50]See, *e.g.*, Munn v. Illinois, 94 U.S. 113, 134 (1877); Silver v. Silver, 280 U.S. 117, 122 (1929); Martinez v. California, 444 U.S. 277, 281–82 (1980).

[51]As I noted above, the Court has explicitly suggested that at least certain common law rights cannot be abrogated unless an adequate substitute remedy has been provided. See cases cited in note 45 *supra*.

[52]See, *e.g.*, Griswold v. Connecticut, 381 U.S. 479, 507–27 (1965) (dissenting opinion).

is not rooted in the Takings Clause or, apparently, any other of the first eight amendments.

In other contexts, of course, the Court has not adopted a strict incorporationist view.[53] And there are powerful objections to such a view.[54] But for present purposes perhaps the decisive answer is that even the strictest incorporationist would not deny that the Due Process Clause prohibits state officials from engaging in outright brutality. That prohibition is substantive due process; no amount of procedure can make police brutality acceptable. Thus the substantive component of the Due Process Clause must include protection for the common law interest in being free from battery. If that much of a departure from the strict incorporation view is acceptable, it is difficult to see why the next step—saying that the interest in freedom from battery receives as much protection as the interest in freedom from trespass—is not acceptable.

An additional, more speculative answer to the incorporationist argument—and an additional basis for the conclusion that the Constitution requires the government to provide some level of protection against private batteries—is that the Fourth Amendment is a textual source for the right to a minimum level of government protection against private batteries. Just as the government can effect a "taking" by withdrawing tort remedies against trespass, so it can effect a "seizure" by withdrawing tort remedies against battery.

The argument that the Fourth Amendment establishes such a requirement is as follows. Suppose the government sought to capture fugitives by declaring them to be outlaws—that is, persons wholly outside the protection of both tort and criminal law. Private parties would then have an incentive to pursue the fugitives and either kill them or turn them over to the government.[55]

Before declaring a fugitive to be an outlaw, the government would of course have to satisfy the procedural requirements of the Due Process Clause.[56] But in addition, the government would surely have to

---

[53]See, *e.g.*, Moore v. City of East Cleveland, 431 U.S. 494 (1977); Roe v. Wade, 410 U.S. 113 (1973).

[54]See, *e.g.*, Ely, Democracy and Distrust, ch. 1 (1980).

[55]In order to avoid questions about when a private party becomes a government agent, I will assume that the government does not set a bounty; private persons are rewarded by plundering the outlaw, and their incentive to turn the outlaw over to the government is that they want him behind bars.

[56]That in itself is a challenge to *DeShaney*, since arguably when the government declares a person to be an outlaw it does not act at all but just withdraws protection.

satisfy the substantive requirement of the Fourth Amendment, the requirement that seizures be reasonable. The government could not strip an alleged criminal of all protections against private wrongs in order to facilitate his or her capture without at least some level of justified suspicion. Just as the government cannot negate the Takings Clause by withdrawing tort remedies so that private parties can directly accomplish the government's purposes, so the government cannot effectively nullify the reasonableness requirement of the Fourth Amendment by removing the legal barriers to private actions that serve the government's purposes.

In this example, the government is enforcing the criminal laws. But while the requirements of reasonableness are sometimes more strict when the government is enforcing the criminal laws, searches and seizures must be "reasonable" whatever the government's purpose.[57] This includes instances in which the government seizes people in order to save resources. If, for example, the government decided that the most economical way to conduct a medical experiment was to seize subjects, the Fourth Amendment would surely apply. This suggests that if the government sought to remove all protection against private batteries, for whatever purpose—even if the purpose were simply to save the costs of enforcing tort law—it would have to satisfy the reasonableness requirement of the Fourth Amendment.

3. My argument so far establishes only that the Due Process Clause requires the government to provide some level of protection against private batteries. Nothing I have said suggests what level of protection is sufficient. Nor are the cases helpful; since the end of the *Lochner* era, the Court has not invalidated a state measure on the ground that it abrogated common law rights.

As a matter of first principles, it is possible to argue that the government has a duty, enforceable in damages (but not by specific relief), to protect its citizens against every tort. The effect of this rule would be that any victim of a tort could recover damages from the government. Since the government would be free to proceed against the tortfeasor, the effect would be that the government would pro-

---

[57]See, *e.g.*, Skinner v. Railway Labor Executives' Association, 109 S. Ct. 1402 (1989); National Treasury Employees Union v. Von Raab, 109 S.Ct. 1384 (1989); New Jersey v. T.L.O., 469 U.S. 325 (1985). See generally Schulhofer, On the Fourth Amendment and the Law-Abiding Public, 1989 Supreme Court Review 87.

vide compensation when the tortfeasor was judgment proof. This regime would be practicable; many governments have voluntarily established compensation programs for the victims of crimes.

This regime would raise several complex policy issues. Forcing the government to internalize all the costs of its law enforcement decisons in this way would have some advantages; the government would be less able to save on enforcement costs by permitting politically powerless groups to be victimized by private violence at an especially high rate. The moral hazard problem would be mitigated because of administrative costs and because standard measures of compensation substantially undercompensate for many torts. On the other hand, so long as the government can define the conduct that constitutes a tort, this regime would create an incentive for the government to make more conduct lawful. For that reason, it might be better to confine the requirement of compensation to certain categories of torts. In general, while the policy implications of such a regime would have to be worked out, it is not unthinkable as a matter of first principles. It was, however, rejected by the Supreme Court even before *DeShaney*,[58] and its rejection in *DeShaney* cannot be viewed as dictum.

The alternative is to require some level of protection short of complete protection. (As I noted, the government in *DeShaney* did provide a significant level of protection; thus one should regard as dictum the broad statements in *DeShaney* suggesting that the state need not provide even minimal protection.) Under this approach, the government is not responsible (even in damages) for all private wrongs, or even all private violence, but it cannot withdraw all remedies. Obviously it is difficult to specify a position between those two poles. But this difficulty is not a reason to reject the conclusion that the government has some obligation to provide a minimum level of protection against private wrongs.

The problem is analogous to that of determining whether Congress has provided adequate remedies for constitutional violations. Congress has broad latitude to prescribe remedies for constitutional violations. For example, Congress need not provide a compensatory remedy for every constitutional wrong.[59] But there must be some

---

[58]See Turner v. United States, 284 U.S. 354 (1919); National Board of Y.M.C.A. v. United States, 369 U.S. 85 (1969); *id.* at 95 (Harlan, J., concurring).

[59]See Bush v. Lucas, 462 U.S. 367 (1983); Harlow v. Fitzgerald, 457 U.S. 800 (1982).

limit on Congress's power to deny remedies for constitutional wrongs. Otherwise, Congress could effectively nullify the substantive constitutional provision.

The Supreme Court has never specified where this limit might be. In general, the Court seems concerned with whether a remedial scheme reflects a rational, comprehensive effort to remedy the relevant category of constitutional violations.[60] This suggests that, by analogy, it might be sensible to require that governments satisfy a standard akin to the arbitrary and capricious rule in their decisions about the level and allocation of resources devoted to combatting private wrongdoing.

In practice, such a standard would require little more than what well-established equal protection standards would require, if they were seriously enforced. Every government provides law enforcement services to some degree, and political pressures ensure that they will continue to do so. The controversies arise not over the total abrogation of all systems of law enforcement but over selective failures to enforce the law. There are claims, for example, that local governments, without adequate reasons, do not vigorously enforce laws against certain crimes (such as domestic violence) or in certain geographical areas (such as low-income areas inhabited by minorities).

These claims are cognizable under the Equal Protection Clause. Even if the government need not provide a minimum level of law enforcement, it may not enforce the laws in an arbitrary or discriminatory way. That is a core requirement of the Clause, which refers to "protection." It will of course not be easy for courts to enforce this requirement. They will have difficulty both in determining whether governments have allocated resources arbitrarily and in remedying any violations. But in view of the centrality of this requirement to both the Equal Protection Clause and, if my arguments are correct, the Due Process Clause, these difficulties will have to be great indeed to justify the courts in not attempting the task.

B

The second issue, squarely raised by the facts of *DeShaney*, is: assuming that there exists a government program to provide some pro-

---

[60]See Schweiker v. Chilicky, 108 S. Ct. 2460, 2468–70 (1988); Bush v. Lucas, 462 U.S. 367, 388–89 (1983). But *cf.* Spagnola v. Mathis, 809 F.2d 16 (D.C. Cir. 1986) (interpreting federal statute to permit a private civil action on the ground that administrative remedy explicitly granted by statute was constitutionally inadequate).

tection against private wrongdoing, under what circumstances do errors in the administration of the program violate the Due Process Clause? The Court's broad language in *DeShaney* suggests that maladministration cannot violate the Due Process Clause when it takes the form of government inaction.

The hypothetical examples I offered earlier—those involving police inaction and judicial bias in a suit brought by a private plaintiff— show that this view is implausible. The Court has said on many occasions, including *DeShaney* itself, that the Due Process Clause "was intended to prevent government 'from abusing [its] power.'"[61] As the hypothetical examples show, government officials can abuse their power by wrongfully withholding government services or protection, as well as by wrongfully inflicting harm on citizens. Indeed, the Supreme Court traces the "abuse of power" notion to the origins of the Due Process Clause in Magna Carta, which forbade deprivations of liberty and property "other than by the law of the land."[62] This suggests that an abuse of power consists of a failure to administer the law. It suggests no reason to exclude failures that consist of a refusal to extend protection.

The Court should, therefore, have ruled in *DeShaney* that an official abuse of power (a term that obviously must be defined) violates the Due Process Clause, irrespective of whether it takes the form of "action" or "inaction." Such a rule would produce no obviously implausible results and would avert the wholly implausible results of the police inaction and judicial bias hypotheticals.

In addition, a rule that all abuses of power violate the Due Process Clause would obviate the need to define a category of state-created "custodial" institutions in which, alone, the government has a duty to act. Recall that in *DeShaney* the Court placed prisons, government hospitals, and possibly government-sponsored foster families in this category. I argued that the category is arbitrary. There no material sense in which a "natural" family—or, for that matter, the situation of any individual in society—is different from the institutions in this category.

It is unnecessary to make a distinction between custodial institutions and other social arrangements if the question is simply whether

---

[61]109 S.Ct. at 1003, quoting Davidson v. Cannon, 474 U.S. 344, 348 (1986) (brackets in *DeShaney*). See also Daniels v. Williams, 474 U.S. 327, 331 (1986); Parratt v. Taylor, 451 U.S. 527, 549 (1981) (Powell, J., concurring).

[62]Murray's Lessee v. Hoboken Land & Improvement Co., 18 How. 272, 276 (1856); see, *e.g.*, Daniels v. Williams, 474 U.S. 327, 331–32 (1986).

a government official has abused his or her power. The standard for what constitutes an abuse of power may vary, of course. A degree of protection against private wrongs that might be acceptable on the part of a social worker dealing with a family might not be acceptable on the part of a prison official.[63] But in each context, the question is whether the government action or omission constituted an abuse of power.

Two questions remain. First, when a government official abusively witholds affirmative government protection, what is the liberty or property interest that is infringed?[64] This question is significant because, as I will explain, the answer requires that current understandings of "liberty" and "property" under the Due Process Clause be modified. Second, how should "abuse of power" be defined?

At first glance it might appear that when the government wrongfully fails to protect a citizen against battery (as in the police inaction case and allegedy in *DeShaney*) or trespass (as in the judicial bias hypothetical), the government has invaded a common law interest. On further examination, however, this appears to be incorrect. Judicial bias violates the Due Process Clause even if the plaintiff seeks vindication of an interest not protected by the common law. Official abuses of power can occur in connection with any regulatory or ben-

---

[63]The Court in *DeShaney* expressed concern for the dilemma that would be faced by government employees if "inaction" were held to violate the Due Process Clause: they could be held liable either for intervening too readily in a possibly abusive family situation or for failing to intervene. 109 S.Ct. at 1007. It is true that the possibility of damages liability for both "action" and "inaction" makes life more difficult for officials; they no longer have a sure way of avoiding liability.

But why is it bad for society that government employees are confronted with this dilemma? Asymmetrical damages liability might distort officials' decisions in the direction that protects them from personal liability. *DeShaney* might give employees like the defendants too little incentive to provide adequate levels of protection. See generally Schuck, Suing Government (1983).

The question how to structure government employees' incentives is very complex: other incentives besides personal liability (such as formal and informal sanctions imposed by the employer and other employees) are relevant, as are the effects of different systems of sanctions on individuals' willingness to accept the job. The proper way to deal with the dilemma is to design substantive and immunity doctrines that produce the correct incentives for employees, not arbitrarily to immunize a category of government "inaction."

[64]The Court in *DeShaney* suggested that the word "deprive" denotes an affirmative act, not a withholding of protection. Although the word does seem to suggest government action as opposed to inaction, it does not unduly stretch the term to apply it to an abusive government failure to intervene to prevent private harm, as in the hypothetical cases I described. Certainly such an interpretation is warranted to prevent the anomaly of saying that the Due Process Clause permits the conduct described in those hypotheticals. In any event, even the Court in *DeShaney* had to accept that "deprive" can include government inaction in "custodial" institutions.

efit program, not just government programs designed to protect common law interests.[65]

If, in the judicial bias hypothetical, the plaintiff is not deprived of a common law interest in property, of what interest is he or she deprived? Under current understandings, the general rule is that apart from common law interests, a property interest exists only when state law prescribes an entitlement in terms that limit the discretion of the officials administering the program.[66] But a plaintiff seeking to enforce a statutory interest is entitled to an impartial judge even if the statute does not limit the judge's discretion.[67] Suppose, for example, that a statute provides for an award of attorney's fees in the sole discretion of the judge. A claimant under the statute who was denied fees by a blatantly biased judge would surely have been deprived of property without due process. But neither a common law interest nor a nondiscretionary statutory entitlement would have been at stake.

Perhaps the best way to understand this situation is that the statutes creating a government program—even a highly discretionary government program—always implicitly create one property interest: an entitlement to a fair decision. That is, roughly speaking, even a fully discretionary program creates an interest, protected by the Due Process Clause, in a decision based on the government's agenda rather than the private agenda of the responsible official. This is certainly a reasonable inference from the establishment of a government program; when the legislature creates a program, it intends that the program be administered in a way that furthers governmental interests, not the personal interests of the administrators.

Thus, in the case of a judge, the jurisdictional statutes alone create an entitlement to a judge who satisfies at least minimal standards of impartiality. In the police inaction hypothetical, the statutes establishing a program of police protection implicitly entitle citizens to decisions that are not abusive in the manner I hypothesized. This entitlement exists even if, as will usually be the case, the statute imposes no express limitations on the officials' discretion to deploy law enforcement resources. The implicit entitlement is not to any specific pattern or level of law enforcement; it is simply to having law enforcement decisions made in a way that is not abusive. It follows

---

[65]See Logan v. Zimmerman Brush Co., 455 U.S. 422, 428–33 (1983).

[66]See, *e.g.*, Board of Regents v. Roth, 408 U.S. 564 (1972).

[67]Indeed, as a matter of first principles, it might be argued that the need for an impartial judge is greatest in such cases.

that the laws in *DeShaney* that established a program of child protective services also created a property interest in having decisons made in connection with that program in a fair, non-abusive way.

The final question is how to define an abuse of power for purposes of this branch of the analysis. The current state of the law is as follows. A state official does not violate the Due Process Clause by simply erring in the interpretation of state law[68] or "negligently" administering state law, even if the effect of the negligent action is to invade a liberty or property interest.[69] On the other hand, it has never been disputed that an "intentional" infringement of such an interest violates the Clause.[70] The Court has held that "deliberate indifference" can be sufficient to show a violation of the Cruel and Unusual Punishment Clause of the Eighth Amendment,[71] and in *DeShaney* the Court suggested that the Due Process Clause should be interpreted in a parallel fashion, at least when applied to "custodial" institutions.[72] The Court has left open the question whether "gross negligence" or "recklessness" is sufficent to constitute a "depriv[ation]" under the Due Process Clause.[73] The courts of appeals are divided over where to draw the line in this theoretically narrow, but practically quite significant, space.

This framework might simply be extended to cases of so-called inaction. Indeed, the notion of "deliberate indifference" suggests inaction. Sometimes, of course, it will be difficult to decide whether a refusal to provide protection against private wrongs was reckless or merely negligent (assuming that is the point where the line is to be drawn). But such difficult judgments are necessary even in cases of government "actions"—that is, government invasions of common law interests. The common problem of determining whether police have used excessive force in arresting a suspect is an example.

Courts reviewing government "inaction" may have to consider an additional category of concerns, because often a failure to protect against private violence will be justified on the ground that scarce government resources were better used in other ways.[74] But not all cases of "inaction" depend on difficult decisions about resource al-

---

[68]*E.g.*, Snowden v. Hughes, 321 U.S. 1, 11 (1944).
[69]Daniels v. Williams, 474 U.S. 327 (1986); Davidson v. Cannon, 474 U.S. 344 (1986).
[70]See, *e.g.*, Davidson v. Cannon, 474 U.S. at 331.
[71]Estelle v. Gamble, 429 U.S. 97, 105–6 (1976).
[72]109 S.Ct. at 1005–6.
[73]Daniels v. Williams, 474 U.S. at 334 n.3.
[74]See generally Heckler v. Chaney, 470 U.S. 821, 831–32 (1985).

location. In addition, courts already assess government decisions defended on this ground—both in the cases involving "custodial"
institutions in which the Court acknowledges that inaction can violate the Due Process Clause[75] and in reviewing federal agencies' failures to act under the federal Administrative Procedure Act and other
statutes.[76] There will often be reason for courts to give substantial
deference to government decisions about resource allocation. But
there is no need to define an arbitrary and essentially indefensible
category of "inaction" that is entirely off-limits.

Alternatively, the Supreme Court's current approach to defining
an "abuse of power" for purposes of the Due Process Clause—the
approach that distinguishes between intentional and deliberately indifferent acts, on the one hand, and simple negligence, on the
other—may be mistaken in more fundamental respects. (These issues go well beyond *DeShaney*, which was decided on the ground that
no "inaction" can ever constitute an abuse of power, and my discussion at this point is meant to be tentative.) The framework may rest
on an incorrect analogy to the law of torts; it does not adequately take
into account the role of state remedies; and it relies too heavily on the
Due Process Clause and not enough on other, specific constitutional
provisions.

First, the framework the Court now uses is borrowed from the law
of torts. Indeed, the term "constitutional tort" has become commonplace. But tort law regulates behavior between strangers. The
relationship between government and governed is more nearly a
fiduciary relationship. Government employees are entrusted with
power that they are to use to serve the public interest (as defined by
the law), not their private interests. The clearest violations of the
Due Process Clause occur when an official (like a biased judge)
breaches that trust and uses his or her power for private purposes.
Those purposes need not be pecuniary; the source of the breach

---

[75]See, *e.g.*, Youngberg v. Romeo, 457 U.S. 307, 319–25 (1982); Whitley v. Albers, 475 U.S.
312 (1986).

[76]See, *e.g.*, Dunlop v . Bachowski, 421 U.S. 560 (1975); Heckler v. Chaney, 470 U.S. at 850
n.7 (Marshall, J., concurring in judgment) (citing cases). See also Marshall v. Jerrico, Inc., 446
U.S. 238, 249 (1980). The Court in Heckler v. Chaney ruled that certain difficulties inherent in
reviewing agency decisions not to take enforcement actions, such as the difficulty of reviewing
agency decisions about the allocation of enforcement resources, warrant a presumption against
review of agency inaction; but the Court explicitly left open the possibility of review of agency
inaction in certain categories of cases. See, *e.g.*, 470 U.S. at 825 n.2; *id*. at 833 n.4. See generally Sunstein, Reviewing Agency Inaction After Heckler v. Chaney, 52 U. Chi. L. Rev. 653,
675–80 (1985).

might be the official's decision to avoid the inconvenience and effort of acting in the way demanded by his or her duties.

This suggests that the proper standard for determining when an official has abused his or her power should be borrowed from the law of trusts. The central duty of a trustee is to administer the trust with the degree of prudence that an ordinary person would show in conducting his or her own affairs.[77] Officials who do not show that degree of concern with the exercise of their official responsibilities are guilty of an abuse of power: they have used their official position to promote their own interests.

Under this approach, government employees' errors of judgment would not be deprivations within the meaning of the Due Process Clause, but most of what is now considered negligence should be considered a deprivation of liberty or property. This approach might seem to lead to the consequences that caused the Court to hold that negligent action cannot constitute a "deprivation"—in particular, that a variety of ordinary torts by state officals would become federal constitutional claims.

The way to solve that problem, however, is not to narrow the substantive protection of the Due Process Clause but to consider the adequacy of state remedies in deciding whether there has been a violation. The Due Process Clause prohibits deprivations by the "State," not by state officials. If one element of the state effects a deprivation of property but another—such as a court entertaining a suit for a remedy—restores the property or its equivalent (in the case of liberty, it can only be an equivalent), then arguably the state has effected no deprivation. If the state refuses to restore the property or liberty equivalent but does so only after affording due process, then arguably the state has not effected a deprivation without due process.

In a few enigmatic decisions, the Court has endorsed this approach, suggesting that conduct that might otherwise violate the Due Process Clause does not do so if the state provides an adequate after the fact remedy.[78] But the Court has not explained how these cases can be squared with the fundamental rule of *Monroe v. Pape*[79] and *Home Telephone and Telegraph Co. v. City of Los Angeles*.[80] Those

---

[77] See Restatement of Trusts §174.

[78] See Parratt v. Taylor, 451 U.S. 527 (1981); Ingraham v. Wright, 430 U.S. 651, 674–82 (1977); Hudson v. Palmer, 468 U.S. 517 (1984); see also Williamson County Regional Planning Commission v. Hamilton Bank, 473 U.S. 172 (1985).

[79] 365 U.S. 167 (1961).

[80] 227 U.S. 278 (1913). This apparent inconsistency is the subject of Monagahan, State Law Wrongs, State Law Remedies, and the Fourteenth Amendment, 86 Colum. L. Rev. 979 (1986).

cases held that a party complaining of a constitutional violation by
state officials may sue in federal court irrespective of whether the
state provides a remedy for the violation. That holding is the foundation of the current widespread litigation under Section 1983.

In fact the inconsistency is only apparent. The only constitutional
violation that can be "remedied" by providing additional state procedures is a violation of the procedural aspect of the Due Process
Clause. The First, Fourth, and Eighth Amendments, for example,
prohibit certain official actions outright, not just when the actions
are unaccompanied by due process (or just compensation). Consequently, unreasonable seizures, cruel and unusual punishments, and
abridgements of freedom of speech or religion violate the Constitution no matter how much of an after the fact remedy the state provides. The same is true, by definition, of violations of substantive
due process.

Many wrongs now viewed as violations of the Due Process Clause
should instead be seen as violations of more specific constitutional
provisions. Physical abuse by a state official, for example, is an unreasonable seizure of the person. Destruction of a prisoner's property
should be analyzed, in the first instance at least, as a seizure of personal effects. The Supreme Court, perhaps because of advocates'
weaknesses, is insensitive to this distinction.[81]

Thus the better approach may be not to try to decide whether
"reckless" action, somehow defined, constitutes a "depriv[ation]"
within the meaning of the Due Process Clause. Instead, the first step
is to determine whether another constitutional provision, such as the
Fourth Amendment, has been violated. (I suggested earlier that the
government's refusal to protect an individual against private violence
might constitute an unreasonable seizure.) If it is, then state remedies
are irrelevant. If the only alleged violation is of the procedural aspects of the Due Process Clause, then state remedies are highly relevant. If a state provides an adequate remedy for an official's deprivation of liberty or property, then the state has not effected a deprivation and the Due Process Clause has not been violated. Should
the Court follow this approach, one important practical consequence
should be that states may no longer be able to escape liability by im-

---

[81]Hudson v. Palmer, 468 U.S. 517 (1984), for example, seems incorrect. The claim was that
a sheriff had maliciously destroyed property belonging to a jail inmate. The Court held that the
existence of an after-the-fact state tort remedy meant that there was no violation of the Due
Process Clause. But the claim alleged not just a deprivation of property without due process but
an unreasonable seizure of personal effects. The Fourth Amendment forbids unreasonable seizures whatever "process" is provided.

posing anachronistically low limits on recovery against the state or state officials. (In Wisconsin, for example, the limit is $50,000.[82]) Such a limit arguably means that the "deprivation" has not been remedied and continues to exist.

These issues, however, go well beyond *DeShaney*. *DeShaney* was not decided on the ground that the defendants were merely negligent, nor on the ground that the state remedy was adequate. Whatever state of mind is needed to establish a "depriv[ation]" within the meaning of the Due Process Clause, and whatever the role of state remedies, the supposed distinction between state action and state inaction should play no role.

There is an ancient antinomy between justice, viewed as the unyielding, logical application of settled rules, and mercy, viewed as making exceptions to those rules for cases where they produce heartless results. But it is a mistake—perhaps an increasingly common one—to think that any argument for results that immediately appeal to one's sympathy must be based on sentiment or emotion rather than reason. The Court in *DeShaney*, making this mistake, insisted that the logic of the law compelled it to rule against the sympathetic plaintiffs.[83] The errors in the Court's analysis make its insistence especially ironic.

---

[82]See note 9 *supra*.

[83]"Judges and lawyers, like other humans, are moved by natural sympathy in a case like this to find a way for Joshua and his mother to receive adequate compensation for the grievous harm inflicted upon them. But before yielding to that impulse, it is well to remember once again that the harm was inflicted not by the State of Wisconsin, but by Joshua's father." 109 S.Ct. at 1007.

STEPHEN J. SCHULHOFER

ON THE FOURTH AMENDMENT
RIGHTS OF THE LAW-ABIDING
PUBLIC

The much debated question of urinalysis drug-testing reached the
Supreme Court in two cases decided during the 1988–89 Term, *National Treasury Employees Union v. Von Raab*[1] and *Skinner v. Railway Labor Executives' Ass'n.*[2] The Court upheld both the drug-testing plans
and embraced a rationale that placed little emphasis on the restrictive
scope of the two programs. As a result, the Court further widened
the "administrative search" exception to normal Fourth Amendment
requirements and laid the basis for approving broader programs of
mandatory urinalysis without individual suspicion.

Already millions of employees in public service and the private
sector are affected. Most federal departments and agencies, including such administrative bureaucracies as the Department of Education and the General Services Administration, now have drug testing
programs. In the transportation industry alone, 4 million workers
face random testing.[3] The Mayor of New York City has proposed a
program to test half of the city's 300,000 employees, in positions
ranging from crane operators to juvenile counselors.[4] Urinalysis

Stephen J. Schulhofer is Frank and Bernice J. Greenberg Professor of Law, and Director of
the Center for Studies in Criminal Justice, The University of Chicago.

AUTHOR'S NOTE: Research support for this article was provided by the Kirkland and Ellis
Faculty Research Fund and the Russell J. Parsons Faculty Research Fund. I am grateful for the
comments of Albert Alschuler, Walter Blum, James Holzhauer, Yale Kamisar, Larry Kramer
and Geoffrey Stone, and for the research assistance of Grace Whittenberg.

[1] 109 S.Ct. 1384 (1989).
[2] 109 S.Ct. 1402 (1989).
[3] New York Times, Aug. 21, 1989, p. A15.
[4] New York Times, Nov. 17, 1989, p. B3.

drug-testing could soon become a fact of life for the majority of working Americans. And regulators stand invited to invoke other search and surveillance techniques, in the workplace and beyond, under the ever-more permissive administrative search rubric. To control drug-related crime, the Chicago Housing Authority will conduct suspicionless sweeps of apartments in public housing projects, over the protest of residents who demand "kinder, gentler home invasions."[5] A suburban school district will require urinalysis drug-testing for high school athletes.[6] The drug-testing cases of the past Term lay a foundation for accepting and possibly encouraging these trends.

Of course, forebodings of this sort are triggered by a fair percentage of the criminal procedure decisions of any recent Term. The difference between the drug-testing cases and other law enforcement victories is fundamental, for the constitutional claims in the drug cases were not put forward by defendants obviously guilty of heinous crimes who were seeking to "hide behind" procedural complexities or to exclude reliable evidence of the true facts. Rather, the Court had one of its rare opportunities to hear face-to-face, as Fourth Amendment claimants, those law-abiding citizens for whose ultimate benefit the constitutional restraints on public power were primarily intended.[7] The claimants had not been accused of crime or suspected of crime, and the searches had not turned up evidence of wrongdoing. Yet the law-abiding public fared no better, indeed it fared worse, than those whose criminal activities prompt traditional police searches and seizures.

To assess this bizarre turn of doctrinal events, we must reexamine fundamentals. The Fourth Amendment has been understood to establish presumptive requirements of probable cause and a warrant, but "administrative" or regulatory inspections, including work-related searches of government employees, have sometimes been exempted from this framework. The Court's treatment of regulatory inspections has always bristled with inconsistency. Contradictions leap from the pages of the U.S. Reports, providing grist for endless academic criticism. But at bottom the Court's ambivalence is under-

---

[5]Chicago Tribune, Nov. 15, 1989, §2, p. 1.

[6]Id. The testing program is financed by a $30,000 gift from an anonymous donor; a school official cautioned that the district would "never" use taxpayer funds for the purpose.

[7]Even the §1983 suits that come before the Court have often involved claims of unreasonable police seizure of individuals who did not appear to be law-abiding citizens. E.g., Tennessee v. Garner, 471 U.S. 1 (1985); Brower v. Inyo County, 109 S.Ct. 1378 (1989). The Court upheld damage claims on behalf of such individuals in both Garner and Brower.

standable, for administrative searches evoke two highly plausible but incompatible intuitions.

Regulatory inspections seem necessary for the orderly management of a complex industrial society, and—because they are ordinarily not aimed at those suspected of crimes—they seem less threatening to the citizen and less subject to the abuses that prompt judicial oversight of ordinary searches and seizures. Yet the security of "persons, houses, papers and effects" guaranteed by the Fourth Amendment cannot be a privilege only of those suspected of crime; it cannot be that criminal suspects may shield their privacy through the probable cause and warrant requirements while law-abiding citizens must open to regulatory scrutiny their homes, their papers and even (as in many urinalysis testing procedures) the genital areas of their bodies. It should not be surprising that the Court often loses its bearings, or wavers about whether the absence of a law enforcement objective justifies fewer restrictions on the power to search. We cannot assess drug testing, therefore, without a wider perspective on the proper scope of regulatory inspections. The doctrinal incoherence seems to have three sources: the Court's inability to frame the relevance of "diminished" privacy expectations; its inability to discriminate among distinct sorts of non-law-enforcement objectives; and its ambivalence about close scrutiny of means-ends relationships once a legitimate regulatory objective has been identified.

To make sense of conflicting intuitions a re-ordering of administrative search doctrine is required. I propose that a "diminished" privacy interest should not support administrative treatment and that a highly sensitive privacy interest should not prevent it. The other distinction which has preoccupied the Court, between regulation and "normal" law enforcement, should also be recognized as chimerical and irrelevant. Administrative searches should escape the presumptive requirements of probable cause and a warrant only when they respond to pressing health and safety concerns or to the internal governance imperatives of a self-contained public activity. Inspections that meet those criteria still require an independent judicial assessment of reasonableness, but other regulatory inspections normally should have to satisfy the traditional probable cause and warrant limitations.

In this Article I develop these principles and apply them to the problem of employee drug testing. With respect to both the specific (but pervasive) drug-testing question and the more general problem of non-law-enforcement searches, I suggest redirecting the focus of

Fourth Amendment analysis and reinvigorating the privacy protections that are most relevant to citizens in their daily lives.

I. THE FOUNDATIONS OF THE "ADMINISTRATIVE" SEARCH

A. FRANK AND CAMARA

In 1959 the Court held, in Frank v. Maryland,[8] that a city health inspector, who had cause to suspect the presence of a dangerous nuisance in a private home, could demand entry without a warrant. Although the Fourth Amendment ordinarily requires both probable cause and (except in exigent circumstances) a warrant issued by a neutral magistrate, the Court held these requirements inapplicable to a search not in aid of criminal prosecution but intended merely to abate conditions threatening the public health.

The Court emphasized several factors to support its result—the long history of acceptance of health inspections, the increasing need for them under modern conditions, the virtual impossibility of adequately identifying and abating dangerous latent conditions under the constraints of a traditional warrant, the limited nature of the intrusion, and the homeowner's absence of a concern about "self-protection" against criminal prosecution—a concern that the Court thought central to the rationale for Fourth Amendment protection.[9] Although the city ordinance in *Frank* permitted warrantless health inspections only on "cause to suspect" that a nuisance existed, the Court's discussion made clear that neither probable cause nor any individualized suspicion was necessary.[10]

Camara v. Municipal Court,[11] decided in 1967, overruled *Frank*. Although recognizing that a health inspection is "a less hostile intrusion than the typical policeman's search for the fruits and instrumentalities of crime," the Court rejected "*Frank*'s rather remarkable premise" that the absence of a self-protection concern rendered "the Fourth Amendment interests at stake . . . merely 'peripheral.'"[12] Justice White wrote for the Court:[13]

---

[8]359 U.S. 360 (1959).

[9]See *id*. at 365.

[10]*Id*. at 372.

[11]387 U.S. 523 (1967).

[12]*Id*. at 530–31.

[13]*Id*. at 530. See also Barrett, Personal Rights, Property Rights, and the Fourth Amendment, 1960 Supreme Court Review 46, 74: "[N]either history nor policy can justify a doctrine which accords special protections to the privacy of lawbreakers which are not enjoyed by citizens generally."

> It is surely anomalous to say that the individual and his private
> property are fully protected by the Fourth Amendment only
> when the individual is suspected of criminal behavior.

Having said that homeowners should be *"fully protected* by the
Fourth Amendment,"[14] the Court held that health inspectors could
obtain a warrant without showing traditional probable cause or any
individual suspicion. The Court said that "probable cause" exists, in
the context of municipal code enforcement, if "reasonable legislative
or administrative standards for conducting an area inspection are satisfied."[15] Such standards are of course antithetical to the traditional
conception of "probable cause": they are based on the age or condition of a neighborhood, the time elapsed since prior inspection, or
some other criterion directed to the status of an area rather than the
condition of a particular home.

The Court gave three reasons for upholding as "reasonable" an
area warrant not based on individual suspicion. First was the long
history of public and judicial acceptance of area inspection programs. Second, the Court doubted whether any other canvassing
technique would insure an "acceptable" level of success in abating
dangerous conditions. Finally, "because the inspections are neither
personal in nature nor aimed at the discovery of evidence of crime,
they involve a relatively limited invasion of the urban citizen's privacy."[16]

Despite *Camara*'s forceful rhetoric condemning the *Frank* result, it
was apparent that the Court had not given homeowners anything approaching the "full" protection of the Fourth Amendment. Commentators quickly noted imprecision and illogic in the Court's three
reasons and resultant ambiguity about what other inspection programs might qualify for a flexible *Camara*-type warrant based on
general administrative criteria rather than individualized cause.[17]

Nonetheless, *Camara*'s factual context and the Court's unfocussed
but suggestive reasoning indicated that the *Camara* exception to the
probable cause requirement was, at its inception, a narrow one. A
diluted warrant standard for health and fire inspection programs can
fairly be considered a necessity. True, one could also say, para-

---

[14]*Camara*, 387 U.S. at 530 (emphasis added).

[15]*Id.* at 538.

[16]*Id.* at 537.

[17]See especially LaFave, Administrative Searches and the Fourth Amendment: The *Camara*
and *See* Cases, 1967 Supreme Court Review 1.

phrasing *Camara*, that "the public interest demands that [murder and drug distribution] be prevented or abated, yet it is doubtful that any other canvassing technique would achieve acceptable results."[18] The *Camara* Court never indicated why incomplete enforcement of municipal codes is a more serious problem than incomplete enforcement of the criminal law. But however "unacceptable" our present level of homicide and drug dealing, some level of enforcement is possible with traditional investigative techniques. This is not the case with respect to many of the dangerous or unsanitary conditions of heating, plumbing and wiring for which inspection is most needed. As Professor LaFave notes, conduct in violation of the criminal law "usually leaves a trail of discernible facts," while "most housing code violations occur within private premises and cannot be detected from outside."[19] Thus, if housing code inspections require probable cause, such inspections may not be possible at all.[20]

This point may come closest to explaining why there is broad agreement about the "necessity" for area inspection in the context of *Camara*, while there is no consensus about the "necessity" of an area-wide inspection for cocaine in the Greenwich Village or Wall Street sections of New York. *Camara*'s notion of what "the public interest demands" did not assume that alternatives consonant with traditional probable cause would be merely inconvenient or less effective. It reflected a widely shared sense that alternative procedures are not workable at all.

Camara's exception to the probable cause requirement can thus be understood as analogous to the exigent circumstances exception to the warrant requirement. In both instances there is a compelling public need and a lack of less intrusive alternatives for meeting it. The exception to the probable cause requirement for searches incident to arrest has a comparable rationale. So understood, the *Camara*

---

[18]*Camara*, 387 U.S. at 537.

[19]3 LaFave, Search and Seizure §10.1(b) at 604–5 (1987). At the fringes of both generalizations, counterexamples are available. Some "victimless" crimes occur in private (though undercover investigations provide a window), and housing code violations occasionally leave a visible (or olefactory) trace. The point still holds for most cases and goes far toward fleshing out the *Camara* Court's intuition.

[20]The principal weakness in this analysis is the possibility of consent searches, which are at best a lucky break in a homicide or drug investigation but would remain common (some argue, almost universal) even if housing inspections required probable cause. Probably, the *Camara* Court assumed that a need to rely on consent would eventually cripple housing code enforcement. The assumption is debatable but by no means implausible. (Housing code inspections, though intended to benefit the occupant, may pinpoint violations that are expensive to correct.)

exception was, at the outset, reconcilable with the Fourth Amendment's strong but rebuttable presumption against searches on less than probable cause.

The *Camara* Court considered not only the need to search but the limited nature of the intrusion: the searches were "neither personal in nature nor aimed at the discovery of evidence of crime."[21] The reference to what the searches were "aimed at" is surprising, because, only a few pages before, the Court had said forcefully that lack of a prosecutorial motivation should not diminish the safeguards against search.[22] Presumably, therefore, the Court meant to stress not motivation but effects.[23] The search is not "personal in nature" because its focus is on heating, plumbing, and wiring rather than on evidence of the occupant's activities. Moreover, the lack of a prosecutorial objective affects the nature of the intrusion. The homeowner is unlikely to oppose the inspector by force; armed officers are seldom present or necessary; no anxiety or "damage to reputation result[s] from an overt manifestation of official suspicion of crime";[24] and nothing is seized. Thus, although housing inspections are undeniably intrusive, the intrusion is qualitatively different and markedly less serious than that involved in a typical police search. The essence of the difference lies not in the absence of a prosecutorial objective *per se* but in the way the officer's remedial objective interacts with the subject matter of the search to diminish the intrusive character of the inspection.

At its birth, therefore, the "administrative search" exception was narrow and not out of harmony with traditional Fourth Amendment principles. The exception came into play only when there was a comprehensive, neutral administrative plan, a compelling need to search, a complete absence of workable alternatives to the dilution of probable cause, and a substantially diminished intrusion on privacy.

B. POST-CAMARA DEVELOPMENTS

The two decades since *Camara* have seen an explosion of administrative search litigation. The elements on which *Camara* had relied to uphold an administrative search on less than probable cause (neutral plan, compelling governmental need, absence of less restrictive

---

[21]*Camara*, 387 U.S., at 537.
[22]*Id*. at 530.
[23]See LaFave, note 19 *supra*, at 606–7.
[24]*Ibid*.

alternatives and greatly diminished intrusion on privacy) are no longer essential. The "tests" have been reformulated, qualifications have been stripped away, and the elements that remain have been applied ever less strictly. But the result has been less a linear relaxation of restrictions than a complex transformation of principles.

What structure there is to administrative search doctrine can be sketched along two dimensions: the nature of the search target and the doctrinal prerequisites to a valid search of that kind of target. Among search targets, the most important categories (each now the subject of its own detailed body of precedent) include commercial premises, prisoners and probationers, students, border areas, fire scenes and government employees. As to each kind of target, the doctrinal issues are whether a search requires a warrant, and—with or without a warrant—whether the search requires probable cause, individual suspicion short of probable cause, or some other factual predicate. I will not review the precedents in detail, a task that requires a lengthy treatise.[25] My objective here is to suggest the many twists and turns that have deprived this field of its unity.

1. *The 1970s. Colonnade Catering Co. v. United States*,[26] decided in 1970, involved a warrantless inspection by Treasury agents who forcibly entered a locked storeroom and seized untaxed liquor. The Court held the seizure illegal but in dictum indicated its approval of statutory provisions for nonforcible entry and for fining owners who refuse to permit inspection. The Court rested its approval for the statutory scheme on the long history of Congressional authorization for warrantless inspection in aid of alcohol revenue enforcement. The necessity for deviation from ordinary Fourth Amendment prerequisites was quite different here than in *Camara*, since no health or safety concerns were present.[27] But the Court devoted no attention to this implicit broadening of the *Camara* exception, possibly because it held the search illegal and ordered the seized liquor suppressed.

In *Biswell v. United States*,[28] decided in 1972, the Court upheld a warrantless search in connection with a program for the inspection of federally licensed firearms dealers. The Court's opinion, by Justice White, stressed two points: (1) the business had long been subject to

---

[25] See LaFave, note 19 *supra*.

[26] 397 U.S. 72 (1970).

[27] The inspection program apparently served only to insure that applicable liquor taxes had been paid.

[28] 406 U.S. 311 (1972).

pervasive regulation, implying a diminished expectation of privacy, even relative to other commercial premises,[29] and (2) a warrant requirement was unworkable given the importance of unannounced, surprise inspections. Because a warrant requirement need not be inconsistent with surprise, *Biswell* cast a cloud over the strict necessity principles implicit in *Camara*. But warrant procedures could conceivably render a program of frequent, unannounced inspections unworkable in the context of firearms regulation.[30] Thus, *Biswell* suggested at most only a modest softening of the strict necessity approach.

Marshall v. Barlow's, Inc.,[31] decided in 1978, reinforced this impression by insisting upon a warrant for an OSHA inspection to determine compliance with workplace safety regulations. Distinguishing *Biswell* and *Colonnade*, the Court stressed the absence of "a long tradition of close governmental supervision," so that "[only in] the most fictional sense . . . can voluntary consent to later searches be found."[32] In addition, the Court held, a warrant requirement would not seriously burden the program, despite the need for surprise inspections, because warrants could be obtained *ex parte*. *Barlow's*, again written by Justice White, reaffirmed *Camara's* strict necessity approach and treated *Biswell* and *Colonnade* as unusual exceptions to the presumption in favor of warrants.[33]

Barlow's did not, however, require probable cause. As in *Camara*, a "general administrative plan" for targeting certain areas or types of industries sufficed to support the warrant. This branch of *Barlow's* is less satisfactory, because dilution of the probable cause standard may not be necessary. Workplace safety hazards, often visible to employees, are unlike the latent plumbing and wiring defects that make a probable cause requirement unworkable in the context of housing inspections.[34] *Barlow's* therefore marked a step away from strict necessity on the probable cause issue, and in effect required no more than a showing of inconvenience.

---

[29]406 U.S. at 316. But see LaFave, note 19 *supra*, §10.2(c) at 639–40.

[30]If inspections must be unannounced and frequent, and if inspectors must obtain a warrant for every inspection, a large administrative burden might ensue. *Id.*, §10.2(e), at 653–54.

[31]436 U.S. 307 (1978).

[32]*Id.* at 313–14.

[33]See *id.* at 313.

[34]Indeed, 29 U.S.C. §657(f)(1) provides explicitly that employees may notify the government of suspected OSHA violations and request an inspection. See *Barlow's*, 436 U.S. at 320 n.16.

In terms of convenience, of course, dilution of the probable cause standard could easily be justified in criminal investigations. The distinction between such investigations and an OSHA inspection must lie in the lesser intrusion of a search that, in the words of *Camara*, is "neither personal in nature nor aimed at the discovery of evidence of crime."[35] If so, *Barlow's* stripped away one of *Camara's* prerequisites to dilution of probable cause. The need to show the unworkability of a probable cause requirement was replaced by a requirement that the probable cause limitation be burdensome or inconvenient, a characteristic that is universally present. What remained of *Camara* was nonetheless significant—a required showing of strong safety-related needs for inspection, together with circumstances suggesting that the intrusion on privacy interests is limited.

Delaware v. Prouse,[36] decided in 1979, again evidenced the Court's desire to restrain the administrative search. The Court struck down discretionary traffic stops for spot check of vehicle license and registration papers. The Court conceded the importance of the State's interest in highway safety and its need to ensure that registration requirements are observed.[37] But the Court held that the spot check was not a "*sufficiently productive* mechanism to justify the intrusion upon Fourth Amendment interests."[38]

Crucial to this conclusion was the Court's view that stops triggered by individual suspicion could achieve most of the State's purposes. "Drivers without licenses are presumably less safe drivers whose propensities may well exhibit themselves," and officers can therefore enforce safety regulations by "acting upon observed violations."[39] Compared to that approach, spot checks offered only a "marginal contribution to roadway safety."[40]

The *Prouse* Court also treated the intrusion as a serious one. Vehicle stops inconvenience the traveller only momentarily and probably less significantly than a fire inspector's visit inconveniences the homeowner (although the homeowner can usually require the housing inspector to return at a more convenient time). The inspection itself is directed only to the license and vehicle registration papers, state-issued documents in which the driver can have no right of

---

[35] 387 U.S. at 537.
[36] 440 U.S. 648 (1979).
[37] *Id.* at 658.
[38] *Id.* at 659 (emphasis added).
[39] *Ibid.*
[40] Id. at 661.

privacy against official inspection. The Court therefore might have chosen to regard the intrusion as minimal. Instead, the Court stressed that automobile travel is often necessary, that travellers retain a reasonable expectation of privacy while driving, and that the standardless nature of the spot check raised "[t]he 'grave danger' of abuse of discretion."[41] The opinion rejected, as had *Camara*, the notion that a regulatory motivation diminishes the intrusive quality of the search.[42]

> [I]f the government intrudes . . . the privacy interest suffers whether the government's motivation is to investigate violations of criminal laws or breaches of other statutory or regulatory standards.

Through the end of the 1970s, the administrative search exception thus remained bounded and reasonably defensible in terms of actual results.[43] The Court had required a warrant, except in cases of unusual necessity and remained cautious about relaxation of probable cause. Above all, the Court had not permitted personal searches of individuals in the absence of objectively founded suspicion or, more often, probable cause.[44]

2. *Dewey*. Matters began to unravel with *Donovan v. Dewey*,[45] decided in 1981. *Dewey* upheld the constitutionality of warrantless safety inspections of mines and stone quarries. The Court found a substantial regulatory interest and concluded that warrantless inspections were "necessary" because advance notice of an inspection would permit concealment of hazardous conditions. As in *Biswell*, the Court failed to explain why a warrant would prevent unannounced inspection, and it ignored its holding in *Barlow's* that a warrant requirement was compatible with the need for surprise. Another departure from *Barlow's* was more basic, for there the Court

---

[41]*Id.* at 662, quoting United States v. Martinez-Fuerte, 428 U.S. 543, 559 (1976).

[42]*Prouse*, 440 U.S. at 662, quoting *Barlow's*, 436 U.S. at 312–13.

[43]Other decisions of that period are, broadly speaking, consistent with this analysis. In South Dakota v. Opperman, 428 U.S. 364 (1976), the Court upheld self-protective inventory searches of impounded vehicles pursuant to standard caretaking procedures. In United States v. Brignoni-Ponce, 422 U.S. 873 (1975), the Court struck down random stops by roving immigration patrols near the international border but held that temporary stops would be permissible on individualized suspicion. In United States v. Martinez-Fuerte, 428 U.S. 543 (1976), the Court upheld an administrative plan for systematic, brief stops of all vehicles passing through a fixed Border Patrol checkpoint.

[44]But *cf.* United States v. Robinson, 414 U.S. 218 (1973) (search of the person incident to lawful arrest); Bell v. Wolfish, 441 U.S. 520 (1979) (search of pretrial detainees after contact visits upheld on the basis of their diminished expectations of privacy).

[45]452 U.S. 594 (1981).

had stressed that inspections of commercial property would generally require a warrant and that "the closely regulated industry of the type involved in *Colonnade* and *Biswell* is the exception."[46] Yet the *Dewey* Court treated *Barlow's* as the exception and repeatedly cited *Colonnade* and *Biswell* as representative of a general rule condoning warrantless inspection of commercial premises.[47]

Dewey did introduce one cautionary note, for the opinion did not rest with its finding that warrantless inspections are necessary. Rather, the Court said, when this is true, the issue becomes "whether the statute's inspection program, in terms of the certainty and regularity of its application, provides a constitutionally adequate substitute for a warrant."[48] The Court viewed the warrant requirement in *Barlow's* as resting on the absence of such a substitute: the Act there failed to specify the scope and frequency of inspections and gave "almost unbridled discretion"[49] to officers in the field. In the Mine Safety Act context, the Court found the statute a "constitutionally adequate substitute" primarily because regulation was so pervasive that the owner "cannot help but be aware" that he will be subject to inspection on a predictable basis.[50]

The Court's insistence on an adequate substitute for the warrant was a useful corrective, but its application of this new requirement was flaccid. The Act required that every mine be inspected at specified frequencies, but nothing in the federal scheme insured that the warrantless inspector had followed the guiding principles identified in the statute or that his choice of a particular site was "pursuant to an administrative plan containing specific neutral criteria."[51] The *Dewey* Court's conclusion that "it is difficult to see what additional protection a warrant requirement would provide"[52] was simply incorrect.[53]

---

[46]436 U.S. at 313.

[47]In a rewriting of administrative search history, the Court asserted that its *Barlow's* holding had been "expressly limited . . . to the inspection provisions of the Occupational Health and Safety Act." 452 U.S. at 599.

[48]*Id.* at 603.

[49]*Id.* at 601, quoting *Barlow's*, 436 U.S., at 323.

[50]*Id.* at 603.

[51]As required by *Barlow's*, 436 U.S. at 323.

[52]*Dewey*, 452 U.S., at 605.

[53]Professor LaFave suggests that the warrant procedure gave no benefit to the mine owner because the statute affords him "the superior procedure" of a pre-search adversary hearing. LaFave, note 19 *supra*, §10.2(e) at 659. But at such a hearing the mine owner can only attempt to show that a search of his mine would fall outside the scope of federal regulatory authority. He cannot insist on a showing that the site selection conforms to a neutral plan. See 30 U.S.C.

The permissive character of the Court's analysis was especially surprising in view of its authorship. The *Dewey* opinion, by Justice Marshall, was the first important administrative search case not written by Justice White. Rather than shoring up the loose language that had cropped up in the course of the restrictive holdings in *Camara*, *Barlow's*, and *Prouse*, Justice Marshall's opinion in *Dewey* hastened the process of relaxation and made the departure from traditional Fourth Amendment requirements the rule rather than the exception for regulatory inspections of commercial premises.

3. *Loosening the restraints after Dewey: T.L.O.* The decisions through *Dewey* had expanded administrative search authority primarily for commercial searches. Authority to conduct personal searches of individuals on less than probable cause was granted only under limited circumstances: an outer patdown for weapons on objectively founded suspicion,[54] and searches without suspicion at the international border[55] or incident to a lawful arrest on probable cause.[56] The cases remained largely faithful to *Camara*'s requirement that an administrative search be "neither personal in nature nor aimed at the discovery of evidence of crime,"[57] and in *Prouse* the Court had disapproved suspicionless stops of individuals in connection with an undoubtedly important regulatory objective.

New Jersey v. T.L.O.,[58] decided in 1985, marks a watershed. Eighteen years after *Camara*, the Court for the first time approved a personal search for evidence, not motivated by an immediate need for self protection, not justified by a warrant, by exigent circumstances, or by a systematic administrative plan, and not supported by probable cause.

In *T.L.O.* a high school assistant principal, who had cause to believe that a student had been smoking in violation of school rules, searched the student's purse for cigarettes. After finding a pack of cigarettes and rolling papers that he associated with illegal drugs, he searched the purse more thoroughly, found marijuana, and turned the drugs over to police.

The Supreme Court ruled that the seizure was not illegal. Its opin-

---

§818(a). Elsewhere in his treatise, Professor LaFave recognizes some of the shortcomings of the statutory hearing. LaFave, note 19 *supra*, §10.2(d) at 651.

[54]Terry v. Ohio, 392 U.S. 1 (1968).

[55]United States v. Ramsey, 431 U.S. 606 (1977).

[56]United States v. Robinson, 414 U.S. 218 (1973); *cf.* Bell v. Wolfish, 441 U.S. 520 (1979) (suspicionless search of prisoners after contact visits).

[57]*Camara*, 387 U.S., at 537.

[58]469 U.S. 325 (1985).

ion, by Justice White, held that the determination of reasonableness under the Fourth Amendment "requires 'balancing the need to search against the invasion which the search entails.'"[59] The Court concluded that school officials need not obtain a warrant before searching a student and that such searches would be valid in the absence of probable cause, "when there are reasonable grounds for suspecting that the search will turn up evidence that the student has violated . . . either the law or the rules of the school."[60]

Whether the Court should have imposed stricter limits on school searches is debatable.[61] The problems of maintaining discipline in the school setting render at least plausible the Court's view that school searches can be "reasonable" within the meaning of the Fourth Amendment on individual suspicion short of probable cause. Yet *T.L.O.* sounded two ominous notes. First, the Court left open the possibility that some school searches might be permissible without individual suspicion.[62] Second, the Court's methodology bypassed the presumption in favor of probable cause and proceeded directly to the balancing of government needs against privacy interests. Justice Blackmun, who concurred in the result, noted the need to rein in this aspect of the Court's analysis. "Only," he wrote, "in those exceptional circumstances in which special needs, beyond the normal need for law enforcement, make the warrant and probable-cause requirement impracticable, is a court entitled to substitute its balancing of interests for that of the Framers."[63]

The Blackmun caveat provides a measure of how far the Court had come since *Camara*. His plea for showing some "special needs" is a far cry from the four elements that justified departure from the Fourth Amendment framework in *Camara*—a neutral plan, a compelling need to search, an absence of workable alternatives to the dilution of probable cause, and a substantially diminished intrusion on privacy. None of these elements was satisfied in *T.L.O.*—there was no neutral plan for systematic inspection; the student's cigarettes, even if she possessed them, posed no threat to anyone; the relevant disciplinary violation was easily investigated under traditional probable cause

---

[59]*Id*. at 337, quoting *Camara*, 387 U.S., at 536–37.

[60]*Id*. at 342.

[61]Justice Stevens, for example, argued that the power to search students on less than probable cause should be confined to searches for evidence of unlawful or seriously disruptive behavior, categories that do not encompass cigarette smoking in the lavatory.

[62]*Id*. at 342 n.8.

[63]*Id*. at 351.

standards; and the inspection was both personal in nature and (as it moved on to a search for marijuana) aimed at the discovery of evidence of crime. Justice Blackmun was willing to embark on de novo balancing (and ultimately to uphold the search) on the more slender basis of "special needs" that render the probable cause requirement merely "impracticable." And the Court's majority seemed to ignore the need for satisfying even this weaker limitation.

4. *The 1986 Term.* Three decisions of the 1986 Term accomplished further doctrinal changes. In the first, *O'Connor v. Ortega*,[64] the Court extended the *T.L.O.* authority for personal searches on less than probable cause from the student context to that of government employees suspected of work-related misconduct. A plurality of four justices, in an opinion by Justice O'Connor, viewed the employee's privacy interest in workplace areas (offices, desks, file cabinets) as diminished (though still sufficient to trigger some Fourth Amendment protection). Both Justice Scalia, who concurred in the result, and Justice Blackmun, for the four dissenters, recognized more substantial employee privacy interests in workplace areas. And significantly, even the plurality stressed that the diminution of privacy expectations in workplace areas did not extend to "closed personal luggage, a handbag or a briefcase that happens to be within the employer's business address."[65] *Ortega* thus seemed to commit all nine Justices to a view that presumably applies, *a fortiori*, to the contents of an employee's bladder.

In its application of Fourth Amendment standards, *Ortega* seemed to narrow the administrative search exception. The plurality structured its analysis around the test Justice Blackmun had formulated in criticism of *T.L.O.*: only when special needs beyond the ordinary requirements of law enforcement make the warrant and probable cause requirements impracticable, the plurality said, was the Court free to depart from the normal Fourth Amendment framework and to undertake *de novo* balancing. But this analytic restriction was only cosmetic. The plurality, relying on factors such as those *T.L.O.* had considered under the rubric of "reasonableness," found that workplace searches did involve "special needs" justifying warrantless searches and a standard of suspicion lower than probable cause. Justice Blackmun, for the four dissenters, agreed that some employer

---

[64]480 U.S. 709 (1967).
[65]*Id.* at 716.

searches could be valid under a diluted standard, but found no "special need" in *Ortega* itself.

Although *Ortega* involved a search on amply founded suspicions, the plurality, like the *T.L.O.* Court, left open the possibility of approving at least some employer searches without individual suspicion. And Justice Scalia's concurring opinion expressly argued that workplace searches for work-related reasons are always reasonable. A better view, surely, would require some objective basis for search. At stake is the privacy of desks, files, and other non-exposed areas where employees reasonably (as all the Justices agree) commingle business and personal material. For even so routine a matter as a search to retrieve a file, it is not impractical, indeed it is only sensible, to require some basis for belief that the file is there. Absent unusual circumstances, my employer should not be free to search through my desk and papers simply because someone in the building has lost a file. But however that open issue may be resolved, it encompasses only searches of workplace areas. Nothing in *Ortega* supports searches on less than objectively founded suspicions or indeed on less than full probable cause, when the object to be searched is some wholly personal item that "happens to be within the employer's business address."[66]

New York v. Burger,[67] also decided in the 1986 Term, widened the administrative search power by another important notch. *Burger* upheld warrantless, random police searches of automobile junk yards that had been subjected to record-keeping requirements under a state regulatory regime. In an opinion by Justice Blackmun, the Court focused mainly on the question whether the search required an administrative warrant (as in *Camara* and *Barlow's*) or no warrant (as in *Dewey*). The Court accurately restated the criteria laid down by precedent but applied them loosely. The Court said that vehicle dismantlers were "closely regulated." Yet the statutory limitations on their activities were slender; in *Barlow's*, far more significant OSHA regulations had been held insufficient to make the business "closely regulated." The Court said that the New York statute informed the dismantler that he will be inspected "on a regular basis."[68] Yet the statute in *Burger* specified no patterns for inspection, laid down no criteria to guide inspectors in choosing inspection sites, and imposed

---

[66]*Ibid.*
[67]482 U.S. 691 (1987).
[68]*Id.* at 711.

no mandate that particular businesses be inspected at any regular intervals.[69] Nothing in the *Burger* scheme could fairly be compared to the predictable inspection intervals mandated in *Dewey*. Instead, *Burger* involved all the vices of discretionary police action that were present, and had proved fatal, in *Prouse* only eight years before.

It is difficult to know what to make of this branch of *Burger*. The prerequisites for avoiding the warrant requirement remained verbally unaltered but were drained of content.

A second important question in *Burger* was whether the search should qualify as "administrative" at all. The avowed purpose of the New York statute was to oversee a business linked to the receipt and distribution of stolen property. No public health or safety hazard was presented, no inadequacy of ordinary law enforcement techniques was involved, and no systematic, neutral plan for inspection was identified. None of the elements that had justified administrative treatment in *Camara*[70] was present. Even in terms of Justice Blackmun's "special needs" formulation, it seems difficult to say that there are "special needs *beyond the normal need for law enforcement*, that render the warrant and probable cause requirements impracticable."[71] Although the statute helped assure that dismantlers are legitimate business persons and helped trace stolen vehicle parts, inspections were carried out solely by police and their main focus was on catching the receiver of stolen property. In *Burger* itself the defendant, by telling the policeman-inspectors that he had not registered or kept the required records, had admitted violating every one of the "administrative" requirements. Yet the police searched anyway, and the Court treated their action as an administrative inspection even though it had no purpose except to gather evidence of crime.

The Court responded to these concerns by observing that penal and regulatory objectives may co-exist and that inspection by police rather than "administrative" officials should not render illegal an otherwise proper administrative regime.[72] These observations are largely valid[73] but beside the point. A genuine scheme of admin-

---

[69]See N.Y. Vehicle & Traffic Law, §415–a5(a) (McKinney 1986).

[70]See text at note 24 *supra*.

[71]*T.L.O.*, 469 U.S. at 351 (concurring opinion) (emphasis added).

[72]*Burger*, 482 U.S. at 712–13.

[73]The commingling of penal and administrative sanctions, together with the use of police as inspectors, does, however, alter many of the circumstances that support the *Camara* Court's conclusion that administrative searches are only minimally intrusive. See text at note 24 *supra*.

istrative regulation may, in part, be designed to prevent criminal harms and may be backed by criminal sanctions. But the question in *Burger* is whether the scheme was genuinely regulatory in the first place.

The Court was willing to find "regulation" in little more than the statute's requirement that operators preserve proof that their materials had a legal source. In the Court's view, such a statute not only creates a "regulatory" regime; it also renders such businesses "closely regulated," puts them on notice that inspections will be on a "regular basis," and provides a "constitutionally adequate substitute for a warrant." The Fourth Amendment invalidates (presumably) a statute providing that particular businesses or activities are subject to unannounced, warrantless inspection at will. But what lies in the space between what the Fourth Amendment forbids and what *Burger* permits? While the Court does not intend a legislative *carte blanche*, neither *Burger* nor its predecessors provide a basis for identifying the remaining boundaries.

The third case of the 1986 Term, *Griffin v. Wisconsin*,[74] lowered administrative search barriers from still another direction. The Court upheld the search of a probationer's home on the basis of a slender tip that fell short of probable cause and fell short of even the founded suspicion necessary for a *Terry*-type stop. *Griffin*, like *Ortega*, gave prominence to Justice Blackmun's *T.L.O.* concurrence and identified the "special needs" formula as the governing test for the administrative search. Yet this restriction again made little difference in practice. The same considerations that led the Court's "balance" to tip in favor of government needs also served to satisfy the threshold test that the probable cause requirement be "impracticable" in the context of the "special" needs of probation supervision. And the Court gave next to no consideration to the possibility that once probable cause was abandoned, some intermediate level of suspicion might be workable. Instead, Justice Scalia, writing this time for the Court, followed the approach he had proposed for government employees only a few months before (and with no takers) in *Ortega*: once "special needs" are deemed to render the probable cause requirement impracticable, then a search can be deemed reasonable without any objective suspicion.

Again the spokesman for a more careful approach, Justice Blackmun wrote for the four dissenters in *Griffin*. In response to the legiti-

---

[74]107 S.Ct. 3164 (1987).

mate needs of probation supervision, he would permit searches of
the home on less than probable cause. But he would require at least
the same objective basis that the Court requires for a temporary
Terry-type stop.

Griffin presented a second issue—whether, as in cases like *Camara*,
the "administrative" search of the home must be authorized by a warrant. In previous cases, the Court had analyzed this issue in shifting
terms but had focused primarily on such factors as the extent to which
a warrant would provide added privacy protection and whether costs
and delays incident to the warrant mechanism would defeat the regulatory program. In *Griffin*, the Court by-passed these questions and
focused instead on the wording of the warrant clause ("no Warrants
shall issue, but upon probable cause"). If probable cause is not mandated, the Court said, the warrant requirement necessarily becomes
inapplicable. A requirement of a judicial warrant issued on less than
probable cause is, the Court asserted, "a combination that neither the
text of the Constitution nor any of our prior decisions *permits*."[75]

The Court's textual point is understandable, but its claim about
precedent is extremely jarring. What about *Camara*? What about *Barlow's* and other Supreme Court cases along the same lines?[76] In a
monumentally obfuscating passage, the Court said that the administrative warrants required by such cases "may but do not necessarily
have to be issued by courts," and that the Court had never permitted
less than full probable cause for "constitutionally mandated judicial
warrants."[77]

As a description of prior decisions, the Court's statement was inaccurate. *Camara* and *Barlow's* had required precisely what *Griffin*
describes as unprecedented—warrants that "*have to be* issued by
courts." *Griffin* seems to reach for a distinction between warrants issued merely by a magistrate or neutral "officer" and "constitutionally
mandated *judicial* warrants."[78] But that effort is untenable. The argument is especially odd as a textual one because the Fourth Amendment does not say that "*judges* shall not issue warrants on less than
probable cause." Written in the passive voice, the Amendment states
that "*no* Warrants shall issue, but upon probable cause." And nothing

---

[75]Id. at 3169 (emphasis added).

[76]*E.g.*, See v. City of Seattle, 387 U.S. 541 (1967).

[77]*Griffin*, 107 S.Ct. at 3170.

[78]*Ibid.* (emphasis added). See also *id.* at 3170 n.5, arguing that the "'neutral magistrate' [cit-
ing *Camara*, 387 U.S. at 532] or 'neutral officer' [citing *Barlow's*, 436 U.S. at 323] envisioned by
our administrative search cases is not necessarily [a] 'neutral judge' . . . ."

in subsequent Fourth Amendment development supports a distinction between warrants issued by magistrates and "constitutionally mandated judicial warrants." *Camara* warrants are rooted in "the warrant machinery contemplated by the Fourth Amendment";[79] such administrative warrants must be issued "by courts."[80] Conversely, criminal search warrants can be issued by magistrates;[81] like administrative warrants, they "may but do not necessarily have to be" issued by a judge.

Are we here confronting anything more than the inartful analysis of a confused or sloppy law clerk? One must hope not. If there were anything to the Court's supposed separation of magistrate warrants from judicial warrants, it would have to consider why Griffin himself should not be protected by the kind of "magistrate warrant" that was held constitutionally imperative in *Camara* and *Barlow's*. The *Griffin* Court devotes not one word to this question.

Yet this line of thought is only minimally reassuring. It merely reinforces the initial impression that the Court is withdrawing the constitutional status of all administrative warrants, not just "judicial" ones. Indeed, at the center of its analysis the *Griffin* Court placed language from *Frank v. Maryland* reasoning that "[i]f a search warrant be constitutionally required, the requirement cannot be flexibly interpreted to dispense with the rigorous constitutional [probable cause] restrictions for its issue."[82] But *Camara* expressly overruled *Frank* on this point. The *Griffin* Court omits this detail. And in a final and supreme irony, the Court follows its *Frank* quotation by chiding Justice Blackmun, whose dissent pressed for a warrant requirement, on the ground that he "neither gives a justification for departure from that [*Frank*] principle nor considers its implications for the body of Fourth Amendment law."[83]

Griffin's holding on the warrant issue, if taken at face value, wipes out the entire body of doctrine concerned with the need for administrative warrants. What *Dewey* did for administrative searches of commercial premises, on condition that there be a constitutionally adequate substitute for a warrant, *Griffin* now does for administrative searches of private homes, and does *without* a requirement of any

---

[79]*Camara*, 387 U.S. at 532.
[80]Coolidge v. New Hampshire, 403 U.S. 443 (1971).
[81]Shadwick v. City of Tampa, 407 U.S. 345 (1972).
[82]*Griffin*, 107 S.Ct. at 3170, quoting Frank v. Maryland, 359 U.S. at 373.
[83]*Griffin*, 107 S.Ct. at 3170.

substitute mechanism to serve the functions of the warrant. Only the fact that *Griffin* accomplishes this result almost (but not fully) *sub silentio* can be almost (but not fully) reassuring for the future of the warrant requirement in this area.

C. THE CURRENT STATUS OF ADMINISTRATIVE SEARCH DOCTRINE

Doctrinal growth or decay is no new phenomenon, in the Fourth Amendment or elsewhere, and is not necessarily a bad thing. Obfuscation, inconsistency, and disingenuous treatment of facts or precedent are not to be defended, but we know that they too have their uses and that Justices have sinned in these ways throughout history. Like many of its predecessors, the present Court does convey an overall sense of direction, in this case one of relaxing Fourth Amendment restrictions generally and administrative search limitations particularly. The Court has upheld nearly all the administrative searches it has considered since 1980 and often has gone out of its way to contemplate standards even less restrictive than those that had been satisfied on the facts before it. Yet this appearance of basic consistency—in the result—is misleading. A closer look reveals a Court fundamentally in disarray.

1. *The Justices.* Of the Justices participating in the cases through the 1986 Term, only three—Powell, Rehnquist, and White— provided reliable votes for upholding administrative searches. Justices Brennan and Marshall were predictable dissenters, though Marshall wrote and Brennan joined the opinion in *Dewey.* The other four Justices, several of whom will be essential to any majority, present a puzzle:

• Justice Stevens joined both *Dewey* and *Burger.* Indeed he has suggested overruling *Camara* and authorizing searches without any warrant for regulatory inspections.[84] Yet Justice Stevens dissented in *T.L.O.*, *Griffin*, and *Ortega*, all involving personal searches in a non-law-enforcement context.

• Justice Scalia joined in *Burger*, wrote for the Court in *Griffin*, and concurred in the result in *Ortega*, where he suggested an approach even more flexible than the plurality's. Yet in *Arizona v. Hicks*,[85] a traditional (non-administrative) search case, Justice Scalia wrote the

---

[84]See *Barlow's*, 436 U.S. at 325 (Stevens, J., dissenting); *Dewey*, 452 U.S. at 606 (Stevens, J., concurring).
[85]107 S.Ct. 1149 (1987).

Court's opinion invalidating on rather technical grounds a very limited police search. And as we shall see, Justice Scalia wrote an impassioned dissent in one of the cases upholding drug testing.

• Justice O'Connor joined in *T.L.O.* and *Griffin*, and she wrote for the plurality in *Ortega*. But her opinion in the latter case suggests a much more cautious approach than the one she adhered to in *Griffin*. And she dissented from the no-warrant holding in *Burger*.

• Justice Blackmun's votes seem virtually the mirror image of Justice O'Connor's. He concurred only in the result in *T.L.O.*, and dissented in *Griffin* and *Ortega*. But Justice Blackmun wrote the Court's opinion upholding the dubious commercial search *Burger*.

Under these conditions, there can be no guarantee that efforts to invoke the administrative search rubric will inevitably garner five approving votes. Nor can one hope to identify the variables likely to move the large "swing" group, which comprises nearly half the Court. On the one hand, the opinions, taken at face value, appear to dismantle virtually every one of the analytic barriers to warrantless search of individuals or commercial property. On the other hand, each of the cases presents, on its facts, some special feature that may explain the intuitive pull to approval for at least a few of the Justices. There may yet be value, therefore, in sifting the decisions with an eye toward imposing some coherence on the sorry state of administrative search doctrine.

2. *The doctrine*. An attempt to recapitulate the twists and turns just canvassed entails obvious risks, but we can summarize the approximate state of the law. First, what prerequisites must be satisfied in order to escape the traditional Fourth Amendment framework (a warrant supported by probable cause) and qualify for the "administrative" rubric? *Camara* relied upon four features—(1) a neutral plan for systematic inspection; (2) a compelling governmental need, linked to a pressing concern for public health or safety; (3) an absence of workable, less restrictive alternatives to the dilution of probable cause; and (4) a greatly diminished intrusion on privacy, resulting from the fact that the search is neither personal in nature nor aimed at discovering evidence of crime. A different point of departure was suggested by *Prouse*. The Court could have said that the Delaware program for spot checks satisfied *Camara's* second and fourth elements but not the others. Instead, the Court jumped immediately to balancing law enforcement needs against the degree of the privacy intrusion. The change of focus was not immediately consequential,

however, because the balancing inquiry produced the same result as *Camara's* four-pronged test.

The major shift occurred in *T.L.O.* The search of the student's purse for cigarettes flunked every one of *Camara's* threshold tests. The Court was able to uphold the search by relying on open-ended balancing as the only necessary threshold inquiry. In effect, the Court broadened the "administrative" rubric to encompass cases not involving systematic, neutral inspection plans and not involving any regulatory features of the usual sort. Justice Blackmun reached the same result but used a stricter threshold test. The Court, he said, should ask first whether "special needs, beyond the normal need for law enforcement, make the warrant and probable cause requirements impracticable." This "special needs" approach has become, for now, the official formulation of the threshold inquiry, having been identified as "the" test by a majority of the Court in *Ortega, Burger,* and *Griffin.*

Second, once the threshold is crossed, what degree of judicial scrutiny is appropriate in determining reasonableness? *Barlow's* looked skeptically at the asserted need for warrantless inspection to insure surprise, and *Prouse* questioned the need for random stops unsupported by individual suspicion. Subsequent decisions have been more deferential. Although *Prouse* carefully weighed the incremental value of additionally intrusive program features, the Court wrote only four years later that "[t]he reasonableness of any particular government activity does not necessarily turn on the existence of alternative 'less intrusive' means."[86] *Dewey* found warrantless inspection necessary to insure surprise. *T.L.O.* and *Ortega* suggested (in dicta) that inspections without objectively grounded suspicion might be supportable, and *Griffin* held such inspections reasonable, without questioning the asserted needs or considering alternative ways to meet them. Deference to alleged governmental interests now appears to be the rule followed in practice, though the Court has generally reached its conclusions about "necessity" and "reasonableness" without acknowledging the absence of serious de novo review.

3. *An assessment.* (a) *The scope of the "administrative" category.* Justice Blackmun is surely correct that some threshold inquiry must precede open-ended analysis of reasonableness. What is wrong, after all,

---

[86]Illinois v. Lafayette, 462 U.S. 640, 647 (1983).

with a warrantless police entry into of a boarded-up slum building for a cursory visual inspection, on the basis of an unsupported tip that the premises constitute a "crack house"? On a balance of law enforcement needs (acute) against privacy interests (diminished), there is nothing *a priori* unreasonable about such a search, and the Fourth Amendment prohibits only "unreasonable searches and seizures." But those words cannot be severed from their history. Insofar as we can ever know the mind and world of the Framers, a search not supported by probable cause was for them presumptively unreasonable. The structure, spirit and history of the Fourth Amendment oblige the Court to identify some exceptional feature before it can substitute its own judgment for the Amendment's basic premise about what ordinarily makes a search reasonable.

What "special" features should qualify? It would be foolhardy to attempt an all-inclusive list. Exigent circumstances, searches incident to arrest, border searches and others have been legitimated by precedent and experience. The *Camara* tests identify another group of searches that certainly deserve exceptional treatment. But when should the Court go beyond the *Camara* formulation?

(i) Systematic, neutral criteria. Both *Camara* and *Dewey* approve administrative treatment in large part because of reliance upon neutral criteria for systematic selection of inspection sites. The *Prouse* Court disapproved non-systematic spot checks but implied that it would uphold a fixed checkpoint for stopping all cars or a subset randomly designated by neutral criteria.[87] The irony is that broad, neutral selection systems (area inspections and fixed vehicle checkpoints) tend to expand the class subjected to invasions of privacy. The approach seems to imply that "misery loves company."[88]

Several considerations explain this paradox. Neutral criteria or systematic random selection prevent abuses of discretion such as harassment of particular individuals. The routine character of neutral selection removes much of the stigma and fear that accompany searches based on individual suspicion. And the breadth of the class subject to search helps mitigate the barriers to an effective political check on unproductive programs.

Nonetheless, the Court has often extended administrative treat-

---

[87] 440 U.S. at 663 & n.26. See also United States v. Martinez-Fuerte, 428 U.S. 543 (1976), upholding fixed vehicle checkpoints designed to stem illegal immigration.

[88] *Prouse*, 440 U.S. at 644 (Rehnquist, J., dissenting).

ment to searches not bounded by neutral, semi-automatic criteria. Both *Biswell* and *Burger* seem to treat the need for frequent, unannounced searches as rendering a systematic inspection plan impracticable. And in upholding searches on less than probable cause, *T.L.O.* and *Ortega* treat the presence of focused suspicion as a factor strengthening the reasonableness of the search.

The administrative search cases are thus plagued by unresolved tension between the virtues of systematic, neutral rules and individualized discretion. Neutral criteria mitigate the subjective distress accompanying an inspection and prevent unjustified selectivity and harassment, but they tend to expand the scope and frequency of administrative searches. Discretion can avoid the unnecessary intrusions that accompany sweeping inspection dragnets and can promote a better means-ends fit by focusing administrative effort on the most worthwhile targets, but it is susceptible to abuse.

The Court can choose to work either side of this dilemma without acknowledging the existence of the other. In the area of vehicle stops it has preferred systematic stops at fixed checkpoints to discretionary roving patrols. But it has approved discretionary inspections of students and employees. And it has permitted discretionary inspections on a mere hunch (the regulatory equivalent of a roving vehicle patrol) in the context of *Biswell*, *Burger*, and *Griffin*.

Clearly, the neutral plan envisioned by *Camara* is no longer essential. But in its absence, some founded suspicion ordinarily is needed to limit the class subject to search and to control discretion. Although individual suspicion is not an irreducible minimum (as sobriety checkpoints and airport metal detectors attest), the Court was ill-advised to suggest in *T.L.O.* and *Ortega* (and to hold in *Griffin*) that administrative inspections can sometimes be valid with neither a neutral plan nor individual suspicion.

A converse question is whether a neutral plan affords sufficient protection without individual suspicion. Since control of discretion is not the only Fourth Amendment concern, neutrality is not necessarily adequate to protect relevant privacy interests.

Systematic suspicionless inspection has been upheld for safety inspections of homes and metal detector screening at airports. Both contexts involve limited intrusions on privacy and dangerous conditions that will seldom present outward manifestations. Sobriety checkpoints are slightly different; the intrusion on privacy is relatively minor but behavior indicating intoxication is often observable.

As the invasion of privacy becomes more significant, it becomes correspondingly more important to limit the size of the class subject to that invasion. And as the condition to be identified becomes more readily observable, it becomes more feasible to achieve the desired limitation by requiring individual suspicion as a prerequisite to search. Systematic metal-detector screening of courthouse visitors is therefore permissible. But body-cavity searches of students entering school should not be. For the same reason, direct observation urinalysis of public employees remains problematic even when conducted according to a neutral plan. In the last two cases the intrusion on privacy is serious, suggesting the need to minimize the number of citizens unnecessarily searched, and a narrower regime of inspection tied to individual suspicion may be feasible.

(ii) Safety and privacy concerns. There are several other ways in which searches may satisfy some but not all of *Camara*'s elements. An inspection regime may meet the diminished-expectation-of-privacy requirement but present no imperative health or safety concerns. Conversely, a situation may involve a pressing public safety concern but require a highly personal search.

The second case certainly should qualify for "administrative" treatment. Indeed, a safety-based exception from traditional Fourth Amendment requirements now seems uncontroversial even in standard law enforcement searches of the person (stop and frisk, search incident to arrest). In this regard the *Camara* elements are undoubtedly too strict.

The first case is less clear. Should a diminution of affected privacy interests be sufficient by itself to trigger reduced Fourth Amendment protection? The problem is that such an approach would turn the constitutional framework into "one immense Rorschach blot."[89] Indeed, the Court expressly rejected a "comparative privacy" approach in *Arizona v. Hicks*, where the search involved only the slight displacement of a stereo turntable so that the officer could observe its serial number.

Hicks tests the argument for a "comparative privacy" analysis in its most attractive setting. But that approach is hopelessly unworkable.

---

[89] Amsterdam, Perspectives on the Fourth Amendment, 58 Minn. L. Rev. 349, 393 (1974). Compare Alschuler, Bright Line Fever and the Fourth Amendment, 45 U. Pitt. L. Rev. 227 (1984), arguing the feasibility of a general "reasonableness" approach.

Relative to some imaginable state of pure privacy, the real-world privacy interests infringed by regulation or law enforcement are always somewhat diminished. The factory work floor (*Barlow's*) is less private than an employee's desk and files (*Ortega*), but these are less private than luggage or a purse at the office. A purse carries diminished privacy expectations when it is taken to school (*T.L.O.*), and in any event is less private than one's physical person or dwelling. A probationer's dwelling, however, is less private (*Griffin*) than an ordinary citizen's, and even the latter is less private in regard to its plumbing and wiring (*Camara*) than in its sleeping quarters (except where these have wiring too). Except when police enter the conjugal bedroom in the dead of night without knocking, the privacy expectations they violate are always substantially diminished, by comparison to something else.

Though diminished privacy alone cannot support administrative treatment, *Camara* suggests that diminished expectations of privacy might still be relevant as a necessary (though not sufficient) element—that a pressing public need to search should not by itself justify an administrative exception. But this approach breaks down whenever safety concerns are acute. Body-cavity searches of prisoners after contact visits present one context in which personal searches seem justifiable without probable cause, on an administrative rationale.[90] If it became necessary to subject air travellers (including flight crew members holding job security) to body search for plastic explosives, such searches also might be justifiable without individual suspicion. One could posit that legitimate expectations of privacy are diminished in these contexts because of the pressing need to search. But that move saves the *Camara* formulation by emptying it of content. Functionally, the safety concern alone supports administrative treatment.

The nature of the affected privacy interest remains relevant in one sense. The relative strength of that interest must be weighed if a case falls within an area that requires an inquiry about "reasonableness." But to cite diminished expectations as a basis for entering that domain and escaping the presumption of probable cause is to invoke intuitively plausible considerations at the wrong place.

For these reasons, diminished (even greatly diminished) expecta-

---

[90]Bell v. Wolfish, 441 U.S. 520 (1979).

tions of privacy cannot be sufficient, by themselves, to liberate a regulatory program from the traditional Fourth Amendment requirements of probable cause and a warrant. In contrast, a pressing safety concern should be. By this criterion, *Camara, Barlow's, Prouse,* and *Dewey* all qualify for an open-ended balancing inquiry. But on this approach most of the Court's recent administrative search cases would be wrongly decided. School officials might have searched T.L.O.'s purse for a weapon (or for a plastic explosive that could evade metal detectors), but they could not search for cigarettes. Nor could officials properly conduct an administrative search on the various non-safety rationales invoked in *Ortega, Burger,* and *Griffin.*

(iii) Needs other than law enforcement. A defense of *T.L.O., Ortega, Burger,* and *Griffin* can be built on the Blackmun test, which converts safety concerns from an essential prerequisite to an example of the broader category of "special needs, beyond the normal need for law enforcement." But why should special needs, other than those involving health and safety, be "special"? What is it about a non-law-enforcement objective that warrants diminished control over official action and reduced protection for privacy?

Unfortunately, Justice Blackmun's concurrence and the Court opinions based on it never attempt to justify the permissive side of his test. Launching a caveat to an even less bounded analysis, Justice Blackmun explained his reasons for refusing to jump directly to balancing but had no occasion to consider whether the threshold inquiry should be stricter than his. Subsequent cases used the caveat for what it authorized rather than for what, at its inception, it was intended to restrain. And they cited his formulation as one already accepted and in no need of defense.

Under these conditions we must speculate about possible justifications for the "special needs" approach. Its most surprising feature is its return to what the Court has called the "remarkable premise" of *Frank v. Maryland,* namely, that the absence of a law enforcement objective renders "the Fourth Amendment interests at stake merely 'peripheral.'"[91] In case after case the Court has approved the *Camara* view that "[i]t is surely anomalous to say that the individual and his private property are fully protected by the Fourth Amendment only when the individual is suspected of criminal activity."[92] Yet the

---

[91]*Camara,* 387 U.S. at 530–31.

[92]*Ibid.,* quoted in *T.L.O.,* 469 U.S. at 335; *Ortega,* 480 U.S. at 715. See also *Barlow's,* 436 U.S. at 312–13: "[T]he privacy interest suffers whether the government's motivation is to investigate violations of criminal laws or breaches of other statutory or regulatory standards."

"special needs" approach has precisely the effect of leaving the law-abiding citizen more vulnerable to invasions of privacy than the criminal suspect is.

Despite this anomaly, the "special needs" formulation proceeds from a plausible intuition. The Fourth Amendment is primarily about law enforcement; "special needs" inspections are about something else. A school teacher's search for a water pistol or noise-maker is not (one would guess) what the Framers intended to restrain by the Fourth Amendment.

Yet this intuition does not fully fit the historical evidence. Of immediate concern to the Framers, in fact the central preoccupation in the area of searches and seizures, was the writ of assistance (a blanket warrant authorizing search of any location without probable cause) used by royal customs officers to search warehouses and cellars for undutied imports. Such searches, which the Court has described as "one of the potent causes of the Revolution,"[93] were not in aid of criminal prosecution or "law enforcement" in the traditional sense, since they apparently had as their sole objective the seizure and forfeiture of untaxed goods.[94] Whatever the Framers might have thought of the teacher's search for a water pistol, they could not have agreed broadly that constitutional inquiry should turn to balancing whenever "special needs, beyond the normal need for law enforcement" render a warrant "impracticable." It was precisely in the area of the Crown's "special needs" for import regulation and revenue forfeitures, in a context of massive evasion and civil disobedience, that the Framers were most insistent upon a warrant issued on particularized probable cause.

This perspective suggests that what may be wanted is a formulation more nuanced than the "special needs" test, with both "normal" law enforcement and quasi-criminal regulatory action separated from inspections that (like the water pistol search) seem to have a fundamentally different character. What makes the latter category different remains to be unpacked.

(iv) Prosecutorial purpose. One distinctive feature of a water pistol search is that the lack of a law enforcement objective mitigates the intrusion on privacy. But this element is problematic. A non-law-enforcement objective may mitigate intrusiveness if it affects the way

---

[93]Chimel v. California, 395 U.S. 752, 761 (1969); Arkansas v. Sanders, 442 U.S. 753, 759 n.5 (1979), both quoting United States v. Rabinowitz, 339 U.S. 56, 69 (1950)(dissenting opinion).

[94]See Levy, Original Intent and the Framers' Constitution 221, 224, 226–27 (1988).

the search is carried out. It may be that a regulatory inspection will not seek evidence of personal activities; will not require armed, hostile officers; will not be opposed by force; will not damage reputation or manifest official suspicion; and will not require that anything be seized. But these elements cease to be present when a regulatory program combines remedial and law-enforcement objectives. Features mitigating the intrusion on privacy were largely missing, for example, in *Griffin* and *Ortega* and were entirely absent in *Burger*. At best, therefore, "special needs" can entail a diminished privacy impact only when remedial goals are cleanly disentangled from law enforcement objectives, a rare occurrence. And in any event, as we learn from *Hicks*, a diminished impact on privacy cannot, by itself, justify a diminished regime of Fourth Amendment protection.[95]

Does there remain, then, any defensible basis for the intuition that "special needs" justify a less restrictive regime of Fourth Amendment protection? Health and safety concerns explain *Camara*, *Biswell*, *Barlow's*, and *Dewey*. But this approach cannot account for *T.L.O.*, *Ortega*, *Burger*, and *Griffin*. And we cannot account for the still more universal intuition that supports the schoolteacher's warrantless seizure of a water pistol.

(v) Internal governance objectives. I suggest that the distinctive feature of the water pistol situation, as well as cases such as *Ortega*, *Griffin*, and *T.L.O.*, is the use of inspection as a tool for the internal governance of a self-contained government activity. One would have to be naive, of course, to believe that terms like "internal" and "external" are self-defining or capable of resolving problems categorically. Nonetheless, these terms come closer to identifying the important features of the administrative search cases than does the contrast, which has so preoccupied the Court, between regulation and "normal" law enforcement. Indeed, the fundamental difficulty in the Court's effort to identify the administrative search is that the contrast between regulation and law enforcement is illusory.

In the context of cases such as *Camara*, *Barlow's*, and *Burger*, we cannot hope to differentiate law enforcement from "administrative" regulation, for these are overlapping categories. While law enforcement and regulation theoretically differ in the sanctions they deploy, they both aim to oversee the conduct of the general public or some sub-group engaged in a particular kind of activity. And in doing so,

---

[95]Note 85 *supra*; see text following not 89 *supra*.

government ordinarily uses both regulatory and penal sanctions. Since this will generally be the case, the presence of penal sanctions cannot by itself defeat an administrative scheme, if the administrative category is to exist at all. The Court correctly noted this point in *Burger*.[96] The converse is also true—the use of regulatory methods cannot by itself qualify a scheme as administrative, at least not if the administrative category is to remain the exception.

Whether government proceeds through the penal or regulatory approach, the important point for present purposes is that both approaches involve control of private activity. Government is not a participant but an adversary whose mission is to constrain the way the activity is pursued, for reasons extrinsic to the goals of the activity itself. I suggest that it was this situation that the Framers "had in mind" when they struck the balance embodied in the Fourth Amendment's probable cause and warrant requirements. The effort to control private activity for public purposes, however worthy, does not permit intrusions on individual privacy in the absence of probable cause and prior judicial approval.

There are exceptions to the presumptive balance struck by the Fourth Amendment, but these exceptions should never turn on the supposed distinction between law enforcement and regulation. Exigent circumstances justify an exception to the warrant requirement in both contexts. Similarly, safety concerns produce exceptions to the warrant and probable cause requirements in the context of both traditional law enforcement (*Terry*, *Chimel*[97]) and administrative regulation (*Biswell*, *Dewey*).

A different situation is presented when government inspects for reasons internal to the governance of a public enterprise. *T.L.O.* and *Ortega* are cases of this sort. Both the investigating authority and the person searched are participants in a shared mission. And the search serves to promote that mission rather than to control activities outside the scope of the enterprise.

The point is not that the person searched, as a participant in the enterprise, has "consented." To argue that line of thought would be simply to restate the issues in terms of "unconstitutional conditions." In any event, that argument is scarcely available in answer to a military draftee or to the *T.L.O.* student, who was obliged to attend public school.

[96]480 U.S. at 712.
[97]Terry v. Ohio, 392 U.S. 1 (1968); Chimel v. California, 395 U.S. 752 (1969).

A different consideration is at work. I suggest that the Fourth Amendment's presumption in favor of probable cause and a warrant was intended for, and makes sense for, striking a balance between the individual interest in the security of private activity and the public interest in effective social control. It was not intended for, and will seldom make sense for, striking a balance between the privacy interests and internal management imperatives of parties who—whether by choice or by legitimately imposed duty—share interdependent roles within an enterprise organized to pursue a governmental mission.

Not that the Fourth Amendment is inapplicable in these contexts. The search or inspection of students and public employees must still be "reasonable." The point here is only that the context permits striking a balance *de novo*. It does not demand presumptive adherence to the probable cause-and-warrant formula, which reflects a balance appropriate mainly to cases in which private activity and public controls are poised in conflict.[98]

This perspective does not resolve all our cases, but it casts them in a different light. Both *T.L.O.* and *Ortega* involved searches in aid of the internal governance objectives of public enterprises, a school in *T.L.O.* and a hospital in *Ortega*. The problem is not that the managers in such contexts are unschooled in "the niceties of probable cause,"[99] and unequipped to seek warrants; these difficulties, which the Court emphasized, would be addressed quickly if the cases had gone the other way. Rather, the fundamental point is that internal governance should not have to await, as does external social control, the accumulation of evidence rising to the level of probable cause. Internal governance searches should be subject only to the more fluid dictates of *ad hoc* "reasonableness."

Griffin is a less obvious case. The issue cannot be whether probation supervision constitutes mere "regulation" or "ordinary law enforcement," a meaningless inquiry. Rather, the central question should be whether probation supervision is simply a rubric under which the state reduces privacy (and increases its power of intervention) for those recently convicted of crime, or whether it instead represents an enterprise of substance, pursuing an identifiable mission

---

[98]For development of a related argument with respect to the regulation of speech in public forums, see Post, Between Governance and Management: The History and Theory of the Public Forum, 34 UCLA L. Rev. 1713, 1767–93 (1987).

[99]*Ortega*, 480 U.S. at 724, quoting *T.L.O.*, 469 U.S. at 343; see also *T.L.O.*, 469 U.S. at 353 (Blackmun, J., concurring).

(*e.g.*, rehabilitation), with meaningful activity in support of that mission and needs for internal governance devices to make that activity effective. Many overloaded state courts routinely place first offenders on one or more years of "non-reporting" probation. Such offenders, who may never see a probation officer, clearly fall under the former type of regime. A search of their homes or personal effects cannot be viewed as an "internal governance" matter and should therefore require probable cause. In *Griffin* itself, however, the defendant had an assigned probation officer and may have been engaged in a substantial program of rehabilitation. (The opinions are silent on this question.) If so, the search could properly by-pass the Fourth Amendment's probable cause framework.

Burger is a different matter. In no sense are we presented with an internal governance search. The New York regime calls for oversight and control of private activity. Although the lower court and the dissenters pressed the point that the scheme was not "truly administrative," it should not matter whether the regime was in some sense administrative or not. Nor should it matter whether "special needs" rendered the probable cause and warrant requirements impractical: Once a state establishes a system to regulate suspected receivers of stolen goods, "unannounced, even frequent, inspections"[100] will be sensible, and they will be incompatible with a probable cause requirement. But to permit officials to inspect under such a regime is simply to reinvent the writs of assistance.[101]

Since New York's regulatory regime was one for external social control rather than internal governance, it should have escaped the Fourth Amendment's presumption of probable cause only if it addressed a pressing health or safety concern. From that perspective, however, *Burger* was worlds apart from *Camara*, *Biswell*, *Barlow's*, and *Dewey*, regardless of whether genuine regulatory or remedial purposes with respect to vehicle dismantlers existed. The same objection applies to the liquor inspection program in *Colonnade*,[102] a regime of discretionary searches strikingly reminiscent of the Crown's colonial raids on untaxed imports, a regime against which the Fourth Amendment was specifically directed. The inspections in *Burger* and

---

[100]*Biswell*, 406 U.S. at 316.

[101]See Levy, note 94 *supra*, at 221–27.

[102]397 U.S. 72 (1970). Since the inspection program was designed solely for revenue enforcement, the health concerns that might apply to some liquor licensing regimes were not applicable.

probably in *Colonnade* [103] should have required probable cause and a warrant.

(vi) *Summary.* The preceding discussion suggests a restructuring of administrative search analysis, with some difference in results. Neither of the factors that have usually preoccupied the Court—the relative expectations of privacy and the presence of a regulatory motivation—should in themselves be controlling or even relevant. Rather, the first question to be addressed is whether pressing health or safety concerns render unworkable the Fourth Amendment's warrant-and-probable cause framework. If not, "balancing" would be permissible only when the inspections at issue are matters of internal governance rather than external social control. Although both safety inspections and internal governance inspections escape the presumptive requirement of probable cause, they remain subject to the Fourth Amendment's dictate of reasonableness.

(b) *Determining reasonableness.* The Court's balancing analysis in administrative search cases swings wildly and without explanation from skeptical scrutiny of asserted needs to respectful deference with little attention to alternatives. Both impulses are understandable. Courts cannot second-guess agency judgments with respect to every detail of a regulatory regime. But neither can they delegate their Fourth Amendment responsibility to insure that an independent "judicial mind"[104] passes on the question of reasonableness.

In a variety of contexts the Court has chosen to defer to judgments of reasonableness made by law enforcement personnel. That solution must seem even more natural in a regulatory context that lacks law enforcement motivation, with its distinctive risk of overreaching. But law enforcement is normally constrained by the threshold requirements of probable cause and a warrant or exigent circumstances. Even when those prerequisites are satisfied, a traditional search still may be constitutionally unreasonable if it is unnecessarily intrusive[105]

---

[103] In both *Colonnade*, *id.* at 76, and Boyd v. United States, 116 U.S., 616, 623–24, the Court asserted an historically based exception to the Fourth Amendment for warrantless seizures of goods subject to forfeiture for breach of the revenue laws. But whatever the rule with respect to warrantless seizure of contraband lawfully discovered, warrantless entry into private premises for the purpose of seizing contraband believed to be present involves different considerations.

[104] McCray v. Illinois, 386 U.S. 300, 307 (1967). *Cf.* Illinois v. Gates, 462 U.S. 213, 239 (1983): "Sufficient information must be presented to the magistrate to enable that [judicial] official to determine probable cause; his action cannot be a mere ratification of the bare conclusions of others."

[105] A valid search must be not only justified at its inception but reasonably limited in scope to the circumstances justifying the initial intrusion. See, e.g., Terry v. Ohio, 392 U.S. 1 (1968); Ybarra v. Illinois, 444 U.S. 85 (1979).

or if the invasion of privacy is necessary but disproportionate to legitimate benefits.[106] If the Court does not always insist upon close proportionality and tight means-ends relationships, the primary reason is
that the probable cause framework or some other threshold requirement already serves the Fourth Amendment's twin purposes of controlling official discretion and limiting the class of citizens subject to
search.

Judicial deference is more problematic in the context of administrative searches. The absence of the Fourth Amendment's normal
threshold framework makes this paradox comprehensible. Regulatory motivation offers to free the inspection regime from the presumptive requirement of probable cause and at the same time argues
for a deferential assessment of reasonableness. But what safeguards
would then remain to control official discretion, to limit the class of
citizens subject to search, and to assure a reasonable balance between
governmental benefits and privacy costs?

As in law enforcement searches, regulatory inspections are the creature of agencies with a distinct mission and with little or no framework for internalizing the full costs of their activities. Judicial control, mandated by the Fourth Amendment, is a necessary corrective
because in both cases the political process provides only a halting and
ineffective mechanism for registering externalities.[107] And particularly in time of apparent "crisis," political actors tend to underestimate the cumulative long-run consequences of compromising
previously recognized privacy interests. The role of the courts, as in
other areas of constitutional adjudication, is to safeguard protected
liberties against the visissitudes of a political process focused on the
very short term.

The problem is somewhat different for internal governance searches. Here the privacy costs fall upon joint participants in a public
mission. But even in such matters the judgment about reasonableness cannot be left entirely to the agency. Here too, preoccupation
with the short run can prevent recognizing the cumulative societal
impact of incursions on protected liberties. And in any event, public

---

[106]In Winston v. Lee, 470 U.S. 753 (1985), the Court held that surgical removal of a bullet
would violate the Fourth Amendment. Although the proposed surgery was supported by
probable cause and a court order, the Court held that such a search would be unreasonable: the
severity of the intrusion outweighed the governmental need because the evidence sought,
though relevant and useful, was not essential to the state's case. See also Tennessee v. Garner,
471 U.S. 1 (1985); Welsh v. Wisconsin, 466 U.S. 740 (1984).

[107]See Schulhofer, Criminal Justice Discretion as a Regulatory System, 17 J. Legal Studies
43, 63–66 (1988).

agencies typically operate outside the market constraints that tend to force internalization of costs and benefits. To the extent that there is effective competition, "the marketplace will punish a [private] firm or individual that demands information beyond the point where the value of the information exceeds the price of obtaining it. In the absence of market discipline, there is no presumption that government will strike an appropriate balance."[108]

Although the judicial inquiry into reasonableness for administrative searches cannot be deferential, not every detail of a regulatory program should be reconsidered de novo by the courts. The focus of attention must be on the Fourth Amendment concerns normally handled by the probable-cause-and-warrant framework but omitted from the threshold criteria for administrative treatment: controlling official discretion, limiting the class subject to search, and assuring a reasonable relationship of program benefits to privacy costs. Regimes for blanket inspection or systematic random selection can satisfy the concern about discretion. But the need remains for scrutinizing the significance of the violations likely to be found or prevented, relative to the severity of the intrusion and the number of non-violating citizens subjected to search.

From this perspective the Court's recent distaste for close scrutiny of suspicionless personal inspections seems particularly inapt. Because the administrative rubric can be invoked without attention to the scope of the class subject to search, the "judicial mind" cannot certify Fourth Amendment reasonableness without careful attention to the justification for suspicionless inspection and its incremental benefits in relation to the large numbers of unsuspected citizens subjected to search. In this regard, the level of scrutiny exemplified by *Delaware v. Prouse* strikes exactly the right note.

The foregoing discussion suggests threshold criteria for administrative treatment (public safety and internal governance concerns), together with areas warranting particularly close judicial scrutiny in connection with the determination of reasonableness. These principles frame many of the central issues in the drug-testing debate, but they caution against resolving cases without attention to specifics. Drug-testing can be seen as an isolated corner of the administrative search phenomenon, and many of its features are unique. Nonetheless, urine testing programs may soon affect the privacy of more citi-

---

[108]Posner, The Uncertain Protection of Privacy by the Supreme Court, 1980 Supreme Court Review 173, 176.

zens than do all other types of administrative searches combined. I now turn to the analysis of drug testing.

II. The Drug-Testing Cases

A. AN OVERVIEW OF WORKPLACE DRUG-TESTING

Prompted by increasing political attention to drug abuse and concern about the impact of drugs on worker productivity, urinalysis drug-testing of private-sector employees spread rapidly in the early 1980s. By 1986, 25 percent of the Fortune 500 corporations and many smaller businesses had instituted urinalysis to screen applicants and, in some instances, existing employees for use of illegal drugs.[109] Unlike blood analysis, which registers drug use only within a few hours of the test, urinalysis can identify drug metabolites for many days after ingestion. The sensitivity of urinalysis proves both its blessing and its curse.

Test results can mislead in several ways. First is the risk of inaccurate laboratory findings. Reported error rates have been high. The Brooks Air Force Base testing laboratory, a major site for analysis of military urine samples, was found to have an error rate of 60 percent.[110] A 1981 study of 13 major testing laboratories by the Centers for Disease Control found that 90 percent had unacceptable results—error rates exceeding 75 percent.[111] For amphetamines and cocaine the false negative rate (the percentage of positive samples incorrectly reported as negative) averaged 69 percent and 64 percent, respectively; the false positive rates (the percentage of negative samples reported positive) averaged only 3 percent and 1 percent, respectively, but some laboratories had false positive rates as high as 37 percent.[112] This problem is, in principle, curable through technological improvement and quality control. A more basic problem concerns the interpretation of "true" positive results.

Because urinalysis registers metabolized by-products of drug ingestion, rather than the drug itself, positive tests can result from

---

[109]Kaufman, The Battle over Drug Testing, New York Times, Oct. 19, 1986, §6 (Magazine), at 52.

[110]See, *e.g.*, Waple, Drug Tests: Issues Raised in Defense of a Positive Result, 11 Nova L. Rev. 751, 753 (1987).

[111]Hansen, Caudill & Boone, Crisis in Drug Testing: Results of CDC Blind Study, 253 J. Am. Med. Ass'n 2382 (1985).

[112]*Id.* at 2386.

ingestion of legal substances whose metabolites mimic those of the psychoactive drugs. The EMIT test commonly used for initial screening of urine samples cannot reliably distinguish metabolites of heroin or morphine from those of codeine, or the metabolites of illegal amphetamines from those of common over-the-counter decongestants, prescription appetite suppressants and other widely available legal drugs.[113] Standard anti-inflammatory drugs available over-the-counter, including Advil and Motrin, trigger positive findings for marijuana.[114] A poppy seed bagel can trigger positive findings for morphine.[115] A related problem is a true positive triggered by innocent or accidental ingestion of illegal drugs, such as passive inhalation of marijuana smoke (on a bus, for example).[116] Accurate findings therefore require follow-up testing by the more sophisticated (and hard-to-interpret) "GC/MS" test,[117] together with disclosure of employee medical information which can reveal private physical and psychological problems.

Positive findings confirmed by follow-up tests can still be misleading. The employer's ultimate concern is with employee performance. An accurate positive finding for drug metabolites is not necessarily a true positive in the sense that it shows impaired capabilities. Illegal drug use does not necessarily indicate current drug impact, because urinalysis picks up drug metabolites long after psychomotor effects have dissipated.[118] And current drug impact does not necessarily indicate impaired capacity. Many drugs are performance enhancing, from caffeine (used legally and routinely in nearly every workplace) to steroids (for athletic strength), amphetamines (for alertness), and even cocaine (for energy).[119] The relation between drugs and perfor-

---

[113]See Zeese, Drug Testing: Legal Manual, §3.01(2)(6), at 3–6, 3–7 (1988).

[114]Ibid.

[115]See Nat'l Federation of Federal Employees v. Carlucci, 680 F.Supp. 416, 428 (D.D.C. 1988).

[116]See Waple, note 110 supra, at 760–62. It appears, however, that at the sensitivity levels presently used in screening tests, unusually intense exposure to marijuana smoke would be necessary to trigger a positive finding. See Schwartz & Hawks, Laboratory Detection of Marijuana Use, 254 J. Am. Med. Ass'n 788, 791 (1985).

[117]Gas chromatography combined with mass spectrometry (GC/MS) is considered the most accurate test methodology and, if performed properly, it can yield highly reliable results. Because of its complexity, "analysts and interpreters must possess high levels of skill, competence, attention to detail, experience with these techniques and the particular instrument systems in use." Dubowski, Drug-Use Testing: Scientific Perspectives, 11 Nova L. Rev. 415, 483 (1987).

[118]See Wisotsky, The Ideology of Drug Testing, 11 Nova L. Rev. 761, 770–71 (1987).

[119]Id. at 772–76.

mance depends upon the particular drug, the way in which it is used (or abused), and the skill required for a given task.

Urinalysis is thus problematic as a guide to productivity and performance because of its inherently overinclusive character. Positive test results may not signal the presence of drug metabolites; drug metabolites may not signal illegal drug use; illegal drug use may not signal current drug influence; and current drug influence may not signal impaired performance.

Drug-testing is also underinclusive. Performance skills such as alertness, dexterity, and judgment are affected by many circumstances independent of drug use. Lack of sleep, marital problems, and personal preoccupations can substantially impair worker safety and productivity. The underinclusiveness of drug-testing does not by itself render testing suspect, especially since an attempt to discipline an employee for having had a sleepless night raises problems obviously not presented by a discharge for illegal drug use. Quantitative estimates suggest that drug abuse alone has enormous consequences for workplace performance. One rough estimate places the social cost of employee drug abuse at $33 billion in reduced productivity.[120] A defender of drug testing notes that "employees with a drinking or drug use problem have an absentee rate 16 times greater than the average employee, and an accident rate four times greater."[121] But data of that sort mask the underinclusiveness of drug testing because they unify "a drinking or drug use problem." Alcohol, ignored in urinalysis testing, is by every measure a far larger problem than illegal drugs. The same study that estimated a $33 billion productivity loss from drug abuse estimated costs of more than $65 billion from reduced productivity due to alcohol abuse.[122]

Testing advocates nonetheless urge random urinalysis as a sensible step in efforts to address employee impairment. Absenteeism and inattention are costly in the most innocuous job positions, and no traveller wants an impaired pilot flying his or her plane. Does drug-testing remain a plausible, if imperfect, solution for the conscientious employer?

Part of the answer is that there is another, less crude way to test for

---

[120]The Conference Board, Corporate Strategies for Controlling Substance Abuse 13 (Axel ed. 1986).

[121]Miller, Mandatory Urinalysis Testing and the Privacy Rights of Subject Employees: Toward a General Rule of Legality Under the Fourth Amendment, 48 U. Pitt. L. Rev. 201, 203–4 (1986).

[122]The Conference Board, note 120 *supra*, at 13; see also Wisotsky, note 118 *supra*, at 768–70.

impairment. That is to test for impairment. Skills testing, whether on a typing exercise, marksmanship range, or flight simulator, is quick, inexpensive, non-intrusive, and directly responsive to legitimate employer concerns. The imperfections of random testing are stark because less intrusive and much more effective alternatives are readily available.

Another source of underinclusiveness is the vulnerability of drug testing to false negatives, reports indicating no drug use when illegal drugs (and perhaps impaired skills) are present. Employees can substitute vials of untainted urine for their own.[123] They can also go "clean." Advance notice of the test date (as occurs in pre-employment or annual physicals and other programs that avoid unsettling surprise tests) enables the "innocent" employee to switch from poppy seed rolls and forego problematic decongestants to prevent a misleading positive result; it also enables the chronic drug abuser to modify his behavior. Unless severely addicted (a condition likely to be observable without testing), that employee presumably will forego illegal drugs temporarily; several days of vigorous physical exercise with heavy consumption of fluids reportedly can purge the body of tell-tale metabolites.

These problems have spawned elaborately spiraling stratagems of evasion and counter-evasion. Unscheduled testing can defeat temporary abstinence or purge, at the cost of unsettling innocent employees who are unexpectedly tested. Heat testing was used to prevent substitution, until employees learned how to warm substitute samples to the proper temperature. Observation from the rear or listening for "normal sounds" apparently can be defeated by a pouch or balloon with tubing that permits substitute fluid to emerge from the desired location. The last resort, inevitably, is direct frontal observation, an especially intrusive and degrading procedure.[124] And even this approach fails to solve the problem completely, since entrepre-

---

[123]See Dan Collins, "Drug-Test Fakery: Free Enterprise Rushes to Fill a Delicate Need," U.S. News & World Report, Feb. 23, 1987, p. 10, reporting a "brisk" business (hundreds of orders per month) in samples of pure urine selling from $19.95 to $49.95 per sample.

[124]See Taylor v. O'Grady, 669 F. Supp. 1422, 1434 (N.D. Ill. 1987) where Judge Getzendanner described the testimony of one public employee subjected to frontal observation testing: "McNeal testified that her experience was humiliating and hateful. I found it painful to listen to her testimony when it was so obvious how embarrassing it was for her . . . ."; see also "Did This Company Go Too Far," Business Week, March 28, 1988, p. 62, describing emotional impact of direct observation testing on female employee who subsequently sued a private employer for damages.

neurial genius apparently has discovered a method to implant pure urine directly into the bladder via catheter.[125]

Like many technological cure-alls, drug testing, once touted as a miraculous panacea (instant, painless identification of drug abusers), now emerges as a complex and imperfect solution. Though often compared to urine sampling that is routinely accepted and valued in physical examinations, employment drug testing assumes an entirely different character, because its objective is not solely to provide information to and for the patient. The chemistry of the process remains the same, but the personal and social context does not. Truly effective testing becomes highly intrusive and alienating to employees. Testing that respects employee dignity and collects samples from a discrete distance will produce many false or misleading positives while enabling true abusers to evade detection. Though not intrinsically useless, drug testing is caught between ineffectiveness and intrusiveness.

The many problems of urinalysis—overinclusiveness, underinclusiveness, and intrusiveness—emerged gradually over the last decade but are now widely understood. Enthusiasm for drug-testing is waning in the private sector, where its great costs and meager benefits are beginning to be appreciated.[126] Tests are so easily evaded that "[s]ome employers . . . refer to them as IQ tests."[127] *Business Week* reports:[128]

> Although screening of new applicants is up, companies may be cutting back on the most controversial practice—random tests of current workers without reasonable cause. "Even friends of testing are ready to write off random checks."

Given these difficulties, why the persistent attraction to testing in private companies, and the enthusiasm for it in the public sector?

---

[125]See Stone, Mass Round-Up Urinalysis and Original Intent, 11 Nova L. Rev. 733, 742 (1987).

[126]See Wessel, "Evidence Is Skimpy That Drug Testing Works, but Employers Embrace Practice," Wall St. J., Sept. 7, 1989, p. B1, col. 3.

[127]*Id.* at B5, col. 1, quoting Mark DiBernardo, director of labor law at the U.S. Chamber of Commerce.

[128]Katie Hafner, "Testing for Drug Use: Handle with Care," Business Week, March 28, 1988, p. 65, quoting Robert L. DuPont, former director of the National Institute on Drug Abuse. For other critical appraisals of drug testing from the enterprise perspective, see "When Business Should Mind its Own Business" (editorial), Business Week, March 28, 1988, p. 106; Nilla Dudley Childs, "Drug Testing: No Quick Fix," Property and Casualty (National Underwriter), June 26, 1989, p. 21. But see Wessel, note 126 *supra*, reporting that some private employers continue to consider drug testing useful.

Part of the explanation is that testing is not only a way to enhance productivity but also a way to weed out "bad" people and help fight the War on Drugs. Private employers subject to marketplace constraints may have limited ability to make pro bono contributions to a national cause. Nonetheless, if their statements can be credited, the pro bono element seems to play a significant role in the adoption of testing programs that are now seen as part of good corporate citizenship. A hospital in Georgia stopped pre-employment testing when it found no significant link between test results and job performance. But a few years later it resumed testing because "[t]hey felt they had to do their part in the war against drug use."[129] Similarly, when Coca-Cola recently adopted periodic drug testing for existing employees it mentioned safety and productivity concerns but gave primary emphasis to the public service aspects of the program. Its press release began:[130]

> Answering President Bush's challenge to the private sector to eliminate drugs from the workplace, Charlotte-based Coca-Cola Bottling Co. Consolidated has begun drug testing for all of its 2200 employees.
> "The drug crisis threatens to destroy the very fabric of our society," Coca-Cola Consolidated Chairman J. Frank Harrison, III said. "Business can no longer stand on the sidelines in the war on drugs. Coca-Cola Consolidated is prepared to take the lead in encouraging all businesses to eradicate illegal drug use from the workplace."

Government agencies, free of the profit constraint but driven by the political will to "do something" about drugs, are even more likely to jump on the drug-testing bandwagon. Defense Secretary Frank Carlucci made no secret of this motivation when he explained a proposal for requiring defense contractors to test their employees:[131]

> Mr. Carlucci suggested that one "area where the Department of Defense can have a major impact on the demand for illegal drugs is throughout the defense contracting community," which he notes involves some 3.2 million people.

---

[129]Wessel, note 261 *supra*.

[130]"Coca-Cola Consolidated Institutes Drug Screening; Answers Call to Eliminate Drugs from Workplace," Nexis PR Newswire, Sept. 9, 1989. The same theme is stressed in the closing sentence of the press release: "'We want to set an example and do our part to solve this heartbreaking national tragedy,' [the Chairman] said."

[131]Brown, "Carlucci to Order Defense Companies to Test for Drugs," Wall St. J., June 16, 1988, p. 27, col. 4.

Seen from the prospective of this altered set of goals, the ineffectiveness of drug testing dissipates. Testing threatens millions of Americans with the speedy, inexpensive infliction of a sanction—unemployment—that has far more sting than the criminal penalties usually imposed for casual drug use. As a deterrent, employment testing can be extremely effective, regardless of its relation to on-the-job performance.

If they wish, private employers may contribute in this way to the War on Drugs. For public employers, the objectives of testing are crucial to the Fourth Amendment analysis. If the real value and motivation for testing—its general deterrent effect—is what gives these programs their effectiveness and renders comprehensible their proliferation, then testing, however useful, must be understood not as a technique of internal agency management but as a tool of external social control. Drug-testing programs that are "reasonable" only from this perspective should not qualify as "administrative" searches at all.

The judicial response to specific drug-testing programs was seldom cast in these terms. Prior to Supreme Court consideration of the issue, dozens of lower courts had passed upon the constitutionality of drug-testing.[132] Neither the analysis nor the results of the cases were uniform, but consensus emerged on three points. First, although urine can be characterized as a bodily waste product, drug testing (unlike collection and analysis of garbage[133]) constitutes a "search" because of both the manner in which samples are collected and the information revealed by urinalysis. Second, such searches need not be supported by probable cause or a warrant; they were held permissible when they met the reasonableness standard applicable to "administrative" searches. Third, "[v]irtually all the reported cases . . . concluded that such testing is unconstitutional in the absence of some reasonable individualized suspicion."[134] There were exceptions to this generalization, for positions involving some unusually pressing safety or security concern, such as corrections officers in direct contact with medium and maximum security prisoners,[135] util-

---

[132]For discussion of the cases, see, *e.g.*, Miller, note 121 *supra*; Adler, Probative Value and the Unreasonable Search: A Constitutional Prospective on Workplace Drug Testing, 1988 U. Chi. Legal Forum 113.

[133]California v. Greenwood, 108 S.Ct. 1625 (1988).

[134]Fraternal Order of Police v. City of Newark, 216 N.J. Super. 461, 524 A.2d 430, 436 (1987).

[135]McDonell v. Hunter, 809 F.2d 1302 (8th Cir. 1987).

ity employees with access to the "vital areas" of a nuclear power plant,[136] or narcotics officers with dangerous undercover assignments.[137] But suspicionless testing was generally rejected for public employees with less unusual responsibilities, including ordinary police officers.[138]

B. SKINNER AND VON RAAB

1. *The federal drug testing programs.* For federal employees, large-scale drug testing was largely confined to the armed forces until the early 1980s.[139] An impetus for wider testing came with the 1986 report of the President's Commission on Organized Crime, which recommended "suitable" drug-testing programs for all employees of federal, state and local government and all employees of federal contractors.[140] Shortly thereafter, in September 1986, President Reagan issued an Executive Order calling for a "Drug-Free Federal Workplace."[141] The Order required the head of each executive agency to establish a program to test all job applicants and current employees in "sensitive positions," as well as any employee reasonably suspected of illegal drug use. Most federal departments and agencies now have drug testing programs covering large numbers of civilian employees.

The drug testing programs that reached the Supreme Court in its 1988 Term predated the President's Executive Order. The Federal Railway Administration (FRA) plan at issue in *Skinner* was adopted in 1985. It requires railroad employers to take blood and urine samples from train crew members in the event of a train accident or any incident involving fatality to an on-duty employee.[142] The regulations also authorize (but do not require) testing of covered employees "for Cause" in specified circumstances, including cases in which a supervisor has "reasonable suspicion" that an employee contributed to an accident or violated specified rules (by speeding, for example).

---

[136]Rushton v. Nebraska Public Power District, 844 F.2d 562 (8th Cir. 1988).

[137]Caruso v. Ward, 72 N.Y.2d 433, 530 N.E.2d 850 (1988).

[138]*E.g.*, *Fraternal Order of Police*, note 134 *supra*; Capua v. City of Plainfield, 643 F.Supp. 1507 (D.N.J. 1986) (firefighters). But see, Shoemaker v. Handel, 795 F.2d 1136 (3d Cir. 1986), upholding random urine testing of jockeys.

[139]As to military testing programs, see, *e.g.*, Committee for GI Rights v. Callaway, 518 F.2d 466 (D.C. Cir. 1975).

[140]President's Commission on Organized Crime, America's Habit: Drug Abuse, Drug Trafficking and Organized Crime 483 (1986).

[141]Exec. Order No. 12,564, 51 Fed. Reg. 32,889 (1986).

[142]49 C.F.R. §219.201(a) (1987).

Medical personnel collect the samples at a facility independent of the railroad. The FRA's Field Manual specifies that the urine samples are to be obtained "under direct observation by the physician/technician ."[143]

Under the FRA program, primary reliance is placed on blood samples, as blood is "the only available body fluid . . . that can provide a clear indication [of] current impairment effects."[144] Urine samples are also used, however, because testing is sometimes impossible within the time that drug traces are eliminated from the bloodstream. In such cases, the urine test, together with information about the employee's behavior and the circumstances of the accident, is used to determine the cause of the accident.[145] Test results may be used in employee disciplinary procedures. Samples are retained for six months and "may be made available to . . . a party in litigation,"[146] presumably including a prosecutor.

The Customs Service program at issue in *Von Raab* is structured differently. Urinalysis testing is made a condition for appointment to three kinds of positions—those involved in drug interdiction or enforcement , those requiring the employee to carry firearms and those in which the employee must handle classified material. Employees who qualify for promotion to a covered position are notified that final selection is contingent on successful completion of drug screening. An independent contractor contacts the employee to fix a time for collecting the sample and affords the employee at least five days' notice of the scheduled test date.[147] The employee can give the sample in a private bathroom stall. But to guard against adulteration or substitution, a monitor remains close by "to listen for the normal sounds of urination." [148] Employees who offer no satisfactory explanation for a positive result are subject to dismissal. But test results are not available to any other agency, including the prosecutor's office, without the employee's consent.

Both the FRA and Customs programs permit testing without individual suspicion. But they present different rationales for testing, and they utilize different testing procedures with different impacts

---

[143]Federal Railway Admin., U.S. Dept. of Transp., Field Manual: Control of Alcohol and Drug Use in Railway Operations D-5 (1986), cited in *Skinner*, 109 S.Ct. at 1428 (dissenting opinion).

[144]49 Fed. Reg. 24291 (1984).

[145]*Ibid.*

[146]49 C.F.R. §219.211 (d) (1987).

[147]See *Von Raab*, 816 F.2d 170, 173 (5th Cir. 1987), vacated, 109 S.Ct. 1384 (1989).

[148]*Von Raab*, 109 S.Ct. at 1388.

on employee privacy. These distinctive features require separate discussion of the two cases.

2. *The Skinner opinions.* The Ninth Circuit had ruled the FRA testing program unconstitutional. The Supreme Court reversed. Justice Kennedy's opinion for the Court held first that the taking and analysis of blood or urine samples constitute a "search" governed by the Fourth Amendment. Blood tests had long been held a search.[149] And the Court stressed that "[t]here are few activities in our society more personal or private than the passing of urine."[150]

Analyzing Fourth Amendment requirements, the Court acknowledged the presumptive requirements of probable cause and a warrant, but noted the exception "when [there are] 'special needs, beyond the normal need for law enforcement.'"[151] In such situations, the Court said, "we have not hesitated . . . to assess the practicality of the warrant and probable cause requirements in the particular context."[152]

The majority held that a warrant was impracticable. The delay involved in procuring a warrant would prevent detection of drug and alcohol traces that are rapidly eliminated from the bloodstream and could also permit dissipation of metabolite traces in urine. Moreover, a warrant would serve little purpose since the circumstances justifying testing and the permissible test procedures are narrowly defined in the regulations and will be well known to covered employees.

The Court also held that neither probable cause nor any individual suspicion was a necessary prerequisite to testing.[153] The Court characterized blood tests as involving only a "limited"[154] intrusion on privacy. And it concluded that even the more intrusive urine tests should be viewed as raising only "minimal" privacy concerns[155] because: (1) protective safeguards were implicit in the FRA regulations; and (2) given the lethal potential of railroad operations and the long-standing regulatory concern with employee impairment, "logic and history show that a diminished expectation of privacy attaches to information relating to the physical condition of covered employees."[156]

---

[149]Schmerber v. California, 384 U.S. 757 (1966).
[150]*Skinner*, 109 S.Ct., at 1413, quoting *Von Raab* , 816 F.2d at 175.
[151]109 S.Ct. at 1414, quoting Griffin v. Wisconsin, 107 S.Ct. 3164, 3167 (1987).
[152]109 S.Ct. at 1414.
[153]*Id.* at 1417.
[154]*Ibid.*
[155]*Id.* at 1418, 1419.
[156]*Id.* at 1419.

In contrast, the Court found "compelling" the government's interest in testing without individual suspicion. The Court viewed the FRA testing procedure as "an effective means of deterring employees engaged in safety-sensitive tasks from using controlled substances or alcohol,"[157] and as a means to "help railroads obtain valuable information about the causes of major accidents."[158] Neither objective would be served if post-accident testing were restricted to employees who were the focus of particularized suspicion.

Justice Marshall, in an opinion joined by Justice Brennan, dissented. He objected first to the majority's use of the "special needs" formula to evade the probable cause and warrant requirements. He would permit exceptions to those requirements only for "routinized, fleeting, and nonintrusive encounters conducted pursuant to regulatory programs which entailed no contact with the person."[159] Drug-testing, like the searches in *T.L.O.*, *Ortega*, and *Griffin*, clearly does not fall into that category. Indeed, Justice Marshall argued, the FRA program went further than cases like *T.L.O.* because it focused on the human body, not just personal effects. Under Justice Marshall's approach, the FRA program would be analyzed under the traditional Fourth Amendment framework. Testing would be permissible only on probable cause. Although blood and urine samples could be collected without a warrant (because of exigent circumstances), the analysis of those samples would be treated as a distinct search requiring prior judicial authorization.

Justice Marshall also argued that the FRA program should be impermissible even under the majority's balancing test, because it was needlessly intrusive. Since a positive urine test cannot establish impairment, urine sampling could be confined to cases in which a blood test suggests impairment and requires confirmation. Similarly, he claimed, both blood and urine testing could be confined to cases involving particularized suspicion, since objective indications of suspicion are needed in any event, in order to connect evidence of employee impairment with actual causation of an accident. Finally, test samples need not be left available for criminal prosecution.

Though *Skinner* represents an extension of administrative search doctrine, the dissenters' objections were not convincing. The administrative search exception was properly held available in this context,

---

[157]*Ibid.*
[158]*Id.* at 1420.
[159]*Id.* at 1424.

and the majority's conclusions with respect to reasonableness were essentially sound.

(*a*) *Was this an administrative search?* Blood and urine tests, both involving a personal and intrusive procedure, seem remote from the context in which administrative search doctrine was born (*Camara's* plumbing and wiring inspections) and even from the searches of personal effects approved on an administrative rationale in *T.L.O.*, *Griffin*, and *Ortega*. Indeed, in holding that urine testing was a "search," the *Skinner* Court itself had stressed the strong privacy interests at stake. Having said that "few activities in our society are more personal or private than the passing of urine,"[160] the Court held only a few pages later that the privacy interests involved were "minimal."[161] Such reasoning highlights what the dissenters called the "shameless manipulability" of ad hoc balancing.[162]

But the dissenters' approach, prohibiting all personal searches in the absence of probable cause, is even more problematic. The distinctions it requires (between "fleeting, . . . nonintrusive" encounters and personal searches, or between searches of personal effects and searches of the body) are elusive and unprincipled. An "impersonal" inspection of home wiring (*Camara*) can be more disruptive and intrusive than a workplace search for job-related personal effects (*Ortega*). A search of personal effects for evidence (the papers in *Ortega*, the purse in *T.L.O.*, or the entire home in *Griffin*) can be more disruptive and intrusive than the bodily invasion involved when a doctor's needle briefly penetrates the skin to draw blood. Not only are areas of diminished privacy contestable and hard to mark out in advance, but all across the spectrum, "comparative privacy" concerns fail to capture the considerations that make the administrative search distinctive. The public interest in railway safety calls for Fourth Amendment limitations more flexible than those of the traditional law enforcement framework.

(*b*) *The reasonableness inquiry.* How should the balance be struck? In defense of testing without suspicion, the Court's opinion commits many unnecessary sins. Its effort to minimize the privacy interests at stake was particularly strained.

(i) Employee privacy interests. The Court recognized that the privacy interests implicated in urine testing are not minimal "in most

---

[160]*Id.* at 1413, quoting *Von Raab*, 816 F.2d. at 175.
[161]109 S.Ct. at 1418, 1419.
[162]*Id.* at 1429.

contexts" but said that the FRA regulations "endeavor to reduce the intrusiveness of the collection process."[163] Three factors were cited in support of this conclusion. One, that the process is "not unlike similar procedures encountered often in the context of a regular physical examination,"[164] was tautologically correct but misleading. Regular physical examinations, because they are performed for the benefit of the patient, present none of the concerns about evasion which prompt adversarial surveillance. The privacy issue is largely a function of the one feature of urine testing not found in the routine physical exam. To say that one is "similar" to the other is to assume away the problem.

The Court's second point was that the regulations do not require direct observation by the monitor. But the FRA's "endeavor" to reduce intrusiveness was half-hearted or short-lived: the regulations are simply silent on the subject of direct observation, and the FRA's Field Manual requires it.[165] Oddly, the Court even referred to the importance of direct observation (citing the Field Manual) to suggest that the regulations, by comparison, were restrained.[166]

The final factor relied upon to show that urine testing presented "minimal" privacy concerns was that covered employees enjoyed a "diminished expectation of privacy" with respect to information concerning their physical condition.[167] The reason for this diminished expectation was the long history of government concern about railway safety. As a result, urine testing poses "only limited threats to the *justifiable* expectations of privacy of covered employees."[168]

There is a problem here. History cannot support the Court's conclusion that employees have a diminished privacy expectation: until recently, employees entering the industry had no reason to anticipate mandatory drug testing.[169] The safety concern, in contrast, is relevant. Indeed, it gets much attention when the Court considers the government interests on the opposing side of the "balance." But to draw on safety concerns a second time—to depreciate the privacy interests at stake—creates confusion (not to mention double-count-

---

[163]*Skinner*, 109 S.Ct. at 1418.

[164]*Ibid.*

[165]Federal Railway Admin., note 143 *supra*.

[166]*Skinner*, 109 S.Ct. at 1418.

[167]*Ibid.*

[168]*Id.* at 1419 (emphasis added).

[169]But *cf.* Consolidated Rail Corp. v. Railway Labor Executives Ass'n. 109 S.Ct. 2477 (1989) (Conrail program in effect since 1976 required periodic urinalysis for blood sugar and albumin, and arguably included right to test for drugs).

ing). Observers have often worried that the Court approaches balancing in administrative search cases with its thumb on the government's side of the scale. The *Skinner* Court's analysis amounts to putting the thumb down on one side of the scale and using the fingers to push up on the other.

These problems cloud *Skinner*'s implications for other urine testing programs. On the one hand, the Court referred to the great privacy concerns raised by urine testing and stressed that it "would not characterize these additional privacy concerns as minimal in most contexts."[170] It cautioned, "[W]e do not suggest that the interest in bodily security enjoyed by those employed in a regulated industry must always be considered minimal."[171] On the other hand, the three ostensibly special features invoked by the Court seem likely to be present "in most other contexts," especially if the intrusiveness of direct observation can be mitigated simply by locating that requirement in a field manual rather than in the main body of regulations.

The idea that seems to reconcile these conflicting perspectives is one the Court never articulates. At bottom, the Court may not truly believe that urinalysis is so terribly intrusive. Notwithstanding its rhetoric about an exceptionally intimate bodily function, the Court seems to have in mind an experience of semi-private or quasi-public urination that is routine not only in medical examinations, but in gymnasium locker rooms, public restrooms, and the rest areas of airport terminals and interstate highways. If this idea is not implicit in *Skinner*, the Court's intuitions are difficult to account for. Yet if this is *Skinner*'s core idea, it departs sharply from commonly shared expectations, especially among women, whose intensely adverse reactions to frontal observation testing seem to get no weight in the balancing analysis.

The Court should have said, more candidly, that urinalysis testing is quite intrusive and becomes extremely so when, as in *Skinner*, it requires direct observation. The proper question is whether this great burden on the employee is warranted by the unusual public interests presented by the need for diagnosis and prevention of railway accidents. Proceeding in this fashion, the Court might have justified urinalysis for the distinctive setting of the FRA program, perhaps with minor modifications.

(ii) Governmental needs. Two government interests were asserted:

---

[170]*Id*. at 1418.
[171]*Id*. at 1418–19.

the FRA's need to deter drug and alcohol use by covered employees and its need to ascertain responsibility for accidents. The deterrence benefits are slender. As in *Prouse*,[172] impairment is likely to leave objectively identifiable traces that would support testing on individual suspicion. The increased benefits of intruding without suspicion seem too marginal to justify the extreme intrusion of direct observation urine sampling. Of course, testing on individual suspicion will not deter "recreational" drug use so far removed from duty hours that impairment will have passed. But that goal cannot support an administrative search in any event, as it involves neither safety nor internal governance concerns.

The other justification for the FRA program was the need to ascertain responsibility for accidents. Here the regulatory interest is compelling, for no one questions the importance of diagnosing causes and taking prompt remedial action, whether by altering equipment and procedures or by removing unreliable personnel from safety-sensitive positions.

The dissenters' argument that testing on individual suspicion could adequately meet this need is difficult to take seriously. They noted, correctly, that diagnosis of accident causation requires eyewitness reports and other information that would meet an individual suspicion standard. But such information may take hours or days to assemble. In the meantime traces of drug use in blood and urine will dissipate. The same problem defeats the dissenters' suggestion that urinalysis be delayed until after blood tests pinpoint potentially impaired suspects. If accident diagnosis warrants blood and urine testing at all, then tests must be administered promptly to all whose physical and mental condition could become relevant to the causal inquiry. There is thus a strong need to test *without* awaiting individual suspicion.

This strong government interest must be balanced against the employee privacy interests, which are also strong. The question whether there are less intrusive means for accomplishing government objectives becomes crucial at this point.

(iii) Less intrusive alternatives. Apart from the possibility of requiring individual suspicion, which fails for the reasons just canvassed, the dissent suggested only one means to mitigate intrusiveness—barring use of test results in criminal prosecution. But if com-

---

[172]440 U.S. 648 (1979).

pelled participation in testing and chemical analysis of the samples
are themselves permissible, the employee's privacy will be defeated
regardless of the use made of test results. It would be perverse to hold
that innocent employees can be subjected to these indignities while
drug abusers caught by the test are shielded from prosecution. Thus,
it is difficult to see why the Court should bar use of results in the
penal context.

The Court did suggest that "routine use in criminal prosecutions"
might require a different result.[173] Routine law enforcement involvement, together with slender or half-hearted regulatory and remedial
goals, would indicate that the administrative features of the program
were merely pretextual. If so, the program would not involve "special needs, beyond the normal need for law enforcement," and the
probable cause requirement would have to apply. But having determined that the FRA program does involve compelling safety-related
concerns, the Court would have no reason to reverse field and invalidate the program upon discovering that a cocaine-intoxicated employee responsible for a fatal train wreck was prosecuted on the basis
of test results.[174]

Although the limitations proposed by the dissenters seem inappropriate, the FRA program may have been unnecessarily intrusive
for a different reason. Apparently, the program requires direct observation of the employee providing the sample.[175] Visual observation is important in the case of scheduled or predictable urine testing,
because of the risks of substitution and adulteration. Whether these
risks are significant in unexpected post-accident testing is unclear.
Given the demeaning effects of direct observation, the Court should
have held this aspect of the program unreasonable, or at least remanded for additional evidence on the need for direct observation.

Subject to this qualification, the FRA program was appropriately
regarded as an administrative search. And the Court properly found
it to be "reasonable," within the meaning of the Fourth Amendment.
In contrast, the Customs Service program upheld in *Von Raab* proves
difficult to defend.

3. *The Von Raab opinions.* The Fifth Circuit had upheld the Customs
testing program. With one important reservation, the Supreme

---

[173]*Skinner*, 109 S.Ct. at 1415 n.5.

[174]*Cf. Burger*, note 67 *supra*, upholding admissibility in criminal prosecution of evidence
seized by police officers during alleged regulatory search.

[175]*Federal Railway Admin.*, note 143 *supra*.

Court agreed. Writing for five members of the Court, Justice Kennedy held first that the Customs Service program qualified for administrative search treatment. Because the program's purposes were to deter drug use among employees eligible for promotion to sensitive positions and to prevent promotion of drug users to those positions, the Court concluded that the program was "not designed to serve the ordinary needs of law enforcement,"[176] and that its constitutionality was governed by the standard of *ad hoc* reasonableness.

The Court ruled that a warrant was not required for two reasons. First, the process of obtaining one would "divert valuable agency resources from the Service's primary mission."[177] Second, a warrant would provide no added privacy protection because the testing of covered employees (those eligible for promotion to sensitive positions) was automatic; hence "there are simply 'no special facts for a neutral magistrate to evaluate.'"[178]

The Court also held that government needs justified testing without suspicion. Because drug users might be indifferent or hostile to the Service's mission, subject to bribery, or affected by impaired judgment and perception in using weapons, the Court found a compelling interest in assuring that front-line interdiction personnel and those who carry firearms are drug free. And the Court held that Customs employees in those positions have a diminished expectation of privacy because they "cannot reasonably expect to keep from the Service personal information that bears directly on their fitness."[179] Conceding that urine tests "doubtless infringe some privacy expectations," the Court held these expectations insufficient to outweigh "the Government's compelling interests in the safety and in the integrity of our borders."[180]

The Court took a different view with respect to the third category of employees covered by the Customs program—those required to handle classified material. The Court indicated that employees who handle "truly sensitive information"[181] could be tested, but expressed doubt about whether that characterization applied to all covered employee positions, which included "Accountant," "Animal

---

[176]109 S.Ct. at 1390.

[177]*Id.* at 1391.

[178]*Ibid.*, quoting South Dakota v. Opperman, 428 U.S. 364, 383 (1976) (Powell, J., concurring).

[179]109 S.Ct. at 1394.

[180]*Ibid.*

[181]*Id.* at 1396.

Caretaker," "Attorney (All)" and "Electrical Equipment Repairer."[182] Because the Service might have defined the category of covered employees more broadly than necessary to meet legitimate concerns about sensitive information, the Court remanded for clarification of both the nature of the information to which covered employees have access and the privacy expectations of those employees.

Justices Marshall and Brennan dissented, largely for the reasons outlined in their *Skinner* dissent. They would insist on probable cause for a search of the person, and would find the Customs program unreasonable even under a balancing approach.

Justice Scalia, joined by Justice Stevens, also dissented. Although both had joined the Court's opinion in *Skinner*, they argued that the Customs program was fundamentally different, because it did not rest on a demonstrated drug or alcohol problem in the agency. Justice Scalia emphasized that the Commissioner of Customs had characterized the agency as "largely drug-free" and had admitted that "[t]he extent of illegal drug use by Customs employees was not the reason for establishing this program."[183] He dismissed the Court's concerns about employee indifference, bribe taking, impaired judgment and faulty perception as "nothing but speculation, and not very plausible speculation at that."[184] He suggested that the real motivation for the Customs program was to "show to the world that the Service is 'clean,'" and concluded that this justification was unacceptable: "the impairment of civil liberties cannot be the means of making a point; . . . symbolism, even symbolism for so worthy a cause as the abolition of unlawful drugs, cannot validate an otherwise unreasonable search."[185]

(a) *Was this an "administrative" search?* The FRA program in *Skinner* easily met the threshold requirement that it serve "special needs" distinct from ordinary law enforcement. In one sense *Von Raab* presents a stronger case for administrative treatment because law enforcement use of test results was prohibited. *Von Raab* appears to involve a purely employment-related program. But this appearance is deceptive. The "special needs" invoked in *Von Raab* are so abstract that they raise doubt about the real motivation for the program.

Although the Service has an interest in assuring that its person-

---

[182]*Id.* at 1397.
[183]*Id.* at 1400.
[184]*Id.* at 1399.
[185]*Id.* at 1401.

nel are "physically fit, and have unimpeachable integrity and judgment,"[186] every employer can legitimately claim the same interest. Moreover, illegal drug use is not the only unlawful activity that implicates this interest. Virtually all unlawful conduct casts doubt, by definition, on the offender's character.

But how can government's ever-present interest in the "integrity and judgment" of its employees constitute a "special" need supporting searches of persons and property without probable cause or any individual suspicion? How can the ever-present possibility of employee disloyalty or theft support suspicionless searches of cars, homes, and personal effects? Government's interest in the probity and good judgment of its employees cannot suffice by itself to avoid the Fourth Amendment's preference for probable cause and a warrant.

The same must be said for the even more abstract claim that testing will reassure the public that the Service is drug free. Every employer has legitimate reasons for wanting to foster public confidence in the competence of its employees. But if image enhancement constitutes a "special" need, every public agency will have special needs vis-à-vis every employee. And the probable cause requirement will always stand in the way of satisfying those needs. The administrative search "exception" cannot be stretched this far without engulfing the Fourth Amendment.

The government also argued in *Von Raab* that drug screening would "set an important example in our country's struggle [against drugs],"[187] and that "if a law enforcement agency and its employees do not take the law seriously, neither will the public . . . ."[188] But these needs lack even abstract or speculative links to the employment relationship and the internal management of the agency. The effort to "set an . . . example," which Justice Scalia called the real "driving force" behind the program,[189] reflects the desire to induce other employers to initiate testing, so that the threat of unemployment will be more widely available to help deter drug use.

But these exemplary goals are not the goals of internal agency governance. These are the goals of law enforcement and its equivalent— external regulation in the form of surveillance and civil sanctions

[186]*Id.* at 1393.
[187]*Id.* at 1401, quoting Customs Commissioner's memorandum announcing test program.
[188]*Ibid.*, quoting Brief for United States [in *Von Raab*], at 36.
[189]109 S.Ct. at 1401.

to bring private activity into compliance with law. Those goals, however laudable, can be pursued only within traditional Fourth Amendment limitations, which bar invasions of privacy in the absence of probable cause. Like the Crown's desire to seal the colonial borders against undutied imports and to forfeit offending goods, government's desire to deter drug use and to delegitimate the drug culture cannot by itself justify suspicionless searches.

This analysis does not, however, extend to Customs positions requiring the use of firearms or access to sensitive information. Concern about the fitness and good judgment of employees with special safety and security responsibilities constitutes a "special need" of the now-traditional sort.[190] With respect to this more specific concern, the issue is whether the government's interest outweighs legitimate employee privacy concerns.

(b) *The reasonableness inquiry.* (i) Government interests. Whether the focus is on the Customs Service's interest in the general fitness and integrity of its employees, or on its more specific interest in the fitness of employees who have access to firearms and confidential information, the slender and speculative nature of its concerns should have posed a fatal obstacle to a finding of reasonableness. Previous "special needs" cases, including *Skinner*, had rested on well-documented problems in areas of major social concern. In contrast, *Von Raab* finds "compelling" the agency's abstract interest in employee integrity and its speculative concerns about misuse of firearms and confidential information.

But *Von Raab* does not necessarily indicate that speculative extrapolation will always suffice to establish a "compelling" governmental interest. The Court stressed several considerations that it thought lent special weight to the Customs Service's concerns and distinguished them from those commonly present in public employment. First, accepting the current wisdom that imported drugs pose an unprecedented threat to national welfare, the Court viewed the fitness of drug interdiction personnel as a matter of distinctive importance.[191] In addition, the Court commented that "the Govern-

---

[190]Justice Scalia denied that testing would help deter drug use by employees who carry firearms. He argued that such employees are more likely to be governed by "knowledge that, if impaired, they may be shot dead in unequal combat with unimpaired smugglers—unless, again, their addiction is so severe that no urine test is needed for detection." *Id.* at 1399. The argument, like other standard moves in the economic analysis of law, assumes rational, self-interested behavior. It cannot be accepted as a satisfactory answer in an area such as drug abuse, where concern focuses on irrational, self-destructive behavior.

[191]*Id.* at 1395.

ment's interest here is at least as important as its interest in searching travelers entering the country. We have long held that travelers seeking to enter the country may be stopped and required to submit to a routine search without probable cause, or even founded suspicion . . . ."[192]

The Court's reliance on a border-search analogy is startling and, at first blush, appalling. Apart from the minor point that urine testing is not a "routine search" of the kind ordinarily permitted without suspicion at the border,[193] a Customs employee reporting for work is not crossing an international boundary. The considerations of history and national self-protection that made routine border searches acceptable have no application to the problem of verifying what Customs officers or other public employees bring with them to the job. If the Court means to equate the act of crossing an international border with the act of entering the workplace, then the Fourth Amendment, often said to be "shrinking,"[194] will have virtually disappeared for most Americans.

What the *Von Raab* Court must have meant is not that urine testing at the workplace threshold is a self-protective border search, but rather that the Customs Service's testing program was an adjunct to its special responsibilities for policing the international border. The importance of effective interdiction at the border, evidenced by the unusual breadth of the authority to search travelers, underscores the importance of assuring the fitness of the personnel charged with that mission. Indeed, the Court referred at one point to "the almost unique mission of the [Customs] Service."[195] Thus, Customs employee responsibilities are distinctive, not only in comparison to public employees generally, but in comparison to other law enforcement personnel, including even drug police and drug prosecutors.

The Court's unwillingness to approve testing for employees who handle "classified" material, except when such material involves "truly sensitive information," confirms this narrow reading of *Von Raab*. The Court did not regard the Service's generalized interests in employee fitness, integrity and good judgment, or its symbolic and exemplary interests in a drug-free workforce as sufficient to warrant suspicionless testing of all accountants, attorneys and animal

---

[192]*Id*. at 1393.

[193]See LaFave, note 19 *supra*, §10.5, at 723–24, 726, 733–34.

[194]Wasserstrom, The Incredible Shrinking Fourth Amendment, 21 Am. Crim. L. Rev. 257 (1984).

[195]109 S.Ct. at 1395.

caretakers. The Court's approach suggests that conceivable effects of drug abuse on employee fitness and integrity will not suffice when less distinctive public service responsibilities are at issue.

(ii) Employee privacy interests. The Court suggested that Customs employees "have a diminished expectation of privacy," and that because of the unique importance of their duties, they "should expect effective inquiry into their fitness and probity . . . . [They] cannot reasonably expect to keep from the Service personal information that bears directly on their fitness."[196] This point is crucial for assessing the Von Raab result because, as the Court itself recognized, the privacy interest in an especially intimate bodily function would otherwise have to be regarded as compelling. Yet the Court's "diminished privacy" point cannot be sound.

Although the Court said that Customs officers were "[u]nlike most private citizens or government employees in general,"[197] the claim about diminished expectations is easily extendable to any employee doing important or sensitive work. The point is also extendable from the context of urine testing to other employer searches of the person, personal effects, financial records, and even the home.[198] Apart from its seemingly limitless character, the Court's "diminished privacy" analysis obscures the relevant issue. Even for employees with unusual security responsibilities, the question is not whether they can "keep from the Service personal information" but whether they have a diminished expectation of privacy in the *places* where such information might be found. Can it be that employees with important responsibilities "cannot reasonably expect" to keep free from warrantless search the intimate areas of person and property where information bearing on fitness and probity might be discovered?

The Court's language presumably is not to be taken at face value. Two limitations are evident in the opinion. First, as we have seen, the Court regarded the Custom's Service's mission as "almost unique." Second, the Court noted that the testing procedures in Von Raab "significantly minimize the program's intrusion on privacy interests."[199] Customs testing affects only employees who qualify for a covered position, and they are tested only once, in what amounts to preemployment screening. Moreover, employees avoid the "'unsettling

---

[196]*Id*. at 1394.

[197]*Ibid*.

[198]*Cf*. Griffin v. Wisconsin, 483 U.S. 868 (1987) (search of probationer's home without objectively grounded suspicion).

[199]109 S.Ct. at 1394 n.2.

show of authority' . . . associated with unexpected intrusions on privacy,"[200] because they receive advance notice of the test date. Direct observation is prohibited, and employees need not disclose personal medical information unless the test result is positive.

So unintrusive is this testing program that one wonders what it can accomplish. With advance notice, freedom from direct observation, and insulation from subsequent, post-employment tests, neither casual nor committed drug abusers seem likely to get caught in the Customs Service's porous dragnet. The Court responded to this argument by noting that avoidance techniques are "fraught with uncertainty and risks."[201] But the danger that evasion efforts could miscarry seems unlikely to weigh heavily with drug abusers, especially since the strongly risk-averse individual is not likely to abuse drugs in the first place.

Two problems are presented here. First is the general question of reasonableness in terms of the balance of affected interests. As in *Prouse*, the inspection procedure offers at best "marginal" benefits, and it therefore does not seem a "sufficiently productive mechanism"[202] to warrant the intrusion on the many innocent citizens subjected to it. The second problem returns us to the question whether the program reflects genuine administrative needs. The narrowly crafted Customs procedure seems well-designed only if its goals are to maintain the momentum of the national drug-war strategy and to provide a relatively inoffensive setting for the test case that would set the first urinalysis precedent. The agency's alleged internal governance interest—in catching drug users and deterring them from seeking promotion—fulfills a verbal formula but has little real content.

(iii) Less intrusive alternatives: testing only on individual suspicion. Having found the government needs "compelling" and the employee privacy interests less weighty, the *Von Raab* Court jumped directly to a conclusion of reasonableness. In *Skinner* Justice Kennedy had paused to explain why the FRA could not be expected to await individual suspicion. Yet in *Von Raab*, this question, which had been the focus of decisions in the lower courts, was passed in silence.

One justification for testing without suspicion may be implicit in the Court's comment that "[d]etecting drug impairment can be a dif-

---

[200]*Id.*, quoting *Prouse*, 440 U.S. at 657.
[201]109 S.Ct. at 1396.
[202]*Prouse*, 440 U.S. at 659.

ficult task [because] it is not feasible to subject employees and their work-product to the kind of day-to-day scrutiny that is the norm in more traditional office environments."[203] But neither the Customs Service nor other modern employers lack effective means to evaluate performance for employees who work outside the "traditional office environment." The Court's view about the infeasibility of evaluating employee performance seems to have been reached in a vacuum, without regard to the available literature or the circumstances of the case.[204]

Another justification for testing without suspicion could be drawn from the government's desire to prevent covered employees from "us[ing] drugs even off-duty, for such use creates risks of bribery and blackmail . . . ."[205] From this perspective, "recreational" drug use would be a legitimate agency concern even when no symptoms are observable on the job.

But the risk of bribery or blackmail as a result of off-duty behavior is serious in every other position of responsibility in the public service. Unless all responsible government officials are to be subject to random urinalysis testing, a concern about bribery or blackmail must be assessed in terms of both the likelihood of drug-related corruption and the seriousness of its consequences. The Customs Service's "almost unique mission"[206] suggests that the consequences of corruption could be significant—the escape of a drug kingpin or the failure to intercept millions of dollars worth of drugs. But given the nature of the "war on drugs" and the constant flow of replacement supplies and suppliers, a single incident of this kind has only a marginal effect on the drug market. The prospects for irreparable injury are remote. And the likelihood of drug-related bribery or blackmail must be rated quite low, given the Custom Service's inability to identify any episode of this sort.

In light of these problems, the Court's failure to consider the alternative of testing on individual suspicion seems to rest on the fact that the Customs program applies only to employees about to enter new and more sensitive positions. In this respect, the program is analo-

---

[203] 109 S.Ct. at 1395.

[204] Compare Taylor v. O'Grady, 669 F. Supp. 1422 (N.D. Ill. 1987), modified, 1989 U.S.App. LEXIS #16581 (7th Cir., Nov. 1, 1989), where the court credited expert testimony concerning the techniques of "trained supervision" and their effectiveness in detecting drug abuse among corrections officers.

[205] 109 S.Ct. at 1395.

[206] Ibid.

gous to the widely accepted practice of routine pre-employment screening.[207]

The analogy is arguably incomplete. Two factors support routine pre-employment screening—the employer's inability to observe the applicant long enough to develop individual suspicion, and the applicant's "waiver" or "consent" implied by seeking a job to which she has no entitlement. Both factors are only partially applicable to the Customs program. Since the program covers existing employees who seek new positions, supervisors will have had ample opportunity for observation; it would be very odd if detailed performance evaluations were not part of every applicant's file. In addition, while covered employees have no entitlement to promotion, the employee's "consent" to testing is attenuated when her only alternative is to forego promotion in a career where she has already invested considerable human capital and acquired protected Civil Service status.

Despite these qualifications, the focus on employees about to assume positions of significantly different responsibility renders the analogy to pre-employment screening sufficiently close. The result in *Von Raab* would therefore be plausible for the Customs program's pre-appointment setting, to the extent that testing effectively serves some important purpose.

The *Von Raab* holding remains problematic because of the strikingly poor means-ends fit in the Customs program. The government's general integrity concerns are insubstantial and its more serious concerns about employees who handle firearms or sensitive information are addressed by porous, easily evaded test procedures.

At its core, the Customs program was not a convincing effort to address internal governance concerns. Rather it was part of a broad social and governmental attempt to bring employment sanctions to bear in the battle to stigmatize drug usage and reduce consumer demand for illegal drugs. However worthy these goals, they are the goals of external social control. Their pursuit, whether through penal or regulatory sanctions, should be constrained by the Fourth Amendment's traditional safeguards of probable cause and a warrant. On balance, the Court should have been willing to strike down the Customs program.

---

[207]See Miller, note 121 *supra*, at 236–37; LaFave, note 19 *supra*, §10.3 at 62 (1988 Supp.); *cf.* Jones v. McKenzie, 833 F.2d 335 (D.C. Cir. 1987) (routine annual medical examination for existing employees).

III. Future Prospects

A. THE REACH OF SKINNER AND VON RAAB

Skinner and *Von Raab* bring to a close the first round of drug testing litigation. There is surely more to come. For now the principal question concerns how broadly the two opinions should be read.

Both cases evaluated drug testing under the totality of the circumstances and offered no framework for determining the relative importance of particular elements. Lower courts will have difficulty extracting guidance from the opinions. On the one hand, much of the Court's language and logic is extendable to virtually every public employment context. Examples include the Court's recognition of a legitimate agency concern for general "fitness and integrity," its refusal to insist on a showing of concrete problems in these areas, its willingness to find employee privacy expectations diminished because the agency has reason to prefer law-abiding personnel, and the Court's disinterest in less intrusive methods for meeting the asserted government needs. Even the more focused concern about employees who carry firearms has implications extending to pilots, bus and truck drivers, and possibly ordinary motorists.

On the other hand, the FRA and Customs programs both present unusual features that the Court at several points stressed. *Skinner* is especially narrow in its implications. The FRA program grew out of a well-documented concern about the role of alcohol and drugs in causing catastrophic railway accidents. Although the Court approved testing without individual suspicion, the triggering circumstances (accidents or rule violations) limited the group subject to test and provided objective, undeniably important reasons for investigating that group. In effect, the FRA program required predicate circumstances roughly comparable to objectively grounded suspicion. And as the Court emphasized, the need for prompt action provided strong reason for declining to await an individually focused basis to test.[208] Both on its facts and on its reasoning, *Skinner* therefore offers no support for random or blanket pre-accident testing, even in safety-sensitive settings.

The language and reasoning of *Von Raab* prevent similarly confident conclusions about its reach. With its broad logic and ostensibly narrow holding, the opinion presents an interpretive Rubik's Cube,

---

[208]*Skinner*, 109 S.Ct. at 1420.

an *Escobedo* for the Eighties.[209] *Von Raab* could become the basis for a discriminating approach or the jumping-off point for blanket approval of intrusive drug testing on the flimsiest pretext. For now the latter prognosis seems overly pessimistic. Since the Court's narrow, five-to-four majority included Justice Blackmun, a consistent voice for restraint in cases involving "administrative" searches of individuals, the tone of *Von Raab's* more cautious passages must be taken seriously.

In addition, much of the evidence internal to the opinion suggests that limiting factors were important to the result. Although the Court's failure to make more use of these limiting factors has led some to consider a narrow reading unrealistic,[210] special features of the Customs program are emphasized at several crucial steps in the analysis. First, *Von Raab* focused on an agency with leading responsibility for stemming the flow of drugs (currently perceived as our "number one" national problem), and involved a border control function which, the Court stressed, implicates a traditionally special concern for national self-protection. Second, the Customs program was narrow in scope. Although individual suspicion was not required, a triggering circumstance (promotion to a covered position) served to limit the group tested and to justify background investigation in terms comparable to those applicable to pre-employment screening. Third, the Customs program was of limited intrusiveness. It afforded advance notice of the test, prohibited visual observation, and barred use of the results in criminal prosecution. Finally, the Court was unwilling to approve even non-intrusive testing for Customs personnel who handle classified but non-sensitive material.

Thus, despite its potentially broad implications, *Von Raab* is best read as approving suspicionless testing *only* in the context of pre-appointment screening, by modestly intrusive test procedures, for personnel in an acutely sensitive government mission. Even for positions with strong public safety overtones, the Court has not upheld random testing of existing employees. And the Court has not upheld any sort of testing for less sensitive government positions.

Many of the lower court decisions since *Skinner* and *Von Raab* have properly stressed these limiting elements of the two cases. In *Ameri-*

---

[209]See Escobedo v. Illinois, 378 U.S. 478 (1964).

[210]*E.g.*, Kamisar, "The Drug Testing Cases," Prepared Remarks at U.S. Law Week's Eleventh Annual Constitutional Law Conference, p. 18 (1989).

can Federation of Government Employees v. Thornburg,[211] a federal district court, holding *Von Raab* inapplicable to random testing of all Federal Bureau of Prisons employees, emphasized the agency's failure to target job functions presenting specific needs for testing. In *Hartness v. Bush*,[212] a district court enjoined random testing of federal employees in the General Services Administration and in the Executive Office of the President; the court noted that there was no evidence that bribery or compromise of classified information had ever occurred in the agencies, that the incidence of drug abuse was minimal, and that unlike the "front-line" drug interdiction personnel in *Von Raab*, these employees were not confronted in their daily work with suspects likely to resort to bribery or violence. In *Harmon v. Thornburg*,[213] the U.S. Court of Appeals for the District of Columbia Circuit held *Von Raab* inapplicable to random testing of all Justice Department employees involved in criminal prosecutions; since the targeted employees were not necessarily specialized in drug cases, the agency had not shown, as in *Von Raab*, a distinctive need beyond the integrity and confidentiality concerns intrinsic to almost any employment relationship.[214]

Yet many recent decisions underestimate the narrowing features of *Skinner* and *Von Raab*. *Harmon*, though it disapproved testing of all prosecutors, implied that testing would be permissible if confined to prosecutors responsible for drug cases.[215] And the court upheld the testing of Justice Department employees who have top secret security clearances. The court recognized that such employees, working in a "traditional office environment,"[216] present a weaker case for suspicionless testing than did the employees in *Von Raab* but said simply that this difference was insufficient to change the result.

The *Harmon* opinion failed to scrutinize DOJ's need to dispense

[211] N.D. Cal., Sept. 11, 1989, LEXIS #10792.

[212] 712 F. Supp. 986 (D.D.C. 1989).

[213] 878 F.2d 484 (D.C. Cir. 1989).

[214] See also Nat'l Federation of Federal Employees v. Cheney, 1989 U.S.App. LEXIS #12963, Slip Op. at 29–37 (D.C. Cir., Aug. 29, 1989) (impermissible to test civilian staff which administers Defense Department urinalysis program; concerns about integrity and misplaced sympathies not comparable to those applicable to drug interdiction personnel in *Von Raab*); Dimeo v. Griffin, 1989 U.S. Dist. LEXIS #10781 (N.D. Ill., Aug. 25, 1989) (impermissible for state racing board to require random testing of jockeys); *cf.* United Steelworkers of America v. USS, 1989 U.S. Dist. LEXIS #3246 (E.D. Pa., March 29, 1989) (private employer's proposal for suspicionless testing of steelworkers in safety-sensitive positions enjoined pending arbitration; *Von Raab* distinguishable because proposed direct observation test procedure is much more intrusive than that in *Von Raab*).

[215] 878 F.2d at 490–91.

[216] *Id.* at 492.

with individual suspicion. It characterized the testing program as merely "somewhat" more intrusive than that upheld in *Von Raab*,[217] even though the DOJ program covered existing as well as new employees and provided for repeated post-employment testing on a mere two hours' notice. Although the DOJ program requires unwilling employees to surrender present jobs rather than merely an opportunity for promotion, the court dismissed the significance of this contrast to *Von Raab*'s pre-appointment setting by observing (incorrectly) that the Supreme Court's discussion of that factor was "confined to a footnote."[218] The D.C. Circuit's willingness to take such an approach, in an opinion by Chief Judge Patricia Wald, suggests how easily *Von Raab* can be read for more than it fairly requires or supports.

Similarly, in *Guiney v. Roache*,[219] the First Circuit upheld random testing of Boston police officers who carry firearms or participate in drug interdiction. In a brief per curiam opinion the court found *Von Raab* controlling "since we can find no relevant distinction between a customs officer and a police officer."[220]

This oversimplification ignores the distinctive border control responsibilities that *Von Raab* stressed. It omits to mention that in *Guiney* (unlike *Von Raab*) the district judge had found that the relevant personnel "are under constant observation by superiors and co-workers," so that reliance on an individual suspicion standard was feasible.[221] And it ignores the contrast between *Von Raab*'s pre-promotion screening and the Boston program for repeated post-employment testing of personnel seeking only to retain existing jobs.

To similar effect, several other recent cases uphold random post-employment testing for police officers and employees in even less sensitive positions.[222] In *Taylor v. O'Grady*,[223] the Seventh Circuit

---

[217]*Ibid.*

[218]*Id.* at 489. The pre-appointment setting of *Von Raab* is made clear in the Court's statement of the facts, 109 S.Ct. at 1388, and is mentioned several times in connection with discussion of the government interest in "prevent[ing] the promotion" of covered employees. *Id.* at 1393, 1395.

[219]873 F.2d 1557 (1st Cir. 1989).

[220]*Id.* at 1558.

[221]*Guiney*, 686 F. Supp. 956, 962 (D. Mass. 1988), rev'd, 873 F.2d 1557 (1st Cir. 1989).

[222]*E.g.*, Am. Federation of Government Employees v. Skinner, D.C. Cir. Sept. 8, 1989, LEXIS #13567 (Department of Transportation employees with health and safety responsibilities); Seelig v. Koehler, N.Y. App. Div., Oct. 12, 1989, Lexis #12427 (N.Y. City corrections officers); Am. Federation of Government Employees v. Cavazos, D.D.C., July 26, 1989, Lexis #8656 (Department of Education employees in specified "sensitive" positions, including motor pool drivers); Brown v. City of Detroit, 715 F. Supp. 832 (E.D. Mich. 1989) (Detroit police officers).

[223]1989 U.S. App. LEXIS #16581 (7th Cir., Nov. 1, 1989)

upheld once-a-year surprise testing of sheriff's deputies who have regular contact with prisoners. The Court found the government interests in testing and the affected privacy interests identical to those in *Von Raab*. Giving no weight to the post-employment setting, or to the greater frequency and intrusiveness of the testing program, ignoring trial court findings that degrading direct observation procedures had been employed, and omitting all reference to the trial court's conclusion that trained supervision afforded a workable, less restrictive alternative, the Seventh Circuit held that approval of the program was "compelled by *Von Raab*."[224]

Decisions such as *Harmon*, *Guiney*, and *Taylor* are doubly disappointing. Not only do they approve testing programs of dubious "reasonableness," but they treat such results as mandated by *Von Raab*, a conclusion that is surely incorrect. However far the Court may ultimately extend *Von Raab*, it has so far refused to approve either random testing of existing employees or any sort of testing for employees not occupying positions with distinctive safety and security responsibilities. For now, therefore, the law requires case-specific evaluation of each testing program under the totality of its particular justifications and effects.

The prospect of proliferating litigation under a highly fact-specific standard suggests that judges, fearing for their dockets, may view a case-by-case approach as unwieldy. An impetus toward judicial acceptance of the employer's determinations of need may be expected. But the essence of the Fourth Amendment is access to an independent judicial mind for the determination of reasonableness. When employers or other administrators claim the right to invade reasonable expectations of privacy without probable cause or any objective suspicion, they should have to present case-specific justifications for their action. The fact that thousands of employers may soon initiate testing programs ought to be ground for more rather than less judicial scrutiny.

I now turn to the factors that, under *Von Raab*'s general principles, should determine reasonableness in several common urine testing situations. I conclude that suspicionless testing is reasonable in many pre-employment screening programs. For post-employment programs, I conclude that testing should generally require individual suspicion, in the absence of special circumstances.

---

[224]*Id.*, slip. op. at 30.

B. PRE-EMPLOYMENT DRUG-TESTING

The logic of *Von Raab* clearly implies approval for pre-employment drug screening, provided that a distinctively important social interest is present. Blanket pre-employment screening seems permissible for pilots, officers who carry weapons, and probably other police and prosecutors. Pre-employment screening without individual suspicion seems more doubtful for teachers, clerks, accountants, and garbage collectors. Even new employees, who of course have no entitlement to public employment, cannot be required to surrender their constitutional protection against unreasonable search and seizure as a condition of obtaining governmental benefits. If the intrusiveness of testing procedures outweighs legitimate government concerns, as the *Von Raab* Court suggested with respect to Customs employees who handle "classified" but non-sensitive information, then testing should be impermissible even as a pre-employment screening device. Supervisors will have opportunities for observation (and then testing on individual suspicion) during the initial probationary employment period.

C. SUSPICIONLESS TESTING OF EXISTING EMPLOYEES

After *Von Raab*, controversy is likely to center on plans to test existing employees without individual suspicion. From blanket pre-promotion testing of drug interdiction personnel and those with access to weapons or national security information, it is but a small step to suspicionless post-appointment testing of the same personnel. The governmental interest in their fitness and probity is the same, and the test procedures are no more degrading than they would be at the time of appointment. As we have seen, two federal courts of appeals have upheld, under *Von Raab*, random post-employment testing of personnel with top-secret security clearances and police who carry firearms;[225] one has implied that federal drug prosecutors can likewise be subject to random post-employment testing.[226] And if suspicionless testing is permissible in those contexts, many other public employment positions will be treated in analogous fashion.

But the post-employment setting changes both the employer's need for testing and the effect on employee privacy interests. Nor-

---

[225]Harmon v. Thornburg, 878 F.2d 484 (D.C. Cir. 1989); Guiney v. Roache, 873 F.2d 1557 (1st Cir. 1989).
[226]*Harmon*, note 225 *supra*. See also cases cited in note 222 *supra*.

mally, employers have no opportunity to observe prospective employees on a daily basis prior to appointment; post-employment, the employer has available a constant flow of information about employee appearance, demeanor, punctuality and job performance . From the employee's perspective, post-employment testing means the prospect of repeated tests over the course of a career. It also means, for practical purposes, an inability to opt out. An employee who is offended by urinalysis procedures can choose not to apply for jobs or promotions subject to pre-employment screening. This burden, though significant, is in no way comparable to that of abandoning an existing job.[227]

Post-employment testing differs, too, because it covers employees who are not self-selected for their willingness to endure urinalysis testing procedures. No doubt many citizens are troubled little or not at all by official inspections, and they are willing to consent to warrantless search of their homes by housing inspectors or even by police. The Fourth Amendment, however, is designed to protect the more sensitive among us, provided only that their expectations be reasonable. For such individuals post-employment screening is a radically different proposition from the Customs program approved in *Von Raab*.

With these distinctions in mind, the reasonableness of post-employment testing should remain subject to skeptical scrutiny, even for employee positions most like those at issue in *Von Raab*. One general issue concerns the intrusiveness of urine collection procedures. A second, concerning ways to meet government needs without urine testing, varies with the employer interests at stake in different public employment contexts.

1. *Sample collection procedures.* Even when supported by probable cause and a warrant, a traditional search will be constitutionally unreasonable if the search procedure is unnecessarily invasive or if the intrusion is disproportionate to legitimate benefits.[228] *A fortiori*, the presence of legitimate employer needs short of probable cause does not insulate urinalysis programs from scrutiny of test procedures.

---

[227] *Cf.* Wygant v. Jackson Board of Education, 476 U.S. 267, 282–83 (1986), reasoning that affirmative action hiring plans are preferable to plans involving layoffs, because "[d]enial of a future employment opportunity is not as intrusive as loss of an existing job."

[228] See text at notes 105–6 *supra*.

Testing in an uncleanly environment, as in *Taylor v. O'Grady*,[229] is never necessary and should be unreasonable *per se*.

More difficult to assess is unannounced testing under sanitary conditions but with direct observation. Neither *Skinner* nor *Von Raab* approves direct observation testing.[230] Should the added intrusiveness of visual observation render it unconstitutional? Or does direct observation actually *enhance* the effectiveness and hence the reasonableness of a testing program?

The problem here, as previously discussed, is that drug-testing inherently wavers between intrusiveness and ineffectiveness. If a relatively unintrusive and ineffective program is reasonable (*Von Raab*), perhaps a highly intrusive but highly effective program should also be reasonable.

The resolution of this dilemma should depend in part on the government needs at stake. In *Skinner* compelling safety concerns justify a highly reliable (and therefore intrusive) search. The safety requirements of nuclear power plants likewise justify intrusive searches, if the alternatives are not equally effective. But a low level of intrusiveness should be essential to the validity of testing that, like the Customs program, rests on non-safety concerns. Speculation about possible connections between drug abuse and employee absenteeism or theft should not be sufficient to warrant the degrading experience of frontal observation testing.[231] A minimally intrusive program might still fail for ineffectiveness, but it should not be possible to save such a program by adding more intrusive features in pursuit of abstract or secondary goals.

Where employer concerns are sufficiently important to warrant some sort of testing, the value of adding more intrusive test procedures must be assessed in context for each workplace. If there is evidence of extensive drug use in the workforce and an objectively grounded concern about evasion, testing without advance warning would be a reasonable precaution. And lack of notice probably does

---

[229]669 F. Supp 1422 (N.D. Ill. 1987), modified, 1989 U.S. App. LEXIS #16581 (7th Cir., Nov. 1, 1989).

[230]In *Von Raab*, the Customs program granted employees the right to use a private bathroom stall. In *Skinner*, the FRA Field Manual called for direct observation, but the Court ignored this point and instead stated that intrusiveness had been mitigated because the FRA regulations did not require direct observation. See *Skinner*, 109 S.Ct. at 1418.

[231]*Cf.* Welsh v. Wisconsin, 466 U.S. 740 (1984) (exigent circumstances do not excuse warrantless entry to investigate drunk driving offense classified as civil forfeiture offense for which no imprisonment authorized).

not by itself represent a major infringement of employee privacy interests.

Once an employee faces surprise testing, the opportunities for evasion are much reduced. The need for direct observation diminishes accordingly. In the absence of case-specific proof about why that precaution is needed, direct observation should be considered unnecessary or "not a sufficiently productive mechanism" in the context of surprise tests. And surprise testing without observation is probably a less intrusive and degrading experience than advance-notice testing with direct observation. Thus, even when strong government needs support a testing program, direct observation is likely to be unreasonable in most contexts. In this connection a useful benchmark for the reasonableness inquiry is provided by regulations issued by the Department of Health and Human Services. These regulations, which now govern the urine testing of most civilian federal employees, prohibit visual observation except when there is "reason to believe that a particular individual may alter or substitute the specimen."[232]

2. *The government needs.* (*a*) *Safety-sensitive positions.* A natural context for approval of testing is that in which lives are directly at risk. The crucial question is whether testing can adequately meet public safety needs if delayed until individual suspicion arises. In some safety-sensitive jobs, such as those of pilots and air traffic controllers, testing on founded suspicion may come too late. After the first observable mistake, irreparable damage may be done.[233]

But concern about irreparable consequences is inapplicable to many safety-sensitive positions. Police officers carrying firearms, for example, would likely betray evidence of intoxication or impaired judgment in speech, driving, and other observable conduct long before manifesting impairment in misuse of a weapon.[234] For such positions, random testing means subjecting large numbers of unsuspected, law-abiding employees to degrading procedures, on the off-chance of catching a drug abuser whose condition is not manifest and is not, in any event, likely to cause irreparable injury before it

---

[232]§2.2(e), 53 Fed. Reg. 11980 (1988).

[233]See LaFave, note 19 *supra*, §10.3 at 61 (1988 Supp.): "Perhaps there are a few forms of public employment in which the hazards of even a momentary lapse of attention or judgment are so substantial . . . and in which the opportunities for preventive close supervision are so limited that only random or blanket testing will suffice."

[234]See Taylor v. O'Grady, 669 F. Supp. 1422, 1438 (N.D. Ill. 1987) (corrections officers); Guiney v. Roache, 686 F. Supp. 956, 962 (D. Mass. 1988), rev'd, 873 F.2d 1557 (1st Cir. 1989).

can be detected. Under such conditions, random testing is unreasonable, even considering the significant public safety overtones.

Since there is usually no reason why testing cannot await the development of individual cause, the First Circuit's decision in *Guiney v. Roach*[235] seems incorrect. Although there is "no distinction between a customs officer and a police officer,"[236] there is a crucial distinction between the pre-employment and post-employment settings. The situation parallels that in *Delaware v. Prouse*.[237] Because impairment is likely to be observable in most cases, random testing is not a "sufficiently productive mechanism" to warrant its privacy costs.

Even for positions involving acute safety responsibilities (pilots and air traffic controllers), drug testing is not the only way to test perception, dexterity, and judgment. Indeed, drug testing is among the most intrusive and least effective means to do so. Both for positions where any mistake can have catastrophic consequences and for positions with more modest safety dimensions, a simple performance test (on a flight simulator or marksmanship range) is the best way to allay safety concerns. And, whether routine and periodic or random and unannounced, such tests violate no Fourth Amendment privacy interests.

Of course, an employer might hesitate to discipline or fire an employee who fails a single performance test. The result might be due to a bad night's sleep. But whatever the explanation, such an employee should not be flying a plane while impaired. And the unsatisfactory performance test normally would establish objective suspicion warranting an immediate drug test.

For these reasons, suspicionless drug testing of existing employees should rarely be permissible on a safety rationale, even in the case of acutely sensitive positions.

(b) *Positions involving law enforcement, national security and public trust.* When government concerns center not on the immediate protection of human life but on less tangible interests, "impairment" is no longer a simple matter of alertness and dexterity. Drug use, even if confined to off-duty hours, can render the employee vulnerable to bribery, blackmail, or careless revelation of secrets. No test of physical dexterity or quick judgment can bring such vulnerability to light.

---

[235] *Ibid.*
[236] *Id.* at 1558.
[237] 440 U.S. 648 (1979).

Under these conditions, the case for suspicionless testing becomes, paradoxically, stronger than when concern focuses on an immediate threat to public safety. Performance testing can no longer meet governmental concerns. Yet the broad reach of concern for employee integrity and the inadequacy of ordinary performance testing highlights the need for a cautious approach to this rationale. Unless courts assess the strength of the particular government interest and the likely value of suspicionless testing, this rationale would soon grow broad enough to support random testing of almost all public employees. *Von Raab*'s treatment of employees who handle classified information indicates that a discriminating approach is essential to keep this rationale within the bounds of Fourth Amendment reasonableness.

Military personnel present a special case because of the premise, now widely accepted, that military life brings with it greatly reduced expectations of privacy.[238] For the civilian sector, a strong situation for testing would be Defense Department or CIA positions involving daily contact with top-secret national security matters, especially if the affected employees, like those in *Von Raab*, work outside a "traditional office environment" and are thrust into direct contact with opposing forces likely to resort to blackmail, bribery, or violence.

For positions in a traditional office environment, observation by supervisors usually will be adequate to detect signs of drug use.[239] Agencies such as the CIA presumably have extensive experience in monitoring personnel and use sophisticated methods to guard against blackmail or bribery, which in any event can occur for many reasons other than drug abuse. The incremental value of testing employees not suspected of drug involvement is bound to be small. Unless the agency can establish with particularity why testing cannot await objective indications of drug use,[240] suspicionless testing seems *prima facie* unreasonable.

In *Harmon v. Thornburg*,[241] the D.C. Circuit reached a contrary result on this point. The court upheld random testing for Department of Justice employees holding top secret security clearances. Al-

---

[238]Committee for GI Rights v. Calloway, 518 F.2d 466 (D.C. Cir. 1975).

[239]See, *e.g.*, the expert testimony on this point described in Taylor v. O'Grady, 669 F. Supp. 1422, 1431–33 (N.D. Ill. 1987), modified 1989 U.S. App. LEXIS #16581 (7th Cir., Nov. 1, 1989).

[240]See Transport Workers' Local 234 v. Southeastern Pennsylvania Transp. Authority, 678 F. Supp. 543, 549 (E.D. Pa. 1988) (testing on suspicion proved inadequate over two-year period).

[241]878 F.2d 484 (D.C. Cir. 1989).

though the employees worked in a "traditional office environment" (and apparently had no direct contact with "the enemy"), the court found this difference insufficient to change the result. The court's opinion, perhaps a hasty reaction to the apparent breadth of *Von Raab*, failed to consider the lessened need for suspicionless testing in the post-employment context, the greater impact on employees already holding the affected positions, and the need to focus on the small incremental value of testing at random a seemingly innocent, low-risk population.

The justification for testing is still weaker in connection with law enforcement positions involving exposure to confidential but less sensitive material. The DOJ program just mentioned also called for random testing of "[a]ll attorneys responsible for conducting grand jury proceedings," and "[a]ll incumbents whose . . . duties include the prosecution of criminal cases." As to these two categories, the D.C. Circuit held the DOJ program impermissible.[242] The court relied on the *Von Raab* opinion's statement that Customs employees engaged in drug interdiction were "[u]nlike most private citizens or government employees in general."[243] The Justice Department had failed to distinguish its integrity and confidentiality concerns from those intrinsic to almost any employment relationship.

This approach is surely correct. To allow broader scope for the "integrity" rationale would expose to random drug-testing virtually all Americans except the homeless unemployed. Yet the court clouded its analysis by suggesting that the Justice Department might succeed in defending random tests for employees engaged primarily in drug prosecution.

Von Raab poses a difficult predicament in this regard. In terms of integrity and confidentiality concerns, it is difficult to distinguish drug prosecutors from "front-line"[244] drug interdiction personnel. Yet once government concerns are held sufficient with respect to drug prosecutors, why not organized crime prosecutors, homicide prosecutors, and police working in these areas or perhaps further afield? The rationale cannot be extended indefinitely; no amount of imagination can bring DOJ's antitrust prosecutors within its scope. But the symbolic nexus between drug enforcement responsibility and drug use seems too fragile to contain the realm of integrity and confidentiality concerns.

---

[242]*Id*. at 496.
[243]*Id*. at 490.
[244]*Von Raab*, 109 S.Ct. at 1393

A better approach, therefore, would be to assess the likely incidence of drug abuse in the relevant employee population, the incremental value of random testing, and its costs in terms of the intrusion upon drug-free employees subjected to the tests. Federal drug prosecutors seem a most unlikely target for productive random testing. Similarly, individual suspicion seems a necessary prerequisite for post-employment testing, on an integrity rationale, of police officers and, *a fortiori*, public school students, teachers, and most other public employees.

Suspicionless testing of existing employees remains defensible under these criteria in particular job settings. Examples include drug agents who work undercover or who have direct responsibility for handling controlled substances. [245] Customs agents with border control assignments also fall in this category, because of the remedial and national self-protective functions (as distinguished from law enforcement functions) involved in their interdiction responsibilities. Attention should focus on whether trained supervision offers inadequate opportunities for detecting drug use, and whether the irreparable consequences of employee error render the risks of delayed testing intolerable. Absent such considerations, post-employment testing on an integrity rationale should normally be considered unreasonable in the absence of individual suspicion.

D.   TESTING OF EXISTING EMPLOYEES ON INDIVIDUALIZED SUSPICION

Cases prior to *Von Raab* tended to approve urinalysis testing when objectively grounded suspicion was a prerequisite. *Von Raab* will not reverse this trend, but the Court's analysis suggests that testing programs may sometimes be vulnerable even when they require individual suspicion.

Von Raab holds that urinalysis testing is ordinarily an intrusive personal search. And it reaffirms that personal searches normally require probable cause. Thus, although individual suspicion is a more restrictive prerequisite than the limitations approved on the facts of *Von Raab*, it remains a more permissive standard than the usual Fourth Amendment norm.

Precedent for exceptions to this norm is slender and context-

---

[245] See, *e.g.*, Caruso v. Ward, 72 N.Y.2d 433, 530 N.E.2d 142 (1988) (members of elite voluntary corps of police officers engaged in hazardous operations, such as infiltrating underworld drug trafficking organizations).

specific. *Terry v. Ohio*[246] held permissible, on less than probable cause, a limited outer patdown of the person, but *Terry* requires objectively grounded suspicion that the individual is armed and dangerous, and it allows this limited search only for weapons, not for evidence. *T.L.O.* and *Ortega* allow searches for evidence on less than probable cause, but both cases involved only searches of personal effects.

The Court has not yet approved intrusive personal searches, on an administrative rationale, outside of contexts presenting specially acute needs, such as railway safety (*Skinner*), drug interdiction (*Von Raab*), or prison security (*Bell v. Wolfish*[247]). And in its only other pronouncement on work-related searches of employees (*Ortega*), the Court stressed that the employee's privacy expectations are not necessarily diminished with respect to "closed personal luggage" or other personal items that "happen[] to be within the employer's business address."[248]

The question still open after *Skinner* and *Von Raab* is whether testing on less than probable cause is justifiable when it involves intrusive procedures and a context which presents only routine non-safety concerns. Some commentators argue that objectively grounded suspicion about drug-related absenteeism or theft is insufficient, that testing in response to those concerns should require probable cause.[249] But because of the employer's internal governance concerns in such situations, the usual Fourth Amendment presumption in favor of probable cause is not applicable.[250] For such situations an individual suspicion requirement strikes a fair balance between the employee's privacy rights and the employer's interest in effective management of the agency. When the intrusiveness of test procedures is mitigated, for example by advance notice and freedom from direct observation, individual-suspicion testing related to genuine employer concerns should be considered reasonable, as the majority of the pre-*Von Raab* cases held.[251]

Surprise testing and direct observation present more difficult

---

[246]392 U.S. 1 (1968).
[247]441 U.S. 520 (1979).
[248]480 U.S. at 716.
[249]See, *e.g.*, Miller, note 121 *supra*, at 217–18; LaFave, note 19 *supra*, at 56–58 (1988 Supp.). Similarly, Justices Brennan and Marshall would permit urine testing only on probable cause. See *Skinner*, 109 S.Ct. at 1422 (Marshall, J., dissenting).
[250]See text at notes 96–99 *supra*.
[251]See text at notes 134–38 *supra*.

questions. As we have seen, the existence of individual suspicion and even the existence of probable cause do not insulate search procedures from scrutiny for unnecessary or disproportionate intrusiveness.[252] But once individual suspicion develops, advance notice of a drug test may interfere with employer needs for prompt action or provide excessive opportunities for evasion. Surprise testing therefore will normally be reasonable.

Once surprise testing is authorized, the likelihood of successful evasion is greatly diminished. The additional intrusion of direct observation is likely to bring little if any improvement in the effectiveness of testing.[253] Even in the context of programs requiring individual suspicion, therefore, direct observation testing will generally be unreasonable.

E. SUMMARY

Because a balanced concern for employer needs and employee privacy interests requires close attention to detail in evaluating urinalysis programs, the criteria of reasonableness cannot be reduced to a single rule of thumb. The preceding analysis suggests general guidelines. Surprise testing is often justifiable, but direct observation ordinarily is not. Suspicionless testing normally will be reasonable in pre-employment screening programs for positions with significant safety or security implications. But for post-employment programs, testing should generally require individual suspicion, in the absence of unusual circumstances.

IV. CONCLUSION

An "administrative" exception to traditional Fourth Amendment requirements is desirable, historically justifiable, and in any event here to stay. I have suggested refocusing the prerequisites for administrative treatment, but those prerequisites, however conceived, will remain fluid. Public agencies, unconstrained by effective economic or political checks on their appetite for information, are understandably drawn to the suspicionless inspection as a convenient and efficient device (from their internal perspective) for acquiring knowledge. They have had and will continue to have little

---

[252]See text at notes 105–6 *supra*.
[253]See text at notes 231–32 *supra*.

difficulty touching the verbal bases necessary to qualify their programs as both administrative and reasonable.

The result is not only untidy and ineffectual doctrine but a social problem of wide dimensions. We have survived decades of experience with essentially discretionary government power to conduct safety inspections of homes. But such inspections are uncontrovertably necessary, of limited import for the physical and behavioral privacy of the occupant, and a rare experience for most homeowners. In recent years the administrative category has gradually expanded to more debatable areas. With urinalysis testing we enter a new era.

Millions of Americans, and perhaps the majority of public employees, now face the prospect of "regulatory" inspection of the most intimately private aspect of their bodies and bodily functions, along with analysis that will signal personal behavior (legal and illegal) and physical, mental, and emotional problems. With supple threshold requirements for administrative treatment and judicial deference on the question of reasonableness, only the restraint of executive officers and agencies now stands between official power to search and the privacy of the ordinary householder, business owner, and public employee.

This is not the regime contemplated by the Framers of the Fourth Amendment. But the problem cannot be obviated by stricter doctrinal tests. A solution requires a change in judicial attitude.

I have suggested that health, safety, and internal governance inspections should qualify for administrative treatment. Urinalysis programs, like other regulatory inspection regimes, can be defended in these terms. But a close look often reveals that their inspiration and objective is not to serve safety or internal governance concerns but solely to express disapproval of drug use and to deploy employment sanctions to deter illegal conduct.

Only if courts look skeptically at asserted program motivations and consider alternative means to achieve asserted goals can the threshold criteria for administrative treatment separate genuine programs from those that simply short-circuit Fourth Amendment limitations in order to exert more effective social control. Only if courts conduct the reasonableness inquiry with a commitment to careful de novo review can the judicial checking function that lies at the core of the Fourth Amendment play its intended role in safeguarding the dignity and security of the law-abiding public.

JOSEPH L. HOFFMANN

THE SUPREME COURT'S NEW VISION OF FEDERAL HABEAS CORPUS FOR STATE PRISONERS

In a 1981 law review article, Sandra Day O'Connor, then an Arizona appellate judge, suggested that our judicial system could be improved by limiting federal review of adjudications of federal constitutional questions by state courts:[1]

> If our nation's bifurcated judicial system is to be retained, as I am sure it will be, it is clear that we should strive to make both the federal and the state systems strong, independent, and viable. State courts will undoubtedly continue in the future to litigate federal constitutional questions. State judges in assuming office take an oath to support the federal as well as the state constitution. State judges do in fact rise to the occasion when given the responsibility and opportunity to do so. It is a step in the right direction to defer to the state courts and give finality to their judgments on federal constitutional questions where a *full* and *fair* adjudication has been given in the state court.

Judge O'Connor singled out federal habeas corpus review of state convictions as a notable example of our system's "strange" and "imperfect" duplication of judicial time and effort.[2] Unfortunately, ac-

Joseph L. Hoffmann is Associate Professor of Law, Indiana University—Bloomington.

AUTHOR'S NOTE: I thank Terry Bethel, Ellen Boshkoff, Craig Bradley, Larry Kramer, Rhonda Long-Sharp, Lauren Robel, and the participants in the Indiana University faculty workshop for their assistance.

[1]O'Connor, Trends in the Relationship Between the Federal and State Courts from the Perspective of a State Court Judge, 22 Wm. & M. L. Rev. 801, 814–15 (1981).

[2]*Id*. at 801.

cording to Judge O'Connor, "[c]hanges and improvements come very slowly, if at all, and, more often than not, incrementally, in small case by case adjustments."[3]

In 1989, as a Justice of the United States Supreme Court, Sandra Day O'Connor was able to help frustrate her own prediction about the slow pace of reform of federal habeas. Justice O'Connor's lead opinions for a plurality of the Court in *Teague v. Lane*,[4] and for a majority in the followup case of *Penry v. Lynaugh*,[5] significantly narrowed the scope of federal habeas by excluding claims based on "new constitutional rules of criminal procedure," or rules that are announced after a defendant's conviction becomes "final."[6] The only exceptions to the *Teague* rule, that "new law" does not apply retroactively to habeas cases, are decisions placing a certain defendant or conduct beyond the reach of the substantive law of crimes or punishments, and decisions recognizing a procedural right so fundamental that, without it, the "likelihood of an accurate conviction is seriously diminished."[7]

Teague generated surprisingly little reaction, perhaps because it was only a plurality decision, and perhaps because it involved the complex and seemingly "technical" issue of habeas retroactivity. Properly understood, however, and in view of its endorsement by a majority in *Penry*, *Teague* represents a watershed decision in the history of federal habeas. Put simply, *Teague* articulates a new vision of federal habeas that, if not overturned by the Court or by Congress,[8] will eventually reshape the entire area of the law. *Teague* may be the most important habeas decision since *Fay v. Noia*.[9]

The impact of *Teague* will be felt on four different levels. First, *Teague* has obvious and immediate significance at the doctrinal level.

---

[3] *Ibid.*

[4] 109 S. Ct. 1060 (1989). Although several parts of Justice O'Connor's *Teague* opinion were joined by a majority of the Court, the parts of the opinion most important to the subject of this article were joined only by Chief Justice Rehnquist and Justices Scalia and Kennedy.

[5] 109 S.Ct. 2934 (1989).

[6] See *Teague*, 109 S.Ct. at 1075.

[7] *Id.* at 1075–77.

[8] In *Teague*, Justice White wrote an opinion concurring in the judgment in which he invited Congress to "correct" the Court, should it feel that the case was wrongly decided. See *id.* at 1079 (White, J., concurring in the judgment). At least one effort to address by legislation some of the issues raised by *Teague* is already under way. See Hoffmann, Retroactivity and the Great Writ: How Congress Should Respond to Teague v. Lane, 1990 B.Y.U. L. Rev. (forthcoming).

[9] 372 U.S. 391 (1963).

Although the precise meaning of terms like "new law" and "final" remains to be worked out in future cases, *Teague* clearly changes the rules of the habeas game, and substantially restricts the availability to federal habeas petitioners of new constitutional decisions.

Second, the doctrinal changes set forth in *Teague* reflect a major change at the theoretical level. *Teague* shifts the focus of federal habeas from the correction of constitutional errors affecting the conviction of an individual defendant to the deterrence, by means of reversing state criminal convictions, of constitutional errors by state courts. This theoretical shift is reminiscent of the Burger Court's latter-day view that the Fourth Amendment exclusionary rule is a tool for deterring police misconduct, and not an individual right of a criminal defendant.[10]

In addition to its doctrinal and theoretical implications, *Teague* will have a significant impact on habeas practice. After *Teague*, the lower federal courts will see more habeas petitions claiming that the state courts misapplied existing federal law, and fewer petitions asking for new constitutional rules or new interpretations of existing rules. The lower federal courts also will be much less likely to find merit in a second or subsequent habeas petition. And the Supreme Court will not review habeas cases at all, except for an occasional case in which the petition for certiorari is filed by a losing state warden, or in which an issue arises about the scope of the *Teague* exceptions. This is because, after *Teague*, almost all certiorari petitions filed by state prisoners will be either uncertworthy, because they do not raise novel legal issues, or unreviewable, because they raise issues that cannot be decided in the petitioner's favor.

Finally, and perhaps most importantly in the long run, *Teague* will have an effect on the development of federal constitutional rules of criminal procedure. The institutional impact of *Teague*—the extent of which can be perceived only dimly at present—will mean that the federal courts will render fewer constitutional criminal procedure decisions and the state courts will render more. This will lead to greater variation in the way federal constitutional rules of criminal procedure are interpreted and applied in the states, and may alter the sensitive balance between the societal interest in preventing and punishing crime and the rights of criminal defendants.

---

[10]See, *e.g.*, Stone v. Powell, 428 U.S. 465 (1976) (holding that Fourth Amendment claims are not cognizable on federal habeas unless the petitioner was denied a "full and fair opportunity for a hearing" in the state courts); United States v. Leon, 468 U.S. 897 (1984) (holding in favor of a "good faith" exception to the Fourth Amendment exclusionary rule).

I. Teague, Penry, and the Supreme Court's New Doctrine of Habeas Retroactivity

In *Teague*, the petitioner, a black man, appealed his state convictions on the ground that the prosecutor's use of peremptory challenges to remove black prospective jurors denied him a jury representing a fair cross-section of the community, in violation of the Sixth Amendment. The Illinois Appellate Court rejected the fair cross-section claim,[11] the Illinois Supreme Court denied leave to appeal, and the Supreme Court denied certiorari.[12]

The petitioner then filed a petition for a writ of habeas corpus in federal district court, repeating his fair cross-section claim and adding an equal protection claim based on the prosecutor's allegedly discriminatory use of peremptory challenges. The district court denied the petition, but a panel of the Court of Appeals for the Seventh Circuit reversed, and the case was taken *en banc*.[13] The *en banc* rehearing was postponed pending the Supreme Court's 1986 decision in *Batson v. Kentucky*,[14] in which the Court held that an equal protection claim could be based on improper use of peremptory challenges in a single case. After *Batson* was decided, the *en banc* Seventh Circuit ruled that the petitioner could not benefit from the *Batson* equal protection holding, since *Batson* did not apply retroactively to habeas cases.[15] The Seventh Circuit rejected the petitioner's fair cross-section claim on the merits.[16]

The Supreme Court granted certiorari, presumably for the purpose of deciding whether the fair cross-section requirement should apply to the petit jury, or more specifically to the use of peremptory challenges. When the decision was finally handed down, however, a majority of the Court declined to reach the merits of the fair cross-section claim. Instead, Justice O'Connor, who wrote the lead opinion in support of the Court's judgment affirming the Seventh Cir-

---

[11]108 Ill. App. 3d 891, 895–97, 439 N.E.2d 1066, 1069–71 (1982).

[12]464 U.S. 867 (1983).

[13]779 F.2d 1332 (7th Cir. 1985) (en banc).

[14]476 U.S. 79 (1986).

[15]See Allen v. Hardy, 478 U.S. 255 (1986) (per curiam) (holding *Batson* does not apply retroactively to habeas cases).

[16]820 F.2d 832 (7th Cir. 1987) (en banc). Judge Cudahy dissented. *Id*. at 844.

cuit, used the case to reconsider "how the question of retroactivity should be resolved for cases on collateral review."[17]

The retroactivity problem posed by *Teague* was difficult: When a federal court reviews a habeas petition filed by a state prisoner, should it apply the law which existed at the time the prisoner was convicted, or the law which exists at the time of the habeas proceeding? Or, to put the same issue differently, when the Court's view of "the law" has changed between the time the prisoner's conviction became "final" on direct review and the time of the federal habeas proceeding, should the "new law" apply "retroactively" to the habeas case?

Before *Teague*, these questions were answered on a rule-by-rule basis, using the three-part balancing test set forth in the Court's 1965 decision in *Linkletter v. Walker*.[18] The *Linkletter* test examined (1) the purpose of the new rule, (2) the reliance placed on the old rule, and (3) the effect on the administration of justice of retroactive application of the new rule.[19] The *Linkletter* decision was criticized almost immediately by commentators,[20] and within a few years by several members of the Court as well.[21] But the *Linkletter* test continued to serve

---

[17]109 S.Ct. at 1069 (opinion of O'Connor, J., writing in part for the Court and in part for a plurality of the Court).

[18]381 U.S. 618 (1965).

[19]See *id*. at 629.

[20]See Beytagh, Ten Years of Non-Retroactivity: A Critique and a Proposal, 61 Va. L. Rev. 1557, 1558 & n. 3 (1975) (citing examples); see also Haddad, The Finality Distinction in Supreme Court Retroactivity Analysis, 79 Nw. U. L. Rev. 1062 (1985). For general discussions of the retroactivity issue, see, *e.g.*, Schaefer, The Control of "Sunbursts": Techniques of Prospective Overruling, 42 N.Y.U. L. Rev. 631 (1967); Schwartz, Retroactivity, Reliability, and Due Process: A Reply to Professor Mishkin, 33 U. Chi. L. Rev. 719 (1966); Mishkin, The Supreme Court, 1964 Term Foreword: The High Court, the Great Writ and the Due Process of Time and Law, 79 Harv. L. Rev. 56 (1965); Currier, Time and Change in Judge-Made Law: Prospective Overruling, 51 Va. L. Rev. 201 (1965); Freund, New Vistas in Constitutional Law, 112 U. Pa. L. Rev. 631 (1964); Meador, Habeas Corpus and the "Retroactivity" Illusion, 50 Va. L. Rev. 1115 (1964); Amsterdam, Search, Seizure and Section 2255: A Comment, 112 U. Pa. L. Rev. 378 (1964); Traynor, Mapp v. Ohio at Large in the Fifty States, 1962 Duke L.J. 319; Torcia & King, The Mirage of Retroactivity and Changing Constitutional Concepts, 66 Dick. L. Rev. 269 (1962); Redlich, Constitutional Law, 1962 Survey of New York Law, 14 Syr. L. Rev. 167 (1962); Bender, The Retroactive Effect of an Overruling Constitutional Decision: Mapp v. Ohio, 110 U. Pa. L. Rev. 650 (1962); Levy, Realist Jurisprudence and Prospective Overruling, 109 U. Pa. L. Rev. 1 (1960).

[21]See, *e.g.*, Desist v. United States, 394 U.S. 244, 256 (1969) (Harlan, J., dissenting) (criticizing *Linkletter* approach on grounds of inconsistency with judicial role); Mackey v. United States, 401 U.S. 667, 675 (1971) (Harlan, J., dissenting and concurring in the judgment) (same); *id*., at 713 (Douglas, J., joined by Black, J., dissenting) (criticizing *Linkletter* approach on grounds that all new rules should apply retroactively in habeas cases).

as the benchmark for habeas retroactivity, until the Court decided to reexamine the issue in *Teague*.

Although Justice O'Connor's lead opinion in *Teague*, which was joined in full by three Justices and in part by two others, addressed several issues, for present purposes I shall discuss only four portions of the opinion, each of which was joined by a four-member plurality of the Court that included Chief Justice Rehnquist and Justices Scalia and Kennedy. For clarity's sake, I will also rearrange the order of the discussion.

In the most important portion of her opinion, Justice O'Connor declared that "new constitutional rules of criminal procedure will not be applicable to those cases which have become final before the new rules are announced."[22] She identified several reasons for adopting a general rule of non-retroactivity on habeas, including the inconsistent and confusing results often produced by the *Linkletter* test and the fact that the *Linkletter* test occasionally led to the disparate treatment of similarly situated habeas petitioners. The most important reason for the new habeas retroactivity rule, however, was Justice O'Connor's contention that the purpose of federal habeas is to deter state courts from ignoring or erroneously construing federal constitutional standards. According to Justice O'Connor, "[i]n order to perform this deterrence function, the habeas court need only apply the constitutional standards that prevailed at the time the original proceedings took place."[23] Justices Stevens and Blackmun, although they did not join this portion of Justice O'Connor's opinion, agreed with her view that "new law" generally should not apply retroactively to habeas cases.[24]

In another significant portion of her opinion, Justice O'Connor discussed the meaning of the term, "new law," for purposes of applying the *Teague* retroactivity rule. She admitted that deciding whether a case announces a "new rule" is difficult, but concluded that, in general, "a case announces a new rule when it breaks new ground or imposes a new obligation on the States or the Federal Government."[25] As examples of "new law," she cited the Court's decisions in *Rock v.*

---

[22] 109 S.Ct. at 1075 (opinion of O'Connor, J.).

[23] See *Desist*, 394 U.S. at 262–63 (Harlan, J., dissenting).

[24] 109 S.Ct. at 1080 (Stevens, J., joined by Blackmun, J., concurring in part and concurring in the judgment).

[25] *Id.* at 1070.

Arkansas,[26] holding that *per se* exclusion of hypnotically refreshed testimony violates a defendant's right to testify on his own behalf, and *Ford v. Wainwright*,[27] holding that the Eighth Amendment prohibits the execution of insane persons. In sum, "a case announces a new rule if the result was not *dictated* by precedent existing at the time the defendant's conviction became final."[28]

Next, Justice O'Connor identified two exceptions to the *Teague* retroactivity rule. The first exception allows for retroactive application of new rules that place "certain kinds of primary, private individual conduct beyond the power of the criminal law-making authority to proscribe."[29] The second exception permits retroactive application of new rules "without which the likelihood of an accurate conviction is seriously diminished,"[30] such as rules barring the domination of trials by mob violence, a prosecutor's knowing use of perjured testimony, and the use of confessions coerced by "brutal methods."

Finally, Justice O'Connor stated that retroactivity is a threshold question that should be resolved prior to a decision on the merits. According to Justice O'Connor, if a habeas court were to declare a new constitutional rule of criminal procedure, without applying it on behalf of the petitioner, the court would be issuing an advisory opinion. But if the court were to announce a new rule and apply it on behalf of the petitioner, then the principle of equal treatment would require that all other habeas petitioners also benefit from the new rule, eliminating any possibility of non-retroactivity. The better view, therefore, is that the habeas court must resolve the retroactivity issue first, deciding the merits of the petitioner's claim only if the new rule sought is one that would apply retroactively to habeas cases.

Applying these principles to Teague's fair cross-section claim, Justice O'Connor, writing for the same four-member plurality, concluded that the claim was based on "new law," that it was governed by the *Teague* retroactivity doctrine, and that it did not fit within either of the exceptions that would have warranted retroactive applica-

---

[26]483 U.S. 44 (1987).
[27]477 U.S. 399 (1986).
[28]109 S.Ct. at 1070.
[29]See *Mackey*, 401 U.S. at 692 (Harlan, J., dissenting and concurring in the judgment).
[30]*Teague*, 109 S.Ct. at 1077.

tion. Accordingly, because Teague would not be entitled to relief even if his interpretation of the law were to prevail, the Seventh Circuit properly denied Teague's habeas petition. Justices White, Stevens, and Blackmun concurred in the judgment, although Justices Stevens and Blackmun disagreed with Justice O'Connor on the scope of the second *Teague* exception and on the threshold nature of the retroactivity issue. Justices Brennan and Marshall dissented.

In *Penry v. Lynaugh*,[31] a case decided four months after *Teague*, Justice O'Connor was able to clarify some of the language in *Teague* and obtain a fifth vote for some of the views she expressed there. *Penry* involved a mentally retarded Texas man who had been convicted of capital murder and sentenced to death. On appeal, the Texas courts rejected Penry's claims that the jury was inadequately instructed at the sentencing phase of the trial, that the Texas death penalty system improperly limits the jury's consideration of mitigating circumstances, and that the imposition of the death penalty against mentally retarded persons violates the Eighth Amendment.[32] The Supreme Court denied certiorari.[33]

Penry then filed a habeas petition in federal district court, alleging that the Eighth Amendment requires jury instructions on mitigating circumstances in capital sentencing, and that the use of the death penalty against mentally retarded persons violates the Eighth Amendment. The district court denied relief, and the Court of Appeals for the Fifth Circuit affirmed.[34] The court stressed, however, that it did not believe the jury that sentenced Penry to death could have given full effect to the mitigating evidence of Penry's mental retardation, in light of the Texas death penalty system and the jury instructions at sentencing. On the jury instruction claim, the court based its affirmance on Circuit precedent.

On certiorari, the Supreme Court first had to decide whether the *Teague* retroactivity doctrine applies to capital sentencing. In a portion of her lead opinion that was joined by a majority of the Court including Chief Justice Rehnquist and Justices White, Scalia, and Kennedy, Justice O'Connor explained that finality concerns are as relevant to capital sentencing as they are to convictions. She con-

[31] Note 5 *supra*.

[32] Penry v. State, 691 S.W.2d 636 (Tex. Crim. App. 1985).

[33] Penry v. Texas, 474 U.S. 1073 (1986).

[34] Penry v. Lynaugh, 832 F.2d 915 (5th Cir. 1987).

cluded that the *Teague* rule, along with its two exceptions and the requirement that retroactivity be treated as a threshold issue, applies to
new constitutional rules in the context of capital sentencing.[35]

Having held that *Teague* applies to capital sentencing, the Court
faced two retroactivity issues. Penry's jury instruction claim was
based on *Lockett v. Ohio*[36] and *Eddings v. Oklahoma*,[37] both decided
well before Penry's trial, in which the Supreme Court ruled that a
defendant has an Eighth Amendment right to present any and all
mitigating evidence that might cause a sentencer to return a life verdict. But the Court had also upheld the facial validity of the Texas
death penalty system in several cases, noting that the Texas system
seems to allow full consideration of mitigating circumstances by the
sentencing jury despite the absence of any reference to such circumstances in the jury instructions.[38] Thus, the first question was
whether Penry's jury instruction claim would require the Court to
make "new law" in his behalf.

Justice O'Connor, writing for a majority including Justices Brennan, Marshall, Blackmun, and Stevens, reiterated her *Teague* definition that a "new rule" is one that is not *"dictated* by precedent existing
at the time the defendant's conviction became final."[39] The Court's
decisions upholding the Texas death penalty system, most of which
predated Penry's conviction, had emphasized that the Eighth Amendment requires full consideration of mitigating circumstances by a
capital sentencing jury. These decisions, along with *Lockett* and
Eddings, effectively "dictated" that Texas sentencing juries must,
upon a defendant's request, be given instructions that permit full
consideration of mitigating circumstances. Moreover, the Court's decisions upholding the Texas death penalty system were premised on
assurances that the system allowed full consideration of mitigating

---

[35]The same portion of Justice O'Connor's opinion also reiterated her *Teague* view that retroactivity should be treated as a threshold issue, and that a habeas court should address the merits
of a petitioner's "new law" claim only if it finds that the "new law" would apply retroactively on
habeas. Justices Brennan, Marshall, Blackmun, and Stevens declined to join this portion of
Justice O'Connor's opinion. However, Justices Brennan and Marshall joined another portion
of Justice O'Connor's opinion in which she made the same point about the threshold nature of
the habeas retroactivity issue. It is not clear whether the decision to join Justice O'Connor on
the threshold point was intentional or a mistake on the part of Justices Brennan and Marshall.

[36]438 U.S. 586 (1978).

[37]455 U.S. 104 (1982).

[38]See, *e.g.*, Lowenfeld v. Phelps, 484 U.S. 231 (1988); Adams v. Texas, 448 U.S. 38 (1980);
Jurek v. Texas, 428 U.S. 262 (1976).

[39]109 S.Ct. at 2944.

circumstances. Penry's jury instruction claim thus did not seek to "impos[e] a new obligation" on the State of Texas. Instead, Penry's claim was simply that "those assurances [made by the state in prior cases] were not fulfilled *in his particular case*,"[40] given the unique nature of his mitigating evidence and the language of the jury instructions. In short, the claim was not based on a "new rule," and the Court could consider it on its merits.

The second habeas retroactivity issue in *Penry* dealt with the scope of the *Teague* exceptions. Penry's claim that the Eighth Amendment bars the use of the death penalty against mentally retarded persons obviously would require the Court to adopt a "new rule." Thus, in the absence of an exception, the Court would be unable to consider the claim on its merits, since the "new rule" would not apply retroactively to Penry's case.

Justice O'Connor, writing for Justices Brennan, Marshall, Blackmun, and Stevens, focused on the exception for "new rules" that place "certain kinds of primary, private individual conduct beyond the power of the criminal law-making authority to proscribe."[41] The purpose of this exception, according to Justice O'Connor, is to allow retroactive application of new rules based on "substantive categorical guarantees" contained in the Constitution. The Court had previously found such guarantees in the Eighth Amendment, at least with respect to punishments, as well as in the Due Process Clause. Thus, Justice O'Connor held, the exception should include "not only rules forbidding criminal punishment of certain primary conduct but also rules prohibiting a certain category of punishment for a class of defendants because of their status or offense."[42] As a result, the Court again could consider Penry's claim on its merits.

A majority of the Court ultimately rejected Penry's claim that the Eighth Amendment bars the death penalty for mentally retarded persons, although Justice O'Connor split with Chief Justice Rehnquist and Justices White, Scalia, and Kennedy on the reasons for this rejection. A different majority of the Court reversed Penry's death sentence, however, and ordered a new sentencing hearing based on the jury instruction claim, with Justices Brennan, Marshall, Blackmun, and Stevens joining the portion of Justice O'Connor's opinion announcing and explaining the reversal. Justice Scalia, joined by the

---

[40] *Id.* at 2947.

[41] See *Mackey*, 401 U.S. at 692 (Harlan, J., dissenting and concurring in the judgment).

[42] 109 S.Ct. at 2953.

Chief Justice and Justices White and Kennedy, dissented on the ground that the jury instruction claim was based on "new law" and therefore should not have been heard on the merits under *Teague*.

II. TEAGUE AND THE COURT'S NEW THEORY OF FEDERAL HABEAS

The doctrinal changes set forth in *Teague* and *Penry* are closely linked to the Court's view about the underlying theory of federal habeas. Because the Court in *Teague* lacked meaningful historical guidance on the issue of habeas retroactivity, it was compelled to resolve the issue by reference to theoretical considerations. The doctrine announced in *Teague*, and adopted by a majority of the Court in *Penry*, was the product of a theory of habeas which was first articulated by Justice Harlan in the late 1960s,[43] but which before last Term had never been adopted by the Court. The theory, which holds that the purpose of habeas is to deter the state courts from committing constitutional errors, emerged in *Teague* and *Penry* as an attractive choice for those Justices who, like Justice O'Connor, were concerned about the proper allocation of responsibility between the state and federal courts in the area of constitutional criminal procedure.

A. THE LACK OF HISTORICAL GUIDANCE ON THE HABEAS RETROACTIVITY ISSUE

Habeas retroactivity was not addressed by the Supreme Court before *Linkletter v. Walker* because, as a practical matter, the issue almost never arose.[44] Until the mid–20th century, the Court narrowly

---

[43]See Desist v. United States, 394 U.S. 244, 256 (1969) (Harlan, J., dissenting); see also *Mackey*, 410 U.S. at 675 (Harlan, J., dissenting and concurring in the judgment).

[44]In a footnote to the majority opinion in *Linkletter*, 381 U.S., at 628–29 n. 13, Justice Clark cited several examples of pre-*Linkletter* cases in which the Court applied "new law" to habeas cases without discussing the issue of retroactivity: "*Eskridge* v. *Washington Prison Board*, 357 U.S. 214 (1958), applied the rule of *Griffin* v. *Illinois*, 351 U.S. 12 (1956), requiring the State to furnish transcripts of the trial to indigents on appeal, to a 1935 conviction. The rule in *Gideon* v. *Wainwright*, 372 U.S. 335 (1963), that counsel must be appointed to represent an indigent charged with a felony, was actually applied retrospectively in that case since *Gideon* had collaterally attacked the prior judgment by post-conviction remedies. See also *Doughty* v. *Maxwell*, 376 U.S. 202 (1964). *Jackson* v. *Denno*, 378 U.S. 368 (1964), involving a coerced confession, was also applied to the petitioner who was here on a collateral attack. See also *McNerlin* v. *Denno*, 378 U.S. 575 (1964). It is also contended that *Reck* v. *Pate*, 367 U.S. 433 (1961), supports the conclusion of absolute retroactivity in the constitutional area since the petitioner convicted in 1937 was released after a finding that the confession was coerced when judged by standards set forth in our cases decided subsequent to his conviction. See *United States ex rel. Angelet* v. *Fay*, 333 F.2d 12, 24 (dissenting opinion of Marshall, J.)."

limited the Act of 1867, which first authorized federal habeas review of state criminal convictions, to challenges to the jurisdiction of the state court.[45] Even where the Court stretched the concept of jurisdiction to consider claims of constitutional error, it would not hear such claims on the merits if the state court had provided the defendant a "fair opportunity" to litigate the claims.[46] Federal habeas, in short, was rarely available to state prisoners. And, of course, until the 1960s and the rise of the incorporation doctrine, the Court simply did not have much constitutional law to apply to state criminal proceedings.

In *Brown v. Allen*,[47] in 1953, the Court expanded the availability of the statutory writ, for the first time reaching the merits of a petitioner's constitutional claim without even attempting to link those claims to the jurisdiction of the state court. Nevertheless, even after *Brown*, the habeas retroactivity issue did not arise often, because habeas petitioners were still required to have raised their constitutional claims properly in state court in order to obtain later habeas relief.[48]

Habeas retroactivity first became important in 1963, when the Court issued its landmark decision in *Fay v. Noia*.[49] In *Fay*, the Court, per Justice Brennan, held that in some cases habeas relief could be granted even though the petitioner had failed to raise his constitutional claim in the state courts. After *Fay*, prisoners were free to file habeas petitions based on "new law" that did not exist at the time of their trials. And, at the same time, the Court's move toward incorporation of the Bill of Rights spurred the development of new constitutional rules of criminal procedure. This combination of the expansion of the scope of federal habeas and the changes in federal constitutional rules of criminal procedure triggered the first wave of habeas retroactivity cases, including *Linkletter*.

Habeas retroactivity, in other words, is an issue that is less than

---

[45]See Friedman, A Tale of Two Habeas, 73 Minn. L. Rev. 247, 262–63 (1988); Mayers, The Habeas Corpus Act of 1867: The Supreme Court as Legal Historian, 33 U. Chi. L. Rev. 31, 54 n. 89 (1965).

[46]See Bator, Finality in Criminal Law and Federal Habeas Corpus for State Prisoners, 76 Harv. L. Rev. 441, 462 (1963).

[47]344 U.S. 443 (1953).

[48]As Justice Harlan pointed out in *Desist*, "[i]t was the rare case in which the habeas petitioner had raised a 'new' constitutional argument both at his original trial and on appeal." 394 U.S. 244, 261 (1969) (Harlan, J., dissenting).

[49]372 U.S. 391 (1963).

thirty years old. Moreover, although *Linkletter* was a case of statutory construction, and although *stare decisis* is normally at its strongest in such cases, *Linkletter* was an unusual case of statutory construction. The post–Civil War history of federal habeas reveals that Congress either has followed the lead of the Supreme Court in defining the scope of federal habeas, or has remained completely silent in the face of the Court's numerous decisions interpreting the Act of 1867. As a result, the Court has come to view the construction of the Act of 1867 as a subject almost completely within its own domain.[50]

Nor has Congress chosen to address habeas retroactivity during the quarter-century since the Court first dealt with the issue in *Linkletter*. The only hint of Congressional intent on the subject is contained in a 1966 amendment to 28 U.S.C. Section 2244 (c), which deals with the res judicata effect of a decision in a habeas case on a later case filed by the same petitioner. The circumstances identified by Congress that would warrant relief on a new federal habeas petition filed by the same petitioner, where the Supreme Court had affirmed the denial of the previous petition, include "the existence of a material and controlling *fact* which did not appear in the record of the proceeding in the Supreme Court."[51] Congress did not mention, as a legitimate reason for filing a new petition, a change in the governing law. And it seems unlikely that Congress would have limited new petitions in this way, if it believed that claims based on changes in the governing law should be cognizable in a petitioner's first habeas petition. In any event, however, this single, indirect treatment of the retroactivity issue does not permit the conclusion that Congress has established a policy on the issue.

B. THE COMPETING THEORIES OF FEDERAL HABEAS

Not surprisingly, given this lack of historical guidance, the debate about habeas retroactivity in *Teague* was transformed into a debate about the theory of federal habeas. Justice O'Connor, for the plurality, argued that a general rule of non-retroactivity, and not the *Linkletter* balancing test, was consistent with the theory that the purpose of federal habeas is to provide an incentive for state judges "to

---

[50]In Wainwright v. Sykes, for example, the Court referred to its "historic willingness to overturn or modify its earlier views of the scope of the writ, even where the statutory language authorizing judicial action has remained unchanged." 433 U.S. 72, 81 (1977).

[51]28 U.S.C. §2244(c) (1964 ed., Supp. V) (emphasis added).

conduct their proceedings in a manner consistent with established constitutional principles."[52] If state judges fail to do so, then the federal courts will grant writs of habeas corpus, overturning convictions and releasing prisoners from state custody. Presumably state judges do not wish to see their judgments upset in the federal courts, and do not wish to see persons convicted in their courtrooms set free. Federal habeas thus operates as a deterrent, ensuring that state judges will "toe the constitutional mark."[53]

Justice Brennan, in his *Teague* dissent, relied upon the competing theory of federal habeas that he had articulated with great force and conviction in his opinion for the Court in *Fay v. Noia.*[54] There, Justice Brennan wrote that the common-law history of the writ shows that "its function has been to provide a prompt and efficacious remedy for whatever society deems to be intolerable restraints."[55] Federal habeas ensures that imprisonment "conform[s] with the fundamental requirements of law," and provides "a mode for the redress of denials of due process of law."[56] About the Act of 1867, Justice Brennan wrote that Congress "was anticipating resistance to its Reconstruction measures," and made federal habeas available to prisoners in state custody so that "federal constitutional rights of personal liberty shall not be denied without the fullest opportunity for plenary federal review."[57] In short, according to Justice Brennan, federal habeas is available "whenever a person's liberty is unconstitutionally restrained."[58]

Which of these two competing theories of federal habeas articulated in *Teague*, the "deterrence of state courts" theory or the "vindication of federal rights/protection of liberty" theory, is correct as a matter of legislative intent? In the overwhelming majority of federal habeas cases, the answer is "both." In the typical habeas case, the federal rights of the defendant are violated by an error committed by the state court, and a grant of habeas relief thus serves both purposes:

---

[52]109 S.Ct. at 1073, quoting Desist v. United States, 394 U.S. 244, 262–63 (1969) (Harlan, J., dissenting).

[53]Mackey v. United States, 401 U.S. 667, 687 (1971) (Harlan, J., dissenting and concurring in the judgment).

[54]Note 9 *supra.*

[55]372 U.S. at 401–2.

[56]*Id.* at 402.

[57]*Id.* at 415, 424.

[58]*Teague*, 109 S.Ct. at 1084 (Brennan, J., dissenting).

It vindicates the petitioner's federal rights, and by doing so it serves to deter the state courts from ignoring or misconstruing such rights in the future.

Nor could the Congress that adopted the Act of 1867 have distinguished between the purpose of protecting the federal rights of defendants and the purpose of deterring state court misconduct. As Justice Brennan noted in *Fay*, the Act of 1867 was adopted in an effort to ensure that state courts would faithfully enforce Reconstruction-era legislation, primarily those laws providing federal rights to freed slaves. This interpretation of the legislative intent, on the surface, seems consistent with the theory that the purpose of habeas is to deter state courts from ignoring or misapplying federal law. Of course, the Reconstruction Congress would also have willingly agreed that the purpose of the Act of 1867 was to protect the persons in whose behalf those federal laws had been, or were about to be, enacted. From the point of view of the Congress in 1867, the two theories of federal habeas would have been functionally equivalent.

Only with the Court's expansion of the scope of federal habeas in *Brown* and *Fay* did the "deterrence of state courts" and "vindication of federal rights/protection of liberty" theories of federal habeas become at least potentially separable. As soon as prisoners were permitted to raise claims of error based on the adoption of new constitutional rules, then it began to matter which of the two theories of federal habeas prevails. The "new law" cases raised, for the first time, the issue whether habeas relief should be granted solely for the purpose of vindicating current interpretations of federal law, even though the state courts had decided the case properly under the federal law as it existed at the time and therefore did not need or deserve to be sent a deterrence "message."

Cases such as *Teague* and *Penry* represent a crucial theoretical fork in the habeas road. They are the only class of habeas cases in which a defendant's federal constitutional rights, as understood at the time of the habeas proceeding, might have been violated, even though the state court conducted the defendant's trial in compliance with all then-applicable federal constitutional standards.

Interestingly, there is another class of habeas cases that presents a "mirror image" of the *Teague* retroactivity problem. That is the class of cases like *Stone v. Powell*,[59] in which the Court held that Fourth

---

[59]428 U.S. 465 (1976).

Amendment claims are not cognizable on federal habeas. The *Stone* Court wrote that the Fourth Amendment exclusionary rule is not a personal right of the defendant, but instead exists solely as a tool to deter police misconduct. Under *Stone*, when a state court violates existing Fourth Amendment law, the court may need a deterrence "message,"[60] but the defendant has no personal right that needs to be vindicated. Once one treats the Fourth Amendment exclusionary rule as a prophylactic device, then the Fourth Amendment context, like the *Teague* "new law" context, is one in which the two purposes of habeas can be separated.[61]

C. THE DEFINITION OF "NEW LAW"

The Court's adoption of the "deterrence of state courts" theory of federal habeas, in *Teague* and *Penry*, has important doctrinal consequences. For example, because the theory holds that the purpose of habeas is to provide an incentive for state judges to do what the Court believes they are supposed to do, the definition of "new law," which determines the scope of federal judicial oversight of a state judge's decision, becomes the crucial element of the *Teague* rule. Beneath this definition lurks the following question: What is the appropriate standard of care for state judges deciding federal constitutional issues? Or, more to the point, what is the standard of care to which state judges should be held by their federal counterparts?

These are, to say the least, questions without easy answers. One approach, suggested by Justice Scalia in his *Penry* opinion, is that a state judge should be expected to do no more than act "reasonably" and "in good faith."[62] This "reasonable good faith" standard of care would shield most kinds of constitutional error in state criminal trials from federal habeas review. In a case where a state judge is faced with "palpable uncertainty as to what the [Supreme Court's] rule might

---

[60]See Bradley, Are the State Courts Enforcing the Fourth Amendment? A Preliminary Study, 77 Geo. L.J. 251 (1988).

[61]The *Stone* Court held, in effect, that a grant of habeas relief to fulfill the "deterrence of state courts" purpose, if such a grant of relief would not also serve the "vindication of federal rights/protection of liberty" purpose, is inappropriate. This, of course, does not compel the conclusion that a grant of habeas relief to fulfill the "vindication of federal rights/protection of liberty" purpose, if it would not also serve the "deterrence of state courts" purpose, is likewise inappropriate.

[62]109 S.Ct. at 2964 (Scalia, J., concurring in part and dissenting in part).

be,"[63] for example, any careful, good faith attempt to decipher the meaning of the Supreme Court's precedents would insulate the state judge's ruling from reversal by a federal habeas court. Even a later decision by the Supreme Court replacing such "palpable uncertainty" with a clearer rule would not trigger habeas review of the conviction.

The only kind of case that can be reversed on federal habeas, under Justice Scalia's "reasonable good faith" standard, is one in which the state judge misapplies clear, binding federal precedent. Justice Scalia's view is therefore analogous to the minimal duty imposed on a police officer in a search warrant case under the current construction of the Fourth Amendment exclusionary rule.

At the opposite extreme is the functional equivalent of "strict liability," under which a state judge is subject to reversal by a federal habeas court any time the judge gets a federal issue wrong, regardless of how reasonable the judge's conclusion may have seemed at the time. This is, in effect, a doctrine of full habeas retroactivity. The few judges and commentators who have held this view, such as Justice Douglas, are not concerned about "deterring" state judges at all.[64] As is true of strict liability in other contexts, such as tort law and criminal law, strict liability in the habeas context provides no greater deterrence than a rule requiring a minimal degree of fault or culpability on the part of the actor involved.[65] Rather, the "strict liability" approach is concerned with providing a remedy for the injured party, or in this context, the defendant whose conviction was tainted by constitutional error.

In *Teague*, and again in *Penry*, Justice O'Connor unfortunately treats the "new law" issue as if it could be resolved simply by consulting an appropriate legal dictionary. "New law," to repeat the words of Justice O'Connor in *Teague*, is the end result of any case that "breaks new ground or imposes a new obligation on the States or the Federal Government,"[66] or in which "the result was not *dictated* by precedent existing at the time the defendant's conviction became final."[67]

---

[63] *Ibid.*

[64] See *Mackey*, 401 U.S. at 713 (Douglas, J., joined by Black, J., dissenting).

[65] See Packer, Mens Rea and the Supreme Court, 1962 Supreme Court Review 107, 109.

[66] 109 S.Ct. at 1070.

[67] *Ibid.*

Based on her application of the "new law" standard in *Teague* and *Penry*, Justice O'Connor's view of "new law" appears to lie somewhere between "reasonable good faith" and "strict liability." Nevertheless, there is reason for concern about where Justice O'Connor, as the swing vote, stands on this issue. According to Justice O'Connor, state judges should not have been expected to anticipate the Supreme Court's decisions in *Rock v. Arkansas*[68] and *Ford v. Wainwright*,[69] the two examples of "new law" cited in *Teague*. Her citations to *Rock* and *Ford* are most curious. *Rock* involved a relatively minor extension of long-standing federal constitutional precedent to a narrow factual situation. And *Ford* was a case in which several centuries of common law, as well as the statutes of virtually every state, already recognized the right at issue. The only question in *Ford* was whether the Court would find the right within the Eighth Amendment as well.

The citations to *Rock* and *Ford* suggest that, in Justice O'Connor's view, state judges need not be expected to do any more than fill in the most obvious interstitial gaps in the existing federal precedents in order to avoid reversal on habeas. This represents, however, an inappropriately crabbed view of the duties of a state judge when interpreting federal constitutional law. As Justice Fortas wrote in a dissent to an early habeas retroactivity decision, "it is proper for a habeas court to require 'conceptual faithfulness' to our opinions and 'not merely decisional obedience' to the rules they announce."[70]

Justice O'Connor's definition of "new law" in *Teague* is much broader, and thus less favorable for defendants, than the standard previously used to decide whether a retroactivity issue exists. Before *Teague*, a new rule was considered "new law" only if it represented a "clear break with the past,"[71] or if it "overrule[d] clear past precedent, or disrupt[ed] a practice long accepted and widely relied upon."[72] Given the tendency of all courts to characterize new rules as mere incremental changes in the law, the "clear break" standard was not often met. After *Teague*, however, almost all new rules will qual-

---

[68] 483 U.S. 44 (1987).

[69] 477 U.S. 399 (1986).

[70] Desist v. United States, 394 U.S. 244, 277 (1969) (Fortas, J., dissenting).

[71] *Id.* at 248.

[72] Milton v. Wainwright, 407 U.S. 371, 381 n.2 (1972) (Stewart, J., dissenting).

ify as "new law," since it will be difficult to say that such rules are "*dictated* by prior precedent."[73]

It is ironic that the Court's definition of "new law," as expressed by Justice O'Connor in *Teague*, places so little responsibility on a state judge to anticipate changes in the governing federal law. The standard of care for state judges under *Teague* is substantially less burdensome than that applicable to a defendant and his attorney under the Court's procedural default doctrine of *Wainwright v. Sykes*.[74] The Court expects a defense attorney, or even a *pro se* defendant, to raise at trial any legal challenges that have been made to courts in other cases, or that have been accepted by another court anywhere in the country. If the attorney or defendant fails to raise such an issue at trial, in violation of a state procedural rule, then the issue is generally unavailable as a basis for later habeas relief.

The *Teague* doctrine does not change the way in which the procedural default rule works against habeas petitioners. But *Teague* does effectively overrule the Court's decision in favor of the petitioner in *Reed v. Ross*,[75] where the petitioner was allowed to raise a procedurally defaulted claim on federal habeas because the claim was sufficiently "novel" at the time of the petitioner's trial that his attorney could not be faulted for failing to raise it. After *Teague*, any claim as "novel" as the one in *Reed v. Ross* will not apply retroactively to habeas cases anyway, so procedural default becomes irrelevant.

Of course, the role of a state judge differs from that of a defense attorney or defendant. We do not want a judge to decide a case in a defendant's favor based on the mere fact that the same issue was raised in another case or accepted by another judge. Instead, we want state judges to decide cases based on their best judgment about what the applicable law is, and how that law applies to the case at bar.

---

[73]In *Teague*, Justice Brennan supported this conclusion by citing nineteen recent Supreme Court habeas cases in which the requested new rule would have been "new law" under Justice O'Connor's definition. 109 S.Ct. at 1088–1090 (Brennan, J., dissenting). Many of the 19 cases did not give rise to retroactivity issues under the pre-*Teague* "new law" standard. The "new law" definition in *Teague* retains some flexibility, as evidenced by the lengthy discussion of the "new law" issue in *Penry*. See 109 S.Ct. at 2944–47 (opinion of O'Connor, J.); *id.* at 2964–65 (Scalia, J., concurring in part and dissenting in part). This flexibility would permit a future Court to narrow the definition without explicitly overruling it. Nevertheless, the *Teague* definition clearly increases the likelihood that a new rule will be held to be "new law" for retroactivity purposes.

[74]433 U.S. 72 (1977).

[75]468 U.S. 1 (1984).

There is something unseemly, however, about adopting a definition of "new law" for habeas retroactivity purposes that does not require a state judge conscientiously to weigh and consider the likelihood that a defendant's federal claim is part of a developing trend.

D. THE DEFINITION OF "FINAL"

In *Teague*, Justice O'Connor defined "new law" as any rule that was not dictated by precedent existing "at the time the defendant's conviction became final."[76] Unfortunately, Justice O'Connor did not resolve the issue of when a state conviction becomes "final." At one point in *Teague*, she quoted Justice Powell's statement in *Solem v. Stumes*[77] that the governing law should be the law "in effect at the time of the conviction."[78] Later, she suggested that the test should be whether the "trials and appeals conformed to then-existing constitutional standards."[79] Finally, in *Penry*, she declared that the petitioner's conviction "became final . . . when this Court denied his petition for certiorari on direct review."[80]

Because *Teague* was premised on the theory that federal habeas serves to deter constitutional errors by state judges, the appropriate time to "fix" the applicable federal law for purposes of habeas review is when the state judges have rendered their final decision on direct review of the case. Any change in the governing federal law between the last state-court decision affirming a defendant's conviction and the Supreme Court's denial of certiorari, perhaps a year or more later, is as irrelevant to the "deterrence" theory as a change in the governing federal law occurring after the denial of certiorari. In either case, the propriety of the state court's decision is unaffected.

In addition to the theoretical argument, practical concerns support defining finality in terms of the last state court decision on direct review. A retroactivity rule focusing on the law in existence at the time of the Court's denial of certiorari would create a strong incentive for defendants to file certiorari petitions, hoping that some beneficial new rule might be announced during the pendency of the petition.

---

[76] 109 S.Ct. at 1070.

[77] 465 U.S. 638 (1984).

[78] 109 S.Ct. at 1073, quoting *Stumes*, 465 U.S. at 653 (Powell, J., concurring).

[79] 109 S.Ct. at 1075.

[80] 109 S.Ct. at 2944.

This would simply transfer work from the lower federal courts to the Supreme Court.

III. TEAGUE AND FEDERAL HABEAS PRACTICE

A. THE IMPACT ON HABEAS PRACTICE IN THE FEDERAL DISTRICT COURTS AND COURTS OF APPEALS

In the district courts, the most obvious practical impact will be that prisoners will quickly learn to conform their habeas petitions to the new rule set out in *Teague*. Prisoners learned not to allege Fourth Amendment violations after the Court excluded such claims from habeas review in *Stone v. Powell*,[81] and to recast Fourth Amendment claims as ineffective assistance of counsel claims after *Kimmelman v. Morrison*.[82] Similarly, prisoners after *Teague* will learn to allege that the state courts violated existing federal law, and not to allege claims based on "new law" declared after their convictions became "final," or on requests for adoption of such "new law" by the district court.

The method of reviewing habeas petitions in the district courts will also change as a result of *Teague*. Whenever a habeas petition is based on an alleged violation of existing federal law, the district court will first have to decide what the law was at the time of the original state proceeding. Under *Teague*, this inquiry will focus on the existing Supreme Court precedent and any other rules that would have been "dictated" by the precedent. Of course, *Penry* demonstrates just how difficult such an inquiry can be for a lower court; with respect to Penry's jury instruction claim, the Supreme Court split five-to-four over whether the claim was based on existing law or "new law."

Although the inquiry into the existing federal law will not always be easy, the district courts may find consolation in the fact that there will be very few meritorious second or subsequent petitions. The fact that *Teague* "freezes" the federal law applicable to a petitioner, coupled with existing habeas doctrines concerning successive petitions and abuse of the writ,[83] effectively establishes a "one petition"

---

[81]428 U.S. 465 (1976).

[82]477 U.S. 365 (1986). See Manville & Brezna, Post-Conviction Remedies: A Self-Help Manual, 60–61 (1988) (discussing how state prisoners may recast Fourth Amendment claims as ineffective assistance claims).

[83]See Rule 9(b) of the Rules Governing Section 2254 Cases in the United States District Courts; Sanders v. United States, 373 U.S. 1 (1963).

rule. In essence, any claim in a second or subsequent petition based on a new rule that is sufficiently "dictated" by prior precedent to avoid the label, "new law," will be barred because it either was or should have been raised in the first petition. Thus, although *Teague* may not reduce the total number of federal habeas petitions, it will reduce the burden that review of such petitions imposes on the district courts, because in most instances only a petitioner's first habeas petition will require substantial judicial time and effort.

Of course, a petitioner who can show that his claim fits within one of the exceptions to *Teague* for certain categories of "new law" will be entitled to relief on a second or subsequent habeas petition, assuming all of the usual procedural requirements are satisfied. But the exceptions have been defined so narrowly that only a handful of "new law" decisions will fit within one of them. The first exception, for substantive rules dealing with the validity of crimes or punishments, will apply to very few decisions outside the context of the death penalty. And, as Justice O'Connor noted in *Teague*, it is unlikely that many new rules would fit within the second exception, because most rules that might be considered essential to an accurate conviction have already been declared.[84]

The habeas practice in the courts of appeals is likely to change in much the same way that it will change in the district courts. Federal appellate courts will face either claims that the state courts have misapplied existing federal law, or claims that the district courts have misinterpreted some aspect of the *Teague* rule, such as the scope of "new law" or one of the exceptions to the doctrine. The determination of the existing federal law will often be problematic, but the appellate courts will need to pay little attention to most second or subsequent habeas petitions.

B.   THE IMPACT ON HABEAS PRACTICE IN THE SUPREME COURT

In the Supreme Court, *Teague* will have a major impact on the habeas caseload. The new retroactivity rule will dramatically reduce the likelihood that a habeas petitioner will obtain a writ of certiorari to challenge the denial of habeas relief by a federal court of appeals. This is because most habeas petitioners who lose in the court of appeals will have only two choices when considering possible certiorari review. The petitioner can file a petition for certiorari alleging that

---

[84]109 S.Ct. at 1077.

the state courts misapplied the existing federal law, which is not likely to be viewed by the Supreme Court as an issue worthy of a grant of certiorari.[85] Alternatively, the petitioner can file a petition for certiorari raising a "new law" issue that might interest the Court, but *Teague* will prevent the Court from taking such a case to resolve the "new law" issue, unless one of the two exceptions applies. After *Teague*, therefore, the Court will be likely to review only two kinds of habeas cases: those in which the state warden lost in the court of appeals, and those in which the petitioner lost, but which present a certworthy issue involving the definition of "new law" or the applicability of one of the exceptions to the *Teague* rule.

Attorneys who represent many habeas petitioners, such as legal clinics or public defenders, will soon realize that they have very little to gain, and perhaps much to lose for their other habeas clients, by seeking to take a habeas case from the court of appeals to the Supreme Court. This is because, absent an applicable exception, the Court can only rule against a "new law" claim in a habeas case. In the vast majority of cases, the Court cannot adopt "new law" in a habeas petitioner's favor. Once the futility of filing a certiorari petition in a habeas case becomes understood, the number of such filings will likely decrease.

C. THE SPECIAL CATEGORY OF CAPITAL CASES

One of the most significant effects of the *Teague* doctrine will be felt in capital cases. The *Teague* rule will shorten federal habeas litigation in capital cases by reducing the time spent in reviewing second or subsequent habeas petitions.

The lengthy delays incurred as a result of federal habeas litigation in capital cases have been documented and criticized.[86] The problem is that a capital defendant, unlike all other defendants, has little or no

---

[85] See Rule 17, Rules of the Supreme Court of the United States.

[86] As one recent federal report noted, "[t]he problem of delay [due to habeas litigation] has been particularly acute in capital cases. In such cases, the continuation of litigation prevents the sentence from being carried out." Office of Legal Policy, Report on Federal Habeas Corpus Review of State Judgments 37 (1988) (Truth in Criminal Justice Report No. 7). See also Robbins, Rationalizing Federal Habeas Corpus Review of State Court Criminal Convictions in Capital Cases, Background and Issues Paper, A.B.A. Criminal Justice Section Task Force on Death Penalty Habeas Corpus 8–9 (1989) ("[F]ederal habeas corpus review of [capital] cases appears to most observers to be both chaotic and protracted. . . . Despite the frantic pace of some of these proceedings, death penalty litigation in most cases is quite protracted. It is rare for a death sentence to be carried out within five or six years of its imposition").

incentive to speed up the pace of habeas review of his conviction and sentence. Quite the contrary—for prisoners on death row, the longer the review process takes, the better.

In recent years, two major reform initiatives have been instituted to deal with this problem.[87] In September 1989, the Ad Hoc Committee on Federal Habeas Corpus in Capital Cases, also known as the Powell Committee, proposed amendments to the federal habeas statute that would apply only to habeas petitions filed in capital cases.[88] Under the proposal, if a state provides qualified counsel to handle state post-conviction proceedings in capital cases, then capital defendants in that state would be (1) subjected to a 180-day statute of limitations for filing their federal habeas petitions, with a possible 60-day extension for good cause, (2) limited to one federal habeas petition absent a claim that raises serious doubt about the defendant's guilt, and that was not raised previously because of a valid excuse, such as newly discovered evidence, and (3) prevented from challenging the effectiveness of their state post-conviction attorneys.

The Powell Committee's proposal to provide state post-conviction counsel for capital defendants is laudable, but the remainder of the proposal is misguided. The proposal reduces the delay in capital cases attributable to habeas litigation by forcing capital defendants to file their first federal habeas petitions sooner than is required of other defendants. The proposal also bars, in capital cases only, all second or subsequent federal habeas petitions that do not raise a serious doubt about factual guilt. These aspects raise serious questions about the actual and perceived fairness of the Powell Committee's proposal. Perhaps not surprisingly, the proposal has drawn fire from commentators who, while agreeing with the provision of state post-conviction counsel, object strenuously to "singling out" capital cases for accelerated review.

The *Teague* doctrine will also have an effect on the problem of lengthy habeas litigation in capital cases, although it will do so with-

[87] The American Bar Association has set up a State-Federal Task Force on Death Penalty Habeas Corpus to address the concerns raised by the "chaotic and protracted" federal habeas litigation in capital cases. See Robbins, note 86 *supra*, at 8–9, 13. In addition, Chief Justice William H. Rehnquist in January, 1988, requested the Conference of Chief Justices to study ways to deal with the problems of federal habeas litigation in capital cases. See *id.* at 12. This request led to the creation of the Ad Hoc Committee on Federal Habeas Corpus in Capital Cases, an organ of the Judicial Conference of the United States chaired by retired Justice Lewis F. Powell, Jr. The Committee has come to be known as the Powell Committee.

[88] See 45 Crim. L. Rep. (BNA) 3239–3245 (September 27, 1989).

out "singling out" capital cases for special treatment. What must be recognized is that the delay caused by habeas litigation in capital cases is often a direct product of habeas retroactivity. A common scenario looks like this: The state sets an execution date. A few days before the scheduled execution, the defendant files a federal habeas petition in the district court, raising one or more colorable constitutional claims in an effort to get a stay of execution. Unable to resolve the merits of the habeas petition before the scheduled execution, the district court or court of appeals grants a stay.[89] The standard review process, including a petition for certiorari to the Supreme Court, takes a year or more. Meanwhile, a year's worth of new constitutional criminal procedure decisions have been issued by the federal courts. Certiorari is denied, and the state sets a new execution date. Now the cycle begins again, with the defendant raising all of the "new law" claims based on the intervening year's decisions.

This potentially endless cycle of habeas review will be cut short, in most capital cases, by the *Teague* doctrine. Because the definition of "new law" in *Teague* is so broad, the federal courts will find it easy to dismiss second or subsequent habeas petitions on the ground that the claims contained therein are based on "new law." Alternatively, petitions raising claims not based on "new law" will be easily dismissed as a successive petition or an abuse of the writ. Either way, the courts will be able to dismiss such petitions quickly enough to avoid the need for a stay of execution. Without a stay of execution, the cycle ends.

The only "new law" claims that will entitle a capital defendant to relief on a second or subsequent habeas petition will be those that fit within one of the exceptions to the *Teague* doctrine. Thus, the only second or subsequent petitions that will require a stay of execution will be those raising a substantial claim that likely fits within one of the exceptions. Of course, one of the exceptions, after *Penry*, includes all substantive Eighth Amendment challenges to the validity of the death penalty for particular classes of defendants or crimes. And the exception for claims based on procedures without which there is a substantial likelihood that an innocent defendant would be

---

[89]In Barefoot v. Estelle, 463 U.S. 880 (1983), the Supreme Court authorized the lower federal courts to adopt procedures for expedited review of capital habeas cases on motions for stays of execution. However, a stay will be granted where the defendant makes a "substantial showing of the denial of [a] federal right" and where a stay is required to prevent the case from becoming moot. *Id.* at 893.

convicted will also be triggered by some "new law" decisions in the capital context. But these exceptions will likely apply to only one or two decisions each Term, and not all capital defendants will be entitled to relief under such decisions. In most capital cases, the *Teague* doctrine will eliminate the need for federal courts to spend much time reviewing second or subsequent petitions, and will thereby avoid the cycle of habeas review.

IV. Teague and the Development of Federal Constitutional Rules of Criminal Procedure

Perhaps the most far-reaching consequence of *Teague* will be its institutional effect on the development of federal constitutional rules of criminal procedure. The extent of this effect cannot be estimated with precision at the present time. Nevertheless, it is quite possible that *Teague*, because of its relocation of responsibility among the various institutions that participate in the development of constitutional criminal procedure, will tip the sensitive criminal procedure balance toward the societal interest in preventing and punishing crime, and away from the rights of the individual criminal defendant.[90]

The constitutional criminal procedure "revolution" of the 1960s and 1970s took place almost exclusively in the federal courts. The Supreme Court, of course, during and even after Chief Justice Warren's tenure, led the way. But the lower federal courts played an important role as well, advancing the "revolution" directly by interpreting and applying the Court's new precedents, and indirectly by framing many criminal procedure issues for the Court's subsequent consideration.[91]

Today, the "revolution" has ended, and federal constitutional rules of criminal procedure are evolving at a much more leisurely pace. But it is still true that the federal courts, and particularly the lower courts, play a central role in the development of constitutional criminal procedure.

Meanwhile, the inclinations of state courts to expand, or to protect vigilantly, the rights of defendants vary widely. In recent years, when many federal courts have become less sympathetic to defendants' rights, some state courts have interpreted their state constitutions to

---

[90]See Packer, The Limits of the Criminal Sanction, 149–73 (1968).

[91]See Cover & Aleinikoff, Dialectical Federalism: Habeas Corpus and the Court, 86 Yale L.J. 1035 (1977).

provide greater protection for defendants than the comparable federal constitutional provisions.[92] Other state courts, however, continue to construe both their state constitutions and the federal constitution narrowly, recognizing defendants' claims only when compelled to do so by controlling precedent.[93] The views of these courts may reflect hostility toward defendants or simply the inevitable effect of institutional differences between the federal and state courts.[94]

After *Teague* and *Penry*, the lower federal courts will find themselves significantly less capable of participating meaningfully in the development of federal constitutional rules of criminal procedure. Outside the context of the Fourth Amendment, most of the opportunities for the lower federal courts to declare "new rules" of constitutional criminal procedure, or to expound on the meaning or application of such "new rules," arise in federal habeas cases. This is because there are many more state criminal prosecutions than federal ones, and because state procedures vary more than do federal procedures, thus raising more interesting and difficult criminal procedure issues.

The institutional effect of *Teague* will be to deprive the lower federal courts of most of their opportunities to make "new law" in federal habeas cases, or at least to make "new law" in a criminal defendant's favor. And, of course, the lower federal courts do not have the power to review state criminal cases on direct appeal. Thus, *Teague* will shift the primary responsibility for the development of federal rules of constitutional criminal procedure, in the sense of interpreting and applying new Supreme Court precedents and framing issues for the Court's consideration, from the lower federal courts

---

[92]See Latzer, Limits of the New Federalism: State Court Responses, 14 Search & Seizure L. Rep. 89 (1987) (listing state courts that have rejected narrow Supreme Court interpretations of the Fourth Amendment); see generally Brennan, State Constitutions and the Protection of Individual Rights, 90 Harv. L. Rev. 489 (1977).

[93]See Bradley, Are State Courts Enforcing the Fourth Amendment? A Preliminary Study, 77 Geo. L.J. 251 (1988) (suggesting that state courts in Georgia, and perhaps in Arizona and South Carolina, have stopped enforcing the Fourth Amendment since Stone v. Powell, 428 U.S. 465 (1976), removed such claims from federal habeas review).

[94]See Neuborne, The Myth of Parity, 90 Harv. L. Rev. 1105, 1115–28 (1977); see also Chemerinsky, Parity Reconsidered: Defining a Role for the Federal Judiciary, 36 U.C.L.A. L. Rev. 233 (1988); Redish, Judicial Parity, Litigant Choice, and Democratic Theory: A Comment on Federal Jurisdiction and Constitutional Rights, 36 U.C.L.A. L. Rev. 329 (1988); Chemerinsky, Federal Courts, State Courts, and the Constitution: A Rejoinder to Professor Redish, 36 U.C.L.A. L. Rev. 369 (1988).

to the state courts. Only the Court itself will be able to "converse" with the state courts on issues of constitutional criminal procedure.[95]

The increase in recent years in prosecutions for federal crimes, such as drug and white-collar offenses, will provide the lower federal courts with some opportunities to declare "new law." This will be true especially in areas of constitutional criminal procedure that are likely to arise in federal criminal cases, such as constitutional rules relating to grand jury practice. And the exceptions to the *Teague* rule will allow some federal habeas cases involving "new law" issues to get into the lower federal courts. Nevertheless, by removing from the scope of federal habeas most claims of state prisoners that are based on "new law," *Teague* will greatly reduce the opportunities for the lower federal courts to advance the development of constitutional criminal procedure.

The shifting of primary responsibility for the development of constitutional criminal procedure from the lower federal courts to the state courts will likely produce two long-term effects. First, it will produce more conflicts in the interpretation and application of criminal procedure rules, because the lower federal courts will no longer be able to use federal habeas to discourage the states in a single federal circuit from adopting different points of view. Second, and more importantly, it will alter, at least in some states, the degree of procedural protection afforded defendants. In states where the state courts are more sympathetic to defendants than the federal courts, there will be no such effect, because those state courts can already provide added protection under their state constitutions. But where the state courts are less sympathetic than their federal counterparts, defendants will suffer, because the unsympathetic state courts will control the interpretation and application of both the state *and* the federal constitutions. It is in this sense that *Teague* may tip the criminal procedure balance toward crime control and away from the rights of the individual defendant.

IV. Conclusion

In *Teague v. Lane* and *Penry v. Lynaugh*, the Supreme Court did what commentators have been suggesting for a long time—a majority of the Court agreed upon a single, coherent theory that explains

---

[95] See Cover & Aleinikoff, note 91 *supra*, at 1052–54.

the purpose of federal habeas corpus review of state criminal convictions. As I have explained in this article, the full impact of the Court's
new vision of federal habeas may surprise a great many people. Perhaps the Court, or Congress, will ultimately decide to modify the
Teague habeas retroactivity rule and ameliorate some of the effects I
have identified. In the meantime, however, the *Teague* rule will likely
force courts, litigants, and commentators to rethink their entire approach to issues of habeas law and practice.

HENRY P. MONAGHAN

HARMLESS ERROR AND THE
VALID RULE REQUIREMENT

Nearly a decade ago in the pages of this journal, in discussing the
nature of overbreadth challenges, I drew attention to what may be
characterized as the "valid rule requirement." A defendant in a coercive action always has standing to challenge the rule actually applied
to him. This means that he can resist sanctions unless they are imposed in accordance with a constitutionally valid rule, whether or not
his own conduct is constitutionally privileged.[1] The valid rule requirement focuses upon the rule as applied to the defendant by the
jury instructions.[2] In *Pope v. Illinois*[3] the Court held that harmless error analysis could be applied to jury instructions that contained a
constitutionally infirm liability-imposing rule. Four dissenting justices thought that this result violated the defendant's Sixth Amendment right to trial by jury.[4] For me, the difficulty is elsewhere, and
Pope provides an occasion for further reflection on the valid rule re-

---

Henry P. Monaghan is Harlan Fiske Stone Professor of Constitutional Law, Columbia University.

[1] Monaghan, Overbreadth, 1981 Supreme Court Review 1, 4–14. See also Monaghan,
Third Party Standing, 86 Colum. L. Rev. 277 (1984). The Supreme Court has referred to this
proposition approvingly but only in a passing manner in a footnote in New York v. Ferber, 458
U.S. 747, 768 n. 21 (1982).

[2] See, for example, Terminiello v. Chicago, 337 U.S. 1 (1949); Stromberg v. California, 283
U.S. 359 (1931). See also DeJonge v. Oregon, 299 U.S. 353, 362 (1937). The death penalty
cases provide particularly good examples of the point that the issue is how a reasonable jury
would have interpreted the instructions. Penry v. Lynaugh, 109 S.Ct. 2934, 2945–49 (1989).

[3] 481 U.S. 497 (1987).

[4] *Id.* at 507–11. *Pope* arose in the state courts. For convenience, however, I refer to the Sixth
Amendment, because the substance of that requirement is imposed on the states by the Four-
teenth Amendment. See Apodaca v. Oregon, 406 U.S. 404, 411 (1972); Blanton v. City of
North Las Vegas, 109 S.Ct. 1289, 1291 n. 4 (1989).

quirement. Is harmless error analysis ever appropriate when a state court conviction rests upon a constitutionally infirm rule? My conclusion is that it is not. This paper is an account of my difficulties in addressing this seemingly rather straightforward question.

I. The Valid Rule Requirement

The claim that the Constitution forbids the imposition of sanctions except in accordance with a constitutionally valid rule, whether or not the defendant's conduct is itself constitutionally privileged seems to me embedded in our conception of the "rule of law." Its operation can be illustrated by reference to the Due Process Clauses.[5] Settled doctrine has it that these Clauses prohibit substantively unreasonable legislation. Of course, determinations of this nature take their content from our social context. Thus, for us, "[g]overnment control of harmless actions like whistling in one's room" could not be justified as a "technique to induce unquestioning obedience to government authority."[6] Accordingly, a statute that prohibited "whistling in any building" would have a substantial number of invalid applications. Suppose that a defendant were charged under such a statute and the evidence showed that he intentionally whistled in the middle of a judicial proceeding and materially interfered with the proceeding. While this conduct is not itself independently privileged, the conviction would be constitutionally infirm were the state courts to affirm jury charges that stated that the fact of whistling sufficed to violate the statute.[7]

From this premise, I argued that neither need nor justification exists for treating the First Amendment overbreadth doctrine as a special standing doctrine. In an overbreadth challenge, the litigant invokes only his own right; he insists upon the application of a sub-

---

[5]The Equal Protection Clause provides perhaps an even better illustration of the thesis. It is no answer to an equal protection challenge to argue that the conduct regulated is not independently privileged.

[6]Greenawalt, Free Speech Justifications, 89 Colum. L. Rev. 119, 121 (1989).

[7]This is not a "no-evidence" case within the compass of Thompson v. Louisville, 362 U.S. 199 (1960), See Hart & Wechsler's The Federal Courts and the Federal System (3rd ed., 1988) (Bator et al., eds.) at 677–82 (cited below as Hart & Wechsler). Like *Thompson*, I assume that the conduct is not independently privileged, Hart & Wechsler, *id.* 679; but unlike *Thompson*, I accept the fact that the terms of the regulatory rule, as defined by state law, *id.* at 679, violate the Due Process Clause. For an elaborate discussion, see Neumann, The Constitutional Requirement of "Some Evidence," 25 San. Diego L. Rev. 633 (1988).

stantive constitutional rule that requires a high degree of specificity and substantial congruence between means and ends.[8]

The undemanding nature of rational basis review and the presumption of separability deprive the valid rule requirement of significant operational bite.[9] But being clear on the underlying theory is quite important where heightened scrutiny is required. The Supreme Court is not, and the reason is its frequently expressed belief that an overbreadth litigant invokes a special rule of standing. For the Court, when the defendant asserts an overbreadth challenge, he is in effect private attorney general—or perhaps a bounty hunter—who invokes a judicially fashioned license to raise the rights of others (imaginary others, at that). This understanding has led to much puzzling and unstable doctrine.[10] Moreover, this understanding has led the Court to revoke its license when the challenged statute has been repealed or amended. Indeed, *Pope* itself rejected an overbreadth challenge on this ground.[11]

The consequences of the Court's attitude surfaced in stark terms in *Massachusetts v. Oakes*,[12] decided late in the last term. The defendant had been charged with taking photographs of his partially nude physically mature fourteen-year-old stepdaughter. The highest state court reversed the conviction on the ground that the statute was substantially overbroad. After the grant of certiorari, the statute was amended. Justice O'Connor's four-person opinion declined to permit an overbreadth challenge. She characterized overbreadth challenges as an "exception to the general rule" that a litigant can raise only his own rights,[13] and concluded that such challenges were "inappropriate if the statute being challenged has been amended or repealed."[14] Justice O'Connor saw nothing "unconstitionally offensive" in such a conclusion, because the former statute "cannot chill protected ex-

---

[8]Monaghan, Overbreadth, note 1 *supra*.

[9]The looseness in fit between ends and means tolerated by the rational basis test and the frequent use of the separability technique reduce the importance of the requirement that the rule actually applied to the defendant be constitutional.

[10]See, for example, Hart and Wechsler, note 7 *supra*, at 189, 194–95, and note 5 (discussing the rise and fall of the claim that a litigant whose own conduct is constitutionally privileged cannot mount an overbreadth challenge). For other examples of confusion, see Monaghan, Overbreadth, note 1 *supra*, at 23–24, 27–30.

[11]481 U.S. at 501–502.

[12]109 S.Ct. 2633 (1989).

[13]*Id.* at 2637. My article was cited for this proposition.

[14]*Ibid.*

pression in the future."[15] For her, "overbreadth question . . . become[s] moot as a practical matter."[16] Justice O'Connor's plurality concluded that a remand was in order to permit the defendant to make an as applied challenge.

Part I of the concurring and dissenting opinion of Justice Scalia, joined by four other Justices on this point, rejected Justice O'Connor's analysis:[17]

> I do not agree with the plurality's conclusion that the overbreadth defense is unavailable when the statute alleged to run afoul of that doctrine has been amended to eliminate the basis for the overbreadth challenge. It seems to me strange judicial theory that a conviction initially invalid can be resuscitated by postconviction alteration of the statute under which it was obtained. Indeed, I would even think it strange judicial theory that an act which is lawful when committed (because the statute that proscribes it is overbroad) can become retroactively unlawful if the statute is amended *preindictment*.

Justice Scalia's view is without citation of authority or indeed analysis. But it should be noted that his intuitions are not premised on some crude cost/benefit assessment about whether the supposed deterrence underpinnings of overbreadth challenges would be marginally impaired if the overbreadth challenge is denied here. He seems to be seeking far more fundamental ground. Yet less than one week later Justice Scalia wrote an opinion for the Court in which he insisted both that overbreadth is a special rule of standing and that as applied standing is the equivalent of a claim of constitutionally privileged conduct.[18] I think both propositions are wrong.

This brings me to *Pope* itself. That case arose out of the conviction of a part-time adult book store attendant for violating the Illinois obscenity statute. Earlier, in *Miller v. California*,[19] the Court had reformulated its well-known tripartite test for determining whether material is obscene. *Miller*'s "social value" prong requires a deter-

---

[15]*Id.* at 2638.

[16]*Ibid.*

[17]*Id.* at 2639. However, in Part II of his opinion, *id.* at 2640–41, Justice Scalia, writing for himself and Justice Blackmun, rejected the overbreadth challenge on the merit. Both Justices concurred that remand on the as applied challenge was appropriate.

[18]For example, Justice Scalia's opinion in Board of Trustees of State University v. Fox, 109 S.Ct. 3028, 3036 (1989), contains both assertions.

[19]413 U.S. 15 (1973).

mination "whether the work, taken as a whole, lacks serious literary, artistic, political, or scientific value."[20] The *Pope* jury was instructed to make this determination based upon state-wide community standards.[21] This instruction was erroneous: "The proper inquiry," said the Court, "is not whether an ordinary member of any given community would find serious [social value], but whether a reasonable person would [so] find."[22]

After having found that "[t]he instruction at issue in this case . . . unconstitutional," the Court divided sharply over whether the conviction was nonetheless "subject to salvage if the erroneous instruction is found to be harmless error."[23] A bare majority concluded that in the circumstances such an analysis was appropriate, and it ordered a remand on that basis.[24]

---

[20]413 U.S. at 24. The other requirements are (*a*) an appeal to prurient interests (*b*) that is patently offensive when measured by contemporary community standards.

[21]481 U.S. at 499.

[22]481 U.S. at 500–501. Justice Scalia concurred with regard to harmless error because he saw no real difference between the instruction given and the Court's substantive standard. *Id.* at 504. See also Allen, Unexplored Aspects of the Theory of the Right to Trial by Jury, 66 Wash. U. L. Q. 33, 40 (1988) (describing the Court's standard as "virtually incomprehensible . . . [or] inordinately silly [because] the values of the reasonable person from the community and community values will be virtually indentical.").

[23]481 U.S. at 501. This disposition limits Marks v. United States, 430 U.S. 188 (1977), not discussed in *Pope*. There, as in *Pope*, the jury was misinstructed on the social value test. The government argued that the error was harmless because the court of appeals had concluded that, under any standard, the material was obscene. The Supreme Court's response was a judicial conclusion "is not an adequate substitute for the decision in the first instance of a properly instructed jury as to this important element of the offense under 18 U.S.C. §1465," *id.* at 196–97 n.12.

[24]The Court's attention was focused entirely on the Sixth Amendment aspects of the problem. No attention was given to the "constitutional fact" dimensions of the case. Bose Corp. v. Consumers Union, 466 U.S. 485 (1984). See Monaghan, Constitutional Fact Review, 85 Colum. L. Rev. 229 (1985). Whether viewed as a question of law, or of law-application (constitutional fact), the question whether a book possesses social value in the eyes of a "reasonable person" seems to be a constitutional fact upon which the defendant is entitled to the Court's independent judgment. See Monaghan, First Amendment Due Process, 83 Harv. L. Rev. 518, 530–31 (1970).

In *Pope*, the Court began its opinion by stating that *Miller* had mandated a three prong determination by the "trier of fact." 481 U.S. at 498. It is customary to submit the issue of social value to the jury, as one of the elements of the state law offense, and such a submission may very well be required by the Sixth Amendment. But surely it is not evident that the First Amendment requires submission to the jury of an issue that the jury cannot authoritatively resolve (subject to conventional standards on post-verdict motions), at least if that issue is not inextricably intertwined with issues that must be submitted to the jury. See Dennis v. United States, 341 U.S. 494, 511–15 (1951), a criminal prosecution where the judge refused to submit the issue of whether the speech constituted a clear and present danger, and over two dissents, his decision was affirmed on appeal.

II. Harmless Error

Harmless error doctrine reflects the general perception that "the well-being of the law encompasses tolerance for harmless error in an imperfect world."[25] The doctrine has received its closest examination in the jury trial context. Here, special concern exists that judicial toleration of harmless error is not a license for judicial invasion of the issue-resolving province constitutionally reserved to the jury.[26] Nonetheless, here too the Court's animating principle is that error free proceedings cannot be an inexorable demand.[27]

Of course, errors of constitutional dimension might have been treated differently and understood to require automatic reversal. Over two decades ago, in *Chapman v. California*,[28] the Supreme Court formally rejected that view: most constitutional errors were subject to harmless error analysis.[29] But, as a prominent judge writing shortly after the decision noted, the standard articulated by the Court for determining whether a constitutional error was harmless came very "close to [stating a rule of] automatic reversal:"[30] "Before [such an] error can be held harmless, the court must be able to declare a belief that it was harmless beyond reasonable doubt."[31] While by no means free from ambiguity, the Court's formulation seemed decidedly jury oriented. Error that increased the likelihood of a guilty verdict by a reasonable jury could not be disregarded, whatever the strength of the untainted evidence of guilt.[32]

---

[25]Traynor, The Riddle of Harmless Error, Introduction (1970).

[26]See Harte-Hanks Communications v. Connaughton, 109 S.Ct. 2678 (1989).

[27]See U.S.C. §2111, and Fed. R. Cr. Proc. 52(a), Fed. R. Civ. Proc. 61, and Fed. R. Ev. 103(a), all of which require use of harmless error analysis.

[28]386 U.S. 18 (1967).

[29]*Id.* at 21–22.

[30]Traynor, note 25 *supra*, at 43. In *Chapman*, the Court assumed that it had the duty to specify the actual content of the harmless error rule, despite the existence of the statute and rules mentioned in note 27 *supra*. Moreover, the Court rejected Justice Harlan's view that the issue was one of state law. *Id.* at 20–21. See Monaghan, Constitutional Common Law, 89 Harv. L. Rev. 1, 21 (1975) (*Chapman* should be viewed as a federal common law rule).

[31]*Id.* at 24.

[32]The conclusion that only constitutional errors that have only marginal impact on the jury's guilt-determining deliberations may be ignored follows from *Chapman*'s endorsement of the standard expressed in Fahey v. Connecticut, 375 U.S. 85, 86–87 (1963): "There is little, if any, difference between our statement in Fahey v. Connecticut about 'whether there is a reasonable possibility that the evidence complained of might have contributed to the conviction' and requiring the beneficiary of a constitutional error to prove beyond a reasonable doubt that the error complained of did not contribute to the verdict obtained." 386 U.S. at 24. See also Traynor, note 25 *supra*, at 43–44; Field, Assessing the Harmlessness of Federal Constitutional

But *Chapman* did not evolve into a rule of nearly automatic reversal; over time the Court's cases reflected increased tensions, as the Court moved uncertainly among such variables as the nature of the error, the error's probable impact on the jury's ultimate determination, and the Court's own independent assessment of guilt. Increasingly, the last factor assumed a dominant role.[33]

Almost two decades after *Chapman*, the Court undertook a major restatement and reformulation of doctrine in *Rose v. Clark*.[34] First, the Court reinforced *Chapman's* holding that harmless error analysis should be applied to most claims of constitutional error, stating that given "an impartial adjudicator," "a strong presumption" exists to that effect. Then, while still professing a strict adherence to *Chapman*, *Rose* reformulated the operative standard:[35]

> The thrust of the many constitutional rules governing the conduct of criminal trials is to ensure that those trials lead to fair and correct judgments. Where a reviewing court can find that the record developed at trial establishes guilt beyond reasonable doubt, the interest in fairness has been satisfied and the judgment should be affirmed.

Operationally, *Rose's* "correct judgment" is judge centered: the relevant judicial inquiry is the sufficiency of the evidence on guilt.[36] The question is whether (assuming a fair trial) a directed verdict against the defendant would have been proper on the basis of the evidence untainted by the constitutional error.[37] This reformulation mirrored

---

Error—A Process in Need of a Rationale, 125 U. Pa. L. Rev. 15, 16 (1976) (whether the error contributed to the result should be decisive, not the sufficiency of the other evidence of guilt).

[33]For example, Stacy & Dayton, Rethinking Harmless Constitutional Error, 88 Colum. L. Rev. 79, 80 (1988) (noting tendency of the Court to invoke harmless error analysis when satisfied of factual guilt).

[34]478 U.S. 570 (1986).

[35]481 U.S. at 579. Justice Powell, the author of *Rose*, prefigured this guilt-oriented approach in his dissenting opinion in Connecticut v. Johnson, 460 U.S. 73, 97 n.5 (1983). Saltzburg, The Harm of Harmless Error, 59 Va. L. Rev. 988 (1973). See also Kornstein, A Bayesian Model of Harmless Error, 5 J. Legal Studies 121, 131 (1976). It is of course possible to formulate harmless error doctrine so that both probable impact and reasonable doubt analysis are required rather than only one of the two. LaFave & Israel, Criminal Procedure 1008 (1985).

[36]This leaves open the question of whether the "other" evidence should be viewed from the prosecution's perspective or the defendant's. Although concerned with an analytically distinct issue, Jackson v. Virginia, 443 U.S. 307 (1979), suggests that that the proper perspective is that of the verdict-winner, the prosecutor. But this seems wrong. Defendant's right to trial by jury is compromised unless the evidence is considered from the defendant's perspective. See Stacy & Dayton, note 33 *supra*, at 131–38.

[37]To be sure, *Rose* itself acknowledged that a judge cannot direct a verdict in a criminal case. 478 U.S. at 578. Nonetheless, that seems to be the general standard to be applied in determin-

the Court's general concern with preserving the results of a fair trial.[38]

Rose also sought to give a principled explanation for the existing per se cases—"exceptional"[39] situations in which the nature of the constitutional violation alone precludes inquiry into the sufficiency of the evidence concerning defendant's guilt. The Court sorted the exceptions into two categories: first, errors that compromised the defendant's right to a fair trial. The explanation—only partially convincing—is that here the criminal trial "cannot reliably serve its function as a vehicle for determination of guilt or innocence."[40] Interestingly, the Court's "reliability" explanation seems to give the "fair trial" exception very limited independent content; operationally, judicial concern with reliability invites focus on the adequacy of the record, with the question being whether that record is sufficient to leave reviewing court convinced of defendant's guilt. If so, there was a fair trial.[41]

Second, the Court explained that because of the Sixth Amendment's clear command to afford jury trials in serious criminal cases, judicial action that is the equivalent of directing a verdict for the prosecution cannot be harmless because "the wrong entity judged the defendant guilty."[42] Unless further elaboration is provided, the

---

ing whether to set aside the jury's verdict because of constitutional error. See also Burger v. Kemp, 483 U.S. 776, 783–87 (1987).

[38]See in particular Strickland v. Washington, 466 U.S. 668 (1984) (demonstration of prejudice an element of establishing violation of Sixth Amendment assistance of counsel); Murray v. Carrier, 477 U.S. 478 (1986) (impact of procedural defaults in state courts on availability of habeas corpus). See also Teague v. Lane, 109 S.Ct. 1060 (1989), and Penry v. Lynaugh, 109 S.Ct. 2934 (1989), limiting habeas corpus challenges.

[39]See Rose v. Clark, 478 U.S. at 578. These situations "are the exception and not the rule."

[40]*Id.* at 577–78. See also Satterwhite v. Texas, 108 S.Ct. 1792, 1797 (1988) (concern with errors that "pervade the entire proceeding"). Reliability is the key word here. I recognize that in many cases the prejudice from fair trial errors is often hard to detect, and thus the record will be too infirm to permit the appellate court to check that fact finding by a directed verdict standard. Surely, any doubt on this score would favor the defendant. But to acknowledge the existence of high risk situations provides only limited explanatory power: on many occasions the record will not be compromised, and guilt may be still plain beyond a rational doubt. Nonetheless, the Court has long been resolute on this point. For example, a litigant has a right to an impartial tribunal "no matter what the evidence was against him." Tumey v. Ohio, 273 U.S. 510, 535 (1927).

[41]Indeed, the equivalence of fair trial and reliable trial seems to be the situation in *Rose* itself. See 478 U.S. at 579 n.7 (". . . error in this case did not affect the composition of the record"). Note should be made here of the Court's tendency to define rights themselves in terms of reliable outcomes. *E.g.*, Strickland v. Washington, 466 U.S. 668, 686–87 (1984) (effective assistance of counsel guarantee satisfied if "a trial whose result is reliable"); Pennsylvania v. Ritchie, 108 S.Ct. 989, 1002 (1987) (discovery); United States v. Bagley, 473 U.S. 667, 678 (1985).

[42]478 U.S. at 578.

Court's "wrong entity" analysis provides little more than a description of the error, not an explanation of why the error cannot be harmless. After all, judges can fairly determine guilt.[43] Nonetheless, the "wrong entity" exception possesses a strong grip on the judicial imagination. It was twice endorsed in strong language at the close of the 1988 term.[44]

Statterwhite v. Texas,[45] a death penalty case, contains the Court's most recent extended discussion of harmless error. *Rose* was drawn upon for the proposition that harmless error analysis is applicable to Sixth Amendment violations except where "the violations pervade the entire procedure."[46] Interestingly, however, when it came time to define the meaning of harmless error, the Court ignored *Rose* and cited *Chapman*: "The question, however, is not whether the legally admitted evidence was sufficient to support the death sentence, which we assume it was, but rather, whether the State has proved 'beyond a reasonable doubt that the error complained of did not contribute to the verdict obtained.'"[47] The long-term significance of this aspect of *Satterwhite* outside the death penalty remains to be seen.

Seemingly, both the jury-centered *Chapman* and the judge—centered *Rose* formulations exclude the "value" of any specific constitutional right from being assessed as an independent variable in its own right, except for rights that bear upon a fair trial before a "proper adjudicator."[48] Accordingly, the third party deterrence rationale of the Fourth Amendment's exclusionary rule receives only incidental and erratic vindication.[49] Nonetheless, a small but significant category of decisions quite clearly make the "value" of the con-

---

[43]It is a commonplace that judges and jurors are not interchangeable institutions. But the move from that observation to no harmless error requires explication. See United States v. Kerley, 838 F.2d 932, 937 (7th Cir. 1988) (Posner, J.).

[44]See Carella v. California, 109 S.Ct. 2419, 2421–22 (1989) (concurring opinion). The wrong entity analysis is apparently not limited to the jury. In Gomez v. United States, 109 S.Ct. 2237 (1989), the Court held that a magistrate could not preside over the selection of a criminal jury. The court rejected a harmless error claim: "Equally basic is a defendant's right to have all critical stages of a criminal trial conducted by a person with jurisdiction to preside." *Id.* at 2248.

[45]108 S.Ct. 1792 (1988).

[46]*Id.* at 1797.

[47]*Id.* at 1798.

[48]See *Rose*, 478 U.S. at 586–89 (Stevens, J., concurring); see generally Stacy & Dayton, note 33 *supra*.

[49]Error in admission of evidence obtained in violation of the Fourth Amendment is harmless if the other evidence suffices to establish guilt. Chambers v. Maroney, 399 U.S. 42, 52–53 (1970), cited in Rose v. Clark, 478 U.S. at 576–77. See generally Loewy, Police Obtained Evidence and the Constitution: Distinguishing Unconstitutionally Obtained Evidence from Unconstitutionally Used Evidence, 87 Mich. L. Rev. 907 (1989).

stitutional right alone determinative.[50] Race discrimination in selecting the grand and petit juries is a striking example.[51] So, too, is the Court's categorical refusal to treat admission of a coerced confession as harmless.[52] Other examples can be cited. *Penson v. Ohio*,[53] involving a violation of the *"Anders"* rule on the responsibilities of a indigent's appellate counsel,[54] is the most recent such instance.[55] We shall see that the overbreadth doctrine itself is an excellent illustration of this category, at least in the Court's mind.

My view is that the real explanation for most of these per se cases, as well as for much of the fair trial and "wrong entity" exceptions recognized in *Rose*, is not that prejudice from the violation is hard to detect. No doubt that is part of it.[56] But precisely the opposite perception seems more to the point: in these situations the Court all too frequently is faced with a case where the defendant's guilt is plain beyond contradiction. Thus, application of harmless error analysis might effectively render the relevant constitutional commands judicially unenforceable.

III. The Sixth Amendment and Harmless Error

Pope drew upon *Rose* not only for its general guilt-oriented approach to harmless error, but also for an even closer parallel.[57] *Rose* itself involved a defective jury instruction, one that was assumed to

---

[50]Hart & Wechsler, note 7 *supra*, at 637 n.6 states: "Note that a harmless error rule not only measures the degree of risk that a particular error actually had an adverse effect; it also defines the extent to which such a risk is accepted as permissible. Isn't this latter judgment a function of the importance attached to vindicating the underlying constitutional right? . . . If so, is not the definition of 'harmless error' inseparable from the task of defining the scope of that constitutional right?"

[51]Vasquez v. Hillery, 474 U.S. 254, 262 (1986) (rejecting harmless error analysis in connection with racial discrimination in selection of grand jury).

[52]The Court's effort in *Rose*, 478 U.S. at 578 n.6, to treat the admission of such a confession as invariably "abor[ting] the basic trial process . . ." is wholly unpersuasive. See Stacy and Dayton, note 33 *supra*, at 102–104. See Colorado v. Connelly, 479 U.S. 157 (1986) (involuntary confession admissible absent police misconduct).

[53]109 S.Ct. 346 (1988).

[54]Anders v. California, 386 U.S. 738 (1967).

[55]See also McKaskle v. Wiggins, 465 U.S. 168, 177 n.8 (1984), suggesting that violation of right to self representation is not subject to harmless error analysis; Gray v. Mississippi, 107 S.Ct. 2045, 2056 (1987) (plurality opinion) (exclusion of "death qualified juror" from sentencing jury).

[56]For example, *Vasquez*, note 51 *supra*, purports to rest on the difficulty of ascertaining prejudice, 474 U.S. at 263–64. See also *Rose*, 481 U.S. at 579 n.7, but this claim seems quite strained.

[57]478 U.S. 570 (1986). *Pope* is not a case where taken as a whole the instructions provide a

have impermissibly shifted the burden of proof on the issue of malice.[58] Harmless error analysis was thought acceptable because the instruction "did not entirely preclude the jury from considering the element of malice," and given the predicate facts that the jury was required to find, "no rational jury," properly instructed, could have failed to find malice.[59] In *Pope*, both elements were equally present:

> Similarly, [here] the jurors were not precluded from considering the question of value: they were informed that to convict they must find, among other things, that the magazines petitioners sold were utterly without redeeming social value[60] . . . . [I]f a reviewing court concludes that no rational juror, if properly instructed, could find value in the magazines, the convictions should stand.[61]

Justice Stevens's dissenting opinion objected that in a criminal case no court is free to decide that, if asked, a jury would have found something it did not find. For him, harmless error analysis "may enable a court to remove a taint from proceedings in order to *preserve* a jury's findings, but it cannot constitutionally *supplement* those findings."[62]

The difference between the Court and the dissent on the Sixth Amendment is exceedingly narrow. For both, the jury is a federally mandated mechanism to adjudge substantive claims defined by state or federal law,[63] and no state may pursue a policy of subverting the

---

constitutionally valid rule—that is, where it is plain beyond doubt that any alleged defects in a particular aspect of the instructions were adequately cured by the instruction considered as a whole. Mistakes, even of consitutional dimension, are properly ignored in the latter case. Greer v. Miller, 483 U.S. 756, 766 (1987); Curtis Publishing Co. v. Butts, 388 U.S. 130 (1967), seems explicable on that basis.

[58]In *Rose* the Court assumed that this was the effect of the instruction. 478 U.S. at 576 n.5. For a replay of *Rose*, see Carella v. California, 109 S.Ct. 2419 (1989).

[59]*Rose*, 478 U.S. at 580–81.

[60]In this respect, the jury was given a charge more favorable than that required by *Miller*, note 19 *supra*. *Miller* rejected the "utterly with redeeming social value" standard, a standard that had considerable support in the case law.

[61]481 U.S. at 503.

[62]481 U.S. at 509–10; 109 S.Ct. 2419 (1989). At the end of the last term the *Rose/Pope* issue was revisited. Carella v. California, note 58 *supra*, like *Rose*, involved an instructional error that unconstitutionally shifted the burden of proof. Largely on the authority of *Rose*, the case was remanded for harmless error analysis. Four justices concurred in an opinion by Justice Scalia, emphasizing that for them impermissible burden-shifting instructions are bad because they amount to a directed verdict; like Justice Stevens, Justice Scalia looked askance at judicial authority to supplement jury finding in criminal cases. Turning to *Pope*, Justice Scalia said that the effect of "misdescription of an element of the offense. . . deprives the jury of its fact finding role. . ." 109 S.Ct. at 2423.

[63]For the entire Court in *Pope*, in assessing whether the error was harmless, nothing whatever turns on the fact that the error complained of was itself of independent constitutional di-

jury's constitutionally prescribed role by withdrawing elements of the offense from its consideration. (The majority's emphasis in both *Rose* and *Pope* that the jury was not entirely precluded from consideration of the relevant issues responds to that concern.) Moreover, the Sixth Amendment requires that the jury be properly instructed on the essential elements of the offense,[64] and presumably, the "failure to charge correctly is not harmless [when] the verdict may have resulted from the incorrect instruction."[65]

To my mind, the dissent's complete rejection of harmless error analysis is unpersuasive. Surely it is too late to argue that the protection of the jury as a constitutionally mandated institution[66] calls for the elimination of all harmless error analysis.[67] Nor is the argument more compelling if viewed from the defendant's perspective. Any right based claims seem weak because of the law's fundamental ambivalence toward the jury. For example, the rules of evidence are infused with a pervasive distrust of the jury's intelligence and emotion.[68] Yet courts, particularly appellate courts, presume a rational jury that will act in accordance with the instructions given it.[69] They do not care very much about how a particular jury reached its

---

mension. Indeed, this seems generally true in harmless error analysis. Compare *Rose* and *Pope* with United States v. Lane, 474 U.S. 438, 444–50 (1986), and United States v. Mechanik, 475 U.S. 66, 71–72 (1986), and Traynor, note 25 *supra*, at 55.

[64]Cabana v. Bullock, 474 U.S. 376, 384–85 (1986). Of course, *Pope* imposes some limit on *Cabana*. See *Pope*, 481 U.S. at 503–4 n.7 (*Cabana* "no longer good authority" to the extent that it excludes harmless error analysis). See also Judge Posner's discussion United States v. Kerley, 838 F.2d 932, 938–39 (7th Cir. 1988).

[65]Brotherhood of Carpenters v. United States, 330 U.S. 395, 409 (1947).

[66]See also Matthews v. United States, 108 S.Ct. 883 (1988); Tull v. United States, 481 U.S. 412 (1987) (jury and civil liability).

[67]In Rose v. Clark, the Court pointed out that harmless error analysis had been applied to evidentiary rulings that affected the jury's decision-making role. 478 U.S. at 582 n.11. Moreover, other institutional changes should be noted. In light of the inroads already made on the traditional state criminal jury by decisions sanctioning nonunanimous verdicts by less than 12 persons, it is hard to believe that so inflexible a rule is necessary to protect the jury. In addition, both the civil and criminal juries have lost much of their constitutionally intended significance with the rise of administrative adjudication.

[68]Note, 98 Yale L.J. 187 n.1 (1989) (collecting sources).

[69]"[T]he theory under which jury instructions are given by trial courts and reviewed on appeal is that juries act in accordance with the instructions given them." City of Los Angeles v. Heller, 106 S.Ct. 1571, 1573 (1986); Mills v. Maryland, 108 S.Ct. 1860, 1867 (1988). See also Tanner v. United States, 107 S.Ct. 2739, 2745–51 (1987) (verdict cannot be impeached by proof of internal dynamics of jurors' conduct). Compare Resnik, On the Bias: Feminist Reconsideration of the Aspirations for Our Judges, 61 So. Cal. L. Rev. 1877, 1899–1903, 1937–38 (1988), with Alschuler, The Supreme Court and the Jury: Voir Dire, Peremptory Challenges, and the Review of Jury Verdicts, 59 U. Chi. L. Rev. 153, 221–29 (1989).

conclusion; in large measure, they care only about how their artifact—the rational jury—would act.[70] This premise may be challenged, but it is difficult to see how any other premise could be employed in a systematic way as a basis for judicial reasoning.[71] If that be true, *Pope*'s restrained "no rational juror" approach to jury instructions is an attractive one in the Sixth Amendment context.[72] But it does not dispose of a different objection, namely, that the state cannot impose sanctions except in accordance with a constitutionally valid rule.

IV. Harmless Error and the Valid Rule Requirement

Can a valid rule requirement claim complete immunity from harmless error analysis? The argument against such a proposition is that the right involved is not visibly more important than other rights that are subject to harmless error analysis. Moreover, the policies supporting a valid rule requirement are not rendered empty if harmless error analysis is let in: the requirement already receives significant indirect protection from other constitutional sources, such as

---

[70]Harrington v. California, 395 U.S. 250, 254 (1969) ("We of course do not know the jurors who sat. Our judgment must be based on . . . the minds of an average jury"). Schneble v. Florida, 405 U.S. 427, 432 (1972). See also Satterwhite v. Texas, 108 S.Ct. 1792 (1988); Mills v. Maryland, 108 S.Ct. 1860, 1866 (1988). Stacy and Dayton argue that on occasion the Court seems concerned with the particular jury, note 33 *supra*, at 128 and note 195, but the materials relied on strike me as unpersuasive.

[71]Professor Alschuler notes that the Court's positive attitude toward the jury is at its highest at the "back end" of the jury trial: when the verdict is in. Alschuler, note 69 *supra*, at 154. The "no rational juror" approach does not impinge upon the power of the jury (illustrated in the highly publicized North trial) to disregard the instructions and refuse to convict whatever the evidence. No right of the defendant is implicated: jury nullification is simply a situation where we prefer to be or necessarily must be not governed by rules. Strickland v. Washington, 466 U.S. 668, 695 (1984). Compare Stacy & Dayton, note 33 *supra*, at 138–42, arguing that jury nullification serves a more limited and structured function of implementing "legally irrelevant [but] fundamental community values." *Id.* at 142.

[72]The acceptability of the Court's analysis in *Pope* seems to me *a fortiori* in civil cases. Despite the Seventh Amendment command that "no fact tried by jury, shall be otherwise re-examined in any Court of the United States, than according to the rules of the common law," the issue resolving role of the jury has in fact been subjected to very considerable judicial interference. Judges can take the case entirely away from the jury on the the evidence both before and after its deliberations—on summary judgment, directed verdict, and judgment n.o.v. Moreover, the judge can order a new trial or a remittitur if sufficiently dissatisfied with the jury's verdict. See Schnapper, Judges against Juries—Appellate Review of Federal Civil Jury Verdicts, 1989 Wisc. L. Rev. 237 (persuasively arguing that current federal appellate review undercuts Seventh Amendment). Against this background, limited use of a "no rational juror" approach to jury instructions does not seriously compromise the institutional role of the jury, nor in any strong sense deny to a civil litigant a fundamental right.

the Sixth Amendment (as construed in both *Rose* and *Pope*), the due process requirement of fair warning, and, as will be shown, from First Amendment overbreadth doctrine.

These objections have force. Nonetheless, in the end I believe the harmless error analysis in this context is unsatisfying. Accordingly, conviction resting upon an invalid rule should be set aside.

First. Harmless error is centrally concerned with the question whether a court should vacate a jury finding that defendant's conduct violated a rule. But the rule itself is not the subject of dispute and the implications of saying that harmless error can be applied to a constitutionally infirm rule are unsatisfactory.[73] What does it mean to say to the defendant: "You were convicted under an unconstitutional rule, but it was only a little bit unconstitutional. Anyway, given the evidence before the trier of fact, you would certainly have been convicted under a valid rule"? To my mind, there are intractable difficulties with both the intelligibility and the containability of any such proposition.[74]

Surely a conviction under a constitutionally infirm provision cannot be saved as harmless error because the conduct shown would have justified defendant's conviction under another statutory provision.[75] Accordingly, the Court has consistently invalidated convictions when liability might have been predicated on the violation of either or both of two rules, one valid, the other not. For example, in

---

[73]Bollenbach v. United States, 326 U.S. 607, 615 (1946) (misdirection with respect to "the standard of guilt is not harmless").

[74]We are not considering a case where separation of a valid from an invalid basis of decision is possible. In those circumstances, something like harmless error analysis is followed. Thus, a good verdict on one count need not be annulled simply because it is joined with a bad one. The same principle can be applied in administrative law. Syracuse Peace Council v. F.C.C., 867 F.2d 654, 657 (D.C. 1989). Moreover, the Court's "causation" cases provide additional support for a separation approach, when separation of the good from the bad is possible. In Mount Health School District v. Doyle, 429 U.S. 274, 286–87 (1977) the plaintiff was discharged on two grounds, one of which was consitutuionally infirm under the First Amendment. The Court stressed the need "to formulate a test of causation which distinguishes between a result caused by a constitutional violation and one not so caused." *Id.* at 286. The Court's remand instructed the district court to determine "whether the Board had shown by the preponderance of the evidence that it would have reached the same decision as to respondent's employment even in the absence of the protected conduct." *Id.* at 287. See also Village of Arlington Heights v. Metropolitan Housing Dev. Corp., 429 U.S. 252, 270–71 n.21 (1977) (defendant could prove "that the same decision would have resulted even if the [racially] impermissible purpose had not been considered"); Price Waterhouse v. Hopkins, 109 S.Ct. 1775 (1989).

[75]DeJonge v. Oregon, 299 U.S. 353, 362 (1937), settled that long ago: "We must take the indictment as thus construed [by the state court]. Conviction upon a charge so made would be sheer denial of due process." Of course, the principle applies whether or not one of the statutes is infirm. See Cole v. Arkansas, 333 U.S. 196, 200–202 (1948), 338 U.S. 345, at 347–52.

Bacheldar v. Maryland[76] the jury returned a conviction after having been charged in three different forms, one of which contained a constitutionally defective rule under the First Amendment. The Court set aside the conviction because it was at least likely that the "convictions may have rested on the unconstitutional ground."[77] More recently, the Court said, "With respect to findings of guilt on criminal charges, the Court consistently has followed the rule that the jury's verdict must be set aside if it could be supported on one ground but not another, and the reviewing court was uncertain which of the two grounds was relied upon by the jury in reaching the verdict."[78] These cases cannot be said to foreclose all discussion, because they do not involve claims that harmless error analysis could be used to insulate the conviction under a constitutionally infirm rule from attack, that is, that even assuming the jury acted upon the constitutionally infirm ground, this error was harmless because no rational jury would have reached a different result under a valid rule. But the underlying principle of the decisions seems to me inconsistent with use of harmless error analysis. Their focus is on the content of the rule applied to the defendant, and their premise is that legitimate government requires application of a valid rule if sanctions are to be imposed.

Second. Close attention to *Pope*'s First Amendment aspects supports the perception that no room exists for a "the rule is only a wee bit unconstitutional" approach. The Court was satisfied that harmless error analysis would not "pose[ ] a threat" to First Amendment values because the offending statute had been replaced on the state's statute books.[79] But, of course, the deep premise of this reasoning is that (despite the guilt-oriented approach of *Rose v. Clark*) the First

---

[76]397 U.S. 564, 569–71 (1970).

[77]*Id.* at 571. This does not mean that the rule need be the same as that applied to defendant's neighbor. These state law deviations are immaterial unless they are so glaring as to invoke the line of authority generated by Yick Wo v. Hopkins, 118 U.S. 356 (1886).

[78]Mills v. Maryland, 108 S.Ct. 1860, 1866 (1988). See also Penry v. Lynaugh, 109 S.Ct. at 2949 (uncertainty in death penalty instruction).

[79]481 U.S. at 501. Invalidation "would not serve the purpose of preventing future prosecutions under a constitutionally defective standard." *Id.* at 501–2. Moreover, the Court observed that Pope could have been retried under the now-repealed statute "provided that the erroneous jury instruction was not repeated." *Id.* at 502. The dissenting justices offered no challenge to this analysis. Rather, to avoid its force, they urged a complete revamping of *Miller*'s criteria when adult obscenity was at stake. *Id.* at 511–13. The Court noted that the defendant "could not plausibly claim that the repealed statute failed to give them notice that the sale of obscene materials would be prosecuted." *Id.* at 502.

Amendment generally does forbid harmless error analysis in over-breadth cases.[80] Why this should be is not clear to me, if overbreadth is only a judge-fashioned, deterrence-oriented standing rule. Indeed, several of the Court's fighting words decisions seem particularly inviting candidates for harmless error analysis: the discrepancy between liability imposing rules invoked by the state courts and what the First Amendment permits seems thin. Nonetheless, there is not even a suggestion that the state court save a conviction on a "no rational trier of fact" approach. Why not? The deterrence rationale said to underpin overbreadth is, to say the least, open to challenge, at least with respect to hot-tempered fighting words.[81] More generally, it is not evident that some limited form of harmless error analysis invariably conflicts with overbreadth's deterrence rationale, any more than does the now generally acknowledged power of state courts to narrow statutes to constitutionally acceptable boundaries.[82] Of course, for me, the overbreadth challenges are best understood as illustrations of the valid rule requirement.

Appendix

The claim that the Supreme Court cannot apply harmless error analysis to sustain a state court conviction resting upon a constitutionally infirm rule invites consideration of a closely related problem. What is the relationship between the valid rule requirement and the firmly recognized power of state (and federal) courts to narrow statutes to constitutionally prescribed boundaries? I am by no means clear in my own mind about all the matters potentially raised in this question, and this is fairly a topic that warrants a separate comment. I do have some preliminary views, however. I do not understand the valid rule requirement to be inconsistent with recog-

---

[80]Gooding v. Wilson, 405 U.S. 518, 521 (1972) ("It matters not that the words appellee used might have been prohibited under a narrowly and precisely drawn statute"). See also Lewis v. City of New Orleans, 415 U.S. 130 (1974).

[81]Hart and Wechsler, note 7 *supra*, at 192–93.

[82]*E.g.*, Ward v. Illinois, 431 U.S. 767, 773–76 (1977).

[83]Suppose that after a full evidentiary hearing a state court issued an injunction on the basis of statute that, as construed by that court, contained a constitutionally infirm rule. Surely an appellate court could uphold the injunction on the basis of a different, but constitutionally valid construction, if the evidence otherwise supported such an order. Yet the appellate court here is engaged in a kind of harmless error analysis. But in conventional understanding this is a penalty-free determination; the order is prospective in character and constitutes a sanction free determination of what defendant obligations are.

nition of a large power in the state courts to narrow legislative commands to constitutional boundaries.[83]

Even in criminal cases, it is plain that state courts can reshape legislative commands to satisfy the valid rule requirement.[84] The Supreme Court has repeatedly recognized that a limiting construction "may be applied to conduct prior to the construction, . . . provided such application affords fair warning. . . ."[85] Of course, the reshaping will not suffice if in the Court's judgment, the reshaping was not reasonably foreseeable.[86]

For me, a bothersome issue occurs when sanctions are imposed in the first instance by a trial court pursuant to a constitutionally infirm rule. The decisions seem to assume an appellate court preserve the conviction by reformulating the rule, and then essentially applying harmless error analysis: "our construction was clearly foreseeable and embraces the conduct shown beyond rational doubt."[87] My doubts are not grounded in fair notice or First Amendment considerations but because of the implications of the valid rule requirement.[88] Perhaps doubt is unwarranted, particularly because sanctions are seldom actually imposed before completion of the appellate process. In any event, I do not think that the Supreme Court can invoke harmless error principles to sustain the imposition of sanctions when the highest state court has itself proceeded on the basis of the invalid rule.

Nor do I see my claim as involving any challenges to the practice of imposing sanctions simply because of a change in law by the appellate court. Particularly in the civil context, appellate courts support the award on the evidence while making more or less explicit changes in the rules applied by the trial court. But in these contexts all the liability rules seem permissible under the constitution.

[84]Ward v. Illinois, 431 U.S. at 773–76. See Hamling v. United States, 418 U.S. 87, 115–16 (1974) (judicial narrowing simply added a "clarifying gloss"); Monaghan, Overbreadth, note 1 *supra.*

[85]Dombrowski v. Pfister, 380 U.S. 479, 491 n.7 (1965), cited with approval in Massachusetts v. Oakes, 109 S.Ct. at 2638 (plurality).

[86]*Ibid.*

[87]See notes 84 & 85 *Supra.* Of course, when reshaping comes at the appellate level, the fair notice requirement may be a demand that becomes more visible. But the foreseeability cases do not turn on whether the unforeseeable construction is at the trial or appellate level. Bouie v. City of Columbia, 378 U.S. 347 (1964); Dombrowski v. Pfister, note 85 *supra.* Douglas v. Buder, 412 U.S. 430, 432 (1973); Marks v. United States, 430 U.S. 388 (1977).

[88]In the First Amendment area the Court has expressed special concern over judicial narrowing at the appellate level, Monaghan, First Amendment Due Process, 83 Harv. L. Rev. 518, 540–43 (1980). Indeed, in Ashton v. Kentucky, 384 U.S. 195, 198 (1986), could be read to prohibit narrowing at the appellate level (except prospectively) when the First Amendment is implicated. But that view is foreclosed by such decisions as *Ward* and *Hamling.*

GEOFFREY C. HAZARD, JR.

AFTER PROFESSIONAL VIRTUE

Mallard v. United States District Court for the Southern District of Iowa[1]
involved the question whether a statute empowering a federal judge
to "request" an attorney to represent an indigent in a civil case[2]
meant to create an obligation on the part of the attorney. Five Justices, speaking through Justice Brennan, held that an attorney could
decline such a request.

Four Justices—Marshall, Blackmun, and O'Connor dissenting
with Justice Stevens—thought the statute was using polite language
to describe an order. Hence, they thought an attorney had a legal
obligation to accept an appointment. Both opinions cited history, not
only the deliberations preceding the enactment of the statute in 1892
but more ancient antecedents as well. Both opinions acknowledged
the tradition that members of the bar have an obligation to represent
indigents. The majority relied on Professor David Shapiro's admi-
rable study of the question.[3] The dissent quoted Justice Field from
over a century ago: "Counsel are not considered at liberty to reject
. . . the cause of the defenseless, because no provision for their compensation is made by law."[4]

The dissent also thought that the statute expressed: "the congressional design of ensuring the poor litigant equal justice whether the
suit is prosecuted in federal or state court . . . ."[5]

Geoffrey C. Hazard, Jr., is Sterling Professor of Law, Yale Law School.

[1] 109 S.Ct. 1814 (1989).

[2] 28 U.S.C. §1915(d), which provides: "The court may request an attorney [to represent the indigent]."

[3] See Shapiro, The Enigma of the Duty to Serve, 55 N.Y.U. L. Rev. 735 (1980).

[4] 109. S.Ct. at 1824–25, quoting from Rowe v. Yaba County, 17 Cal. 61, 63 (1860).

[5] 109 S.Ct. at 1825.

The majority seemed equally cognizant of the ideal of equal justice for the poor. They observed: "In a time when the need for legal services among the poor is growing and public funding for such services has not kept pace, lawyers' ethical obligation to volunteer their time *pro bono publico* is manifest."[6]

But the majority concluded that the term "request" in the statute did not seem to denote "order," "direct," or "appoint."

Both opinions happily were free of internecine zaps and zingers. Indeed, the opinions manifest a similar sadness that the "congressional design" notwithstanding, "public funding for such services has not kept pace." While questing equal justice, the law also has responsibility to decide, authoritatively and coherently, what to do inasmuch as equal justice cannot be realized. *Mallard* encapsulated that dilemma. Imagaining myself a member of the Court, I would have empathized with the minority but voted with the majority.

The case arose out of the refusal of Attorney John E. Mallard of the Iowa bar to accept appointment by a United State Magistrate to represent inmates of a state prison in their civil suit against prison officials seeking redress for brutalities and other wrongs. The inmates had filed the suit *in forma pauperis*. The Magistrate evidently thought the allegations were not frivolous. A meritorious claim of brutality perpetrated on incarcerated people surely qualifies for publicly-provided assistance of counsel. Attorney Mallard, however, refused the appointment. The Magistrate ordered him to comply. Mallard still refused and appealed to the District Judge. The District Judge ordered him to comply. Continuing his refusal, Mallard sought mandamus from the Court of Appeals for the Eighth Circuit. The Eighth Circuit denied the application. Mallard's petition for certiorari was granted by the Supreme Court, which then reversed.

Mallard's eligibility for appointment came from a list of attorneys admitted to practice before the United States District Court for the Southern District of Iowa. Becoming a member of a federal court bar is a step beyond admission to practice in the state and nominally entails special qualifications and special responsibilities. Mallard evidently got admitted to the federal court because his areas of practice included bankruptcy, which is within the exclusive federal jurisdiction, and securities law, which is primarily within the federal do-

---

[6]*Id.* at 1823.

main. The question was whether admission entailed a legally enforceable responsibility to represent indigents.

The court's appointment system involved an organization called the Volunteer Lawyers Project. This organization was jointly sponsored by the Legal Services Corporation of Iowa, a federally funded legal assistance organization, and the Iowa State Bar Association. The Volunteer Lawyers Project, as the name implies, evidently began as a group of lawyers volunteering to accept indigent appointments. However, the system had become mandatory. Every lawyer on the federal court rolls was subject to a call to serve, which worked out to one appointment about every three years.

The system was conceived as giving effect to professional virtue, a lawyer's obligation to represent the poor. Such an obligation is a classic canon of the legal profession. The canon contemplates practitioners ready to provide services to whomever may be in need of legal assistance. The clients pay if they are able, but will be served nonetheless if they cannot. This vision accordingly contemplates practitioners competent to handle practically whatever matter may come through the door, whether it be a will, a deed, the replevin of a cow, or a criminal charge such as horse stealing.

The classic canon also assumes a limited number of practitioners, not simply "the bar" but *the* bar. Members of such a bar constitute an oligopoly. This economic position provides its members an income that is steady and large enough to permit them to maintain respectability and to afford professional beneficence. Also contemplated is a fellowship of the bar—a common identity, reciprocal obligations to each other, and a shared sense of duty to others. Every lawyer is supposed to share the burden of representing the poor and anyone who shirks is subject to tacit but forceful peer disapproval. This traditional vision is, of course, romantic. The bar of the past to which it relates had features that constrained practice of its ideals. These features include the following.

Members of the bar were always concerned primarily, if not exclusively, with matters involving fees, the more lucrative the better. Most lawyers had been strivers who had endured a long and precarious apprenticeship that could drain charitable instincts. Successful lawyers usually had differentiated themselves into specialties such as mortgage finance, wills and estates, business law, and maintaining relations with the county commissioners and the state legislature. Whatever technique in advocacy they once possessed had atrophied, many of them had not been in a courthouse for years, and some had never actually tried a case.

The social structure of the bar was another impediment to free legal services. Lawyers recognized that their status in practice was largely a function of the status of their clientele, and generally wanted no truck with impecunious felons. Relationships among members of the bar were shaped by professional status. The trial bar had something of a fellowship, bound together in chronic apprehension over unpredictability of juries and idiosyncrasy of judges, these being the primary subjects of their professional conversation. The mortgage, probate, and corporation lawyers found their way into sub-circles identified by where they took luncheon and played golf. Within each group there were great individual differences in competence, efficiency, sense of responsibility, and disposition toward public service. However, most were known to be very conserving of their time and advice, which after all, as Lincoln said, was their stock in trade.

The bar not only was divided along practice lines but also was riven by social division and personal animosities. Where entrance to the bar had been achieved by ethnic and religious minorities, for example Irish Catholics and Jews, there were additional divisions along such lines. The bar was a human institution embedded in local society. This meant that notions of professional virtue, though firmly proclaimed, were only tenuously shared. All these considerations militated against providing legal services to people lacking means to pay.

The community and the bar nevertheless held together more or less. Social peace is a blessing in itself and a necessary predicate for pursuit of property and happiness. Most people realize this truth, not least the lawyers. Their calling involves canalization of conflict into peaceful and stable resolutions. That task includes seeing to it that cries of injustice not go unheeded, at least sharp cries about manifest specific injustice. Ignoring such cries embarrasses the legal system's pretension to just ordering of relations within the community, and that in turn threatens the community's very fabric. A community whose fabric is torn apart offers no vocation for lawyers. There is thus an element of long term professional self-interest in the obligation to serve indigents who are accused of crime or in other kinds of legal trouble.

Persons in positions of authority in the traditional community generally acted in a sensible way. Otherwise, they did not remain in such positions. This was true in particular of authorities in the administration of justice. Accordingly, in criminal cases by and large the prosecutor did not bring charges except on good ground. Good ground required that the accused be either provably guilty or probably guilty and socially marginal. Whether a defense would be interposed was up to the accused. An affluent accused, for example, a bank officer charged with defalcation, could retain counsel as he would have in a will contest or litigation over an easement. While there was a right to retain counsel, however, there was no right to have counsel.

Appointing counsel for an indigent accused criminal was therefore not a necessary practice, except in unusual cases. From time to time a judge would think the basis of a prosecution was doubtful, perhaps because the prosecutor was on a tear or because the police seemed to have bungled the investigation. Counsel then had to be appointed. In a heavy case, the judge would ask an experienced member of the trial bar to undertake the representation. In other cases one of the firms was asked to send over one of the young fellows.

The appointments would be accepted. These occasional undertakings were needed in order to maintain respect for the system of justice and to guard against injustice in the case of a defendant who was actually innocent. The bar understood that such appointments had to be made and that the judge would be sensible in distributing them. The burden on a leading lawyer of being appointed in a capital case or other heavy assignment was offset by the professional recognition implied in the appointment. Tendering the service of juniors solidified the leading law offices' commitment to professionalism. Accepting an appointment also banked good will with the judiciary.

An essentially similar system took care of civil legal assistance, but appropriately at a lower level of regularity and intensity. In the first place, injustice in civil matters generally was considered to have less severe and obvious consequences than injustice in criminal matters. In the second place, it was assumed that when poor people came to a lawyer's office with a substantial meritorious legal problem, they would get help. Legal assistance would be provided either directly by the lawyer or by referral to a legal aid office, which would have been established in larger communities. In this way the poor were assisted in dealing with unjust evictions, repossessions, marital discord such as spousal assault, and juvenile court proceedings. Unmeritorious cases were not given assistance. A competent lawyer could tell an unmeritorious case when he saw one, especially if he was free to decline it. Occasionally the poor were wrongly turned away, or intimidated from seeking legal help in the first place.

Sometimes an indigent would take a civil matter directly to court, appearing *in propia persona*. If the indigent was a defendant, the court tried to assure itself that the claim was at least facially valid. Judicial scrutiny was sometimes superficial and was difficult to give effect in matters prosecuted by lawyers over whom the court had no effective leverage, such as sleazy collection attorneys. Nevertheless, it provided a safeguard against serious abuse.

Pro per plaintiffs presented much greater difficulty for the court. Most *pro per* claims had poor legal foundation, even if they might be morally worthy. The judge would accurately conjecture that a *pro per* plaintiff had been turned down by lawyers on this very ground. Few claimants understood court procedure or the limitations of the judge's role and powers. However, now and then a case appeared that had something to it. A substantial non-frivolous civil claim by a poor person is entitled to the judicial system's attention on a par with criminal cases. The system did not give an indigent civil claimant a right to counsel for that would clog the courts with frivolous cases and put the administration of justice in disrepute. It therefore required the judge to assess whether a case had such apparent merit that a lawyer should be prevailed on.

Appointment of counsel in this classic situation rested on essentially the same institutions as appointments in criminal cases. The judge exercised prudent restraint in asking lawyers to serve and lawyers exercised prudent alacrity in responding, both guided by a professional narrative concerning law and justice.[7] Lawyers who were unwilling or unfit to serve simply remained outside the system, unburdened by professional obligation but also unbenefited by judicial and professional approbation. The system thus depended on reciprocity, the medium of exchange being elemental political currency, which is to say standing and influence.

Circumstances gradually changed. The appellate courts came to lay it down that counsel had to be provided in every significant criminal case. First, it was capital cases where the particular facts indicated that an acquittal might well have resulted if the defendant had had the assistance of counsel. Then cases involving serious procedural irregularity. Then felony prosecutions generally. Then all cases where jail was a possibility. The state appellate courts in politi-

---

[7]See The Supreme Court, 1982 Term—Cover, Foreword: Nomos and Narrative, 97 Harv. L. Rev. 4 (1983).

cally liberal states pointed the way, but the weight of authority was provided in Supreme Court decisions making appointment of counsel a matter of due process.[8]

Congress ratified the requirement that counsel be appointed in criminal cases in federal court. The states that had public defender systems, many since the early part of the century, enlarged those systems. States that previously depended on the appointment system created defender systems for the cities and larger towns. Other states continued to rely on the appointment system but required that appointed counsel be compensated.

Requiring that a criminal defendant have legal representation made hostage of the public's concern that criminals be put in jail. Criminals could not be put in jail except according to due process; due process, so held the Supreme Court, now required that defense lawyers be provided; since the public wanted criminals put in jail, defense lawyers had to be provided. It was inconceivable that the Supreme Court would recede from *Gideon* in the foreseeable future. It was also inconceivable that criminal prosecutions should abate for want of defense lawyers. Conservatives and liberals would join in voting appropriations. Public provision for criminal legal aid might be grudging and insufficient but there was no getting around it.

Civil legal aid was something else. The notion that due process meant lawyer-assisted process never took hold in civil matters. For one thing, there was a long tradition, exemplified in workman's compensation proceedings, juvenile court, and small claims, that legal dispute resolution could be more just, more expeditious and less expensive if lawyers were kept out. For another thing, in civil cases there was no apparatus of legal assistance provided by the state to assist one side, as was provided for the prosecution in criminal cases.[9]

There was a more fundamental difficulty in fixing the provision of civil legal aid. The measure of necessary legal aid in criminal cases was the quantum provided the prosecution. There was no similar measure for civil legal aid. To provide a lawyer to an indigent civil grievant was in effect to confer a subsidy in the amount of nuisance

---

[8]The seminal case is of course Gideon v. Wainwright, 372 U.S. 335 (1963).

[9]In Gideon v. Wainwright, *id.* at 344, the Court observed: "Governments, both state and federal, quite properly spend vast sums of money to establish machinery to try defendants accused of crime. Lawyers to prosecute are everywhere deemed essential . . . That government hires lawyers to prosecute and defendants who have the money hire lawyers to defend are the strongest indications of the widespread belief that lawyers in criminal courts are necessities, not luxuries."

settlement value to beneficiaries arbitrarily selected in terms of income or wealth and self-selecting in terms of disposition to litigate. Implicitly recognizing this, the courts were willing to say that due process required legal aid only in narrowly limited civil categories.[10] In other civil matters provision of legal aid would have to remain dependent on someone's exercise of discretion to calibrate demand with a supply.

The old system rationed supply through waiting lines at lawyers' chambers, courthouses, and legal-aid offices, and judicial discretion in *pro per* cases. This arrangement constituted charity, which was considered obnoxious by champions of the poor, and depended on grace, which is always in short and erratic supply. But it did the job of rationing justice.[11] The authority to allocate those means was widely diffused and low in visibility and accountability. In terms of the system as it existed, however, it was exercised by politically responsible authority.

In the late 1960s an attempt was made through the Great Society program to make civil legal aid a matter of legal right or at least political right. It was to be a matter not of the bar's professional responsibility but of entitlement under public law. However, the scope of potential entitlement was to be defined by budgetary constraints, not in terms of legally specified categories. The causes for which legal aid might be provided thus were limited only by fiscal resources and legal imagination. In time, that imagination would embrace racial equality, gender equality, a pollution-free environment, a drug-free America, the right to live for the unborn, the right to die for the afflicted, the right of association, the right of privacy, the right to see, the right not to see. In aggregate, civil legal aid was seen as a writ of entry into the New Jerusalem. Skeptics thought these possibilities could not be realized; conservatives feared that they might be.

The result has been continuous political struggle over legal aid.[12] Public funding of civil legal aid has been held nominally static for a decade, and in real terms has been cut about in half through inflation. Conflict over the scope and aims of legal aid can be found even in the more confined domain of legal assistance in criminal cases. The pay-

---

[10]See, *e.g.*, Lassiter v. Dept. of Social Service, 452 U.S. 18 (1981).

[11]See Hazard, Rationing Justice, 8 J. Law & Econ. 1 (1965)

[12]See generally Cramton, Crisis in Legal Services for the Poor, 26 Villanova L. Rev. 521 (1981).

ment rates authorized by Congress for appointed counsel in the federal criminal cases have rapidly eroded through inflation. The payment rates authorized for appointed counsel in the state systems have been generally worse than the federal allowances. Public defender systems are kept spare in professional staff, sparer still in paralegal staff and wage scales. None of the systems adequately provides for expenses such as necessary investigations. Those responsible for appropriations at the federal, state and local level generally begrudge the money, and understandably so. There are many other poor and unfortunates—mothers with dependent children, old people, homeless, bed-ridden, sick, abused, ill-housed, uneducated, and just poor—who are just as badly off and much more deserving.

Among the signs of strain has been the attempt to make the appointed counsel system work notwithstanding the burdens imposed on it, as in the Southern District of Iowa. A system of voluntary service can work if the providers are few in number and have sustaining relationships with each other. Everyone can scrutinize how burdens are shared and can effectively inflict the sanction of disapproval on the shirkers. When the system becomes large, informality is no longer sustainable. Participants have to be identified by list, assignments have to be made according to systematic selection, and those who fail to comply have to be brought to book with formal legal sanctions.

Although the service in the Southern District of Iowa was still called the Lawyer's Volunteer Project, a compulsory procedure determined the number and schedule of needed appointments, selected the appointees, approved compensation in criminal cases, and imposed sanctions against the uncooperative. The bar provided sponsorship, but the local profession had long ceased to be a fellowship of similarly accomplished practitioners of a commonly understood craft. The transformation of the profession in the Southern District of Iowa was starkly illustrated in Attorney Mallard's plea of avoidance from service.[13]

> In his motion to withdraw from the appointment petitioner's stated that he had no familiarity with the legal issues presented in the case, that he lacked experience in deposing and cross-examining witnesses, and that he would willing volunteer his ser-

---

[13]109 S.Ct. at 1817.

vices in an area in which he possessed some expertise, such as bankruptcy and securities law.

It is difficult to dispute that Attorney Mallard had a strong point. It is perhaps more difficult to deal with the implications of the point. Alasdair MacIntyre's *After Virtue* concludes with the thought that: "In a society where there is no longer a shared conception of the community's good . . . the alternatives become those of defining justice in terms of some sort of equality . . . or in terms of legal entitlement."[14]

Mallard memorializes our situation after professional virtue has ceased to be a plausible foundation for legal assistance to the poor. But where is the shared conception of the community's good that would enable us to formulate coherent terms of entitlement to such assistance?

---

[14]MacIntyre, After Virtue 217–18 (1981).

WALTER HELLERSTEIN

STATE TAXATION AND THE SUPREME COURT

The Supreme Court's outpouring of significant state tax decisions in recent years has elicited little more than a yawn from most constitutional scholars. The nation's preeminent law reviews, which once were filled with articles examining the Court's state tax opinions,[1] pay scant attention to them today. Leading constitutional law casebooks make only passing reference to state taxation.[2] Indeed, the Court itself has expressed ennui over the prospect of adjudicating a seemingly endless stream of state tax controversies.[3]

The lack of academic interest in the Court's state tax jurisprudence may be attributable to several factors. Matters of greater cosmic significance—abortion, affirmative action, and capital punishment, to name a few—may have crowded state tax questions off scholarly

---

Walter Hellerstein is Professor of Law at the University of Georgia.

AUTHOR'S NOTE: I wish to thank Milner Ball, Robert Brussack, Paul Kurtz, and James Smith for their helpful comments on an earlier draft of this article.

[1]See, *e.g.*, Bittker, The Taxation of Out-of-State Tangible Property, 56 Yale L.J. 640 (1947); Dunham, Gross Receipts Taxes on Interstate Transactions, 47 Colum. L. Rev. 211 (1947); Lowndes, The Tax Decisions of the Supreme Corut, 1938 Term, 88 U. Pa. L. Rev. 1 (1939); Traynor, State Taxation and the Supreme Court, 1938 Term, 28 Calif. L. Rev. 1 (1939); Developments in the Law—Federal Limitiations on State Taxation of Interstate Business, 75 Harv. L. Rev. 953 (1962).

[2]See Stone, Seidman, Sunstein & Tushnet, Constitutional Law 210–12, 262, 287–93 336–37, 521–22 (1986); Gunther, Constitutional Law 331–34 (11th ed. 1985). In earlier editions, Professor Gunther devoted considerable attention to state taxation. See Gunther, Constitutional Law 684–765, 771–75 (8th ed. 1970).

[3]See, *e.g.*, American Trucking Ass'ns, Inc. v. Scheiner, 483 U.S. 266, 268 (1987) ("[a]gain we are 'asked to decide whether state taxes applied to an interstate motor carrier run afoul of the commerce clause'"); Container Corp. of America v. Franchise Tax Bd., 463 U.S. 159, 162 (1983) ("[t]his is another appeal claiming that the application of a state taxing scheme violates the Due Process and Commerce Clauses of the Federal Constitution").

agendas. The complex and technical rules that often inform state tax disputes may have led other scholars to embrace the view of a distinguished student of constitutional law: "pursuit of the intricacies of state taxation . . . would require more time and space than the undertaking warrants."[4] And the disrepute into which conventional doctrinal analysis has fallen in certain quarters may have induced still other scholars to avoid an area in which doctrinal concerns drive the judicial process and political and social considerations play a distinctly secondary role.

Whatever the reason, the fact remains that the Court's output in this domain has been extraordinary, and its opinions have had an enormous theoretical and practical impact.[5] The Court's 1988 Term was no exception: it considered eleven state tax cases and handed down full-dress opinions in eight,[6] confronting issues arising under the Commerce, Due Process, Equal Protection, and Supremacy Clauses, the First and Eleventh Amendments, and the intergovernmental and Indian immunity doctrines. The constitutional landscape in the state tax field deserves some re-mapping in light of the Court's recent decisions.

---

[4] Gunther, note 2 *supra*, at 332–33.

[5] See Hellerstein, Is "Internal Consistency" Foolish?: Reflections on an Emerging Commerce Clause Restraint on State Taxation, 87 Mich. L. Rev. 138 (1988); Hellerstein, Commerce Clause Restraints on State Taxation: Purposeful Economic Protectionism and Beyond, 85 Mich. L. Rev. 758 (1987); Hellerstein, Complementary Taxes as a Defense to Unconstitutional State Tax Discrimination, 39 Tax Law. 405 (1986); Hellerstein, State Income Taxation of Multijurisdictional Corporations, Part II: Reflections on ASARCO and Woolworth, 81 Mich. L. Rev. 157 (1982); Hellerstein, Constitutional Limitations on State Tax Exportation, 1982 Am. Bar Found. Res. J. 1; Hellerstein, State Income Taxation of Multijurisdictional Corporations: Reflections on Mobil, Exxon, and H.R. 5076, 79 Mich. L. Rev. 113 (1980); Hellerstein, State Taxation and the Supreme Court: Toward a More Unified Approach to Constitutional Adjudication?, 75 Mich. L. Rev. 1426 (1977); Hellerstein, Michelin Tire Corp. v. Wages: Enhanced State Power to Tax Exports, 1976 Supreme Court Review 99; Hellerstein, State Taxation and the Supreme Court, 1974 Term: Standard Pressed Steel and Colonial Pipeline, 62 Va. L. Rev. 149 (1976).

[6] Shell Oil Co. v. Iowa Dep't of Revenue, 109 S.Ct. 278 (1988); Goldberg v. Sweet, 109 S.Ct. 582 (1989); Allegheny Pittsburgh Coal Co. v. County Comm'n, 109 S.Ct. 633 (1989); Texas Monthly Co. v. Bullock, 109 S.Ct. 890 (1989); Davis v. Michigan Dep't of Treasury, 109 S.Ct. 1500 (1989); Amerada Hess Corp. v. Director, Div. of Taxation, 109 S.Ct. 1617 (1989); Cotton Petroleum Corp. v. New Mexico, 109 S.Ct. 1698 (1989); California State Bd. of Equalization v. Sierra Summit, Inc., 109 S.Ct. 2228 (1989). The Court heard oral argument in two companion cases, involving the question whether taxpayers have a federal constitutional right to a refund of state taxes held to be unconstitutionally discriminatory under the Commerce Clause, McKesson Corp. v. Division of Alcoholic Beverages and Tobacco, cert. granted, 109 S.Ct. 389 (1988) and American Trucking Ass'ns, Inc. v. Smith, cert. granted, 109 S.Ct. 389 (1988), but subsequently set the cases for reargument during its 1989 Term. 109 S.Ct. 3238 (1989). In a brief per curiam opinion, the Court held that a suit by Oklahoma against an Indian Tribe for failure to collect state excise taxes on cigarette sales and bingo receipts was improperly removed from state to federal court. Oklahoma Tax Comm'n v. Graham, 109 S.Ct. 1519 (1989).

I. THE COMMERCE CLAUSE

The Commerce Clause has long been the linchpin of the Court's state tax jurisprudence. Despite Justice Scalia's skepticism over the existence "of any clear theoretical underpinning for judicial 'enforcement' of the Commerce Clause,"[7] the Court's interpretation of the Commerce Clause remains the most significant constitutional restraint on state tax power—as it has been for more than a century.[8] In its 1977 opinion in *Complete Auto Transit, Inc. v. Brady*,[9] the Court sought to "clear up the tangled underbrush of past cases"[10] by articulating a four-part test to govern the validity of state taxes under the Commerce Clause. A tax must be applied to an activity that has a substantial nexus with the state; it must be fairly apportioned to activities carried on by the taxpayer in the state; it must not discriminate against interstate commerce; and it must be fairly related to services provided by the state. In opinions subsequent to *Complete Auto Transit*, the Court has faithfully adhered to this four-part test, which it has characterized as a "consistent and rational method of inquiry" that looks to "the practical effects of a challenged tax" on interstate commerce.[11]

The Court reiterated its commitment to the analytical framework established in *Complete Auto Transit* in both of the Commerce Clause opinions it rendered during the 1988 Term. In *Goldberg v. Sweet*,[12] involving a challenge to Illinois' telecommunications excise tax, the Court observed:[13]

> This Court has frequently had occasion to consider whether state taxes violate the Commerce Clause. The wavering doctrinal lines of our pre-*Complete Auto* cases reflect the tension between two competing concepts: the view that interstate commerce enjoys a "free trade" immunity from state taxation; and the view that businesses engaged in interstate commerce may be required to pay their own way. *Complete Auto* sought to resolve this tension

---

[7]Tyler Pipe Industries, Inc. v. Washington Dep't of Revenue, 483 U.S. 232, 260 (1983) (Scalia, J., concurring and dissenting).

[8]See generally Hellerstein, State Taxation of Interstate Business: Perspectives on Two Centuries of Constitutional Adjudication, 41 Tax Law. 37, 40–45 (1987).

[9]430 U.S. 274 (1977).

[10]Spector Motor Service, Inc. v. O'Connor, 340 U.S. 602, 612 (1951) (Clark, J., dissenting).

[11]Mobil Oil Corp. v. Commissioner of Taxes, 445 U.S. 425, 443 (1980).

[12]109 S.Ct. 582 (1989).

[13]*Id*. at 587–88 (citations omitted).

by specifically rejecting the view that the States cannot tax interstate commerce, while at the same time placing limits on state taxation of interstate commerce. Since the *Complete Auto* decision we have applied its four-prong test on numerous occasions. We now apply it to the Illinois tax.

Similarly, in *Amerada Hess Corp. v. Division, Director of Taxation*,[14] involving a challenge to New Jersey's denial of a state corporate income tax deduction for federal windfall profit taxes, the Court declared:[15]

> In *Complete Auto Transit, Inc. v. Brady*, this Court sustained a state tax "against Commerce Clause challenge when the tax is applied to an activity with a substantial nexus with the taxing State, is fairly apportioned, does not discriminate against interstate commerce, and is fairly related to services provided by the taxing State." We repeatedly have applied this principle in subsequent cases, most recently this Term in *Goldberg v. Sweet*. Appellants do not dispute the soundness of the *Complete Auto* standard . . . . Rather they argue that the . . . Tax . . . fails each of the four prongs of the *Complete Auto* test.

The Court's ritualistic invocation of a verbal formula for adjudicating Commerce Clause challenges to state taxes cannot provide easy answers to hard questions. Nevertheless, in an area of the law in which hundreds of cases had left "much room for controversy and confusion and little in the way of precise guides to the States in the exercise of their indispensable power of taxation,"[16] the Court's effort to analyze the issues in a "consistent and rational"[17] manner has helped to delineate the controlling constitutional principles governing state taxation of interstate commerce.

A. NEXUS

The nexus requirement reflects the fundamental notion that there must be "some definite link, some minimum connection between a state and the person, property, or transaction it seeks to tax."[18] In recent years, the Court has been quite indulgent in finding the requi-

---

[14]109 S.Ct. 1617 (1989).

[15]*Id.* at 1621 (citations omitted).

[16]Northwestern States Portland Cement Co. v. Minnesota, 358 U.S. 450, 457 (1959).

[17]See note 11 *supra*.

[18]Miller Bros v. Maryland, 347 U.S. 340, 344–45 (1954). While *Miller Brothers* was decided under the Due Process Clause, the nexus requirement has been incorporated into the Court's Commerce Clause doctrine. See text at note 15 *supra*.

site nexus to justify the exercise of state tax power. The Court has sustained a state's power to impose a use tax on catalogs shipped from outside the state directly to the taxpayer's in-state customers.[19] It has also sustained a state's power to tax all the receipts derived by an out-of-state supplier from sales to an in-state purchaser on the basis of the presence of the supplier's single resident employee.[20] And, while rejecting the notion that the "slightest presence" of an out-of-state vendor constitutes a sufficient nexus to require the vendor to collect use taxes,[21] the Court has nevertheless sustained use tax collection liability on the basis of in-state activities that many would regard as insubstantial.[22]

The most hotly debated nexus issue in the state tax field today, on which more than a billion dollars of tax revenues ride,[23] is whether the states may require an out-of-state mail-order vendor to collect use taxes on catalog sales. In 1967 the Court held in *National Bellas Hess, Inc. v. Department of Revenue*[24] that a state lacks the constitutional power[25] to require an out-of-state mail order vendor, whose only contacts with the state are by mail or common carrier, to collect the state's use tax on goods sold and shipped to customers in the state. After chafing under the decision for the past two decades, the states now assert that subsequent developments have undermined the factual and legal premises underlying *National Bellas Hess*.

The states contend that the economic environment in which *National Bellas Hess* was decided has changed dramatically. They point to the spectacular growth in the mail-order industry, now estimated

---

[19]D. H. Holmes Co. v. McNamara, 108 S.Ct. 1619 (1988).

[20]Standard Pressed Steel Co. v. Department of Revenue, 419 U.S. 560, 562 (1975).

[21]National Geographic Soc'y v. State Bd. of Equalization, 430 U.S. 551 (1977).

[22]See *ibid.* (magazine employed four in-state employees at two offices to solicit advertising unrelated to mail-order sales on which tax was imposed); Scripto, Inc. v. Carson, 362 U.S. 207 (1960) (company used ten in-state independent contractors to make sales).

[23]U.S. Advisory Commission on Intergovernmental Relations, State and Local Taxation of Out-of-State Mail Order Sales 31 (1986).

[24]386 U.S. 753 (1967).

[25]The Court referred to both the Commerce and the Due Process Clauses in reaching its decision, but the decision was rooted in the Commerce Clause. See Interstate Sales Tax Collection Act of 1987 and the Equity in Interstate Competition Act of 1987: Hearings on H.R. 1242, H.R. 1891, and H.R. 3521 Before the Subcomm. on Monopolies and Commercial Law of the House Comm. on the Judiciary, 100th Cong., 2d Sess. 347–48 (1988) (testimony of Walter Hellerstein). The question whether the Court's decision was based on the Due Process Clause as well as the Commerce Clause may be significant with respect to the power of Congress to overrule *National Bellas Hess*, an option it is presently considering. *Ibid. passim*.

to generate sales of more than $50 billion per year,[26] as well as to striking changes in marketing techniques that permit mail-order sellers to reach consumers through toll-free (800) telephone numbers and computer terminals. They also assert that technological advances in communications, including automated accounting systems, should dispel the Court's concern voiced in *National Bellas Hess* that imposing a use tax collection obligation on a mail-order seller would create a "welter of complicated obligations to local jurisdictions"[27]that would frustrate the Commerce Clause purpose of ensuring "a national economy free from such unjustifiable local entanglements."[28]

The states also point to changes in the legal environment. They claim that since *National Bellas Hess* was decided, the Court has discredited the idea underlying the decision that physical presence in the state is a *sine qua non* of the state's authority to assert its coercive power over an out-of-state resident or business. They find support for their position in cases such as *Burger King v. Rudzewicz*,[29] sustaining personal jurisdiction over nonresident defendants without physical presence in the state. "[I]t is an inescapable fact of modern commercial life," the Court there observed,[30]

> that a substantial amount of business is transacted solely by mail and wire communications across state lines, thus obviating the need for physical presence within a State in which business is conducted. So long as a commercial actor's efforts are "purposefully directed" towards residents of another State, we have consistently rejected the notion that an absence of physical contacts can defeat personal jurisdiction there.

The Court's opinion in *Goldberg v. Sweet* is certain to fuel the debate over the continuing vitality of *National Bellas Hess*. In *Goldberg*, the Court addressed the question whether Illinois' Telecommunications Excise Tax Act[31] violated the Commerce Clause. The tax was im-

[26]U.S. Advisory Commission on Intergovernmental Relations, note 23 *supra*, at 4. The intermediate estimate for 1985 was $44.9 billion, with industry estimates well in excess of $100 billion. *Id*. at 3.

[27]*National Bellas Hess*, 386 U.S. at 759–60.

[28]*Id*. at 760. See Hartman, Collection of the Use Tax on Out-of-State Mail-Order Sales, 39 Vand. L. Rev. 993, 1011–12 (1986).

[29]471 U.S. 462 (1985).

[30]*Id*. at 476. See also Keeton v. Hustler Magazine, Inc., 465 U.S. 770 (1984) (sustaining personal jurisdiction over out-of-state defendant based on circulation within the state of the defendant's magazines).

[31]Ill. Rev. Stat. ch. 120, 2001–2021 (1987).

posed on the "act or privilege" of "originating" or "receiving" interstate telecommunications in the state at the rate of 5 percent of the
gross charge for the telecommunications.[32] The tax applied only to
calls charged to an Illinois service address,[33] which the Court understood to mean the address where the telephone equipment was located,[34] regardless of where the telephone call charge was billed or
paid. An identical 5 percent tax was also imposed on intrastate telecommunications by another section of the Act. To avoid multiple
taxation of the call by more than one state, the Act provided a credit
to any taxpayer upon proof that the taxpayer had paid a tax to another state on the same interstate telecommunication taxed by Illinois.[35] The tax was collected by the retailer of the taxable
telecommunication (i.e., the telecommunications provider) from the
consumer whose service address was charged.[36]

The parties agreed that Illinois had a substantial nexus with the
interstate telecommunications taxed by the Act,[37] so the Court was
not compelled to address the first prong of its Commerce Clause test.
Nevertheless, in considering the question whether the Illinois levy
threatened to expose the taxpayer to multiple taxation in violation of
the Commerce Clause's fair apportionment requirement,[38] the
Court focused on the possibility that more than one state would have
the requisite nexus, and hence the requisite power, to impose a tax on
the same telephone call that was subject to tax in Illinois.

In finding that the taxpayers had overstated the risk of multiple
taxation, the Court expressed "doubt that States through which the
telephone call's electronic signals merely pass have a sufficient nexus
to tax that call."[39] The Court likewise expressed "doubt that termi-

[32]Ill. Rev. Stat. ch. 120, 2004, § 4 (1987).
[33]Ill. Rev. Stat. ch. 120, 2002, § 2(a), 2(b) (1987).
[34]109 S.Ct. at 586 n.6.
[35]Ill. Rev. Stat. ch. 120, 2004, § 4 (1987).
[36]Ill. Rev. Stat. ch. 120, 2005, § 5 (1987).
[37]109 S.Ct. at 588.
[38]This issue is considered more fully below. See text accompanying notes 59–74 infra.
[39]109 S.Ct. at 589. The Court cited United Air Lines, Inc. v. Mahin, 410 U.S. 623, 631
(1973) and Northwest Airlines, Inc. v. Minnesota 322 U.S. 292, 302–04 (1944) (Jackson, J.,
concurring) for the proposition that a state has no nexus to tax an airplane based solely on its
flight over the state. The holding of neither case actually supports the proposition for which it
is cited. In Mahin, the Court sustained a state's power to apply its fuel use tax to aviation fuel
stored temporarily in the state prior to loading aboard aircraft for consumption in interstate
flights. In Northwest Airlines, the Court held that the state of an airline's incorporation, principal place of business, and major repair base could impose a property tax on the entire value of

nation of an interstate call, by itself, provides a substantial enough nexus for a State to tax a call."[40] For this proposition, the Court cited *National Bellas Hess* with the parenthetical comment that "receipt of mail provides insufficient nexus."[41] Hence the good news from *Goldberg* for out-of-state vendors is that the Court harbors serious reservations about the power of states to tax out-of-state firms who exploit a state's market solely through electronic media[42] or the mail and that *National Bellas Hess* remains good law.

There is also bad news from *Goldberg* for out-of-state vendors, however. For the Court, in assessing the risk of multiple taxation arising from the Illinois taxing scheme, identified two states that do have sufficient nexus to tax a consumer's purchase of an interstate telephone call: a state like Illinois which taxes the origination or termination of an interstate telephone call charged to a service address within that state, and a state which taxes the origination or termination of an interstate telephone call billed or paid for within that state.[43] While the Court's dicta thus suggest that neither the receipt of a telephone call nor the receipt of mail by itself creates a taxable nexus under the Commerce Clause, the two events in combination do create such nexus. Otherwise the Court could not have declared that a state which taxes the termination of an interstate telephone call billed within the state would have nexus to tax such call. Under the Court's reasoning, only the out-of-state vendor which carefully structures its operations so as to communicate with its customers exclusively through electronic media or exclusively through the mails would retain Commerce Clause immunity from collecting the state's use tax.[44]

---

its fleet of planes without apportionment. The Court's dictum in *Goldberg* may cast a shadow over the holding of state tribunals that sales and use taxes may be imposed on the in-flight sale of liquor on flights that merely pass over the state, Republic Airlines, Inc. v. Department of Revenue, Wis. Tax Appeals Comm'n, May 4, 1989, reported in [Wis.] State Tax Rptr. (CCH) ¶203–058, and that overflight time may be taken into account in apportioning an airline's aircraft to the state. Alaska Airlines, Inc. v. Department of Revenue, 307 Ore. 406, 769 P.2d 193 (1989).

[40] 109 S.Ct. at 589–90.

[41] *Id.* at 590.

[42] This assumes that one can draw a reasonable analogy between the requisite nexus for taxing an interstate service (the telecommunication) and the requisite nexus for requiring an out-of-state vendor to collect a tax on a transaction generated by that service.

[43] *Id.* at 109.

[44] This assumes that the requisite nexus for taxing an interstate phone call is substantially the same as the requisite nexus for requiring an interstate vendor to collect the tax on a sale generated by the phone call. See note 42 *supra*. Even on this assumption, however, it might be argued

Though less tantalizing than its dicta in *Goldberg*, the Court's disposition of the nexus issue in *Amerada Hess* was not without significance. In *Amerada Hess*, most of the nation's major integrated oil companies attacked the constitutionality of New Jersey's denial of a deduction for federal windfall profit taxes from the state corporate income tax base. The windfall profit tax is an excise tax imposed on the "windfall profit" from the production of crude oil.[45] Because the windfall profit tax is an expense attributable to the production of oil, and because the oil companies engaged in no oil production in New Jersey, they claimed that denying a deduction for an expense attributable to out-of-state production, while including income from that production in their apportionable tax base,[46] was equivalent to imposing a tax on such out-of-state production. In so doing, New Jersey was allegedly imposing a tax on a transaction with which it lacked nexus.

The Court gave this argument less attention than it deserved. Seizing on the fact that the oil companies were admittedly carrying on an integrated "unitary business"[47] in New Jersey, the Court ob-

---

that no nexus would be created under the typical telephone order that is filled by mail. The customer would ordinarily make a toll-free call that would be billed to the vendor's location. The Court gave no indication that the mere origination of a telephone call by an in-state customer would provide nexus over the out-of-state vendor when the call was billed to the out-of-state vendor. The fulfillment of the customer's order by mail would likewise fail to provide sufficent nexus under *National Bellas Hess*. The Court's position, however, that a state has nexus to tax the origination of an interstate telephone call billed within the state, 109 S.Ct. at 590, undercuts this argument, unless there is some basis for not considering the contact with the out-of-state vendor resulting from the origination of the telephone call in conjunction with the resulting mail-order sale for purposes of establishing nexus over the out-of-state vendor. The claim that the mail-order sale must be viewed in isolation from other contacts the out-of-state vendor has with the taxing state for purposes of establishing the out-of-state vendor's obligation to collect use taxes cannot be sustained in light of National Geographic Society v. State Board of Equalization, 430 U.S. 551 (1977) (nexus over out-of-state vendor created by in-state activities unrelated to mail-order sales).

[45]26 U.S.C. §4986–4998 (1982). The levy is imposed on taxable crude oil removed from the premises after February 29, 1980. Broadly speaking, the "windfall profit" associated with any particular barrel of oil is the difference between the market price of the barrel and the adjusted base price of the barrel, which generally reflects the barrel's price prior to the expiration of federal price controls. *Ibid.*

[46]The taxpayers conceded that the inclusion of their out-of-state production income in their apportionable tax base was appropriate under the "unitary business" principle. Reply Brief for Appellants 3, *Amerada Hess*, 109 S. Ct.1617; see text at notes 47–48 *infra* & note 47 *infra*.

[47]A "unitary business" is an enterprise carried on across state lines in which the enterprise's in-state activities are sufficiently integrated with its out-of-state activities to give the state nexus with all the activities and to justify a state's tax upon an apportioned share of all the income generated by those activities. See Container Corp. of America v. Franchise Tax Bd., 463 U.S. 159, 163–69 (1983); Hellerstein, State Income Taxation of Multijurisdictional Corporations: Reflections on Mobil, Exxon, and H.R. 5076, 79 Mich. L. Rev. 113, 140–53 (1980).

served that New Jersey had a substantial nexus with the activities that generated the oil companies' net income, including their out-of-state oil-producing activities.[48] New Jersey's denial of a deduction for costs attributable to such out-of-state activity did not "alter the fact that New Jersey has a substantial connection to the oil-producing activity by virtue of the determination that this activity is conducted by a unitary business."[49]

By relying on the undisputed fact that the oil companies were conducting a unitary business in New Jersey and focusing on the question whether New Jersey had a sufficient nexus with the oil companies' income, the Court failed to confront squarely the tax-payers' point. To be sure, from a technical standpoint, the denial of the windfall profit tax deduction simply increased the oil companies' unitary income tax base with which New Jersey had a sufficient nexus. From a practical standpoint, however, the denial of the windfall profit tax deduction was essentially indistinguishable from a tax imposed by New Jersey on a share of the windfall profit from the oil companies' out-of-state production.[50]

The critical nexus question, then, was whether "the practical effect" of the challenged tax, which purportedly informs the Court's Commerce Clause analysis,[51] was more akin to an effort by New Jersey to tax out-of-state oil production or to the routine inclusion of income from a unitary business in the state's tax base. The answer to that question lies in the appropriate characterization of the windfall profit tax. If it is truly analogous to a severance tax, as the oil companies claimed, then there is force to their assertion that, by denying

---

[48]109 S.Ct. at 1621.

[49]*Ibid.*

[50]For example, assume that a taxpayer's federal windfall profit tax liability is $1 million and that New Jersey's apportionable share of the taxpayer's income is 20 per cent. Under the New Jersey corporate income tax, the taxpayer was required to add $1 million to its apportionable tax base, which is generally patterned after its federal income tax base, because the $1 million had been subtracted from its federal tax base pursuant to I.R.C. §164(a)(5). Twenty percent of the $1 million, or $200,000 would be apportioned to New Jersey and New Jersey's 9 percent corporate income tax rate would be applied to produce an increased tax liability of $18,000. If New Jersey had simply adopted its own "apportioned" windfall profit tax at 9 percent of the federal rate, the taxpayer's tax liability would be increased by 9 percent of the $1 million federal tax liability or $90,000. New Jersey's apportioned share of this figure would be 20 per-cent of $90,000 or $18,000, precisely the same increase in tax liability resulting from the add-back of federal windfall profit taxes under the statutory procedure. See Brief for Appellants at 37 n.16, *Amerada Hess,* 109 S.Ct. 1637.

[51]See *Complete Auto Transit,* 430 U.S. at 279; text at note 10 *supra.*

a deduction for the windfall profit tax, New Jersey was in substance taxing out-of-state transactions under the guise of taxing unitary business income. Indeed, the Court has indicated that only the state in which mineral production occurs has sufficient nexus to impose a severance tax on such production: "'the severance can occur in no other state' and 'no other state can tax the severance.'" [52] On the other hand, if the windfall profit tax may fairly be characterized as a levy on the oil companies' unitary income rather than as a site-specific expense, as New Jersey contended,[53] then the Court was fully warranted in concluding that New Jersey's denial of a deduction for a cost associated with the earning of that income did not amount in substance to a tax on an activity with which New Jersey lacked nexus.

Whatever the "true" nature of the federal windfall profit tax, an issue over which much ink has been spilled,[54] the Court's holding without further explanation in *Amerada Hess* is troublesome. If a state as a matter of law has a substantial nexus with any expense associated with income derived from a unitary business carried on in the state, then states may be free to deny deductions which relate to exclusively out-of-state activity while at the same time taxing (under the unitary business principle[55]) income derived from those very same activities. This raises the specter of states skewing their denial of deductions so as to permit deductions for in-state activities while denying deductions for out-of-state activities. The objectionable aspects of such a practice may more appropriately be analyzed under the Commerce Clause's fair apportionment or nondiscrimination criteria.[56] Nevertheless, the Court could have limited the possibility of geographic skewing of deductions had it been willing to say that the Commerce Clause requires that states must have nexus with ac-

---

[52]Commonwealth Edison Co. v. Montana, 453 U.S. 609, 617 (1981).

[53]Brief for Appellee at 26–33, *Amerada Hess*, 109 S.Ct. 1617; *id*. at 1622 n.7.

[54]See, *e.g.*, Attermeier & Reveley, Characterizing the Windfall Profit Tax for State Income Tax Purposes, 32 Oil & Gas Tax Q. 465 (1984); Robison, The Misnamed Tax: The Crude Oil Windfall Profits Tax of 1980, 84 Dick. L. Rev. 589 (1980). As noted below, see text accompanying notes 80–81 *infra*, the oil companies had the better of the argument over the question whether the windfall profit tax should be characterized as a site-specific cost, even though the Court found it unnecessary to resolve the issue. *Amerada Hess*, 109 S.Ct. at 1622 n.7.

[55]See note 46 *supra*.

[56]These issues are addressed below. See text accompanying notes 75–82 and notes 96–100 *infra*.

tivities whose costs are deducted from unitary income as well as with the unitary income itself.

B. APPORTIONMENT

The requirement that a tax affecting interstate commerce be fairly apportioned to the taxpayer's activities in the taxing state is venerable.[57] It has acquired greater significance, however, as the Court's decisions have broadened the states' taxing powers. With the abandonment of the formal criteria that once created an irreducible zone of tax immunity for interstate commerce,[58] the Court's emphasis has shifted from the question whether interstate commerce may be taxed at all to the question whether interstate commerce is being made to bear its fair share—or more than its fair share—of the state tax burden. If a tax is fairly apportioned to the taxpayer's activities in the taxing state, there is no risk, at least in principle, that a tax will subject a taxpayer engaged in interstate commerce to more than its fair share of the tax burden and expose it to a risk of multiple taxation not borne by local commerce.

Both of the Commerce Clause decisions rendered by the Court during its 1988 Term raised significant apportionment issues. In *Goldberg*,[59] the taxpayers[60] contended that Illinois' telecommunications tax violated the Commerce Clause's fair apportionment requirement because it was levied on the gross charge of each telephone call. They argued that the fair apportionment requirement compelled Illinois to include within its tax base only the portion of the gross charge of each interstate telecommunication that reflected the ratio of in-state activity to total activity associated with the telecommunication. They pointed to the apportionment formulas that the states have developed and the Court has approved for apportioning the tax bases of other instrumentalities of interstate commerce en-

---

[57]See, *e.g.*, Pullman's Palace Car Co. v. Pennsylvania, 141 U.S. 18, 26 (1891); Maine v. Grand Trunk Ry., 142 U.S. 217, 278 (1891).

[58]See *Complete Auto Transit*, 430 U.S. 274; Hellerstein, State Taxation and the Supreme Court: Toward a More Unified Approach to Constitutional Adjudication?, 75 Mich. L. Rev. 1426, 1441–46 (1977).

[59]The facts of *Goldberg* are set out at text accompanying notes 31–36 *supra*.

[60]The named plaintiff, Goldberg, was a taxpayer whose liability arose out of the telephone calls charged to his service address. However, GTE Sprint Communications Corporation, whose challenge to the Illinois tax was also before the Court in a companion case (GTE Communications Corp. v. Sweet), was technically a tax collector rather than a taxpayer. For sake of simplicity, all challengers to the tax will be referred to as taxpayers.

gaged in land, water, and air transportation, based on such factors as track mileage,[61] barge line mileage,[62] and revenue tons.[63] By analogy, they claimed, Illinois was required to apportion taxable gross receipts from the interstate telecommunications by some equivalent ratio, such as the miles the electronic signals traveled within Illinois to the total miles traveled.[64]

The short answer to the taxpayers' claim was that Illinois did apportion its tax. By taxing only the receipts from calls originating or terminating in Illinois that were charged to an Illinois service address,[65] Illinois effectively taxed only half the universe of interstate telecommunications originating or terminating in Illinois. This assumes, quite reasonably I believe, that roughly half of the calls originating or terminating in Illinois are charged to an Illinois service address with the other half charged to the service address of the caller in the other state in which the call originated or terminated. Since no states other than the state of origination or termination have the power to impose a tax on an interstate telecommunication—a fact made clear in the Court's nexus discussion[66]—Illinois' "charged-to-an-Illinois-service-address" limitation on its tax effected a 50 percent apportionment of the tax base to Illinois. Such an apportionment should satisfy constitutional strictures in a domain in which "rough approximation" rather than "precision" is the controlling standard.[67]

The Court, however, took a more circuitous route to the same conclusion. Invoking the language of *Container Corp. of America v. Franchise Tax Board*,[68] the Court viewed the fair apportionment requirement as triggering an inquiry into the question whether a tax is "internally and externally consistent."[69] The Court's "internal consistency" test, which the Court has recently grafted onto the body of its Commerce Clause doctrine,[70] requires that a tax "be structured so

---

[61]See, *e.g.*, Pittsburgh, C., C. & St. L. Ry. v. Backus, 154 U.S. 421 (1894).

[62]See, *e.g.*, Ott v. Mississippi Valley Barge Line Co., 336 U.S. 169 (1949).

[63]Braniff Airways, Inc. v. Nebraska State Bd. of Equalization, 347 U.S. 590 (1947).

[64]109 S. Ct. at 588.

[65]See text accompanying notes 33–34 *supra*.

[66]See text accompanying notes 37–42 *supra*.

[67]Illinois Central R.R. v. Minnesota, 309 U.S. 157, 161 (1940).

[68]463 U.S. 159, 169–70 (1983).

[69]109 S.Ct. at 588.

[70]See generally Hellerstein, Is "Internal Consistency" Foolish?: Reflections on an Emerging Commerce Clause Restraint on State Taxation, 87 Mich. L. Rev. 138 (1988).

that if every State were to impose an identical tax, no multiple taxation would result."[71] The Illinois levy plainly satisfied this standard. If every state confined its telecommunications tax levy to receipts from interstate telephone calls that were charged to an in-state service address, only one state would tax the receipts from each interstate call.

The Court then turned to the "external consistency" standard, which reflects familiar Commerce Clause doctrine requiring fair apportionment. Here the Court confronted a thornier problem. The Illinois tax was clearly unapportioned, in the sense that the tax applied to the gross charge of an interstate activity, and there was no formulary apportionment of the tax base to reflect in-state activity. The Court responded to this objection on several—and not wholly consistent—grounds. The tax was like a sales tax and did not need to be apportioned; the tax was fairly apportioned because it created little risk of multiple taxation; the tax created some risk of multiple taxation, but provision of a tax credit eliminated the possibility of actual multiple taxation; and true apportionment of the tax base, on a mileage or other geographic basis, was administratively and technologically impossible in light of the complexity of contemporary telecommunications networks.[72]

As indicated above, I have no quarrel with the Court's conclusion that the Illinois tax was fairly apportioned.[73] It is unfortunate, however, that the Court failed to embrace the most straightforward response to the fair apportionment claim. Each of the justifications the Court advanced for its conclusion that the Illinois tax was fairly apportioned has weaknesses,[74] and they may come back to haunt the

---

[71]*Goldberg*, 109 S.Ct. at 589.

[72]*Id.* at 589–91.

[73]See text accompanying notes 65–67 *supra*.

[74](1) *The tax was like a sales tax and did not need to be apportioned.* It is true that the tax had many of the characteristics of a retail sales tax in that it was assessed on the individual consumer, it was measured by the price of the service sold, and it was collected by the retailer. It is also true that retail sales taxes generally are not apportioned. As I have explained in detail elsewhere, however, our tolerance of unapportioned sales taxes is largely a creature of administrative necessity and represents no more than a second-best solution to the fair apportionment of receipts from an interstate transaction over which more than one state may legitimately exercise taxing power. See Hellerstein, note 70 *supra*, at 170–88. Moreover, the Court has unjustifiably extended its tolerance of unapportioned retail sales taxes to unapportioned business gross receipts taxes. *Ibid.* Because the line between retail sales taxes and general business gross receipts taxes is not always clear (at least to the Court), and because there is a risk that the Court may extend its analysis of the retail gross receipts tax in *Goldberg* to the business gross receipts taxes that many states impose on telecommunications and other public service companies, it would have been better if the Court had not put its imprimatur upon an unapportioned levy in this context.

Court in other contexts. As some of us instruct our law students on exams, a good short answer will receive a higher grade than an equally good longer answer.

The Court did give a short answer to the apportionment question raised by *Amerada Hess*.[75] Unfortunately, this question required a longer answer. The gravamen of the oil companies' claim was that New Jersey, by denying a deduction for an out-of-state expense (the windfall profit tax), geographically skewed their apportionable income to assign more income to New Jersey than was fairly attributable to their activities in the state. The Court's response was essentially a reiteration of its rationale for rejecting the taxpayer's nexus claim:[76] "[F]or apportionment purposes, it is inappropriate to consider the windfall profit tax as an out-of-state expense. Rather, just as each appellant's oil-producing revenue as part of a unitary business is not confined to a single State, so too the costs of producing this revenue are unitary in nature."[77]

The problem with the Court's answer is that it assumes, as a matter of federal constitutional law, that all expenses of a unitary busi-

---

(2) *The tax was fairly apportioned because it created little risk of multiple taxation.* As I have explained elsewhere, see Hellerstein, note 70 *supra*, at 185, this is essentially a non sequitur. While it is true that the fair apportionment requirement is designed to prevent multiple taxation, it does not follow that any tax that does not create the risk of multiple taxation is fairly apportioned. Wholly apart from its role in preventing multiple taxation, the fair apportionment criterion serves to limit the territorial reach of state tax power by requiring that the state's tax base correspond to the taxpayer's in-state presence. Norfolk & Western Ry. v. Missouri State Tax Comm'n, 390 U.S. 317, 323–35 (1968). There may be cases in which a state's tax creates no risk of multiple taxation but nevertheless involve unquestioned extraterritorial taxation (*e.g.*, if a state sought to tax the unapportioned income of all corporations doing business in the state, but granted a credit for other states' taxes). In such cases, it is important that we not lose sight of the fact that there is more to the fair apportionment criterion than avoiding the risk of multiple taxation. The Court's opinion is unhelpful in that respect.

(3) *The tax created some risk of multiple taxation, but provision of a tax credit eliminated the possibility of actual multiple taxation.* As suggested in (2) above and as I have argued elsewhere, see Hellerstein, note 70 *supra*, at 182–88, the provision of a tax credit does not make an unapportioned tax "fairly apportioned," even though it may deal with the multiple taxation issue. The Court's opinion may lead some readers to the opposite conclusion.

(4) *True apportionment of the tax base, in the sense of division of the tax base on a mileage or other geographic basis, was administratively and technologically impossible in light of the complexity of contemporary telecommunications networks.* As noted above, see text accompanying notes 65–67 *supra*, this conclusion is essentially untrue in light of the possibility of dividing the tax base on a fifty-fifty split between the state of the calls' origin and destination. Moreover, it may encourage states to adopt crude approaches to apportionment of technologically complex industries (*e.g.*, financial services) when in fact more precise ways of measuring in-state presence are feasible. See, *e.g.*, the Multistate Tax Commission's Proposed Regulations for Apportioning the Income of the Financial Services Industry, 1989 Multistate Tax Comm'n Rev. 17 (March 1989).

[75]The facts of *Amerada Hess* are set out at text accompanying notes 44–45 *supra*.

[76]See text accompanying notes 47–49 *supra*.

[77]109 S. Ct. at 1622.

ness bear the same relationship to that business as does the income from the business. By hypothesis, then, such expenses are deemed to constitute an inextricable component of the unitary business that cannot be separately identified on a geographic basis.[78] But this assumption is unwarranted. It may well be that unitary income, as the Court effectively defined it in the very first case challenging the constitutionality of formulary apportionment, is generated by a "series of transactions" beginning with "manufacture" or production in one state and "ending with sale in other states" so that[79]

> [t]he Legislature, in attempting to put upon this business its fair share of the burden, of taxation was faced with the impossibility of allocating specifically the profits earned by the processes conducted within its borders.

It does not follow, however, that all the expenses of producing that income are equally difficult to identify on a geographic basis. To be sure, many expenses, such as the costs of centralized services or interest payments on company-wide debt, would generally be as difficult to segregate on a geographic basis as the income these expenses helped to generate. Other expenses, however, such as local real estate taxes, clearly can be so segregated.

The mere fact that some expenses can be identified on a geographic basis does not mean that a denial of a deduction for those expenses raises concerns about unfair apportionment. For example, if a state denied a deduction for local real estate taxes no matter where incurred, the increase in the apportionable tax base, and hence in taxable income, would not implicate the fair apportionment criterion. There is nothing in the disallowance of such a deduction that would systematically distort the relationship between the income apportioned to the state and the activities carried on there.

When, on the other hand, an expense can be identified on a geographic basis and that expense is associated exclusively with out-of-state activity, the denial of a deduction for the expense from unitary income does raise serious concerns about unfair apportionment. The inexorable effect of denying the expense deduction is to increase the portion of unitary income attributable to out-of-state activity. When the income is apportioned to the deduction-denying state, the result is the inclusion of a disproportionate component of out-of-state

---

[78]See note 47 *supra*.

[79]Underwood Typewriter Co. v. Chamberlain, 254 U.S. 113, 120 (1920).

values in the tax base and the taxation of income that is necessarily greater than can fairly be attributed to in-state business activities.

If, then, the windfall profit tax constitutes an exclusively out-of-state expense, a persuasive case can be made that New Jersey's denial of a windfall profit tax deduction violated the fair apportionment criterion. The Court never reached this question because of its view that "[f]or fair apportionment purposes, the relevant question is whether the windfall profit tax is a cost of a unitary business, rather than what the attributes of that cost may be."[80] Nevertheless, the taxpayers had the better of the argument over the question whether the windfall profit tax is in fact is a site-specific cost that is incurred exclusively outside of New Jersey. It is imposed on a specific activity—the removal of taxable crude oil—that occurs at a geographically identifiable location, and it has many of the earmarks of a severance tax, which the Court itself has characterized as site-specific.[81]

Does this mean that the Court erred in failing to strike down New Jersey's tax as unfairly apportioned? Not necessarily. First, even if the Court had recognized the flaws in New Jersey's taxing scheme, it might still have concluded (as it did in *Amerada Hess*) that the taxpayers failed to carry the burden of proving unfair apportionment by demonstrating "that there is no rational relationship between the income attributed to the State and the intrastate values of the enterprise."[82]Second, the Court may have declined to adopt a rule condemning the disallowance of out-of-state expense deductions for sound institutional reasons. Adoption of such a rule would have required courts to determine whether a whole array of routine tax deductions pass constitutional muster (such as deductions for depletion or for intangible drilling costs). Moreover, unless the Court had limited its holding to cases involving exclusively out-of-state expenses, courts would have been saddled with the task of determining the level of disallowed in-state expense deductions that would insulate the disallowance of an out-of-state expense deduction from constitutional attack. The mere prospect of overseeing the development of such a body of case law may have dissuaded the Court from authorizing an inquiry into these questions.

---

[80]*Amerada Hess*, 109 S.Ct. at 1622 n.7.

[81]See text at note 52 *supra*.

[82]*Amerada Hess*, 109 S.Ct. at 1622 (quoting *Container*, 463 U.S. at 180).

C. DISCRIMINATION

The rule forbidding state taxes that discriminate against interstate commerce has been a central tenet of the Court's Commerce Clause doctrine ever since the Court invoked the Clause more than a century ago as the basis for invalidating a state tax.[83] Although the concept of discrimination is not self-defining and the Court has never precisely delineated the scope of the prohibition against discriminatory taxes, the essential meaning of discrimination as a criterion for adjudicating the constitutionality of state taxes affecting interstate commerce emerges unmistakably from the Court's numerous decisions addressing the issue: a tax that by its terms or operation imposes greater burdens on out-of-state goods, activities, or enterprises than on competing in-state goods, activities, or enterprises will be struck down as discriminatory under the Commerce Clause.

In *Goldberg*, the taxpayers claimed that Illinois' 5 percent tax on the gross receipts from interstate telecommunications discriminated against interstate commerce, despite the existence of an identical 5 percent tax on intrastate telecommunications, because interstate calls bore a relatively heavier tax burden than intrastate calls. The argument can best be understood by illustration, which Justice Stevens provided in his concurring opinion:[84]

> A call originating in and terminating in Illinois that costs $10 is taxed at full value at 5%. A second call, originating in Illinois but terminating in Indiana, costs the same $10 and is taxed at the same full value at the same 5% rate. But while Illinois may properly tax the entire $10 of the first call, it (technically) may tax only that portion of the second call over which it has jurisdiction, namely, the intrastate portion of the call (say, for example, $5). By imposing an identical 50¢ tax on the two calls, Illinois has imposed a disproportionate burden on the interstate call.

The Court's reasoning dismissing the taxpayers' argument was unpersuasive. The Court first noted that the Illinois tax was distinguishable from Pennsylvania's flat trucking taxes it had recently invalidated because the levies bore more heavily on interstate trucks than intrastate trucks.[85] The former traveled fewer miles on state highways than the latter and, as a consequence, interstate trucks were subjected to a higher per-mile charge than the intrastate trucks

---

[83]See Welton v. Missouri, 91 U.S. 275 (1876).

[84]109 S.Ct. at 593 (Stevens, J., concurring).

[85]American Trucking Ass'ns, Inc. v. Scheiner, 483 U.S. 266 (1987).

for exercising the same privilege. The point of distinction the Court perceived between the Pennsylvania and Illinois taxes was that Pennsylvania's taxes burdened out-of-state truckers, who would have difficulty effecting legislative change, whereas Illinois' tax burdened local consumers, who presumably had access to the political process.[86] "It is not the purpose of the Commerce Clause," the Court declared, "to protect state residents from their own state taxes."[87]

Surely the Court cannot have meant what it said. If Illinois had imposed a tax on state residents' purchases of out-of-state but not in-state goods, the tax would have been struck down in short order. A more blatant discrimination against interstate commerce in violation of the "free trade" principles underlying the Commerce Clause is difficult to imagine. It is a cardinal purpose of the Commerce Clause to protect state residents from their own state taxes when those taxes discriminate against interstate Commerce. Justice Stevens recognized this point in his concurring opinion.[88] One would hope that upon further reflection, the Court will repudiate its careless remark.

The Court's second ground for dismissing the taxpayers' discrimination claim was that, in contrast to the measurable indicia of local presence reflected by the trucks' mileage on state highways which provided the Court with a basis for finding that the Pennsylvania highway taxes bore more heavily on out-of-state than local trucks, "the exact path of thousands of electronic signals can neither be traced nor recorded."[89] It "therefore" followed that the tax did not discriminate against interstate commerce.[90] Despite the Court's professed inability to identify the amount of discrimination, if any, that resulted from the Illinois levy, one suspects that there is in fact some discrimination if one analyzes the issue in terms of the example set forth above.[91] Moreover, the Court has declared that "we need not know how unequal the Tax is before concluding that it unconstitutionally discriminates."[92]

The more compelling response to the discrimination claim was that the taxpayers' argument proceeded on a false premise, namely,

---

[86]109 S.Ct. at 591.

[87]*Ibid.*

[88]*Id.* at 592–93.

[89]*Id.* at 591.

[90]*Ibid.*

[91]See text at note 84 *supra.*

[92]Maryland v. Louisiana, 451 U.S. 725, 760 (1981).

that the discrimination issue should be analyzed solely in terms of calls that Illinois actually seeks to tax because they are charged to an Illinois service address. If one instead analyzes the issue in terms of the entire universe of calls originating and terminating in Illinois, only about one-half of which Illinois seeks to tax, the discrimination claim evaporates.[93] Justice Stevens, referring to the example set forth above,[94] put it this way:[95]

> Although Illinois taxes the entirety of every call charged to an Illinois number, it does not tax any part of the calls that are received at an Illinois number but charged elsewhere. Thus, although Illinois taxes the entire Illinois-Indiana $10 call, it taxes no part of the reciprocal Indiana-Illinois $10 call. At the 5% rate, Illinois receives 50¢ from the two calls combined, precisely the amount it receives from one $10 purely intrastate call. By taxing half the relevant universe of interstate calls at full value, Illinois achieves the same economic result as taxing all of those calls at half value would achieve. As a result, interstate phone calls are taxed at a lower effective rate than intrastate calls, and accordingly bear a proportional tax burden.

In *Amerada Hess*, the taxpayers' constitutional attack on New Jersey's denial of a windfall profit tax deduction was easily cast in the form of an argument that the tax discriminated against interstate commerce. The alleged effect of the statutory scheme was to single out for special tax burdens a form of business activity that is conducted only in other jurisdictions. The levy therefore imposed a discriminatorily higher effective tax burden on out-of-state than on local business.[96]

Thus framed, however, the taxpayers' argument suffered from a lack of evidence that New Jersey had intentionally or explicitly singled out the windfall profit tax for invidious treatment. Indeed, the statute, which denied a deduction for "[t]axes paid or accrued to the United States on or measured by profits or income,"[97] was drafted long before the windfall profit tax was enacted in 1980. Moreover, it was applied to deny a deduction for federal income taxes. Hence it

[93]The fair apportionment claim collapsed in a similar fashion when it was viewed in the context of the entire universe of interstate telephone calls originating and terminating in Illinois. See text accompanying notes 65–67 *supra*.

[94]See text at note 84 *supra*.

[95]109 S.Ct. at 593 (Stevens, J., concurring).

[96]See Brief for Appellants 41–49, *Amerada Hess*, 109 S.Ct. 1617.

[97]N.J. Stat. Ann. § 54:10A–4(k) (West 1986).

could not be argued that the statute by its terms or by design discriminated against interstate commerce.

It is well settled, of course, that the Commerce Clause proscribes taxes that, though nondiscriminatory on their face, nevertheless discriminate against interstate commerce by their practical operation.[98] If denying the windfall profit tax deduction in practical effect disallows the deduction of an out-of-state expense, and there is no comparable in-state expense whose deduction is disallowed, then it would seem that a prima facie case of state tax discrimination has been stated. The Court found, however, that no such claim had been stated. Its determination rested largely on the basis of the questionable conclusion that the windfall profit tax was comparable to the federal income tax—or at least that it was not "irrational or arbitrary" for New Jersey so to consider the tax.[99] If the windfall profit tax is viewed as comparable to the federal income tax, it undermines the contention that out-of-state expense and business activity has been singled out for discriminatory treatment because the federal income tax is not an exclusively out-of-state expense. Once the Court rejected the taxpayers' premise that the New Jersey statute singled out the windfall profit tax for a deduction denial, it could leave for another day the question "whether a statute that did so would impermissibly discriminate against interstate commerce."[100]

D. FAIR RELATION BETWEEN THE TAX AND THE SERVICES PROVIDED BY THE STATE

The first three prongs of the Court's contemporary Commerce Clause standard—substantial nexus, fair apportionment, and nondiscrimination—were familiar concepts deeply embedded in the Court's doctrine for years before *Complete Auto Transit* was handed down in 1977. By contrast, the fourth prong—the requirement that

[98]See, *e.g.*, Nippert v. City of Richmond, 327 U.S. 416, 431 (1946); Best & Co. v. Maxwell, 311 U.S. 454, 456 (1940).

[99]*Amerada Hess*, 109 S.Ct. at 1623 n.9. The Court based its conclusion on the facts that the windfall profit tax was intended to reach only the excess income derived from oil production as a result of decontrol, that the "net income limitation" assured that the tax was imposed only on receipts above cost, and that the Internal Revenue Service characterized the structure of the tax as more akin to an income tax than to an excise tax. *Ibid.* Most other observers, however, including the Solicitor General, are of the view that the windfall profit tax more closely resembles an ordinary severance tax than the federal income tax. See Brief for the United States as Amicus Curiae in support of Juris. Statement 24–27; Attermeier & Reveley, note 54 *supra*; Robison, note 54 *supra*.

[100]*Amerada Hess*, 109 S.Ct. at 1624.

a tax be "fairly related to the services provided by the State"[101]—was an uncertain, if not an unknown, quantity when the Court articulated it along with the other three Commerce Clause criteria in *Complete Auto Transit*. Read literally, the Court's language could have been taken as contemplating a detailed factual investigation into the specific benefits the state provided to the taxpayer to ascertain whether the value of the benefits bore a reasonable relationship to the amount of the tax imposed. With the exception of cases involving state-imposed user charges,[102] however, no such detailed factual investigation had ever been required by the Court in determining the validity of a tax under the Commerce Clause. Moreover, language in several of its opinions following on the heels of *Complete Auto Transit* suggested that the "fairly related" standard would be satisfied so long as the state provided the taxpayer with "the benefits of a trained work force and the advantages of a civilized society."[103]

In *Commonwealth Edison Co. v. Montana*,[104] which considered a challenge to Montana's 30 percent coal severance tax, the Court lifted the shroud of uncertainty that had obscured the meaning of the "fairly related" test and made it clear that the test was not an invitation to judicial review of taxes for excessiveness. The Court held that the relevant inquiry under the "fairly related" test is whether the tax is reasonably related to the extent of the taxpayers' contact with the state, "since it is the activities or presence of the taxpayer in the State that may properly be made to bear a 'just share of state tax burden.'"[105] Justice Blackmun, the author of *Complete Auto Transit*, vigorously dissented from the Court's view of the meaning of the "fairly related" test, asserting that the Court had "emasculated" the fourth prong and left it utterly without meaning.[106]

Cases following *Commonwealth Edison* vindicate Justice Blackmun's complaint. The "fairly related" test appears to have little independent significance as a restraint on state tax power. Any tax held to violate the "fairly related" test is likely to flunk some other portion of

---

[101]*Complete Auto Transit*, 430 U.S. at 279.

[102]See, *e.g.*, Evansville-Vanderburgh Airport Authority District v. Delta Airlines, 405 U.S. 707 (1972).

[103]Japan Line, Ltd. v. County of Los Angeles, 441 U.S. 434, 445 (1979); see also Department of Revenue v. Association of Washington Stevedoring Cos., 435 U.S. 734, 750–51 (1978).

[104]453 U.S. 609 (1981).

[105]*Id.* at 626 (quoting Western Live Stock v. Bureau of Revenue, 303 U.S. 250, 254 (1938)).

[106]*Id.* at 645 (Blackmun, J., dissenting).

the Court's Commerce Clause standard as well.[107] And it is hard to conceive of any tax that would satisfy the substantial nexus, fair apportionment, and nondiscrimination criteria that would not also satisfy the "fairly related" test.[108]

Goldberg and *Amerada Hess* reinforce this conclusion. The Court had little difficulty in concluding that both levies, which had already passed the first three prongs of the Court's Commerce Clause test, likewise passed the fourth. In *Goldberg*, the Court observed that "[t]he fourth prong of the *Complete Auto* test focuses on the wide range of benefits provided to the taxpayer, not just the precise activity connected to the interstate activity at issue."[109] Illinois telephone consumers received numerous benefits from Illinois, including "police and fire protection as well as the other general services provided by the State."[110] The Illinois telecommunications tax therefore survived constitutional scrutiny, if it can be called that, under the "fairly related" test. The Court similarly concluded that New Jersey's corporate income tax was "fairly related" to the services provided by the state in light of the benefits provided by New Jersey "'which include police and fire protection, the benefits of a trained work force and "the advantages of a civilized society."'"[111]

---

[107]Thus in American Trucking Associations, Inc. v. Scheiner, 483 U.S. 266, 291 (1987), the only case in which the Court has invoked the "fairly related" test in striking down a state tax, the flat tax on trucks was also held to violate the Commerce Clause's nondiscrimination requirement.

[108]None exists to my knowledge.

[109]109 S.Ct. at 592.

[110]*Ibid.*

[111]*Amerada Hess*, 109 S.Ct. at 1624 (quoting Exxon Corp. v. Wisconsin Department of Revenue, 447 U.S. 209, 228 (1980) (quoting Japan Line, Ltd, 441 U.S. at 445)).

The only other case touching on the Commerce Clause during the Court's 1988 Term was Cotton Petroleum Corp. v. New Mexico, 109 S. Ct. 1698 (1989), where the Court held that New Mexico could validly impose severance taxes on oil and gas extracted from Indian lands by non-Indian lessees despite the fact that the Indian tribe imposed similar taxes on the same oil and gas production. In so holding the Court rejected the argument that the tax imposed a multiple burden on interstate commerce. It reasoned that until Congress provides otherwise, both the tribe and the state had taxing jurisdiction over the taxpayer's oil and gas leases. *Id.* at 1714. It also rejected the claim that the state tax exceeded the benefits provided to the taxpayer, observing that "there is no constitutional requirement that the benefits received from a taxing authority by an ordinary commercial taxpayer—or by those living in the community where the taxpayer is located—must equal the amount of its tax obligations." *Ibid.* Finally, the Court held that a tribe should not be treated as a state under the Commerce Clause for purposes of determining whether the state's tax must be fairly apportioned: "[T]he fact that States and tribes have concurrent jurisdiction over the same territory makes it inappropriate to apply Commerce Clause doctrine developed in the context of commerce 'among' States with mutually exclusive territorial jurisdiction to trade 'with' Indian tribes." *Id.* at 1716.

II. The Due Process Clause

The Supreme Court has construed the Due Process Clause as a limitation on the territorial reach of the states' taxing powers.[112] The Due Process Clause, like the Commerce Clause, has been construed to require that the state have a minimum connection or nexus with the person, property, or transaction it seeks to tax, and that the measure of the tax fairly reflect the taxpayer's activities in the state, *i.e.* that it be fairly apportioned. On numerous occasions the Court has recognized that the requirements of the Commerce and Due Process Clauses in the nexus and apportionment contexts are substantially the same.[113] In *Amerada Hess*, the Court reiterated that "the *Complete Auto* test encompasses due process standards."[114] Thus in the only due process challenge to a state tax it considered during its 1988 Term, the Court declared that because New Jersey's income tax "passes all four prongs of the *Complete Auto* test, we also conclude that it does not violate due process."[115]

III. The Equal Protection Clause

In light of the broad leeway the states enjoy under the Equal Protection Clause in drawing lines for tax purposes "when no specific federal right, apart from equal protection, is imperiled,"[116] it may come as somewhat of a surprise that the Court has invalidated a number of state taxes on equal protection grounds in recent years. In the space of single year, the Court relied on the Equal Protection Clause to strike down a gross premiums tax discriminating against out-of-state insurers,[117] a use tax credit limited to residents for sales taxes paid to other states,[118] and a property tax exemption limited to

---

[112]The Court first invoked the Due Process Clause as a prohibition of extraterritorial taxation in Louisville & Jeffersonville Ferry Co. v. Kentucky, 188 U.S. 385, 398 (1903). See Central Railroad Co. v. Pennsylvania, 370 U.S. 607, 620 (1962) (Black, J., concurring).

[113]See, *e.g.*, National Bellas Hess v. Department of Revenue, 386 U.S. 753, 756 (1967) (nexus); Ott v. Mississippi Valley Barge Line Co., 336 U.S. 169, 174 (1949) (apportionment).

[114]109 S.Ct. at 1625.

[115]*Ibid.*

[116]Lehnhausen v. Lake Shore Auto Parts Co., 410 U.S. 356, 359 (1973); see also Exxon Corp. v. Eagerton, 462 U.S. 176, 196 (1983) ("'[l]egislatures have especially broad latitude in creating classifications and distinctions in tax statutes'").

[117]Metropolitan Life Insurance Co. v. Ward, 470 U.S. 869 (1985).

[118]Williams v. Vermont, 472 U.S. 14 (1985).

Vietnam veterans who were residents of the state prior to a certain date.[119]

Perhaps these decisions can be explained by the fact that they raised serious concerns of interstate federalism and therefore fell within the exception to the Court's generally relaxed oversight of state tax classifications. To be sure, this explanation flies in the face of the Court's position that the Equal Protection Clause should not be construed as an "instrument of federalism."[120] It also runs counter to the Court's declaration that discrimination against out-of-state interests need only be rationally related to a legitimate state purpose to survive equal protection scrutiny.[121] Yet, it is difficult to make sense of these decisions except as heightened judicial scrutiny masquerading as "rational basis" analysis.[122]

The Court's most recent decision striking down a state taxing scheme under the Equal Protection Clause, however, cannot be explained on these grounds. *Allegheny Pittsburgh Coal Co. v. County Commission*[123] involved neither suspect classifications nor fundamental rights, and no specific federal interest, apart from equal protection, was jeopardized. *Allegheny* concerned a challenge to gross disparities in ad valorem property tax assessments resulting from the practice of assessing property based on its recent sales price. Like many taxing jurisdictions across the country, Webster County, West Virginia, relied on sales prices of recently conveyed property in determining its value for ad valorem tax purposes and did not systematically adjust the assessment of unsold comparable properties to reflect current value. So long as property was unsold, it remained on the tax rolls with the same assessment it bore in prior years, with only minor and infrequent adjustments. As a consequence, recently conveyed property was often assessed at a much higher percentage of its fair market value than was comparable property that had not recently been sold. Indeed, the record in *Allegheny* revealed that the taxpayers' property—consisting of coal-bearing lands—was as-

---

[119]Hooper v. Bernalillo County Assessor, 472 U.S. 612 (1985).

[120]Western & Southern Life Ins. Co. v. State Bd. of Equalization, 451 U.S. 648, 667 n.21 (1981).

[121]*Ibid.*

[122]See Cohen, Federalism in Equality Clothing: A Comment on Metropolitan Life Insurance Company v. Ward, 38 Stan. L. Rev. 1 (1985).

[123]109 S.Ct. 633 (1989).

sessed at approximately eight to 35 times more than comparable neighboring properties.[124]

In a brief opinion, the Court sustained the taxpayers' claim that the county's assessment practice violated the Equal Protection Clause. While reiterating the well-entrenched principle that the states have broad powers under the Clause to impose different types of taxes upon different types of taxpayers and property, the Court observed that the county assessor made no attempt to justify the disparities in assessment on the ground that recently sold and unsold property constituted two different classes of property that were to be taxed differently according to deliberate state policy. Indeed, the opposite was true: West Virginia's constitution and implementing statutes provided that all the property in question was to be taxed at a uniform rate throughout the state according to its value. Given the state's own professed adherence to a standard of uniformity and equality of property assessments based on market value, the county assessor's reliance on actual sales prices as the basis for achieving such equality could not be justified as a state-sanctioned classification scheme.

Nor could the practice be viewed as a mere "transitional delay in adjustment of assessed value"[125] or as one of those "occasional errors or state law or mistakes in judgment"[126] that the Equal Protection Clause would tolerate. In contrast to a program of generalized adjustments in property values designed to equalize the value of properties for short periods without the necessity of reappraising every parcel every year, the assessor's occasional adjustments to the assessment of unsold property were "too small to seasonably dissipate the remaining disparity between these assessments and the assessments based on a recent purchase price."[127] Moreover, the assessor's practice that produced the disparate assessments was "intentional"[128] and "systematic"[129] and therefore could not be dismissed as a permissible error in judgment.

From a doctrinal perspective, the Court's opinion in *Allegheny* is unexceptional. It is settled law that "intentional systematic under-

---

[124]*Id*. at 638.

[125]*Ibid*.

[126]*Ibid*.

[127]*Ibid*.

[128]*Ibid*.

[129]*Ibid*.

valuation by state officials of other taxable property in the same class contravenes the constitutional right of one taxed upon the full value of his property."[130] In light of the Court's determination that the discriminatory assessments resulted from "intentional systematic undervaluation" by the county assessor and that the property in question was considered by West Virginia to fall within a single class, it followed as a matter of course that the taxpayers had been denied equal protection.[131]

From a practical perspective, however, the Court's holding has considerable significance. There are hundreds of taxing jurisdictions throughout the nation with "methods" of achieving equality among different parcels that are essentially indistinguishable from that of Webster County, West Virginia. Assessments from such jurisdictions would appear to be vulnerable to equal protection challenge, at least if disparities of the magnitude that were proven in *Allegheny* can be demonstrated elsewhere.[132]

The Court's decision in *Allegheny* also raises serious questions about the constitutionality of California's Proposition 13.[133] Proposition 13 amended the state constitution to limit property taxes to 1 percent of 1975–76 valuations and to prohibit annual increases in valuations of more than 2 percent, unless the property is sold. The Court was well aware of the potential implications of its decision for California's taxing system, and observed in a footnote:[134]

> We need not and do not decide today whether the Webster County assessment method would stand on a different footing if it were the law of a State, generally applied, instead of the aberra-

---

[130]Sunday Lake Iron Co. v. Wakefield, 247 U.S. 350, 352–53 (1918). See also Sioux City Bridge Co. v. Dakota County, 260 U.S. 441, 445–46 (1923); Cumberland Coal Co. v. Board of Revision of Tax Assessments, 284 U.S. 23, 28–29 (1931); Hillsborough v. Town of Cromwell, 326 U.S. 620 (1946).

[131]The Court also held, in line with established precedent, see cases cited in note 130 *supra*, that the taxpayers could not be relegated to the remedy of seeking to have the assessments of the undervalued property raised, as the West Virginia Supreme Court had suggested. In re 1975 Tax Assessments against Oneida Coal Co., 360 S.E.2d 560, 565 (W. Va. 1987). Rather they were entitled under the Equal Protection Clause to have their assessments reduced to the level at which comparable properties were assessed.

[132]See, *e.g.*, Township of West Milford v. Van Decker, 235 N.J. Super. 1, 561 A.2d 607 (1989) (increased assessment of property based on sales price violates federal and state constitutions); Krugman v. Village of Atlantic Beach, 121 A.D.2d 175, 533 N.Y.S.2d 495 (2d Dep't 1988) (assessor's practice of selective reassessment of only those properties in the taxing district that were sold during the prior year contravenes statutory and constitutional mandates).

[133]Cal. Const. art. XIIIA, §2.

[134]109 S.Ct. at 638 n.4.

tional enforcement policy it appears to be. The State of California has adopted a similar policy. . . popularly known as
"Proposition 13.". . . The system is grounded on the belief that
taxes should based on the original cost of property and should not
tax unrealized paper gains in the value of property.

The Court appears to be suggesting that Webster County's discrimination against recently purchased property may be distinguishable from California's because the former reflected the "aberrational"
actions of a single assessor, contrary to the policy of West Virginia to
tax all property equally, whereas the latter reflects the considered
policy of a state. But one has to ask which way that distinction cuts.
Is the Equal Protection Clause less offended by discrimination that
reflects deliberate state policy than by discrimination resulting from
the aberrational conduct of a single individual?

Although as an original proposition one might have thought not,
an affirmative answer to this question is deeply rooted in equal protection doctrine. The Equal Protection Clause, after all, only protects against unjustifiable discrimination. If "rational basis" is the
standard of justification, as it is in the context of tax classifications
that do not implicate federal concerns apart from equal protection,[135] then if the discrimination has a "rational basis," as it arguably does in California, it will pass muster under the Equal Protection
Clause.[136]

Assuming that California's ad valorem property tax system would
survive scrutiny under the Equal Protection Clause,[137] it raises a se-

---

[135]Because the practice of reassessing property based on recent sales will bear dispropor-
tionately on newcomers to the taxing jurisdiction, including those who have moved from other
states, one could argue that such a practice does in fact raise federalism concerns, thus triggering a higher standard of equal protection scrutiny. See Shapiro v. Thompson, 394 U.S. 618
(1969); Indeed, as suggested above, see text accompanying notes 116–22 supra, the Court has
been inclined to strike down taxing schemes that threaten federalism interests even under a
"rational basis" analysis. See cases cited in notes 117–19 supra; see also Zobel v. Williams, 457
U.S. 55 (1982).

[136]But see note 135 supra. Writing without the benefit of the Supreme Court's guidance in
Allegheny, the California Supreme Court dismissed a constitutional challenge to Proposition 13
on equal protection and other grounds. Amador Valley Joint Union High School District v.
State Board of Equalization, 22 Cal. 3d 318, 149 Cal. Rptr. 239, 583 P.2d 1281 (1981). The
Court distinguished the principal cases underlying the Allegheny decision, see cases cited in
note 130 supra, on the ground that those cases "involved constitutional or statutory provisions
which mandated the taxation of property on a current value basis" and they "do not purport to
confine the states to a current value system under equal protection principles." 22 Cal. 3d at
235, 149 Cal. Rptr. at 251, 583 P.2d at 1293. No review of this decision was sought in the
United States Supreme Court.

[137]A definitive resolution of this issue is possible in due course. See Northwest Financial,
Inc. v. San Diego County, Cal. Super. Ct., San Diego Cty., No. 611092, filed April 12, 1989
(challenging the constitutionality of Proposition 13 in light of Allegheny).

ries of additional questions bearing on the relationship between a taxpayer's federal right to equal protection and the underlying state classification scheme. If a state can classify property for ad valorem tax purposes on the basis of sales price, then, as the Court has stated in an analogous context, "the only question relevant for us is whether the state has done so."[138] The Court's conclusion in *Allegheny*, of course, was based on its determination that the state had not done so.[139] Does this mean, however, that if West Virginia tomorrow were formally to adopt an ad valorem tax system based on recent sales prices that the preexisting practice of the Webster County assessor would satisfy equal protection strictures? Apparently so, assuming the constitutionality of Proposition 13.

But why should the result be any different merely because the classification in West Virginia was de facto rather than de jure? As the Court declared in *Nashville, C. & St. L. Ry. v. Browning*,[140] in dismissing an equal protection challenge by a railroad to the valuation of its property which was overvalued by comparison to the valuation of other property in Tennessee:[141]

> If the discrimination of which the Railway complains had been formally written into the statutes of Tennessee, a challenge to its constitutionality would be frivolous. If the state supreme court had construed the requirement of uniformity in the Tennessee Constitution so as to permit recognition of these diversities, no appeal could successfully be made to the Fourteenth Amendment. Here . . . all the organs of the state are conforming to a practice, systematic, unbroken for more than forty years, and now questioned for the first time. It would be a narrow conception of jurisprudence to confine the notion of "laws" to what is found written on the statute books, and to disregard the gloss which life has written upon it. Settled state practice cannot supplant constitutional guarantees, but it can establish what is state law. . . . And if the state supreme court chooses to cover up under a formal veneer of uniformity the established system of differentiation between two classes of property, an exposure of that fiction is not enough to establish its unconstitutionality. . . . the Equal Protection Clause is not a command of candor.

---

[138]Nashville, C. & St. L. Ry. v. Browning, 310 U.S. 362, 369 (1940). The first clause of the sentence quoted in the text reads "[s]ince, so far as the Federal Constitution is concerned, a state can put railroad property into one pigeonhole and other property into another . . ." *Ibid.*

[139]See text following note 124 *supra.*

[140]310 U.S. 362 (1940).

[141]*Id.* at 369.

The Court's answer would presumably be the one it gave in *Allegheny*: "There is no suggestion in the opinion of the Supreme Court of West Virginia, or from any other authoritative source, that the State may have adopted a different system in practice from that specified by statute."[142] But it is difficult to reconcile this view with the West Virginia Supreme Court's declaration that "[t]he uniform use of recent deed values as the basis for appraising property subject to *ad valorem* taxation does not violate *W. Va. Const.*, art X, §1 ['taxation shall be equal and uniform throughout the State']."[143] If the Tennessee Supreme Court may "cover up under a formal veneer of uniformity the established system of differentiation between two classes of property,"[144] why may not the West Virginia Supreme Court do so? Perhaps the evidence of the adoption of an implicit policy applied evenhandedly to all similarly situated property in the state was not as strong in West Virginia as it was in Tennessee.[145] In any event, the Court's opinion in *Allegheny* leaves us with this perplexing question: When does "intentional systematic undervaluation by state officials of property in the same class,"[146] which is nevertheless sanctioned by the highest court of the state as satisfying that state's uniformity and equality requirement, amount merely to a covering up "under a formal veneer of uniformity the established system of differentiation between two classes of property"?[147]

There is one final variation on *Allegheny*'s implications for the relationship between federal and state law that is worthy of consideration, illustrated by a recent decision of the Nebraska Supreme Court.[148] Most personal property in Nebraska is exempt from taxation. The personal property of railroads, pipelines, and other centrally assessed utilities is taxable, however. After the railroads' personal property had been held excludable from ad valorem taxation under a federal statute protecting railroads from discriminatory taxation,[149] the pipelines, which are not protected by the statute,

[142] 109 S.Ct. at 638.

[143] In re 1975 Tax Assessments Against Oneida Coal Co., 360 S.E.2d 560, 564 (W. Va. 1987).

[144] *Nashville, C. & St. L. Ry.*, 310 U.S. at 369.

[145] See *Allegheny*, 109 S.Ct. at 638–39.

[146] *Sunday Lake Iron*, 247 U.S. at 352–53.

[147] *Nashville, C. & St. L. Ry.*, 310 U.S. at 369.

[148] Northern Natural Gas Co. v. State Board of Equalization and Assessment, 232 Neb. 806, 443 N.W.2d 249 (1989).

[149] 49 U.S.C. §11503 (1982).

claimed that they were entitled to the same treatment as the railroads. Relying on both the state uniformity provision and the federal Equal Protection Clause, the Nebraska court sustained the pipelines' claim.

The significant question raised by the Nebraska decision is whether the lowering of assessed property values of some taxpayers pursuant to federal law[150] provides other taxpayers of the same class with a right to the same treatment under the Equal Protection Clause. Although a mechanical application of *Allegheny* could lead to that conclusion, such a conclusion is unwarranted. In *Allegheny* and its predecessors,[151] the states were under no federal obligation to classify. The states' classification scheme, or lack thereof, therefore governed the equal protection inquiry. So long as the states' classification met the loose "rational basis" requirement, the only judicially cognizable equal protection question was whether the state had in fact accorded equal treatment to property it had placed in a particular class.

In the Nebraska case, by contrast, federal law created a classification scheme that is binding on the states. So long as this classification scheme has a rational basis, as the federal legislation plainly does, no substantial equal protection attack can be leveled against the classification. And this is so regardless of how the states might originally have classified the property at issue apart from their obligation to conform to federal law. In short, it would misread *Allegheny* to conclude that the Equal Protection Clause requires that all property the state places in a particular class must be treated alike when federal law dictates that one subclass[152] of such property be assessed at a lower rate than that prescribed by the state for the class in question.[153]

---

[150]There are federal statutes providing motor carriers and air carriers with similar protection to that afforded railroads against discriminatory property taxation. 49 U.S.C. §11503a (1982); 49 U.S.C. App. §1513(d) (1982).

[151]See note 130 *supra*.

[152]As indicated above, the subclassification must be able to survive equal protection scrutiny.

[153]See State v. Colonial Pipeline Co., 471 So. 2d 408 (Ala. Civ. App. 1984), writ. quashed, Ex Parte Colonial Pipeline Co., 471 So. 2d 413 (Ala. 1985), appeal dismissed, 474 U.S. 936 (1985) and Federal Express Corp. v. Tennessee State Board of Equalization, 717 S.W.2d 873 (Tenn. 1986) both of which reached conclusions contrary to the Nebraska Supreme Court on this issue.

The only other equal protection issue addressed by the Court during its 1988 Term was raised by *Amerada Hess*. The Court summarily dismissed the claim, noting that "there is no discriminatory classification" underlying New Jersey's denial of the windfall profit tax deduc-

IV. Intergovernmental Immunity

From the very beginning of our constitutional history, it has been clear that the states may not impose taxes discriminating against the federal government. Indeed, the seminal case articulating the doctrine of federal immunity from state taxation, *McCulloch v. Maryland*,[154] involved a tax that discriminated against the federal government, and the decision could have been read as suggesting that the immunity the federal government enjoyed from state taxation applied only to taxes that discriminated against the federal government.[155] In any event, despite the Court's narrowing of the federal government's immunity in cases involving nondiscriminatory taxes,[156] the Court has steadfastly adhered to the fundamental principle that the Supremacy Clause bars taxes discriminating against the federal government.[157]

The Court revisited the question of the federal government's immunity from discriminatory taxation during its 1988 Term in *Davis v. Michigan Department of Treasury*.[158] Like many other states, Michigan exempted from personal income taxation all retirement benefits paid by the state or its political subdivisions while taxing retirement benefits paid by all other employers, including the federal government. Paul Davis, a former federal employee who argued the case on his own behalf in the Supreme Court, contended that Michigan's exemption for state but not federal employees was barred by federal law. Although the technical question before the Court was whether the state's disparate treatment of state and federal employees violated a federal statute preserving federal employees' immunity from discriminatory taxation,[159] the Court concluded that the immunity

---

tion and that "there is unquestionably a rational basis" for such denial. *Amerada Hess*, 109 S.Ct. at 1625.

[154]4 Wheat. 316 (1819).

[155]*Id.* at 436; First Agricultural National Bank of Berkshire County v. State Tax Commission, 392 U.S. 229, 350 (1968) (Marshall, J., dissenting).

[156]See, *e.g.*, Washington v. United States, 460 U.S. 536 (1983); United States v. New Mexico, 455 U.S. 720 (1982). Broadly speaking, modern case law has narrowed the federal government's immunity from nondiscriminatory taxes to levies whose legal incidence falls on the federal government.

[157]See, *e.g.*, Memphis Bank & Trust Co. v. Garner, 459 U.S. 392 (1983); Phillips Chemical Co. v. Dumas Independent School District, 361 U.S. 376 (1960).

[158]109 S.Ct. 1500 (1989).

[159]The statute at issue, 4 U.S.C. §111 (1988), provides in pertinent part: "The United States consents to the taxation of pay or compensation for personal service as an officer or employee of

guaranteed by the statute was "coextensive with the prohibition against discriminatory taxes embodied in the modern constitutional doctrine of intergovernmental immunity."[160]

Michigan's taxing scheme indisputably discriminated in favor of state retirees and against federal retirees. The state argued, however, that the individual federal retiree was not entitled to claim the protection of the immunity doctrine and, in any event, that the state's differential treatment of state and federal retirees was justified by meaningful distinctions between the two classes of taxpayers. In striking down the levy, the Court rejected both of these arguments.

The state's first contention—that the federal immunity doctrine did not protect the federal retiree—was premised on the notion that the immunity doctrine was designed to protect the federal government, not private entities or individuals. So long as the challenged tax did not interfere with the federal government's ability to perform its governmental functions, the argument continued, there has been no violation of the immunity doctrine. While agreeing with the state's characterization of the overall purpose of the immunity doctrine, the Court disagreed with the inference the state drew from it. In the Court's eyes, it simply "does not follow that private entities or individuals who are subjected to discriminatory taxation on account of their dealings with a sovereign cannot themselves receive the protection of the constitutional doctrine."[161] Indeed, the Court observed that all precedent was to the contrary,[162] and the Court saw no reason to depart from that precedent.

The state's second defense of the less favorable treatment of federal as compared to state retirees was based on the ground that there were significant differences between the two classes of taxpayers. The state argued that its interest in hiring and retaining qualified civil servants through the inducement of exempting retirement benefits justified the preferential treatment of its retired employees. But the Court found this argument beside the point because it merely showed that the state had a rational basis for discriminating between

---

the United States . . . by a duly constituted taxing authority having jurisdiction, if the taxation does not discriminate against the officer or employee because of the source of the pay or compensation."

[160]109 S.Ct. at 1506.

[161]*Ibid.*

[162]See, *e.g.*, cases cited in note 157 *supra*.

two groups of retirees, not that there were significant differences be-tween the classes. [163]

The state found further significant differences between state and federal retirees warranting exemption for the former but not the lat-ter in the fact that state retirees generally received less generous re-tirement benefits than their federal counterparts. The Court again was unpersuaded. Even assuming the state was correct in its evalua-tion of the relative value of state and federal retirement benefits, the discrimination the state practiced did not serve its ostensible purpose: "A tax exemption truly intended to account for differences in retire-ment benefits would not discriminate on the basis of the source of those benefits, as Michigan's does; rather it would discriminate on the basis of the amount of benefits received by individual retirees." [164]

Justice Stevens filed a lone dissent from the Court's opinion in *Davis*. He recognized that there was "discrimination" against federal in favor of state retirees, but he did not regard such discrimination as unconstitutional. "The fact that a State may elect to grant a prefer-ence, or an exemption, to a small percentage of its residents does not make the tax discriminatory in any sense that is relevant to the doc-trine of intergovernmental immunity." [165] In Justice Stevens' view, so long as the tax imposed on federal retirees was imposed on the vast majority of voters in the state, as Michigan's tax was, there is a suffi-cient "political check" against excessive taxation to obviate the con-cerns that underlie the intergovernmental immunity doctrine. [166]

As *Davis* suggests, the critical issue in cases involving allegations of state tax discrimination against the federal government often boils down to the delineation of the appropriate universe of taxpayers with whom the federal taxpayers are to be compared. In *Davis* and other cases [167] in which those who dealt with the federal government were treated like the vast majority of other taxpayers in the state, but less favorably than a small group of taxpayers who dealt with the state,

---

[163]109 S.Ct. at 1508. The Court reiterated the point it had made in response to a similar argument in *Phillips Chemical*, 361 U.S. 376, that the criteria for adjudicating alleged discrimi-nation against the federal government are not the loose standards associated with equal protec-tion analysis but rather the existence of "significant differences" between the classes. *Ibid.*

[164]*Ibid.*

[165]*Id.* at 1511.

[166]*Id.* at 1512–13.

[167]See *Phillips*, 361 U.S. 376 (1960); Moses Lake Homes, Inc. v. Grant County, 365 U.S. 744 (1961); Memphis Bank, 459 U.S. 392 (1983); United States v. City of Manassas, 108 S. Ct. 1568 (1988) aff'g without opinion 830 F.2d 530 (4th Cir. 1987).

the question whether there is unconstitutional discrimination depends entirely on whether one limits the comparison to those who deal with the federal and state governments or whether one takes account of the vast majority of other taxpayers who are treated like those who deal with the federal government. Despite Justice Stevens' plea that the relevant question is whether the vast majority of taxpayers in the state are treated like those who deal with the federal government, thereby providing a "political check" against abuse of the power to tax,[168] the Court's precedents show its strong inclination to strike down taxes that favor those who deal with the state over those who deal with the federal government.[169] However attractive Justice Stevens' position may be in theory, the Court apparently feels more comfortable with the simpler notion that "it does not seem too much to require that the State treat those who deal with the Government as well as it treats those with whom it deals itself."[170]

The Court has not clearly indicated, on the other hand, whether a statute that treats those who deal with public or exempt entities (including the federal government) differently from those who deal with the private sector constitutes unconstitutional discrimination against the federal government. For example, would a statute imposing a gross receipts tax on public contractors be constitutional? In most cases, the issue does not arise because those who deal with the federal government are treated like all other taxpayers in the state, or like all other taxpayers except a favored class of taxpayers who deal with the state. In light of *Davis* and other cases condemning taxes that treat those who deal with the federal government differently from those who deal with the state, one suspects that the Court would invalidate a tax treating those who deal with the federal government differently from taxpayers in the private sector except those who deal with public entities or other exempt property owners.[171]

Whatever the doctrinal significance of *Davis*, its fiscal implications

---

[168]*Davis*, 109 S.Ct. at 1513, 1514; *cf.* United States v. County of Fresno, 429 U.S. 452, 458 (1977).

[169]See note 167 *supra*.

[170]*Phillips*, 361 U.S. at 385.

[171]See United States v. Montana, 437 F. Supp. 354 (D. Mont. 1977), rev'd on other grounds, 440 U.S. 147 (1979) (invalidating gross receipts tax limited to public contractors); Montana v. United States, 440 U.S. 147, 167–72 (White, J., dissenting); *County of Fresno*, 429 U.S. at 471–72 (Stevens, J., dissenting) (tax limited to lessees of publicly owned property unconstitutional); but see Peter Kiewit Sons' Co. v. State Board of Equalization, 161 Mont. 140, 505 P.2d 102 (1973).

for the states are truly staggering. Nearly half the states accorded disparate treatment to state and federal retirees prior to *Davis*.[172] Refund exposure has been estimated at $140–192 million for Arizona, $30–40 million for Iowa, $160 million for Missouri, $66 million for Oklahoma, $142 million for Oregon, $150 million for South Carolina, $370 million for Virginia, and $130 million for Wisconsin, to name just a few of these states.[173] State legislatures across the country have been scrambling to deal with the problem created by *Davis*, either by exempting federal employees, taxing state employees, or some combination of both.[174] And these legislative solutions are certain to spawn additional litigation. As Georgia's state budget director put it on the eve of a legislative session that nobody wanted which was called to adopt a pension plan that nobody likes: "I think we'll probably be sued by the state employees . . ., we'll be sued by the federal employees, and we'll be sued by the general public."[175]

V. Conclusion

During its 1988 Term, the Court harvested another bumper crop of state tax cases. The Court addressed issues ranging across the entire constitutional spectrum,[176] and it rendered decisions of considerable practical significance. One might have thought that the flow of state tax litigation to the Supreme Court would have been the first casualty of the elimination of the Court's mandatory appellate

---

[172]BNA, Daily Tax Report G–1 (August 11, 1989); *cf*. Davis, 109 S.Ct. at 1511 n.3 (Stevens, J., dissenting).

[173]BNA, Daily Tax Report, note 172 *supra*, at G-2–G-3.

[174]*Ibid*.

[175]"Special legislative session called to patch state's pension law," Athens Daily News, p. 1, col. 2, Sept. 10, 1989.
The Court decided two other cases during its 1988 Term involving Supremacy Clause and intergovernmental immunity issues. Both were narrow in scope and of relatively modest import. In Shell Oil Co. v. Iowa Department of Revenue, 109 S. Ct. 582 (1989), the Court held that the provision of the Outer Continental Shelf Lands Act that "State taxation laws shall not apply to the outer Continental Shelf," 43 U.S.C. §1333(a)(2) (1982), did not prohibit Iowa from including in Shell's apportionable tax base income that it derived from a unitary business conducted in part in the Outer Continental Shelf. In California State Board of Equalization v. Sierra Summit, Inc., 109 S. Ct. 2228 (1989), the Court held that California was neither preempted by federal law nor barred by the intergovernmental immunity doctrine from imposing a sales or use tax on bankruptcy liquidation sales.

[176]The 1988 Term cases considered in this article raised issues that are central to the Court's constitutional doctrine limiting state taxes. I leave it to others to untangle Court's state tax cases involving First Amendment and Indian immunity issues. See Texas Monthly, Inc. v. Bullock, 109 S. Ct. 890 (1989); Cotton Petroleum Corp. v. New Mexico, 109 S. Ct. 1698 (1989).

jurisdiction.[177] The Court's grant of plenary consideration to state tax cases shows no sign of abating, however.[178] For those who labor in the state tax field, there remain many rows to plow.

---

[177]28 U.S.C.A. §1257 (Supp. 1989).

[178]At this writing, the Court has five state tax cases on its 1989 Term docket. In addition to the two 1988 Term cases set for reargument, see note 6 *supra*, the Court has agreed to review Jimmy Swaggart Ministries v. Board of Equalization, 204 Cal. App. 3d 151, 250 Cal. Rptr. 891 (1988), prob. juris. noted, 109 S.Ct. 1741 (1989); Franchise Tax Bd. v. Alcan Aluminium, 860 F.2d 688 (7th Cir. 1988), petition for cert. granted, 109 S.Ct. 1741 (1989); Missouri v. Jenkins, 855 F.2d 1295 (8th Cir. 1988), petition for cert. granted, 109 S.Ct. 1930 (1989).

DOUGLAS G. BAIRD

THE SEVENTH AMENDMENT AND JURY TRIALS IN BANKRUPTCY

Twice this decade the Supreme Court has found the structure of the bankruptcy courts constitutionally defective. In both cases, much turned on the contours of bankruptcy jurisdiction in the 18th century. Congress cannot entrust non-Article III bankruptcy judges with the job of adjudicating contractual disputes between a debtor in bankruptcy and a third party, for these disputes "are the stuff of the traditional actions at common law tried by the courts at Westminster in 1789."[1] A creditor has a right to insist on a jury trial when the debtor brings a fraudulent conveyance action against it in large part because of the absence of evidence suggesting that such actions "were typically or indeed ever entertained by English courts of equity when the Seventh Amendment was adopted."[2] In relying on bankruptcy jurisdiction as it existed in the 18th century, however, the Court may have misperceived both it and the shadow it should cast on bankruptcy law today.

I

Bankruptcy law began under the aegis of the Chancellor, and the idea that bankruptcy courts are courts of equity is one that runs

Douglas G. Baird is Harry A. Bigelow Professor of Law, The University of Chicago.

AUTHOR'S NOTE: I thank Russell Eisenberg, Elizabeth Gibson, Robert Ginsberg, Richard Helmholz, John Langbein, Charles Ten Brink, and Martha Decker Wolz for their help.

[1] Northern Pipeline Construction Co. v. Marathon Pipe Line Co., 458 U.S. 50 (1982) (concurring opinion).

[2] Granfinanciera, S.A. v. Nordberg, 109 S.Ct. 2782 (1989). The leading pre-*Granfinanciera* discussion of jury trials in bankruptcy is Gibson, Jury Trials in Bankruptcy: Obeying the Commands of Article III and the Seventh Amendment, 72 Minn. L. Rev. 967 (1989).

deep in our jurisprudence. Hence it is not surprising that the Supreme Court has assumed over the last century that, at their core, bankruptcy disputes sound in equity, not in law, and that only on the periphery do we need to worry about whether someone who is the equivalent of a master in equity can displace the Article III judge and whether chancery methods can replace trial by jury. Reconstructing the past is an uncertain task, however, and the picture is not as simple as it appears to be. *Granfinanciera v. Nordberg*, the case the Court decided this Term, and its use of history illustrate the point.

The Chase & Sanborn Corporation filed a bankruptcy petition in 1983. Its trustee in bankruptcy asserted that within a year of the bankruptcy petition, the corporation, while it was insolvent, had transferred $1.7 million to Granfinanciera, a Colombian financial institution, and had received nothing in return. If the trustee's assertions were true, the transfer of funds was a fraudulent conveyance and could be avoided in bankruptcy.[3] Granfinanciera, however, denied that it had received the money from Chase & Sanborn and given nothing back while Chase & Sanborn was insolvent. It also demanded a jury trial. Because there was no statutory right to a jury trial, Granfinanciera had to rely on the Seventh Amendment, which provides that, "In Suits at common law . . . the right of trial by jury shall be preserved, and no fact tried by a jury, shall be otherwise reexamined in any Court of the United States, than according to the rules of common law."

The Supreme Court held that the fraudulent conveyance action to recover money was a "suit at common law" within the meaning of the Seventh Amendment because the 18th century equivalent of the trustee, the assignee, brought such actions in the common law courts. The Court inferred from the existence of fraudulent conveyance litigation in the common law courts in the 18th century and its apparent absence in Chancery that these disputes fell outside the jurisdiction of the Chancellor. If they had to be heard in common law courts, the Court reasoned, then creditors exposed to fraudulent conveyance attacks always enjoyed the right to a jury trial. The 18th century practice tells us that fraudulent conveyance actions fall outside of those disputes, inherently equitable in nature, that are at the heart of bankruptcy.

The logic that the Court adopted in *Granfinanciera* played out a

---

[3] See 11 U.S.C. §548.

view of bankruptcy jurisdiction that the Court first articulated in dictum almost a century before in *Barton v. Barbour*, a case involving equity receiverships:[4]

> [I]n cases of bankruptcy, many incidental questions arise in the course of administering the bankrupt estate, which would ordinarily be pure cases at law, and in respect of their facts triable by jury, but, as belonging to the bankruptcy proceedings, they become cases over which the bankruptcy court, which acts as a court of equity, exercises exclusive control. Thus a claim of debt or damages against the bankrupt is investigated by chancery methods. The bankruptcy court may, and in cases peculiarly requiring such a course will, direct an action or an issue at law to aid it in arriving at a right conclusion. But this rests in its sound discretion.

The administration of the assets of a debtor in bankruptcy and the determination of claims against those assets are matters that fall within the domain of the Chancellor. Disputes about such matters are therefore not "suits at common law" within the meaning of the Seventh Amendment, even though a similar dispute could arise outside of bankruptcy and even though outside of bankruptcy such disputes must be resolved through a trial by jury. By implication, there may be disputes involving someone in bankruptcy that are not "incidental to administering the bankrupt estate" and that therefore remain "suits at common law" even though one of the litigants is in bankruptcy. Until this Term, however, no court had identified such a dispute. Everything was either part of administering the bankruptcy estate or was a matter for which a jury trial had already been provided by statute.

Under the bankruptcy acts of 1800 and 1841, the jury was used to resolve most disputed questions of fact. Because of the statutory right to a jury trial, the scope of the Seventh Amendment in bankruptcy disputes was never an issue. The question could have been raised under the 1867 Bankruptcy Act. The 1867 Act gave the bankruptcy court sweeping jurisdiction and allowed for jury trials under only narrow circumstances. The 1867 Act, however, was repealed in 1878 and the constitutionality of its jury trial provisions was never confronted in a reported opinion. Under the 1898 Act, which survived

---

[4]*Barton v. Barbour*, 104 U.S. 126, 134 (1881). The question of the Seventh Amendment right to a jury trial was unlikely to arise before 1867, because a statutory right to a jury trial existed in virtually all bankruptcy disputes before that time. The question does not appear to have been litigated under the 1867 Act.

until 1979, the jurisdiction of the bankruptcy courts was cut back sharply. The bankruptcy court could hear a dispute only if it was connected with the administration of the bankruptcy estate. If a dispute were not connected with the administration of the bankruptcy estate, the bankruptcy court could hear it only with the consent of the parties.[5] Courts consistently held each time someone asserted a right to a jury trial in bankruptcy that the dispute was incidental to the administration of the bankruptcy estate and hence the dispute was not a "suit at common law" within the meaning of the Seventh Amendment. The jurisdiction of the bankruptcy court was defined in such a way that, whenever the bankruptcy court had the power to resolve a dispute, no right to a jury trial existed under the reasoning of *Barton*.[6]

The Court did look at the Seventh Amendment twice under the 1898 Bankruptcy Act. In *Schoenthal v. Irving Trust Co.*,[7] a trustee sought to recover a voidable preference. A voidable preference is an action the trustee may sometimes be able to bring against a creditor of the debtor in bankruptcy if it was paid shortly before the filing of the bankruptcy petition. The creditor in *Schoenthal*, however, had not filed a claim for a share of the assets in the bankruptcy court. Under the 1898 Act, the bankruptcy court did not have jurisdiction over those who did not file claims. The trustee was required to pursue them outside of bankruptcy court. In *Schoenthal*, the trustee brought a suit in equity in the District Court and the defendants sought to have the suit converted to a common law action and have the question tried before a jury.

The Court held that under §267 of the Judicial Code, the defendants should be given a jury trial because there was a "plain, adequate, and complete remedy at law." In the course of its opinion, the Court observed that this section[8]

> serves to guard the right of trial by jury preserved by the Seventh Amendment and to that end it should be liberally construed. . . . In England, long prior to the enactment of our first

---

[5]Because the courts developed an expansive notion of "consent" under the 1898 Act, courts could have held that consent sufficient to give the bankruptcy court jurisdiction was not sufficient to waive the Seventh Amendment right to a jury trial. The Court, however, declined to pursue this tack in Katchen v. Landy, 382 U.S. 323 (1966).

[6]Lower courts adopted the dictum in *Barton* without discussion under the 1898 Bankruptcy Act. Carter v. Lechty, 72 F.2d 320 (8th Cir. 1934); In re Rude, 101 F. 805 (D. Ky. 1900); In re Christensen, 101 F. 243 (N.D. Iowa 1900).

[7]287 U.S. 92 (1932).

[8]287 U.S. at 94.

Judiciary Act, common law actions of trover and money had and received were resorted to for the recovery of preferential payments by bankrupts.

The lesson of *Schoenthal* is a narrow one. A common law action brought in a common law court must be heard by a jury. *Schoenthal* does not confront the question whether a dispute that had to be heard by a jury if it were brought in a common law court could nevertheless be resolved without a jury if brought before the bankruptcy court. It does not tell us whether a common law cause of action can be resolved by "chancery methods" in bankruptcy or what causes of action lose their common law character when the Chancellor is called upon to resolve them.

Katchen v. Landy[9] involved the trustee's efforts to recover a preference from someone who had filed a claim against the estate. Under §57(g) of the 1898 Act, a creditor could not share in the assets the trustee gathered for the benefit of creditors if it had received a preferential payment and had not surrendered it to the trustee. The Court in *Katchen* held that deciding how to divide the assets of the bankrupt was a matter of bankruptcy administration within the meaning of *Barton* and that the bankruptcy court could resolve that question without conducting a jury trial. Moreover, because the resolution of this question would be res judicata in any subsequent dispute, the bankruptcy court had the power to resolve the entire preference issue, even if the preference were larger than the creditor's share of the assets of the bankruptcy estate.

Schoenthal and *Katchen* did not identify those disputes that, because they were not incidental to the administration of the bankruptcy estate, gave rise to a right to a jury trial even if they were heard in the bankruptcy court. In *Granfinanciera*, the Court concluded that a fraudulent conveyance action against a party who had not filed a claim in bankruptcy court was one for which the right to a jury trial could be invoked. *Granfinanciera*, like the earlier cases, determines what is incidental to the administration of the bankruptcy estate by looking at bankruptcy practice as it existed in 1789. The Seventh Amendment requires us to identify those bankruptcy matters that the Chancellor could decide on his own (but might in some cases refer the matter to a jury if he chose) and those for which he had to defer to the common law courts (and was obliged to refer a question to a jury).

---

[9]382 U.S. 323 (1966).

II

Granfinanciera, like the cases before it, is built upon a doubtful premise. For over a century, the Court has assumed that there were bankruptcy disputes in 1789 that had to be heard by a jury and other cases that did not have to be. The use of the jury was widespread in bankruptcy cases in the 18th century, even for matters, such as whether and the extent to which a given creditor was entitled to share in the bankruptcy estate, that have always been thought to be "incidental to the administration of the bankruptcy estate." The Court, explicitly in *Barton* and implicitly in other cases, assumes that of those matters referred to juries, the Chancellor had discretion in some, but not in others. It is hard, however, to find such a distinction between the discretionary and nondiscretionary use of the jury in 18th century bankruptcy cases, and nothing suggests that the question turns on whether the matter is "incidental to administering the bankruptcy estate."

Juries frequently heard bankruptcy disputes in the 18th century. A casual search through the reporters discloses common law juries answering the question of whether a debtor was a "merchant" and therefore fell within the class of those who could be put into bankruptcy by their creditors and the question of both the amount and the validity of a particular debt.[10] There are cases in which the issue for the jury is whether the debtor had committed an act of bankruptcy,[11] whether a person was entitled to come in as a creditor and participate in the distribution of the bankrupt's assets,[12] or whether a particular claim was provable in bankruptcy.[13] One treatise on bankruptcy law noted in 1801: "Wherever facts are in dispute, the usual way is to direct an issue at law, to bring the question of fact before a jury. Of this, the instances in the books are too numerous to be cited."[14]

---

[10]Hankey v. Jones, 2 Cowp. 745 (K.B. 1778). The issue in that case was whether a clergyman can have a bankruptcy commission taken out against him. For a case in which the Chancellor allows the commissioners to proceed against a clergyman, see Ex parte Meymot, 1 Atkyns 196, 26 Eng. Rep. 127 (1747). In this case, however, the Chancellor allows the commissioners to proceed "but so as not to prejudice any remedy the petitioner may have by an action at law." 1 Atkyns at 201, 26 Eng. Rep. at 130.

[11]Worseley v. Demattos & Slader, 1 Burrow 467 (K.B. 1758).

[12]Ex parte Cottrell, 2 Cowp. 742 (K.B. 1778).

[13]Utterson v. Vernon, 3 T.R. 539 (K.B. 1790).

[14]Cooper, The Bankrupt Law of America Compared With the Bankrupt Law of England 118 (1801). Like the few other lawyers of the period who commented on the jury trial in bankruptcy, Thomas Cooper may have had political axes to grind. (He wrote this book while serving a sentence under the Alien and Sedition Act.)

To the modern bankruptcy lawyer, the idea that the eligibility of a debtor for bankruptcy or the validity of a creditor's claim should be resolved outside of the bankruptcy court by a jury is a strange one. We tend to assume the jurisdiction of the Chancellor matches the summary jurisdiction of the bankruptcy court under the 1898 Bankruptcy Act. This assumption, however, does not always hold. Indeed, one of the few 18th century bankruptcy disputes in which the Chancellor explicitly found he had no jurisdiction was a matter over which the bankruptcy court did have jurisdiction under the 1898 Act.[15] Moreover, the boundaries between Chancery and the courts of law were not clearly drawn in the 18th century and were frequently overlapping, especially in a bankruptcy case, which by its nature gives rise to multiple disputes.

In the 18th century, a bankruptcy proceeding began when a creditor petitioned the Chancellor to appoint a group of commissioners to investigate the affairs of a debtor. The creditor had to show that the debtor was a merchant and had committed "an act of bankruptcy," such as keeping to his house, fleeing to parts unknown, making a fraudulent conveyance, or doing some other act that had the effect of thwarting ordinary common law methods of debt collection. After this petition for the appointment of commissioners, the debtor could in turn petition the Chancellor and ask him to supersede the commission on the ground that he was not a merchant or that he had not committed an act of bankruptcy.

The case of William Gulston was a typical one.[16] Gulston had left England for the Barbados. Dale, one of his creditors, asserted that Gulston tried to evade his creditors by hiding himself from his creditors before he left. If he had, Gulston had committed an act of bankruptcy and could be put in bankruptcy involuntarily. Gulston, through his lawyers, contended that he had gone to the Barbados to manage his estate there and that he had made no secret of his plans before he left. Because Gulston had not tried to evade his creditors and thus had not committed an act of bankruptcy, his lawyer argued, the Chancellor should supersede the bankruptcy petition that Dale had sworn out against him.

The reported decision suggests that the Chancellor had three op-

---

[15] See Clarke v. Capron, 2 Ves. Jun. 667, 30 Eng. Rep. 832 (1795) (Chancellor lacks power to hear dispute in which a creditor claims he was not given the dividend from the estate to which he thought he was entitled; the creditor's recourse was a common law action called an action on a dividend).

[16] In re Gulston, 1 Atkyns 193, 26 Eng. Rep. 125 (1743); Ex parte Gulston, 1 Atkyns 139, 26 Eng. Rep. 91 (1753).

tions. He could supersede the petition on the basis of what he knew; he could refer the matter back to the commissioners and have them decide the question; or he could direct the parties to resolve the dispute in a common law court. The Chancellor chose the last course. The dispute came to the common law courts through a device known as the "feigned" issue. Dale was ordered to bring an action in assumpsit against Gulston in which he asserted that he wagered Gulston a nominal amount that Gulston had hid himself from his creditors. Dale would allege that because Gulston had in fact hid himself, Gulston had lost the bet and he, Dale, had the right to sue Gulston in assumpsit for the amount of the wager. For his part, Gulston was ordered not to deny that he had made the wager, but to deny that he had evaded his creditors. When Dale brought his action on this fictional wager and Gulston offered this defense, the jury had to decide the factual question that was before the Chancellor. It had to decide whether Gulston had tried to evade his creditors to determine whether Dale won his bet. The jury found against Dale and hence that Gulston had not tried to evade his creditors and therefore had not committed an act of bankruptcy. The case then returned to the Chancellor, who superseded the petition and decided, among other things, how costs should be borne.

The device of the feigned issue overcame a practical problem that the Chancellor faced in the 18th century. There were many more factual disputes than one judge could resolve. Moreover, the Chancellor was obliged to resolve all controversies through written depositions. Given all the other matters before him and given the difficulties of resolving through writings many factual disputes such as the one posed in the bankruptcy of Gulston, the feigned issue was an effective way of delegating to others the job of resolving a straightforward factual question.[17] The Chancellor may have had the power to decide all factual disputes, but he delegated this power in many cases to others in the first instance. One can draw this inference from the conclusion of *In re Gulston* in which the Chancellor says that "after the trial shall be had, any of the parties are to be at liberty to apply to his Lordship for further directions."[18]

---

[17] See Langbein, Fact Finding in the English Court of Chancery: A Rebuttal, 83 Yale L.J. 1620 (1974).

[18] 1 Atkyns at 196, 26 Eng. Rep. at 127. Similarly, in Smith v. Jameson, 5 Durnford & East 601 (K.B. 1794), in an action brought in the King's Bench by an order of the Chancellor for money had and received, one of the judges noted that "[i]t is unnecessary to consider whether or not this Action be right in point of form, because it is brought under an order of the Court of

If one were to define "suits at common law" within the meaning of
the Seventh Amendment as those disputes ordinarily decided in the
common law courts in the 18th century, questions ranging from
whether a debt was dischargeable to the size and amount of each debt
would require a jury trial. Much of the practice under the 1898 Act as
well as the 1978 Bankruptcy Reform Act would have to be struck
down. Cases such as *In re Gulston*, however, suggest that although the
Chancellor may have usually ordered a jury trial, he did not have to.
The litigants may have had no right to a jury trial. In *Gulston*, the
Chancellor had the right to decide the matter himself or to ask the
commissioners to do it. He was not obliged to direct an issue at law,
and thus disputes over whether a person had committed an act of
bankruptcy could not be considered "suits at common law." The
Court may have been too quick to assume in *Granfinanciera* that a
bankruptcy dispute routinely resolved in the common law courts was
a "suit at common law." The cases it cited in which assignees that
brought trover actions against those who had allegedly received
fraudulent conveyances may have been brought only because the
Chancellor chose to refer them to the common law courts rather than
resolve them himself.[19]

Whether the Chancellor always had the power to decide questions
of fact in bankruptcy cases is not clear, however. *Gulston* does strongly suggest that in some kinds of cases the Chancellor had the discretion to resolve factual disputes in bankruptcy, but ordinarily sent
them to the common law courts. This is not to say, however, that the
Chancellor had such discretion with respect to all matters that came
before him. Indeed, there is some suggestion that in the case of
fraudulent conveyance actions more was at issue than taking advantage of the common law jury to decide disputed facts.

Fraudulent conveyance law was first put in statutory form in 1571,
the same year as the first comprehensive English bankruptcy statute.[20] At its core, fraudulent conveyance law allows creditors to void

---

Chancery, and it is to abide the future directions of that Court, where care will be taken that
Justice is finally administered to all the parties." *Id.* at 603.

[19] As noted above, the Chancellor typically ordered the parties to resolve a factual dispute by
using the device of the feigned issue, and the fraudulent conveyance actions in the common law
reporters are typically trover actions. The form of the action, however, does not itself tell us
whether the Chancellor had ordered that it be brought. When a factual dispute before the
Chancellor could be couched in the form of an ordinary writ, such as trover or money had and
received, he would direct that such an action be brought, rather than insist on using the device
of the feigned issue. See Bourne v. Dodson, 1 Atkyns 154, 158, 26 Eng. Rep. 100, 102 (1740).

[20] The first English bankruptcy statute, enacted some 30 years earlier in 1542–43, was much
more skeletal. For the comprehensive statute, see 13 Eliz. c. 7 (1571), discussed in VIII Hold-
sworth, History of English Law 236f. (1925).

any transfer their debtor makes with actual intent to delay, hinder, or defraud them. In the 18th century, the fraudulent conveyance statute was thought to embody common law principles, and a fraudulent conveyance action was ordinarily an action at law. Because making a fraudulent conveyance is itself an act of bankruptcy, deciding whether creditors could put a debtor into bankruptcy often required deciding whether the debtor had made a fraudulent conveyance. Hence, the Chancellor was frequently called upon to apply fraudulent conveyance law in bankruptcy matters. When the Chancellor directed the parties to the common law courts in these cases, he did defer to the common law courts rather than to decide himself a matter that sounded at law. In doing so, however, he was not necessarily conceding that his power to decide such questions was limited.

In *Bourne v. Dodson*,[21] the debtor transferred two ships to one of his creditors on account of an antecedent debt nine months before the filing of a bankruptcy petition against him. The debtor's assignee argued that the transfer was void as a fraudulent conveyance and relied in particular on the debtor having remained in possession of the ships and their cargo after the transfer. Fraudulent conveyance law, then as now, looked askance at any transfer of ownership that was not accompanied by an immediate transfer of possession. In this case, however, the ships and their cargo of tobacco were at sea. The idea of "possession" under these circumstances was elusive. The Chancellor did not want to discourage secured creditors who took interests in ships that were at sea. On the other hand, he did not want to give carte blanche to debtors to transfer assets and then continue to behave toward other creditors as if they still had them. Instead of resolving this question himself, however, the Chancellor directed that it be tried at law.[22] In the course of reaching this decision, the Chancellor noted his reluctance to decide a question that was in the first instance a legal (as opposed to an equitable) one: "for if it is a void assignment, it is void at law, and then I shall not take upon me in equity, absolutely to decide a matter which is properly triable at law."[23]

Nevertheless, the Chancellor did have the power to resolve such questions. For example, six years later, the Chancellor decided in a bankruptcy case to uphold an assignment of a ship at sea as collateral

---

[21] 1 Atkyns 154, 26 Eng. Rep. 100 (1740).

[22] He considered ordering a trover action, but rejected that course because of a second issue that also needed to be put before a jury for which trover would not lie.

[23] 1 Atkyns at 157, 26 Eng. Rep. at 101.

to a creditor. This was a case in which the assignment was not made on account of an antecedent debt and in general seemed less suspicious than the earlier one: "I am of opinion, as this appears to be a fair transaction, and money actually paid, and not an old creditor endeavouring to get an undue preference, that it ought to be supported in equity."[24]

These two cases raised a problem to which the Chancellor returned again several years later. Bankruptcy law has its own fraudulent conveyance provisions. In particular, 18th century bankruptcy law made void any transfer of ownership if the bankrupt retained possession and remained the "reputed owner." Most cases in which a transfer fell afoul of this provision would also run afoul of fraudulent conveyance law as well. In interpreting both provisions, one has to decide the crucial question of whether nonpossessory security interests are themselves fraudulent conveyances. In *Ryall v. Rolle*,[25] the Chancellor called upon the Lord Chief Justice of King's Bench, the Lord Chief Baron of the Court of the Exchequer, and a justice of the Court of Common Pleas to assist him in resolving another dispute in which there was a separation of ownership and possession. That the Chancellor would have judges from other courts sit with him suggests that the separation between the courts was not complete during this period.

Together, these three cases do suggest that the Chancellor paused before interpreting or applying laws that outside of bankruptcy ordinarily fell within the domain of the common law courts. These cases from the first half of the 18th century also show us the common law jury before it assumed its modern role as a finder of fact. The jury during this period determined not only what the facts were, but also had a role in deciding what facts were necessary for a transaction to be a fraudulent conveyance. The Chancellor would find it difficult to determine whether a transfer was a fraudulent conveyance at law if the touchstone was whether a jury would find it fraudulent. Nevertheless, the cases suggest only that the Chancellor exercised restraint when confronting questions of fraudulent conveyance law and other common law matters, not that the Chancellor lacked power to resolve them in the first instance. The Chancellor might abstain, but he did not have to.

In *Granfinanciera*, the Court focused on one kind of fraudulent con-

---

[24]Brown v. Heathcote, 1 Atkyns 160, 163, 26 Eng. Rep. 103, 105 (1746).
[25]1 Atkyns 165, 26 Eng. Rep. 107 (1749).

veyance action. These were "fraudulent preference" actions. In the late 18th century, the assignee could set aside transfers a debtor made to a creditor on account of an antecedent debt if the debtor knew it was going to commit an act of bankruptcy and deliberately choose to circumvent the bankruptcy rule of pro rata distribution and instead preferred one creditor over another. Before this period, the assignee could not set aside transactions that took place before the act of bankruptcy. After this period, what mattered was not the animus of the debtor who made the payment, but rather the animus of the creditor who obtained it. These cases are not the most promising ones to examine for the Chancellor's power in the case of fraudulent conveyances generally. The crucial question in a fraudulent preference case was the state of mind of the debtor. One needs to answer questions such as whether the debtor made the transfer because he knew he was going to commit an act of bankruptcy shortly after the transfer or whether he was simply acting in the ordinary course of his business. Because these are essentially factual disputes, one would expect them to be referred to a common law jury. As noted, juries ordinarily resolved factual disputes in bankruptcy in the 18th century, even when there was no question of law that commended restraint or deference. Hence, these cases are unlikely to tell us much about the scope of the Chancellor's power in fraudulent conveyance actions, quite apart from the fraudulent preference action itself having disappeared from bankruptcy law in this country.

Two fraudulent preference cases, however, do cast some light on the question. The Court focused on one in *Granfinanciera*. In *Ex parte Scudamore*,[26] a creditor named Haverfield persuaded his debtor to assign to him as collateral the proceeds the debtor was to receive from the dissolution of a partnership he had with another man. The assignees sought to have this transfer declared void. In considering the case, the Chancellor was of two minds. On the one hand, it appeared that the creditor simply demanded and received security for what he was owed, in which case the assignment would not be preferential as the law was then understood.[27] On the other, the debtor in assigning his share of the partnership may have conveyed all of his assets. This was evidence that the debtor was making a transfer in anticipation of failing and was deliberately favoring one creditor over others:[28]

[26] 3 Ves. Jun. 85, 30 Eng. Rep. 907 (1796).
[27] It would, of course, be preferential under modern bankruptcy law. See 11 U.S.C. §547.
[28] 3 Ves. Jun. at 88, 30 Eng. Rep. at 908–9.

The creditor comes with a pressing demand upon the feelings and conscience of the man. He presses for a security. The debtor gives him a particular security. Suppose in this case it was a mortgage: I cannot conceive any ground to defeat it. The petitioners rely upon the nature of the security; a letter of attorney to receive debts generally. That is a circumstance. It approaches a little nearer to contemplation of bankruptcy: but I do not think it sufficient. I cannot take it for granted, he had nothing but his share of the debts due to the partnership.

Thus far, the opinion focuses on the merits, something one would not expect if the matter were one that were beyond the Chancellor's jurisdiction. The next part of the opinion, however, makes matters less clear:[29]

You are applying on behalf of the assignees desiring me to direct the money to be paid over. I do not think, I can make that order. If you can recover it, you may. My opinion inclines upon the facts before me, that *Haverfield* [the creditor allegedly preferred] is right. Let an action be brought against Haverfield, if the parties shall think proper.

In *Granfinanciera*, the Court drew the inference (from the Chancellor's statement that he could not make the order) that he lacked the power to void such transfers. The Chancellor's words, however, are subject to at least one other interpretation: he was not satisfied from the state of the record that there had been a fraudulent preference, but he would permit the parties to resolve the question through a common law action.

Jacob v. Sheppard[30] is another fraudulent preference action in which the Chancellor turned to the common law courts, but in which it is at least plausible to think that the matter was within his discretion. In this case, Leigh conveyed goods to one of his creditors in June. Leigh and this creditor agreed that the proceeds from the sale of the goods would go first to paying this creditor what he was owed and then to another creditor. The surplus would then be returned to Leigh. Leigh became a bankrupt by no later than the following February,[31] and his assignees brought a bill against those who had enjoyed the proceeds from the sale of the goods on the ground that the transfer of

---

[29]3 Ves. Jun. at 88, 30 Eng. Rep. at 909.

[30]The best account of the case is contained in Worseley v. Demattos, 1 Burrow K. B. Reports 467, 479–81 (1758). *Jacob* was litigated in 1726. It was not cited in *Granfinanciera*.

[31]The transfer was made in June 1709 and the commission was taken out in February 1709. (At this time, the new year did not begin until March.)

the goods and the resulting deed of trust were fraudulent. The Master of the Rolls found the transfer was not itself an act of bankruptcy, but was fraudulent. The Chancellor reversed this decree. Whether the transfer was fraudulent was a question of nonbankruptcy law. Moreover, if it were fraudulent outside of bankruptcy, then the transfer would itself have been an act of bankruptcy. Hence the master's decision was internally inconsistent: the transfer could not be void unless it was also an act of bankruptcy.[32] At this point, the Chancellor directed an issue at law to determine when the debtor became a bankrupt. The jury found that the first act of bankruptcy did not take place in June, but rather in the following February. At this point, the Chancellor upheld the June transfer.[33]

Although this is another case in which the Chancellor does not actually void a transfer, there is much in the opinion that suggests that he had the power. The assignees sought to set aside the deed of trust by first going to the Chancellor. The matter was referred to a master. The master failed to understand the link between the making of a fraudulent conveyance and an act of bankruptcy, but there is no suggestion that he lacked jurisdiction. The Chancellor did not tell the assignees that they had to try to set aside the transfer in the common law courts because he himself lacked power to resolve the question. Rather, he directed them to use these courts to find out when the act of bankruptcy took place. At that point, he would decide whether to avoid the transfer.

Eighteenth century bankruptcy opinions do show an awareness of the overlap between equity and law, and fraudulent conveyance disputes show this overlap better than any other. The concerns evidenced both by the Chancellor and the common law judges (most prominently Lord Mansfield), however, do not seem focused on jurisdiction proper. First and foremost, there is widespread acceptance of the idea that the common law jury was the sensible place in which to resolve largely factual disputes. Second, there is the concern that bankruptcy law be in harmony with the common law. Unless a particular statute directed otherwise,[34] bankruptcy law should track

---

[32]1 Burrow at 480 ("[A] court of equity could not decree it to be fraudulent, unless it was fraudulent *at law*; in which case it would constitute an *act* of bankruptcy, of itself. . . . [N]o deed made by a trader can be fraudulent in Chancery, which is not fraudulent in a court of law, and an act of bankruptcy. Therefore he directed an issue.").

[33]*Ibid.* ("Upon the equity reserved, Ld. King *established* the deeds: held the plaintiffs to be only intitled to the surplus *after* the trusts in the deeds were performed . . . .").

[34]A good example is the fraudulent conveyance provision of the bankruptcy law that focused on separation of ownership and possession. 21 James c.19. This provision was the focal point of the disputes in *Ryall, Bourne,* and *Brown.*

nonbankruptcy law. The easiest way to ensure that bankruptcy law tracked nonbankruptcy law in the case of a fraudulent conveyance was to turn the dispute over to a jury. In a world in which it made so much sense to have a jury hear the question, the issue of whether the Chancellor had the power to do it differently might not arise. English judges in the late 18th century never had to ask whether there was a right to a jury trial in these cases.

III

American bankruptcy law must be seen against English experience, but the relationship between the Bankruptcy Clause of the Constitution and the Seventh Amendment must also be seen against the relationship between debtor-creditor law and the national government in this country in the 1780s. The Framers appear to have omitted the right to a jury trial in civil cases in the Constitution because of the difficulties of embodying the right in a single principle. The separation between law and equity differed from one state to the next.[35] The Anti-Federalists, however, read the omission in conjunction with the decision of the Framers to give the Supreme Court appellate jurisdiction as to questions of both fact and law in all federal cases. If the Supreme Court could review questions of fact, the civil jury would not be the final arbiter of facts in the federal system.[36] In part, the Anti-Federalists feared that citizens would not have the protection of jury trials in cases in which the government was a party in a civil action.[37] Another part of the story, however, lies in the link between jury trials and debtor-creditor law.

---

[35] See 2 Farrand, The Records of the Federal Convention of 1787 at 587, 628 (rev. ed. 1937). For example, Nathaniel Gorham of Massachusetts argued that "[i]t is not possible to discriminate equity cases from those in which juries are proper," *id*. at 587, and later "[t]he constitution of the Juries is different in different States and the trial itself is *usual* in different cases in different States," *id*. at 628.

[36] See Essay of a Democratic Federalist, Pennsylvania Herald (October 17, 1787), reprinted in 3 Storing, The Complete Anti-Federalist 3.5.6, at 60 (1981) ("[W]hat is meant by the *appellate* jurisdiction as to law and *fact* which is vest in the superior court of the United States? . . . The word *appeal*, if I understand it right, in its proper legal signification includes the *fact* as well as the *law*, and precludes every idea of a trial by jury.").

[37] See Essays of An Old Whig, Philadelphia Independent Gazetter, reprinted in 3 Storing, *id*., 3.3.16, at 28; Essay of a Democratic Federalist, Pennsylvania Herald (October 17, 1787), reprinted *id*., 3.5.6, at 60 ("Suppose therefore, that the military officers of congress, by a wanton abuse of power, imprison the free citizens of America . . . Suppose, I say that they commit similar, or greater indignities, in such cases a trial by jury would be our safest resource, heavy damages would at once punish the offender, and deter others form committing the same: but what satisfaction can we expect from a lordly court of justice, always ready to protect the officers of government against the weak and helpless citizen, and who will perhaps sit at the distance of many hundreds of miles from the place where the outrage was committed?").

Debtor-creditor relations were in many ways at the heart of what happened in Philadelphia in 1787 and in the ratification debates that followed. The Constitution in a number of ways protected creditors from the biases and vicissitudes of local law.[38] States no longer had the power to issue bills of credit, coin money, or make anything legal tender other than gold or silver. They had to give full faith and credit to judgments in other states. Moreover, giving the federal courts jurisdiction over disputes between citizens of different states or between a citizen of a state and a foreign state was intended in part to protect foreigners.[39] Of the 445 civil actions brought in the Virginia Circuit Court between 1790 and 1797, 329 were brought by citizens of Great Britain.[40] During the ratification debate in Virginia, the connection between the absence of a jury trial right and the favored treatment of British creditors was made explicitly.[41]

The debates over the Federal Constitution and the later adoption of the Seventh Amendment cast some light on the role that the Seventh Amendment was supposed to serve in the federal system. In these debates we find some discussion of when and under what circumstances a jury trial existed under English law. A Democratic Federalist responded to James Wilson's argument that the courts of equity did not conduct jury trials with the following observation:[42]

---

[38]The "economic" interpretation of the Constitution was first set out (and overstated) in Beard, An Economic Interpretation of the Constitution of the United States (1913). For a discussion of debtor-creditor relations and the Seventh Amendment, see Wolfram, The Constitutional History of the Seventh Amendment, 57 Minn. L. Rev. 639, 677–78 (1973).

[39]See Friendly, The Historic Basis of Diversity Jurisdiction, 41 Harv. L. Rev. 483, 496–97 (1928). It has also been argued that the diversity and alienage jurisdictions were put into the Constitution to permit federal courts to enforce the peace treaty with Great Britain that required that British creditors "meet with no lawful impediment to the recovery of the full value in sterling money, of all bona fide debts heretofore contracted." Definitive Treaty of Peace with Great Britain, September 3, 1783, art. IV, 8 Stat., T.S. No. 104. See Wolfram, note 38 *supra*, at 675–76.

[40]See Henderson, Courts for a New Nation 76 (1971).

[41]See 3 Elliot, The Debates in the Several State Conventions on the Adoption of the Federal Constitution 566 ("I have ever been an advocate for paying British creditors, both in Congress and elsewhere. But here we do injury to our own citizens. It is a maxim in law, that debts should be on the same original foundation they were on when contracted. . . . The procrastination and delays of our courts were probably in contemplation by both parties. . . . *Trial by jury* must have been in the contemplation by both parties, and the *venue* was in favor of the defendant. From these premises it is clearly discernible that it would be wrong to change the nature of the contracts. . . . The treaty of peace with Great Britain does not require that creditors should be put in a better situation than they were, but that there should be no hinderance to the collection of debts. It is therefore unwise and impolitic to give those creditors such an advantage over the debtors.") (comments of Mr. Grayson). The best discussion of the relationship between debtor-creditor law and the Seventh Amendment is Charles Wolfram's. See Wolfram, note 38 *supra*, at 678–79.

[42]Storing, as cited note 36 *supra*.

I must also directly contradict Mr. Wilson when he asserts that
there is no trial by jury in the courts of chancery—It cannot be
unknown to a man of his high professional learning, that whenever a difference arises about a matter of fact in the courts of equity in America or England, the fact is sent down to the courts of
common law to be tried by a jury, and it is what the lawyers call a
feigned issue.

Alexander Hamilton responded in *Federalist No. 83*:[43]

It has been erroneously insinuated, with regard to the court of
chancery, that this court generally tries disputed facts by a jury.
The truth is, that references to a jury in that court rarely happen,
and are in no case necessary, but where the validity of a devise of
land comes into question.

The question of whether the jury trials that commonly took place in
bankruptcy cases were available as of right was never resolved during
this period. In the few discussions of the question of the right to a
jury trial in equity cases, there is no effort to draw the line more
finely than Hamilton did between those cases for which a jury trial
was mandatory and those for which it was discretionary.

Those most likely to argue that such a right existed, however,
would be most likely to focus on the way in which it protected debtors from the harshness of bankruptcy law as it existed at the time.
The jury trial in bankruptcy protected a debtor against creditors
who asserted he had committed an act of bankruptcy, even when he
had not. What would matter to them is not the need to ensure that
bankruptcy law tracked the common law where they overlapped, but
rather that the common law jury be generally available to protect
debtors from the collection efforts of overzealous creditors. In short,
they would treat a case such as *In re Gulston* as of a piece with *Jacob v.
Sheppard*, even though the first case involved a purely factual question
and the second required interpretation of nonbankruptcy law.

To the extent that, as applied to debtor-creditor relations, the purpose of the Seventh Amendment was to offer debtors the protection
of the jury against the overzealous creditors, particularly British
creditors, one might argue that, at its core, the Seventh Amendment
protected the right to a jury trial in those cases in which the rights of
the individual debtor were at issue. An individual debtor could not

---

[43]The Federalist Papers (Meridian Books ed. 1961), No. 83, at 565 n.*. Hamilton may only
address the question of whether a jury trial could take place in a court of equity, not whether
the Chancellor was obliged to direct an issue to a common law court. Hamilton does, however,
explicitly focus on the idea that the Chancellor ultimately decided whether a jury should resolve a particular dispute.

be put into bankruptcy involuntarily without a jury trial.[44] Such a jury trial right was granted by statute in this country until 1978. On the other hand, an action brought against a creditor or someone who received a fraudulent conveyance might stand on a different footing. *Granfinanciera* was a case in which the jury trial right exists when a local debtor is pursuing a foreign creditor, rather than when a foreign creditor is pursuing a local debtor. The idea that creditors, and in particular foreign creditors, should enjoy a right to a jury seems at odds with the concerns that led to the passage of the Seventh Amendment.

The absence of a jury trial guarantee in civil cases was one of the chief objections to the original Constitution, but those who supported the Constitution were not opposed to the jury. The Federalists in the first Congress promulgated the Bill of Rights and provided for extensive jury trial rights in the Judiciary Act of 1789. Moreover, when Congress passed the first bankruptcy act in 1800, it also provided for jury trials on the threshold questions of whether a debtor was the kind of person to whom the act applied and whether he had committed an act of bankruptcy[45] as well as on any dispute involving the size or the allowance of a claim a creditor might have against the estate.[46] The judge could in his discretion order the resolution of any other factual dispute through a jury trial after a party in interest requested it.[47]

In short, during the crucial period that forms the baseline for determining the constraints that the Constitution places upon jury trials in bankruptcy, jury trials were both widespread and uncontroversial. Few gave thought to the question of whether jury trials were required in bankruptcy cases because no one doubted that they would exist. The likely line that would have been drawn would have focused on the protection of the individual debtor, but the argument in favor of drawing this line turns on the protections long afforded debtors under American law,[48] not on English chancery practice.

It was not until 1867 that Congress passed a bankruptcy statute

---

[44]There were no voluntary bankruptcies in the 18th century, and insisting that there is a jury trial right for such things as a discharge would be harder than arguing for the right when a debtor is threatened with involuntary bankruptcy.

[45]See 2 Stat. 19, ch. §3 (1800).

[46]*Id.* §58.

[47]*Id.* §52.

[48]For a discussion of the laws that protected American debtors during the colonial period, see Coleman, Debtors and Creditors in America: Insolvency, Imprisonment for Debt, and Bankruptcy, 1607–1900, at 9–15 (1974).

that failed to provide for jury trials to resolve disputed questions of fact.[49] In the 19th century, of course, the federal courts had to take account of Chancery's extensive use of jury trials in many other contexts to resolve the scope of the Seventh Amendment in equity cases. By and large, however, these courts assumed that if a case was properly before the Chancellor in the first instance, the Chancellor could direct an issue at law or not as he chose. Bankruptcy cases were different in that every case can give rise to multiple disputes. To say that the bankruptcy commissioners acted under the aegis of the Chancellor is not to say that every dispute involving a bankrupt for that reason alone is something other than a "suit at common law." The early use of jury trials in bankruptcy, the short life of the 1867 Act, and the narrow jurisdiction of the 1898 Act combined to postpone until last Term a dispute that put the question before the Court.

IV

The Supreme Court suggested in *Crowell v. Benson*[50] that Congress could remit matters involving public rights to tribunals whose adjudicators did not have to have life-tenure. The question then arose whether, when such tribunals heard issues that would otherwise be tried at law before a jury, a jury trial was still necessary. The Court held in *Atlas Roofing Co. v. Occupational Safety & Health Review Commission*[51] that even where a party could insist on a jury trial if Congress had put it under the jurisdiction of a federal court, that party may not be able to insist on a jury when the right in issue was a "public right" whose resolution Congress has entrusted to "an administrative forum with which the jury would be incompatible."[52]

At this point, there is a linkage between Article III doctrine and Seventh Amendment doctrine. If what is at issue is a statutorily created "public right," there may not be a Seventh Amendment right to a trial by jury if the matter is adjudicated in a non-Article III forum even though the cause of action is "legal" in nature. The justification rests in Congress's power to craft new causes of action. The doctrine

---

[49]The 1841 Bankruptcy Act, like the 1800 Act, made extensive use of the jury. See 5 Stat. 440, §1 (on the question of whether debtor can be put in bankruptcy involuntarily), §4 (on eligibility for discharge), §7 (right of assignee and creditor to jury trial on validity and amount of debt) (1841).

[50]285 U.S. 22 (1932).

[51]430 U.S. 442 (1977).

[52]See 430 U.S. at 450.

is puzzling given that the debates leading up to the enactment of the Seventh Amendment focused so squarely on the role the jury played in protecting citizens from arbitrary actions of the government. One might argue that actions that were legal in nature and that involved public rights (with perhaps the government as a party) would be cases in which the need to have a jury would be particularly strong.

Given this connection between Article III and the Seventh Amendment, however, the Court in *Granfinanciera* had to ask whether by virtue of assigning fraudulent conveyance actions to a non-Article III tribunal, the need for a jury trial that would otherwise exist could be eliminated. The Court concluded that in this case there needed to be a jury trial because the right involved was "legal" in nature and was "private," rather than "public." Fraudulent conveyance actions were not "public rights" because "they more nearly resemble state-law contract claims brought by a bankrupt corporation to augment the bankruptcy estate than they do creditors' hierarchically ordered claims to a pro rata share of the bankruptcy res." In reaching this conclusion, the Court observed that:[53]

> [I]f a statutory cause of action . . . is not a "public right" for Article III purposes, then Congress may not assign its adjudication to a specialized non-Article III court lacking "the essential attributes of the judicial power."

Taken out of context, this observation might seem to suggest that bankruptcy judges have no power to conduct a jury trial in a fraudulent conveyance dispute. A bankruptcy judge may decide only those matters that were "public rights." Adjudication of other rights (through trial by jury if the right were legal in nature) had to take place before an Article III judge, not the bankruptcy judge. At the end of its opinion, however, the Court went out of its way to say that it did not[54]

> express any view as to whether the Seventh Amendment or Article III allows jury trials in such actions to be held before non-Article III bankruptcy judges subject to the oversight provided by the district courts pursuant to the 1984 Amendments.

To reconcile these two observations, one must draw the inference that in the first case, the court was referring to non-Article III tribunals that were independent of Article III courts. Bankruptcy

---

[53] 109 S.Ct. at 2796, quoting Crowell v. Benson, 285 U.S. at 51.
[54] 109 S.Ct. at 2802.

judges, by contrast, operate under the aegis of the district courts. The oversight provided by the district courts may satisfy Article III's requirement that the adjudication of private rights be in the control of judges with life tenure. The Seventh Amendment gives the defendant in a fraudulent conveyance action the right to insist on a jury trial, and Article III requires that a fraudulent conveyance action be passed upon by an Article III judge. But the Court did not rule that conducting a jury trial is itself an exercise of the judicial power that only an Article III judge can do. It is possible that a bankruptcy judge can conduct a jury trial (thus satisfying the Seventh Amendment) and a judge with life tenure can review the actions of the bankruptcy judge (thus satisfying Article III).

To reach this conclusion, however, the Court must worry about the second half of the Seventh Amendment as well. The decision in the bankruptcy court by the District Court may not "be otherwise reexamined in any Court of the United States, than according to the rules of common law." Article III seems to require de novo review in the district court of matters not central to the administration of the bankruptcy involving private as opposed to public rights, but the last part of the Seventh Amendment seems to forbid de novo review of jury verdicts. One might argue, however, that when there is a jury trial, the district court could review de novo decisions of the bankruptcy judge de novo on questions of law and apply a deferential standard of review to the jury verdict. Article III requires supervision only of what the judge does below, not of what the jury does. Hence, one can satisfy Article III by scrutinizing the decisions of the judge on questions of law, but satisfy the Seventh Amendment by applying a deferential standard of review on matters of fact.

Whether this argument is sound turns on whether the sum of these two parts (the legal questions passed on by the bankruptcy judge and subject to de novo review on the one hand and the fact questions passed on by the jury on the other) equals the whole. *United States v. Raddatz*[55] suggests that whatever the non-Article III judge does must be subject to de novo review. Under one view, all the judge does in a trial by jury is pass on questions of law. Hence to the extent that the introduction of a jury reduces the scope of judicial decision making, the scope of review Article III requires is reduced correspondingly.

But one could take a different view. *Raddatz* may require that an Article III judge have the power to do everything over again (at least

---

[55] 447 U.S. 667 (1980).

in theory). This protection disappears if a case is subject only to appellate review. Under this argument, one mistakes the role a court plays in a jury trial if one thinks that a case can be separated neatly into questions of law and questions of fact. The jury's deliberations are strongly influenced by much that is not reviewable—the tone of the jury instructions, the questioning of witnesses. These things may themselves constitute the "exercise" of the "judicial power" that must be done by someone who enjoys life tenure.

Ultimately, however, the Supreme Court may try to link the question of whether bankruptcy judges must have life tenure with the 18th century experience just as it linked the Seventh Amendment question with its origins. If Court upholds the broad powers of bankruptcy judges under existing law notwithstanding *Marathon*, *Granfinanciera* suggests that it may rely on the idea that bankruptcy judges work under and are subject to the control of the district courts, just as special masters were under the control of the Chancellor. If one were to complete the historical link, the Court might well go on to say that once in chancery, one must follow "chancery methods." If bankruptcy judges can survive as non-Article III judges only to the extent they retain the character of special masters, they lose protection when they conduct jury trials.

Such a use of history, however, would be unfortunate. The concerns of the English judges in bankruptcy disputes in the 18th century were rarely about turf. Their twin concerns were that disputes be resolved in the most practical way and that common law disputes in bankruptcy be settled as they would be outside of bankruptcy. The Americans who pressed for the jury trial right were, in this context, concerned not about copying lines the Chancellor drew in England, but rather in giving debtors protections they had traditionally enjoyed in this country. A world in which creditors can transplant bankruptcy disputes to forums ill-equipped to resolve them is not true to the English or American experience in the 18th century.

JOHN SHEPARD WILEY Jr.

BONITO BOATS: UNINFORMED BUT MANDATORY INNOVATION POLICY

The Supreme Court's opinion in *Bonito Boats* declared that the
federal patent code preempted a state law that protected an unpatented industrial design.[1] Given the precedents, this result seems
ordinary. But in fact it is striking, for the opinion extended earlier
decisions that were controversial when decided and that time has cor-
roded further. The Court's extension of precedent potentially imperils a good deal of previously secure state law—a remarkable result
for the Rehnquist Court. Indeed, it is difficult to believe the Court
was alert to the array of interpretations its rhetoric invites. This potential is particularly arresting because the opinion offers no convincing rationale for its result.

I. PREEMPTION: UNANIMOUS AND SURPRISING

Bonito Boats concerned intellectual property. (Unfortunately
this pretentiously self-congratulatory phrase, which makes fights
over beer labels sound high-minded, has no prosaic synonym.) A
Florida statute outlawed one, but only one, particular way of manufacturing a fiberglass boat: the "direct molding process."[2] To make

John Shepard Wiley Jr. is Professor of Law, UCLA School of Law.

AUTHOR'S NOTE: I gratefully thank Ralph Brown, Harold Demsetz, Rochelle Dreyfuss,
Frank Easterbrook, Julian Eule, Terry Fisher, James Fitzpatrick, Edmund Kitch, Bill Klein,
Paul Mishkin, Bill Page, Shelley Saxer, Richard Stewart, Mark Ramseyer, and Steve Yeazell
for criticisms and suggestions. This gratitude does not necessarily imply their agreement. I
also thank the Dean's Fund for support.

[1] Bonito Boats, Inc. v. Thunder Craft Boats, Inc., 109 S.Ct. 971 (1989).

[2] Fla. Stat. §559.94 (2) (1987).

fiberglass boat hulls, one needs a mold. Bonito Boats made its mold the old fashioned way: from trees. It designed a hull shape, built the shape in hardwood, covered the hardwood with fiberglass, and finally removed the hardwood when the surrounding fiberglass mold had solidified. Bonito's competitor, Thunder Craft Boats, made its mold a different old fashioned way: by copying. Rather than monkey around with a hardwood creation, Thunder Craft simply cast a Bonito hull. Copying by any method other than direct molding would have avoided the statute's reach. But Thunder Craft's direct molding prompted Bonito to sue. Three state courts agreed with Thunder Craft, however, that federal patent law preempted the Florida statute. The United States Supreme Court also agreed—unanimously.

Unanimous opinions seem unremarkable. Think of the differences among the nine justices. If they all agree on something, then that thing must be obvious. One might regard the *Bonito Boats* opinion as simple agreement on an obvious proposition—stare decisis. The Court decided the *Sears* and *Compco* cases a quarter century ago.[3] These cases arose when firms like Bonito tried to protect themselves from low-priced imitators like Thunder Craft. In both cases, lower courts used state unfair competition law to prohibit the imitation. But in *Sears* and *Compco*, the Supreme Court announced a preemptive federal right to copy. State efforts to prevent copying, the Court said, extended patent-like protection to unpatented articles and thereby contravened federal patent law. In the intervening 25 years, the Court has neither overruled nor even expressly questioned these opinions. On the contrary, in every subsequent case the Court has nominally treated them as governing law. *Bonito Boats* thus called for a plain application of the rule from *Sears* and *Compco*: states may not extend federal patent policy beyond the limits that Congress has set down. Simple. No dissent.

This account is superficial in the extreme. *Bonito Boats* is a great surprise largely because *Sears* and *Compco* decisions themselves were so distinctive. As the *Bonito Boats* Court itself noted,[4] the *Columbia Law Review* had found *Sears* and *Compco* sufficiently remarkable to convene what has become a much-cited symposium of experts in the

---

[3]Sears, Roebuck & Co. v. Stiffel Co., 376 U.S. 225 (1964); Compco Corp. v. Day-Brite Lighting, Inc., 376 U.S. 234 (1964).

[4]109 S.Ct. at 979.

field.[5] One declared Justice Black's theory of preemption to be "rather startling."[6] Another forecasted that the rulings "may portend revolutionary changes in the law of unfair competition."[7] A third said with the release of the decisions "it seemed, at first glance, that the law of unfair competition and related fields had become 'disaster areas.' The roof had seemingly fallen in . . . ."[8]

A more serene view in this symposium cited Justice Brandeis' famous *Nabisco* opinion from 1938 and stressed that *Sears* and *Compco* "only reinforce[d *Nabisco*'s] fundamental principle that anyone is free to copy an unpatented article, subject to some concessions to avoid confusion of source."[9] *Sears* and *Compco* indeed did continue the policy of *Nabisco*. But Brandeis had authored *Erie* only seven months before, and noted in *Nabisco* that its right to copy existed as a matter of state common law.[10] States control their common law, and can amend it at their pleasure. It would have startled Brandeis—perhaps the century's leading critic of adopting state policies as federal law simply because those policies appeal to a federal judge—to learn that his *Nabisco* opinion provided precedent for a later preemptive dictate that barred states from deviating from its policy about copying.

The preemptive feature of *Sears* and *Compco* thus was notably new in the post-*Erie* world. But *Sears* and *Compco* applied substantive policy that, beyond being precedented at common law, also was characteristic of the era. The Warren Court continued a tradition that was suspicious and fearful of monopolies of any kind, and that was impatient with arguments in their defense.[11] Just two years later, for instance, a dissenting Justice Stewart complained that the Court's application of the federal law against mergers was so aggressive that "[t]he sole consistency that I can find is that . . . the Government

---

[5]Product Simulation: A Right or a Wrong? 64 Colum. L. Rev. 1178 (1964).

[6]Leeds, *id*. at 1180.

[7]Handler, *id*. at 1184.

[8]Derenberg, *id*. at 1192. See also McCarthy, Important Trends in Trademark and Unfair Competition Law During the Decade of the 1970s, 71 Trademark Reporter 93, 95 (1981) ("[t]he federal glacier had lurched forward").

[9]Brown, *id*. at 1227 (earlier and later citing Kellogg Co. v. National Biscuit Co., 305 U.S. 111 (1938)); see also Bender, 64 Colum. L. Rev. at 1241–42 (stressing aspects of common law continuity, sympathizing with the Court's concern, but decrying "the Court's obscurity in disposing of the problem").

[10]305 U.S. at 113 n.1 (noting jurisdictional basis of diversity and citing *Erie*).

[11]*Cf*. Jungerson v. Ostby & Barton C., 335 U.S. 560, 572 (1949) (Jackson, J., dissenting) ("the only patent that is valid is one which this Court has not been able to get its hands on").

always wins."[12] The following Term the Court delivered its *Utah Pie* decision, which Professor Ward Bowman lampooned as manifesting an antitrust hatred of monopoly so intense that the Court—for fear that one competitor might actually win—nearly outlawed competition altogether.[13] *Sears* and *Compco*'s hostility to state-created monopolies was entirely consistent with this resolute stance.

The Burger and Rehnquist Courts have tended to view this stance as more rigid than resolute. They have softened many of the Warren Court's harsh per se rules of antitrust.[14] The Reagan Administration moved even more aggressively to blunt the edges of a legal tool that it viewed as demonstrably unsafe. At a time when the country has felt vulnerable due to loss of an international competitive edge, this concern extended from modifying antitrust to promoting innovation as well. Congress strengthened the scope of intellectual property protection in a series of actions uniformly favorable to creators.[15] Probably most significant was the 1982 creation of the new Court of Appeals for the Federal Circuit (CAFC), which has markedly fortified patent protection—even to the extent of in effect overruling earlier Supreme Court decisions hostile to patents.[16] The Reagan administration abandoned the hostility that earlier administrations had expressed for intellectual property and proclaimed a new-found enthusiasm for patents.[17]

---

[12]United States v. Von's Grocery Co., 384 U.S.270 (1966). See also Robert Bork's comments on the landmark merger case of Brown Shoe Co. v. United States, 370 U.S. 294 (1962), in his chapter entitled "The Crash of Merger Policy." Bork, The Antitrust Paradox (1978).

[13]See Bowman, Restraint of Trade by the Supreme Court: The Utah Pie Case, 77 Yale L.J. 70 (1967).

[14]See, *e.g.*, Page, The Chicago School and the Evolution of Antitrust: Characterization, Antitrust Injury, and Evidentiary Sufficiency, 75 Va. L. Rev. 1221 (1989).

[15]See, *e.g.*, Pub. L. 92–140, 85 Stat. 391 (1971 extension of copyright to sound recordings); Copyright Act of 1976, 17 U.S.C. §101 *et seq.* (extension of copyright duration and coverage); Piracy and Counterfeiting Amendments Act of 1982, Pub.L. 97–180, 96 Stat. 91; Drug Price Competition and Patent Term Restoration Act of 1984, Pub.L. 98–417, 98 Stat. 1585; Semiconductor Chip Protection Act of 1984, 17 U.S.C. §901–14, Trademark Counterfeiting Act of 1984, Pub.L. 98–473, 98 Stat. 2178; Berne Convention Implementation Act of 1988, P.L. 100–568, 102 Stat. 2853.

[16]Compare Sakraida v. Ag Pro, Inc., 425 U.S. 273, 282 (1976) (invalidating patent because invention does not produce a "synergistic" effect), with Stratoflex, Inc. v. Aeroquip Corp., 713 F.2d 1530, 1540 (Fed. Cir. 1983) (reference to synergism requirement constitutes "error of analytical inclusion"); see also Dreyfuss, The Federal Circuit: A Case Study in Specialized Courts, 64 N.Y.U. L. Rev. 1, 26 (1989) ("[t]he CAFC has taken a decidedly pro-patent bias"); Merges, Commercial Success and Patent Standards: Economic Perspectives on Innovation, 76 Calif. L. Rev. 803, 822 ("the Federal Circuit appears to be a 'pro-patent' court").

[17]See, *e.g.*, Andewelt, Recent Revolutionary Changes in Intellectual Property Protection and the Future Prospects, 50 Albany L. Rev. 509, 512 (1986) ("[Antitrust Division attitudes]

The Burger and Rehnquist Courts also have taken a different attitude toward preemption than did the Warren Court. The later Courts have decided a series of preemption cases that followed *Sears* and *Compco* in empty citation alone. Apart from their facade of respect, these cases broke with the result and rejected the logic of *Sears*.

The first such case was *Goldstein v. California*, which presented the situation of *Sears* and *Compco* in the copyright rather than the patent context.[18] *Sears* and *Compco* had reasoned that the patent code's list of requirements prohibited states from protecting inventions that failed to qualify. The patent in *Compco* was invalid, for instance, because the invention was beyond the subject matter of patent law.[19] Like the patent code, the federal copyright code lists requirements for protection. Like the patent code, it had no explicit preemption clause (at that time[20]). And as did *Sears*, *Goldstein* evaluated a state law that sought to protect items—here, sound recordings—that had failed to qualify for federal protection.[21]

The Burger Court simply refused to apply the *Sears* logic to the formally identical *Goldstein* setting. The Court reiterated that patent law's list of requirements "indicated . . . which configurations [Congress] wished to remain free" for copying. But flatly and cryptically it announced that copyright law was different than patent law; for copyright, "Congress has drawn no balance; rather it has left the area unattended, and no reason exists why the State should not be free to act."[22] Yet the two statutes were materially identical; each listed requirements for protection and said nothing expressly about state power. *Goldstein* rejected the logical core of *Sears* and *Compco* by drawing the contrary conclusion from the same situation. Despite its stated "reaffirm[ation]"[23] of the two earlier precedents, then, *Gold-*

---

have changed in two areas—intellectual property protection and intellectual property licensing. In both areas we used to be hostile, but now we are promoters.").

[18]Goldstein v. California, 412 U.S. 546 (1973).

[19]See Day-Brite Lighting, Inc. v. Compco Corp., 311 F.2d 26, 28 (7th Cir. 1962) (design was functional); compare Choate, Francis, & Collins, Patent Law 642 (3d ed. 1987) ("[t]he subject matter of an ornamental design should not be the result of purely functional requirements"); *cf.* Stiffel Co. v. Sears, Roebuck & Co., 313 F.2d 115, 117–18 & n.5 (7th Cir. 1963) (patents invalid for want of novelty).

[20]See note 46 and accompanying text *infra*.

[21]See 412 U.S. at 566 (1909 Copyright Act established that "composers were to have no control over the recordings themselves").

[22]*Id.* at 569–70.

[23]*Id.* at 571.

stein's reasoning implied that *Sears* and *Compco* now reigned in appearance but not reality.

The opinion in *Kewanee Oil Co. v. Bicron Corp.* reinforced *Goldstein*'s conclusion.[24] A trial court had enjoined ex-employees' use of their former employer's trade secrets, which related to a product that, as the dissent said, "could be patented but was not."[25] The Supreme Court held that the federal patent code did not preempt the state trade secret law from which the injunction had issued. Thus the Court again permitted state law to afford exclusive protection for one competitor against others—despite the lack of patent protection for the disputed information. The *Bonito Boats* Court modestly called *Kewanee* "decidedly less rigid" than *Sears*,[26] while the *Kewanee* dissent claimed flatly that the "decision is at war with the philosophy of *Sears* . . . and *Compco*."[27] Professor Paul Goldstein concluded in this *Review* that *Kewanee* "overrode the two precedents with that most effective vehicle of judicial restraint, benign neglect."[28]

Sears and *Compco* suffered a further indignity in 1979. The opinion in *Aronson v. Quick Point Pencil Co.* declined to preempt state law that enforced a royalty contract for use of an unpatented design for a key ring.[29] The *Aronson* Court distinguished *Sears* and *Compco* because "[e]nforcement of Quick Point's agreement does not prevent anyone from copying the keyholder. It merely requires Quick Point to pay the consideration which it promised . . . ."[30] But *Sears* and *Compco* had enforced free copying of unpatented ideas. To allow state laws that required royalty payments to circumvent the two opinions was logically to permit every kind of state intellectual property right, for creators always can waive their rights for a fee.

At least a decade ago, then, *Sears* and *Compco* appeared to be drained of meaningful content. Their reiteration today thus is notable—and all the more so because of the expansion that the reiteration implies.

---

[24]416 U.S. 470 (1974).

[25]*Id*. at 495 (Douglas, J., dissenting).

[26]109 S.Ct. at 980

[27]416 U.S. at 495.

[28]Goldstein, Kewanee Oil Co. v. Bicron Corp.: Notes on a Closing Circle, 1974 Supreme Court Review 81, 81; see also *id*. at 82 (opinion does not "attemp[t] to distinguish Sears or to come to grips with its preemptive logic"); Abrams, Copyright, Misappropriation, and Preemption: Constitutional and Statutory Limits of State Law Protection, 1983 Supreme Court Review 509, 512 (1983) (*Goldstein* and *Kewanee* "an abrupt about-face" from *Sears* and *Compco*).

[29]440 U.S. 257 (1979).

[30]*Id*. at 264.

II. Preemption: Far Reaching?

Bonito Boats possibly strengthens *Sears* and *Compco* in two ways. First, it is unanimous, which neither *Sears* nor *Compco* was. Justice Harlan had concurred only in the result of the earlier cases, complaining that the states deserved "more leeway in unfair competition 'copying' cases than the Court's opinion would allow."[31] Justice Harlan's difference with the earlier majorities in fact was rather minor. His brief concurrence took issue only with the extent of injunctive relief appropriate in cases of "palming off" or consumer confusion—situations as to which the majority agreed with him that states had "the power to impose liability."[32] Nevertheless, the Court's unanimity in *Bonito Boats* perhaps may suggest a more forceful expression of principle.

Second and more important, *Bonito Boats'* facts are less confined than were those of *Sears* or *Compco*. Bonito had never tried to patent any aspect of its boat.[33] The creations in *Sears* and *Compco*, on the other hand, both had won patents from the federal Patent and Trademark Office (PTO), only to have lower courts later declare the patents to be invalid.[34] Before *Bonito Boats*, therefore, one could have described *Sears* and *Compco* as suppressing state efforts to protect that which federal patent courts had decided was unprotectable.[35] After *Bonito Boats*, this limited description no longer is tenable.

This difference might differ mightily. Few things are the subject of an expired patent: the invention must have impressed a Patent and Trademark Office (PTO) bureaucrat and must have avoided or survived judicial challenge for the next 17 (or 14) years. So too are the subjects of an invalidated patent relatively rare. Although only 30 percent of design patents survived judicial challenge from 1964–83,[36] for instance, still very few product designs win a patent in the first place. Vastly more common are creations that are wholly unpatentable. Your drawing of John Wayne's face, for example. Or the

---

[31]376 U.S. at 239.

[32]*Id.* at 238; see also *id.* at 232.

[33]109 S.Ct. at 974 and 982.

[34]See note 19 and accompanying text *supra*.

[35]See, *e.g.*, Kitch & Perlman, Legal Regulation of the Competitive Process 48 (3rd ed. 1986). *Cf. Bonito Boats*, 109 S.Ct at 985.

[36]Lindgren, The Sanctity of the Design Patent: Illusion or Reality? 20 Years of Design Patent Litigation since Compco v. Day-Brite Lighting, Inc. and Sears, Roebuck & Co. v. Stiffel Co., 10 Okla. City U.L. Rev. 195, 261 (app. II) (1985).

Associated Press's news stories. Or your imitative but not confusing usage of the mark "Tiffany" to describe your movie theater in Kansas City. A federal rule that preempts state protection of unpatented and unpatentable creations will be far more active and intrusive than one dealing only with state protection for patented innovation. Under this analysis, then, *Bonito Boats* makes a much bigger preemptive splash than did either *Sears* or *Compco*.

This analysis survives two possible objections. First, one might argue that *Bonito Boats* involved a process that was the subject of an expired patent after all. The *Bonito Boats* Court described the process in Patent No. 3,419,646 (issued to one Robert Smith in 1968 for "a method for the direct molding of boat hulls") as "similar" to Bonito's process.[37] This observation does not dictate that the Smith patent anticipated or made obvious the Bonito's process, however, for two ideas can be similar even though one does not make the other obvious. Nor could the fact of Smith's process patent have denied Bonito the possibility of a patent on its particular boat design.

Second, no language in *Sears* or *Compco* ascribed significance to the presence of invalidated patents. In other words, the rule stated by *Sears'* and *Compco's* wording was thus perhaps as broad as the one described by the *Bonito Boats* facts. Yet I already have described how opinions after *Sears* failed to follow its broad theory.[38] Given this later reluctance, *Bonito Boats* remains noteworthy as holding that *Sears* and *Compco* really mean what their broad language had implied.

If this interpretation succeeds in suggesting that the preemptive scope of *Bonito Boats* is broader than that of *Sears* and *Compco*, the next question is obvious. How much broader? The *Bonito Boats* opinion was careless on the topic. The collection of phrases the opinion used to describe its own scope is varied. Perhaps its broadest formulation declared that "States may not offer patent-like protection to intellectual creations which would otherwise remain unprotected as a matter of federal law."[39] What is "patent-like protection"? A common sense interpretation might say that it is the exclusive right to "make, use, or sell" something.[40] What are "intellectual creations"? Every-

---

[37] 109 S.Ct. at 984.

[38] See text accompanying notes 18–30 *supra*.

[39] 109 S.Ct. at 980. *Cf. id.* at 978; 986.

[40] 35 U.S.C. §271. *Cf.* 109 S.Ct at 981 ("Like the patentee, the beneficiary of the Florida statute may prevent a competitor from 'making' the product in what is evidently the most efficient manner available and from 'selling' the product when it is produced in that fashion.").

day usage might say they are any intangible protected by "intellectual property" law.

So interpreted, *Bonito Boats* mandates the preemption of state anti-dilution laws;[41] state rights of publicity;[42] state misappropriation laws that survive copyright preemption;[43] and state idea protection statutes[44]—none of which has a federal counterpart. The fact that states might have drafted some of these laws with a careful eye to avoid federal copyright preemption would be irrelevant under the different threat of patent preemption. Indeed, current copyright law might well have tolerated Bonito's use of the Florida law to defend against Thunder Craft's technique of copying. The law of modern copyright preemption is engagingly baroque.[45] One certainly can argue, however, that all state protection of fiberglass boats should escape copyright preemption under the 1976 Act because these utilitarian designs do not enjoy copyright protection under the general subject matter of "sculptural works."[46] But the *Bonito Boats* Court preempted the Florida statute with no mention of the copyright issues that counsel on both sides had urged upon it. This decision to preempt on patent grounds without bothering about copyright issues implies that patent and copyright preemption are two distinct and unrelated questions for this Court—a conclusion that lengthens the decision's preemptive shadow.

Thus we see an aggressive but conceivable interpretation of *Bonito Boats* that makes suspect every state doctrine of intellectual property not protected by one of the opinion's three express safe harbors. The first saved state trademark and trade dress protection that operates

---

[41]See, *e.g.*, Mead Data Central v. Toyota Motors, 875 F.2d 1026 (2d Cir. 1989).

[42]See, *e.g.*, Haelan Laboratories, Inc. v. Topps Chewing Gum, Inc., 202 F.2d 866 (2d. Cir. 1953); *cf.* Zacchini v. Scripps-Howard Broadcasting Co., 433 U.S. 562 (1977) (First Amendment does not invalidate a state's right of publicity).

[43]See, *e.g.*, International News Service v. Associated Press, 248 U.S. 215 (1918); Baird, Common Law Intellectual Property and the Legacy of International News Service v. Associated Press, 50 U. Chi. L. Rev. 411 (1983); Abrams, note 28 *supra*.

[44]See, *e.g.*, Calif. Civ. Code §980 (protecting works of authorship not fixed in a tangible medium of expression).

[45]See, *e.g.*, Abrams, note 28 *supra*, at 548.

[46]See 17 U.S.C. §301(b)(1) (no preemption of any state remedy with respect to subject matter not within the subject matter of copyright); *id.* §102(a)(5) (copyright subject matter includes "sculptural works"); *id.* section 101 (protection for "sculptural works" does not extend to their "utilitarian aspects"). See also *id.* §102(b) (no copyright protection for any process). Contra, Brown, Design Protection: An Overview, 34 UCLA L. Rev. 1341, 1381, 1392–93 n.230 (1987).

"to prevent consumer confusion as to source."[47] The second safe harbor reiterated *Kewanee*'s allowance of state trade secret law,[48] while the third affirmed *Aronson*'s sanction of state contract law relating to unpatented intellectual property.[49] Later in the opinion the Court emphasized that its ruling did not infringe the domain of the three cases that had narrowed *Sears* and *Compco* (although today only *Kewanee* and *Aronson* guarantee practical jurisdiction for states, for in 1976 Congress supplied exclusive protection for sound recordings such as those at issue in *Goldstein*[50]). The opinion finally declared that "where 'Congress determines that neither federal protection nor freedom from restraint is required by national interest,' *Goldstein* . . . the States remain free to promote originality and creativity in their own domains."[51] This apparent generosity to the states is not very helpful to them, however, for determining just where Congress has so determined and thus where states remain free is precisely the question at hand. Under this most militant interpretation, then, *Bonito Boats* leaves to states in matters of intellectual property the sure validity only of their trademark, trade secret, and contract enforcement.

The same logic imperils state trademark law extending beyond *Bonito Boats*'s first safe harbor, which approved only of trademark law that aims "to prevent consumer confusion as to source."[52] Courts infrequently but occasionally formulate trademark law to serve different goals, like that of encouraging innovation.[53] Should state trademark law now venture upon this divergent[54] path, however, it would replicate conduct that the *Bonito Boats* Court condemned.[55]

---

[47]109 S.Ct. at 979.

[48]*Id.* at 979–80.

[49]*Id.* at 980.

[50]See *Goldstein*, 412 U.S. at 551–52; 17 U.S.C. §102(a)(7) & 114.

[51]See 109 S.Ct. at 985.

[52]See note 47 *supra* and accompanying text.

[53]See, *e.g.*, LeSportsac, Inc. v. K Mart Corp., 754 F.2d 71, 77 (2d Cir. 1985) (trademark law should provide an incentive for firms to develop imaginative and attractive designs); Boston Professional Hockey Ass'n, Inc. v. Dallas Cap & Emblem Mfg., Inc., 510 F.2d 1004, 1011 (5th Cir.), cert. denied, 423 U.S. 868 (1975) ("tilt[ing]" trademark protection "from the purpose of protecting the public to the protection of the business interests of the plaintiff").

[54]See, *e.g.*, International Order of Job's Daughters v. Lindeburg & Co., 633 F.2d 912 (9th Cir. 1980) (reaching opposite result as cases in note 53 *supra* after rejecting their goal).

[55]See 109 S.Ct. at 984 (condemning the state law because its "very purpose . . . is to 'reward' the 'inventor' by offering substantial protection against public exploitation of his or her idea embodied in the product").

The analysis of the previous paragraph suggests that defenders of such a state law could find no defense in a claim of the law's validity under the federal trademark statute—the Lanham Act.[56]

One thus might interpret *Bonito Boats* to reveal an imperial federal patent code striding across the entire field of state intellectual property protection and permitting only three narrow state initiatives: trademark, trade secret, and contract protection. This interpretation is extreme—a reading for the biggest preemptive bang. It is certainly not the only possible reading of *Bonito Boats*, and I do not maintain that it in some sense is the most likely. My point so far rather has been that the decision contains some logic and language suggestive of a surprisingly broad rule of preemption. For those seeking to minimize the excitement, the Court also includes language suggestive of narrower readings. The dissonance is perplexing.

For instance, sometimes the Court differently described the scope of its ruling as "federal pre-emption of state regulation of the subject matter of patent."[57] This definition would narrow the opinion's preemptive field, and may strike many as the most reasonable or credible. But if patentable subject matter is supposed to be an important boundary, then *Bonito Boats* silently overruled *Compco* even while purporting to apply it.[58] Moreover, it is baffling why the Court failed both to define that subject matter precisely as well as to describe Bonito's boat as within that subject matter rather than as merely "unpatentable."[59]

Alternatively, one might fasten on the opinion's references to "design and utilitarian ideas,"[60] which again would narrow the preemptive field but in a different way. This definition of a preemptive limit in turn raises many puzzles, however—for instance, why Congress

---

[56]*Cf.* 36 BNA Patent Trademark & Copyright Journal, at 762 (10/27/88) ("I would like to make clear that sec. 43(a) should not be construed to preempt State unfair competition laws.") (floor comment by Moorhead, who did not author the 1988 Lanham Act amendment).

[57]109 S.Ct. at 979. *Cf. id.* ("articles or processes which fall within the broad scope of patentable subject matter" and "potentially the subject of design patents").

[58]See note 19 *supra* and accompanying text.

[59]See note 33 *supra*; compare *Kewanee*, 416 U.S. at 479–93 (lengthy analysis of significance of patentability).

[60]109 S.Ct. at 974, 981. See also *id.* at 978 ("publicly known design and utilitarian ideas which were unprotected by patent"); *id.* at 980 ("publicly known, unpatented design and utilitarian conception"); *ibid.* ("unpatented utilitarian or design conception which has been freely disclosed by its author to the public at large"); *id.* at 981 ("design and utilitarian conceptions"). *Cf. Goldstein*, 412 U.S. at 569–70 (distinguishing between "mechanical configurations" and "writings").

would oppose state rewards for creation only when the rewarded inventions actually were useful.[61]

The opinion offers still more phrases that could serve as different definitions of its preemptive scope.[62] But by now it is plain that to settle the question of *Bonito Boats*'s boundary, we need the usual—a clear and persuasive theory of the case. Of all the cargo in *Bonito Boats*, however, that one item is missing.

III. Preemption: Unjustified

The logic in *Bonito Boats* is frail and incomplete. I consider and reject six possible rationales for its result.

A. LITERALISM

Supposing such a thing to exist, simple literalism in statutory interpretation fails badly as justification for the *Bonito Boats* result. The patent code was the ostensible basis for the decision. Tellingly, the Court never got around to naming a specific section, for good reason: the Court could not have. This federal statute simply lists a variety of requirements that inventors must satisfy to win their patent. It contains no section that bounds or even addresses state power.

The federal Constitution does specify that the "exclusive Right[s]" given to inventors shall be but for "limited Times."[63] This provision addresses its restraint to Congress, however, and not to states, and so offers no support for *Bonito Boats*: a federal judicial limitation of a state's policy. It is true that the Court sometimes has applied to states other constitutional restrictions whose language refers exclusively to Congress. Concerning this portion of the Constitution, however, the Court's past precedents uniformly have rejected such a proposed expansion.[64]

---

[61]*Cf.* Brenner v. Manson, 383 U.S. 519 (1966) (patent law requires inventions be useful).

[62]See 109 S.Ct. at 976 ("unpatented article"); *id.* at 977 ("that which is already available to the public, or that which may be readily inferred from publicly available material"); *id.* at 982 ("all ideas in general circulation . . . unless they are protected by a valid patent") (quoting Lear, Inc. v. Adkins); *id.* at 984 ("an intellectual creation"); *id.* at 986 ("useful shapes and processes for which patent protection has been denied or is otherwise unobtainable").

[63]Art. I, §8, cl. 8, gives Congress the power "[t]o promote the Progress of Science and useful Arts, by securing for limited times to Authors and Inventors the exclusive Right to their respective Writings and Discoveries."

[64]*Goldstein*, 412 U.S. at 555–61; *Kewanee*, 416 U.S. at 478–79.

B. CANONS OF INTERPRETATION

Nor do the usual background assumptions or interpretive canons make sense of the result: indeed, they contradict it. In preemption cases, the most common of these assumptions is professed regard for state autonomy.[65] Testimonials endorsing states' rights open rather than end the conversation, for to mistake them as decisive is to conclude erroneously that the Court never preempts upon mere implication. But although regard for states' rights does not always decide cases, it does throw into relief the result in *Bonito Boats*.

A different maxim that might seem, but in fact is not, helpful is "inclusio unius est exclusio alterius": the inclusion of one is the exclusion of another. The logic in *Bonito Boats* (as in *Sears* and *Compco*) amounts to the notion that silence in the federal patent code should exclude supplementary state protection for inventors.[66] But it is a non sequitur to reason that congressional silence on a topic—without more—implies a desire to block state activity in that field. The federal constitutional structure suggests just the contrary, for that structure created a federal government of limited power against the backdrop of plenary state authority. Indeed, precisely this contrary implication appealed to a unanimous Court a mere two months later, when it deployed such reasoning to state an inadvertent but precise critique of *Bonito Boats*:[67]

> It is one thing to consider the congressional policies identified [by case law] in defining what sort of recovery federal . . . law authorizes; it is something altogether different, and in our view inappropriate, to consider them as defining what federal law allows States to do under their own . . . laws. . . . Ordinarily, state causes of action are not pre-empted solely because they impose liability over and above that authorized by federal law . . . .

C. LEGISLATIVE HISTORY

The Court has never suggested that the legislative history of the Patent Code discloses a whiff of preemptive intent. This legislative

---

[65]See, *e.g.*, Puerto Rico Dept. of Consumer Affairs v. Isla Petroleum Corp., 108 S.Ct. 1350, 1353 (1988).

[66]See, *e.g.*, 109 S.Ct. at 977; 978; 984–85.

[67]California v. ARC America Corp., 109 S.Ct. 1661, 1666–67 (1989). See also *id.* at 1665 ("presumption against finding preemption of state law in areas traditionally regulated by the States"); *cf. Goldstein*, 412 U.S. at 557 n.13 (offering examples of state tradition from 1751 of granting patents).

silence normally would be prominent for a body professing interest in legislative intent.[68] Yet the *Bonito Boats* opinion left the omission unremarked.

The Court did mention the scanty constitutional history of relevance, but only to misconstrue it. It cited Federalist No. 43 to support a claim that a "fundamental purpos[e] behind the Patent and Copyright Clauses of the Constitution was to promote national uniformity in the realm of intellectual property."[69] But *Sears* had recounted that "when the Constitution was adopted provision for a federal patent law was made one of the enumerated powers of Congress because, as Madison put it in The Federalist No. 43, the States 'cannot separately make effectual provision' for either patents or copyrights.'"[70] Madison's rationale for federal protection suggests that the federal role arises, not because state protection is undesirable as *Bonito Boats* maintained, but because individual states lack the ability to offer enough effective protection.[71]

Justification for *Bonito Boats'* displacement of state authority thus must be on grounds other than literalism, standard presumptions, or legislative history. The opinion hinted at three different substantive federal policies that it might have served. None of these hints proves very helpful.

D. A FEDERAL POLICY TO CORRECT R&D INCENTIVES?

One can speak in at least two different languages about law, patent or otherwise. In the vocabulary of moral entitlement, patents defend inventors' just desserts. But in the vernacular of instrumental social engineering, patents encourage research and development and ultimately improve consumer welfare. Conversations in these different tongues can—but do not necessarily—reach similar conclusions, but each almost always proceeds in its own distinct style.

The authors of intellectual property law have never entirely banished the discourse of moral entitlement, but *Bonito Boats* continued a tradition of suppressing it in favor of utilitarian policy analysis. Here

---

[68]*Cf.* Goldstein v. California, 412 U.S. at 566 (drawing significance from a congressional report that "[n]owhere . . . indicate[s]" that Congress intended particular intellectual property "to be free from state control").

[69]109 S.Ct. at 983.

[70]376 U.S. at 228.

[71]See also Goldstein v. California, 412 U.S. at 556 & n.12 ("In effect, [the national system that Madison supported] allows Congress to provide a reward greater than any particular State may grant . . . .").

the Court spoke without discomfort or self-consciousness about
"spur[s] to the inventor" and "balanc[ing] between the need to encourage innovation and the avoidance of monopolies which stifle
competition . . . ."[72] But it balked when a lower court condemned
Thunder Craft's copying as "unscrupulous." This "conclusory label," the Court declared, "merely endorses a policy judgment [that]
the patent laws do not leave the States free to make."[73] So *Bonito Boats*
talked economics, not philosophy.[74] Some will dispute this normative premise,[75] but I accept it for present purposes. Thus we turn to
an economic analysis of innovation incentives.

Efficiency analysis of intellectual property is long on jargon but
short on concrete advice. Depending on one's assumptions about the
state of the world, one can use the relevant theory either to support or
to oppose legal protection. In the escapist phrase, the crucial issue
remains "an empirical question." And to no one's astonishment, the
empirical question turns out to be unanswered and to have no answers in sight.

The efficiency case for intellectual property protection begins by
talking about public goods and transactions costs. New boat hull designs, innovative machines, fresh fiction, the latest shape of Michael
Jackson's face—such products of human ingenuity are to economists
but information, and information is a "public good." That is, the
firm producing such a good cannot—absent legal protection—stop
others from using it. If I sell my improved mousetrap in a patentless
world, you are free to copy the design and to compete with me. According to the standard prediction, I get discouraged just thinking
about the situation, and a market without legal protection for costly
innovations thus fails to produce the optimal amount of them.

---

[72]109 S.Ct. at 982 & 975.

[73]*Id.* at 984.

[74]Accord, Kellogg Co. v. National Biscuit Co., 305 U.S. 111, 119 (1938) (Brandeis, J.); International News Service v. Associated Press, 248 U.S. 215, 262 (1918) (Brandeis, J., dissenting); Graham v. John Deere Co., 383 U.S. 1, 9 (1966); Breyer, The Uneasy Case for
Copyright: A Study of Copyright in Books, Photocopies, and Computer Programs, 84 Harv.
L. Rev. 281, 284–91 (1970); compare Hettinger, Justifying Intellectual Property, 18 Philosophy & Public Affairs 31, 51 (1989).

[75]See, *e.g.*, International News Service v. Associated Press, 248 U.S. at 239–40; Mazer v.
Stein, 347 U.S. 201, 219 (1954); San Francisco Arts & Athletics v. United States Olympic
Committee, 107 S.Ct. 2971, 2979, 2982–83 (1987); Gordon, An Inquiry into the Merits of
Copyright: The Challenges of Consistency, Consent, and Encouragement Theory, 41 Stan. L.
Rev. 1343, 1438–69 (1989); Hughes, The Philosophy of Intellectual Property, 77 Geo. L. J.
287 (1988); *cf.* Harper & Row Publishers Inc. v. Nation Enterprises, 471 U.S. 539, 546, 562
(1985) (O'Connor, J.).

Consumers would be willing to pay for these advances. Indeed, in a frictionless world they would organize and pay creators directly— but on Planet Earth the costs of such transactions are prohibitive. Thus patent and copyright law employ a policy of exclusive rewards for creators to bring consumers otherwise unavailable innovations.[76] The sort of exclusivity that prompts innovation creates efficiency, benefits consumers, and contrasts with federal antitrust law's usual (and sensible) distaste for inefficient and undesirable monopoly pricing.

The efficiency case against protecting intellectual property accepts the foregoing, but elaborates by introducing the notion of "lead-time exclusivity" or "first mover advantage." Innovation remains desirable. But the incentive that prompts it could be simply the first mover's jump on complacent competitors. Law could reduce this time lag nearly to zero, by requiring significant innovators to "predisclose" their new ideas to their competitors. Indeed, antitrust law briefly toyed with this notion, only to reject it for fear that it might deter all invention.[77] Even without such an extreme policy, however, free riders eventually appear to copy an innovator's accomplishments for profit. It simply takes longer. Copycats generally copy only successful products—the ones that (by definition) already have earned their makers some reward. Added to the time copyists require even to identify worthwhile targets can be a lag due to their actual manufacturing and marketing, if these tasks turn out to be time consuming because data are secret, experience is valuable, and so forth. In theory, this period of lead-time exclusivity might be long enough to support the innovator's original investment.[78] If so, then this situation is a happy one for consumers because they enjoy the best of both worlds: an ample supply of new products, followed (sooner or later) by low competitive pricing.

This framework of analysis does permit one to rationalize some case law. We now can reconcile optimal federal innovation policy with state laws that also aim to promote efficiency or consumer welfare through different means. For instance, Holmes suggested that

---

[76]See Coase, The Problem of Social Cost, 3 J. Law & Econ. 1 (1960); Demsetz, Some Aspects of Property Rights, 9 J. Law & Econ. 61 (1966); Demsetz, The Private Production of Public Goods, 13 J. Law & Econ. 293 (1970).

[77]Berkey Photo v. Kodak, 603 F2d 263, 276, 281 (2d Cir. 1979).

[78]See, *e.g.*, Scherer, Industrial Market Structure and Economic Performance 443–50 (2d ed. 1980).

trade secret law aims not to offer a "monopoly subsidy" for innovation[79] but rather seeks to protect confidential or trusting relations[80]—which in the rubric of efficiency are desirable as less costly alternatives to self-help or to formal and intricate contracts.[81] Or again, state contract law becomes consistent with efficient federal innovation policy because contracts also promote efficiency by allowing parties to enforce bargains.[82]

Apart from providing a way to mesh innovation law with trade secret and contract law, however, this framework of analysis fails to specify the practical content of the ideal federal innovation policy. Its different versions offer opposing advice to policymakers: give, or else do not give, an exclusive right to a creator. To choose between them, we must know how much reward innovators truly need before they will innovate. Law should give them that amount of protection, and no more.

The central difficulty is severe ignorance. In some markets, the promise of a lead-time exclusivity and nothing more does seem enough to sustain a good deal of innovation. For instance, this policy governs nearly all American industrial design.[83] We have no proof that this world has been the best of all possible, but Ford did design his Model T, Loewy his rotary telephone, Eames his chair, and Iacocca his Mustang. On the other hand, it may be that with legal design protection we would have had designs that today remain invisible as unimagined. And since the very earliest days of the Republic, it has been Congress's opinion that inventors of novel, nonobvious, and original inventions require a far longer period of exclusive rights than offered by their manufacturing jump on rivals.[84] Economic research suggests that exclusive and across-the-board reliance on lead-time exclusivity would deter innovation in some industries.[85] And it is quite clear that the importance of legal

---

[79]Goldstein, note 28 *supra*, at 83.

[80]See E.I. DuPont De Nemours Powder Co. v. Masland, 244 U.S. 100 (1917).

[81]Compare notes 24–28 *supra* and accompanying text.

[82]Compare notes 29–30 *supra* and accompanying text.

[83]See generally Brown, note 46 *supra*.

[84]See Patent Act of 1790, 1 Stat. 109; 35 U.S.C. §154 & 173 (17-year term for utility patents and 14-year term for design patents).

[85]See, *e.g.*, Nelson, Peck & Kalacheck, Technology, Economic Growth and Public Policy 159–60 (1967).

protection for what economists call "appropriability" differs from one industry to another.[86]

In sum, we know that innovation protection sometimes is important, but sometimes not, and that one cannot generalize in a way that ignores such differences. The trouble is that we know hardly any more than these meager facts. The famous economist Fritz Machlup confessed a fairly spectacular degree of ignorance by advising Congress that "[n]o economist, on the basis of present knowledge, could possibly state with certainty that the patent system, as it now operates, confers a net benefit or a net loss upon society."[87] In commenting on a survey of the literature by Steven Cheung,[88] George Priest summarized:[89]

> What does the patent system give us, and at what cost? According to Cheung, Bentham claims something for nothing; Taussig responds nothing for nothing, Plant rejoins nothing for something, Arrow replies something (but not enough) for something; Cheung concludes that they all fail to take into account transaction costs. The ratio of empirical demonstration to assumption in this literature must be very close to zero. . . . Cheung has demonstrated quite persuasively that, in the current state of knowledge, economists know almost nothing about the effect on social welfare of the patent system or of other systems of intellectual property.

Ignorance is a drawback. It also is an unavoidable fact of life. Congress in the last couple of centuries has been unwilling to wait for academic consensus before inventing the patent and copyright codes. Nor has Congress in the last few decades feared to adjust—repeatedly—the extent and duration of such policy coverage.[90] Given our ignorance, the standards by which a legislative body ought to decide to tinker with such policy coverage is a pretty problem.

There is reason to mistrust the most likely evidence of a need for

---

[86]Levin, Klevorick, Nelson & Winter, Appropriating the Returns from Industrial Research and Development, 3 Brookings Papers on Economic Activity (1987).

[87]Senate Subcomm. on Patents, Trademarks, and Copyrights, Senate Comm. on the Judiciary, 85th Cong., 2d Sess., An Economic Review of the Patent System 79 (Study No. 15, Comm. Print 1958). See also Markham, Inventive Activity: Government Controls and the Legal Environment, in The Rate and Direction of Inventive Activity 598–99 (1962) ("studies have developed relatively little information on the social costs at which these positive benefits of the patent system are obtained").

[88]Cheung, Property Rights and Invention, 8 Research in Law & Economics 5 (1986).

[89]Priest, What Economics Can Tell Lawyers About Intellectual Property, 8 Research in Law & Economics 19, 19 & 21 (1986).

[90]See, e.g., note 15 supra.

increased protection: industry whining. If all firms expect to innovate about the same amount, the entire industry has an incentive to
complain that its creative acts deserve more exclusive protection, irrespective of the minimum reward necessary to trigger a given research and development (R & D) investment. These answers are as
credible as those my dean would receive if she asked all faculty
whether they need raises. On the other hand, the industry may be
divided between firms that innovate and those that clone the innovations.[91] Presumably the former would support protection and latter
oppose it—both categorically and irrespective of the truth.

A different legislative standard might withhold added protection
for intellectual property until industry members produced some
documented evidence of innovation expenditures they had considered but rejected for fear of free riders. But most decisions not to
act leave little documentation, while well-counseled firms often can
manipulate such tests through the creative building of records. Still a
different standard would adopt new protection only after experience
abroad had shown its worth, although problems of analysis and possibly national preeminence dog this idea as well. Legislatures—
federal as well as state—thus face a difficult decision when they
ponder whether added intellectual property protection will benefit
consumers.

Judges can bring little to this controversy. Nonetheless, the Court
mused about the question—in revealingly conditional language. It
said that "duplication *may* be an essential part of innovation in the
field of aquadynamic design."[92] It may be. But the premise of patent
law is that free riders deter, not promote, patentable innovation, at
least under some circumstances. We have no contrary analysis of the
data regarding unpatentable innovation or under different circumstances, because we have no data. Or again, "the competitive reality
of reverse engineering may act as a spur to the inventor, creating an
incentive to develop inventions that meet the rigorous requirements
of patentability."[93] It may so act. But reverse engineering also may
discourage innovation—both patentable and unpatentable—by increasing the risk and decreasing the expected return to innovation investment. The *Bonito Boats* Court offered no contrary facts because it

---

[91] See, *e.g.*, Brown, note 46 *supra*, at 1399 ("the most vigorous support for [the proposed
federal design protection law] came from original parts manufacturers").

[92] 109 S.Ct. at 982.

[93] *Ibid.*

had no facts to support its empirical hypothesis that boat consumers do better to allow free riders than to bar them.

The Court may have been influenced by briefs that offered examples of expired design patents that the Florida law and other similar design statutes would have locked up forever—at least as against the economical "direct molding process." It indeed might seem a lamentable loss to consumers to withdraw from their competitive suppliers the most efficient way to reproduce an already-available design. Consumers then lose a competitive price for a monopoly one (supposing that the design really has no ready substitutes and that other means of copying are prohibitively expensive—extreme assumptions that are useful for exposition). This ex post analysis, however, ignores the ex ante consumer benefit of increased innovation. With a greater reward for doing so, designers may well spend more to innovate in the future. This future increase in available designs is the very point of laws like Florida's, and any analysis ignoring this aim errs by dwelling on costs and ignoring benefits. Some may be confident that the design increase will not be big enough to be worthwhile, or that it will not occur at all. But scholars investigating this question have yet to reach so firm a conclusion.[94]

It thus is possible to see the *Bonito Boats* decision as expressing a federal policy to enforce an optimal regime of innovation incentives. Given the Court's professed enthusiasm for the premise of state autonomy, however, the *Bonito Boats* opinion cannot justify itself on these grounds because we have no reason to consider federal courts to be better judges than state legislators of when added protection is efficient. Florida legislators may well have been comically unaware of the true reward necessary to induce innovation by boat makers. But they scarcely could have been less informed about the boat business than nine judges in Washington, D.C.

E. A FEDERAL POLICY TO COMBAT STATE CAPTURE?

I have argued that the Court had no factual basis for believing it could improve upon the Florida legislature's design of an innovation policy beneficial to consumers. Together with everyone else, the Court and the Florida legislature lacked information about innovators' responsiveness to the bait of intellectual property protection. And presumably the Florida legislators at least had listened to the relevant industry.

---

[94]See text accompanying notes 87–89 *supra.*

But that very industry contact may have been just the problem, in the Court's eyes, and hence its rationale for federal preemption. The *Bonito Boats* opinion offered that "[a]bsent [a preemptive] federal rule, each State could afford patent-like protection to particularly favored home industries, effectively insulating them from competition from outside the State."[95] The suggestion is that state parochialism justifies federal preemption.

The facts possibly manifested parochialism. The statute was specific to a single industry, and indeed to a single industry process. The state supreme court remarked the legislation "is intended to protect the original manufacturers of boat hulls . . . ."[96] Bonito was a Florida company, and Thunder Craft was from Tennessee. Bonito sold its boats in "a broad interstate market."[97] Although the matter is quite speculative, it is conceivable that Bonito Boats itself had prompted the Florida legislature to enact Florida's anti-boat molding law. The timing was suggestive: Bonito developed its hull design in 1976, the Florida legislature passed its law in 1983, and Bonito sued its competitor Thunder Craft about 18 months after the statute's effective date. In sum, a local company used and perhaps even obtained a state law for the purpose of suppressing competition from out of state.

Bonito Boats' concern with local industry capture of parochial state legislation sounds a note that the *Sears* and *Compco* opinions had not, perhaps because they had reviewed state law as created by ostensibly insulated federal diversity courts rather than by seemingly capture-prone state legislators.[98] The capture concern also was absent from the *Goldstein* opinion, even though the facts in that case disclosed a more likely instance of capture: a California law that protected California's powerful recording industry. This concern about parochial capture is familiar, however, in a different Supreme Court context. Nearly endlessly the antitrust community has discussed and litigated the problem under the heading of the "state action" or "*Parker v. Brown*" problem.[99] That problem is to define the conditions

---

[95] 109 S.Ct. at 984. See also *id*. at 983 ("The prospect of all 50 States establishing similar protections for preferred industries without the rigorous requirements of patentability prescribed by Congress could pose a substantial threat to the patent system's ability to accomplish its mission of promoting progress in the useful arts.").

[96] Bonito Boats, Inc. v. Thunder Craft Boats, Inc., 515 So.2d 220, 223 (Fla. 1987).

[97] 109 S.Ct. at 974.

[98] See *Sears*, 376 U.S. at 227 n.2; *Compco*, 376 U.S. at 236 n.3.

[99] See Parker v. Brown, 317 U.S. 341 (1943).

under which the national competition policy of the Sherman Act should preempt state or local efforts to shield industry from competition. In more than a dozen cases judges have struggled to formulate a doctrinal response. Commentators have criticized that doctrine and have offered a barrage of supposedly improved alternatives. From every one of these varying perspectives, the *Bonito Boats* approach looks wrong.

The simplest statement of the Court's response to the state action problem is that it permits anticompetitive state regulations if they are, first, "clearly articulated and affirmatively expressed as state policy," and, second, "actively supervised by the State itself."[100] The first prong of this test would reverse the *Bonito Boats* result, for the Florida statute indeed was "clearly articulated." The Court has expressed some uncertainty about the applicability of the second "active supervision" requirement.[101] If the second "active supervision" prong were also to apply, the *Bonito Boats* Court again would be wrong to hold that Florida *never* can impede competition in this way, for this rule would instead defer to Florida action that exhibited sufficient circumspection.

Commentators have attacked this doctrine on a variety of reasons. Their alternative proposals suggest other criticisms of *Bonito Boats*. Judge Frank Easterbrook, for instance, argues that the state action doctrine ought to invalidate those state laws that exploit consumers beyond the state's borders.[102] Florida's law might have been of this character. To decide the issue, Easterbrook would have the Court determine whether Florida's law permitted Florida boat makers to export a monopoly overcharge to boat consumers outside the state—an inquiry that *Bonito Boats* might have required but in fact did not. Easterbrook criticizes preemption in the absence of such an inquiry as unjustified invasion of state economic autonomy. Unsurprisingly, Judge Easterbrook also is critical of the *Bonito Boats* opinion.[103]

One may fault Judge Easterbrook's position as insufficient to do

---

[100]California Retail Liquor Dealers Ass'n v. Midcal Aluminum, Inc., 445 U.S. 97, 105 (1980).

[101]See Hoover v. Ronwin, 466 U.S. 558 (1984); Page, State Action and Active Supervision: An Antitrust Anomaly, Antitrust Bulletin (forthcoming) (urging abandonment of the second "active supervision" test).

[102]Easterbrook, Antitrust and the Economics of Federalism, 26 J. Law & Econ. 23 (1983).

[103]See Easterbrook, Intellectual Property is Still Property, 13 Harv. J.L. & P.P. (forthcoming 1990).

much about the problem of parochial industry capture.[104] But that objection does not lend support to an urge to invalidate every state action supported by its beneficiaries.[105] Self interest drives our system of government. To disable a state from helping those who appeal to it would be to insist upon some selfless republicanism that is utopian, certainly insofar as the patent code is able to affect the national personality.

Courts could remedy the overreach of this approach by asking whether the purchased legislation deserves preemption because it harms the public interest (as the relevant federal statute defines it), or whether the legislation instead ought to survive as consonant with the public interest. If we accept *Bonito Boats* as establishing an efficiency goal for the patent code,[106] this inquiry returns us to the substantive question of the last section: whether the Florida law was efficient. I argued there that this question is unanswerable as a matter of scholarly evidence and consensus. It merits emphasis here that states nonetheless can make goodhearted and pragmatic effort to improve the world. Their work in this field is not automatically suspect as capture, any more than Congress's is.

No one has ever accused the federal patent system of perfection. Before creation of the CAFC in 1982, many (eventually including Congress) thought that differences among the circuit courts about the proper definition of patentable invention had created debilitating uncertainty for patent law.[107] After 1982, some have argued that the CAFC law on this crucial point unwisely favors commercially successful innovators to the neglect of technological breakthroughs that for irrelevant reasons garner little immediate profit.[108]

One either ground—or for some other equally sober, disinterested, public regarding, and high minded reason—Florida might have seen a need to supplement the federal patent incentive in a particular market: the boat business. The state might have reasoned that boat makers like Bonito could have contracted validly with their customers that the boat was not to be used for molding clones, but that

---

[104]See Wiley, A Capture Theory of Antitrust Federalism, 99 Harv. L. Rev. 713, 740 n.133 (1986).

[105]See Wiley, A Capture Theory of Antitrust Federalism: Reply to Professors Page and Spitzer, 61 S. Calif. L. Rev. 1327 (1988), and cited authorities.

[106]See text accompanying note 74 *supra*.

[107]See, *e.g.*, Dreyfuss, note 16 *supra*, at 6–7.

[108]See, *e.g.*, Merges, note 16 *supra*, at 837–60.

the practical difficulties of enforcing such a contractual regime made the Florida law the best practical alternative for the public. Or Thunder Craft's method of direct molding might have decimated the lead time that innovators traditionally had enjoyed in the boat industry. The statute thus might have been Florida's effort to maintain a proven status quo arising from traditional means of copying—means that the Florida statute permitted to continue.

A Court concerned with attacking industry capture ought to care deeply if the Florida law was such an honest attempt to help boat consumers by maintaining or spurring boat innovation rather than a simple sop to Bonito-the-generous-campaign-contributor. But the *Bonito Boats* Court lacked interest in examining the bath water for babies. In its only remotely relevant analysis, the Court recited Florida legislative history that "indicates that [the law] was intended to create an inducement for the improvement of boat hull designs."[109] The law indeed might have had this apparently efficient and proconsumer effect. The Court offered no reason to doubt it. Moreover, counsel alerted the Court that eleven other states had also passed similar statutes. Yet the Court showed even less interest in the provenance or consequences of these laws while issuing an opinion fatal to them. The *Bonito Boats* Court thus cannot justify its holding as a sensible effort to defeat parochial state decision making.

One might doubt the Court's competence ever to do a better job of classifying state laws as efficient or captured. One then could retreat into procedure. As an alternative test, the Court could erect a requirement that states accompany all patent-like legislation with a "Consumer Impact Statement" demonstrating serious and sustained deliberation in support of a conclusion that the law was an efficient benefit to consumers. But then "[a] regulation whose justification was too plain to require explication would be vulnerable; a questionable one could be immunized if it proponents had the skill or influence to generate a proper legislative history."[110]

In sum, the positions on antitrust's analogous state action problem are various. The one approach that no one favors is the one that *Bonito Boats* adopted: to ban all state initiatives regardless of their asserted and possible benefit to consumers.

---

[109]109 S.Ct. at 981. See also *id.* at 974.

[110]Cantor v. Detroit Edison Co., 428 U.S. 579, 610 (1976) (Blackmun, J., concurring in the judgment); see also Wiley, note 104 *supra*, at 744–45 & nn. 145–48 (further criticism of this approach).

F. A FEDERAL POLICY TO PROMOTE NATIONAL UNIFORMITY?

Embrace of "national uniformity" is the last refuge of every tottering preemption argument.[111] The simple tautology of the plea is both its great strength and its obvious weakness. Every preemption crushes diversity, so the uniformity argument is reliable. But the proof is too strong, for diversity is inevitable and indeed the very point of our federal system. The national uniformity argument in *Bonito Boats* shares just these qualities.

Justice O'Connor said that to allow laws like Florida's "would lead to administrative problems of no small dimension."[112] She pointed out that "[t]he federal patent system provides a basis for the public to ascertain the status of the intellectual property embodied in any article in general circulation."[113] She then used two (not entirely explicit) premises to reach her conclusion: (1) no central repository of data about freedom to duplicate products would exist if the patent system were not exclusive; (2) the costs of uncertainty absent such a central repository would be unacceptable; and therefore federal exclusivity is needed to avoid unacceptable costs. Both premises are doubtful.

Centralized repositories indeed can exist if patent law is not preemptive, for private services will supply information when demand is sufficient. To appreciate that private firms in fact can supply data to buyers (and can do so faster than the relevant federal agency), one need look only to Supreme Court citations throughout this volume—which all would be to *U.S. Reports* rather than to West's *Supreme Court Reporter*, if only they could be. CCH, BNA, and other commercial publishers make a business of summarizing relevant law for particular clienteles. That firms need information about legal rights does not support that the PTO can be the only one to give those rights.

Neither is the cost of uncertainty unacceptable, absent an exclusive federal information repository. Business regularly tolerates the costs of diversity in a federal system. Varying commercial regulation is the norm. Fifty states grant trademark rights, yet few argue that the federal trademark regime of the Lanham Act ought to stamp out state trademark law. Warranty and product liability law varies between jurisdictions. Contract law, blue sky regulation, corporation

---

[111]My argument here follows Mishkin, The Variousness of "Federal Law," 105 U. Pa. L. Rev. 797, 812–14, 821–23, & 830–32 (1957).

[112]109 S.Ct. at 983.

[113]*Ibid.*

law, antitrust and unfair competition law, consumer protection, advertising and product disparagement regulation, trade secret law, tortious interference with contract and prospective advantage, rights of privacy and publicity—all these commercially significant doctrines are creatures of state law and hence can differ from one state to the next. The UCC, national securities regulation, federal bankruptcy law, and other forces of uniformity have done much to reduce balkanization of the economy. But our federal system never has been and is not now so completely national in character that the Court can simply cite the prospect of local diversity and conclude that therefore it ought to be abolished.

Justice O'Connor also made a different argument in favor of national uniformity: that federal jurisdiction in patent matters is exclusive and therefore supplementary state rights are void.[114] But exclusive federal patent jurisdiction simply shows Congress' desire for uniform federal patent law—not its aim to exclude supplementary state law. The error of *Bonito Boats'* non sequitur is most apparent from this Term's *ARC America* opinion, which recited that federal antitrust jurisdiction is exclusive but nonetheless concluded unanimously that federal antitrust law did not preempt the ability of state antitrust law to offer supplementary protection.[115] One might differ with this conclusion for reasons of substantive policy,[116] but not because federal antitrust jurisdiction is exclusive.

In short, *Bonito Boats'* claim that national uniformity necessitated the elimination of the Florida law failed to distinguish that law from the thousands of others that constitute the normal diversity of our federal system. One might well believe the very notion of fifty different legal systems is but a historical curiosity, and that every step toward its elimination is progress. Such a view would applaud *Bonito Boats'* uniformity argument. But it would be remarkable to find the Rehnquist Court espousing that position.

IV. Conclusion

The *Bonito Boats* opinion unanimously endorsed a Warren Court precept—one jarringly out of character with a Term otherwise

---

[114]*Ibid.*

[115]*ARC America*, note 67 *supra*, 109 S.Ct. at 1666.

[116]See Sullivan & Wiley, Recent Antitrust Developments: Defining the Scope of Exemptions, Expanding Coverage, and Refining the Rule of Reason, 27 UCLA L. Rev. 265, 297–99 (1979).

marked by partisan strife over a conservative shift.[117] The opinion is all the more notable for its vague scope and lack of credible justification. Perhaps the Court, like many, begins to snooze at the mere mention of the patent code. Whatever the explanation, the opinion watered a withered vine that now will cause doctrinal uncertainty until the Court either convincingly explains the case's taxonomy or culls it as a weed. Meanwhile, the opinion deserves only the respect that nine votes can give to unpersuasive assertion.

---

[117]See, *e.g.*, Greenhouse, The Year the Court Turned to the Right, New York Times, July 7, 1989, p. 1, col. 3.

GERHARD CASPER

CHANGING CONCEPTS OF CONSTITUTIONALISM: 18TH TO 20TH CENTURY

When one considers the nature of constitutional government in the developed Western democracies at the end of the 20th century, one cannot help but be impressed by how much these democracies have in common. All adult citizens have the right to vote. In most countries governments are regularly turned out of office. Many countries have institutionalized judicial review. But even without judicial review, basic rights—such as freedom of speech or religion—are reasonably respected and protected. There have been gains in the area of equal rights for women. Economic activities can be pursued in relative freedom. While welfare systems have not succeeded in eliminating poverty, they represent at least an acknowledgment of the obligation to moderate poverty. Apart from poverty, stark social differences remain, but equality of opportunity, not infrequently, is more than a mere aspiration.

To be sure, differences exist among Western democracies, and each has its pockets of hard to solve problems. At present, we in the United States seem to be plagued by more of them than other advanced democracies and some of these concern the very essence of our society. The black underclass and the pervasiveness of crime are

Gerhard Casper is William B. Graham Distinguished Service Professor of Law and Provost, The University of Chicago.

AUTHOR'S NOTE: This paper was originally presented at a conference entitled Constitutionalism: The American Experiment in a Wider Perspective, held at Harvard Law School, April 6–9, 1989.

perhaps the most notorious examples. Yet, if it is considered plausible to talk about convergence of market economies and socialist
systems, how much more plausible would it be to stipulate the convergence of the mature Western democracies.

Max Horkheimer, one of the original members of the "Frankfurt
School," in his later years, seemed much dispirited by the phenomenon of convergence. He lamented the worldwide weakening of the
"sense for differences." According to Horkheimer, European countries, especially after World War II, instead of going about arranging
a "truer life" ("Einrichtung des richtigeren Lebens") and concentrat-
ing on the freedom of the individual and justice, merely followed the
United States in stressing the standard of living and business.[1]
Horkheimer's lament suggests that there was a European alternative
to the American way grounded in differences that existed before
World War II. In this paper I should like to explore the question of
what those differences might have been and whether, or to what extent, we are experiencing a convergence of concepts of constitutionalism.

While some convergence has indeed taken place, it is my thesis
that this convergence does not eliminate basic differences between
the United States and Western Europe, especially in their respective
attitudes toward the responsibility of government for "arranging," in
Horkheimer's words, "a truer life." Since the late 18th century, both
the authoritarian—let us say Prussian—and the democratic—let us
say French—strand in European constitutionalist thought have
known constitutional *duties* as well as constitutional *rights* on the part
of the citizen as well as on the part of government. Put differently, the
notion of the *state* and its functions remains an important element
in understanding European constitutionalism. American constitutionalism, on the other hand, continues to be primarily caught up in
the language of rights. For American constitutionalism the concept
of the state has little denotative or connotative meaning. My paper is
a modest effort to remind us of the forest, as we study the trees.

In 1844 the young Marx, in exile in Paris, published an article entitled "On the Jewish Question." It was written at a time when the
German constitutions continued to withhold full political status
from Jewish citizens and Marx could characterize the German states
as "Christian" and, therefore, the "Jewish question" as a "theologi-
cal" rather than a secular issue. In his article Marx argued that re-

[1]Horkheimer, Notizen 1950 bis 1969 und Dämmerung 104 (1974).

ligious freedom in the United States, the abolition of property qualifications for the right to vote, the protection of private property rights, and other delineations between state and society constituted the modern "political" state. "The state, after its own fashion, abolishes the distinctions of birth, status, education, occupation when it declares birth, status, education, occupation to be nonpolitical distinctions."[2]

While Marx viewed this political emancipation as "great progress"[3] and the United States as the "most perfect example of the modern state,"[4] political emancipation to him was not the final form of human emancipation. All it had done was to displace from the state to private law and bourgeois society matters that had previously been directly political. The sphere of society, as distinguished from that of the state, was, of course, in his eyes, the sphere of egoism and the war of everybody against everybody. However, by relating the human world back to the human being as such, political emancipation made possible the ultimate emergence of the human being as a true member of the human species. This final form of emancipation would eventually overcome the modern state, which defined politics merely in terms of abstract generalities and emancipation in terms of individual freedom.

Marx's treatment of the United States in the second part of his essay depicts American society as crassly commercial, money-oriented, in short, capitalistic. For this he relies on the 1833 travel account of Thomas Hamilton. The picture of the United States that Marx conveys is not altogether atypical for the period. The European vision of America was becoming more complicated than it had been in earlier decades, as some disappointed emigrants returned and as the travel literature about the United States created controversy.[5]

A colorful example of the critical reverberations is provided by Schopenhauer. A few years after Marx—though we must assume independently of him—Schopenhauer also discussed the theory and practice of American constitutionalism in terms which were similar to those of Marx. His premise was, of course, different. Schopen-

---

[2]Marx & Engels, 1 Werke 354 (1957).

[3]*Id*. at 356.

[4]Marx & Engels, 3 Werke 62 (1957).

[5]See, for instance, Duden, Die nordamerikanische Demokratie und das v. Tocqueville'sche Werk 84*ff* (1837).

hauer's Hobbesian view of humanity led him to argue for a completely irresponsible ruler. "A constitution which embodied no more than the abstract rule of law would be a splendid thing for beings other than man."[6] He contrasts his ideal of a Hobbesian sovereign with the United States where one encounters, according to Schopenhauer, an attempt at the rule of pure, abstract law. Alas, the result was not enticing to the austere philosopher: in the United States base utilitarianism went hand in hand with ignorance, bigotry, mockery of the law, repudiation of public indebtedness, slavery, lynchlaw, murder, invasion of a neighboring country, and many other vices. "Thus this model of a constitution based on pure law speaks little in favor of republican government."[7]

What these two views of American constitutionalism have in common is the contrast between the "abstract" rule of law and a society characterized by the war of everybody against everybody. While Marx appreciates the emancipatory progress represented by the United States on the way to "true" emancipation, Schopenhauer's pessimistic view of human nature sees the American example as confirming the need for monarchical rule. Both authors stress American materialism, a point made with such frequency by European travelers that it had already become a cliché.[8] Neither critic is much concerned with the details of American institutions or their historical and theoretical underpinnings. For instance, the emphasis both writers place on the abstract rule of law in the United States seems oblivious to the fact that the Americans' choice of constitutions as the means for anchoring the organization of their governments and the protection of their rights had its formal and substantive antecedents in the colonial charters and fundamental orders of the 17th century which, in turn, reflected the traditions of the common law.[9]

Nevertheless, the emphasis on "abstractness" characterizes American constitutionalism in a manner that would have been understood by the Framers and that continues to be invoked by both its critics and its supporters. Morton Horwitz, for instance, has for a long time

---

[6] Schopenhauer, 2 Parerga und Parapolimena: kleine philosophische Schriften 260, in 5 Arthur Schopenhauer's Sämtliche Werke (Grisebach ed., 2d ed.).

[7] *Id.* at 261.

[8] Tocqueville, 2 Democracy in America (Reeve & Bowen trans., 1945). For other foreign travel accounts, see White, The Marshall Court and Cultural Change, 1815–35 31–33 (1988).

[9] Casper, Constitutionalism, in 2 Encyclopedia of the American Constitution 473, 476 (1986).

criticized the dominance of the process-orientation of American political thought.[10] Public choice theorists, on the other hand, with their skepticism about efforts to define the public interest and "organic" conceptions of the state, see this same process-orientation of the "American experiment in constitutional democracy" as attesting to the "genius" of the Framers.[11]

Implicit in all this is a juxtaposition of American constitutionalism with other traditions. At the time Marx and Schopenhauer wrote, i.e., in the mid–19th century, these differences were indeed marked, though, I think, it is fair to say that the American example and experience were hardly an omnipresence in the European sky. The watershed year for the Europeans was 1789, not 1787 or 1776. It is of course the case that the events of 1789 had been influenced by the American Revolution and the revolutionary constitutions of France display this influence. Yet, there is considerable dispute about the strength of that influence[12] and, in any event, the very course of the French Revolution had, early on, made it seem desirable to the European admirers of the American Revolution to emphasize discontinuities rather than continuities. A Viennese observer, Sartori, writing in the mid 1790s, almost stood matters on their head when he suggested that the difference was to be found in the French reliance on written constitutions: "[T]he North American Revolution was carried out under the rule of closest unity, without a constitution, and always with moderation against a recognized enemy, whereas the French Revolution was marked by the most horrible cruelties under the shield of the constitutions."[13]

However strange this summary of the American Revolution may sound to students of American constitutionalism, it does have a point. After all, the bills of rights in those American revolutionary constitutions which contained them harked back to the privileges and liberties of the unwritten English constitution, the colonial charters and theories of natural rights. Rights and liberties were acknowledged whether written down or not. Yet, the American revolution-

---

[10]See, most recently, Horwitz, The Warren Court: Rediscovering the Link Between Law and Culture, 55 U. Chi. L. Rev. 450, 454 (1988).

[11]Buchanan & Tullock, The Calculus of Consent 301 (1962).

[12]For a skeptical view, see Tocqueville, L'Ancien Régime et la Révolution 239 (1964).

[13]As quoted in Dippel, Germany and the American Revolution 1770–1800 300 (Uhlendorf trans., 1977). Compare Palmer, 1 The Age of Democratic Revolution 240 (1959).

ary assumption of popular sovereignty found its foremost expression in the notion of consent based written constitutions superior to legislation with representative institutions and separation of powers.

While the concept of a constitution had been long in the making, the American development expressed a normative conception. It did not simply refer to having a constitution but to having a particular kind of constitution. Prior to this normative theory of constitutional first principles, it was assumed that all legitimate polities, absolute and mixed alike had constitutions "and the issue of unlimited versus limited forms of governments was a practical choice between more or less preferable constitutional alternatives equally grounded in history."[14]

The new normative concept of a constitution[15] established the beginning of that way of thinking that we refer to as constitutionalism. The new normative concept finds one expression in the famous Concord resolve of 1776: "[We] Conceive that a Constitution in its Proper Idea intends a System of Principles Established to Secure the Subject in the Possession and enjoyment of their Rights and Privileges, against any encroachments of the Governing Part."[16] It finds another expression in Article 16 of the French Declaration of Rights: "A society in which the guarantee of rights is not assured, nor the separation of powers provided for, has no constitution."[17] It is present in, finally, Kant's critique of Hobbes which develops the argument for representative government—however ambiguous Kant's concept of representation was in practice[18]—on the basis of a priori principles. Constitutionalist reservations concerned, in Kantian terms, rights that the people could not surrender, because to surrender them would be contrary to the very purpose and nature of humanity. Even a unanimous decision to give up freedom and equality Kant viewed as null and void.[19]

---

[14]Krieger, An Essay on the Theory of Enlightened Despotism 71 (1975).

[15]See generally Stourzh, Fundamental Law and Individual Rights in the 18th Century Constitution (1984).

[16]Handlin & Handlin, The Popular Sources of Political Authority: Documents on the Massachusetts Constitution of 1780 153 (1966).

[17]Godechot, Déclaration des droits de l'homme et du citoyen du 26 août 1789, in Les Constitutions de la France Depuis 1789 35 (cited below as Godechot).

[18]See Krieger, The German Idea of Freedom 120 (1957).

[19]Kant, Über den Gemeinspruch: Das mag in der Theorie richtig sein, taugst aber nicht für die Praxis, 6 Werke 125, 143*ff* (1964).

France, in her early revolutionary constitutions, adopted a modern, normative understanding, losing sight of it, however, as the country, in the short period of a quarter century, rushed from constitutional monarchy to republic to dictatorship to empire and, finally, restoration. France went through seven constitutions as these changes occurred. The French example taught France and the rest of continental Europe a number of lessons which remained important throughout the nineteenth century and which had far-reaching implications.

The first of these lessons was that the new constitutional ethos had a long way to go before it could take hold. The form of constitutions and the substance of constitutionalism remained separate. The theme of the constitution as an empty shell found one of its most literate treatments in Karl Marx's ironic analysis of the 1848 French Constitution in his *The Eighteenth Brumaire of Louis Bonaparte*, first published in New York in 1852.[20] Dicey, at the turn of the century, made a similar point when he contrasted the French constitution of 1791 with the realities at the height of the French Revolution.[21] In discussing one of the most celebrated liberal constitutions of the nineteenth century, that of Belgium, Dicey expressed profound skepticism about the whole constitutionalist enterprise: "The matter to be noted is, that where the right to individual freedom is a result deduced from the principles of the constitution, the idea readily occurs that the right is capable of being suspended or taken away."[22]

The second lesson taught by the French example was to be found in the fact that the French nation-state was not defined primarily by the constitutions. This is also true for other European countries for whose definition history, a monarchically controlled state apparatus, and relative ethnic homogeneity have been important elements. The French constitutions did not constitute France in the manner in which the American Constitution had constituted the "new" United States. While the French Revolution had changed the meaning of the term "la nation,"[23] whatever it now meant remained antecedent to

---

[20]Marx & Engels, 8 Werke 111 (1957).

[21]Dicey, The Law of the Constitution 198–99 (10th ed., 1964).

[22]*Id.* at 201.

[23]Art. 3 of the Declaration of the Rights of Man: "The source of all sovereignty resides essentially in the nation." Godechot, note 17 *supra*, at 33–34. Compare Goubert, The Ancien Régime: French Society 1600–1750 3–4 (Cox trans., 1973).

and independent of the varying constitutions. The point is made most clearly in the Preamble to the 1848 Constitution which begins with the words: "France constitutes herself as a republic."[24] What seems missing here is the adverb "now," or, as history suggests, the phrase "for the time being." In our days, the Constitution of the Fifth Republic lists among the functions of the president that he ensures "the continuity of the state" ("a continuité de l'Etat").[25]

The difference between state and constitution has been crucial for much of Europe, even though, in the 19th century, the differentiation was less pronounced in countries with relatively strong parliaments.[26] Among instances, such as Belgium, Switzerland, and Italy, where state-formation and constitution-making went hand in hand, only the 1848 constitution of Switzerland has provided a continuous basis for the legitimacy of the Swiss state and the definition of its democracy.

In the United States the state, an "uneasy" state for that,[27] was formed by its constitution and continues to be tied up in constitutional terms to this very day. The continuing differences between Great Britain and continental countries are in part traceable to a similar phenomenon. Britain has been defined by the law of the unwritten constitution as this law has developed over centuries.[28] The continuity of the British constitution has made it unnecessary to differentiate between state and constitution. As Nettl puts it, the English tradition got along well without any native theory of the state until Harold Laski.[29]

To this date the term "state," in Anglo-Saxon countries, is rarely used as identifying that corporate ensemble which is made up of citizens but has an identity all its own[30] (as in the formulation "the citizen and the state"). Only economists seem at ease with the concept. Economists apart, English speakers, rather tellingly, come closest to

---

[24]"La France s'est constituée en République," Constitution du 4 Novembre 1848, Godechot, note 17 supra, at 263.

[25]See Luchaire, La Protection Constitutionnelle des Droits et des Libertés 11–14 (1987).

[26]See Fioravanti, The Study of Public Law in Italy: The Liberal State, Fascism, and the New Democratic Constitution (1861–1948) 8 (unpublished paper, 1988).

[27]Karl, The Uneasy State (1983).

[28]See Dicey, note 21 supra.

[29]Nettl, The State as a Conceptual Variable, 20 World Politics 559, 561–62 (1968).

[30]Compare id. at 564.

the European usage when they identify functions of government as the "administrative state" or the "welfare state."[31]

The third lesson taught by the French example between 1789 and 1815 was that constitutions could be used not only "to Secure the Subject[s] in the possession and enjoyment of their Rights and Privileges, against any encroachments of the Governing Part,"[32] but also to establish the duties of citizens. The French Revolution assigned moral programmatic tasks to constitutions which, in the manner in which they were executed, had no equivalents in American state constitutions. The seeds of this approach can be found in the most revolutionary of the early French constitutions, that of 1793. Its version of the Declaration of Rights began with the statement that the end of society was the common happiness—not its pursuit, but its achievement. Rights were summarized as equality, liberty, safety, and property. By contrast with 1789, liberty took second place. In accord with 1789, liberty was defined as the power to do all that did not harm the rights of others, supplemented by a "moral limitation" expressed as the negative version of the golden rule. Positively, the Constitution stated that it was the "sacred duty" of society to provide public aid in the form of work or subsistence to those citizens who were "malheureux," unfortunate.[33]

These positive rights were dropped again by the Constitution of 1795, which mostly reflected the bourgeois reaction to the revolutionary excesses of the preceding year. Its Declaration of the Rights of Man (defined as the "obligations" of the legislators) was, however, supplemented by a declaration of the *duties* of man which included the negative and positive version of the golden rule as well as a duty to defend and serve society and obey the letter and the spirit of the laws.[34] The theme of "reciprocal" duties of the citizens toward the republic and of the republic toward the citizens was also voiced in

---

[31]President Bush, in his innaugural address, employed the term "state" as referring to what I call the corporate ensemble, but, characteristically, in a negative fashion: "We know how to secure a more just and prosperous life for man on earth: through free markets, free speech, free elections, and the exercise of free will *unhampered by the state*." New York Times, Jan. 21, 1989, at 10 (Midwestern ed.) (emphasis added).

[32]Handlin & Handlin, note 16 *supra*, at 153.

[33]La Constitution de 1793, Art. 6, 21, in Godechot, note 17 *supra*, 80–82. The Constitution of 1793 also emphasized society's responsibility for making instruction available to all citizens in the interest of furthering the progress of "la raison publique" (public reason).

[34]Constitution du 5 Fructidor An III (22 aout 1795), *id.* at 102–3.

the 1848 Constitution.[35] It is perhaps worth recalling that the Declaration of the Rights of Man of 1789 and its subsequent versions always referred to the rights of man "and of the citizen." The concept of the citizen as the bearer of rights easily leads to the question what concomitant obligations might be.

The issue of obligations was not altogether absent from the early American constitutions, though more often than not they couched obligations in terms of Christian ethics. The Virginia Bill of Rights of 1776, for instance, proclaimed it to be the "mutual duty of all to practice Christian forbearance, love, and charity towards each other."[36] Virginia's constitution, but also others, invokes "justice, moderation, temperance, frugality, and virtue."[37] The New Hampshire Bill of Rights of 1784 refers to "that chain of connections that binds the whole fabric of the constitution in one indissoluble bond of union and amity."[38] On the whole, however, the American constitutions speak the language of rights. Furthermore, these rights are essentially "negative" rights.[39]

Finally, there was a fourth lesson to be drawn from the French revolutionary experience. The Napoleonic code was promulgated in 1804. It, for the first time, imposed the same "civil" law on all of France and, in a myriad of ways, secured the new equality of civil capacity with respect to property and the freedom of contracts. While the French Civil Code underwent some changes as regimes changed, in its essentials it has remained in force since 1804 as, in René David's words, "the most lasting and the only true constitution of France."[40] Furthermore, it has some claim to being at least part of the constitution of those countries in Europe, such as Italy,[41] and in Latin America that followed its model. It even lasted for almost a century in those sections of western Germany that did not relinquish it after the defeat of Napoleon. The constitutional aspect of "private" law is, of course, well familiar to students of the common law.[42] The case of the Napoleonic Code gains a dramatic quality

---

[35]Constitution du 4 Novembre 1848, *id.* at 264.

[36]Virginia Constitution of 1776, §16, reprinted in Thorpe, 7 The Federal and State Constitutions and Other Organic Laws 3812, 3814 (1909) (cited below as Thorpe).

[37]Virginia Constitution of 1776, §15, *ibid.*

[38]New Hampshire Constitution of 1784, Art. XXXVII, 4 Thorpe, *id.*, at 2457.

[39]Currie, Positive and Negative Constitutional Rights, 53 U. Chi. L. Rev. 864 (1986).

[40]David, French Law: Its Structure, Sources, and Methodology 111 (Kindred trans., 1972).

[41]See Fioravanti, note 26 *supra*, at 14.

[42]See Epstein, The Classical Legal Tradition, 73 Cornell L. Rev. 292, 296 (1988).

from the contrast between its permanence in the face of ever changing constitutions.

Less dramatic, but of similar significance, is the earlier example of the General Code for the Prussian States, a product of the enlightened absolutism of Frederick II who desired a comprehensive, natural law based codification. The draft was completed in the year of Frederick's death, 1786, and, after some reactionary changes, eventually promulgated by his successor in 1794.[43] It remained in force until supplanted by the German Civil Code of 1900. Where Napoleon's code, to some extent, ratified the egalitarian accomplishments of the French Revolution, the Prussian Code, which covered both private and public law, did not tamper with the prerogatives of king and nobility.[44] It nevertheless reflected constitutionalist impulses in its comprehensive effort clearly to define the rights (and, of course, obligations) of the subject. For instance, the rights of property were spelled out, but also expressly limited in terms of the interests of others and the interests of "the state."

More significantly, the code included a title headed "Of the Rights and Duties of the State in general."[45] Its first section states that these rights and duties are united in its "head," meaning the monarch. The head is responsible for external and internal peace and security, but also for the protection of the individual in "his own." It is his task to make arrangements that provide the inhabitants with the means and opportunity to develop their abilities and strengths so that they may apply these to further their fortunes. To be sure, Frederick II did not usher in the welfare state, and expectations on the part of the subjects remained limited,[46] yet the seeds for later developments were planted with this conception of the functions of the state.

Leonard Krieger identifies the modernization of absolutism as "the conjunction of absolutism and constitutionalism." He writes that "the law was now general, natural, and rational, organizing government and individuals in a single order of natural society, complementary in their interests but separate in their functions." "The characteristic mode of action of government was the enforcement of

---

[43] See Wieacker, Privatrechtsgeschichte der Neuzeit 328–31 (2d ed., 1967).

[44] See Rosenberg, Bureaucracy, Aristocracy and Autrocracy: The Prussian Experience 1600–1815 190 (Beacon ed., 1966).

[45] Allgemeines Landrecht für die Preussischen Staaten, Part 2, Title 13 (1835) (cited below at ALR).

[46] Denninger, Der Präventions-Staat, 21 Kritische Justiz 1, 12 (1988).

the order in the natural order; the characteristic mode of action outside government was the assertion of natural rights by individuals."[47] Or, as R. R. Palmer puts it: "What was wanted on the Continent was an enlightened authority strong enough to recast existing institutions. Government itself should replace special privilege with more equal rights, make the law more equitable and more respected, apportion taxes more fairly and collect them more efficiently, develop education to produce useful citizens, and raise more people from servility and localism into membership in an enlarged modern community."[48]

Governmental functions began to be carried out by a modern cadre of administrators who "were subject to general norms and prescribed procedures and committed to impersonal efficiency."[49] Frederick the Great thought of himself as "the first servant of the state." The principles governing this new system of administration were first codified in the title about "The Rights and Duties of the Servants of the State" in the Prussian General Code[50] with its emphasis on the separation of office and incumbent, hierarchical authority structures, rule based administration, and professional qualifications.[51] Similar principles were put in place by Napoleon in France leading to the development of that body of administrative law that proved so fascinating to Dicey. England did not reform its civil service before the 1850s.

During the revolutionary periods of the 19th century, the overriding constitutionalist theme in Germany (putting aside the issue of national unification) was the dispute over the participation of the new bourgeois-democratic forces in the government of the state.[52] The constitutional monarchies that emerged in the first half of the 19th century were characterized by what became known as the "monarchische Prinzip," the monarchic principle. It continued to unite in the monarch, as the head of the state, essentially those rights and duties that the Prussian General Code attributed to the state. The new parliamentary institutions served a limiting function. As Dieter

---

[47]Krieger, note 14 *supra*, at 76.

[48]Palmer, Turgot: Paragon of the Continental Englightenment, 19 J. Law & Econ. 607, 609 (1976).

[49]Rosenberg, note 44 *supra*, at 48.

[50]Part 2, Title 10, ALR, note 45 *supra*.

[51]See Bendix, Nation-Building and Citizenship 109 (1964).

[52]Böckenförde, Staat, Gesellschaft, Freiheit 93 (1976).

Grimm puts it in his recent book on German constitutional history: "Given the monarchic principle and the monarchic prerogative, the legislative representation of the people does not actually become part of the state. More accurately it can be described as a representation of society at the level of the state looking after certain interests of the subjects and asserting them at least negatively."[53] Francis Sejersted makes a similar point about the Norwegian constitution of 1814 and the Storting as "a controlling power acting on the part of the Constitution."[54] About the last third of the century Sejersted says: "As the position of the Storting was thus gradually changed from negative control into positive power, the problem of controlling positive state power changed from the problem of controlling the king into the problem of controlling the legislator."[55]

The details of constitutional arrangements are not the subject of this paper. In the case of Germany the arrangements varied greatly from the more liberal constitutions of Southern Germany to the more conservative ones in the north. The most ambitious constitutional undertaking in 19th century Germany, the 1849 Frankfurt Constitution for the Reich as a whole, with universal franchise, an extensive bill of rights, and judicial review,[56] floundered on the very unwillingness of Frederick William IV of Prussia to become head of a Reich that was not based on the monarchic principle.[57]

In the long run, the actual importance of the monarchic principle was bound to diminish, as laws and constitutions stressed equal civil capacity and liberties for all citizens and redefined the boundaries of the public and the private sphere in favor of the latter through the protection of private property, inheritance, freedom of contract, and the deregulation of occupations.[58] Furthermore, as the franchise in Western Europe was gradually extended, the significance of the representative bodies grew in the direction of parliamentarianism.[59]

---

[53]Grimm, Deutsche Verfassungsgeschichte 1776–1866 122 (1988).

[54]Sejersted, Democracy and the Rule of Law, in Elster & Slagstad, eds., Constitutionalism and Democracy 131, 136 (1988).

[55]*Ibid.*

[56]It was the German constitution that most directly displayed American influences. See Steinberger, 200 Jahre amerikanischer Bundesverfassung 16 (1987).

[57]See Grimm, note 53 *supra*, at 204–5.

[58]A good summary of these developments may be found in Habermas, Strukturwandel der Öffenlichkeit 86–91 (2d ed., 1965).

[59]For an account of these developments in Western Europe, see Bendix, note 51 *supra*, at 55–104.

While the constitutions that reflected these developments generally lacked enforcement procedures on the model of American judicial review and could often be amended or fleshed out by statutes,[60] they nevertheless had a programmatic significance that defined political culture and the consensus and could be employed in political debate as basic directives.[61] Yet neither the conception of the state nor the conception of its functions depended on these constitutions in the way in which this was the case in the United States. This was especially true of the influential concept of the *Rechtsstaat* with its varying emphasis on individualism in purpose and lawfulness in form as essential requisites of all modern states. As Krieger points out with respect to Robert von Mohl, the main theoretician of the *Rechtsstaat*: "Mohl's first systematic development of the *Rechtsstaat* idea was designed to defend rather than combat the positive welfare activities of the state in terms of individual liberty."[62]

You did not have to be a Hegelian to believe in the dualism of state and society, seeing the latter as the system of private interests, and the former as a separate system of overarching public reason and responsibilities, the res publica.[63] While the differences between Rousseau's "general will" and Hegel's notion of the state as "self-conscious ethical substance" were considerable, their implications for the conception and authority of government were similar in their emphasis on the separateness of the state.[64]

Hegel took a dim view of too much societal power. His comments on England are telling: "Take the case of *England* which, because private persons have a predominant share in public affairs, has been regarded as having the freest of all constitutions. Experience shows that that country—as compared with the other civilized states of Europe—is the most backward in civil and criminal legislation, in the laws and liberty of property, in arrangements for arts and science, and that objective freedom or rational right is rather *sacrificed* to formal right and particular private interest."[65] The point of the quo-

---

[60]See, for instance, Art. 107 of the Prussian Constitution of 1850, in Huber, 1 Dokumente zur Deutschen Verfassungsgeschichte 401, 413 (1961).

[61]Wahl, Der Vorrang der Verfassung, 20 Der Staat 485, 496 (1981).

[62]Krieger, note 18 *supra*, at 260. See von Mohl, Die Polizei-Wissenschaft nach den Grundsätzen des Rechtsstaates (3rd ed., 1866 (1st ed., 1832)).

[63]See, *e.g.*, Hauriou, Précis de Droit Constitutionnel 83–97 (2d ed., 1929).

[64]See, *e.g.*, de Jouvenel, Sovereignty 302 (Huntington trans., 1957).

[65]Hegel, Philosophy of Mind, in Encyclopedia of the Philosophical Sciences §544 at 273 (Wallace trans., 1971).

tation is the differentiating perception rather than its accuracy. Hegel saw the work of the state as having a double function: first, it maintains the individuals as persons, "thus making right a necessary actuality, then it promotes their welfare, which each originally takes care of for himself, but which has a thoroughly general side; it protects the family and guides civil society."[66] While this "guidance of civil society" in continental Europe was carried out in different ways and pursued different approaches, it nevertheless had the notion of the state as a common element.

In the second half of the 19th century, as the conflict between working class and capitalism sharpened, one of the most "modern" writers on the subject of state and society was Lorenz von Stein who, in his monumental work, attempted to safeguard the autonomous sphere of society and private property while at the same time insisting on confronting the problem of actual inequalities through ameliorating state action and by means of state economic policy.[67] "The interaction of these principles brings about the totality of laws and measures for the capitalistic social order and its administration which constitute the social administration and its public law."[68] Böckenförde sums it up correctly when he refers to the legitimation of the state "not so much through its constitution as through the active, welfare-providing administration."[69]

There were differences to be sure. One could argue, for instance, that once France became a parliamentary democracy in the last decades of the 19th century in which middle-class politicians held power, France resembled the United States more than it resembled Germany.[70] Yet, there was a "single generic process" which had profound consequences for the relationship between the working class and the state, well identified by Zolberg:[71]

> Wherever the state had historically emerged as a highly differentiated political actor—that is, where a monarchy succeeded in achieving absolutism—and managed to survive as such into the

---

[66]*Id.* §537 at 264. On Hegel's concept of right, see recently Smith, What is "Right" in Hegel's Philosophy of Right, 83 Am. Pol. Sci. Rev. 3 (1989).

[67]Arndt, Gesellschaftlicher Bedingungsrahmen und staatlicher Handlungsspielraum, in Schnur, ed., Staat und Gesellschaft: Studien über Lorenz von Stein 149, 153–55 (1978).

[68]von Stein, 3 Handbuch der Verwaltungslehre 36 (3rd ed., 1888).

[69]Böckenförde, note 52 *supra*, at 147.

[70]Zolberg, How Many Exceptionalisms? in Katznelson & Zolberg, Working-Class Formation 397, 449 (1986).

[71]*Id.* at 448.

period of the industrial revolution, liberalization did not lead to a
sharp separation of politics and economics into mutually exclusive institutional spheres along the lines of the British and especially American development. The resulting configuration also
imparts a distinctive character to public policy, whereby any col-
lective action by workers to improve their lot entails of necessity a
confrontation with central political authority as well as with employers.

Modern social historians have begun to compare the social developments in the United States and Europe as a whole, looking at such
measures as family structure, industrialization, mobility, social inequalities, the nature of cities, and the like. Many of the data generated suggest European characteristics that differ from those of
American society. The most prominent among these is the earlier
emergence of the welfare state in Europe. The first, though modest,
state sponsored insurance schemes against workplace accidents, ill-
ness, and old age poverty were put into effect in Germany, Austria,
and Hungary in the 1880s. By World War I almost all European
countries had some such programs.[72] In this respect, beginning with
Disraeli, even England followed a statist course.

Dicey, in the introduction to the 1914 edition of his *Law and Public
Opinion in England* noted that the current of opinion had, for between
thirty and forty years, been running in the direction of "collectiv-
ism," and the doctrine of laissez faire, "in spite of the large element of
truth which it contains," had more or less lost its hold upon the English people. He listed the Workmen's Compensation Act of 1897,
the whole line of Factory Acts, the Old Age Pensions Act of 1908, the
National Insurance Act of 1911, the Trade Union Act of 1913, and
the minimum wage laws, among others.[73]

After World War I, the Weimar Constitution of 1919, the most celebrated constitutional document of its time, attempted to constitu-
tionalize the welfare state. Part 2 spelled out "basic rights *and basic
duties*." It was subdivided into sections entitled "The Individual,"
"The Life of the Community," "Religion and Religious Corporations," "Education and Schools," and "Economic Life." There was
hardly an aspect of life for which the constitution did not include governing principles of a programmatic nature, placing it all under the

---

[72]Kaelble, Auf dem Weg zu einer europäischen Gesellschaft 73 (1987).

[73]Dicey, Law and Public Opinion in England XXX–XXXIII (2d ed., 1914). For a modern
analysis, see Mommsen, ed., The Emergence of the Welfare State in Britain and Germany
(1981).

overarching care of the state. It reads at times as if it were the democratic version of Frederick the Great's General Code, and it left little doubt that the regulatory powers of the state were comprehensive indeed.

In addition, however, the Weimar Constitution formulated values that were supposed to guide the democratic legislature. Hans Kelsen, who had made major contributions to Austria's democratic constitution of 1920, was exceedingly critical of attempts to identify democracy with substantive notions about the social order. To him, democracy was a method to produce a social order, not a particular content.[74] Yet, as the West passed through the turmoil of the depression and the challenges posed by Communism, Fascism, and National Socialism, issues of social ordering were increasingly translated into constitutional issues. This occurred on two rather different planes.

The first of these was the constitutional formulation of substantive ordering principles. In the wake of the universal franchise, the concept of citizenship was expanding from the formal equality of sharing capacities to the substantive equality of sharing goods. "The political, economic, and social forces which caused this extension of the public into the private realm easily invoked the seeming contradiction between political equality, on the one hand, and social and economic inequalities on the other. 'Second-class citizenship' is a concept well-known to contemporary ears."[75] The Weimar Constitution provides one illustration of this phenomenon. Other illustrations can be found in the section on social and economic rights of the declaration of rights in the Constitution of the French Fourth Republic,[76] and in the part on the "Rights and Duties of Private Citizens" of the 1948 Italian Constitution which, in Weimerian terms, is subdivided into titles on "civil relations," "ethical and social relations," "economic relations," and "political relations."[77] It is my argument that, in the case of Europe, this development was part of a continuum going back all the way to the late 18th century and intimately connected to the very notion of the state.

[74]Kelsen, Vom Wesen und Wert der Demokratie 94 (2d ed., 1929). Also see his critique of efforts to establish a necessary connection between democracy and capitalism: Kelsen, Democracy and Socialism, in Conference on Jurisprudence and Politics, 15 U. Chi. L. School Conf. Ser. 63 (1954).

[75]Casper, Social Differences and the Franchise, Daedalus 103, 105 (Fall 1976).

[76]Le Projet de Constitution du 19 Avril 1946, in Godechot, note 17 *supra*, at 374–76.

[77]Blaustein & Flanz, eds., 8 Constitutions of the Countries of the World: Italy 50 (1987).

Of course, we encounter the constitutional formulation of social ordering principles also in the United States during the first part of the 20th century. The debate over economic substantive due process was, after all, a constitutional debate concerning the line between the public and the private realm. Since its authoritative forum was the Supreme Court, it did not involve changes in the constitutional document itself. Indeed, the resolution of the conflict in favor of social rights was achieved by the deconstitutionalization of laissez faire and by the redistribution of legislative powers away from the states to the federal government. The Supreme Court has summarized this development in the following words: "It is . . . well established that legislative Acts adjusting the burdens and benefits of economic life come to the Court with a presumption of constitutionality, and the burden is on one complaining of a due process violation to establish that the legislature has acted in an arbitrary and irrational way."[78]

In the crisis of the 1930s the United States fell back, to use Kelsen's terminology, on democracy as a method for producing a social order within constitutional bounds set by the equal protection clause and, more recently, by procedural due process limitations on the manner in which the welfare state operates. Otherwise the Constitution is not viewed as providing ordering principles. This latter point has been dramatically, almost programmatically, emphasized by the Supreme Court in the recent *DeShaney* case. Speaking about the Due Process Clause of the Fourteenth Amendment (and by implication its counterpart in the Fifth Amendment) Chief Justice Rehnquist wrote (for a majority of six justices): "Its purpose was to protect the people from the State, not to ensure that the State protected them from each other. The Framers were content to leave the extent of governmental obligation in the latter area to the democratic political processes. Consistent with these principles, our cases have recognized that the Due Process Clauses generally confer no affirmative right to governmental aid, even where such aid may be necessary to secure life, liberty, or property interests of which the government itself may not deprive the individual."[79] It is very difficult to imagine any European court possessed of the power of judicial review to make a stark statement of this kind.

In the United States the line between the public and the private

---

[78]Usery v. Turner Elkhorn Mining Co., 428 U.S. 1, 15 (1976).

[79]DeShaney v. Winnebago Co. Dept. of Social Services, 109 S.Ct. 998, 1003 (1989).

realm is mostly drawn by legislation, subject to perceptions about the severity of various crises. Because regulation in the United States more often than not occurs as crisis management, it is also more readily reexamined as a crisis recedes and the usual distrust of the state[80] and rent seeking by private interest groups reasserts itself. This, too, is part of a continuum going back all the way to the late 18th century.

The second constitutional plane is organizational and concerns the separation of powers. It has different aspects. One involves the structure of government, the other the role of the judiciary. Most European democracies have been, or have once again become, parliamentary. Between the wars, the Weimar Constitution provided for a popularly elected president with significant powers, especially in emergencies (though, as in the constitutional monarchies, the presidential powers could not be exercised without the countersignature of the responsible minister).[81] Hugo Preuss, the main framer of the Weimar constitution, explicitly rejected "parliamentary absolutism," along French lines, but also the American model of an independent executive branch.[82] In 1958 France herself restructured government in favor of executive authority.

While parliamentary democracy in Europe underwent questioning and eventually, in some countries, dictatorial dissolution, the United States entered a period, which has not yet ended, during which it searched for more effective administration. Barry Karl opens his recent book, *The Uneasy State*, with the following paragraph:[83]

> I[n] S[eptember] 1932, as Americans awaited an election they prayed would save them from the seemingly endless Depression, the president of Dartmouth said, in a letter to a recent graduate, "I don't believe we can go on much longer without a very major change in our form of government." He hoped that the alternative might be a parliamentary form, but he was willing to accept even more revolutionary changes—changes that would involve picking strong leaders and giving them the authority to lead "rather than having them [be] street-runners to whom we signal our will and from whom we expect immediate obedience."

---

[80]*Cf.* Karl, note 27 *supra*.

[81]Mommsen, Max Weber and German Politics 1890–1920 351 (Steinberg trans., 1984).

[82]Preuss, Staat, Recht und Freiheit 426–7 (1926).

[83]Karl, note 27 *supra*, at 9.

The theme of this search has been executive reorganization and the costs and benefits, as well as the proper understanding of, the American doctrine of separation of powers.[84]

The other aspect has been the increasing importance of the judiciary, especially after World War II. Austria had adopted judicial review as part of its 1920 constitution, with institutional precursors in the 19th century. Germany's solutions, in 1919, tended in the same direction, though they were exceedingly complex.[85] After World War II and in reaction to the perversions of the dictatorships, judicial review came into its own in countries such as the Federal Republic, Italy, Greece, Spain, Portugal, and even, though in a modified form, France, and, in 1984, Belgium. It also found an expression in the European Convention on Human Rights. In addition, courts have become a major, if not the main mechanism for the oversight of complex and depersonalized governmental agencies and for the implementation of legislative or administrative compromises which often provide little guidance. In Europe these issues have become even more pronounced, because, in the European Community, legislative powers are in the hands of government representatives from the member states who work in a diplomatic setting without much direct accountability. In this situation the protection of individual rights becomes the task of judges who must develop a common law of basic rights by reference to exceedingly vague notions of shared values.[86] What the French call "le gouvernement des juges" and the Germans highlight as "Justizstaat" is indeed a common characteristic of 20th century constitutionalism on both sides of the Atlantic. Even Canada has yielded.

Where does all of this leave us? First of all, it is obvious that the welfare state, whether constitutionally anchored or not, is a permanent feature of developed western democracies. In the United States its basis is statutory and regulatory, but even where purely regulatory, changes tend to be marginal, rather than fundamental. In countries where constitutions or constitutional jurisprudence contain programmatic social principles their very vagueness places a premium on the details of statutory and regulatory implementation and

---

[84]See Sunstein, Constitutionalism after the New Deal, 101 Harv. L. Rev. 421 (1987); see also Karl, Executive Reorganization and Presidential Power, 1977 Supreme Court Review 1.

[85]Casper, Guardians of the Constitution, 53 So. Cal. L. Rev. 773, 776–78 (1980).

[86]See Weiler, Eurocracy and Distrust, 61 Wash. L. Rev. 1103 (1986).

notions of judicial deference and legislative discretion limit the otherwise enhanced power of the courts.[87]

Nevertheless, differences exist in terms of the actual scope of state functions and in terms of constitutional theory. In some way, these differences have become more salient since Europe has accepted the American "higher law" concept of constitutions while integrating into it prior notions about the responsibilities of the state. I may quote from a leading German textbook on constitutional law whose author, Konrad Hesse, is a former, highly distinguished, justice of the Federal Constitutional Court: "[The] constitution is viewed as a substantive whole. Its contents are frequently designated as fundamental values which are prior to the positive legal order. With the integration of the traditions of liberal and representative parliamentary democracy, the liberal *Rechtsstaat*, and the federal state, and with the introduction of newer principles, especially the welfare state, the framers of the constitution connected these fundamental values to a 'value system' and constituted a state which is neutral as to Weltanschauung but not as to values."[88]

The concept of constitutionalism represented by this quotation reflects a trend which is in no way restricted to Germany, indeed, it can also be found in the modern American literature on constitutional law. I confess that I view it with reserve. My objections are not primarily based on the fact that it lacks theoretical rigor. No one theory can resolve disputes about the appropriate scope of government. Which is precisely why we should be reluctant to make constitutions carry more weight than they can bear. Two consequences flow from the comprehensive ordering approach to constitutionalism. First, political restrictions and moral obligations become sanctified as constitutional law.[89] The state takes over the constitution rather than the constitution the state. Second, since every social issue becomes a constitutional issue (especially, in the modern regime of judicial review), law and its oracles will be severely overtaxed.

Europe has had a concept of the state which has much to recommend itself to the extent to which it acknowledges common causes and responsibilities of the political community toward its less fortu-

---

[87]Currie, note 39 *supra*, at 889.

[88]Hesse, Grundzüge des Verfassungsrechts der Bundesrepublik Deutschland 4 (16th ed., 1988).

[89]Denninger, note 46 *supra*, at 13.

nate members. The United States has had (with interruptions) a concept of the constitution which has much to recommend itself to the extent to which it views "the governing part" with suspicion, but nevertheless places great responsibility on the democratic process. The differences have become more subtle, but they are still conceptual differences which make a difference—for better or for worse.

DAVID P. CURRIE

LOCHNER ABROAD: SUBSTANTIVE DUE PROCESS AND EQUAL PROTECTION IN THE FEDERAL REPUBLIC OF GERMANY

> [T]here exists some strange misconception of the scope of this [due process] provision . . . . [I]t would seem, from the character of many of the cases before us, and the arguments made in them, that the clause . . . is looked upon as a means of bringing to the test of the decision of this court the abstract opinions of every unsuccessful litigant . . . of the justice of the decision against him, and of the merits of the legislation on which such a decision may be founded.[1]

As Justice Miller's famous lament suggests, wishful thinkers have sought since the beginning to find a way of making the United States Supreme Court ultimate censor of the reasonableness of all governmental action. Justice Chase thought he had discovered the magic wand in natural law,[2] Justice Bradley in the Privileges or Immunities

David P. Currie is Harry N. Wyatt Professor of Law, The University of Chicago.

AUTHOR'S NOTE: I wish to thank the Law Faculty of the University of Heidelberg, where the research leading to this paper was begun; the Kirkland & Ellis Faculty Research Fund, and the Mayer, Brown & Platt Faculty Research Fund, which helped support its continuance; Eberhard Schmidt-Assmann, Helmut Steinberger, and Cass Sunstein, who furnished invaluable advice; Donald Kommers, who graciously permitted use of translations from his excellent casebook, The Constitutional Jurisprudence of the Federal Republic of Germany (Duke Univ. Press, 1989), and David Lyle, who provided indispensable research assistance.

[1]Davidson v. New Orleans, 96 U.S. 97, 104 (1878) (Miller, J.). This and other American decisions noted in this article are discussed in Currie, The Constitution in the Supreme Court: The First Hundred Years (1985) (cited below as The First Hundred Years), and Currie, The Constitution in the Supreme Court: The Second Century (forthcoming Univ. of Chicago Press 1990) (cited below as The Second Century).

[2]Calder v. Bull, 3 Dall. 386, 387 (1798) (separate opinion).

Clause,[3] Justice Goldberg in the Ninth Amendment.[4] Miller battled bravely, but he had lent significant support to the enemy with his freewheeling opinion in *Loan Association v. Topeka*.[5] The fire was kept flickering in dissent[6] and in majority opinions upholding laws against due process and equal protection challenges only because they were reasonable.[7] It burst into full flame in *Lochner v. New York*[8] in 1905, and for the next quarter century the Supreme Court was indeed what Justice Miller had denied it should be: ultimate censor of the reasonableness of all governmental action.[9]

In the mid-1930s substantive due process went into eclipse. As Justice Stone predicted in his celebrated footnote,[10] for the next half century the Supreme Court limited itself largely to enforcement of the specific provisions of the Bill of Rights, protection of the integrity of the political process, and defense of discrete and insular minorities.[11]

In the days of Chief Justice Warren, however, general reasonableness review began a cautious comeback—sometimes without much attention to the textual basis of the decision[12] or behind such smokescreens as cruel and unusual punishment[13] and the "penumbras" of actual constitutional provisions.[14] The once dreaded specter of substantive due process was trotted out of the closet in *Roe v. Wade*,[15] while serious enforcement of the equality principle was extended beyond race to other more or less "suspect" classifications such as sex, alienage, and illegitimacy,[16] and to those affecting such "fundamental" interests as voting, free expression, and interstate travel.[17]

So far the genie has been kept partly in the bottle by the Court's

[3]Slaughter-House Cases, 83 U.S. 36, 116–24 (1873) (dissenting opinion).
[4]Griswold v. Connecticut, 381 U.S. 479, 486–93 (1965) (concurring opinion).
[5]87 U.S. 655 (1875).
[6]*E.g.*, Munn v. Illinois, 94 U.S. 113, 136–54 (1877) (Field, J.).
[7]*E.g.*, Mugler v. Kansas, 123 U.S. 623, 661–72 (1887); Missouri Pac. Ry. v. Mackey, 127 U.S. 205, 208–10 (1888).
[8]198 U.S. 45.
[9]See The First Hundred Years, chs. 2, 4, 5, 7.
[10]United States v. Carolene Products Co., 304 U.S. 144, 152–53 n.4 (1938).
[11]See generally The Second Century, chs. 8–16.
[12]*E.g.*, Slochower v. Board of Higher Education, 350 U.S. 551, 558–59 (1956). See also the earlier decision in Wieman v. Updegraff, 344 U.S. 183, 190–92 (1952).
[13]Robinson v. California, 370 U.S. 660, 666–68 (1962).
[14]Griswold v. Connecticut, 381 U.S. 479, 484–86 (1965).
[15]410 U.S. 113, 152–56 (1973).
[16]Craig v. Boren, 429 U.S. 190 (1976); Graham v. Richardson, 403 U.S. 365 (1971); Levy v. Louisiana, 391 U.S. 68 (1968).
[17]Reynolds v. Sims, 377 U.S. 533 (1964); Carey v. Brown, 447 U.S. 455 (1980); Shapiro v. Thompson, 394 U.S. 618 (1969).

relative restraint in defining what is suspect or fundamental. Justice White may have sounded a welcome call for retreat with his reminder that "the Court is most vulnerable and comes nearest to illegitimacy when it deals with judge-made constitutional law having little or no cognizable roots in the language or design of the Constitution."[18] Yet the debate over general judicial oversight is far from over, despite the once apparent finality of the New Deal resolution. It may therefore prove enlightening to examine the experience of another modern nation with somewhat similar constitutional traditions in wrestling with the same issue—the Federal Republic of Germany.

The Basic Law (Grundgesetz) of the Federal Republic was forty years old in 1989. It establishes a democratic federal state with a parliamentary system, judicial review by independent judges, and a bill of rights.[19] In many fundamental respects it is similar to the Constitution of the United States, and the resemblance is not purely coincidental.[20] At the same time there are a great many differences in detail, which help to make the Basic Law a fertile field for comparative study.

The Bill of Rights (Grundrechtskatalog) is central to the Basic Law.[21] It is more detailed than ours. In addition to familiar articles guaranteeing freedom of religion (Art. 4) and expression (Art. 5) and the sanctity of the home (Art. 13),[22] there are specific provisions codifying some of the rights our Supreme Court has protected under more open-ended provisions: marriage and the family (Art. 6), private schools (Art. 7), travel (Art. 11), occupational freedom (Art. 12). I shall discuss some of these latter provisions at the outset.

More interesting from the standpoint of the judicial function are decisions of the German Constitutional Court (Bundesverfassungsgericht) doing what our Supreme Court did in *Lochner*: protecting additional substantive rights on the basis of general provisions that correspond to our Due Process and Equal Protection Clauses.

There are several such provisions. Article 2(2) contains a general

---

[18]Bowers v. Hardwick, 478 U.S. 186, 194 (1986).

[19]Art. 1–20, 28, 93, 97, 100(1) GG.

[20]See, *e.g.*, Steinberger, 200 Jahre amerikanische Bundesverfassung 32–39 (1987); Golay, The Founding of the Federal Republic of Germany (1958), *passim*.

[21]See, *e.g.*, Schulz, Ursprünge unserer Freiheit 217 (1989), citing remarks by Carlo Schmid in the debates of the constitutional convention.

[22]See also Art. 8 (freedom of assembly), 9 (freedom of association), 10 (privacy of telecommunications), 17 (right of petition).

guarantee of life, limb, and (physical) liberty.[23] Article 14 not only imposes familiar limits on condemnation but also includes a general guarantee of property. Article 3 provides both general and specific assurances of equality. Article 1, which is commonly described as the central provision of the entire constitution[24] and which is explicitly protected from amendment,[25] declares that "[t]he dignity of man shall be inviolable." Most interesting of all for present purposes is Article 2(1)'s enigmatically phrased right to "free development of personality," which has been interpreted to embrace everything not dealt with more specifically elsewhere.

From these open-ended provisions, in conjunction with even more general conceptions derived from other articles of the Basic Law—in particular the "social state" (Sozialstaat) and what may be literally but incompletely translated as the rule of law (Rechtsstaat)[26]—the Constitutional Court has fashioned a set of tools that constitute it as that which, notwithstanding Justice Miller's warning, our Supreme Court was for the first third of this century: ultimate censor of the reasonableness of governmental action.

I. Marriage, the Family, and Private Schools

"Marriage and the family," says Article 6(1), "shall enjoy the special protection of the state." The paragraphs that follow contain specific provisions for parents and children, motherhood, and persons born out of wedlock. Thus Article 6 provides explicit protection for some of the interests our Supreme Court has accorded the benefits of heightened scrutiny under the Fourteenth Amendment.[27]

Article 6 is commonly applied in conjunction with the general equality provision of Article 3 to assure intensive scrutiny of classifications disfavoring marriage or the family.[28] Sometimes Article 6 is applied independently to strike down discrimination against the classes it protects, as a more specific equality provision. Married cou-

---

[23]Detailed procedural protections for those taken into custody or accused of crime are provided in Articles 103 and 104.

[24]See, *e.g.*, 6 BVerfGE 32, 41 (1957); Häberle, Die Menschenwürde als Grundlage der Staatlichen Gemeinschaft, in Isensee & Kirchhof, eds., 1 Handbuch des Staatsrechts der Bundesrepublik Deutschland 815, 860 (1987) (cited below as Handbuch des Staatsrechts).

[25]Art. 79(3) GG.

[26]See Art. 20, 28 GG.

[27]See, *e.g.*, Moore v. City of East Cleveland, 431 U.S. 494 (1978); Zablocki v. Redhail, 434 U.S. 374 (1977); Levy v. Louisiana, 391 U.S. 68 (1968).

[28]See text at notes 266–67.

ples may not be assessed higher income taxes than if they were single;[29] orphans may not be denied welfare benefits simply because they are married;[30] a broker who helps a prospective renter find an apartment may not be denied a fee because she is married to the landlord's manager.[31]

Although Article 6(5) appears to entrust protection of illegitimates to the legislature,[32] it was understood from the beginning to embody a principle that bound the courts in their interpretation of existing laws,[33] and more recently the Court has begun to determine the consistency of statutory measures with the constitutional provision itself.[34] In accordance with its language, Article 6(5) has been held not only to limit outright discrimination against illegitimates[35] but also to justify[36] and even to require[37] special privileges to compensate for the disadvantages with which illegitimates are saddled; for otherwise they could not enjoy the actual equality of opportunity to which Article 6(5) entitles them.

The rights conferred by Article 6, moreover, go beyond mere protection against discrimination. Article 6(1) has been interpreted to permit parents who are separated to opt for joint custody of their children[38] and to allow people to visit relatives in jail.[39] Article 6(2)'s guarantee of parental rights has been read to ensure parents a significant role in determining which school their children attend and what course of study they pursue[40] as well as access to information about

---

[29] 6 BVerfGE 55, 70–84 (1957).

[30] 28 BVerfGE 324, 347–61 (1970). See *id.* at 356, finding in Art. 6(1) a "strict prohibition of differentiation respecting government benefits according to family status alone."

[31] 76 BVerfGE 126, 128–30 (1987). See *id.* at 128: "Article 6(1) forbids [the state] to disadvantage married persons simply because they are married."

[32] "Illegitimate children shall be provided *by legislation* with the same opportunities . . . as are enjoyed by legitimate children." Not until 1969, under a threat by the judges to implement article 6(5) themselves, did the legislature comply with its mandate. See 25 BVerfGE 167, 172–88 (1969); BGBl. I, 1243 (1969). *Cf.* Art. 117(1) GG, which provided a four-year grace period for legislative correction before Article 3's provisions for sex equality became enforceable. See 3 BVerfGE 225 (1953), discussing these latter provisions.

[33] See 8 BVerfGE 210, 217 (1958).

[34] See, *e.g.*, 44 BVerfGE 1, 22 (1976).

[35] *E.g.*, 74 BVerfGE 33, 38–43 (1986) (inheritance). *Cf.* the line of cases beginning with Levy v. Louisiana, 391 U.S. 68 (1968).

[36] See 17 BVerfGE 280, 283–86 (1964) (longer period of child support from father).

[37] See 8 BVerfGE 210, 214–21 (1958) (judicial proceeding to establish paternity).

[38] 61 BVerfGE 358, 371–82 (1982) (insisting upon a "particular" (besondere) justification for such a limitation of parental rights and finding none). See also 36 BVerfGE 146, 161–69 (1973) (marriage may not be forbidden because of husband's previous sexual relationship with bride's mother). In either of these cases the court could have reached the same result on equality grounds but did not.

[39] 42 BVerfGE 95, 100–103 (1976).

[40] 34 BVerfGE 165, 182–99 (1972).

their educational performance.[41] Furthermore, in the course of concluding that the excusable failure of a pregnant woman to meet a statutory deadline for notification did not justify denying her immunity from loss of employment, the Constitutional Court strongly hinted that Article 6(4)'s provision for the protection and care of mothers might require the state to provide such immunity if it did not do so on its own.[42]

Article 7, which establishes the framework for public and private education in the Federal Republic, explicitly guarantees "the right to establish private schools" (Art. 7(4)).[43] Like the various provisions of Article 6, this paragraph has been invoked to justify intensive scrutiny of classifications affecting the exercise of the right.[44] More notable when viewed from this side of the Atlantic was the conclusion in the same case—in the teeth of contrary legislative history that informed the first half of the opinion—that Article 7(4) required the state to subsidize private schools. Otherwise, said the Court, the explicit right to establish such schools would be hollow; for the requirement of the same paragraph that private institutions not promote "segregation of pupils according to the means of the parents" made it impossible for them to survive without public support.[45]

As some of these examples suggest, Articles 6 and 7 are among several provisions of the Basic Law that have been held to create not merely traditional rights against government intrusion (Abwehrrechte) but positive governmental duties to protect or support the individual (Schutzpflichten) as well. Other examples will be noted as we proceed, but despite their striking contrast with the prevailing understanding of our Constitution[46] they are not the principal focus

[41]59 BVerfGE 360, 381–82 (1982).

[42]52 BVerfGE 357, 366 (1979). See Art. 6(4) GG: "Every mother shall be entitled to the protection and care of the community."

[43]Cf. Pierce v. Society of Sisters, 268 U.S. 510 (1925) (finding such a right protected by the Due Process Clause). For special limitations on private elementary schools in Germany, see Art. 7(5) GG.

[44]See 75 BVerfGE 40, 69–78 (1987), finding preferential treatment of religious schools and the exclusion of subsidies for adult education contrary to Art. 7(4) in conjunction with Art. 3.

[45]Id. at 58–66. Contrast the Court's conclusion, 20 BVerfGE 56, 96–112 (1966), that general subsidies for political parties were inconsistent with Article 21(1)'s guarantee of party autonomy. Our Supreme Court is keenly aware of the danger that conditional subsidies can pose to individual freedoms (see Speiser v. Randall, 357 U.S. 513 (1958)), but it has refused to outlaw spending itself simply because the power might sometime be abused. See Buckley v. Valeo, 424 U.S. 1 (1976). There is some truth in the arguments that underlie both the private school and political party decisions; but there is a certain tension between the conclusions that subsidies are constitutionally forbidden and that they are constitutionally required.

[46]Cf. DeShaney v. Winnebago County Department of Social Services, 109 S. Ct. 988 (1989); Harris v. McRae, 448 U.S. 297 (1980).

of this paper.[47] What is most significant for present purposes is that Articles 6 and 7 explicitly codify some of the rights our Supreme Court has found to be "fundamental" for due process and equal protection purposes and thus add legitimacy to judicial review of governmental action affecting private education and the family.

II. PROPERTY

"Property and inheritance," says Article 14(1), "are guaranteed." Their "content and limits" are determined by statute (*id.*). "Property imposes duties," and its "use should also serve the public weal" (Art. 14(2)). Condemnation is permitted only for the public good and pursuant to statutes providing just compensation (Art. 14(3)).

The right to property occupies a prominent position in German constitutional law. The Constitutional Court put the point most plainly in an important 1968 opinion:[48]

> Property is an elementary constitutional right that is closely connected to the guarantee of personal liberty. Within the general system of constitutional rights its function is to secure its holder a sphere of liberty in the economic field and thereby enable him to lead a self-governing life. . . . The guarantee of property is not primarily a material but rather a personal guarantee.

Thus property rights are by no means relegated to an inferior position in West Germany, as they have been in the United States.[49] Economic independence is understood to be essential to every other freedom,[50] and property rights are taken very seriously. The explicit constitutional references to the social obligations of property have been held to permit considerable regulation. Article 14 has neverthe-

---

[47]For discussion of affirmative government duties under the two constitutions, see Currie, Positive and Negative Constitutional Rights, 53 U. Chi. L. Rev. 864 (1986).

[48]Hamburg Flood Control Case, 24 BVerfGE 367, 389, 400 (1968).

[49]Contrast Murdock v. Pennsylvania, 319 U.S. 105, 115 (1943) ("preferred position" for First Amendment rights); Kovacs v. Cooper, 336 U.S. 77, 95–96 (1949) (Frankfurter, J., concurring) ("those liberties of the individual which history has attested as the indispensable conditions of an open as against a closed society come to this Court with a momentum for respect lacking when appeal is made to liberties which derive merely from shifting economic arrangements"). This is not to deny that even in Germany there are subtle differences in the levels of judicial scrutiny according to how intimately the right in question is bound up with the development of personality. See Denninger, in 1 Kommentar zum Grundgesetz für die Bundesrepublik Deutschland (1984), vor Art. 1, Rdnr. 11, 14 (cited below as Luchterhand), and cases cited.

[50]*Cf.* Hayek, The Road to Serfdom 103–4 (1944).

less been applied not only to prevent unjustified takings in the narrow sense but also to prevent unreasonable limitations of property rights that fall short of a traditional taking.

A. TAKINGS

The Constitutional Court has made clear that takings cannot be justified simply by providing adequate compensation. Article 14 is basically a guarantee of property itself, not of its equivalent in money.[51] Consequently the Court has scrutinized attempted takings carefully to ensure that constitutional limitations other than the compensation provision have been observed.

The requirement that condemnation be authorized by statute (Gesetzesvorbehalt) reflects a fundamental principle that we shall encounter repeatedly in the course of this journey: Individual rights may be restricted, if at all, only in accordance with laws made by the popularly elected legislature. This principle is by no means unknown to Anglo-American law. It informed Justice Black's monumental opinion for the Supreme Court in *Youngstown Sheet & Tube Co. v. Sawyer*,[52] and it represents an early and often neglected aspect of the Due Process Clauses.[53] In Germany it is explicit in a number of bill of rights provisions, and it has been found implicit as a general principle in the rule of law.[54] When takings have been attempted without adequate statutory authority, they have been struck down.[55]

There have been few decisions of the Constitutional Court on the question of what constitutes the "public weal" (Wohl der Allgemeinheit) for which private property may be taken. On its face the term is broader than the "public use" formulation that American courts have so generously construed.[56] The Constitutional Court

[51]See 24 BVerfGE 367, 400 (1968).

[52]343 U.S. 579, 582–89 (1951).

[53]See *id.* at 646 (Jackson, J., concurring) (arguing that the President's duty to take care that the laws be faithfully executed and the Due Process Clause "signify about all there is of the principle that ours is a government of laws, not of men": "One [clause] gives a governmental authority that reaches so far as there is law, the other gives a private right that authority shall go no farther"); Corwin, The Doctrine of Due Process of Law before the Civil War, 24 Harv. L. Rev 366 (1911).

[54]See 49 BVerfGE 89, 126 (1978): "The general principle that lawmaking authority is reserved to the legislature (Gesetzesvorbehalt) requires a statutory basis for executive acts fundamentally (wesentlich) affecting the freedom and equality of the citizen."

[55]56 BVerfGE 249, 261–66 (1981) (cable car); 74 BVerfGE 264, 284–97 (1987) (automobile test track).

[56]See, *e.g.*, Berman v. Parker, 348 U.S. 26 (1954); Hawaii Housing Authority v. Midkiff, 467 U.S. 229 (1984).

had no difficulty in upholding takings for the purpose of refugee settlement[57] and the transmission of private power to serve the general public.[58] More interesting challenges were posed by cases involving a private cable car for recreational purposes[59] and a test track for a private automaker.[60] The first provoked a strongly worded separate opinion deploring years of inattention to the public weal requirement;[61] approval in the second might seriously erode the distinction between private and public interest.[62] Both cases, however, went off on the ground of lack of statutory authority; the limiting case has yet to be decided.[63]

The Constitutional Court has also had little to say on the question of what constitutes just compensation. Article 14 provides that compensation is to be determined by "an equitable balance" between public and private interests;[64] not surprisingly, the Court has taken this to mean that full market value is not necessarily required.[65] More strikingly, the requirement that the statute itself provide for compensation has led the Constitutional Court to reject entirely the familiar American doctrine of inverse condemnation. If government action has the effect of taking property without compensation, the remedy is disallowance, not damages; for otherwise the state would have to pay compensation the legislature had not authorized, contrary to the constitutional allocation of powers.[66] The Constitutional

---

[57]46 BVerfGE 268, 288–89 (1977).

[58]66 BVerfGE 248, 257–59 (1984), explaining (at 257) that condemnation on behalf of a private enterprise was permissible at least "when the enterprise [was] subject to a statutory obligation promoting the general welfare and . . . conducted for the benefit of the public."

[59]56 BVerfGE 249 (1981).

[60]74 BVerfGE 264 (1987).

[61]56 BVerfGE at 266, 269–95 (separate opinion of Böhmer, J.), concluding (at 287) that the condemnation in question was "for the benefit of a private undertaking designed solely for private profit." For Justice Böhmer's narrow view of the permissible scope of condemnation for private companies, see id. at 293.

[62]Cf. Charles Wilson's notorious comment that "what's good for General Motors is good for the country." The argument in the German case was that the test track (for Daimler-Benz) would create jobs and stimulate the economy. "Condemnation for the benefit of private persons . . . that serves the public weal only indirectly and presents an enhanced danger of abuse to the detriment of the weak," the Court observed, "poses particular constitutional problems." 74 BVerfGE at 287.

[63]See generally Papier, in Maunz, Dürig, et al., 2 Grundgesetzkommentar Art. 14, Rdnr. 495–509 (rev. to 1989) (cited below as Maunz/Dürig).

[64]See Art. 14(3) GG: "Die Entschädigung ist unter gerechter Abwägung der Interessen der Allgemeinheit und der Beteiligten zu bestimmen."

[65]See 24 BVerfGE 367, 420–22 (1968). For criticism of this conclusion see Leisner, Eigentum, in 6 Handbuch des Staatsrechts, §149, Rdnr. 180–83 (1989). For an introduction to the extensive jurisprudence of the civil courts on the question of the level of compensation, see Papier in 2 Maunz/Dürig, Art. 14, Rdnr. 510–60.

[66]See 4 BVerfGE 219, 230–37 (1955); 58 BVerfGE 300, 322–24 (1981). For discussion of the

Court therefore tests laws regulating property not under the taking provisions but for their consistency with the general guarantee of property;[67] and nonconfiscatory taxes are generally held not to be limitations on property at all.[68]

Even when the explicit requirements of statutory authority, public weal, and just compensation appear to be met, the Constitutional Court has made clear that condemnation is an exceptional remedy that may be employed only as a last resort. Property may not be taken until efforts to buy it on the open market have failed;[69] property that has been condemned reverts to its former owner when it is no longer needed.[70] Property thus may be condemned only when and to the extent necessary. These results might be justified by narrow interpretation of the explicit term "public weal."[71] It may be more appropriate, however, to view them as applications of the more general principles of proportionality and least burdensome means which—as we shall see—the Court has found implicit in the rule of law.[72]

B. LIMITATIONS ON PROPERTY

Less familiar to those versed in American law than the limitations on actual takings imposed by Article 14(3) are the restrictions on regulation imposed by Article 14(1)'s assurance that "property . . . [is] guaranteed." The provision acknowledging the lawmakers' authority

---

impact of the latter decision upon the civil courts' practice of awarding common-law or statutory compensation for wrongful takings, see Papier in 2 Maunz/Dürig, Art. 14, Rdnr. 597–638; for criticism of the Constitutional Court's position, see Leisner in 6 Handbuch des Staatsrechts § 149, Rdnr. 173–79.

[67]The civil and administrative courts, on the other hand, have developed an extensive jurisprudence for determining when regulation amounts to a taking; the problem has proved as refractory in Germany as it has in the United States. See Papier in 2 Maunz/Dürig, Art. 14, Rdnr. 291–450, arguing (Rdnr. 449) for a test based upon the severity of the restriction (cf. Pennsylvani a Coal Co. v. Mahon, 260 U.S. 393 (1922)); Leisner in 6 Handbuch des Staatsrecht s §149, Rdnr. 148–51, arguing that such a test should be complemented by special concern for those made to bear an undue share of the total burden (Sonderopfertheorie).

[68]See, e.g., 4 BVerfGE 7, 17 (1954) (upholding a special assessment for relief of the troubled iron, steel, and coal industries). Compare the dictum that the state of Hessen could demand free copies of all books published there in the interest of improving its library—so long as the burden of doing so was not disproportionate to the profitability of the publication. 58 BVerfGE 137, 144–52 (1981). See id. at 144, explaining that, like a tax, the law imposed no duty to convey a particular piece of property to the government. See also Hesse, Grundzüge des Verfassungsrechts der Bundesrepublik Deutschland (15th ed., 1985), Rdnr. 447, arguing that taxation is the "exposed flank" of the property guarantee.

[69]45 BVerfGE 297, 335 (1977).

[70]38 BVerfGE 175, 185 (1974).

[71]See Leisner in 6 Handbuch des Staatsrechts §149, Rdnr. 170.

[72]See Papier in 2 Maunz/Dürig, Art. 14, Rdnr. 507–9.

to determine the "content and limits" of property has not been taken to place property rights wholly at legislative disposal; the property guarantee is more than a mere Gesetzesvorbehalt. On the other hand, the further provisions that "property imposes duties" and that "[i]ts use shall also serve the public weal" make clear that property rights are by no means absolute.[73] Not surprisingly in light of the competing public and private interests recognized by the Basic Law itself, the Constitutional Court has applied a balancing test in determining the permissible scope of limitations on property: Like condemnation measures, definitions and limitations of property must conform with the proportionality principle.[74]

As in the United States, the ownership of property does not include the right to cause a public nuisance; the state may prevent mining companies from depleting groundwater supplies[75] and may destroy dogs suspected of rabies.[76] But the social duties of property in Germany, like various public interests in this country, justify limitations that go far beyond the simple case of preventing affirmative harm to others. Renters may be protected from unusual or sudden rent increases[77] as well as against eviction[78] and the diversion of rental property to other uses.[79] Farm and forest lands may be protected against sales that appear detrimental to the interests of agriculture or forestry.[80] For the well-being of the wine industry, the legislature may forbid the growing of grapes on unsuitable soil.[81] To promote recreation it may establish associations to administer private fishing rights and distribute the profits to their former owners.[82] To assure an adequate and safe public water supply it may go so far as

[73] These clauses are viewed as concrete applications of the general Sozialstaat principle of Articles 20 and 28. They were derived from more intrusive limitations in Articles 153–55 of the Weimar Constitution of 1919, in which social provisions were far more prominent. See Schneider, Die Reichsverfassung vom 11. August 1919, in 1 Handbuch des Staatsrechts §3, Rdnr. 37–38 (1987).

[74] See, e.g., 21 BVerfGE 150, 154–55 (1967).

[75] 10 BVerfGE 89, 112–14 (1959).

[76] 20 BVerfGE 351, 355–62 (1966). See also 25 BVerfGE 112, 117–21 (1969) (upholding a prohibition of construction on dike lands). Cf. Mugler v. Kansas, 123 U.S. 623, 661–72 (1887); Miller v. Schoene, 276 U.S. 272 (1928). On the issue of flood-plain zoning in this country, see Sax, Takings, Private Property and Public Rights, 81 Yale L.J. 149 (1971).

[77] 37 BVerfGE 132, 139–43 (1974); 71 BVerfGE 230, 246–51 (1985). Cf. Block v. Hirsch, 256 U.S. 135 (1921).

[78] 68 BVerfGE 361, 367–71 (1985).

[79] 38 BVerfGE 348, 370–71 (1975).

[80] 21 BVerfGE 73, 82–85 (1967); 21 BVerfGE 87, 90–91 (1967); 21 BVerfGE 102, 104–5 (1967).

[81] 21 BVerfGE 150, 154–60 (1967).

[82] 70 BVerfGE 191, 199–213 (1985).

to abolish private rights to the use of groundwater, so long as landowners are given a grace period in which to phase out existing uses.[83] To promote industrial peace and democracy it may give workers the right to participate in management decisions (codetermination)[84]— but so far, at least, only because the owners retain ultimate control.[85] It may even redefine the balance of public and private interests in copyrighted material retroactively, by shortening the statutory period of protection of already copyrighted works from 50 to 25 years.[86]

At the same time, however, the Constitutional Court has found in the general property guarantee substantive limits on regulation reminiscent of those imposed by our Supreme Court during the *Lochner* era. The public interest in protection of renters cannot justify depriving owners of the right to terminate garden leases[87] or to recapture rented premises for their own residential use.[88] The public interest in preserving a viable agricultural economy cannot justify prohibiting the purchase of agricultural land for investment purposes,[89] the breakup of large holdings as such,[90] or the use of trademarked place names on wine bottles.[91]

Of particular interest are decisions concluding, despite initial holdings to the contrary,[92] that government benefits may constitute property for purposes of Article 14.[93] This conclusion is reminiscent of the Supreme Court's position, in the line of cases beginning with *Goldberg v. Kelly*,[94] that certain "entitlements" to state assistance are

---

[83] 58 BVerfGE 300, 338–53 (1981). *Cf.* Goldblatt v. Town of Hempstead, 369 U.S. 590 (1962).

[84] 50 BVerfGE 290, 339–52 (1979) (stressing the social function and the impersonal nature of shareholder interests in industrial facilities).

[85] *Id.* at 351. See Papier in 2 Maunz/Dürig, Art. 14, Rdnr. 430, arguing that the power to decide how property is to be used is central to Art. 14 and thus that the owners must retain the last word. *Cf.* Trustees of Dartmouth College v. Woodward, 4 Wheat. 518 (1819).

[86] 31 BVerfGE 275, 284–85, 291–92 (1971). Retroactive redefinition of the date on which the period of protection began to run, however, was held impermissible. *Id.* at 292–95.

[87] 52 BVerfGE 1, 29–40 (1979).

[88] 68 BVerfGE 361, 374–75 (1985).

[89] 21 BVerfGE 73, 85–86 (1967).

[90] 26 BVerfGE 215, 221–28 (1969).

[91] 51 BVerfGE 193, 216–21 (1979).

[92] *E.g.*, 2 BVerfGE 380, 399–403 (1953) (compensation for victims of Nazi wrongs). Property, said the Court, did not include "claims that the state affords its citizens by statute in fulfillment of its duty to provide for their welfare," for if it did welfare laws could never be repealed. *Id.* at 402.

[93] *E.g.*, 16 BVerfGE 94, 111–18 (1963) (retirement benefits); 53 BVerfGE 257, 289–94 (1980) (same); 69 BVerfGE 272, 298–306 (1985) (health insurance). For justification of this development, see Hesse, Rdnr. 443–45.

[94] 397 U.S. 254 (1970).

protected by the Due Process Clauses. The test for determining which benefits qualify as property mirrors the Supreme Court's insistence that the law give the claimant a right rather than leaving the matter to official discretion,[95] but the German cases are more restrictive; the benefits must also be based upon the claimant's own contributions and must be designed to provide minimum conditions for survival.[96]

The German decisions, however, do not merely insist upon a fair hearing before individuals are deprived of benefits that qualify as property. It is true that the Constitutional Court has found a requirement of fair procedure implicit in the substantive property guarantee.[97] But the decisions sometimes protect welfare rights against unreasonable legislative impairment as well. In one case, for example, the Court held that a new rule doubling the waiting period required to qualify for unemployment benefits could not constitutionally be applied to persons who had already satisfied the original requirement.[98] This is a step our Court has been unwilling to take, although we have had difficulty explaining why. Perhaps the answer is that the legislature meant to limit only administrative and not legislative withdrawal of benefits; the legislature is after all still free under the American cases to define the substantive scope of the right.[99]

---

[95] E.g., 63 BVerfGE 152, 174 (1983). Cf. Board of Regents v. Roth, 408 U.S. 564 (1972).

[96] See 69 BVerfGE 272, 300 (1985). See id. at 305–6 and 72 BVerfGE 9, 18–21 (1986), respectively applying this test to conclude that rights to medical and unemployment insurance constituted property. Cf. Sniadach v. Family Finance Corp., 395 U.S. 337, 341–42 (1969) (limiting pretrial wage garnishment on due process grounds because garnishment of wages may "drive a wage-earning family to the wall").

[97] See, e.g., 46 BVerfGE 325, 333–37 (1977) (transfer of property pursuant to judicial sale must be postponed to permit judicial challenge to adequacy of price); 53 BVerfGE 352, 358–61 (1980) (striking down unreasonable burden imposed upon landlord in showing that increased rent did not exceed prevailing rate). Cf. 35 BVerfGE 348, 361–63 (1973) (adequate opportunity for judicial review, including provision of counsel in cases of poverty, implicit in property provision). Cf. Mapp v. Ohio, 367 U.S. 643 (1961), and Bivens v. Six Unknown Named Agents, 403 U.S. 388 (1971) (both suggesting that judicial remedies may be implicit in substantive constitutional provisions).

[98] 72 BVerfGE 9, 22–25 (1986). As in the case of conventional property, limitations on existing rights are not forbidden outright. See, e.g., 53 BVerfGE 257, 308–11 (1980) (permitting application of a new provision for division of retirement benefits on divorce to persons married under the old scheme, subject to an extended hardship clause); 69 BVerfGE 272, 304–07 (1985) (upholding increase in cost of medical insurance for those already insured). Yet the Court has gone so far as to suggest that the property guarantee may require the state actually to *increase* benefits to counteract inflation, which reduces their real value. See 64 BVerfGE 87, 97–103 (1983) (holding that such adjustments need not be made annually). Contrast the Legal Tender Cases, 79 U.S. 457 (1871) (rejecting due process challenge to inflationary issue of paper money); Atkins v. United States, 556 F.2d 1028 (Ct. Cls. 1977) (concluding that Article III's ban on reduction of judicial salaries did not require cost of living increases).

[99] For doubts as to whether an American legislature *could* bind itself not to revoke a welfare program, see Crenshaw v. United States, 134 U.S. 99, 104–8 (1890) (permitting Congress to

Most interesting from the American point of view is the 1971 decision of the Constitutional Court striking down a statute that authorized schools to use copyrighted material free of charge.[100] This decision was not based upon impairment of preexisting rights conferred by statute or common law. Rather the Court seems to have found the right to profit from the fruits of one's labors secured by the Constitution itself: "In accord with the property guarantee the author has in principle the right to claim compensation for the economic value of his work . . . ."[101] The Constitution of the United States does not create property; the Due Process and Takings Clauses protect only against infringement of property rights created by other laws.[102] The copyright decision suggests that, like "liberty" in our Due Process Clauses,[103] property in the Basic Law has a dimension independent of ordinary law; Article 14, the Court seems to be saying, constitutionalizes the Lockean principle of *Pierson v. Post*.[104]

The text of the Basic Law lends support to this interpretation: Property is not merely protected against "deprivation" or "taking," it is "guaranteed." Of course the creator of economic values does not have an unlimited right to exploit them. The copyright decision itself, invoking the explicit legislative authority to determine the content and limits of property, acknowledged that the author's interests would prevail only "insofar as the interests of the general public do not take priority."[105] Indeed the same opinion held that the public interest justified permitting schools to use copyrighted material without the author's consent so long as adequate royalties were paid.[106] A later decision limited the applicability of Lockean theory by upholding a statute providing for state ownership of archeological

repeal a law providing tenure for federal employees); Stone v. Mississippi, 101 U.S. 814, 815–20 (1880) (permitting modification of a twenty-five-year charter to conduct a lottery on the ground that the state had no power to promise not to exercise its police power). If government benefits are based upon contract, however, they may be protected by the Contracts Clause of Art. I, §10—though under recent decisions only against unreasonable legislative impairments. See United States Trust Co. v. New Jersey, 431 U.S. 1 (1977); Allied Structural Steel Co. v. Spannaus, 438 U.S. 234 (1978) (striking down law impairing private pension contracts).

[100] 31 BVerfGE 229 (1971).

[101] *Id.* at 243. See also *id.* at 240–41 (defining "the essential elements of copyright as property within the meaning of the Constitution"); Rittstieg in 1 Luchterhand, Art. 14/15, Rdnr. 110a.

[102] See Board of Regents v. Roth, 408 U.S. 564, 577 (1972).

[103] See Ingraham v. Wright, 430 U.S. 651, 672–74 (1977) (right to bodily integrity).

[104] 3 Cai. R. 175 (N.Y. Sup. Ct. 1805); see Locke, Second Treatise of Government 15 (Barnes & Noble ed. 1966).

[105] 31 BVerfGE at 243.

[106] *Id.* at 242.

discoveries,[107] and the Court in so holding seemed to say that the Constitution did not create property rights after all.[108] Whatever its current status or justification, however, the copyright case indicates one of several ways in which the German Constitutional Court has gone beyond current American practice in the constitutional protection of property.[109]

III. OCCUPATIONAL FREEDOM

Article 12(1) codifies the occupational freedom once recognized by the Supreme Court in such cases as *Lochner*:

> All Germans shall have the right freely to choose their trade, occupation, or profession, their place of work and their place of training. The practice of trades, occupations, and professions may be regulated by or pursuant to statute.

Like the right to property, occupational freedom is taken very seriously in Germany as an element of individual autonomy and an essential basis of other freedoms.[110] The right extends to preparation for—as well as exercise of—an occupation.[111] Like property, it may be limited basically only in accordance with statute.[112] Even statu-

---

[107]78 BVerfGE 205, 211–12 (1988). *Cf.* the English common law of treasure trove, noted in Casner & Leach, Cases and Text on Property 35 (3d ed. 1984).

[108]78 BVerfGE at 211, citing earlier cases: Art. 14(1) "guarantees only those rights which the owner already has."

[109]See generally Rittstieg in 1 Luchterhand, Art. 14/15, Rdnr. 37, concluding that the judges have become more protective of property interests since the early 1970s; Leisner in 6 Handbuch des Staatsrechts §149, Rdnr. 102–17, 133–42, arguing that the Court has done too little to protect property.

[110]See, *e.g.*, 7 BVerfGE 377, 397 (1958): "[Article 12(1)] guarantees the individual more than just the freedom to engage independently in a trade. To be sure, the basic right aims at the protection of economically meaningful work, but it views work as a 'vocation.' Work in this sense is seen in terms of its relationship to the human personality as a whole: It is a relationship that shapes and completes the individual over a lifetime of devoted activity; it is the foundation of a person's existence through which that person simultaneously contributes to the total social product." *Cf.* text at note 48 *supra*, discussing property.

In recent years our Supreme Court has not seen it that way. See, *e.g.*, Williamson v. Lee Optical Co., 348 U.S. 483 (1955). Serious due process protection of the right to a livelihood in the United States has been limited to instances in which the individual's very existence was threatened, and then to a guarantee of fair hearing. Sniadach v. Family Finance Corp., 395 U.S. 337 (1969).

[111]See, *e.g.*, 33 BVerfGE 303 (1972) (striking down limits on admission to public universities). This case is discussed at notes 140–47 *infra*.

[112]For decisions invalidating limitations on occupational freedom not adequately authorized by statute see, *e.g.*, 22 BVerfGE 114, 119–23 (1967) (disqualification of attorney); 38 BVerfGE 373, 380–85 (1975) (ban on deposit boxes for prescriptions in outlying areas); 41 BVerfGE 251, 259–66 (1976) (expulsion from vocational school); 43 BVerfGE 79, 89–92 (1976) (ban on repre-

tory limitations, moreover, have been subjected to sometimes demanding scrutiny under the pervasive proportionality principle, and quite a number of them have been struck down.

The leading case remains the seminal 1958 *Pharmacy* decision,[113] which established varying degrees of judicial review (Stufentheorie) according to the severity of the intrusion. To begin with, regulation of how a profession is practiced is easier to justify than limitation of entry into the profession itself:[114]

> The practice of an occupation may be restricted by reasonable regulations predicated on considerations of the common good. The freedom to choose an occupation, however, may be restricted only insofar as an especially important public interest compellingly requires . . .—[and] only to the extent that protection cannot be accomplished by a lesser restriction on freedom of choice.

Moreover, entry limitations such as educational requirements designed to protect the public from unqualified practitioners are easier to justify than those irrelevant to individual ability; and the desire to protect existing practitioners from competition, the Court said, could "never" justify an entry restriction.[115] On the basis of this calculus the Constitutional Court has achieved results reminscent of those reached by the Supreme Court during the *Lochner* period.

As under the reign of *Lochner*,[116] a great many limitations of occupational freedom have been upheld—some of them rather intrusive. Compulsory retirement ages may be set for chimney sweeps[117] and midwives.[118] The sale of headache remedies may be restricted to

---

sentation of codefendants by members of same law firm); 54 BVerfGE 224, 232–36 (1980) (ban on doctors' discussing disciplinary proceedings with patients); 63 BVerfGE 266, 288–97 (1983) (exclusion of Communist from bar); 65 BVerfGE 248, 258–64 (1983) (requirement that price be marked on goods offered for sale). The Court has also made clear, however, that limitations may be based upon customary law existing before the adoption of the Basic Law in 1949. 15 BVerfGE 226, 233 (1962). See also Scholz in 1 Maunz/Durig, Art. 12, Rdnr. 315–16.

[113] 7 BVerfGE 377 (1958).

[114] *Id.* at 405.

[115] *Id.* at 406–8. The language of Article 12 might be taken to suggest that the mere exercise of a profession was subject to unlimited legislative regulation, the choice of profession to none at all. Citing the difficulty of drawing clear lines between choice and exercise, the explicit authorization to regulate access to certain professions in Art. 74(19), and the debates of the constitutional convention, the Court found that choice and exercise of an occupation constituted poles of a continuum: Art. 12 guaranteed a unitary freedom of occupational activity that was subject at any point to reasonable regulation, but what was reasonable varied according to the severity of the limitation. See *id.* at 400–403.

[116] See The Second Century, chs. 2, 4, 5.

[117] 1 BVerfGE 264, 274–75 (1952).

[118] 9 BVerfGE 338, 344–48 (1959).

pharmacists,[119] and the latter may be forbidden to own more than one store.[120] Shops may be required to close on Saturday afternoons, Sundays, holidays, and in the evening;[121] nocturnal baking may be prohibited.[122] The legislature may outlaw the erection or expansion of flour mills[123] and limit the amount of flour produced.[124] The state may monopolize building insurance[125] and employment agencies.[126] It may require employers to hire the handicapped,[127] limit the number of notaries,[128] and require them to serve welfare applicants without charge.[129]

At the same time, throughout its history the Constitutional Court has struck down as unwarranted infringements on occupational freedom an impressive array of restrictions that would pass muster without question in the United States today. The state may not limit the number of drugstores on the ground that there are already enough of them[130] or license taxicabs only in cases of special need.[131] It may not require vending machines to be shut down after stores are closed[132] or require barbers who close on Saturday afternoon to shut down on Monday morning too.[133] It may ban neither door-to-door sales of veterinary medicines[134] nor C.O.D. shipments of live animals.[135] It may not require that retailers be competent to practice their trade,[136] forbid doctors to specialize in more than one field or to perform services outside their specialties,[137] or ban the collection of dead birds for scientific purposes.[138] Finally, in perfect contrast to

---

[119] BVerfGE 73, 77–81 (1959).

[120] 17 BVerfGE 232, 238–46 (1964).

[121] 13 BVerfGE 237, 239–42 (1961).

[122] 23 BVerfGE 50, 56–60 (1968).

[123] 25 BVerfGE 1, 10–23 (1968) (stressing that these limitations were a temporary response to a serious glut on the flour market).

[124] 39 BVerfGE 210, 225–37 (1975).

[125] 41 BVerfGE 205, 217–28 (1976) (inferring from the limitation of federal legislative competence to "private" insurance in Art. 74(11) GG that provisions respecting public insurance were not to be measured against Art. 12).

[126] 21 BVerfGE 245, 249–60 (1967).

[127] 57 BVerfGE 139, 158–65 (1981).

[128] 17 BVerfGE 371, 376–81 (1964) (stressing the public functions that notaries performed).

[129] 69 BVerfGE 373, 378–81 (1985) (finding the burden trivial).

[130] 7 BVerfGE 377, 413–44 (1958).

[131] 11 BVerfGE 168, 183–90 (1960). *Cf.* New State Ice Co. v. Liebmann, 285 U.S. 262 (1932).

[132] 14 BVerfGE 19, 22–25 (1962).

[133] 59 BVerfGE 336, 355–59 (1982).

[134] 17 BVerfGE 269, 274–80 (1964).

[135] 36 BVerfGE 47, 56–65 (1973).

[136] 19 BVerfGE 330, 336–42 (1965).

[137] 33 BVerfGE 125, 165–71 (1972).

[138] 61 BVerfGE 291, 317–19 (1982).

the decision that sealed the death of economic due process in the United States, it may not forbid the manufacture and sale of healthful food products on the ground that they might be confused with chocolate.[139]

Here too, as in connection with familial rights and private schools, there are strong indications that the Basic Law may impose affirmative duties on government. The most notable decision is that in the so-called *Numerus Clausus* case,[140] where, despite insisting that it was not deciding whether Article 12(1) required the state to set up institutions of higher learning, the Constitutional Court flatly declared that the right to obtain a professional education was worthless if the state did not provide one, and therefore that access to public education was not a matter of legislative grace. "In the field of education," said the Court, "the constitutional protection of basic rights is not limited to the function of protection from governmental intervention traditionally ascribed to basic liberty rights."[141]

While recognizing that financial constraints limit any constitutional duty to expand educational facilities, and acknowledging the breadth of legislative discretion in this regard,[142] the Court has applied Article 12(1) in conjunction with the general equality provision of Article 3 and the Sozialstaat principle[143] to scrutinize with great

---

[139]53 BVerfGE 135, 145–47 (1980). *Cf.* Carolene Products Co. v. United States, 323 U.S. 18 (1944). The German court did concede that more stringent measures respecting margarine might be permissible to preserve the viability of the crucial dairy industry (53 BVerfGE at 146), but the second *Carolene Products* decision was based on the danger of confusion alone (323 U.S. at 27–31).

The chocolate decision and others noted above demonstrate that, despite the suggestion of Scholz in 1 Maunz/Dürig, Art. 12, Rdnr. 322, that judicial review under Art. 12(1) has become less intensive than it was in the days of the drugstore case, it has by no means lost its bite. None of this is to say that there is actually more occupational freedom in West Germany than in the United States. Notwithstanding the lack of judicial interest in the area, legislators in this country seem somewhat less inclined to inhibit such freedom than their German counterparts, as Americans seem more mistrustful of government in general. In Chicago, for example, it is possible to sell groceries after 2 P.M. on Saturday; it is basically illegal in Germany.

[140]33 BVerfGE 303 (1972).

[141]*Id.* at 330–32. "The more involved a modern state becomes in assuring the social security and cultural advancement of its citizens," the opinion added, "the more the complementary demand that participation in governmental services assume the character of a basic right will augment the initial postulate of safeguarding liberty from state intervention. This development is particularly important in the field of education." *Ibid* . See Scholz in 1 Maunz/Dürig, Art. 12, Rdnr. 63, explaining that where the state has a practical monopoly (as it has of higher education in West Germany), exclusion comes close in practical effect to prohibition.

[142]See 33 BVerfGE at 332–36.

[143]See *id.* at 331. It is common practice for the Constitutional Court to base a decision on the combined effect of two or more provisions. See also Denninger, in Luchterhand vor Art. 1, Rdnr. 23–25, explaining that, although the Sozialstaat principle is not generally directly enforceable by private suit, it places upon the state "shared responsibility for the creation and maintenance of the factual conditions necessary for the exercise of freedoms guaranteed by the Bill of Rights."

care any restrictions on access by qualified applicants to existing facilities. A university in one state is forbidden to discriminate against residents of another.[144] Even relatively poor grades are no excuse for excluding applicants who satisfy minimum standards when there is unused capacity,[145] and the Court has gone so far as to review the adequacy of teaching loads in order to determine whether there is room for additional students.[146] Thus the judges exercise a substantial degree of supervision over university administration in the interest of equal access to professional education.[147]

Closely related to the occupational freedom guaranteed by Article 12(1) is the requirement of Article 33(5) that public employment be regulated "with due regard to the traditional principles of the professional civil service." A major victory of the powerful civil servants' lobby over Allied efforts at reform,[148] this provision preserves to a significant extent the privileged position of the German civil servant.

Article 33(5) requires only "due regard" for traditional principles, not unswerving adherence to them.[149] One of its basic components is "suitable compensation" for public service, which has led to invalidation of insufficient provisions for retirement benefits[150] and to a requirement of extra pay for civil servants with children.[151] The Court has also employed Article 33(5) to reinforce the conclusion that other branches may not be given discretion to limit judicial salaries[152] and to protect traditional prerogatives we might be inclined to think less significant: the right of judges, teachers, and professors to titles befitting their dignified positions.[153]

Not long ago all of this (with the exception of matters affecting judges, whose independence is guaranteed by Article III) would

---

[144]See 33 BVerfGE at 351–56.

[145]39 BVerfGE 258, 269–74 (1975).

[146]54 BVerfGE 173, 191–207 (1980); 66 BVerfGE 155, 177–90 (1984).

[147]Moreover, like other substantive provisions, Article 12(1) has been read to guarantee adequate procedures to assure vindication of the right itself. See, *e.g.*, 39 BVerfGE 276, 294–301 (1975) (right to file complaint protesting rejection of application for university admission); 52 BVerfGE 380, 388–91 (1979) (right to warning as to the importance of answering questions during bar examination).

[148]See Benz, Von der Besatzungsherrschaft zur Bundesrepublik, 113–16, 208–9 (1985).

[149]3 BVerfGE 58, 137 (1953). For criticism of this conclusion see Maunz in 2 Maunz-Dürig, Art. 33, Rdnr. 58.

[150]8 BVerfGE 1, 22–28 (1958); 11 BVerfGE 203, 210–17 (1960).

[151]44 BVerfGE 249, 262–68 (1977) (invoking Art. 33(5) in conjunction with Art. 6 and the Sozialstaat principle).

[152]26 BVerfGE 79, 91–94 (1969) (also invoking the guarantee of judicial independence in Article 97(1)).

[153]38 BVerfGE 1, 11–17 (1974) (judges); 62 BVerfGE 374, 382–91 (1982) (teachers); 64 BVerfGE 323, 351–66 (1983) (professors). See also 43 BVerfGE 154, 165–77 (1976), holding that Article 33(5) required a hearing before dismissal even of probationary public workers.

have been a matter of legislative grace in the United States under the privilege doctrine.[154] Even today it is difficult to see how an American court could have reached any of the results just noted, since none of the provisions struck down by the German Court involved indirect limitations on protected interests such as expression or religion.[155] Thus while Article 12(1) of the Basic Law specifically guarantees the freedom from state interference with private occupations that our Supreme Court once protected under the rubric of substantive due process, Article 33(5) goes beyond anything the Supreme Court ever did by affording significant substantive protections to public employees as well.

IV. LIFE, LIBERTY, DIGNITY, AND PERSONALITY

A. LIFE AND LIBERTY

Article 2(2) contains a general guarantee of life, bodily integrity, and personal liberty:

> Everyone shall have the right to life and to inviolability of his person. Personal liberty (die Freiheit der Person) shall be inviolable. These rights may be encroached upon only pursuant to statute.

The liberty protected by Article 2(2) is freedom from bodily restraint;[156] other liberties are protected by other provisions.

The last sentence of Article 2(2) should by now be familiar; only the legislature may authorize incursions on interests protected by this provision.[157] However, not every law suffices to justify physical restraint or invasion of bodily integrity. Article 104 specifies a number of procedural limitations on arrest and imprisonment. Article 103 requires courts to afford a hearing, permits punishment only on the basis of preexisting statutes that afford fair warning, and forbids double jeopardy. Article 102 abolishes the death penalty. Article 19(2) draws the outer boundary of legislative restriction of any basic right: "In no case may the essential content of a basic right be encroached upon."

Despite early expectations,[158] this last provision has played little

---

[154]*Cf.* Holmes's famous comment in McAuliffe v. New Bedford, 155 Mass. 216, 220, 29 N.E. 517 (1892), that "there is no constitutional right to be a policeman."

[155]Contrast Perry v. Sindermann, 408 U.S. 593 (1972).

[156]See Dürig in 1 Maunz/Dürig, Art. 2(2), Rdnr. 1, 49.

[157]See Lorenz, Recht auf Leben und körperliche Unversehrtheit, in 6 Handbuch des Staatsrechts, §128, Rdnr. 36.

[158]See Dürig in 1 Maunz/Dürig, Art. 2(1), Rdnr. 31–32, 62–63.

part in the decisions. It did form the principal basis of the Court's 1967 conclusion that a person could not be committed to a mental hospital for mere "improvement":[159]

> It is not among the tasks of the state to "improve" its citizens. The state therefore has no right to deprive them of freedom simply to "improve" them, when they pose no danger to themselves or to others . . . . Since the purpose of improving an adult cannot constitute a sufficient ground for the deprivation of personal liberty, [the statute] encroaches upon the essential content of the basic right . . . .

The same opinion went on, however, to state an alternative ground that, because of its greater stringency, has generally made it unnecessary to inquire whether a restriction invades the "essential content" of a basic right. Quite apart from the limitation imposed by Article 19(2), the institutionalization of an individual who endangered neither himself nor others offended "the principle of proportionality (Verhältnismässigkeit), which is rooted in the rule of law."[160]

The Basic Law nowhere mentions the proportionality principle, and the Court has equivocated as to its source. Some early decisions seemed to find it implicit in the basic rights themselves, or in the provisions permitting legislatures to limit them.[161] One prominent commentator attributed it to the guarantee of "essential content" in Article 19(2).[162] As the quotation above suggests, proportionality is now commonly understood to be one aspect of the Rechtsstaat principle implicit in the various provisions of Article 20 and made explicit as to the Länder in Article 28(1).[163]

The basic idea behind the proportionality principle is that, even where the legislature is specifically authorized to restrict basic rights, the restriction s may go no further than necessary.[164] The decisions have broken down this general principle into three elements reminiscent of the American tests both for substantive due process and for

---

[159]22 BVerfGE 180, 218–20 (1967).

[160]*Id.* at 220.

[161]See, *e.g.*, 17 BVerfGE 108, 117 (1963): "Respect for the basic right of bodily integrity demands respect across the board for the principle of proportionality in passing upon the validity of incursions into this right."

[162]See Dürig in 1 Maunz/Dürig, cited in note 158 *supra*.

[163]See also 30 BVerfGE 1, 20 (1970); Hill, Verfassungsrechtliche Gewährleistungen gegenüber der staatlichen Strafgewalt, in 6 Handbuch des Staatsrechts §156, Rdnr. 21.

[164]See 30 BVerfGE at 20. See also Denninger in 1 Luchterhand vor Art. (1), Rdnr. 12, finding in the basic rights and the Rechtsstaat principle protection against unnecessary as well as nonstatutory limitations of protected interests and quoting from a property case that "'the general welfare is not only the basis but also the limit'" of governmental intrusion.

the necessity and propriety of federal legislation: The limitation must be adapted (geeignet) to the attainment of a legitimate purpose; it must be necessary (erforderlich) to that end; and the burden it imposes must not be excessive (unzumutbar).[165] Necessity for this purpose is narrowly defined: As in certain instances of strict scrutiny in the United States, the legislature must choose the least burdensome means of achieving its goal.[166]

The upshot is intensive scrutiny of the reasonableness of measures impinging upon the interests protected by Article 2(2). Pretrial incarceration is permitted only when necessary to investigate the case[167] or when there is a grave risk of recurrence,[168] and it may not last too long.[169] Persons accused of crime may be institutionalized to determine their mental competency[170] and subjected to an electroencephalogram[171] but not to a spinal tap in connection with a relatively minor offense.[172] One may not be punished for another's wrongs,[173] put on trial when dangerously ill,[174] or evicted when suffering from depression.[175]

Article 2(2) has also been the most prolific source of decisions recognizing the affirmative duty of the state to protect the individual from harm inflicted by third parties. The critical case was the famous abortion decision, which produced a result the polar opposite of that our Supreme Court had reached two years earlier in *Roe v. Wade*: Far from giving the woman a right to terminate her pregnancy, the Basic Law demands in principle that abortion be made a crime; the German constitution requires what our Constitution forbids.[176]

---

[165]See 78 BVerfGE 232, 245–47 (1988). *Cf.* McCulloch v. Maryland, 4 Wheat. 316, 421 (1819); Mugler v. Kansas, 123 U.S. 623, 661–62 (1887) (both stressing the legitimacy of the end and the appropriateness of the means).

[166]*Id.* at 245. *Cf.* Shelton v. Tucker, 364 U.S. 479, 488 (1960); Dean Milk Co. v. Madison, 340 U.S. 349, 354 (1951). This general formulation does not exclude varying levels of scrutiny according to the seriousness and intimacy of the intrusion. See Denninger in 1 Luchterhand, cited in note 49 *supra*; text at notes 113–15 *supra*, discussing the *Pharmacy* case.

[167]19 BVerfGE 342, 347–53 (1965).

[168]35 BVerfGE 185, 190–92 (1973).

[169]20 BVerfGE 45, 49–51 (1966).

[170]2 BVerfGE 121, 122–23 (1953).

[171]17 BVerfGE 108, 114–15 (1963).

[172]16 BVerfGE 194, 198–203 (1963). See also 17 BVerfGE 108, 117–20 (1963).

[173]*Cf.* 20 BVerfGE 323, 330–36 (1966), finding a violation of the general freedom of action guaranteed by Article 2(1) in the punishment of a faultless voluntary association, which had no rights protected by Art. 2(2).

[174]51 BVerfGE 324, 343–50 (1979). This decision was based not on fair trial considerations but on the danger to the defendant's health.

[175]52 BVerfGE 214, 219–22 (1979).

[176]See 39 BVerfGE 1 (1975); Roe v. Wade, 410 U.S. 113 (1973).

Two conclusions at variance with the prevailing American understanding inform the German decision. The first is that life begins before birth,[177] the second that fundamental rights are not simply a guarantee against governmental intrusion.[178] Article 1(1) makes the latter point clear with regard to the right of human dignity, which the state is expressly directed to "respect and protect."[179] Article 1(1) was invoked along with Article 2(2) in the abortion case,[180] and since the more specific bill of rights provisions are commonly viewed at least in part as concrete aspects of human dignity,[181] the "protect and respect" clause may well have influenced the interpretation of Article 2(2) as well.[182]

There were dissents in the abortion case, but the dissenting Justices conceded the state's duty to protect fetal life, arguing only that criminal penalties were not an indispensable means to this end.[183] Moreover, subsequent decisions have affirmed the state's constitutional duty to protect against the hazards of nuclear power plants,[184] aircraft noise,[185] terrorism,[186] and chemical weapons.[187] Acutely aware of the danger of constitutionalizing ordinary tort law as well as other matters basically committed to other branches, the Court has afforded legislative and executive organs wide leeway in determining

---

[177]See 39 BVerfGE at 37–42.

[178]*Id.* at 42–51. Contrast DeShaney v. Winnebago County Department of Social Services, 109 S.Ct. 998, 1003 (1989): "[N]othing in the language [or history] of the Due Process Clause . . . requires the State to protect the life, liberty, and property of its citizens against invasion by private actors."

[179]In one of its very first opinions, while taking a narrow view of the protective duty imposed by Article 1(1), the Constitutional Court expressly acknowledged it: "The second sentence [of Article 1(1)] . . . obliges the state indeed to the positive act of 'protection,' but that means protection against attacks on human dignity by other people, such as humiliation, stigmatization, persecution, ostracism, and the like—not protection from material want." 1 BVerfGE 97, 104 (conceding that the social state principle of Art. 20 required the legislature to assure "tolerable living conditions" for the needy but insisting that "only the legislature can do what is essential to make the social state a reality" (*id.* at 105)). Later decisions respecting the government's obligation under more specific bill of rights provisions to support or provide education (see text at notes 44–45 and 140–42 *supra*) have cast considerable doubt upon this narrow interpretation. See generally Denninger in 1 Luchterhand vor Art. 1, Rdnr. 23–28.

[180]39 BVerfGE at 41, 51.

[181]See Art. 1(2) GG, declaring that the German people acknowledge human rights because of the inviolability of human dignity; Dürig in 1 Maunz/Dürig, Art. 1, Rdnr. 10, 55.

[182]See *id.* at Rdnr. 102.

[183]See 39 BVerfGE at 68–95 (Rupp-von Brünneck and Simon, JJ., dissenting). See also Denninger in 1 Luchterhand vor Art. 1, Rdnr. 33–34.

[184]9 BVerfGE 89, 140–44 (1978); 53 BVerfGE 30, 57–69 (1979).

[185]56 BVerfGE 54, 73–86 (1981).

[186]46 BVerfGE 160, 164–65 (1977). *Cf.* 55 BVerfGE 349, 364–68 (1980) (involving the adequacy of German efforts to secure the release of the aged Nazi leader Rudolf Hess from Allied imprisonment).

[187]7 BVerfGE 170, 214–16, 222–30 (1987).

how to fulfill their protective duties; not since the abortion decision has it found government action deficient to protect life and limb.[188] Moreover, even the abortion case permitted destruction of the fetus for medical, eugenic, ethical, and social reasons,[189] and there is reason to think that in practice the "social" exception may largely have swallowed the rule. Yet the positive duty to protect the individual against harm from third parties remains a vital principle of German constitutional law. Notwithstanding their strikingly contrasting outcomes, both *Roe v. Wade* and its German counterpart are prime examples of intrusive judicial review based on open-ended constitutional provisions.[190]

B. HUMAN DIGNITY

Article 2(2) is indeterminate as to the limits of legislative intervention, but not as to the nature of the rights it protects. Articles 1(1) and 2(1) are indeterminate in both respects.

Article 1(1) provides that "[t]he dignity of man shall be inviolable." Obviously this language leaves a great deal of latitude for interpretation. The Constitutional Court attempted to define its essence in a major 1977 opinion:[191]

> It is contrary to human dignity to make the individual the mere tool [blosses Objekt] of the state. The principle that "each person must always be an end in himself" applies unreservedly to all areas of the law; the intrinsic dignity of the person consists in acknowledging him as an independent personality.

If this helps, well and good. Concrete examples may help too.

Earlier cases, the opinion continued, had established that it was inconsistent with human dignity to impose punishment without

---

[188]See also 66 BVerfGE 39, 60–61 (1983) (rejecting an attack on the stationing of nuclear missiles in West Germany on the ground that, to whatever extent German officials were responsible for the decision, the question of how best to defend the country was committed to the discretion of the political branches). One may be tempted to conclude from the later decisions that the Court has effectively withdrawn from the position it took in the abortion case. However, the decisions may all be reconcilable on the merits. It is easy enough to disagree over the proper balance of interests in nuclear-safety cases or the best way to prevent harm to present and future kidnap victims; despite the obvious shortcomings of criminal penalties it is difficult to see how anything less would have a significant impact upon abortion. See 39 BVerfGE at 52–64.

[189]See 39 BVerfGE at 49–50.

[190]See Glendon, Abortion and Divorce in Western Law 33 (1987).

[191]45 BVerfGE 187, 228 (1977) (Life Imprisonment Case). For more detail along the same lines see Dürig in 1 Maunz/Dürig, Art. 1(1), Rdnr. 28.

fault[192] or to inflict cruel or disproportionate penalties.[193] Life imprisonment, the Court concluded, was permissible only on condition that the possibility of release was never foreclosed: "[T]he state strikes at the very heart of human dignity if [it] treats the prisoner without regard to the development of his personality and strips him of all hope of ever regaining his freedom."[194] On other occasions the Court has invoked the dignity clause in conjunction with other bill of rights provisions to protect informational privacy[195] and the right to have birth records reflect the results of a sex-change operation. "Human dignity and the constitutional right to the free development of personality," said the Court in the latter case, "require that one's civil status be classified according to the sex with which he is psychologically and physically identified."[196]

Commentators agree that human dignity also forbids such atrocities as torture, slavery, and involuntary human experiments; not surprisingly, they differ as to such matters as the death penalty (which at present Article 102 expressly forbids), artificial insemination, and suicide.[197] The open-endedness of the dignity provision is compounded by the Court's explicit conclusion that the meaning of human dignity may change over time:[198]

> The history of criminal law shows clearly that milder punishments have replaced those more cruel in character and that the

---

[192]45 BVerfGE at 228, citing 20 BVerfGE 323, 331 (1966), which had based this conclusion on Art. 2(1) in conjunction with the Rechtsstaat principle.

[193]45 BVerfGE at 228, citing 1 BVerfGE 332, 348 (1952); 25 BVerfGE 269, 285–86 (1969).

[194]45 BVerfGE at 245; see also id. at 228–29. As the quotation suggests, this decision was not based entirely on Article 1(1). See id. at 223, noting the obvious involvement of Article 2(2)'s right to personal liberty; id. at 239, concluding that the "interest in rehabilitation flows from Article 2(1) in tandem with Article 1." In early days doubts had been expressed whether Article 1(1) was directly enforceable at all, partly because Article 1(3) made only the "following" basic rights binding on government organs as "directly enforceable law." See, e.g., Dürig in 1 Maunz/Dürig, Art. 1(1), Rdnr. 4, 7 (adding, in Rdnr. 13, 16, that it hardly mattered since the dignity principle had to be employed as a standard in interpreting other constitutional provisions as well as the ordinary law). For the contrary view, see Podlech in 1 Luchterhand, Art. 1(1), Rdnr. 61. To this date the Constitutional Court has never invalidated government action on the basis of Article 1(1) alone.

[195]See, e.g., 27 BVerfGE 1, 6 (1969) (microcensus): "It would be inconsistent with the principle of human dignity to require a person to record and register all aspects of his personality, even though such an effort is carried out in the form of a statistical survey; [the state] may not treat a person as an object subject to an inventory of any kind." The census questions in issue, which pertained to vacation habits, were held permissible.

[196]49 BVerfGE 286, 298 (1978).

[197]Compare Dürig in 1 Maunz/Dürig, Art. 1(1), Rdnr. 30–41, with Podlech, in 1 Luchterhand Art. 1(1), Rdnr. 43–55.

[198]45 BVerfGE 187, 229 (1977). Cf. the discussion of changing standards of cruel and unusual punishment in Furman v. Georgia, 408 U.S. 238 (1972).

wave of the future is toward more humane and differentiated
forms of punishment. Thus any decision defining human dignity
in concrete terms must be based on our present understanding of
it and not on any claim to a conception of timeless validity.

In short, human dignity is a rather flexible concept.

In the cases so far discussed, Article 1(1) was invoked in traditional
fashion to protect the citizen against government intrusion. In the
well-known *Mephisto* decision, on the other hand, the dignity clause
provided the principal justification for permitting government
limitation of the artistic freedom guaranteed by Article 5(3)—an
injunction against publication of a novel impugning the memory of a
deceased actor.[199] The later *Lebach* case took this reasoning a giant
step further: As the abortion case had made clear,[200] Article 1(1) directed the state not only to respect human dignity but affirmatively
to protect it against third parties; it followed that the constitution not
only permitted but required an injunction against publication of information respecting the plaintiff's past crimes.[201]

C. THE DEVELOPMENT OF PERSONALITY

We come now to Article 2(1), which epitomizes substantive due
process in the Federal Republic:

> Everyone shall have the right to the free development of his per-
> sonality insofar as he does not violate the rights of others or of-
> fend against the constitutional order or the moral code.

"Free development of personality" (die freie Entfaltung der Per-
sönlichkeit) is no more self-defining in German than it is in English.
Literally it seems to suggest something akin to a right of privacy, an
intimate sphere of autonomy into which the state is forbidden to in-
trude. Various aspects of privacy are indeed embraced within Article
2(1), but any such limiting construction was firmly rejected in the
seminal *Elfes* decision in 1957. The free development of personality,
the Court argued, could not be limited to "that central area of personality that essentially defines a human person as a spiritual-moral
being, for it is inconceivable how development within this core area

---

[199]30 BVerfGE 173 (1971). See *id*. at 195: "[T]he values embodied in Article 1(1) influence
the guarantee [of artistic freedom.]" All Justices agreed on the general principle that in such a
case the interest in artistic freedom must be balanced against that in reputation; the injunction
itself was affirmed by an equally divided Court.
[200]See 39 BVerfGE 1, 41, 51 (1975); text at notes 175–83 *supra*.
[201]35 BVerfGE 202 (1973) (relying on Art. 1(1) in conjunction with Art. 2(1)).

could offend the moral code, the rights of others, or even the constitutional order . . . ." Rather the Court construed the provision to guarantee a "general right of freedom of action" (allgemeine Handlungsfreiheit)—citing the debates of the constitutional convention for the conclusion that "linguistic rather than legal considerations prompted the framers to substitute the current language for the original proposal" that "'[e]very person is free to do or not to do what he wishes.'"[202] Casting Article 2(1) loose from its restrictive terminology—like the freeing of "liberty" in the Fourteenth Amendment from its history in *Allgeyer v. Louisiana*[203]—opened the door to judicial review of all restrictive governmental action.

What this review would produce in practice depended upon interpretation of the three limits Article 2(1) places upon freedom of action, "the rights of others, . . . the constitutional order, [and] the moral code." The first and last are easy enough to understand, if not always to apply: The rights of others justify banning such activities as arson and trespass; the moral code has been held, as in the United States, to authorize punishment for sodomy.[204] More difficult to determine was the meaning of the second limitation, which leaves unprotected those activities which "offend against the constitutional order."

This term or something very like it appears in several other articles in connection with constitutional limitations on subversive activities.[205] In those articles, in order not unduly to encroach upon legitimate political opposition, it has been given a restrictive meaning.[206] In the quite different context of Article 2(1) "the constitutional order" has been interpreted more broadly. The general right to freedom of action, the Court stated in *Elfes*, was limited both by

---

[202]6 BVerfGE 32, 36–37 (1957), citing the explanation given by Dr. von Mangoldt at the constitutional convention, Parlamentarischer Rat, Verhandlungen des Hauptausschusses 533 (1949). This interpretation has met with some criticism from the commentators. See, *e.g.*, Hesse, Rdnr. 425–28. For a more approving view, see Dürig in 1 Maunz/Durig, Art. 2, Rdnr. 3, 10, 11.

[203]165 U.S. 578 (1897).

[204]See 6 BVerfGE 389, 432–37 (1957); 36 BVerfGE 41, 45–46 (1973). *Cf*. Bowers v. Hardwick, 478 U.S. 186 (1986). For criticism of the German decisions, see Podlech in Luchterhand, Art. 2(1), Rdnr. 64. Contrast 49 BVerfGE 286, 298–301 (1979), upholding the right to have birth records corrected to reflect a sex-change operation: "[T]he sexual change secured by the complainant cannot be considered immoral."

[205]See Art. 9(2), 18, 21(2) GG.

[206]See, *e.g.*, 5 BVerfGE 85 (1956) (Communist Party case). See also Art. 20(3), which in using similar language requires the legislature to follow only the constitution itself. See 6 BVerfGE at 38.

the Basic Law itself and "by every legal norm that conforms procedurally and substantively with the Constitution."[207]

This interpretation, like the decision that the Privileges or Immunities Clause of our Fourteenth Amendment forbade impairment only of rights already protected by other federal laws,[208] provoked the question whether Article 2(1) added anything at all. At a minimum, as the cases have shown, it provided affected individuals with standing to attack laws passed without legislative authority[209] or delegating excessive rulemaking power to the executive.[210] More important and more interesting was the reminder in *Elfes* that a law qualified as part of the constitutional order only if it conformed with "the principles of the rule of law and the social welfare state."[211]

While the Sozialstaat principle standing alone has never yet been held to invalidate govenmental action or inaction, the rule of law has given Article 2(1) much of its bite. As we have seen, even in the absence of express provisions such as those applicable to bodily restraint, condemnation, and occupational freedom, the Rechtsstaat principle has been held to permit restrictions of liberty only in accordance with statute,[212] and limitations on general freedom of action lacking a sufficient legal basis have been struck down.[213] The Rechtsstaat principle also contains a significant limitation on delegation of policymaking authority that goes beyond that made explicit by Article 80(1),[214] requires fair warning[215] and fair procedure,[216]

---

[207]6 BVerfGE 32, 38 (1957). See also *id.* at 38–40, invoking legislative history. For an argument in favor of a narrower interpretation, see Dürig in 1 Maunz/Dürig, Art. 2(1), Rdnr. 18–25.

[208]Slaughter-House Cases, 83 U.S. 36 (1873).

[209]*E.g.*, 26 BVerfGE 246, 253–58 (1969) (striking down statute for want of federal competence to regulate use of the title of Engineer).

[210]*E.g.*, 20 BVerfGE 257, 268–71 (1966) (invalidating a provision for fees in antitrust proceedings for violation of the delegation limits of Art. 80(1)).

[211]6 BVerfGE 32, 41 (1957).

[212]See text at notes 51–54 *supra.*

[213]*E.g.*, 56 BVerfGE 99, 106–09 (1981) (reversing a decision that forbade a lawyer to appear as counsel against a municipality if his partner was a member of the municipal council for want of "a legal basis in the governing provisions of ordinary law").

[214]See, *e.g.*, 8 BVerfGE 274, 324–27 (1958), most pertinently invoking the separation of powers provision of Art. 20(2): "If the authority of the executive is not sufficiently defined, it no longer can be said to execute the law . . . but takes over [the legislature's] function." See also 49 BVerfGE 89, 126–30 (1978), enunciating the strict requirement that the legislature itself make all "essential" decisions regarding the peaceful use of nuclear power. Article 80(1) applies only to the delegation of authority to adopt regulations under federal law. Despite the plain words and purpose of Art. I, §1 of our Constitution, the Supreme Court has struck down none of the numerous essentially unlimited delegations of federal legislative power since Schechter Poultry Corp. v. United States, 295 U.S. 495 (1935).

[215]See 5 BVerfGE 25, 31–34 (1956). *Cf.* United States v. Cohen Grocery Co., 255 U.S. 81 (1921).

[216]*E.g.*, 26 BVerfGE 66, 71–72 (1969) (permitting victim to intervene in criminal proceed-

and imposes meaningful limitations on retroactivity.[217] Most important, as we have also seen, the German conception of the rule of law embodies the pervasive principle of proportionality.[218] It is this principle, in connection with the broad interpretation of "personality" in *Elfes*, that has enabled the German Court to act as censor of the reasonableness of all governmental action.

As in the United States during the *Lochner* era, most challenged measures have passed muster. National security was held to justify the law limiting issuance of passports in *Elfes*;[219] price regulations were upheld because they were reasonable.[220] At the same time, a number of restrictions on the general freedom of action have been struck down for want of proportionality. The state may not prohibit intermediaries from seeking to match willing drivers with people who are looking for rides.[221] A person in pretrial custody may not be denied a typewriter.[222] As noted in connection with the human dignity provision, persons who have undergone sex change operations are entitled to have birth records corrected to reflect their new gen-

---

ing); 38 BVerfGE 105, 111–18 (1974) (affirming a witness's right to counsel under certain circumstances); 57 BVerfGE 117, 120–21 (1981) (relying on the rule of law in conjunction with the explicit guarantee of a judicial hearing in Art. 103(1) to hold that a filing deadline was satisfied when the document arrived at court); 64 BVerfGE 135, 145–57 (1983) (discussing to what extent proceedings must be translated for a defendant who cannot communicate in German); 65 BVerfGE 171, 174–78 (1983) (no appellate argument in the absence of defense counsel). Why these opinions did not rely solely on Article 103(1) was not always made clear. But see 38 BVerfGE at 118: "Art. 103 (1) basically guarantees only a hearing as such, not a hearing with the assistance of counsel"; 64 BVerfGE at 145–46 and cases cited, explaining that the essence of an Article 103(1) hearing was the right to know the basis of the charge and to respond. *Cf.* Goss v. Lopez, 419 U.S. 565 (1965), stressing the same elements in determining what constituted due process in connection with a suspension from school.

[217]See, *e.g.*, 13 BVerfGE 206, 212–14 (1961) (invalidating a law increasing the tax on land sales previously made); 21 BVerfGE 173, 182–84 (1967) (holding that a prohibition on combining tax counseling with certain other activities could not be applied immediately to persons who had been engaged in both before the statute was passed). Retroactivity in the first of these cases was in the Court's terms "genuine" (echt), since the law attached consequences to past acts themselves. In the second it was "spurious" (unecht), since the law merely disappointed expectations by diminishing the value produced by past actions. Not surprisingly, the Court has been considerably more lenient in passing upon spurious than upon genuine retroactivity. See, *e.g.*, 19 BVerfGE 119, 127–28 (1965) (permitting taxation of securities that had been tax-exempt when purchased). Also not surprisingly, there have been difficulties in distinguishing genuine from spurious retroactivity. *E.g.*, 72 BVerfGE 175, 196–99 (1986) (upholding increase in interest payable in the future on preexisting loans). For criticism of the distinction as engendering more confusion than clarity, see 48 BVerfGE 1, 23 (1978) (Steinberger, J., dissenting).

[218]See especially text at notes 159–66 *supra*.

[219]6 BVerfGE 32, 41–44 (1957).

[220]8 BVerfGE 274, 327–29 (1958).

[221]7 BVerfGE 306, 313–18 (1964).

[222]35 BVerfGE 5, 9–11 (1973). A television set, however, is not required. 35 BVerfGE 307, 309–10 (1973) (rejecting a claim based upon the freedom to inform oneself from generally available sources, Art. 5(1)).

der.[223] Parents may not be given power to bind minor children by contract;[224] the filing of criminal charges in good faith may not be treated as a tort.[225] In one of the best known cases of this nature the Constitutional Court found it unreasonable to require those who sought to hunt with falcons to demonstrate competence in the use of firearms. Not only did the required skills have "no connection either with the care of falcons or with the practice of falconry," but any hunter who discharged a weapon during the chase would frighten away his own falcon.[226]

Article 2(1) and the proportionality principle have also been employed on a number of occasions to secure a general right of "informational self-determination" (informationelle Selbstbestimmung), or freedom from unwarranted publicity. First elaborated in the *Microcensus* case in 1969,[227] this right has been held to limit divulgence of divorce files,[228] medical records,[229] and private recordings of conversations.[230] Most recently it has led the Court to require greater restraint and confidentiality in connection with both the census[231] and legislative investigations,[232] and even to forbid general dissemination of the names of individuals who had been stripped of contracting authority as spendthrifts[233]—although one might have thought publicity essential to protection of those with whom the spendthrift might deal. In this as in so many other respects the German Court has gone beyond its American counterpart; while freedom from certain disclosures is afforded in this country by the First, Fourth, and Fifth Amendments,[234] we have as yet no general right to informational privacy—much less a governmental duty to prevent

---

[223]49 BVerfGE 286, 298–301 (1979).

[224]72 BVerfGE 155, 170–73 (1986) (giving a correspondingly narrow interpretation to the countervailing provision for parental rights in Article 6(2)).

[225]74 BVerfGE 257, 259–63 (1987) (making the Lockean argument that the citizen, having surrendered his natural right to self help, is entitled to seek state protection).

[226]55 BVerfGE 159, 165–69 (1980).

[227]27 BVerfGE 1, 6–8 (1969) (finding adequate justification for requiring a cross-section of inhabitants to answer questions pertaining to their vacation habits).

[228]27 BVerfGE 344, 350–55 (1970).

[229]32 BVerfGE 373, 378–86 (1972).

[230]34 BVerfGE 238, 245–51 (1973).

[231]65 BVerfGE 1, 41–70 (1983).

[232]77 BVerfGE 1, 38–63 (1987).

[233]78 BVerfGE 77, 84–87 (1988).

[234]See U.S. Const., Amend. 4 ("The right of the people to be secure . . . against unreasonable searches and seizures shall not be violated"), 5 ("nor shall any person . . . be compelled in any criminal case to be a witness against himself"); NAACP v. Alabama, 357 U.S. 449 (1957).

private revelations of past crimes, such as the German Court established in the *Lebach* case in 1973.[235]

Article 2(1), in conjunction with the proportionality principle, is thus the heart of substantive due process in Germany.

V. EQUALITY

"All persons," says Article 3(1), "shall be equal before the law." Relying on Article 1(3)'s statement that the Bill of Rights binds legislative as well as executive and judicial authorities, the Constitutional Court made clear at the outset that—in contrast to a similarly worded clause in the 1850 Prussian Constitution—Article 3 forbade not only unequal administration of the laws but unequal legislation, too.[236]

It could hardly have been the intention of those who wrote this provision to forbid all distinctions between persons—to require that murderers go unpunished or blind children be allowed to practice brain surgery. Taking a cue from decisions interpreting predecessor provisions, the Court in its very first substantive decision concluded that Article 3(1) required equal treatment only when inequality would be arbitrary (willkürlich).[237] Thus, as in the United States, the equality provision forbids only those classifications which are

---

[235]35 BVerfGE 202, 218–44 (1973), also noted at note 201 *supra*. *Cf*. Briscoe v. Reader's Digest, 93 Cal. 866, 483 P.2d 34 (1971) (permitting but not requiring damages for a strikingly similar disclosure on strikingly similar grounds). It seems questionable whether our Supreme Court would even permit the assessment of damages in such a case after Cox Broadcasting Corp. v. Cohn, 420 U.S. 469 (1975) (holding the state could not forbid publication of the name of a rape victim identified by public judicial record). As in the case of occupational freedom, however, it would be dangerous to conclude from the more extensive constitutional protection of informational privacy in the Federal Republic that Germans are in fact freer than Americans in this regard. Citizens of the Federal Republic are required both to possess identity cards and to register their place of residence; a legislator who voted for either measure in this country might well find himself out of a job. See Gesetz über Personalausweise vom 21. April 1986, BGBl. I S. 548; Velderechtsrahmengesetz vom 16. Aug. 1980, BGBl. I S. 1429, in 1 Sartorius, Verfassungs-und Verwaltungsgesetz der Bundesrepublik Deutschland, Nr. 255–56.

[236]1 BVerfGE 14, 52 (1951) (Southwest Reorganization Case). *Cf*. Constitution for the Prussian State (1850), Art. 4. See also the 1925 decision of the Reichsgericht (111 RGZ 320, 322–23), recounting the earlier understanding and leaving open the question whether the comparable provision in Art. 109 of the 1919 Weimar Constitution should be more broadly construed; Stein in 1 Luchterhand Art. 3, Rdnr. 5–6.

[237]1 BVerfGE 14, 52 (1951). See also 111 RGZ 320, 329 (1925) (reaching the same conclusion under the analogous clause of the Weimar Constitution). For the suggestion that the inspiration for this interpretation came from the United States and from Switzerland, see Stein in 1 Luchterhand Art. 3, Rdnr. 6.

without adequate justification; but the Constitutional Court has taken the need for such justification very seriously.

A. CLASSIFICATIONS EXPRESSLY PROHIBITED

Article 3(3) gives specific content to the general equality requirement by listing a number of bases of classification that basically cannot be justified: "No one may be prejudiced or favored because of his sex, his parentage, his race, his homeland and origin, his faith, or his religious or political opinions."[238] In contrast to the United States, where race decisions have formed the heart of equal protection jurisprudence, the sex discrimination provision is the only one of these specific prohibitions that has played a significant role in the German cases.[239]

There have been many sex discrimination decisions, and they long antedate our Supreme Court's first forays into the field.[240] Article 117(1) gave legislatures until 1953 to eliminate gender distinctions from the civil code and other laws, but in that year the Constitutional Court affirmed its authority to strike down nonconforming provisions as soon as the grace period expired.[241]

The Court has made clear from the beginning that the specific requirement of sex equality demands heightened scrutiny of classifications based on gender. Merely rational grounds that might suffice

---

[238]Article 3(2) reinforces the ban on sex discrimination by adding that "[m]en and women shall have equal rights." See Dürig in 1 Maunz/Dürig, Art. 3(3), Rdnr. 4, equating the meanings of the two sex equality provisions and explaining their origins.

[239]See 2 BVerfGE 266, 286 (1953) (upholding restrictions on travel by East German refugees because based not on their homeland (Heimat) but on the social and economic difficulties presented by a large influx of persons); 5 BVerfGE 17, 21–22 (1956) (permitting reference to East German law to determine age of majority for East German); 48 BVerfGE 281, 287–88 (1978) (permitting relief for Spanish Civil War veterans to be limited to those living in the Federal Republic on the ground that "Heimat" meant geographical origin and "Herkunft" (origin) social class); 63 BVerfGE 266, 302–05 (1983) (Simon, J., dissenting) (complaining that the ban on political discrimination had been largely ignored). See also Dürig in 1 Maunz/Dürig, Art. 3(3), Rdnr. 75, 87, 46, confirming that the "homeland" provision was designed to protect refugees and that "origin" refers to social class, and explaining that the inclusion of "ancestry" forbids nepotism, among other things. Contrast Kotch v. Pilot Commissioners, 330 U.S. 552 (1947) (rejecting an equal protection challenge to a system under which only "relatives and friends" of established pilots were accepted as apprentices). Thus the list of suspect classifications is somewhat longer in West Germany than it is in the United States.

[240]The Supreme Court first invalidated sex discrimination in Reed v. Reed, 404 U.S. 71 (1971) (striking down a preference for males to administer decedents' estates).

[241]3 BVerfGE 225, 237–48 (1953) (rejecting objections, which look strange to American eyes, that judicial enforcement of the constitutional prohibition might offend higher-law principles of predictability and separation of powers). For development of the interesting notion of unconstitutional constitutional provisions, see 1 BVerfGE 14, 32–33 (1951); 3 BVerfGE at 230–36.

under the general equality provision cannot justify sex discrimination; a "compelling" reason is required.[242] Compelling reasons for this purpose have been specifically defined: "Differential treatment of men and women . . . is permissible only if sex-linked biological or functional differences so decisively characterize the matter to be regulated that common elements can no longer be recognized or at least fade completely into the background."[243]

The reference to biological differences is readily understandable and would justify sex distinctions for such purposes as procreation and marriage.[244] Recognition of the legitimacy of "functional" distinctions, on the other hand, seemed to create the risk of perpetuating stereotypes based on traditional male and female roles.[245]

In fact, some early decisions applying the gender provision were not promising. The Court permitted the state to limit the work done by women in the interest of protecting their health,[246] place the primary duty of financial support of illegitimate children on fathers,[247] and require widowers but not widows to prove dependency in order to obtain benefits upon the death of a spouse.[248] In accordance with explicit language now found in Article 12a,[249] the Court upheld a military draft of men only.[250] Most strikingly, in 1957 the Justices went so far as to uphold a law that punished homosexual activity only between men—on the armchair sociological ground that female homosexuals tended to be quiet about it and thus posed less of a threat to society.[251]

---

[242]See, *e.g.*, 15 BVerfGE 337, 343–44 (1963); 48 BVerfGE 327, 337 (1978).

[243]39 BVerfGE 169, 185–86 (1975).

[244]See Dürig in 1 Maunz/Dürig, Art. 3(2), Rdnr. 13; Stein in 1 Luchterhand Art. 3, Rdnr. 81.

[245]See the criticism of the "functional" criterion in Maunz/Dürig, Art. 3(2), Rdnr. 18.

[246]5 BVerfGE 9, 11–12 (1956) (finding differential treatment justified by "the objective biological and functional differences between men and women").

[247]11 BVerfGE 277, 281 (1960).

[248]17 BVerfGE 1, 17–26 (1963). Contrast Frontiero v. Richardson, 411 U.S. 677 (1973) (striking down a similar provision in the United States several years later).

[249]"Men who have attained the age of eighteen years . . . ."

[250]12 BVerfGE 45, 52–53 (1960 (invoking Art. 12(3) and 73 Nr. 1, which then contained the limitation later placed in Article 12a). *Cf.* Rostker v. Goldberg, 453 U.S. 57 (1981) (upholding a similarly selective draft without benefit of such an explicit provision).

[251]6 BVerfGE 389, 420–32 (1957). The Court adhered to this decision as late as 1973. See 36 BVerfGE 41, 45–46 (1973) (upholding ban on homosexual acts between men and boys). Apparently it did not occur to anyone to argue that it was unequal to permit men to have sexual relations with women but not with other men; the distinct contention that the prohibition infringed Article 2(1)'s right to free development of personality was rejected on the ground that "homosexual activity unmistakably offends the moral code." 6 BVerfGE at 434. See text at note 204 *supra*.

From a very early date, however, the Court also began to strike down gender classifications, and the trend has intensified with the passage of time. As early as 1959 the Justices invoked Article 3 in conjunction with the familial rights guaranteed by Article 6 to invalidate a law giving fathers the last word on childrearing;[252] four years later they gave legislators two years to do away with a preference for men in the inheritance of farms.[253] Later decisions have established that mothers must sometimes share the cost of child care,[254] that a father's citizenship cannot determine that of his child,[255] that married couples may elect the wife's maiden name,[256] and that a "housework day" for single workers may not be prescribed for women only.[257] In 1967 the Court struck down a dependency requirement for widowers' benefits in the civil service, distinguishing its earlier decision on the ground that here, in contrast to the private sector, pensions were generally based upon services rendered rather than need.[258] In 1975 it added that changing patterns of women's employment would soon require a similar conclusion in the case of other pensions as well.[259]

Sex classifications continue to be upheld in some cases. A 1976 decision permitted men for the time being to receive greater retirement benefits than women because their wages were higher.[260] Mothers may still be given preferential custody of children born out of wedlock.[261] Most recently, invoking the Sozialstaat principle, the Court has expressly endorsed a variant of affirmative action in this field: Women may be given special benefits to compensate for disadvantages having a biological basis.[262] As in the United States, however, sex is treated as a relatively suspect classification in Germany—

---

[252] 10 BVerfGE 72–89 (1959).

[253] 15 BVerfGE 337, 342–46, 352 (1963).

[254] 26 BVerfGE 265, 273–77 (1969). The Court specifically reaffirmed its earlier decision (see note 247 *supra*) that fathers could generally be required to support illegitimate children as a counterweight to the mother's duty to rear them; but it saw no reason to distinguish between parents when the child lived with neither one.

[255] 37 BVerfGE 217, 244–59 (1974). Nor may it determine the law governing marital property (63 BVerfGE 181, 194–96 (1983)) or divorce (68 BVerfGE 384, 390 (1985)).

[256] 48 BVerfGE 327, 337–40 (1978).

[257] 52 BVerfGE 369, 373–79 (1979).

[258] 21 BVerfGE 329, 340–54 (1967).

[259] 39 BVerfGE 169, 185–95 (1975).

[260] 43 BVerfGE 213, 225–230 (1977). For the limits of this holding, see 57 BVerfGE 335, 342–46 (1981).

[261] 56 BVerfGE 363, 387–90 (1981).

[262] 74 BVerfGE 163, 178–81 (1987) (upholding earlier optional retirement for women on the ground that their traditionally disadvantaged position in the workplace was attributable in part to anticipated and actual interruptions during pregnancy, birth, and childrearing and raising

along with race, religion, and the other bases of distinction enumerated in Article 3(3).

B. THE GENERAL EQUALITY PROVISION

The list of forbidden bases of classification in Article 3(3) is not exhaustive. Despite its initial definition of forbidden distinctions as those that were arbitrary[263] and repeated professions of judicial restraint,[264] the Constitutional Court has also applied the general equality clause of Article 3(1) to strike down an impressive variety of measures.

To begin with, the Court has scrutinized with especial care those classifications affecting interests specifically protected by other provisions of the Basic Law. Often it has done so on the basis of the other provisions themselves.[265] On other occasions the substantive provisions have been drawn upon to give content to the general prohibition of Article 3(1). Thus the Court has been quick to condemn discrimination against married persons[266] or families with children[267] under Article 3(1) in conjunction with the applicable paragraphs of Article 6. It has done the same in cases respecting inequalities affecting the academic[268] and occupational[269] freedoms guaranteed by Articles 5(3) and 12(1), the traditional rights of civil servants under Article 33(5),[270] the right to operate private schools under Article 7(4),[271] and above all the right to participate in elections.[272] In

---

the question whether such a measure might even be constitutionally *required*). *Cf.* the explicit requirement of Article 6(5) (discussed at notes 31–38 *supra*) that the legislature act affirmatively to assure equality of actual opportunity for illegitimate children.

[263]See text at note 237 *supra*.

[264]*E.g.*, 12 BVerfGE 326, 337–38 (1961).

[265]See, *e.g.*, the marriage and family decisions discussed at notes 28–31 *supra*.

[266]*E.g.*, 13 BVerfGE 290, 295–318 (1962) (deductibility of salary paid to owner's spouse); 67 BVerfGE 186, 195–99 (1984) (unemployment compensation when both spouses out of work).

[267]See 61 BVerfGE 319, 343–44, 351–54 (1982) (requiring cost of child care to be considered in determining taxable income).

[268]*E.g.*, 56 BVerfGE 192, 208–16 (1981). See also the cases discussed at notes 142–46 *supra*.

[269]*E.g.*, 37 BVerfGE 342, 352–60 (1974).

[270]56 BVerfGE 146, 161–69 (1981).

[271]75 BVerfGE 40, 71–78 (1987).

[272]*E.g.*, 1 BVerfGE 208, 241–60 (1952) (exclusion of party receiving less than 7.5% of vote from proportional representation in legislature); 3 BVerfGE 19, 23–29 (1953) (requirement of 500 petition signatures for Bundestag candidate of party not already represented); 6 BVerfGE 273, 279–82 (1957) (nondeductibility of contributions to unrepresented parties); 7 BVerfGE 99, 107–08 (1957) (denial of public television time to unrepresented party); 16 BVerfGE 130, 138–44 (1963) (unequal population of election districts); 41 BVerfGE 399, 412–23 (1976) (exclusion of independent candidate from reimbursement of election expenses); 44 BVerfGE 125, 138–66 (1977) (government propaganda for parties in ruling coalition). Some of these decisions were based in part upon the explicit guarantee of "equal" Bundestag elections in Article 38 or

several of these cases,[273] as in those passing upon classifications made suspect by Article 3(3), the Court explicitly required an unusually strong justification for discrimination. In 1986 it expressly generalized the principle: "If the rule to be tested under Article 3(1) affects other interests protected by the Bill of Rights, the legislature's freedom of action is more narrowly circumscribed."[274] These decisions closely resemble those reached under the fundamental rights strand of equal protection analysis in the United States.[275]

As in the United States, there is some tendency to extend this heightened scrutiny to classifications affecting other interests deemed fundamental—such as the right to have birth records altered to reflect a sex-change operation—which are not specifically enumerated in the Basic Law.[276] Indeed it has often been said that classifications made in tax laws require special justification because of the severity of their impact.[277] A surprising number of such distinctions have actually been found wanting: discriminatory taxation of chain stores,[278] preferential treatment of vertically integrated firms under the value-added tax,[279] nondeductibility of partners' salaries[280] and of child-care expenses,[281] to name only a few.[282] These decisions stand in sharp contrast to modern decisions in the United States; the

---

on Article 21(1)'s guarantee of the rights of political parties; others add references to the guarantee of democracy in Articles 20 and 28. *Cf.* Justice Stone's suggestion—which has been followed—of heightened scrutiny of measures impairing the integrity of the democratic process. United States v. Carolene Products Co, 304 U.S. 144, 152–53 n.4 (1938).

[273]*E.g.*, 1 BVerfGE 208, 249, 255, 256 (1952) (elections); 37 BVerfGE 342, 352–54 (1974) (occupational freedom); 67 BVerfGE 186, 195–96 (1984) (marriage).

[274]74 BVerfGE 9, 24 (1986).

[275]See, *e.g.*, Carey v. Brown, 447 U.S. 455, 461–62 (1980) (freedom of speech); Niemotko v. Maryland, 340 U.S. 268 (1951) (free exercise of religion).

[276]60 BVerfGE 123, 133–35 (1982) (striking down a provision limiting this right to persons at least 25 years old). *Cf.* Reynolds v. Sims, 377 U.S. 533, 561–62 (1964) (subjecting limitations on the value of votes to strict scrutiny although the right to vote was nowhere generally guaranteed).

[277]See, *e.g.*, 21 BVerfGE 12, 27 (1966); 35 BVerfGE 324, 335 (1973). For a rare protest against the notion of strict scrutiny in tax cases generally, see 15 BVerfGE 313, 318 (1963).

[278]19 BVerfGE 101, 111–18 (1965). But see 29 BVerfGE 327, 335–36 (1970) (permitting discriminatory taxation of multiply owned saloons).

[279]21 BVerfGE 12, 26–42 (1966).

[280]13 BVerfGE 331, 338–55 (1962).

[281]68 BVerfGE 143, 152–55 (1984).

[282]Note also the intensive scrutiny practiced in an early decision striking down an exaction for support of the fire department that was imposed only upon men between the ages of 18 and 60 who had not served as firemen, 9 BVerfGE 291, 302 (1959): "[A]s a special assessment [the exaction] would have to be limited to those who derived special benefits from the fire department; as a substitute for service it could reach only those under a duty to serve; as a general tax it could not be imposed only on men between 18 and 60 years of age." A revised exaction limited to those who were eligible for fire duty but had not served was later upheld, 13 BVerfGE 167 (1961).

Supreme Court has not scrutinized classifications in tax laws with much care since the New Deal revolution.[283]

Moreover, although the Constitutional Court has sometimes said that legislatures have particularly broad discretion in determining how to spend public funds,[284] one dissenting Justice, in language reminiscent of that of Justice Thurgood Marshall, has argued for heightened scrutiny of discriminatory welfare provisions under the influence of Article 20's social state principle.[285] Indeed, in contrast to the American cases, the German decisions lend her considerable support. Among other things, the Constitutional Court has found fault with the exclusion of unemployment benefits for students[286] and for persons formerly employed by their parents,[287] limitations on aid for the blind[288] or disabled,[289] and the denial of retirement benefits to persons living abroad.[290] Some of these decisions may be explainable on the ground that the classification impinged upon some other fundamental right; but the overall impression is that the Constitutional Court is rather strict in scrutinizing classifications in the distribution of welfare benefits as such.

Indeed, without regard to the various categories of heightened scrutiny already discussed, recent opinions have exhibited a marked tendency to replace the deferential arbitrariness standard originally enunciated with the apparently more aggressive search for a reason "sufficient to justify" the challenged distinction.[291] Decisions in the past few years suggest that, whatever formulation is employed, review under the general equality provision is never as toothless as it has become in economic cases in the United States. In striking down

---

[283]See, e.g, Lehnhausen v. Lake Shore Auto Parts Co., 410 U.S. 356 (1973), upholding a personal property tax imposed on property not owned by individuals without a serious effort to justify the distinction. See generally Gunther, Foreword: A Model for a Newer Equal Protection, 86 Harv. L. Rev. 1, 8 (1972). For a recent exception to this pattern, see Allegheny Pittsburgh Coal Co. v. County Commission, 109 S.Ct. 633 (1989).

[284]E.g., 17 BVerfGE 210, 216 (1964).

[285]See 36 BVerfGE 237, 248–50 (Rupp-von Brünneck, J., dissenting). Cf. Dandridge v. Williams, 397 U.S. 471, 520–23 (1970) (Marshall, J., dissenting).

[286]74 BVerfGE 9, 24–28 (1986).

[287]18 BVerfGE 366, 372–80 (1965) (noting the severity of the exclusion and the impact of the Sozialstaat principle).

[288]37 BVerfGE 154, 164–66 (1974).

[289]39 BVerfGE 148, 152–56 (1975) (finding such a limitation not yet unconstitutional but warning that it soon may be).

[290]51 BVerfGE 1, 23–29 (1979) (holding that they must at least be given their contributions back).

[291]See, e.g., 74 BVerfGE 9, 29–30 (1986) (dissenting opinion) (pointing out the general and unannounced change in the governing standard).

limitations on the assessment and award of agency or court costs[292] without intimating that the distinctions either embodied suspect classifications or impinged upon fundamental rights, for example, the Constitutional Court conjured up memories of the vigorous way in which the Equal Protection Clause was enforced in economic cases during the *Lochner* era in this country.[293]

Furthermore, in more recent decisions the notion of arbitrariness has tended to come loose from its moorings and to enjoy an independent life of its own. Originally a test for the legitimacy of legal distinctions, arbitrariness began to appear, despite cogent warnings in dissent,[294] as a ground for condemning official action—especially judicial action—without mention of inequality at all.[295] Thus the equality clause of Article 3(1) bade fair to become a guarantee of substantive and procedural due process as well—though there was hardly any need for another such provision in view of the broad interpretation already given the right to free development of personality under Article 2.

Finally, although the Constitutional Court has sometimes said that Article 3 imposes no duty to rectify inequalities existing apart from governmental action,[296] other opinions have more than hinted that it may outlaw de facto inequality under some circumstances. The first was an opinion, reminiscent of *Griffin v. Illinois*, relying on Article 3(1) to require the assignment of counsel to an indigent party at state expense[297]—one of the very few areas in which our Supreme Court has come close to recognizing positive rights to government support. Most arresting in this regard was the decision that allowing taxpayers unrestricted deductions for political contributions gave an unfair advantage to wealthy contributors and the parties they tended to

[292]50 BVerfGE 217, 225–33 (1979); 74 BVerfGE 78, 94–96 (1986). See also 54 BVerfGE 277, 293–97 (1980) (holding in contrast to our certiorari practice that the highest civil court could not decline jurisdiction of meritorious cases simply because of its overloaded docket).

[293]*Cf.*, *e.g.*, Gulf, C. & S.F. Ry. v. Ellis, 165 U.S. 150 (1897) (striking down a provision that imposed attorney fees in actions for livestock losses only if the defendant was a railroad). See generally The Second Century, chs. 2, 5, 7.

[294]See 42 BVerfGE 64, 79–83 (1976) (Geiger, J., dissenting).

[295]*E.g.*, 57 BVerfGE 39, 41–42 (1981); 58 BVerfGE 163, 167–68 (1981); 62 BVerfGE 189, 191–94 (1982); 62 BVerfGE 338, 343 (1982); 71 BVerfGE 202, 204–05 (1985). A plausible explanation may be that to deviate from the law in a particular case is to apply it unequally. See 54 BVerfGE 117, 124–26 (1980); Dürig in 1 Maunz/Dürig, Art. 3(1), Rdnr. 52.

[296]See, *e.g.*, 1 BVerfGE 97, 107 (1951).

[297]2 BVerfGE 336, 339–41 (1953). *Cf. Griffin*, 351 U.S. 12 (1956). See also 1 BVerfGE 109, 111 (1952) (finding assignment of counsel required by the more general requirements of democracy and the social state); 54 BVerfGE 251, 266–73 (1980) (requiring state-assigned guardian for ward without funds).

support[298]—with an explicit dictum to the effect that progressive taxation was constitutionally required.[299] This is but one more example of the ways in which the equality clauses, like other provisions of the Basic Law, have been employed to make the Constitutional Court ultimate censor of the reasonableness of all governmental action.

VI. CONCLUSION

What is one to make of all this? What one will; my aims are descriptive and comparative. For better or worse, the German Constitutional Court is in the business of determining the reasonableness of governmental action—and, to a significant degree, of inaction as well. In exercising this authority the Court has delved repeatedly into details of the organization and practices of higher education[300] and broadcasting,[301] passed upon such minutiae as the appropriate titles of teachers and judges, and joined our Supreme Court in composing a detailed (though strikingly different) abortion code. Moreover, while the German court has so far generally been deferential to other branches in determining how and how far to protect citizens against want or third parties, the abortion and private school subsidy cases demonstrate the potential for constitutionalizing vast additional areas of tort, criminal, and welfare law. The tendency of the German decisions has been progressive rather than reactionary, and the notion of affirmative rights to governmental protection is essentially foreign to our jurisprudence; but the basic principle of freewheeling judicial review is reminiscent of that which gave us *Scott v. Sandford*, *Lochner v. New York*, and *Roe v. Wade*.

Whether the German judges were justified in finding that the

---

[298] 8 BVerfGE 51, 63–69 (1958).

[299] *Id*. at 68–69: "[I]n the tax field a formally equal treatment of rich and poor by application of the same tax rate would contradict the equality provision. Here justice requires that in the interest of proportional equality a person who can afford more pay a higher percentage of his income in taxes than one with less economic power."

[300] In addition to the cases on university admissions noted above, see the line of decisions beginning with 35 BVerfGE 79 (1973), invoking Art. 5(3)'s guarantee of academic freedom to assure faculty control of basic questions relating to research and curriculum.

[301] The seminal decision on broadcasting was 12 BVerfGE 205 (1961), where the Court interpreted Art. 5(1)'s provision that "freedom of reporting by means of broadcasts . . . [is] guaranteed" to require the state to regulate broadcasting in such a way that various social and political interests had the opportunity to utilize the medium and to participate in its governance. For later decisions applying and refining these requirements, see, *e.g.*, 57 BVerfGE 295 (1981); 73 BVerfGE 118 (1986).

Basic Law conferred such sweeping judicial authority I leave to those brought up in the system. I have explained at some length elsewhere why I believe our Constitution does not,[302] but both the language and the history of the two documents differ significantly. That familial and occupational rights are entitled to some constitutional protection in Germany, for example, is obvious from the text; so is the disfavored position of discrimination on grounds of sex. Only to a limited extent, therefore, are the German decisions directly relevant to the interpretation of our Constitution.

More important for us is what the German decisions have to say about the desirability of empowering politically insulated judges to make open-ended judgments about the reasonableness of government action. Some may find in the German experience confirmation of the dangers of unchecked judicial intervention , others proof of the need for broad judicial review. Unlike their American counterparts during the *Lochner* years, the German judges do not seem often to have blocked desirable or even fairly debatable reforms; they do seem to have spared their compatriots a flock of unjustified restrictions on liberty and property. Whether this record affords a basis for confidence that either American or German judges would exercise such a power wisely in the long run is another matter; so is the question whether so broad a power, however wisely exercised, is consistent with one's conception of democracy. Phil Kurland had a word for it, as he has on so many important matters: "Essentially because [the Supreme Court's] most important function is anti-majoritarian, it ought not to intervene to frustrate the will of the majority except where it is essential to its functions as guardian of interests that would otherwise be unrepresented in the government of the country."[303] Reasonable people will continue to differ on this fundamental question; their ability to do so is an important aspect of the free democratic order established by the constitutions both of the United States and of the Federal Republic.

---

[302]See generally The First Hundred Years and The Second Century.
[303]Kurland, Politics, the Constitution, and the Warren Court 204 (1970).

MARK TUSHNET

"OF CHURCH AND STATE AND THE SUPREME COURT": KURLAND REVISITED

In 1961 Philip Kurland offered a doctrinal solution to the problem of interpreting the religion clauses of the First Amendment.[1] In the generation since Kurland proposed his solution, the Supreme Court and commentators on its work have continued to address that problem, but no one has yet devised a better solution than Kurland's. I will examine Kurland's solution and some prominent recent alternatives by discussing three important religion clause cases of the 1988 Term, with the goal of sketching some reasons why Kurland's solution has not yet been widely accepted.

I. KURLAND'S PROPOSAL: FORMAL NEUTRALITY

Kurland's solution to the problem of interpreting the religion clauses is simple: "[R]eligion may not be used as a basis for classification for purposes of governmental action." As Kurland noted, this was a doctrine "akin to the reading of the equal protection clause."[2] Kurland did not so much defend his proposal as illustrate its application to all of the religion clause cases decided up to 1961 by the Supreme Court. The nature of his descriptions of the cases, coupled with his brief explicit justification for the proposal, show us why he thought that the proposal made sense.

Mark Tushnet is Professor of Law, Georgetown University Law Center.
[1]Kurland, Of Church and State and the Supreme Court, 29 U. Chi. L. Rev. 1 (1961).
[2]*Id.* at 5.

Kurland's proposal is a doctrinal solution to a problem of constitutional interpretation, rather than, for example, a solution that relies solely on the intent of the framers of the Constitution or solely on whatever norms of political morality might be relevant to the relation between religion and government. Doctrinal solutions have a number of important features. First, although they are not finally justified by historical or directly normative considerations, they must be broadly consistent with acceptable understandings of the origins of the constitutional provision in question, and they must provide normatively acceptable solutions to many of the central problems that the provision addresses.[3] For example, as part of the background for his proposal, Kurland simply assumed that any acceptable doctrine of the religion clauses must produce the result that it is unconstitutional for a government to outlaw the saying of the Catholic Mass or to require attendance at the Mass.[4] The reasons for this assumption are historical and normative: Such legislation was almost precisely the sort that concerned the framers of the First Amendment, and today there is agreement that such legislation is normatively undesirable. In addition to these historical and normative dimensions, a doctrinal solution must answer contemporary problems in ways that are generally acceptable. In the nature of things, however, the answers a doctrinal solution provides on contemporary issues will not be as widely accepted as its answers to the problems that preoccupied the past, precisely because contemporary problems arise when people differ on what is normatively acceptable.

The most important feature of a doctrinal solution, however, is its administrability. By this I mean that doctrinal solutions must be relatively easy to state and to understand. Legal doctrines are applied not by Ronald Dworkin's Hercules but by those relatively ordinary men and women who become judges and justices. The processes by which judges are selected, and the way in which cases are filtered through the political process to the courts, refine both the decisionmakers and the presentation of the problems. But in the end, the degree to which judges are set apart from the wider society is inevitably, and properly, limited. Doctrinal solutions must be capable of being applied by these people in a relatively dispassionate way. Oth-

---

[3]Some aspects of constitutional law have little direct moral content. Separation of powers may be an example. Doctrinal solutions to problems of interpretation in these areas need not touch normative issues at all closely.

[4]Kurland, note 1 *supra*, at 10.

erwise, they simply replicate the decisions made in the political branches. More important, doctrinal solutions should be designed to resist normatively problematic distortions: they should make it more difficult for judges to rely on unstated invidious criteria. Doctrinal solutions, in short, must be relatively easy to state and understand.

Kurland's proposal for the interpretation of the religion clauses offers an attractive doctrinal solution of this sort. The Supreme Court's decisions in this area in recent years, however, cast some light on the viability of his proposal. In particular, the Court's actions, and alternative doctrinal formulations offered by Justices O'Connor and Kennedy, illustrate one of the primary difficulties with all doctrinal solutions. The very administrability of doctrinal solutions, which is perhaps their most important characteristic, makes it difficult to sustain them in the long run.

First, no one, even a judge, who articulates a doctrinal solution can ensure that it will be applied "faithfully" in the future. Later judges can interpret the doctrine in light of the facts of the case in which it was articulated, distinguish it as involving a discrete area of law while the case at hand involves a different area, and, in general, deploy the usual techniques of legal argument to refine or reject the doctrine. This difficulty should not be overstated, however. Certain forms of words resist these transformations more than others; a doctrine that says that governments may never punish people because of disagreement with the content of their speech is somewhat harder to distinguish, though of course not harder to overrule, than a doctrine that says that governments may not unreasonably regulate speech.[5] The more resistant the doctrine is, the less it can be turned to invidious use. Kurland's doctrine is resistant in this way. The alternative proposals to which the Court has been attracted are subject to distortion—in particular, to being transformed into standards that unconsciously incorporate the assumptions of mainstream Christianity.

Second, because they are likely to be simple, doctrinal solutions will almost surely be both under- and over-inclusive.[6] They will lead courts to strike down as unconstitutional legislation widely under-

---

[5]The "never punish because of content" rule can be distinguished, for example, by saying that in the case at hand the government was not concerned with the content of the speech but with the collateral consequences of its utterance. See, *e.g.*, City of Renton v. Playtime Theatres, 475 U.S. 41 (1986).

[6]The present generation's standard presentation of this point is Kennedy, Form and Substance in Private Law Adjudication, 89 Harv. L. Rev. 1685 (1976).

stood to be inoffensive, and to refuse to strike down legislation similarly understood to be normatively troubling.[7] Judges often find it difficult to resist the pressure to accommodate the demands of sympathy in individual cases by devising "exceptions" to the general rule to handle their present difficulties. They may understand that at other times, judges might need simpler lines than the ones they are developing, but they are likely to think that, because they know that they could handle the complexity they are introducing into the doctrine, other judges will be able to do so just as well.

Third, doctrinal solutions tend to become outdated. To the extent that they offer normatively acceptable solutions to contemporary problems, doctrinal solutions are vulnerable from two directions. The nature of the problems presented to the courts may change; or what seems normatively acceptable to a wide enough range of people may change as the public's values change. Both of these types of changes led Kurland's view to lose favor.

These problems, specific to Kurland's proposal but illustrating a more general legal dynamic, suggest that no doctrinal solution will ever be stable. It will require results that are widely believed to be normatively unacceptable, and it may readily be dislodged by legal developments in nearby fields of law. Yet, at least for scholars, there is a real advantage to thinking about doctrinal solutions. Kurland's article deploys his doctrine as a critical standard for evaluating the Supreme Court performance. To the extent that the most important characteristic of a doctrinal solution, its administrability, allows scholars to notice when invidious comparisons have crept into the law, the solution will remain valuable. In the end, of course, one's judgment must be comparative: How well does Kurland's doctrine stand up against alternative doctrines the Court has or might articulate? The burden of this article is that it stands up very well indeed.

Three of the Supreme Court's decisions in religion clause cases in the 1988 Term provide a useful basis for examining the primary competition to Kurland's for an overall analysis of those clauses.[8] The

---

[7] Sager, Fair Measure: The States of Underenforced Constitutional Norms, 91 Harv. L. Rev. 1212 (1978), discusses the ways in which legal standards other than fully enforced doctrines address the problem of underinclusiveness.

[8] The Justices divided over the interpretation of the facts in a fourth case, Hernandez v. C.I.R., 109 S.Ct. 2136 (1989), in a way that makes it less useful for present purposes than the others. According to the dissenters, the facts of the case showed that the law was being enforced in a way that discriminated against a particular religion, which they believed was unconstitutional. The majority did not disagree with their constitutional analysis, but said that the case did not properly present the question of religious discrimination.

cases illustrate what some believe to be the normative problems associated with Kurland's position and, perhaps more important, the changing nature of the issues that have come to the Court since 1961.

II. Mandatory Accommodation and the Free Exercise Clause

It followed directly from Kurland's analysis that exempting the activities of religious believers from generally applicable regulations, solely because of their beliefs, was impermissible. He treated such exemptions as subsidies and wrote: "[T]he first amendment prohibits such a subsidy where it is granted because of the religious nature of the activity conducted."[9] If legislatures could not grant such subsidies without running afoul of Kurland's neutrality principle, of course the Constitution itself could not be the source of a requirement that subsidies be granted.

In *Sherbert v. Verner*,[10] the Court rejected the neutrality approach. South Carolina's unemployment compensation statutes defined as ineligible for compensation someone who was unavailable for work. This interpretation differed from those of most other state courts dealing with comparable provisions. The South Carolina courts held that a person was unavailable for work when she could not obtain a job in her hometown that had a work schedule consistent with her religiously based requirement that she not work on Saturday. The Supreme Court held that the statute, so interpreted, violated the Constitution because it imposed a burden on the free exercise of religion without adequate justification.

Sherbert, a case we would now describe as a disproportionate religious impact case, presented the Court with what appeared to it as a case of unjustifiable unfairness. South Carolina's unemployment compensation statutes did make life particularly difficult for people with a certain set of religious beliefs. The fact that virtually every other state had managed to administer its parallel statute without imposing such a burden undermined any claim that providing compensation for people like Sherbert would be expensive or would create serious problems of administration. In addition, the Court was surely motivated by its judgment that cases like Sherbert's would be rare: most of the time, people would be able to find a job with a schedule that could be juggled to accommodate their religious be-

---

[9]Kurland, note 1 *supra*, at 46.
[10]374 U.S. 398 (1963).

liefs.[11] Taking these factors together, the Court may have felt that in *Sherbert* it was facing a case in which the state was making life difficult for a rather small group of religious believers for no particularly good reason.

The Court might have responded to the problem presented in *Sherbert* by treating it as a gerrymander. That is, at least once the burden on the religious observers was pointed out, and after it became clear that no substantial governmental purpose was served by denying them benefits, the state's adherence to its general rule began to look like intentional discriminat ion.[12] But the Court did not view *Sherbert* this way; instead, *Sherbert* became the origin, and in a sense remains almost the only example, of the doctrine that the Free Exercise Clause of the First Amendment sometimes requires that the government accommodate its general regulations to the religious beliefs of some of its citizens. The Court has required state governments to accommodate religious belief in three cases essentially identical to *Sherbert*.[13] In addition, it required the state of Wisconsin to exempt the children of Amish parents from the state's requirement that children attend school to the age of sixteen.[14] Otherwise, it has rejected claims for mandatory exemption.[15]

Last Term's decision in *Frazee v. Illinois Department of Employment Security*[16] is the most recent in the *Sherbert* line. Frazee refused a temporary sales position offered him by Kelly Services because the job would have required him to work on Sunday. Frazee said that, "as a Christian," he could not work on Sunday. His application for unemployment compensation was denied because, the Department found, Frazee had failed, without good cause, to accept suitable work when offered. The only difference between Frazee's claim and Sherbert's was that Sherbert was a member of an established sect that had

---

[11]See *id*. at 399 n.2.

[12]For a similar suggestion, see Tribe, American Constitutional Law 1257 (2d ed. 1988).

[13]Thomas v. Review Board of Indiana Unemployment Security Div., 450 U.S. 707 (1981); Hobbie v. Unemployment Compensation Appeals Comm'n of Florida, 480 U.S. 136 (1987); Frazee v. Illinois Department of Employment Security, 109 S.Ct. 1514 (1989).

[14]Wisconsin v. Yoder, 406 U.S. 205 (1972).

[15]A majority of the Justices expressed the view in Bowen v. Roy, 476 U.S. 693 (1985), that an exemption was required for religious believers whose beliefs were inconsistent with a federal requirement that recipients of public assistance have Social Security numbers. This view was not, however, expressed in a judgment of the Court because Justices Blackmun and Stevens thought that the issue was not a live one in the case before them. For examples of cases rejecting claims for mandatory accommodation, see United States v. Lee, 455 U.S. 252 (1982); Reynolds v. United States, 98 U.S. 145 (1879).

[16]109 S.Ct. 1514 (1989).

refusal to work as one of its tenets, while Frazee was not associated with such a church but rested his objection to Sunday work on his personal interpretation of the requirements of Christianity.

The Supreme Court, in a unanimous opinion by Justice White, held that this difference was insufficient to justify a different result. In that, it was surely correct. To treat members of established sects who hold religious views in one way, and to treat differently others who hold exactly the same views even though they are not associated with established sects, would be a form of discrimination among religious beliefs that would be precluded by any coherent theory of the religion clauses. Yet, when we put this appropriate concern about discrimination together with the Court's pattern of results in mandatory accommodation cases, especially in view of some of the language in *Frazee*, the doctrine of mandatory accommodation becomes problematic.

The Court's pattern of results is troublesome for a number of reasons. The first, simply, is that *Sherbert* retains vitality only as a case about unemployment compensation but is taken to be a case about mandatory accommodation. As a result, people are led to believe that there is a general doctrine of mandatory accommodation, a belief that the Court's decisions basically belie. A "doctrine" that is not enforced is not a happy thing for the Court to have. It generates litigation, as people present claims for exemption based on the purported "doctrine" of *Sherbert*, only to find that those claims are routinely denied. It also misleads scholars into saying things such as, "Under the doctrine of mandatory accommodation, the free exercise clause requires the states to adopt rules that the establishment clause prevents them from adopting."[17] As an analytic matter this is incorrect,[18] but it is a foolish Court that puts such rhetorical weapons in the hands of its critics.

Finally, the purported existence of a doctrine of mandatory accommodation has led commentators, and members of the Court at least in dicta, to believe that there is, or ought to be, a doctrine of permissible accommodation. After all, if a state can be required to provide what Kurland called a subsidy without violating the Establishment Clause, surely there might be other forms of subsidy that it is permit-

---

[17]See, *e.g.*, Choper, The Religion Clauses of the First Amendment: Reconciling the Conflict, 41 U. Pitt. L. Rev. 673, 674 (1980).

[18]See Tushnet, Reflections on the Role of Purpose in the Jurispridence of the Religion Clauses, 27 W. & M. L. Rev. 997 (1986).

ted to give, again without violating the establishment clause. Again, as an analytic matter, this does not follow, but the Court's language about accommodation suggests that it does. For example, in upholding the constitutionality of a city's support of a nativity scene, the Court wrote: "[The Constitution] affirmatively mandates accommodation, not merely tolerance, of all religions, and forbids hostility toward any."[19] If the doctrine of permissible accommodation is independently troublesome, the Court ought not provide it with rhetorical support through a doctrine of mandatory accommodation.

A second difficulty with the Court's pattern of results is that it rests on distinctions among religions that may well seem invidious. Of course, any doctrine requiring accommodation of religion but not accommodation of political belief or personal preference will require the Court to draw lines between religion and non-religion, and on occasion some adherents of what the Court regards as non-religion will be insulted by that judgment. In addition, to the extent that the state can show that accommodating religion would, on balance, be too difficult—because, for example, there were too many people who would claim unemployment compensation based on their inability to be available for work on Sunday—it need not accommodate. On one level, this balancing test works against religious denominations with large numbers of adherents, because accommodating all of the adherents might indeed be difficult. On other levels, though, it may work in their favor. The more adherents of the denomination there are, the more likely it is that some employer will be found who is willing to accommodate their schedules, for example, and so the less likely it is that they will have any need for a constitutional doctrine of mandatory accommodation.[20] Further, and more subtly, the fewer adherents there are to a denomination or sect, the more likely it is that the Court will unconsciously undervalue the harm done to the individual believer by rigid application of the state's rules. Unfamiliarity, here, may breed not respect but, as is usually the case, insensitivity.[21]

---

[19]Lynch v. Donnelly, 465 U.S. 668, 673 (1984).

[20]At some point, there may be so many of them that they can secure legislation in their favor, requiring all employers to accommodate them. That raises questions about the constitutionality of permissive accommodations, discussed in the next section.

[21]For a good example of insensitivity, see O'Lone v. Estate of Shabazz, 482 U.S. 503 (1987), whose description of the Muslim ritual of *Jumu'ah* suggests that a believer's conscience can accept its absence rather easily; the analogy to the ritual in Judaism is probably something like the *kashruth* requirements, which are not observed by all Jews but which are quite important to those who do observe them.

Finally, the pattern of the Court's results in mandatory accomoda-
tion is troubling because, put bluntly, the pattern is that sometimes Christians win but non-Christians never do. Claims by non-
Christians to exemption have been rejected when they sought exemption from rules requiring all military officers to wear only prescribed headgear,[22] when they sought exemption from rules regarding the scheduling of out-of-prison work that interfered with their
ability to participate in religious services,[23] and when they sought to
require the government to adjust its program of roadbuilding so as to
avoid the destruction of a central object of worship.[24] Each of these
cases can be explained away,[25] but to one who pays attention to bottom line results, the pattern is troubling.[26]

The Court's language has on occasion been even more disturbing.
Other than the unemployment compensation cases, *Wisconsin v. Yoder*
is the only instance when the Court required an accommodation.[27]
One aspect of the mandatory accommodation doctrine is that the
state can escape the requirement by demonstrating that allowing exemptions would, in one way or another, severely impair important
state interests. In the course of rejecting Wisconsin's assertion that
exempting Amish children from the requirement of education up to
age sixteen would "foster ignorance," Chief Justice Burger's opinion
said: "[T]he Amish community has been a highly successful social
unit within our society, even if apart from the conventional 'mainstream.' Its members are productive and very law-abiding members
of our society; they reject public welfare in its usual modern form."
He also emphasized that the case did not involve "a way of life and
mode of education by a group claiming to have recently discovered
some 'progressive' or more enlightened process for rearing their chil-

---

[22]Goldman v. Weinberger, 475 U.S. 503 (1986).

[23]O'Lone v. Estate of Shabazz., note 21 *supra*.

[24]Lyng v. Northwest Indian Cemetery Protective Ass'n, 485 U.S. 439 (1988).

[25]*Goldman* and *O'Lone*, for example, involved the application of First Amendment rules in
what have come to be called special or restrictive environments, and First Amendment rules
about speech too have been adjusted in such environments. See, *e.g.*, Greer v. Spock, 424 U.S.
828 (1976); Houchins v. KQED, 438 U.S. 1 (1978). *Lyng* involved what the Court described as
the government's use of its own property rather than its manipulation of the general regulatory
environment in which religions operate.

Cf. Cornelius v. NAACP Legal Defense Fund, Inc., 473 U.S. 788 (1985).

[26]It should be noted, though, that Jews in particular may be the beneficiarie s of the holding
about unemployment compensation in *Sherbert* even though they may not have benefited from
the supposed general doctrine of mandatory accommodation.

[27]406 U.S. 205 (1972). West Virginia Board of Education v. Barnette, 319 U.S. 624 (1943),
involved a claim founded in religious belief, but the Court treated the claim as falling under
general free speech principles rather than free exercise principles.

dren for modern life."[28] It is not unfair to read this as saying that the claims of the Amish prevailed because they were a "good" religion.

One would like to put aside the invidiousness of Chief Justice Burger's comparisons as the product of a particular insensitivity. Yet, there is a systematic connection between the mandatory accommodation doctrine, at least when the doctrine incorporates a balancing test, and invidious comparisons among religions, to the disadvantage of non-mainstream denominations, sects, and cults. The state is required to accommodate religious beliefs under some circumstances, but, the Court has said, only if those beliefs are sincerely held. To require accommodation without requiring sincerity would, of course, open the way for strategic claims to exemption by those who found the state's regulations merely burdensome. The question of sincerity has not preoccupied the Court, because the cases it has handled have all involved claims conceded to be sincere. In *Frazee*, however, Justice White did discuss sincerity briefly. "Undoubtedly, membership in an organized religious denomination, especially one with a specific tenet forbidding members to work on Sunday, would simplify the problem of identifying sincerely held religious beliefs, but we reject the notion that to claim the protection of the Free Exercise Clause, one must be responding to the commands of a particular religious organization."[29] This suggests that a subtle preference for claims readily understandable by those adherents of mainstream religion who are likely to administer the mandatory accommodation doctrine is built into the doctrine itself.

In part the preference occurs because it is a normal human reaction to be skeptical about the sincerity of a person who claims to hold unconventional beliefs. Further, the preference for conventional religious beliefs may affect not just the determination of sincerity but also the application of the balancing test in the mandatory accommodation doctrine. One difficulty with balancing tests in general is that they are susceptible to overt and, even more important, unconscious manipulation. Those administering them, not excluding the Justices of the Supreme Court, may sincerely believe that they are giving appropriate weight to the individual's claims and the government's interest, but may in fact be assigning erroneous weights. In the present context, *Frazee*'s mention of the role of membership in churches with established doctrines of a particular sort suggests that the mandatory

---

[28]406 U.S. at 235.
[29]109 S.Ct. at 1517.

accommodation doctrine will be administered with a thumb on the scales—or with a hand underneath the scale—when non-mainstream claims are made. The reason is that the less familiar the claim is—that is, the less connected it is to the kinds of worship that the Justices of the Supreme Court are accustomed to—the less likely it is that they will regard infringements on those forms of worship as really serious. The Justices may of course say that they assume that the claims of severe impairment are both sincere and accurate, but there is some distance between saying that and believing it in a way that finds expression in the application of a balancing test.[30]

Kurland said that determining sincerity "may be the insoluble problem under any theory of the first amendment religion clauses."[31] One reason, presumably, is that the determination lends itself to invidious comparisons. And one near-solution to the problem is to reduce the occasions on which such comparisons might arise. Kurland's approach to the religion clauses, by opposing a doctrine of mandatory accommodation, provides that near-solution by refusing to authorize any judicial balancing of the impact on religion of facially neutral state regulations. It does so at a cost, however. By insisting that governmental regulations be cast solely in secular terms, Kurland's approach raises the normative question associated with disparate impact: even if the government's rules are neutral, should not their actual impact on the people of the society matter? We might respond to this question by adopting an "intent" test, not for the administrative reasons the Court has given in the equal protection context,[32] but on the ground that intentional imposition of disadvantages is more unattractive than unintentional imposition of the very same disadvantages. For myself, I find that argument unconvincing. We might, of course, simply accept the cost of disparate impact as the price we have to pay to have an acceptable jurisprudence of the religion clauses.

Another solution, though, would be to allow but not require the state to accommodate religious belief. The Court has been attracted to the doctrine of permissible accommodations in recent years, but it too is problematic.

---

[30]I invite readers to consider their reaction to claims that obtaining Social Security numbers is a form of "soul murder" or that taking photographs is making graven images.

[31]Kurland, note 1 *supra*, at 63.

[32]See text accompanying notes 95–97 *infra*.

III. Permissible Accommodation and the Establishment Clause

Any accommodation of religion occurs when the government adopts a regulation whose aim is to ease the burdens that specific religious beliefs place on people living in an organized pluralistic society. Sometimes those burdens arise when the majority acting through its government has, either unthinkingly or deliberately, adopted burdensome regulations. At other times, however, the burdens occur when the government has failed to act in ways that make adherents of particular religious beliefs more comfortable living among people some of whom disagree with them. For Kurland, it went almost without saying that any sort of accommodation of religion as such was impermissible. In discussing the *Selective Draft Law Cases*, in which draftees challenged, among other things, the exemption from the draft of those with religiously grounded conscientious objections, Kurland simply stated: "It may be more difficult for some than it was for Chief Justice White [the author of the Court's opinion] to see why this classification was not a breach in the high wall of separation."[33] He called the Court's decision in *Hamilton v. Regents of the University of California* "clearly . . . correct" in rejecting an argument for mandatory accommodation of those with religious objections to military training. Then he added, as if it followed inexorably from that rejection: "The one thing that the state legislature ought not to be permitted to do was exactly what the students in these cases demanded: to make exemption turn on religious belief or religious affiliation. . . . If military service be considered a duty of every qualified citizen, exemption grants a benefit to religious adherents because they are religious adherents, a result banned by the separation clause."[34]

More recently, perhaps responding to a perception that expansion of the role of government places more burdens on religious believers than government did in the past, various members of the Court have spoken in terms of permissible accommodation.[35] The precise mean-

---

[33]Kurland, note 1 *supra*, at 22–23.

[34]*Id*. at 26.

[35]One reason to doubt the proposition that concern for permissible accommodations resulted from the increasing intrusiveness of government on religious life is the fact that programs like the military training program in *Hamilton* undoubtedly placed as severe a burden on religious belief as any of the government's more recent activities. For analyses of the doctrine of accommodation of religion, see McConnell, Accommodation of Religion, 1985 Supreme Court Review 1; Tushnet, The Emerging Principle of Accommodation of Religion (Dubitante), 76 Geo. L. J. 1691 (1988).

ing of permissible accommodation, not to mention its specific doctrinal content, remains rather undefined, but discussions in two of
the 1988 Term's cases shed some light on the doctrine and the problems it may entail.

Last Term, *County of Allegheny v. American Civil Liberties Union*[36]
presented the Court with another occasion to visit the problem of
symbolic and relatively passive governmental support for religious
displays around the Christmas holiday season.[37] The county had
placed a creche in the main lobby of its courthouse, and erected a
menorah outside the City-County Building. A majority of the Court
held that the display of the creche violated the establishment clause,
and that the display of the menorah did not. Justice Kennedy, joined
by the Chief Justice and Justices White and Scalia, dissented from
the former holding, and would have upheld the county's support of
both displays on a theory much different from that adopted by the
Court's majority. In the course of elaborating his approach, Justice
Kennedy used the language of permissible accommodation.[38]

Piecing his references to "accommodation" together, we may conclude, though with some hesitation, that Justice Kennedy intends a
relatively broad meaning for permissible accommodation: A permissible accommodation occurs when the government responds to
the religious beliefs of the citizenry in any way so long as its action
does not coerce non-believers.[39]

[36]109 S.Ct. 3086 (1989).
[37]For a more extended discussion, which explains the biased statement of the facts in the
text, see §IV *infra*.
[38]Justice Kennedy's introductory statement of his approach was: "The ability of the organized community to recognize and accommodate religion in a society with a pervasive public
sector requires diligent observance of the border between accommodation and establishment.
Our cases disclose two limiting principles: government may not coerce anyone or participate in
any religion of its exercise; and it may not, in the guise of avoiding hostility or callous indifference, give direct benefits to religion in such a degree that it in fact 'establishes a [state] religion or religious faith, or tends to do so.'" *Id*. at 3136, quoting Lynch v. Donnelly, 465 U.S.
668, 678 (1984). Later references used the phrase "symbolic recognition or accommodation,"
and variants, in ways that suggest an intended distinction between symbolic recognition and
accommodation. See, *e.g.*, *id*. at 3138 ("Non-coercive government action within the realm of
flexible accommodation or passive acknowledgement of existing symbols does not violate the
Establishment Clause unles it benefits religion in a way more direct and more subtantial than
practices that are accepted in our national heritage"). Throughout the opinion, Justice Kennedy referred to widely adopted and seemingly well-settled forms of governmental recognition
of religion. At the conclusion of the opinion, Justice Kennedy wrote: "Obsessive, implacable resistance to all but the most carefully scripted and secularized forms of accommodation requires
this Court to act as a censor, issuing national decrees as to what is orthodox and what is not.
What is orthodox, in this context, means what is secular; the only Christmas the State can acknowledge is one in which references to religion have been held to a minimum. The Court thus
lends its assistance to an Orwellian rewriting of history as many understand it." *Id*. at 3146.
[39]See note 38 *supra*. This conclusion is supported by Justice Kennedy's rejection of the majority's statement that the Court had theretofore allowed accommodation only to remove bur-

Two immediate difficulties arise from this definition of permissible accommodation. First, this definition seems to deprive the Establishment Clause of meaning independent of the Free Exercise Clause, which standing alone would seem to ban government coercion of religious belief or observance. One response to this objection, suggested by Justice Kennedy's opinion, is that the Free Exercise Clause deals with "*direct* coercion" of religious belief[40] while the Establishment Clause deals with the "extreme case," in which the government "benefits religion in a way more direct and more substantial than practices that are accepted in our national heritage."[41]

But this response raises even more pointedly the second difficulty with Justice Kennedy's approach to permissible accommodations. That difficulty can be seen once we note that Justice Kennedy repeatedly refers to "government" decisions to accommodate religious belief, except when he speaks of "traditions of diversity and pluralism [that] allow *communities* to make reasonable judgments respecting the accommodation or acknowledgement of holidays. . . ."[42] The reference to communities makes it clear that, when "government" accommodates religion in the way that Justice Kennedy would permit, a majority of the citizens of a community, acting through their representatives, are simply doing what they want to do. That is, they are simply reflecting their own religious preferences on matters of specifically religious concern.[43] As Justice Blackmun put it, "prohibiting the display of a creche in the courthouse deprives Christians of the satisfaction of seeing the government adopt their religious message as their own, but this kind of government affiliation with particular religious messages is precisely what the Establishment Clause

---

dens the government itself imposed. 109 S.Ct. at 3138 n.2. Justice Kennedy took this to be an assertion that "government 's power to accommodate and recognize religion extends no further than the requirements of the Free Exercise Clause," *ibid.*, which it is not. Significantly, Justice Kennedy cited at this point Justice Scalia's dissenting opinion in Texas Monthly, Inc. v. Bullock, 109 S.Ct. 890 (1989). For a discussion of *Texas Monthly*, see text accompanying notes 47–57 *infra*.

[40] 109 S.Ct. at 3137.

[41] *Id.* at 3137, 3138.

[42] *Id.* at 3146 (emphasis added). I take the possibly implicit limitation to holidays to reflect caution on Justice Kennedy's part, perhaps because, at the end of the Term, the implications of his more general approach were not entirely clear to him. Nothing in his "non-coercion" approach, however, would seem to require, or even support, such a limitation.

[43] This last qualification is designed to remove from consideration decisions by a majority, for religious reasons, to adopt regulations that do not refer to religious belief alone. For an extended discussion of such decisions, see Greenawalt, Religious Convictions and Political Choice (1988).

precludes."[44] Similarly, by relying on the historical record of community acceptance of permissible accommodations to define indirect coercion, Justice Kennedy allows the majority, in this instance the majority of the people of the United States extended over time, to determine the limits on government power. In some ways this is a distinctly anticonstitutional stance, for constitutional limitations are designed precisely because we cannot rely on majorities to restrain themselves.[45]

In effect, Justice Kennedy's approach would simply place a limit of reasonablene ss on government action regarding religion. That limit, of course, exists under the Due Process Clause. More pointedly, even classifications explicitly based on religion would appear to be constitutional, under Justice Kennedy's approach, if they were reasonable. As Kurland perceived, the public's general understanding is that classifications based on race and religion, and perhaps more, need greater justification than that. To that extent, perhaps, the public is itself committed to placing more stringent limits on its own action than Justice Kennedy thinks it is.

The majority in the creche-menorah case agreed that the Constitution permitted some sorts of accommodation of religion. But it limited permissible accommodations to relieving burdens that the government itself imposed.[46] In the 1988 Term, the Court's most extensive confrontation with this approach to permissible accommodations occurred in *Texas Monthly, Inc. v. Bullock*.[47] Although no opinion was joined by a majority of the Court, five Justices adopted an approach that usefully illuminates this notion of permissible accommodation.

Texas Monthly concerned an exemption from a general sales tax for "periodicals that are published or distributed by a religious faith and that consist wholly of writings promulgating the teaching of the faith and books that consist wholly of writings sacred to a religious

---

[44]109 S.Ct. at 3105 n.51.

[45]One standard citation for the general proposition is The Federalist, No. 51 (Madison). A plurality of the Court relied on similar historical validation of a majority judgment in its death penalty cases, Stanford v. Kentucky, 109 S.Ct. 2969 (1989), and Penry v. Lynaugh, 109 S.Ct. 2934 (1989). The problem in those cases is different from that addressed in the text, for the Eighth Amendment, as interpreted by the Court, itself incorporates a historical reference through its reliance on "evolving standards of decency." Even so, the dissenters in the death penalty cases did argue that the plurality's approach was anticonstitutional.

[46]109 S.Ct. 3086, 3105 n.51.

[47]109 S.Ct. 890 (1989).

faith."[48] A general sales tax places some burden on the exercise of religion; it forces people to pay somewhat more than they otherwise would for the books and magazines they use in their religious activities. Texas argued that its exemption of religious writings was a permissible accommodation of religion, aimed at relieving religion of a burden government itself placed on religion. The Court rejected that argument and invalidated the exemption.

The result in *Texas Monthly* was not easy to reconcile with *Corporation of Presiding Bishop v. Amos*,[49] in which the Court upheld an accommodation, finding no constitutional violation in a provision of federal equal employment statutes that exempts religious institutions from certain obligations, imposed on all other employers, to avoid discriminating against employees because of their religion. In *Amos*, the exemption extended even to discrimination that was chosen by the religious employer though not compelled by the employer's religious beliefs. The imposition of the sales tax on the sale of religious articles seems quite similar to the imposition of the antidiscrimination rules on religious employers.[50]

Justice Brennan addressed that claim by offering a more precise formulation of an acceptable principle of permissible accommodation. Such accommodations, he wrote, "involve[d] legislative exemptions that did not or would not impose substantial burdens on nonbeneficiaries while allowing others to act according to their religious beliefs, or that were designed to alleviate government intrusions that might significantly deter adherents of a particular faith from conduct protected by the Free Exercise Clause."[51] For Justice

---

[48]One might argue that the relevant issue for a "burden" analysis is whether the government regulation makes religious exercise relatively more expensive than competing activities. The question would then be, does this government regulation make religious activities differentially more expensive than it makes nonreligious ones? The application of a neutral government regulation of all activities falling under some general description would, on this definition, not raise questions of "burden" at all. Yet, this definition simply transfers the problem to the identification of the general description under which the religious and nonreligious activities fall.

[49]483 U.S. 327 (1987).

[50]Justice Brennan also addressed the accommodation argument by saying that Texas had not shown that "the payment of a sales tax by subscribers to religious periodicals or purchasers of religious books would offend their religious beliefs or inhibit religious activity. The State therefore cannot claim persuasively that its tax exemption is compelled by the Free Exercise Clause in even a single instance, let alone in every case. No concrete need to accommodate religious activity has been shown." 109 S.Ct. at 901. This is, of course, not responsive to Texas's argument, which was not that an exemption was required in order to avoid an actual infringement of the Free Exercise Clause, but was rather than an exemption was permitted to avoid placing some burden on religious exercise.

[51]*Id.* at 901 n.8.

Brennan, an accommodation of religion is permissible in two situations: where the accommodation does not impose substantial burdens on those not exempted, and—apparently independent of the "no substantial burden on nonbeneficiaries" test—where the government's regulation itself makes religious exercise more costly.[52] *Amos* involved the latter condition because it "prevented potentially serious encroachments on protected religious freedom," while Texas's sales tax exemption did not "remove[] a demonstrated and possibly grave imposition on religious activity sheltered by the Free Exercise Clause . . . [and] burdens nonbeneficiaries by increasing their tax bills. . . ."[53]

Formulating the permissible accommodation doctrine in this way does explain why *Amos* and *Texas Monthly* are compatible, but we need some justification for this rather narrow formulation rather than a more expansive one.[54] Justice Brennan provided that explanation, though he did not present his argument in the form developed here. For him, as for Justices Blackmun and O'Connor (who concurred in the result but joined in a separate opinion), the exemption in *Texas Monthly* was an unconstitutional establishment of religion because it was too narrow. It singled out religious activities by name and exempted them from a general statute. Where legislation does that, it cannot "have appeared other than as state sponsorship of religion."[55] If religious activities are to be exempted from general regulations, "the benefits derived by religious organizations [must] flow[] to a large number of nonreligious groups as well."[56]

---

[52] Two points about the latter test should be noted. First, the cost imposed by the government cannot be so great as to constitute a violation of the free exercise clause, for that would make permissible accommodations available only when they were mandatory, and would thereby eliminate any doctrine of merely permissible accommodations. Second, by making the presence of a governmentally imposed burden a trigger for analysis, the test raises the familiar difficulties associated with the state action doctrine. See Tushnet, note 35 *supra*, at 1710.

[53] *Ibid.* See also Estate of Thornton v. Caldor, Inc., 472 U.S. 703 (1985) (invalidating statute requiring employers to grant employees their Sabbath off, in part because of burden on employees who did not observe Sabbath).

[54] It should be noted, however, that because it allows accommodation where infringements on free exercise are "possible" or "potential," the formulation does make permissible accommodations different from mandatory ones, which arise only when there is an actual infringement on free exercise.

[55] 109 S.Ct. at 897.

[56] *Ibid.* Justice Brennan argued that cases such as Walz v. Tax Commission, 397 U.S. 664 (1970), adopted this approach to permissible accommodation. In *Walz* the Court held that granting a property tax exemption to churches did not violate the establishment clause. One reason (not, as Justice Scalia's dissent in *Texas Monthly* effectively showed, a reason central to the Court's analysis) was that the exemption for churches fell within a broader class of exemptions for various charitable and educational institutions. Of course the result in *Walz* is compatible with Justice Brennan's formulation.

Requiring that permissible accommodations be broad enough to encompass a substantial amount of nonreligious activities has several advantages. As Justice Brennan said, an exemption confined to religion must signal government endorsement of religion as such. But a sufficiently broad exemption—one that provides relief from property taxes for property owned by religious, educational, and charitable organizations, for example—signals government endorsement of some activity whose definition encompasses all the exempted categories.[57]

More important, requiring sufficient breadth makes the doctrine of permissible accommodation self-limiting in an important sense. Any exemption from a general regulation impairs the government's—that is, the majority's—ability to promote the substantive goals of the regulation (at least to the extent that those goals can be identified independent of the exemption).[58] Exempting religious employers from antidiscrimination rules, for example, allows there to be more religious discrimination in the society than would otherwise be the case; it has, in Justice Brennan's words, "some adverse effect on those holding or seeking employment with those organizations,"[59] which is a cost that the majority believes worth incurring. A broad exemption from the sales tax increases the taxes the public must raise from other sources. As the breadth of the exemption increases, the costs in terms of promoting the substantive goals also increase. At some point it will become too costly to allow an exemption, which limits the scope of those accommodations that the majority will be willing to enact.[60] In terms of Justice Brennan's test,

---

[57]For a discussion of the problems with the general theory that the establishment clause bars government signals of endorsement of religion, see §IV *infra*.

[58]Such independent identification seems necessary to be in a position to describe something as an exemption in the first place.

[59]109 S.Ct. at 901–2 n.8.

[60]The plurality and Justices Blackmun and O'Connor agreed on this basic analysis, though they disagreed over how broad an exemption would have to be to satisfy the requirement of breadth. For Justice Brennan, the required breadth depended on the state's purposes. If it sought to subsidize groups that contribute to a community's cultural, intellectual, or moral betterment, the exemption might properly encompass religious publications. If it sought to "promote reflection and discussions about questions of ultimate value. . . , then a tax exemption would have to be available to an extended range of associations whose publications were substantially devoted to such matters." 109 S.Ct. at 900. Justice Blackmun appeared to adopt the latter view of Texas's purposes, writing that a statute could exempt the sale of religious books if it also exempted sales "of philosophical literature distributed by nonreligious organizations devoted to such matters of conscience as life and death, good and evil, being and nonbeing, right and wrong." *Id.* at 906. Both opinions agreed that determining the basic purpose of the exemption was a matter for the legislature, and that an exemption for religious publications only was too narrow.

we can determine the substantiality of the burden on nonbenefici-aries by examining the breadth of the accommodation: with a suffi-ciently broad accommodation, the class of nonreligious beneficiaries is so encompassing that the total impact on nonbeneficiaries is rela-tively small.

Justice Brennan's conception of permissible accommodations as those sufficiently broad that they will necessarily be limited in ways that do not threaten the values protected by the establishment clause is undeniably attractive, and limits the concept in a way that Justice Kennedy's does not.[61] It does, however, generate its own difficulties. Justice Brennan's conception has two elements. Accommodations of religion are permissible if they (*a*) "remove burdens on the free ex-ercise of religion,"[62] which can be imposed only by governments (the second situation mentioned earlier), and (*b*) are sufficiently broad, in the sense suggested above of being self-limiting (a reformulation of the first situation). Both elements will produce some doctrinal diffi-culties.

The intuition that justifies the "burden on free exercise" element is straightforward. As the law of mandatory accommodations demon-strates, sometimes general regulations adopted by government make it somewhat more difficult for certain religious adherents to follow their beliefs than it would be were the government not to act at all. A permissible accommodation, according to this first element, lifts the burden the regulation imposes, thereby restoring the incentive structure, as to these believers, that existed before the government acted. In contrast, were the government to "accommodate" religion by directly altering the incentive structure, for example by requiring private employers to take the beliefs of their employees into account, it would be subsidizing religion in a rather direct way.[63]

---

[61]Justice Scalia's dissent, which was joined by the Chief Justice and Justice Kennedy, was devoted primarily to a demonstration that Justice Brennan's approach was incompatible with the precedents on which he relied. He criticized the requirement of breadth as irrelevant in the permissible accommodation context. It arose, he said, in the Court's consideration of cases in which a statute was defended on the ground that it only incidentally benefited religion. But "where accommodation of religion is the justification, by definition religion is being singled out." 109 S.Ct. at 913. He also suggested that an exemption might be required by the Free Exercise Clause, and he interpreted the plurality opinion as eliminating the distinction be-tween permissible and mandatory accommodations. He would have allowed accommodations that demonstrate "promotion" of or "favoritism" to religion, *ibid.*, but he said that exempting religious publications from the sales tax "is not even a close case." *Ibid.*

[62]Allegheny County v. ACLU, 109 S.Ct. at 3105 n.51.

[63]Of course, relieving governmentally imposed burdens, by altering incentive structures as to only those religious believers whose beliefs are indeed accommodated, differentially favors, and thereby subsidizes, some religions. The "breadth" element addresses this problem,

Unfortunately for the theory of permissible accommodations, the most prominent statutory accommodation of religion appears to fail under Justice Brennan's approach.[64] The federal antidiscrimination laws place private employers under a duty to "reasonably accommodate" the religious needs of their employees.[65] Recall that Justice Brennan's approach has two tests. First, does the "reasonable accommodation" requirement impose a "substantial burden on non-beneficiaries"? If the requirement has any bite at all, it will force some adjustments in the work schedules of employees, thereby burdening them to some extent. And, to the degree that it limits the employer's ability to structure work assignments as conditions require, the statute imposes a burden on employers as well. The Court has construed the requirement of reasonable accommodation quite narrowly, with the effect of making it compatible with Justice Brennan's first test while depriving it of substantial significance.[66]

Justice Brennan's test also requires that the accommodation relieve someone of a governmentally imposed burden. The only candidate appears to be the employer, who must comply with the general non-discrimination rule. Yet, on its face, the duty to accommodate does not remove a burden on the free exercise of religion by employers, who, most of the time, are likely to be simply indifferent to the religious needs of their employees. Perhaps the general anti-discrimination norms "burden" the employer, who might fear that a court would find thathe or she had discriminated on the basis of religion, if the employer had not accommodated the employee's religious beliefs. A statutory requirement of reasonable accommodation would, in a sense, relieve that burden, though surely the burden Congress really had in mind was the one placed on the employee by an employer's failure to accommodate.[67] That interpretation of the antidiscrimination rule is hardly inevitable, of course, and in any event, it will be the unusual employer who could fairly claim that

---

though, as discussed in text accompanying notes 72–74 *infra*, it does not does so with complete success.

[64]The general requirement of nondiscrimination in Title VII may be sufficiently broad, in that employers are barred from discriminating on the basis of race, gender, and other grounds, as well as religion. (I acknowledge that, to the extent that religion is not part of some more general category that encompasses the other bases of prohibited discrimination—to the extent, that is, that Title VII is a grab-bag rather than the expression of a single principle—this defense of the prohibition on religious discrimination would fail.)

[65]42 U.S.C. §2000e(j) (1981).

[66]See, *e.g.*, Ansonia Board of Education v. Philbrook, 479 U.S. 60 (1986).

[67]42 U.S.C. §2000e(j) (1981).

requiring him or her to refrain from discriminating on the basis of religion imposed a burden on the employer's free exercise of religion, as the first element requires, rather than on the free conduct of the employer's business.[68]

As a result, to fit the "reasonable accommodation" requirement into the theory of permissible accommodation, we would have to construct some theory according to which the employers' free exercise of religion is burdened by some government regulation.[69] The implications of that effort can be seen more clearly when we consider how one might defend a statute that required schools to provide a "moment of silence" which is designed not to encourage, but only to allow, students to engage in prayer.[70] Although the details might be worked out in a number of ways, the basic defense is that the government, by taking control over so substantial a portion of the lives of young people, strongly structures the opportunities they have to engage in reflective religious activity, and that young people are sufficiently sensitive to the structuring of their lives by other people that they will find it difficult to engage in prayer unless the structures are designed to give them the opportunity.[71]

The point to be noted about this argument, and parallel arguments dealing with the "reasonable accommodation" requirement, is that they present what might be called a "reverse state action" problem. Ordinarily political liberals try to find state action where it is not obvious, in order to authorize the courts to impose constitutional requirements where legislatures have refused to impose them directly. Under Justice Brennan's theory of permissible accommodations, political conservatives will try to find government-imposed burdens where they are not obvious, in order to authorize the legislature to act where it otherwise could not. As a matter of strict doctrine, one could separate the reverse state action problem, as it arises in the context of permissible accommodations, from the state action problem as it arises in its usual context. Yet, as Justice Kennedy's adoption of the language of permissible accommodation suggests, the judges who are asked to apply doctrine may find it difficult to sustain such

---

[68]It may be worth noting, too, that the requirement of reasonable accommodation, seen as related to the nondiscrimination requirement, is a form of affirmative action. Because Title VII does not require affirmative action with respect to race or gender, the reasonable accommodation requirement singles out religion as a ground for special treatment.

[69]It may be, of course, that the "reasonable accommodation" requirement is inconsistent with Justice Brennan's theory of permissible accommodations.

[70]The qualification is necessary to deal with Wallace v. Jaffree, 472 U.S. 38 (1985).

[71]See Tushnet, note 35 supra, at 1711.

analytic distinctions. As we have seen, that is a consideration that counts against any constitutional doctrine.

Justice Brennan's requirement of sufficient scope raises another set of difficulties. *Amos* and the example of school prayer as a permissible accommodation illuminate one. The theory of permissible accommodation almost necessarily results in a problem of disparate impact. Denominations who, as employers, have no religious objections to employing nonmembers of the denomination in the jobs covered by the statutory exemption upheld in *Amos* are not aided by the exemption.[72] Even worse, denominations whose religious principles lead them to oppose that sort of discrimination cannot possibly be benefited by the exemption, and may be insulted by it. Similarly, some religions do not believe that prayer is acceptable outside the confines of the church and under its leadership; providing prayer opportunities in school accommodates the religious beliefs of other religions but not the beliefs of such denominations. In general, given the diversity of religious beliefs in our society, any statutory accommodation of religion will have that sort of disparate impact.

Under the Equal Protection Clause, disparate impact alone is insufficient to invalidate a statute; the disparate impact must be intended. There is a sense in which permissible accommodations are intended to have an impact on religious belief, but there is no obvious intent to have a disparate impact. Further, the requirement of breadth can be seen as effort to diffuse the disparate impact; the broader the permissible accommodation, and therefore the more religious and nonreligious beliefs and activities it encompasses, the smaller the disparate impact.[73]

---

[72]They may in fact be placed at a competitive disadvantage by the exemption, to the extent that the benefited denominations are able to keep within the denomination the salary of these employees, while the others "lose" those salaries, in the sense that the money leaks outside the denomination.

[73]The analogy to equal protection law may still be illuminating. The purpose of permissible accommodations is to ease a burden on religion. In this way they are more akin to statutes that utilize suspect classifications on their face than to the facially neutral statutes that are the primary concern in most disparate impact cases. Such statutes are of course constitutional if they promote compelling state interests better than any alternative, but the Supreme Court has been unsurprisingly reluctant to find that this sort of statute does so. More interesting, in this connection, is the "separate but equal" doctrine of Plessy v. Ferguson, 163 U.S. 537 (1896). That doctrine applies to statutes that use racial or other suspect classifications but do not affect the classes at issue differently: under a true regime of "separate but equal" both blacks and whites are deprived of the opportunity to associate with each other but not deprived of anything else. See Wechsler, Toward Neutral Principles of Constitutional Law, 73 Harv. L. Rev. 1, 34. (1959). It is possible, of course, to deny that there ever can be a true regime of separate but equal, in which case this branch of equal protection law is uninteresting. Brown v. Board of

The "breadth" requirement leads to a difficulty from another direction. Proponents of accommodations support them precisely because they confer benefits, or relieve burdens, on religion. In diluting the religious message an accommodation sends, the breadth requirement deprives accommodations of the religious content that makes them distinctive, and thereby signals to adherents of the religions whose activities are accommodated that their religious beliefs are simply one set of beliefs among many that the government believes it appropriate to accommodate. By subsuming religion into "groups that contribute[] to the community's cultural, intellectual, and moral betterment" or treating it as one of "an extended range of associations" that "promote reflection and discussion about questions of ultimate value," in Justice Brennan's terms, or as a form of "philosophical literature . . . devoted to such matters of conscience as life and death, good and evil, being and nonbeing, right and wrong," in Justice Blackmun's,[74] the doctrine of permissible accommodations with a requirement of breadth ultimately does not really accommodate religion, but rather the relevant set of beliefs encompassed by the broader exemption. In a way this reproduces the problem of disparate impact, though here from the other side: Some denominations may grudgingly accept a permissible accommodation with the string of other exemptions for "similar" groups attached, while others, more insistent on the significance of their specifically religious beliefs, may find such an accommodation more costly to their sense of themselves than it is worth.

A doctrine of permissible accommodations with a breadth require-

---

Education, 349 U.S. 294 (1955), and even more dramatically Shelley v. Kraemer, 334 U.S. 1 (1949), proceeded on the contrary assumption that it was possible for the state to act "through indiscriminate imposition of inequalities," as Chief Justice Vinson put it in *Shelley*, though to do so violated the equal protection clause. If the imposition is indeed indiscriminate, however, what is the equal protection violation? It would seem that the violation occurs, as Charles Black understood in his analysis of *Brown*, because the state uses the suspect classification intentionally, to signal something about the social significance of the classification. Black, The Lawfulness of the Segregation Decisions, 69 Yale L. J. 421 (1960).

How do permissible accommodations fare under this analysis? They use religion as a basis for government classification, and they do so in the strongest sense of intentionally, that is, precisely in order to confer a benefit on some religions that does not flow either to nonbelievers or to all religions. The relevant question would then appear to be, what is the signal intended to be sent by these accommodations? It is difficult to avoid the conclusion that permissible accommodations, with their necessarily disparate impact, indicate some degree of government approval of the practices that benefit from the accommodations—certain types of employment discrimination by religious employers, "unorganized" prayer—in the face of other religions that are indifferent to or even actively disapprove of those practices.

[74]109 S.Ct. at 900 (Brennan, J., announcing judgment of Court), 906 (Blackmun, J., concurring in judgment).

ment differs somewhat from the other doctrines considered so far, because the doctrine may be administered without subconscious bias. Yet, the element that makes it attractive, the breadth requirement with its self-limiting effects, also makes it less attractive than might appear at the outset, by signalling the relative unimportance of religion to the government even as the government acts in the name of accommodating religion.

IV. "No Endorsement" and the Establishment Clause

The Court in *Allegheny County v. ACLU* adopted Justice O'Connor's analysis of the establishment clause, by holding that the clause, "at the least, prohibits government from appearing to take a position on questions of religious belief or from 'making adherence to a religion relevant in any way to a person's standing in the political community.'"[75] The preceding analysis of the necessary disparate impact of permissible accommodations suggests that this formulation cannot be taken entirely at face value. A permissible accommodation with a disparate impact either takes a position or appears to take a position on questions of religious belief—that is, on the propriety of the activity that is accommodated. Even if the formulation is modified in some way, the "no endorsement" analysis leads to doctrinal difficulties that *Allegheny County* itself illustrates.[76]

According to Justice O'Connor's original formulation of the "no endorsement" test, the question is whether the government's action communicates "a message to nonadherents that they are outsiders, not full members of the political community, and an accompanying message to adherents that they are insiders, favored members of the political community." This question has a subjective and an objective component, the subjective one being "the intention of the speaker" and the objective one being what a reasonable person, presumably either an adherent or a nonadherent, would "fairly" understand the government's message to be.[77]

Once we realize that the "no endorsement" question will be an-

---

[75] 109 S.Ct. at 3101, quoting Lynch v. Donnelly, 465 U.S. 668, 698 (1984) (O'Connor, J., concurring).

[76] As Justice Kennedy noted, these difficulties have been discussed before. 109 S.Ct. at 3141, citing Smith, Symbols, Perceptions, and Doctrinal Illusions: Establishment Neutrality and the "No Endorsement" Test, 86 Mich. L. Rev. 266 (1987), and Tushnet, The Constitution of Religion, 18 Conn. L. Rev. 701 (1986)). Justice Stevens responded, appropriately, that by far the majority of scholars who have discussed the "no endorsement" approach have approved it. 109 S.Ct. at 3131 n.6.

[77] Lynch v. Donnelly, 465 U.S. 668, 690 (1984) (O'Connor, J., concurring).

swered by judges who are, inevitably, either adherents or non-adherents, however, difficulties with the doctrine become apparent. These difficulties can be seen through an examination of *Allegheny County*, which involved two displays erected by the county during November and December 1986 and January 1987.[78] One display was a nativity scene placed in the main staircase of the county court-house, while the other included a large "Christmas" tree, a smaller menorah, and a still smaller sign saying, "During this holiday sea-son, the City of Pittsburgh salutes liberty." The Court held that the display of the nativity scene violated the "no endorsement" test, while the display of the menorah did not.

One difficulty with the "no endorsement" test arises at its founda-tion. We are asked to consider what a "reasonable" adherent or non-adherent would understand the government's message to be. Yet, in the context of religious beliefs, to invoke a test requiring one to be "reasonable" is to force religion into a quite peculiar mold. In an im-portant sense, a "reasonable" Jew or Christian is what Michael Sandel calls a radically unsituated person, whose way of understand-ing the world is somehow detached from his or her experience and the historical experience of the religion of which he or she is an ad-herent.[79] To this extent, Justice O'Connor's approach may simply be incoherent.[80]

Of course, no one is radically unsituated, Justices of the Supreme Court included. When they attempt to apply Justice O'Connor's test, mis-steps are inevitable. In the nature of things, most of the Jus-tices of the Supreme Court are likely to be Christians—"adherents," in Justice O'Connor's generalized term. In *Allegheny County* it be-came clear that the principal application of the "no endorsement" test required these adherents to consider how reasonable nonadherents would understand the government's message. Yet, when Justice O'Connor first applied her test to a nativity scene, she found that nonadherents, that is, Jews, would not understand its message to be one of endorsement of Christianity.[81] Even commentators who ap-prove of her test have said, virtually unanimously, that something

---

[78]Some of the difficulties are suggested by the choice in characterizing the facts of the case. If one calls this period "the holiday season," one prejudges the case in one way, while if one calls it "the Christmas holiday season," as the Court did, 109 S.Ct. at 3093 one prejudges it another way.

[79]Sandel, Liberalism amd the Limits of Justice 11–14 (1982).

[80]It may also express her view, and now that of the Court, that the only kind of religion worthy of the name is a "reasonable" one. If so, the sectarianism of the approach is apparent.

[81]Lynch v. Donnelly, 465 U.S. at 692.

went wrong in the application at least.[82] Given that the test asks adherents to project themselves into the minds of "reasonable" nonadherents, this sort of result seems likely to occur with some frequency, as the adherents, seeing themselves as reasonable people who do not find a message of endorsement in the government' s activity, will tend to believe that a reasonable nonadherent would not find one either.

In *Allegheny County*, the Court held that the nativity scene there violated the Establishment Clause. To interpret a reasonable nonadherent's understanding of the message, the Court said, we must look at the nativity scene's setting. In *Lynch v. Donnelly*, the nativity scene was placed in a larger display that included reindeer, Santa Claus, and other symbols of the "holiday" season, while in *Allegheny County* "nothing in the context of the display detracts from the creche's religious message."[83] The concern for items that "detract" from the religious message signals another difficulty in the "no endorsement" test. The new difficulty was more apparent in Justice Blackmun's discussion of the menorah. He began by saying that "the menorah's message is not exclusively religious," and that, in its setting, along with the Christmas tree and the sign, it conveyed a message about the "winter-holiday season, which has attained a secular status in our society." The Christmas tree and the sign were plainly secular, and the tree was "the predominant element" in the display. "[T]he combination of the tree and the menorah communicates, not a simultaneous endorsement of both Christian and Jewish faith, but, instead, a secular celebration of Christmas coupled with an acknowledgement of Chanukah as a contemporaneous alternative tradition."[84]

Justice O'Connor, concurring in the result as to the menorah, understood that Justice Blackmun's analysis devalued the religious content of the menorah, just as, in many ways, her own analysis of the nativity scene in *Lynch* devalued its religious content. As she understood it, the question was whether the combined display endorsed Judaism (a proposition that Justice Blackmun correctly derided as "implausible"[85]), "religion in general," or something else. To Justice

---

[82]See, *e.g.*, Tribe, Seven Deadly Sins of Straining the Constitution Through a Pseudo-Scientific Sieve, 36 Hastings L. J. 155, 162 (1984). For a compilation of comments on Justice O'Connor's use of the test, see Smith, note 76 *supra*, at 274 n.45.

[83]109 S.Ct. at 3103–4.

[84]*Id*. at 3114.

[85]*Id*. at 3113 n.64.

O'Connor, the display celebrated pluralism rather than religion.[86]

Neither of these analyses is satisfactory. Justice Blackmun's approach demonstrates, as *Lynch* had before, that where the Justices feel pressure to validate a religious activity, they are likely to respond by treating it as essentially nonreligious. This is likely to be insulting at least to those who take comfort in the display even if they are unconcerned about whether the government stands behind it. And, to those who indeed support the activity precisely because it implicates the government in the support of religion, upholding it on the ground that they were somehow mistaken may give them momentary comfort, but when they reflect on the message that the Court's decision sends they may find themselves dismayed.[87]

Justice O'Connor's analysis replicates the narrowness of her understanding of the nativity scene in *Lynch*, in the sense that she is able to see a message of pluralism in a display that combines Christian and Jewish symbols, but not, of course, Moslem or Buddhist ones. One might think a reasonable Buddhist would see in the combined display an endorsement of a particular combination of specific religious traditions rather than an endorsement of pluralism.[88] Perhaps we can rely on the political processes in jurisdictions where there are substantial numbers of Moslems or Buddhists to preclude the public display of something whose vision of pluralism is so narrow as to encompass only Christian, Jewish, and purely secular symbols and statements. Yet, the Supreme Court is itself a part of the government that, among its other functions, communicates an understanding of the way in which government operates to the public. In this light, what are we to make of a statement by a Supreme Court Justice that pluralism means Christianity and Judaism?

The distortion of judgment implicit in Justice O'Connor's application of the "no endorsement" test is systematic. Because Supreme Court Justices are either adherents or nonadherents, they must develop an understanding of what a "reasonable nonadherent or adherent" would take to be the message of the government's action. At

---

[86]*Id.* at 3123.

[87]Perhaps Supreme Court opinions, unlike municipal holiday displays, receive so little public attention that they do not convey any message of the sort that concerns Justice O'Connor. If so, a great deal of scholarship in constitutional law, for example, that concerned with the legitimacy of the Court in light of the strength of its opinions, would have to be reconsidered.

[88]I leave to this note the observation that it would be wrong to treat the combined display as an endorsement of the Judaeo-Christian tradition because I do not believe that there is such a tradition, at least from the perspective of Jews.

their best they will be as empathetic as they can be,[89] but they cannot become someone else. Even more, it probably is beyond anyone's ability to stand apart, not just from the actions of the Allegheny County authorities, but from his or her own activities as a Justice of the Supreme Court to discern what message—of endorsement or not—the Court's opinions send.

The difficulties with the "no endorsement" test are doctrinal, just as the difficulties with the mandatory accommodation approach are. That is, when either approach is applied by the relatively ordinary—situated—men and women who are our judges, the fact that they are situated with respect to religion will induce predictable and normatively troubling distortions in outcome.

V. Conclusion

The major contemporary competitors to Kurland's analysis are doctrinally unsatisfying. Further, precisely because Kurland's analysis calls for the invocation of a rigid and easily applied test— "Does the regulation at issue utilize a religious classification?"—it is preferable as doctrine to the competitors; unlike them, it is unlikely to produce distorted outcomes because of the judges' unconscious predilections. If Kurland's analysis remains powerful, though, why has it been ignored by the Supreme Court?

In part, because it does not always yield normatively attractive results. In core applications, where up to the point of litigation legislators have simply overlooked the impact of a neutral rule on some religious believers, the doctrine of mandatory accommodation plainly produces "better" outcomes. Yet, this is simply to say that Kurland's analysis, like any legal doctrine, is inevitably both under- and over-inclusive. It ignores the necessary comparative judgment among doctrinal competitors, in which Kurland's analysis does quite well, and it seeks a perfect Constitution to be administered, alas, by imperfect judges.[90]

Kurland's approach may have fallen by the wayside for another reason. Doctrinal solutions to particular problems of constitutional intepretation are often attractive because they fit together well with solutions to other problems of interpretation.[91] Yet, if those other

---

[89]See Minow, Justice Engendered, 101 Harv. L. Rev. 10 (1987).

[90]See Monaghan, Our Perfect Constitution, 56 NYU L. Rev. 353 (1981).

[91]As a non-random sample, I note that Stone, Seidman, Sunstein & Tushnet, Constitutional Law (1986), uses the same doctrinal structure to present material on the dormant Commerce Clause, the Equal Protection Clause, and the Establishment Clause.

doctrines change, the fit may no longer seem so good, and the doctrinal solution may lose one of its attractive features. Kurland presented his solution as analogous to equal protection doctrine. He identified two forms of un-neutral government action. The first is what we have come to know as facial discrimination, in which the government expressly relies on racial or religious categories to impose burdens or confer benefits. Kurland described the second as "classifications that purport to relate to other matters [but are] really classifications in terms of religion [or race]"[92]—that is, gerrymanders. As the law of equal protection stood in 1961, these forms of non-neutrality almost fully occupied the terrain.[93] A prescient scholar might have anticipated that another form of discrimination would come to preoccupy the Supreme Court in race discrimination cases, the problem of rules that, though stated in terms neutral as to race, have a disproportionate adverse impact on blacks.[94]

The emergence of a new form of discrimination into legal analysis has posed a problem for Kurland's proposal. The Court has developed doctrines that reduce the congruence between equal protection doctrine and Kurland's proposed religion clause doctrine. Relying on concerns about administrability,[95] the Court has refused to invalidate neutral rules with disproportionate racial impact unless the impact was intended in a strong sense,[96] but it has invalidated neutral rules with disproportionate religious impact without regard to intent.[97] It has been skeptical of rules that expressly use racial terms in order to, as their proponents would have it, aid otherwise disadvantaged racial groups,[98] but it has approved rules that expressly use religious terms for similar, though not quite identical, purposes.[99] Kurland's doctrinal solution, in short, no longer fits quite so well into the general legal terrain as it did in 1961.[100]

---

[92]Kurland, note 1 *supra*, at 5.

[93]In light of later developments, I would now distinguish several sub-categories within the category of gerrymanders, to deal separately with rules that perfectly replicate the racial or religious lines for which they are intended to be substitutes, and rules that use non-racial or non-religious terms that are imperfect substitutes and therefore impose burdens or confer benefits on some members of the favored or disfavored groups respectively. Nothing significant in my later analysis turns on sustaining this distinction, however.

[94]Although few realized it at the time, Brown v. Board of Education, 347 U.S. 483 (1954), was such a case. I believe that Herbert Wechsler's discussion, note 73 *supra*, attempted somewhat inelegantly to capture this point.

[95]In the sense of the courts' ability to distinguish between situations made unconstitutional by the test and those permitted under it.

[96]Washington v. Davis, 426 U.S. 229 (1976).

[97]See §II *infra*.

[98]See, *e.g.*, City of Richmond v. J. A. Croson, Inc., 109 S.Ct. 706 (1989).

[99]See §III *infra*.

[100]This occurred because the Court itself has consistently rejected Kurland's proposal, and

402   THE SUPREME COURT REVIEW   [1989

Changing political circumstances have also undermined Kurland's proposal. When he wrote, the pressing issue on the political agenda was public aid to church-related schools. Although Kurland said that "anyone suggesting that the answer, as a matter of constitutional law, is clear one way or the other is either deluding or deluded,"[101] his analysis necessarily implied that a facially neutral program of assistance to nonpublic schools was constitutional . For some, Kurland's proposal deserved to be rejected because it was too sympathetic to the claims being pressed by religious forces in the political arena.

Today the issues those forces are pressing have changed, and Kurland now appears to some to be too unsympathetic to their claims. Fiscal constraints have made public aid to church-related schools an issue that only crops up in connection with questions of expanding public forms of day-care. Instead, the people of the United States, in the midst of one of their periodic upsurges in public religiosity, have begun to seek direct government support of clearly sectarian activities such as organized prayer in the public schools. Kurland found such support simply unthinkable, and perhaps when he wrote it was. The Justices of the Supreme Court are sensitive to their political surroundings, in part because they are selected periodically through a political process. They must therefore take seriously those urges that find substantial expression in the political process even if they ultimately conclude that the Constitution limits the ability of the people to enact what they wish. Kurland's analysis would not let them take those urges seriously.[102] Under contemporary circumstances, there is little reason to believe that the Court will, though it should, adopt Kurland's approach.[103]

---

has thereby created a doctrinal disparity between its religion clause jurisprudence and its Equal Protection Clause jurisprudence. Had the Court followed Kurland's advice from the outset, his proposal would now fit well with current equal protection doctrine.

[101]Kurland, note 1 *supra*, at 96.

[102]My formulation perhaps suggests what I doubt is true, that the Justices feel under some pressure to respond to these popular urges. Rather, because of their political role, the Justices are likely to share those urges though their institutional roles may constrain them to reject what the public wants.

[103]I do not mean to contend that Kurland's solution is a perfect one either. For example, because it requires that judges determine whether a statute is neutral as to religion, it demands that they be able to distinguish between religion and nonreligion, a task that they are unlikely to perform well. However, I believe that the occasions on which this is likely to be a problem are sufficiently less common than the occasions on which the other tests ask the judges to perform well, that Kurland's proposal comes out ahead in the comparison that is the core of any evaluation of competing proposals.